THE VISUAL
DICTIONARY
ENGLISH · FRENCH · GERMAN · SPANISH

Jean-Claude Corbeil • *Ariane Archambault*

THE VISUAL
DICTIONARY

ENGLISH • FRENCH • GERMAN • SPANISH

The Visual Dictionary was created and produced by

 QA International
329, rue de la Commune Ouest, 3e étage,
Montréal, Québec, H2Y 2E1
Tel.: (514) 499-3000 - Fax: (514) 499-3010
www.qa-international.com

We acknowledge the financial support of the Government of
Canada through the Book Publishing Industry Development
Program (BPIDP) for our publishing activities.

Canadä

The Visual Dictionary has been entirely created on Macintosh by
Apple Computer Inc.

10 9 8 7 6 5 4 3 2 1 02 01 00 99

Printed in U.S.A.

ACKNOWLEDGMENTS

The creators of the original edition would like to acknowledge the contribution of the following people and organisations:

A.C. Delco
Aérospatiale (France)
Aérospatiale Canada (ACI) Inc.
Air Canada (Linguistic Policy and Services)
Amity-Leather Products Company
Animat Inc.
Archambault Musique
International Association of Lighthouse
   Authorities (Marie-Hélène Grillet)
Association des groupes d'astronomes amateurs
   (Jean-Marc Richard)
Atlas Copco
Atomic Energy of Canada Ltd. (Pierre Giguère)
Bell Canada
Bell Helicopter Textron
Bellefontaine
Benoît, Richard
Beretta
Black & Decker
Bombardier Inc.
Boutique de harnais Pépin
British Hovercraft Corporation Ltd. (Division of
   Westland Aerospace)
C. Plath North American Division
Caloritech Inc.
Cambridge Instruments (Canada) Inc.
CAMIF (Direction relations extérieures)
Canada Billard & Bowling Inc. (Bernard Monsec)
Canadian National (Information and Linguistic
   Services)
Canadian Kenworth Company
Canadian Coleman Supply Inc.
Canadian Liquid Air Ltd.
Canadian Curling Association
Canadian Coast Guard
Canadian Broadcasting Corporation (Gilles
   Amyot, Pierre Beaucage, Claude L'Hérault,
   Pierre Laroche)
Carpentier, Jean-Marc
Casavant Frères Limitée (Gilbert Lemieux)
Centre de Tissage Leclerc Inc.
Chromalox Inc.
Clerc, Redjean
Club de tir à l'arc de Montréal
Club de planeur Champlain
Collège Jean de Brébeuf (Paul-Émile Tremblay)
Collège militaire royal de Saint-Jean
Communauté urbaine de Montréal (Bureau de
   transport métropolitain)
Complexe sportif Claude-Robillard
Control Data Canada Ltd.
Cycles Performance
David M. Stewart Museum (Philippe Butler)
Department of National Defence of Canada
   (Public Relations)
Detson
Direction des constructions navales
   (Programmes internationaux) (France)
Distributions TTI Inc.
Energy, Mines and Resources Canada (Canada
   Centre for Remote Sensing)
Environment Canada (Atmospheric Environment
   Service, Gilles Sanscartier)
FACOM
Fédération québécoise des échecs
Fédération québécoise de tennis
Fédération québécoise de luge et bobsleigh
Fédération québécoise de canot-camping
Fédération québécoise de boxe olympique
Fédération québécoise de badminton
Fédération québécoise d'haltérophilie

Fédération québécoise d'escrime
Fédération de patinage de vitesse du Québec
Festival des Montolfières du Haut-Richelieu
Fincantieri Naval Shipbuilding Division
Fisher Scientific Ltd.
Ford New-Holland Inc.
Gadbois, Alain
GAM Pro Plongée
G.E. Astro-Space Division
G.T.E. Sylvania Canada Ltd.
General Electric Canada Inc. (Dominion
   Engineering Works, Mony Schinasi)
General Motors of Canada Ltd.
GIAT Industries
Government of Canada Terminology Bank
Gym Plus
Harrison (1985) Inc.
Hewitt Equipment Ltd.
Hippodrome Blue Bonnets (Robert Perez)
Honeywell Ltd.
Hortipro
Hughes Aircraft Company
Hydro-Québec (Centre de documentation, Anne
   Crépeau)
IBM Canada Ltd.
Imperial Oil Ltd.
Institut de recherche d'Hydro-Québec (IREQ)
International Telecommunications Satellite
   Organization (Intelsat)
International Civil Aviation Organization (IATA)
Jardin Botanique de Montréal
John Deere Ltd.
Johnson & Johnson Inc.
La Maison Olympique (Sylvia Doucette)
La Cordée
Le Beau Voyage
Le Coz, Jean-Pierre
Lee Valley Tools Ltd.
Leica Camera
Les Manufacturiers Draco ltée
Les Instruments de Musique Twigg Inc.
Les Équipements Chalin ltée
Les Appareils orthopédiques BBG Inc.
Leviton Manufacturing of Canada Ltd.
Liebherr-Québec
Manac Inc.
Manutan
Marcoux, Jean-Marie
Marrazza Musique
MATRA S.A.
Matra Défense (Direction de la communication)
Mazda Canada
Médiatel
Mendes Inc. (François Caron)
Michelin
MIL Tracy (Henri Vacher)
Ministère des transports du Québec (Sécurité
   routière, Signalisation routière)
Monette Sport Inc.
Moto Internationale
National Oceanic and Atmospheric
   Administration (NOAA) — National
   Environmental Satellite and Information
   Service (Frank Lepore)
National Aeronautics and Space Administration
   (NASA)
Nikon Canada Inc.
Northern Telecom Canada Ltd.
Office de la langue française du Québec
   (Chantal Robinson)
Ogilvie Mills Ltd. (Michel Ladouceur)

Olivetti Systems and Networks Canada Ltd.
Ontario Hydro
Paterson Darkroom Necessities
Petro-Canada (Calgary)
Philips Electronics Ltd. (Philips Lighting)
Philips Electronics Ltd. (Scientific and Analytical
   Equipment)
Pierre-Olivier Decor
Planétarium Dow (Pierre Lacombe)
Plastimo
Port of Montreal (Public Affairs)
Pratt & Whitney Canada Inc.
Quincaillerie A.C.L. Inc.
Radio-Québec
Remington Products (Canada) Inc.
Russell Rinfret
Rodriguez Cantieri navali S.p.A.
S.A. Redoute Catalogue (Relations extérieures)
Samsonite
Secretary of State of Canada (Translation
   Bureau)
Shell Canada
SIAL Poterie
Smith-Corona (Canada) Ltd.
SNC Defence Products Ltd.
Société Nationale des Chemins de Fer français
   (S.N.C.F.) (Direction de la communication)
Société de transport de la Communauté urbaine
   de Montréal
Spalding Canada
Spar Aerospace Ltd. (Hélène Lapierre)
St. Lawrence Seaway Authority (Normand
   Dodier)
Sunbeam Corporation (Canada) Ltd.
Swimming Canada
Teleglobe Canada Inc. (Roger Leblanc)
Telesat Canada (Yves Comtois)
The Coal Association of Canada
The British Petroleum Company p.l.c.
   (Photographic Services)
Thibault
Tideland Signal Canada Ltd.
Transport Canada (Montreal Airports, Gilbert
   L'Espérance, Koos R. Van der Peijl)
Ultramar Canada Inc.
United States Department of Defense
   (Department of the Navy, Office of
   Information)
Université du Québec à Montréal (Module des
   arts, Michel Fournier)
Université du Québec (Institut national de la
   recherche scientifique, Benoît Jean)
Varin, Claude
Via Rail Canada Inc.
Viala L.R. Inc. (Jean Beaudin)
Ville de Montréal (Bureau du cinéma; Service de
   l'habitation et du développement urbain;
   Service de la prévention des incendies,
   Robert Gilbert, Réal Audet; Service des
   travaux publics)
Volcano Inc.
Volkswagen Canada Inc.
Volvo Canada Ltd.
Water Ski Canada
Weider
Wild Leitz Canada ltée
Xerox Canada Inc.
Yamaha Canada Music Ltd.

Oxford University Press would like to acknowledge the contribution of Enrique Gonzalez Sardinero and Robin Sawers.

INTRODUCTION

This world-renowned dictionary is the first comprehensive visual dictionary in full colour. Covering some 600 subjects, it identifies more than 25,000 terms by the use of thousands of detailed and accurate illustrations. The dictionary lets you see, at a glance, the vocabulary of a subject in not one, but four, languages: English, French, German, and Spanish.

A PICTURE/WORD DICTIONARY

The *Visual Dictionary* closely links pictures and words.

The pictures describe and analyze today's world: the objects of everyday life, our physical environment, the animal and vegetable life that surrounds us, the communication and work techniques that are changing our lifestyles, the weapons that preoccupy us, the means of transportation that are breaking down geographical barriers, the sources of energy on which we depend, etc.

Illustrations play a specific role in our dictionary: they serve to define words, enabling dictionary users to "see" immediately the meaning of each term. Users can thus recognize the objects they are looking for and, at a single glance, find the corresponding vocabulary.

The *Visual Dictionary* provides users with the words they need to accurately name the objects that make up the world around them.

The terms in the dictionary have been carefully selected from current documents written by experts in each area. In case of doubt, the vocabulary has been studied by specialists in the corresponding field and cross-checked in encyclopedias and language dictionaries. We have taken these precautions to ensure the accuracy of each word and a high level of standardization.

A DICTIONARY FOR ONE AND ALL

The *Visual Dictionary* is aimed at all persons who participate in one way or another in contemporary civilization and, as a consequence, need to know and use a great number of technical terms from a wide range of fields.

It thus addresses the needs and curiosity of each and every one of us. It is not designed only for specialists.

The depth of analysis varies according to the subject. Rather than arbitrarily providing a uniform breakdown of each subject, the authors have acknowledged that people's degrees of knowledge differ from one field to another, and that the complexity of the topics dealt with varies widely. For example, more people are familiar with clothing and automobiles than with atomic energy or telecommunications satellites, and find the former subjects simpler than the latter. Another aspect of the same problem is that, in describing human anatomy, we are obliged to use medical terminology, even though the terms seem more complicated than those for fruits and vegetables. In addition, our world is changing: photographic vocabulary, for example, has become much more complicated due to camera automation. Similarly, although microcomputer fans are familiar with computer terminology, the field remains a mystery for much of the rest of the population.

The *Visual Dictionary* allows for these phenomena, and reflects the specialized vocabulary commonly used in each field.

AN EASY-TO-CONSULT DICTIONARY

People may use the *Visual Dictionary* in several different ways, thanks to the List of Chapters (page xxxi), the detailed table of contents (page xv), and the index (page 833).

Users may consult the dictionary:

By going from an idea to a word, if they are familiar with an object and can clearly visualize it, but cannot find or do not know the name for it. The table of contents breaks down each subject according to an easy-to-consult, stratified classification system. The *Visual Dictionary* is the only dictionary that allows users to find a word from its meaning.

By going from a word to an idea, if they want to check the meaning of a term. The index refers users to the illustrations, which provide the names for the individual features.

At a glance, by using the List of Chapters. The coloured page edges help users find the chapters they are looking for.

For foreign language equivalents, by browsing through the book or going into depth for particular themes. The objects of the modern world are clearly identified at a glance in four languages.

For sheer pleasure, by flipping from one illustration to another, or from one word to another, for the sole purpose of enjoying the illustrations and enriching their knowledge.

A DICTIONARY WITH A DIFFERENCE

We are all familiar with several types of dictionaries and encyclopedias. It is not always easy, however, to grasp their distinguishing features. The following overview highlights the main differences between the *Visual Dictionary* and other reference works.

a) Language dictionaries

These dictionaries describe the meanings given by speakers to the general vocabulary of their language.

They provide two major types of information: headwords (vocabulary), and a list of the meanings of each term (dictionary entries).

The vocabulary, which comprises all of the words covered by lexicographical descriptions, constitutes the framework of the dictionary. For consultation purposes, the headwords are arranged in alphabetical order. Generally speaking, the vocabulary includes common, contemporary language, archaic words useful for understanding the texts or history of a civilization, and a certain number of widely used technical terms.

Each dictionary entry provides an itemized, semantic description of the corresponding headword. Generally, the entry indicates the part of speech for the headword, its etymology and its various meanings, as well as the word's social usage (familiar, colloquial, vulgar, etc.) according to criteria that, even today, remain somewhat "impressionistic."

In general, language dictionaries are classified according to their target users and the number of terms in the vocabulary, which, in addition to nouns, includes all other parts of speech (verbs, pronouns, adjectives, adverbs, prepositions, conjunctions, etc.). A 5,000-word dictionary is intended for children, one with 15,000 words is suitable for schools and a 50,000 word dictionary covers the needs of the general public.

b) Encyclopedic dictionaries

In addition to the information included in language dictionaries, encyclopedic dictionaries provide details about the nature, functioning, and history of things, thus enabling laymen with solid general knowledge and specialists to understand the scope of a word. They devote much more space to technical terms, and reflect current scientific and technological developments. Generally speaking, pictures play an important role in illustrating the text. The size of encyclopedic dictionaries varies according to the breadth of the vocabulary, the length of the entries, the emphasis placed on proper nouns and the number of fields of specialization covered.

c) Encyclopedias

Unlike the preceding category of reference works, encyclopedias do not deal with language. They are devoted to providing scientific, technical, occasionally economic, historical and geographic descriptions. The arrangement of the entries varies, as all classification systems are valid: alphabetic, conceptual, chronological, by field of specialization, etc. The number of different encyclopedias is virtually unlimited, given the fragmentation of civilization into multiple categories. There is, however, a distinction between universal encyclopedias and specialized encyclopedias.

d) Specialized lexicons and vocabularies

These works usually address specific needs created by scientific and technological progress. They focus on ensuring efficient communication through precise, standardized terminology. They vary in all respects: the method of compilation, the authors' approach to the subject matter, the scope of the vocabulary, the number of languages, and the means of establishing equivalents in the various languages (i.e., by simple translation or by a comparison of unilingual terminologies). Specialized lexicography has become an area of intense activity. The number of works is multiplying in all sectors and in all language combinations.

e) The *Visual Dictionary*

The *Visual Dictionary* is a terminology-oriented dictionary. It is aimed at providing members of the general public with the specific terms they need, in their own or another language, to name the objects of daily life, and helping them grasp the meaning of words through illustrations. The dictionary is an ideal tool for both second-language and mother tongue vocabulary building. Grouped together in interlocking categories, the various elements are interdefined. The dictionary is thus organized according to chapters, subjects, specific objects, and features of these objects. Depending on a person's degree of familiarity with a given chapter, the terminology may seem simple or technical. The fundamental goal, however, is to provide non-specialists with a coherent analysis of useful, necessary vocabulary for each subject.

The *Visual Dictionary* is not an encyclopedia, for at least two reasons: rather than describing objects, it names them; in addition, it avoids listing all the objects in a given category. For example, rather than enumerating the various types of trees, it focuses on a typical representative of the category, and examines its structure and individual parts.

It may even less be considered a language dictionary: like other terminological works, it contains no written definitions and covers only nouns and, in particular, noun phrases.

Nor may it be seen as a compendium of specialized vocabularies, as it avoids terminology used only by specialists, focusing instead on more widespread terms—at the risk of being considered simplistic by experts in specific fields.

The *Visual Dictionary* is the first terminology-oriented dictionary to group together in a single volume the thousands of technical and not-so-technical terms most commonly used in our society, where science, technology, and their end products are part of everyday life.

This is the editorial policy that has guided us in creating this dictionary. Consequently, the number of words it contains does not have the same significance as for a language dictionary, for several reasons: in keeping with our editorial policy, we have deliberately chosen to limit the number of words; unlike conventional dictionaries, this work focuses exclusively on nouns, the most significant words in the language, to the exclusion of adjectives, verbs, prepositions, etc.; and finally no one is sure exactly how to count compound terms!

COMPUTER-PRODUCED ILLUSTRATIONS

The illustrations in the *Visual Dictionary* have been created by computer from recent documents and original photographs.

The use of computers has given the illustrations a highly realistic, almost photographic look, while allowing to highlight the essential features corresponding to the vocabulary. The graphic precision of the *Visual Dictionary* is one of the main sources of its excellence as an encyclopedic and lexicographical reference tool.

In addition, thanks to computers, we have been able to improve the accuracy of the lines joining objects to their names, thus enhancing the clarity of the link between words and the things they describe.

CAREFULLY ESTABLISHED VOCABULARY

In creating the *Visual Dictionary*, we have used the method of systematic and comparative terminological research, which is standard practice among professionals who prepare works of this type.

This method comprises several steps, which follow one another in a logical order. The following paragraphs provide a brief description of each of these steps.

Field delimitation

First of all, on the basis of our objectives, we defined the scope and contents of the proposed work.

We began by choosing the chapters we felt it necessary to cover. We then divided each chapter into fields and sub-fields, taking care to abide by our editorial policy and avoiding overspecialization and the temptation to cover all subjects in detail. This step resulted in a working table of contents, the dictionary framework, which guided our subsequent steps and was refined as the work progressed. The detailed table of contents is the end result of this process.

Documentary research

In keeping with our production plan, we assembled pertinent documents likely to provide us with the required information about words and concepts in each subject matter.

In order of reliability, our documentary sources were as follows:

• Articles and books by experts in the various fields, written in their native language, with an acceptable degree of specialization. Translations of such texts provide revealing information about vocabulary usage, but must be used with due caution;

• Technical documents, such as national standards

or the guidelines of the International Standard Organization (ISO), product instructions, technical documents provided by manufacturers, official government publications, etc.;

• Catalogues, commercial texts, advertisements from specialized magazines and major newspapers;

• Encyclopedias, encyclopedic dictionaries, and unilingual language dictionaries;

• Unilingual, bilingual, and multilingual specialized vocabularies and dictionaries. The quality and reliability of these works, however, must be carefully assessed;

• Bilingual and multilingual language dictionaries.

In all, we consulted four to five thousand references. The selected bibliography included in the dictionary indicates only the general documentary sources consulted, and does not include specialized sources.

Sifting through the documents

A terminologist went through the documents for each subject, in search of specific concepts and the words used to express them by different authors and works. Gradually, a framework was established, as the terminologist noted the use of the same term for a given concept from one source to another, or, on the contrary, the use of several terms for the same idea. In the latter case, the terminologist continued his research until he was able to form a well-documented opinion of each competing term. All of this research was recorded, with reference notes.

Creation of a multilingual terminology base

The English terminology is based on standard British usage; the French terminology on the European French norm; and the Spanish terminology on Castilian usage. The norm for German terminology reflects the criteria used by major German publishing houses. Nothing in this dictionary is the result of translation; all languages have been prepared by renowned specialists and verified by major dictionary houses. Because of this, errors frequently found in other multilingual dictionaries based exclusively on a translation approach have been avoided.

Creation of terminological files

The preceding step enabled us to assemble all of the elements for our terminological files.

Each concept identified and defined by an illustration has been paired with the term most frequently used to describe it by the leading authors or in the most reliable sources. Where several competing terms were found in the reference material, following discussion and consensus between the terminologist and the scientific director, a single term was chosen.

Terminological variants

Frequently, several words may be used to designate virtually the same concept.

We dealt with such situations as follows:

• In some cases, a term was used by a single author or appeared only once in our documentary sources. We retained the most frequently used competing term.

• Technical terms are often compound words with or without a hyphen, or several-word expressions. This results in at least two types of terminological variants:

a) The compound technical term may be shortened by the deletion of one or more of its elements, especially where the meaning is clear in the context. The shortened expression may even become the normal term for the concept. In such cases, we retained the compound form, leaving users the freedom to abbreviate it according to the context.

b) An element of the compound term may itself have equivalents (most often synonyms from the commonly spoken language). We retained the most frequently used form.

Variants may stem from the evolution of the language, without terminological consequences. We therefore retained the most contemporary or well-known form.

TERMINOLOGICAL APPROACH

A few comments about the terminological approach, as compared to the lexicographical approach, are in order.

Language dictionaries have a long history. They are familiar reference works, used by most people since early school age, with a well-established, widely known and accepted tradition. We all know how to consult a dictionary and interpret the information it provides—or fails to provide.

Terminological dictionaries are either very recent or intended for a specialized public. There is no solid tradition to guide those who design and produce such works. Although specialists know how to interpret dictionaries pertaining to their own fields, given that they are familiar with the terminology, the same cannot be said for the layperson, who is confused by variants. Finally, whereas language dictionaries have to a certain extent established standard word usage among their users, specialized vocabularies are characterized by competing terms in new fields of specialization.

Users of a reference work such as the *Visual Dictionary* should take into account these elements in assessing this new type of reference tool.

HEADING •
identifies the topic of each page.

SUBHEADING •
indicates the object depicted.

CHAPTER •
of the dictionary is shown in the side
margin on each page.

**To find the correct term for
something, start by turning to the
table of contents, which lists the
dictionary's chapters, headings,
and subheadings, with the first
page reference for each heading.**

COLOUR ILLUSTRATIONS •
realistically depict the objects and
their component parts.

GOTHIC CATHEDRAL
CATHÉDRALE' GOTHIQUE
GOTISCHER DOM''
CATEDRAL' GÓTICA

CATHEDRAL
CATHÉDRALE'
DOM''
CATEDRAL'

ARCHITEKTUR
ARQUITECTURA

ARCHITECTURE
ARCHITECTURE

transept spire
flèche' de transept''
Vierungsturm''
aguja' del transepto''

belfry
clocheton''
Glockenstube'
campanario''

tower
tour'
Turm''
torre'

flying buttress
arc''-boutant
Strebebogen''
arbotante''

pinnacle
pinacle''
Fiale'
pináculo''

abutment
culée'
Widerlager''
estribo''

side chapel
chapelle' latérale
Seitenkapelle'
capilla' lateral

buttress
contrefort''
Strebepfeiler''
contrafuerte''

crossing
croisée'
Vierung'
crucero''

arcade
arcade'
Arkade'
arcada'

pillar
pilier''
Pfeiler''
pilar''

176

PLAN
PLAN^M
GRUNDRISS^M
PLANO^M

Lady chapel
chapelle' axiale
Chorscheitelkapelle'
capilla' axial

apsidiole
absidiole'
Radialkapelle'
capilla' radial

ambulatory
déambulatoire^M
Chorumgang^M
deambulatorio^M

transept
transept^M
Querschiff^M
crucero^M del transepto^M

aisle
collatéral^M
Seitenschiff^M
nave' lateral

porch
porche'
Portal^M
pórtico^M

chevet
chevet^M
Chorhaupt^M
ábside^M

apse
abside'
Hauptapsis'
ábside^M

choir
chœur^M
Chor^M
coro^M

crossing
croisée' du transept^M
Vierung'
crucero^M

nave
nef'
Mittelschiff^M
nave'

• COLOURED TAB
on the edge of the page corresponds
to the chapter as shown in the List of
Chapters. This colour-coding allows
you to find, at a glance, the subject
you are looking for.

ARCHITECTURE
ARCHITECTURE

ARCHITEKTUR
ARQUITECTURA

VAULT
VOÛTE'
GEWÖLBE^N
BÓVEDA'

traverse arch
arc^M-doubleau^M
Schildbogen^M
nervio^M transversal

formeret
arc^M-formeret^M
Gurtbogen^M
imposta' principal

keystone
clé' de voûte'
Schlußstein^M
clave'

lierne
lierne'
Scheitelrippe'
nervio^M secundario

tierceron
tierceron^M
Tierceron^M
tercelete^M

diagonal buttress
arc^M diagonal
Kreuzrippe'
nervio^M diagonal

Lady chapel
chapelle' axiale
Chorscheitelkapelle'
capilla' axial

apsidiole
absidiole'
Radialkapelle'
capilla' radial

choir
chœur^M
Chor^M
coro^M

• DOTTED LINES
link the terms with the objects they
describe.

• INDICATION OF GENDER
f: feminine
m: masculine
n: neuter

• TERMS
are included in the index, with
references to all pages on
which they appear.

**To see an illustration depicting
a term that you know,
consult the index.**

177

DICTIONARIES

- *Gage Canadian Dictionary*. Toronto: Gage Publishing
  Limited, 1983, 1313 p.
- *The New Britannica/Webster Dictionary and Reference Guide*.
  Chicago, Toronto: Encyclopedia Britannica, 1981, 1505 p.
- *The Oxford English Dictionary*. Second edition. Oxford:
  Clarendon Press, 1989, 20 vol.
- *The New Shorter Oxford English Dictionary*, 1994, 2 vols.
- *Concise Oxford Dictionary*, 1995, 1673 p.
- *The Oxford Illustrated Dictionary*. Oxford: Clarendon Press,
  1967, 974 p.
- *Oxford American Dictionary*. Eugene Ehrlich, et al.
  New York, Oxford: Oxford University Press, 1980, 816 p.
- *The Random House Dictionary of the English Language*.
  Second edition. New York: Random House 1983, 2059 p.
- *Webster's Encyclopedic Unabridged Dictionary of the English
  Language*. New York: Portland House, 1989, 2078 p.
- *Webster's Third New International Dictionary*. Springfield:
  Merriam-Webster, 1986, 2662 p.
- *Webster's Ninth New Collegiate Dictionary*. Springfield:
  Merriam-Webster, 1984, 1563 p.
- *Webster's New World Dictionary of American Language*.
  New York: The World Pub., 1953.

ENCYCLOPEDIAS

- *Academic American Encyclopedia*. Princeton:
  Arete Publishing Company, 1980, 21 vol.
- *Architectural Graphic Standards*. Eighth edition.
  New York: John Wiley & Sons, 1988, 854 p.
- *Chamber's Encyclopedia*. New rev. edition. London:
  International Learning System, 1989.
- *Collier's Encyclopedia*. New York: Macmillan Educational
  Company, 1984, 24 vol.
- *Compton's Encyclopedia*. Chicago: F.E. Compton Company,
  Division of Encyclopedia Britannica Inc., 1982, 26 vol.
- *Encyclopedia Americana*. International Edition, Danbury:
  Grolier, 1981, 30 vol.
- *How It Works, The Illustrated Science and Invention
  Encyclopedia*. New York: H.S. Stuttman, 1977, 21 vol.
- *McGraw-Hill Encyclopedia of Science & Technology*.
  New York: McGraw-Hill Book Company, 1982, 15 vol.
- *Merit Students Encyclopedia*. New York: Macmillan
  Educational Company, 1984, 20 vol.
- *New Encyclopedia Britannica*. Chicago, Toronto:
  Encyclopedia Britannica, 1985, 32 vol.
- *The Joy of Knowledge Encyclopedia*. London: Mitchell
  Beazley Encyclopedias, 1976, 7 vol.
- *The Random House Encyclopedia*. New York: Random
  House, 1977, 2 vol.
- *The World Book Encyclopedia*. Chicago: Field Enterprises
  Educational Corporation, 1973.

TABLE OF CONTENTS

TABLE OF CONTENTS

TABLE OF CONTENTS

TABLE OF CONTENTS

TABLE OF CONTENTS

TABLE OF CONTENTS

TABLE OF CONTENTS

TABLE OF CONTENTS

TABLE OF CONTENTS

TABLE OF CONTENTS

TABLE OF CONTENTS

LIST OF CHAPTERS

ASTRONOMIE
ASTRONOMÍA

ASTRONOMY
ASTRONOMIE

CELESTIAL COORDINATE SYSTEM
COORDONNÉES^F CÉLESTES
KOORDINATENSYSTEM^N DER HIMMELSKUGEL^F
COORDENADAS^F ASTRONÓMICAS

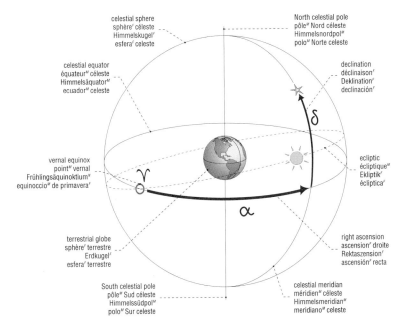

celestial sphere
sphère^F céleste
Himmelskugel^F
esfera^F celeste

North celestial pole
pôle^M Nord céleste
Himmelsnordpol^M
polo^M Norte celeste

celestial equator
équateur^M céleste
Himmelsäquator^M
ecuador^M celeste

declination
déclinaison^F
Deklination^F
declinación^F

vernal equinox
point^M vernal
Frühlingsäquinoktium^N
equinoccio^M de primavera^F

ecliptic
écliptique^M
Ekliptik^F
ecliptica^F

terrestrial globe
sphère^F terrestre
Erdkugel^F
esfera^F terrestre

right ascension
ascension^F droite
Rektaszension^F
ascensión^F recta

South celestial pole
pôle^M Sud céleste
Himmelssüdpol^M
polo^M Sur celeste

celestial meridian
méridien^M céleste
Himmelsmeridian^M
meridiano^M celeste

EARTH COORDINATE SYSTEM
COORDONNÉES^F TERRESTRES
KOORDINATENSYSTEM^N DER ERDKUGEL^F
COORDENADAS^F GEOGRÁFICAS

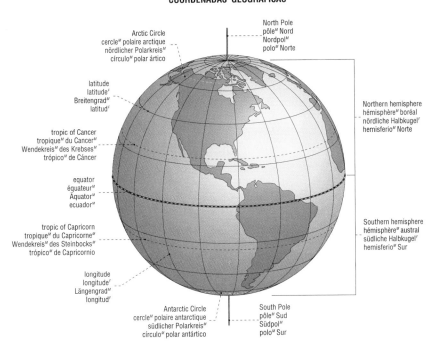

Arctic Circle
cercle^M polaire arctique
nördlicher Polarkreis^M
círculo^M polar ártico

North Pole
pôle^M Nord
Nordpol^M
polo^M Norte

latitude
latitude^F
Breitengrad^M
latitud^F

Northern hemisphere
hémisphère^M boréal
nördliche Halbkugel^F
hemisferio^M Norte

tropic of Cancer
tropique^M du Cancer^M
Wendekreis^M des Krebses^M
trópico^M de Cáncer

equator
équateur^M
Äquator^M
ecuador^M

tropic of Capricorn
tropique^M du Capricorne^M
Wendekreis^M des Steinbocks^M
trópico^M de Capricornio

Southern hemisphere
hémisphère^M austral
südliche Halbkugel^F
hemisferio^M Sur

longitude
longitude^F
Längengrad^M
longitud^F

Antarctic Circle
cercle^M polaire antarctique
südlicher Polarkreis^M
círculo^M polar antártico

South Pole
pôle^M Sud
Südpol^M
polo^M Sur

SOLAR SYSTEM
SYSTÈME^M SOLAIRE
SONNENSYSTEM^N
SISTEMA^M SOLAR

PLANETS AND MOONS
PLANÈTES^F ET SATELLITES^M
PLANETEN^M UND MONDE^M
PLANETAS^M Y LUNAS^F

Phobos
Phobos
Phobos^M
Fobos

Deimos
Deimos
Deimos^M
Deimos

Mars
Mars
Mars^M
Marte

Sun
Soleil^M
Sonne^F
Sol^M

Moon
Lune^F
Mond^M
Luna^F

Earth
Terre^F
Erde^F
Tierra^F

Venus
Vénus
Venus^F
Venus

Mercury
Mercure
Merkur^M
Mercurio

Ganymede
Ganymède
Ganymed^M
Ganimedes

Callisto
Callisto
Callisto^M
Calixto

Europa
Europe
Europa^F
Europa

Io
Io
Io^F
Io

Jupiter
Jupiter
Jupiter^M
Júpiter

ORBITS OF THE PLANETS
ORBITES^F DES PLANÈTES^F
UMLAUFBAHNEN^F DER PLANETEN^M
ÓRBITAS^F DE LOS PLANETAS^M

asteroid belt
astéroïdes^M
Asteroidengürtel^M
zona^F de asteroides^M

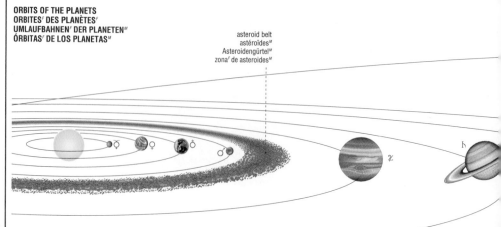

Uranus
Uranus
Uranus*M*
Urano ♅

Pluto
Pluton
Pluto*M*
Plutón ♇

Charon
Charon
Charon*M*
Carón

♄ Saturn
Saturne
Saturn*M*
Saturno

Titan
Titan
Titan*M*
Titán

♆ Neptune
Neptune
Neptun*M*
Neptuno

Triton
Triton
Triton*M*
Tritón

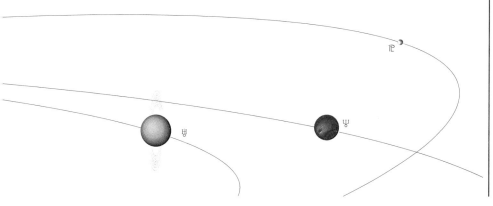

SUN
SOLEIL^M
SONNE^F
SOL^M

STRUCTURE OF THE SUN
STRUCTURE^F DU SOLEIL^M
STRUKTUR^F DER SONNE^F
ESTRUCTURA^F DEL SOL^M

photosphere
photosphère^F
Photosphäre^F
fotosfera^F

spicules
spicule^M
Spikulen^F
espículas^F

chromosphere
chromosphère^F
Chromosphäre^F
cromosfera^F

corona
couronne^F
Korona^F
corona^F

convection zone
zone^F de convection^F
Konvektionszone^F
zona^F de convección^F

radiation zone
zone^F de radiation^F
Strahlungszone^F
zona^F de radiación^F

core
noyau^M
Kern^M
núcleo^M

flare
éruption^F
Flare^M
erupción^F

faculae
facule^F
Fackeln^F
fáculas^F

sunspot
tache^F
Sonnenfleck^M
mancha^F solar

filament
filament^M
Filament^N
filamento^M

prominence
protubérance^F
Protuberanz^F
protuberancia^F

granulation
granulation^F
Granulation^F
granos^M de arroz^M

PHASES OF THE MOON
PHASES^F DE LA LUNE^F
MONDPHASEN^F
FASES^F DE LA LUNA^F

new moon
nouvelle Lune^F
Neumond^M
Luna^F nueva

new crescent
premier croissant^M
Mondsichel^F (zunehmender Mond^M)
creciente^M

first quarter
premier quartier^M
Halbmond^M (erstes Viertel^N)
cuarto^M creciente

waxing gibbous
gibbeuse^F croissante
zunehmender Mond^M
quinto^M octante

MOON
LUNE[F]
MOND[M]
LUNA[F]

LUNAR FEATURES
RELIEF[M] **LUNAIRE**
OBERFLÄCHENFORMATIONEN[F] **DES MONDES**[M]
SUPERFICIE[F] **LUNAR**

bay
baie[F]
Bucht[F]
bahía[F]

cliff
falaise[F]
Felsen[M]
risco[M]

ocean
océan[M]
Ozean[M]
océano[M]

lake
lac[M]
See[M]
lago[M]

sea
mer[F]
Meer[N]
mar[M]

mountain range
chaîne[F] de montagnes[F]
Bergkette[F]
cordillera[F]

crater
cratère[M]
Krater[M]
cráter[M]

wall
rempart[M]
Wand[F]
muro[M]

cirque
cirque[M]
Kar[N]
circo[M]

full moon
pleine Lune[F]
Vollmond[M]
Luna[F] llena

waning gibbous
gibbeuse[F] décroissante
abnehmender Mond[M]
tercer octante

last quarter
dernier quartier[M]
Halbmond[M] (letztes Viertel[N])
cuarto[M] menguante

old crescent
dernier croissant[M]
Mondsichel[F] (abnehmender Mond[M])
menguante[M]

7

SOLAR ECLIPSE
ÉCLIPSE^F DE SOLEIL^M
SONNENFINSTERNIS^F
ECLIPSE^M DE SOL^M

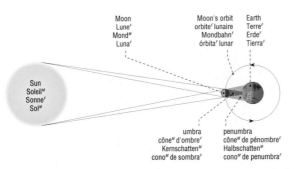

Moon
Lune^F
Mond^M
Luna^F

Moon's orbit
orbite^F lunaire
Mondbahn^F
órbita^F lunar

Earth
Terre^F
Erde^F
Tierra^F

Sun
Soleil^M
Sonne^F
Sol^M

umbra
cône^M d'ombre^F
Kernschatten^M
cono^M de sombra^F

penumbra
cône^M de pénombre^F
Halbschatten^M
cono^M de penumbra^F

TYPES OF ECLIPSES
TYPES^M D'ÉCLIPSES^F
FINSTERNISARTEN^F
TIPOS^M DE ECLIPSES^M

total eclipse
éclipse^F totale
totale Finsternis^F
eclipse^M total

annular eclipse
éclipse^F annulaire
ringförmige Finsternis^F
eclipse^M anular

partial eclipse
éclipse^F partielle
partielle Finsternis^F
eclipse^M parcial

LUNAR ECLIPSE
ÉCLIPSE^F DE LUNE^F
MONDFINSTERNIS^F
ECLIPSE^M DE LUNA^F

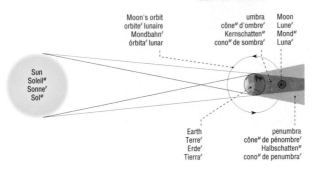

Moon's orbit
orbite^F lunaire
Mondbahn^F
órbita^F lunar

umbra
cône^M d'ombre^F
Kernschatten^M
cono^M de sombra^F

Moon
Lune^F
Mond^M
Luna^F

Sun
Soleil^M
Sonne^F
Sol^M

Earth
Terre^F
Erde^F
Tierra^F

penumbra
cône^M de pénombre^F
Halbschatten^M
cono^M de penumbra^F

TYPES OF ECLIPSES
TYPES^M D'ÉCLIPSES^F
FINSTERNISARTEN^F
TIPOS^M DE ECLIPSES^M

partial eclipse
éclipse^F partielle
partielle Finsternis^F
eclipse^M parcial

total eclipse
éclipse^F totale
totale Finsternis^F
eclipse^M total

SEASONS OF THE YEAR
CYCLE^M DES SAISONS^F
JAHRESZEITEN^F
ESTACIONES^F DEL AÑO^M

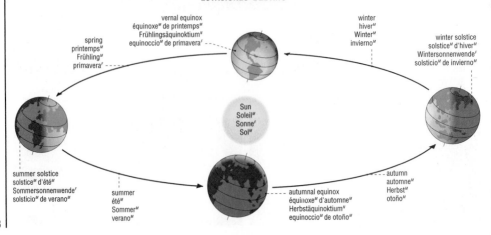

vernal equinox
équinoxe^M de printemps^M
Frühlingsäquinoktium^N
equinoccio^M de primavera^F

winter
hiver^M
Winter^M
invierno^M

spring
printemps^M
Frühling^M
primavera^F

winter solstice
solstice^M d'hiver^M
Wintersonnenwende^F
solsticio^M de invierno^M

Sun
Soleil^M
Sonne^F
Sol^M

summer solstice
solstice^M d'été^M
Sommersonnenwende^F
solsticio^M de verano^M

summer
été^M
Sommer^M
verano^M

autumnal equinox
équinoxe^M d'automne^M
Herbstäquinoktium^N
equinoccio^M de otoño^M

autumn
automne^M
Herbst^M
otoño^M

COMET
COMÈTE^F
KOMET^M
COMETA^M

gas tail
queue^F de gaz^M
Gasschweif^M
cola^F gaseosa

coma
chevelure^F
Koma^F
cabellera^F

nucleus
noyau^M
Kern^M
núcleo^M

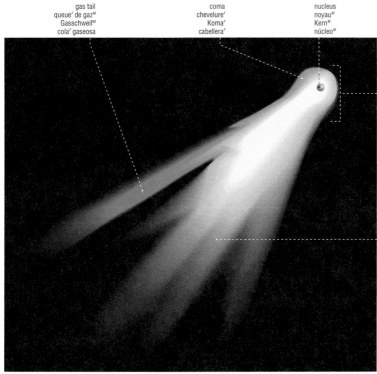

head
tête^F
Kopf^M
cabeza^F

dust tail
queue^F de poussières^F
Staubschweif^M
cola^F de polvo^M

GALAXY
GALAXIE^F
GALAXIE^F
GALAXIA^F

HUBBLE'S CLASSIFICATION
CLASSIFICATION^F DE HUBBLE
HUBBLESCHE KLASSIFIKATION^F
CLASIFICACIÓN^F DE HUBBLE

spiral galaxy
galaxie^F spirale
Spiralgalaxie^F
galaxia^F espiral

elliptical galaxy
galaxie^F elliptique
elliptische Galaxie^F
galaxia^F elíptica

lenticular galaxy
galaxie^F lenticulaire
linsenförmige Galaxie^F
galaxia^F lenticular

irregular galaxy
galaxie^F irrégulière
unregelmäßige Galaxie^F
galaxia^F irregular

barred spiral galaxy
galaxie^F spirale barrée
Balkenspiralgalaxie^F
galaxia^F espiral con barras^F

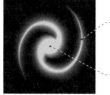

spiral arm
bras^M spiral
Spiralarm^M
brazo^M espiral

nucleus
noyau^M galactique
Kern^M
núcleo^M

CONSTELLATIONS OF THE NORTHERN HEMISPHERE
CONSTELLATIONS*F* DE L'HÉMISPHÈRE*M* BORÉAL
KONSTELLATIONEN*F* DER NÖRDLICHEN HALBKUGEL*F*
CONSTELACIONES*F* EN EL HEMISFERIO*M* BOREAL

1	Fishes Poissons[m] Fische[w] Piscis	**9**	Eagle Aigle[m] Adler[m] Aguila	**25**	Dragon Dragon[m] Drache[m] Dragón
2	Whale Baleine[f] Walfisch[m] Ballena	**10**	Arrow Flèche[f] Pfeil[m] Saeta	**26**	Harp Lyre[f] Leier[f] Lira
3	Ram Bélier[m] Widder[m] Aries	**11**	Swan Cygne[m] Schwan[m] Cisne	**27**	Hercules Hercule Herkules[m] Hércules
4	Triangle Triangle[m] Dreieck[n] Triángulo	**12**	Lizard Lézard[m] Eidechse[f] Lagarto	**28**	Serpent Bearer Ophiucus Schlangenträger[m] Serpentario
		13	Cepheus Céphée Kepheus[m] Cefeo	**29**	Serpent Serpent[m] Schlange[f] Serpiente
		14	Cassiopeia Cassiopée Cassiopeia[f] Casiopea	**30**	Northern Crown Couronne[f] boréale Nördliche Krone[f] Corona Boreal
		15	Giraffe Girafe[f] Giraffe[f] Jirafa	**31**	Herdsman Bouvier[m] Bärenhüter[m] Boyero
		16	Perseus Persée Perseus[m] Perseo	**32**	Berenice's Hair Chevelure[f] de Bérénice Haar[n] der Berenike[f] Cabellera de Berenice
		17	Charioteer Cocher[m] Fuhrmann[m] Cochero	**33**	Hunting Dogs Chiens[m] de chasse[f] Jagdhunde[m] Lebreles
		18	Bull Taureau[m] Stier[m] Tauro	**34**	Great Bear Grande Ourse[f] Großer Bär[m] Osa Mayor
		19	Orion Orion Orion[m] Orión	**35**	Little Lion Petit Lion[m] Kleiner Löwe[m] León Menor
		20	Milky Way Voie[f] lactée Milchstraße[f] Vía Láctea	**36**	Crab Cancer[m] Krebs[m] Cáncer
5	Andromeda Andromède Andromeda[f] Andrómeda	**21**	Twins Gémeaux[m] Zwillinge[m] Géminis	**37**	Little Dog Petit Chien[m] Kleiner Hund[m] Can Menor
6	Pegasus Pégase[m] Pegasus[m] Pegaso	**22**	Lynx Lynx[m] Luchs[m] Lince	**38**	Water Monster Hydre[f] femelle Nördliche Wasserschlange[f] Hidra
7	Little Horse Petit Cheval[m] Füllen[n] Caballito	**23**	Pole Star étoile[f] Polaire Polarstern[m] Estrella Polar	**39**	Lion Lion[m] Löwe[m] Leo
8	Dolphin Dauphin[m] Delphin[m] Delfín	**24**	Little Bear Petite Ourse[f] Kleiner Bär[m] Osa Menor	**40**	Virgin Vierge[f] Jungfrau[f] Virgo

ASTRONOMY
ASTRONOMIE
ASTRONOMIE
ASTRONOMÍA

CONSTELLATIONS OF THE SOUTHERN HEMISPHERE
CONSTELLATIONS^F DE L'HÉMISPHÈRE^M AUSTRAL
KONSTELLATIONEN^F DER SÜDLICHEN HALBKUGEL^F
CONSTELACIONES^F DEL HEMISFERIO^M AUSTRAL

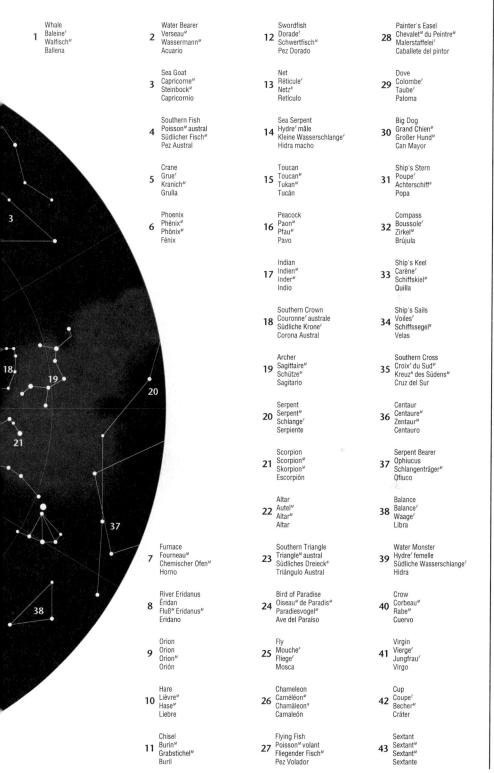

1 Whale
Baleine^f
Walfisch^w
Ballena

2 Water Bearer
Verseau^w
Wassermann^w
Acuario

3 Sea Goat
Capricorne^w
Steinbock^w
Capricornio

4 Southern Fish
Poisson^w austral
Südlicher Fisch^w
Pez Austral

5 Crane
Grue^f
Kranich^w
Grulla

6 Phoenix
Phénix^w
Phönix^w
Fénix

7 Furnace
Fourneau^w
Chemischer Ofen^w
Horno

8 River Eridanus
Éridan
Fluß^w Eridanus^w
Eridano

9 Orion
Orion
Orion^w
Orión

10 Hare
Lièvre^w
Hase^w
Liebre

11 Chisel
Burin^w
Grabstichel^w
Buril

12 Swordfish
Dorade^f
Schwertfisch^w
Pez Dorado

13 Net
Réticule^f
Netz^n
Retículo

14 Sea Serpent
Hydre^f mâle
Kleine Wasserschlange^f
Hidra macho

15 Toucan
Toucan^w
Tukan^w
Tucán

16 Peacock
Paon^w
Pfau^w
Pavo

17 Indian
Indien^w
Inder^w
Indio

18 Southern Crown
Couronne^f australe
Südliche Krone^f
Corona Austral

19 Archer
Sagittaire^w
Schütze^w
Sagitario

20 Serpent
Serpent^w
Schlange^f
Serpiente

21 Scorpion
Scorpion^w
Skorpion^w
Escorpión

22 Altar
Autel^w
Altar^w
Altar

23 Southern Triangle
Triangle^w austral
Südliches Dreieck^v
Triángulo Austral

24 Bird of Paradise
Oiseau^w de Paradis^w
Paradiesvogel^w
Ave del Paraíso

25 Fly
Mouche^f
Fliege^f
Mosca

26 Chameleon
Caméléon^w
Chamäleon^v
Camaleón

27 Flying Fish
Poisson^w volant
Fliegender Fisch^w
Pez Volador

28 Painter's Easel
Chevalet^w du Peintre^w
Malerstaffelei^f
Caballete del pintor

29 Dove
Colombe^f
Taube^f
Paloma

30 Big Dog
Grand Chien^w
Großer Hund^w
Can Mayor

31 Ship's Stern
Poupe^f
Achterschiff^v
Popa

32 Compass
Boussole^f
Zirkel^w
Brújula

33 Ship's Keel
Carène^f
Schiffskiel^w
Quilla

34 Ship's Sails
Voiles^f
Schiffssegel^v
Velas

35 Southern Cross
Croix^f du Sud^w
Kreuz^v des Südens^w
Cruz del Sur

36 Centaur
Centaure^w
Zentaur^w
Centauro

37 Serpent Bearer
Ophiucus
Schlangenträger^w
Ofiuco

38 Balance
Balance^f
Waage^f
Libra

39 Water Monster
Hydre^f femelle
Südliche Wasserschlange^f
Hidra

40 Crow
Corbeau^w
Rabe^w
Cuervo

41 Virgin
Vierge^f
Jungfrau^f
Virgo

42 Cup
Coupe^f
Becher^w
Cráter

43 Sextant
Sextant^w
Sextant^w
Sextante

ASTRONOMICAL OBSERVATORY
OBSERVATOIRE^M ASTRONOMIQUE
STERNWARTE^F
OBSERVATORIO^M ASTRONÓMICO

TELESCOPE
TÉLESCOPE^M
TELESKOP^N
TELESCOPIO^M

prime focus observing capsule
nacelle^F d'observation^F
Primärfokuskabine^F
cabina^F en el foco^M primario

prime focus
foyer^M primaire
Primärfokus^M
foco^M primario

interchangeable end assembly
anneau^M de tête^F amovible
Austauschring^M
anillo^M movible

flat mirror
miroir^M plan rétractable
ebener Spiegel^M
espejo^M plano

horseshoe mount
monture^F en fer^M à cheval^M
Hufeisenmontierung^F
montura^F de herradura^F

hour angle gear
engrenage^M horaire
Stundenwinkelantrieb^M
ángulo^M horario

polar axis
axe^M horaire
Polachse^F
eje^M polar

declination axis
axe^M de déclinaison^F
Deklinationsachse^F
eje^M de declinación^F

hydrostatic pad
patin^M hydrostatique
hydrostatische Lagerung^F
zapata^F hidrostática

primary mirror
miroir^M primaire concave
Hauptspiegel^M
espejo^M primario

telescope base
base^F
Podest^V
base^F del telescopio^M

OBSERVATORY
OBSERVATOIRE^M
STERNWARTE^F
OBSERVATORIO^M

dome shutter
cimier^M mobile
Kuppelspaltabdeckung^F
obturador^M de la cúpula^F

air intake
prise^F d'air^M de ventilation^F
Lufteintritt^M
respiradero^M

arch
arche^F
Bogen^M
arco^M

rotating dome
coupole^F rotative
Drehkuppel^F
cúpula^F giratoria

telescope
télescope^M
Teleskop^N
telescopio^M

crane
treuil^M
Kran^M
grúa^F

airlock
sas^M
Luftschleuse^F
esclusa^F de aire^M

air space
vide^M
Luftspalt^M
cámara^F de vacío^M

windscreen
rideau^M pare-vent^M
Windschutz^M
cortavientos^M

exterior dome shell
enveloppe^F extérieure
äußere Kuppelhülle^F
cubierta^F exterior de la cúpula^F

control room
salle^F de commandes^F
Regieraum^M
sala^F de control^M

rotating dome truck
boggie^M
Kuppelantrieb^M
sistema^M rotativo de la cúpula^F

girder
couronne^F de base^F
Drehschiene^F
estructura^F de base^F

interior dome shell
enveloppe^F intérieure
innere Kuppelhülle^F
cubierta^F interior de la bóveda^F

RADIO TELESCOPE
RADIOTÉLESCOPE^M
RADIOTELESKOP^N
RADIOTELESCOPIO^M

ALTAZIMUTH MOUNTING
MONTURE^F ALTAZIMUTALE
ALTAZIMUTALE MONTIERUNG^F
MONTURA^F ACIMUTAL

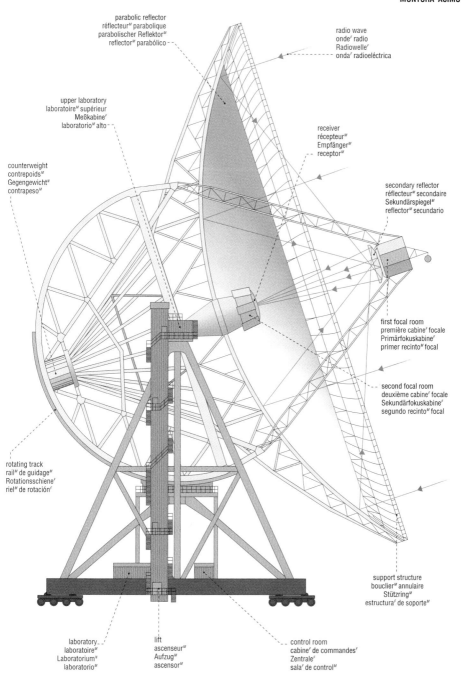

parabolic reflector
réflecteur^M parabolique
parabolischer Reflektor^M
reflector^M parabólico

radio wave
onde^F radio
Radiowelle^F
onda^F radioeléctrica

upper laboratory
laboratoire^M supérieur
Meßkabine^F
laboratorio^M alto

receiver
récepteur^M
Empfänger^M
receptor^M

counterweight
contrepoids^M
Gegengewicht^N
contrapeso^M

secondary reflector
réflecteur^M secondaire
Sekundärspiegel^M
reflector^M secundario

first focal room
première cabine^F focale
Primärfokuskabine^F
primer recinto^M focal

second focal room
deuxième cabine^F focale
Sekundärfokuskabine^F
segundo recinto^M focal

rotating track
rail^M de guidage^M
Rotationsschiene^F
riel^M de rotación^F

support structure
bouclier^M annulaire
Stützring^M
estructura^F de soporte^M

laboratory
laboratoire^M
Laboratorium^N
laboratorio^M

lift
ascenseur^M
Aufzug^M
ascensor^M

control room
cabine^F de commandes^F
Zentrale^F
sala^F de control^M

HUBBLE SPACE TELESCOPE
TÉLESCOPE^M SPATIAL HUBBLE
HUBBLE RAUMTELESKOP^N
TELESCOPIO^M ESPACIAL HUBBLE

aperture door
couvercle^M
Schutzklappe^F
puerta^F

light shield
écran^M protecteur
Tubus^M
protección^F contra la luz^F

antenna
antenne^F
Antenne^F
antena^F

equipment section
case^F d'équipement^M
Geräteteil^M
sección^F para el equipo^M

fine guidance system
système^M de pointage^M fin
Feinnachführungssystem^N
sistema^M afinado de dirección^F

aft shroud
bouclier^M arrière
hinteres Gehäuse^N
recubrimiento^M de la popa^F

solar panel
panneau^M solaire
Sonnensegel^N
panel^M solar

secondary mirror
miroir^M secondaire
Sekundärspiegel^M
espejo^M secundario

primary mirror
miroir^M primaire
Primärspiegel^M
espejo^M primario

scientific instruments
appareils^M scientifiques
Instrumente^N
instrumentos^M científicos

radiator
radiateur^M
Wärmetauscher^M
radiador^M

star tracker
senseur^M stellaire
Nachführsensor^M
rastreador^M de estrellas^F

camera
caméra^F
Kamera^F
cámara^F

PLANETARIUM
PLANÉTARIUM^M
PLANETARIUM^N
PLANETARIO^M

working area
zone^F de manœuvre^F
Wartungsschacht^M
zona^F de trabajo^M

treble loudspeaker
haut-parleur^M d'aigus^M
Hochtonlautsprecher^M
altavoz^M para frecuencias^F altas

zenith
zénith^M
Zenit^M
cenit^M

projection dome
voûte^F de projection^F
Projektionskuppel^F
bóveda^F de proyección^F

midrange loudspeaker
haut-parleur^M de médiums^M
Mitteltonlautsprecher^M
altavoz^M para frecuencias^F medias

auditorium
salle^F de projection^F
Zuschauerraum^M
sala^F de proyección^F

control room
salle^F de contrôle^F
Regieraum^M
cabina^F de control^M

control console
pupitre^M de commandes^F
Schaltpult^N
tablero^M de controles^M

bass loudspeaker
haut-parleur^M de graves^M
Baßlautsprecher^M
altavoz^M para frecuencias^F bajas

planetarium projector
planétaire^M
Planetariumsprojektor^M
proyector^M múltiple

auxiliary projector
projecteur^M auxiliaire
Hilfsprojektor^M
proyector^M auxiliar

SUMMARY

PROFILE OF THE EARTH'S ATMOSPHERE
COUPE^F DE L'ATMOSPHÈRE^F TERRESTRE
PROFIL^N DURCH DIE ERDATMOSPHÄRE^F
CORTE^M DE LA ATMÓSFERA^F TERRESTRE

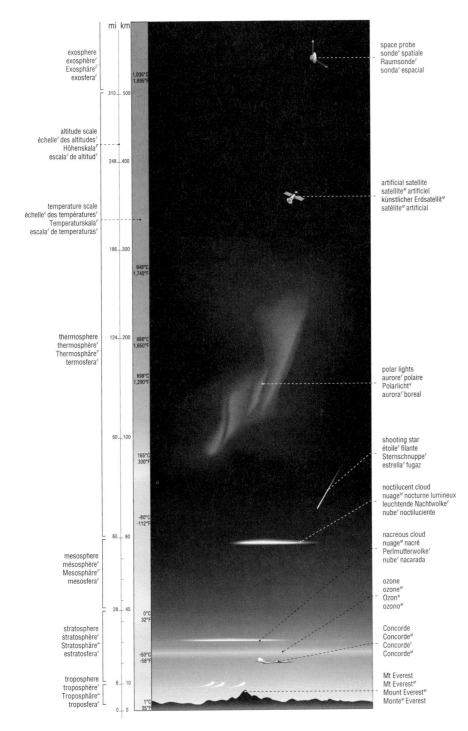

exosphere
exosphère^F
Exosphäre^F
exosfera^F

altitude scale
échelle^F des altitudes^F
Höhenskala^F
escala^F de altitud^F

temperature scale
échelle^F des températures^F
Temperaturskala^F
escala^F de temperaturas^F

thermosphere
thermosphère^F
Thermosphäre^F
termosfera^F

mesosphere
mésosphère^F
Mesosphäre^F
mesosfera^F

stratosphere
stratosphère^F
Stratosphäre^{F-}
estratosfera^F

troposphere
troposphère^F
Troposphäre^{F-}
troposfera^F

mi km
1,035°C
1,895°F
310 500
248 400
186 300
948°C
1,740°F
124 200
898°C
1,650°F
698°C
1,290°F
60 100
165°C
330°F
-80°C
-112°F
50 80
28 45
0°C
32°F
-50°C
-58°F
6 10
1°C
35°F
0 0

space probe
sonde^F spatiale
Raumsonde^F
sonda^F espacial

artificial satellite
satellite^M artificiel
künstlicher Erdsatellit^M
satélite^M artificial

polar lights
aurore^F polaire
Polarlicht^N
aurora^F boreal

shooting star
étoile^F filante
Sternschnuppe^F
estrella^F fugaz

noctilucent cloud
nuage^M nocturne lumineux
leuchtende Nachtwolke^F
nube^F noctiluciente

nacreous cloud
nuage^M nacré
Perlmutterwolke^F
nube^F nacarada

ozone
ozone^M
Ozon^N
ozono^M

Concorde
Concorde^M
Concorde^F
Concorde^M

Mt Everest
Mt Everest^M
Mount Everest^M
Monte^M Everest

CONFIGURATION OF THE CONTINENTS
CONFIGURATION*F* DES CONTINENTS*M*
KONFIGURATION*F* DER KONTINENTE*M*
CONFIGURACIÓN*F* DE LOS CONTINENTES*M*

Arctic
Arctique*F*
Arktis*F*
Ártico*M*

Greenland Sea
mer*F* du Groenland*M*
Grönlandsee*F*
mar*M* de Groenlandia

North America
Amérique*F* du Nord*M*
Nordamerika*N*
América*F* del Norte

Atlantic Ocean
océan*M* Atlantique
Atlantischer Ozean*M*
océano*M* Atlántico

Central America
Amérique*F* centrale
Mittelamerika*N*
América*F* Central

Caribbean Sea
mer*F* des Antilles*F*
Karibisches Meer*N*
mar*M* Caribe

South America
Amérique*F* du Sud*M*
Südamerika*N*
América*F* del Sur

Pacific Ocean
océan*M* Pacifique
Pazifischer Ozean*M*
océano*M* Pacífico

Antarctica
Antarctique*F*
Antarktis*F*
Antártida*F*

North Sea
mer^f du Nord^w
Nordsee^f
mar^w del Norte

Arctic Ocean
océan^w Arctique
Nordpolarmeer^w
océano^w Glacial Artico

Eurasia
Eurasie^f
Eurasien^w
Eurasia^f

Bering Sea
mer^f de Béring
Beringmeer^w
mar^w de Bering

Europe
Europe^f
Europa^w
Europa^f

Asia
Asie^f
Asien^w
Asia^f

China Sea
mer^f de Chine^f
Chinesisches Meer^w
mar^w de la China^f Meridional

Oceania
Océanie^f
Ozeanien^w
Oceanía^f

Africa
Afrique^f
Afrika^w
Africa^f

Indian Ocean
océan^w Indien
Indischer Ozean^w
océano^w Indico

Australia
Australie^f
Australien^w
Australia^z

Caspian Sea
mer^f Caspienne
Kaspisches Meer^w
mar^w Caspio

Black Sea
mer^f Noire
Schwarzes Meer^w
mar^w Negro

Mediterranean Sea
mer^f Méditerranée^f
Mittelmeer^w
mar^w Mediterráneo

Red Sea
mer^f Rouge
Rotes Meer^w
mar^w Rojo

STRUCTURE OF THE EARTH
STRUCTURE^F DE LA TERRE^F
STRUKTUR^F DER ERDE^F
ESTRUCTURA^F DE LA TIERRA^F

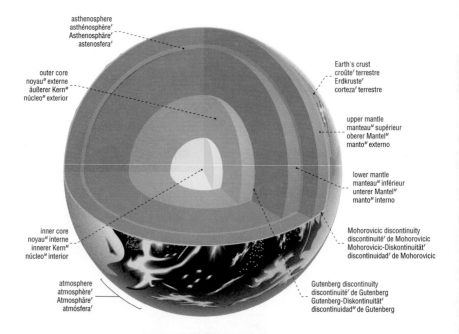

asthenosphere
asthénosphère^F
Asthenosphäre^F
astenosfera^F

outer core
noyau^M externe
äußerer Kern^M
núcleo^M exterior

Earth's crust
croûte^F terrestre
Erdkruste^F
corteza^F terrestre

upper mantle
manteau^M supérieur
oberer Mantel^M
manto^M externo

lower mantle
manteau^M inférieur
unterer Mantel^M
manto^M interno

inner core
noyau^M interne
innerer Kern^M
núcleo^M interior

Mohorovicic discontinuity
discontinuité^F de Mohorovicic
Mohorovicic-Diskontinuität^F
discontinuidad^F de Mohorovicic

atmosphere
atmosphère^F
Atmosphäre^F
atmósfera^F

Gutenberg discontinuity
discontinuité^F de Gutenberg
Gutenberg-Diskontinuität^F
discontinuidad^M de Gutenberg

SECTION OF THE EARTH'S CRUST
COUPE^F DE LA CROÛTE^F TERRESTRE
SCHNITT^M DURCH DIE ERDKRUSTE^F
CORTE^M DE LA CORTEZA^F TERRESTRE

continental shelf
plateau^M continental
Kontinentalschelf^M
plataforma^F continental

sea level
niveau^M de la mer^F
Meeresspiegel^M
nivel^M del mar^M

continental slope
talus^M continental
Kontinentalhang^M
talud^M continental

deep-sea floor
fond^M de l'océan^M
Tiefseeboden^M
lecho^M oceánico

granitic layer
croûte^F granitique
Granitschale^F
capa^F granita

basaltic layer
croûte^F basaltique
Basaltschale^F
capa^F basáltica

Mohorovicic discontinuity
discontinuité^F de Mohorovicic
Mohorovicic-Diskontinuität^F
discontinuidad^F de Mohorovicic

EARTHQUAKE
SÉISME[M]
ERDBEBEN[N]
TERREMOTO[M]

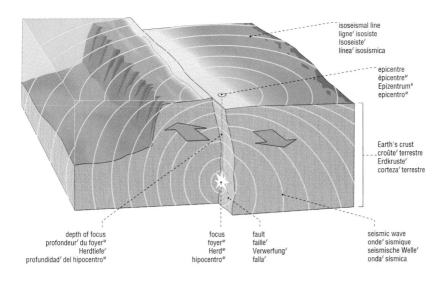

isoseismal line
ligne[F] isosiste
Isoseiste[F]
línea[F] isosísmica

epicentre
épicentre[M]
Epizentrum[N]
epicentro[M]

Earth's crust
croûte[F] terrestre
Erdkruste[F]
corteza[F] terrestre

depth of focus
profondeur[F] du foyer[M]
Herdtiefe[F]
profundidad[F] del hipocentro[M]

focus
foyer[M]
Herd[M]
hipocentro[M]

fault
faille[F]
Verwerfung[F]
falla[F]

seismic wave
onde[F] sismique
seismische Welle[F]
onda[F] sísmica

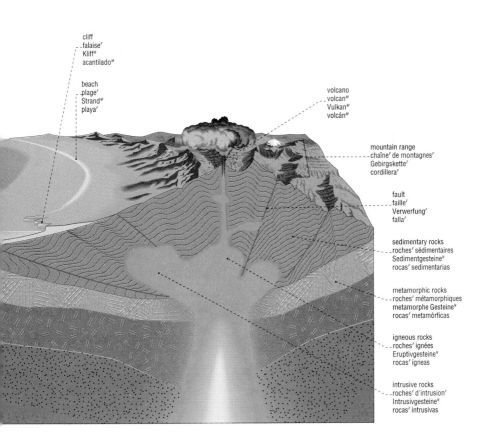

cliff
falaise[F]
Kliff[N]
acantilado[M]

beach
plage[F]
Strand[M]
playa[F]

volcano
volcan[M]
Vulkan[M]
volcán[M]

mountain range
chaîne[F] de montagnes[F]
Gebirgskette[F]
cordillera[F]

fault
faille[F]
Verwerfung[F]
falla[F]

sedimentary rocks
roches[F] sédimentaires
Sedimentgesteine[N]
rocas[F] sedimentarias

metamorphic rocks
roches[F] métamorphiques
metamorphe Gesteine[N]
rocas[F] metamórficas

igneous rocks
roches[F] ignées
Eruptivgesteine[N]
rocas[F] ígneas

intrusive rocks
roches[F] d'intrusion[F]
Intrusivgesteine[N]
rocas[F] intrusivas

CAVE
GROTTE^F
HÖHLE^F
GRUTA^F

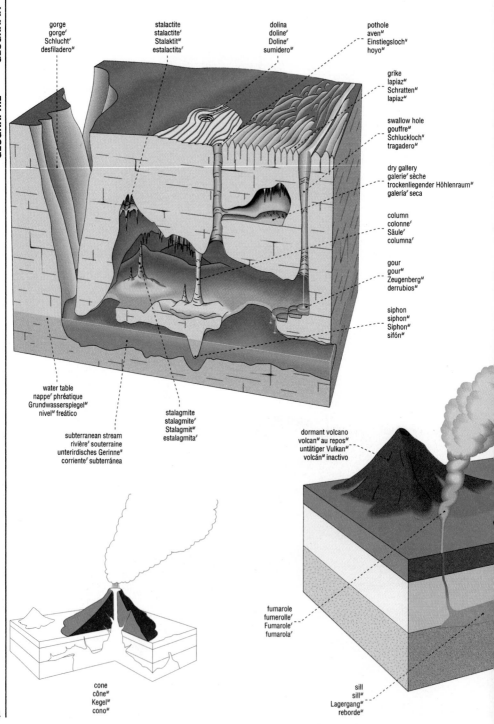

gorge
gorge^F
Schlucht^F
desfiladero^M

stalactite
stalactite^F
Stalaktit^M
estalactita^F

dolina
doline^F
Doline^F
sumidero^M

pothole
aven^M
Einstiegsloch^N
hoyo^M

grike
lapiaz^M
Schratten^M
lapiaz^M

swallow hole
gouffre^M
Schluckloch^N
tragadero^M

dry gallery
galerie^F sèche
trockenliegender Höhlenraum^M
galería^F seca

column
colonne^F
Säule^F
columna^F

gour
gour^M
Zeugenberg^M
derrubios^M

siphon
siphon^M
Siphon^M
sifón^M

water table
nappe^F phréatique
Grundwasserspiegel^M
nivel^M freático

subterranean stream
rivière^F souterraine
unterirdisches Gerinne^N
corriente^F subterránea

stalagmite
stalagmite^F
Stalagmit^M
estalagmita^F

dormant volcano
volcan^M au repos^M
untätiger Vulkan^M
volcán^M inactivo

fumarole
fumerolle^F
Fumarole^F
fumarola^F

cone
cône^M
Kegel^M
cono^M

sill
sill^M
Lagergang^M
reborde^M

VOLCANO
VOLCAN^M
VULKAN^M
VOLCÁN^M

VOLCANO DURING ERUPTION
VOLCAN^M **EN ÉRUPTION**^{F}
VULKAN^M **MIT AUSBRUCHSTÄTIGKEIT**^{F}
VOLCÁN^M **EN ERUPCIÓN**^{F}

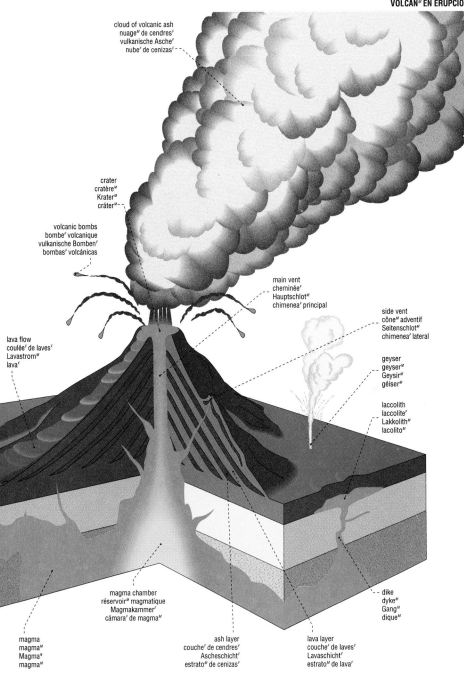

cloud of volcanic ash
nuage^M de cendres^F
vulkanische Asche^F
nube^F de cenizas^F

crater
cratère^M
Krater^M
cráter^M

volcanic bombs
bombe^F volcanique
vulkanische Bomben^F
bombas^F volcánicas

main vent
cheminée^F
Hauptschlot^M
chimenea^F principal

side vent
cône^M adventif
Seitenschlot^M
chimenea^F lateral

lava flow
coulée^F de laves^F
Lavastrom^M
lava^F

geyser
geyser^M
Geysir^M
géiser^M

laccolith
laccolite^F
Lakkolith^M
lacolito^M

magma chamber
réservoir^M magmatique
Magmakammer^F
cámara^F de magma^M

dike
dyke^M
Gang^M
dique^M

magma
magma^M
Magma^N
magma^M

ash layer
couche^F de cendres^F
Ascheschicht^F
estrato^M de cenizas^F

lava layer
couche^F de laves^F
Lavaschicht^F
estrato^M de lava^F

25

GLACIER
GLACIER^M
GLETSCHER^M
GLACIAR^M

bergschrund
rimaye^F
Bergschrund^M
rimaya^F

glacial cirque
cirque^M glaciaire
Kar^N
circo^M glaciar

névé
névé^M
Firn^M
neviza^F incipiente

serac
sérac^M
Serac^M
sérac^M

hanging glacier
glacier^M suspendu
Hängegletscher^M
glaciar^M suspendido

rock basin
ombilic^M
Felsenbecken^N
cuenca^F

rock step
verrou^M glaciaire
Kartreppe^F
escalón^M rocoso

crevasse
crevasse^F
Gletscherspalte^F
grieta^F

glacier tongue
langue^F glaciaire
Gletscherzunge^F
lengua^F glaciar

ground moraine
moraine^F de fond^M
Grundmoräne^F
morrena^F de fondo^M

medial moraine
moraine^F médiane
Mittelmoräne^F
morrena^F central

MOUNTAIN
MONTAGNE^F
BERG^M
MONTAÑA^F

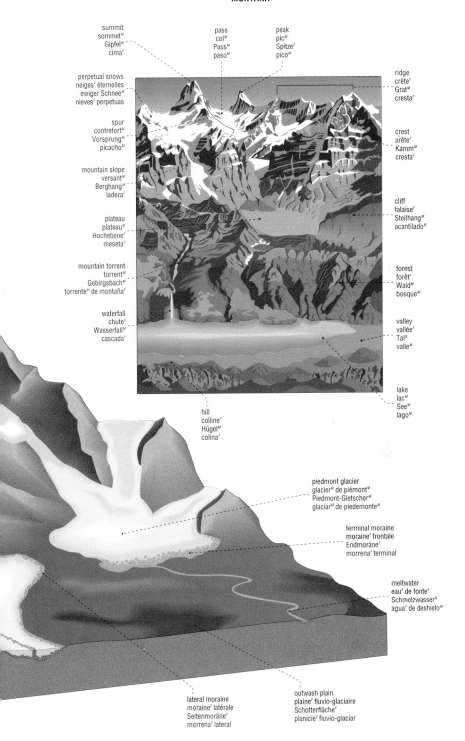

summit
sommet^M
Gipfel^M
cima^F

pass
col^M
Pass^M
paso^M

peak
pic^M
Spitze^F
pico^M

ridge
crête^F
Grat^M
cresta^F

perpetual snows
neiges^F éternelles
ewiger Schnee^M
nieves^F perpetuas

crest
arête^F
Kamm^M
cresta^F

spur
contrefort^M
Vorsprung^M
picacho^M

mountain slope
versant^M
Berghang^M
ladera^F

cliff
falaise^F
Steilhang^M
acantilado^M

plateau
plateau^M
Hochebene^F
meseta^F

forest
forêt^F
Wald^M
bosque^M

mountain torrent
torrent^M
Gebirgsbach^M
torrente^M de montaña^F

waterfall
chute^F
Wasserfall^M
cascada^F

valley
vallée^F
Tal^N
valle^M

lake
lac^M
See^M
lago^M

hill
colline^F
Hügel^M
colina^F

piedmont glacier
glacier^M de piémont^M
Piedmont-Gletscher^M
glaciar^M de piedemonte^M

terminal moraine
moraine^F frontale
Endmoräne^F
morrena^F terminal

meltwater
eau^F de fonte^F
Schmelzwasser^N
agua^F de deshielo^M

lateral moraine
moraine^F latérale
Seitenmoräne^F
morrena^F lateral

outwash plain
plaine^F fluvio-glaciaire
Schotterfläche^F
planicie^F fluvio-glaciar

27

OCEAN FLOOR
FOND*M* **DE L'OCÉAN***M*
MEERESGRUND*M*
LECHO*M* **MARINO**

MID-OCEAN RIDGE
DORSALE*F* **MÉDIO-OCÉANIQUE**
OZEANISCHER RÜCKEN*M*
DORSAL*F* **OCEÁNICA**

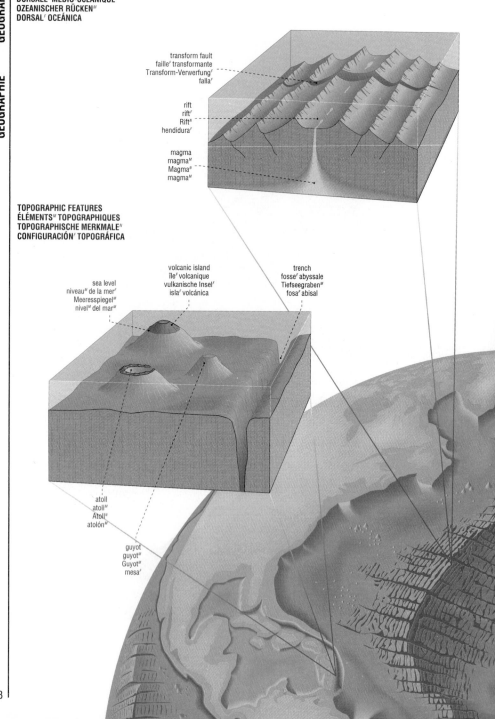

transform fault
faille*F* transformante
Transform-Verwerfung*F*
falla*F*

rift
rift*F*
Rift*N*
hendidura*F*

magma
magma*M*
Magma*N*
magma*M*

TOPOGRAPHIC FEATURES
ÉLÉMENTS*M* **TOPOGRAPHIQUES**
TOPOGRAPHISCHE MERKMALE*N*
CONFIGURACIÓN*F* **TOPOGRÁFICA**

volcanic island
île*F* volcanique
vulkanische Insel*F*
isla*F* volcánica

trench
fosse*F* abyssale
Tiefseegraben*M*
fosa*F* abisal

sea level
niveau*M* de la mer*F*
Meeresspiegel*M*
nivel*M* del mar*M*

atoll
atoll*M*
Atoll*N*
atolón*M*

guyot
guyot*M*
Guyot*M*
mesa*F*

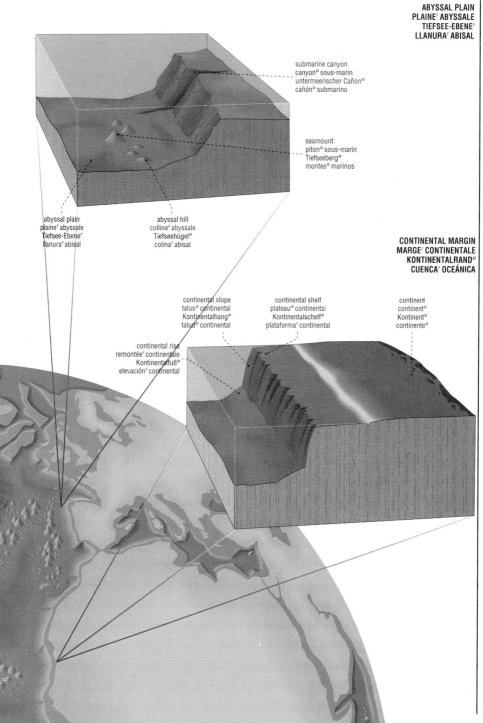

ABYSSAL PLAIN
PLAINE' ABYSSALE
TIEFSEE-EBENE'
LLANURA' ABISAL

submarine canyon
canyon^M sous-marin
untermeerischer Cañon^M
cañón^M submarino

seamount
piton^M sous-marin
Tiefseeberg^M
montes^M marinos

abyssal plain
plaine' abyssale
Tiefsee-Ebene'
llanura' abisal

abyssal hill
colline' abyssale
Tiefseehügel^M
colina' abisal

CONTINENTAL MARGIN
MARGE' CONTINENTALE
KONTINENTALRAND^M
CUENCA' OCEÁNICA

continental slope
talus^M continental
Kontinentalhang^M
talud^M continental

continental shelf
plateau^M continental
Kontinentalschelf^M
plataforma' continental

continent
continent^M
Kontinent^M
continente^M

continental rise
remontée' continentale
Kontinentalfuß^M
elevación' continental

WAVE
VAGUE^F
WELLE^F
OLA^F

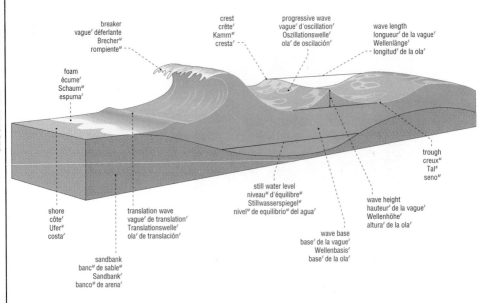

breaker
vague^F déferlante
Brecher^M
rompiente^M

crest
crête^F
Kamm^M
cresta^F

progressive wave
vague^F d'oscillation^F
Oszillationswelle^F
ola^F de oscilación^F

wave length
longueur^F de la vague^F
Wellenlänge^F
longitud^F de la ola^F

foam
écume^F
Schaum^M
espuma^F

trough
creux^M
Tal^N
seno^M

shore
côte^F
Ufer^N
costa^F

translation wave
vague^F de translation^F
Translationswelle^F
ola^F de translación^F

still water level
niveau^M d'équilibre^M
Stillwasserspiegel^M
nivel^M de equilibrio^M del agua^F

wave height
hauteur^F de la vague^F
Wellenhöhe^F
altura^F de la ola^F

sandbank
banc^M de sable^M
Sandbank^F
banco^M de arena^F

wave base
base^F de la vague^F
Wellenbasis^F
base^F de la ola^F

COMMON COASTAL FEATURES
CONFIGURATION^F DU LITTORAL^M
KÜSTENFORMEN^F
CONFIGURACIÓN^F DEL LITORAL^M

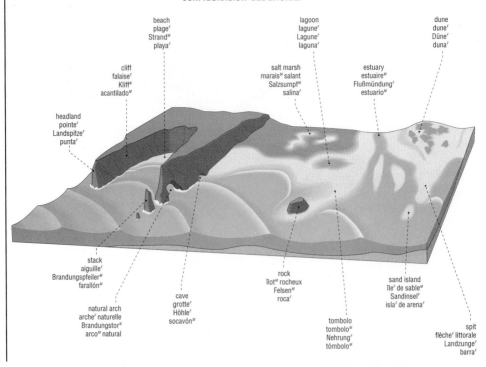

beach
plage^F
Strand^M
playa^F

lagoon
lagune^F
Lagune^F
laguna^F

dune
dune^F
Düne^F
duna^F

cliff
falaise^F
Kliff^M
acantilado^M

salt marsh
marais^M salant
Salzsumpf^M
salina^F

estuary
estuaire^M
Flußmündung^F
estuario^M

headland
pointe^F
Landspitze^F
punta^F

stack
aiguille^F
Brandungspfeiler^M
farallón^M

rock
îlot^M rocheux
Felsen^M
roca^F

sand island
île^F de sable^M
Sandinsel^F
isla^F de arena^F

natural arch
arche^F naturelle
Brandungstor^N
arco^M natural

cave
grotte^F
Höhle^F
socavón^M

tombolo
tombolo^M
Nehrung^F
tómbolo^M

spit
flèche^F littorale
Landzunge^F
barra^F

ECOLOGY
ÉCOLOGIE^F
ÖKOLOGIE^F
ECOLOGÍA^F

STRUCTURE OF THE BIOSPHERE
STRUCTURE^F DE LA BIOSPHÈRE^F
STRUKTUR^F DER BIOSPHÄRE^F
ESTRUCTURA^F DE LA BIOSFERA^F

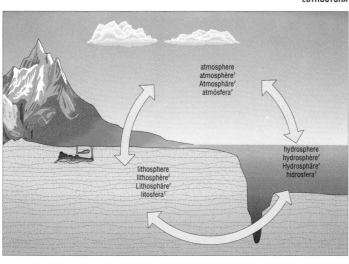

atmosphere
atmosphère^F
Atmosphäre^F
atmósfera^F

hydrosphere
hydrosphère^F
Hydrosphäre^F
hidrosfera^F

lithosphere
lithosphère^F
Lithosphäre^F
litosfera^F

FOOD CHAIN
CHAÎNE^F ALIMENTAIRE
NAHRUNGSKETTE^F
CADENA^F ALIMENTICIA

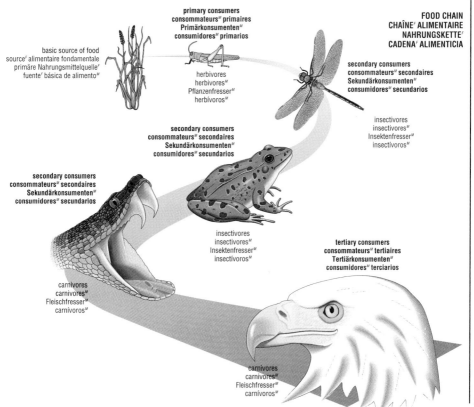

primary consumers
consommateurs^M primaires
Primärkonsumenten^M
consumidores^M primarios

basic source of food
source^F alimentaire fondamentale
primäre Nahrungsmittelquelle^F
fuente^F básica de alimento^M

herbivores
herbivores^M
Pflanzenfresser^M
herbívoros^M

secondary consumers
consommateurs^M secondaires
Sekundärkonsumenten^M
consumidores^M secundarios

insectivores
insectivores^M
Insektenfresser^M
insectívoros^M

secondary consumers
consommateurs^M secondaires
Sekundärkonsumenten^M
consumidores^M secundarios

secondary consumers
consommateurs^M secondaires
Sekundärkonsumenten^M
consumidores^M secundarios

insectivores
insectívores^M
Insektenfresser^M
insectívoros^M

tertiary consumers
consommateurs^M tertiaires
Tertiärkonsumenten^M
consumidores^M terciarios

carnivores
carnivores^M
Fleischfresser^M
carnívoros^M

carnivores
carnivores^M
Fleischfresser^M
carnívoros^M

ECOLOGY
ÉCOLOGIE[F]
ÖKOLOGIE[F]
ECOLOGÍA[F]

POLLUTION OF FOOD ON AND IN THE GROUND
POLLUTION[F] DES ALIMENTS[M] AU SOL[M]
SCHADSTOFFBELASTUNG[F] IM BODEN[M]
CONTAMINACIÓN[F] DE ALIMENTOS[F] EN LA TIERRA[F]

acid precipitation
pluie[F] acide
saurer Niederschlag[M]
precipitación[F] ácida

agricultural pollution
pollution[F] agricole
landwirtschaftliche Verschmutzung[F]
contaminación[F] agrícola

industrial pollution
pollution[F] industrielle
industrielle Verschmutzung[F]
contaminación[F] industrial

POLLUTION OF FOOD IN WATER
POLLUTION[F] DES ALIMENTS[M] DANS L'EAU[F]
SCHADSTOFFBELASTUNG[F] IM WASSER[N]
CONTAMINACIÓN[F] DE ALIMENTOS[M] EN EL AGUA[F]

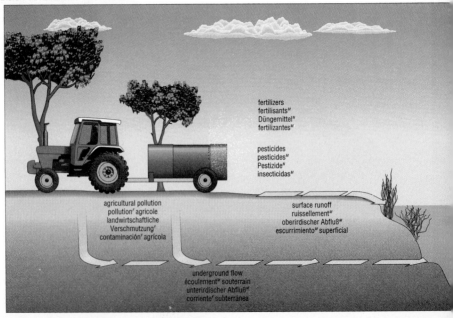

fertilizers
fertilisants[M]
Düngemittel[N]
fertilizantes[M]

pesticides
pesticides[M]
Pestizide[N]
insecticidas[M]

agricultural pollution
pollution[F] agricole
landwirtschaftliche
Verschmutzung[F]
contaminación[F] agrícola

surface runoff
ruissellement[M]
oberirdischer Abfluß[M]
escurrimiento[M] superficial

underground flow
écoulement[M] souterrain
unterirdischer Abfluß[M]
corriente[F] subterránea

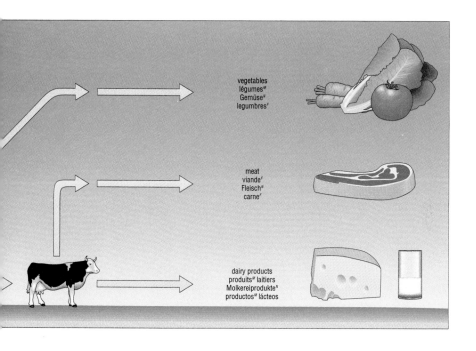

vegetables
légumes^M
Gemüse^N
legumbres^F

meat
viande^F
Fleisch^N
carne^F

dairy products
produits^M laitiers
Molkereiprodukte^N
productos^M lácteos

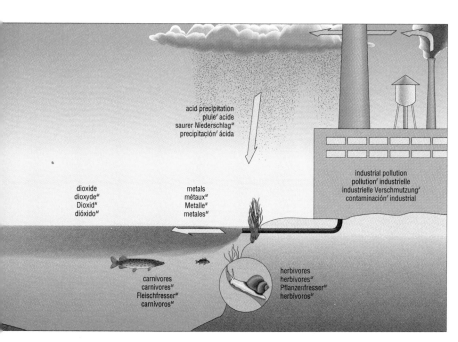

acid precipitation
pluie^F acide
saurer Niederschlag^M
precipitación^F ácida

industrial pollution
pollution^F industrielle
industrielle Verschmutzung^F
contaminación^F industrial

dioxide
dioxyde^M
Dioxid^N
dióxido^M

metals
métaux^M
Metalle^N
metales^M

carnivores
carnivores^M
Fleischfresser^M
carnívoros^M

herbivores
herbivores^M
Pflanzenfresser^M
herbívoros^M

ATMOSPHERIC POLLUTION
POLLUTION*F* DE L'AIR*M*
ATMOSPHÄRISCHE VERSCHMUTZUNG*F*
CONTAMINACIÓN*F* ATMOSFÉRICA

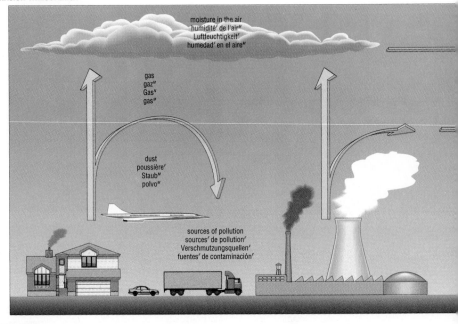

moisture in the air
humidité*F* de l'air*M*
Luftfeuchtigkeit*F*
humedad*F* en el aire*M*

gas
gaz*M*
Gas*N*
gas*M*

dust
poussière*F*
Staub*M*
polvo*M*

sources of pollution
sources*F* de pollution*F*
Verschmutzungsquellen*F*
fuentes*F* de contaminación*F*

HYDROLOGIC CYCLE
CYCLE*M* DE L'EAU*F*
WASSERKREISLAUF*M*
CICLO*M* HIDROLÓGICO

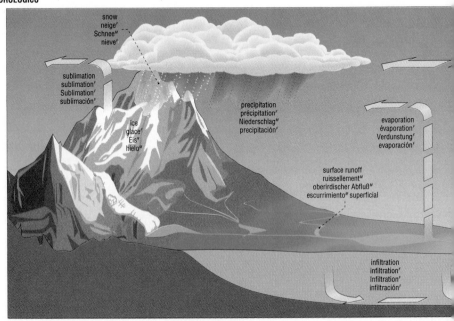

snow
neige*F*
Schnee*M*
nieve*F*

sublimation
sublimation*F*
Sublimation*F*
sublimación*F*

ice
glace*F*
Eis*N*
hielo*M*

precipitation
précipitation*F*
Niederschlag*M*
precipitación*F*

evaporation
évaporation*F*
Verdunstung*F*
evaporación*F*

surface runoff
ruissellement*M*
oberirdischer Abfluß*M*
escurrimiento*M* superficial

infiltration
infiltration*F*
Infiltration*F*
infiltración*F*

action of wind
action^f du vent^M
Wirkung^f des Windes^M
acción^f del viento^M

fallout
retombées^f
Fall-out^M
precipitación^f radiactiva

gas
gaz^M
Gas^N
gas^M

dust
poussière^f
Staub^M
polvo^M

acid precipitation
pluie^f acide
saurer Niederschlag^M
precipitación^f ácida

attack on nature
atteinte^f à la nature^f
Angriff^M auf die Natur^f
acción^f sobre la naturaleza^f

attack on humans
atteinte^f à la personne^f
Angriff^M auf den Menschen^M
acción^f sobre el ser^M humano

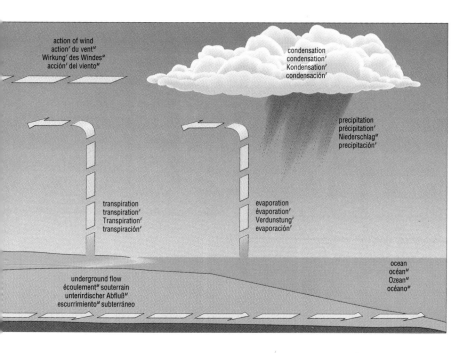

action of wind
action^f du vent^M
Wirkung^f des Windes^M
acción^f del viento^M

condensation
condensation^f
Kondensation^f
condensación^f

precipitation
précipitation^f
Niederschlag^M
precipitación^f

transpiration
transpiration^f
Transpiration^f
transpiración^f

evaporation
évaporation^f
Verdunstung^f
evaporación^f

ocean
océan^M
Ozean^M
océano^M

underground flow
écoulement^M souterrain
unterirdischer Abfluß^M
escurrimiento^M subterráneo

35

PRECIPITATIONS
PRÉCIPITATIONS[F]
NIEDERSCHLÄGE[M]
PRECIPITACIONES[F]

STORMY SKY
CIEL[M] D'ORAGE[M]
STÜRMISCHER HIMMEL[M]
CIELO[M] TURBULENTO

rainbow
arc-en-ciel[M]
Regenbogen[M]
arco[M] iris

cloud
nuage[M]
Wolke[F]
nube[F]

rain
pluie[F]
Regen[M]
lluvia[F]

raindrop
goutte[F] de pluie[F]
Regentropfen[M]
gota[F] de lluvia[F]

lightning
éclair[M]
Blitz[M]
rayo[M]

CLASSIFICATION OF SNOW CRYSTALS
CLASSIFICATION[F] DES CRISTAUX[M] DE NEIGE[F]
KLASSIFIKATION[F] VON SCHNEEKRISTALLEN[M]
CLASIFICACIÓN[F] DE LOS CRISTALES[M] DE NIEVE[F]

plate crystal
plaquette[F]
Plättchen[N]
plaquita[F] de hielo[M]

stellar crystal
étoile[F]
Stern[M]
estrella[F]

column
colonne[F]
Säule[F]
columna[F]

needle
aiguille[F]
Nadel[F]
aguja[F]

spatial dendrite
dendrite[F] spatiale
räumlicher Dendrit[M]
dendrita[F] espacial

mist
brume^F
Dunst^M
neblina^F

fog
brouillard^M
Nebel^M
niebla^F

dew
rosée^F
Tau^M
rocío^M

glazed frost
verglas^M
Rauhreif^M
escarcha^F

capped column
colonne^F avec capuchon^M
bedeckte Säule^F
columna^F con capuchon^M

irregular crystal
cristaux^M irréguliers
irreguläres Aggregat^N
cristales^M irregulares

snow pellet
neige^F roulée
Reif- und Frostgraupel^F
copo^M de nieve^F

sleet
grésil^M
Eiskörnchen^N
cellisca^F

hail
grêlon^M
Hagel^M
granizo^M

37

METEOROLOGY
MÉTÉOROLOGIE^F
METEOROLOGIE^F
METEOROLOGÍA^F

WEATHER MAP
CARTE^F MÉTÉOROLOGIQUE
WETTERKARTE^F
CARTA^F DEL TIEMPO^M

wind direction and speed
direction^F et force^F du vent^M
Windrichtung und -geschwindigkeit^F
dirección^F y velocidad^F del viento^M

barometric pressure
pression^F barométrique
Luftdruck^M
presión^F barométrica

isobar
isobare^F
Isobare^F
isobara^F

depression
dépression^F
Tiefdruckgebiet^N
zona^F de baja presión^F

precipitation area
zone^F de précipitation^F
Niederschlagsgebiet^N
zona^F de precipitación^F

trough
creux^M barométrique
Trog^M
depresión^F barométrica

type of air mass
type^M de la masse^F d'air^M
Luftmasse^F
masa^F de aire^M

anticyclone
anticyclone^M
Hochdruckgebiet^N
zona^F de alta presión^F

STATION MODEL
DISPOSITION^F DES INFORMATIONS^F D'UNE STATION^F
STATIONSMODELL^N
MODELO^M DE CLAVE^F

wind speed
force^F du vent^M
Windgeschwindigkeit^F
velocidad^F del viento^M

type of high cloud
type^M de nuage^M élevé
Art^F der hohen Wolken^F
nube^F alta

type of middle cloud
type^M de nuage^M moyen
Art^F der mittelhohen Wolken^F
nube^F media

station circle
cercle^M de la station^F
Stationskreis^M
círculo^M de la estación^F

air temperature
température^F de l'air^M
Lufttemperatur^F
temperatura^F ambiente

sea-level pressure
pression^F au niveau^M de la mer^F
Luftdruck^M in Meereshöhe^F
presión^F barométrica a nivel^M del mar^M

wind direction
direction^F du vent^M
Windrichtung^F
dirección^M del viento^M

barometric tendency
tendance^F barométrique
Drucktendenz^F
tendencia^F barométrica

present state of weather
état^M présent du temps^M
gegenwärtige Wetterlage^F
estado^M actual del tiempo^M

pressure change
évolution^F de la pression^F
Luftdruckänderung^F
cambio^M de presión^F

temperature of dew point
température^F du point^M de rosée^F
Taupunkttemperatur^F
temperatura^F del punto^M de rocío^M

type of low cloud
type^M de nuage^M bas
Art^F der tiefen Wolken^F
nube^F baja

WIND
VENT^M
WIND^M
VIENTO^M

calm
air^M calme
Windstille^F
calma^F

shaft
hampe^F
Pfeil^F
brisa^F leve

barb
barbule^F
ganzer Querstrich^M
viento^M moderado

wind arrow
flèche^F du vent^M
Windstärkefiederchen^N
flecha^F indicadora de la dirección^F
del viento^M

half barb
demi-barbule^F
halber Querstrich^M
viento^M suave

pennant
fanion^M
Fähnchen^N
tempestad^F

INTERNATIONAL WEATHER SYMBOLS
SYMBOLES^M MÉTÉOROLOGIQUES INTERNATIONAUX
INTERNATIONALE WETTERSYMBOLE^N
SÍMBOLOS^M METEOROLÓGICOS INTERNACIONALES

FRONTS
FRONTS^M
FRONTEN^F
FRENTES^M

surface cold front
front^M froid en surface^F
Kaltfront^F am Boden^M
frente^M frío de superficie^F

surface warm front
front^M chaud en surface^F
Warmfront^F am Boden^M
frente^M cálido de superficie^F

occluded front
front^M occlus
Okklusion^F
frente^M ocluido

upper cold front
front^M froid en altitude^F
Höhenkaltfront^F
frente^M frío en las alturas^F

upper warm front
front^M chaud en altitude^F
Höhenwarmfront^F
frente^M cálido en las alturas^F

stationary front
front^M stationnaire
stationäre Front^F
frente^M estacionario

CLOUD AMOUNT
NÉBULOSITÉ^F
BEDECKUNGSGRAD^M
NUBOSIDAD^F

clear sky
ciel^M clair
wolkenloser Himmel^M
despejado

scattered cloud
ciel^M à nébulosité^F dispersée
Himmel^M mit vereinzelten Wolken^F
nubes^F dispersas

cloudy sky
ciel^M nuageux
bewölkter Himmel^M
medio nublado

very cloudy sky
ciel^M très nuageux
stark bewölkter Himmel^M
muy nublado

overcast sky
ciel^M couvert
bedeckter Himmel^M
completamente nublado

slightly covered sky
ciel^M peu nuageux
heiterer Himmel^M
ligeramente nublado

obscured sky
ciel^M noir
nicht angebbar (z.B. wegen Nebel^M)
obscurecido por contaminación^F

PRESENT WEATHER
MÉTÉORES^M
METEORE^M
FENÓMENOS^M **ATMOSFÉRICOS**

intermittent rain
pluie^F intermittente
Regen^M mit Unterbrechungen^F
lluvia^F intermitente

snow shower
averse^F de neige^F
Schneeschauer^M
chubasco^M de nieve^F

sleet
grésil^M
Schneeregen^M
aguanieve^F

continuous rain
pluie^F continue
anhaltender Regen^M
lluvia^F continua

thunderstorm
orage^M
Gewitter^N
tormenta^F

hail shower
averse^F de grêle^F
Hagelschauer^M
granizada^F

intermittent drizzle
bruine^F intermittente
Sprühregen^M mit Unterbrechungen^F
llovizna^F intermitente

heavy thunderstorm
orage^M violent
starkes Gewitter^N
tormenta^F eléctrica

squall
grain^M
Bö^F
borrasca^F

continuous drizzle
bruine^F continue
anhaltender Sprühregen^M
llovizna^F continua

sandstorm or dust storm
tempête^F de sable^M ou de poussière^F
Sand- oder Staubsturm^M
tormenta^F de polvo^M

freezing rain
pluie^F verglaçante
Eisregen^M
lluvia^F helada

intermittent snow
neige^F intermittente
Schnee^M mit Unterbrechungen^F
nieve^F intermitente

tropical storm
tempête^F tropicale
tropischer Sturm^M
tormenta^F tropical

smoke
fumée^F
Rauch^M
humo^M

continuous snow
neige^F continue
anhaltender Schnee^M
nieve^F continua

hurricane
ouragan^M
Orkan^M
huracán^M

mist
brume^F
Dunst^M
neblina^F

rain shower
averse^F de pluie^F
Regenschauer^M
chubasco^M

slight drifting snow at ground level
chasse-neige^F faible basse
leichtes Schneetreiben^N
acumulación^F baja de nieve^F liviana

fog
brouillard^M
Nebel^M
niebla^F

heavy drifting snow at ground level
chasse-neige^F forte basse
starkes Schneetreiben^N
acumulación^F baja de nieve^F pesada

39

METEOROLOGICAL MEASURING INSTRUMENTS
INSTRUMENTS^M DE MESURE^F MÉTÉOROLOGIQUE
METEOROLOGISCHE MESSINSTRUMENTE^N
INSTRUMENTOS^M DE MEDICIÓN^F METEOROLÓGICA

MEASUREMENT OF SUNSHINE
MESURE^F DE L'ENSOLEILLEMENT^M
MESSUNG^F DES SONNENSCHEINS^M
MEDICIÓN^F DE LA LUZ^F SOLAR

sunshine recorder
héliographe^M
Sonnenscheinautograph^M
actinómetro^M

upper support screw
vis^F de support^M supérieure
obere Halterungsschraube^F
tornillo^M de soporte^M superior

upper sphere clamp
bague^F supérieure de blocage^M de la sphère^F
obere Klemmschraube^F
abrazadera^F superior

sphere support
support^M de sphère^F
Kugelhalterung^F
soporte^M de la esfera^F

glass sphere
sphère^F de verre^M
Glaskugel^F
esfera^F de vidrio^M

card support
porte-cartes^M
Halterung^F für die
Registrierkarten^F
caja^F

lower sphere clamp
bague^F inférieure de blocage^M de la sphère^F
untere Klemmschraube^F
abrazadera^F inferior

latitude scale
échelle^F de latitude^F
Breitengradskala^F
escala^F de latitud^F

check nut
écrou^M de contrôle^M
Kontrollmutter^F
tuerca^F de seguridad^F

lock nut
écrou^M à cabestan^M
Gegenmutter^F
tuerca^F de fijación^F

lower support screw
vis^F de support^M inférieure
untere Halterungsschraube^F
tornillo^M de soporte^M inferior

base plate
base^F
Grundplatte^F
placa^F base^F

levelling screw
vis^F de nivellement^M
Nivellierschraube^F
tornillo^M nivelador

sub-base
socle^M
Sockel^M
pie^M

MEASUREMENT OF RAINFALL
MESURE^F DE LA PLUVIOSITÉ^F
MESSUNG^F DES REGENFALLS^M
MEDICIÓN^F DE LA LLUVIA^F

direct-reading rain gauge
pluviomètre^M à lecture^F directe
selbstschreibender Regenmesser^M
pluviómetro^M de lectura^F directa

rain gauge recorder
pluviomètre^M enregistreur
Niederschlagsschreiber^M
pluviómetro^M

collecting funnel
entonnoir^M collecteur
Sammeltrichter^M
colector^M

measuring tube
éprouvette^F graduée
Meßrohr^M
tubo^M medidor

recording unit
appareil^M enregistreur
Aufzeichnungsgerät^N
unidad^F de grabación^F

tightening band
collier^M de serrage^M
Schelle^F
banda^F de tensión^F

levelling screw
vis^F de réglage^M du niveau^M
Nivellierschraube^F
tornillo^M nivelador

container
récipient^M
Behälter^M
recipiente^M de vertido^M

support
support^M
Ständer^M
soporte^M

collecting vessel
récipient^M collecteur
Auffanggefäß^N
recipiente^M de acumulación^F

MEASUREMENT OF TEMPERATURE
MESURE^F DE LA TEMPÉRATURE^F
MESSUNG^F DER TEMPERATUR^F
MEDICIÓN^F DE LA TEMPERATURA^F

INSTRUMENT SHELTER
ABRI^M MÉTÉOROLOGIQUE
WETTERHÜTTE^F
CASETA^F DE INSTRUMENTOS^M
METEOROLÓGICOS

minimum thermometer
thermomètre^M à minima^M
Minimumthermometer^N
termómetro^M mínimo

maximum thermometer
thermomètre^M à maxima^M
Maximumthermometer^N
termómetro^M máximo

MEASUREMENT OF AIR PRESSURE
MESURE^F DE LA PRESSION^F
MESSUNG^F DES LUFTDRUCKS^M
MEDICIÓN^F DE LA PRESIÓN^F DEL AIRE^M

barograph
baromètre^M enregistreur
Barograph^M
barógrafo^M

mercury barometer
baromètre^M à mercure^M
Quecksilberbarometer^N
barómetro^M de mercurio^M

psychrometer
psychromètre^M
Psychrometer^N
psicrómetro^M

MEASUREMENT OF WIND DIRECTION
MESURE^F DE LA DIRECTION^F DU VENT^M
MESSUNG^F DER WINDRICHTUNG^F
MEDICIÓN^F DE LA DIRECCIÓN^F DEL VIENTO^M

MEASUREMENT OF WIND STRENGTH
MESURE^F DE LA VITESSE^F DU VENT^M
MESSUNG^F DER WINDSTÄRKE^F
MEDICIÓN^F DE LA FUERZA^F DEL VIENTO^M

MEASUREMENT OF HUMIDITY
MESURE^F DE L'HUMIDITÉ^F
MESSUNG^F DER LUFTFEUCHTIGKEIT^F
MEDICIÓN^F DE LA HUMEDAD^F

wind vane
girouette^F
Windfahne^F
veleta^F

anemometer
anémomètre^M
Anemometer^N
anemómetro^M

hygrograph
hygromètre^M enregistreur
Hygrograph^M
higrógrafo^M

MEASUREMENT OF SNOWFALL
MESURE^F DE LA NEIGE^F
MESSUNG^F DES SCHNEEFALLS^M
MEDICIÓN^F DE NEVADAS^F

MEASUREMENT OF CLOUD CEILING
MESURE^F DE LA HAUTEUR^F DES NUAGES^M
MESSUNG^F DER WOLKENHÖHE^F
MEDICIÓN^F DE LA ALTURA^F DE LAS NUBES^F

snow gauge
nivomètre^M
Schneemesser^M
nivómetro^M

theodolite
théodolite^M
Theodolit^M
teodolito^M

alidade
alidade^F
Alhidade^F
alidada^F

ceiling projector
projecteur^M de plafond^M
Wolkenhöhenmesser^M
proyector^M de altura^F máxima

WEATHER SATELLITE
SATELLITE^M MÉTÉOROLOGIQUE
WETTERSATELLIT^M
SATÉLITE^M METEOROLÓGICO

GEOSTATIONARY SATELLITE
SATELLITE^M GÉOSTATIONNAIRE
GEOSTATIONÄRER SATELLIT^M
SATÉLITE^M GEOESTACIONARIO

S-band omnidirectional antenna
antenne^F d'émission^F équidirective
S-Band Rundstrahlantenne^F
antena^F omnidireccional de banda S^F

despun section
dispositif^M contrarotatif
gegengedrehter Teil^M
sección^F antirrotacional

UHF antenna
antenne^F UHF
UHF-Antenne^F
antena^F UHF

S-band high gain antenna
antenne^F d'émission^F à haut gain^M
S-Band hochbündelnde Antenne^F
antena^F de banda S^F de alta ganancia^F

radiometer
radiomètre^M
Radiometer^F
radiómetro^M

magnetometer
magnétomètre^M
Magnetometer^F
magnetómetro^M

sunshade
pare-soleil^M
Sonnenschutzschirm^M
parasol^M

thermal barrier
barrière^F thermique
Wärmeabstrahler^M
muro^M térmico

radial thruster
propulseur^M radial
Radialschubdüse^F
propulsor^M radial

telescope
télescope^M
Teleskop^N
telescopio^M

earth sensor
détecteur^M terrestre
Erdsensor^M
sensor^M terrestre

sun sensor
détecteur^M solaire
Sonnensensor^M
sensor^M solar

hepad
détecteur^M de particules^F
Hepad^M
sensor^M

solar cells
cellules^F solaires
Solarzellen^F
células^F solares

solar array
panneau^M solaire
Solarzellenfläche^F
panel^M solar

solar array drive
commande^F de panneau^M solaire
Steuerung^F der Solarzellenfläche^F
brazo^M del panel^M solar

ORBIT OF THE SATELLITES
ORBITE^F DES SATELLITES^M
UMLAUFBAHN^F DER SATELLITEN^M
ÓRBITA^F DE LOS SATÉLITES^M

geostationary orbit
orbite^F géostationnaire
geostationäre Umlaufbahn^F
órbita^F geoestacionaria

polar orbit
orbite^F polaire
polare Umlaufbahn^F
órbita^F polar

POLAR-ORBITING SATELLITE
SATELLITE^M À DÉFILEMENT^M
POLARUMLAUFENDER SATELLIT^M
SATÉLITE^M DE ÓRBITA^F POLAR

reaction engine
moteur^M-fusée^F
Reaktionstriebwerk^N
motor^M a reacción^F

radiometer
radiomètre^M
Radiometer^N
radiómetro^M

instrument platform
compartiment^M des instruments^M
Instrumentenplattform^F
plataforma^F de instrumentos^M

battery modules
batteries
Batteriemodule^N
módulos^M de batería^F

thermal louvre
volet^M de contrôle^M thermique
Wärmejalousie^F
rejilla^F de control térmico

sun sensor
détecteur^M solaire
Sonnensensor^M
sensor solar

search-and-rescue antennas
capteur^M de signaux^M de détresse^F
Such- und Rettungsantennen^F
antenas^F de exploración^F y rescate^M

infrared sounder
détecteur^M à infrarouge^M
Infrarotsensor^M
resonador^F de rayos^M infrarrojos

earth sensor
détecteur^M terrestre
Erdsensor^M
sensor^M terrestre

earth radiation scanner
scanneur^M de radiations^F terrestres
Erdstrahlungsscanner^M
explorador^M de radiaciones^F
de la tierra^F

microwave scanner
scanneur^M à hyperfréquences^F
Mikrowellenscanner^M
explorador^M de microondas^F

ultraviolet spectrometer
spectromètre^M à ultraviolet^M
Ultraviolett-Spektrometer^N
espectrómetro^M de rayos^M ultravioleta

earth radiation sensor
capteur^M de radiations^F terrestres
Erdstrahlungssensor^M
sensor^M de radiaciones^F de la tierra^F

antenna
antenne^F
Antenne^F
antena^F

S-band antenna
antenne^F d'émission^F
S-Band Antenne^F
antena^F de banda S^F

CLOUDS AND METEOROLOGICAL SYMBOLS
NUAGES^M ET SYMBOLES^M MÉTÉOROLOGIQUES
WOLKEN^F UND METEOROLOGISCHE SYMBOLE^N
NUBES^F Y SÍMBOLOS^M METEOROLÓGICOS

HIGH CLOUDS
NUAGES^M DE HAUTE ALTITUDE^F
HOHE WOLKEN^F
NUBES^F ALTAS

CLOUDS WITH VERTICAL DEVELOPMENT
NUAGES^M À DÉVELOPPEMENT^M VERTICAL
QUELLWOLKEN^F
NUBES^F DE DESARROLLO^M VERTICAL

cirrus
cirrus^M
Zirrus^M
cirros^M

cumulonimbus
cumulo-nimbus^M
Kumulonimbus^M
cumulonimbos^M

cirrocumulus
cirro-cumulus^M
Zirruskumulus^M
cirrocúmulos^M

cirrostratus
cirro-stratus^M
Zirrostratus^M
cirrostratos^M

MIDDLE CLOUDS
NUAGES^M DE MOYENNE ALTITUDE^F
MITTELHOHE WOLKEN^F
NUBES^F MEDIAS

altostratus
alto-stratus^M
Altostratus^M
altostratos^M

altocumulus
alto-cumulus^M
Altokumulus^M
altocúmulos^M

stratocumulus
strato-cumulus^M
Stratokumulus^M
estratocúmulos^M

LOW CLOUDS
NUAGES^M DE BASSE ALTITUDE^F
TIEFE WOLKEN^F
NUBES^F BAJAS

nimbostratus
nimbo-stratus^M
Nimbostratus^M
nimbostratos^M

stratus
stratus^M
Stratus^M
estratos^M

cumulus
cumulus^M
Kumulus^M
cúmulos^M

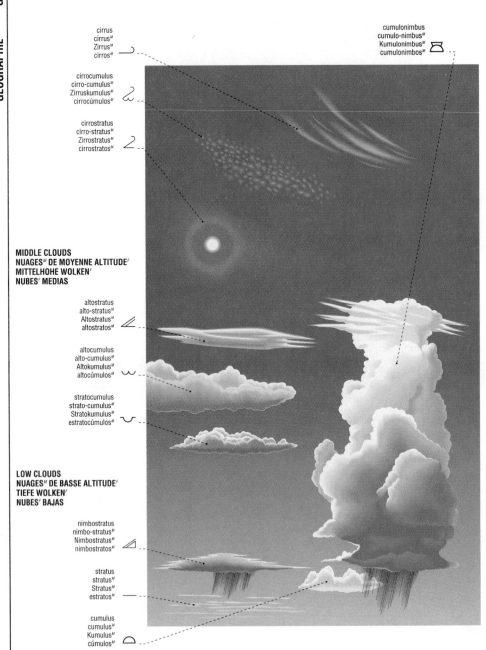

44

CLIMATES OF THE WORLD
CLIMATS*ᴹ* DU MONDE*ᴹ*
KLIMATE*ᴺ* DER WELT*ᶠ*
CLIMAS*ᴹ* DEL MUNDO*ᴹ*

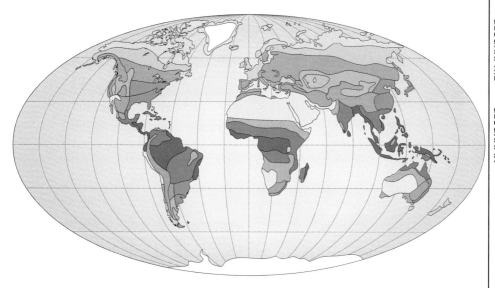

TROPICAL CLIMATES
CLIMATS*ᴹ* TROPICAUX
TROPISCHE KLIMATE*ᴺ*
CLIMAS*ᴹ* TROPICALES

tropical rain forest
forêt*ᶠ* tropicale
tropischer Regenwald*ᴹ*
tropical lluvioso

tropical savanna
savane*ᶠ*
tropische Savanne*ᶠ*
sabana*ᶠ*

steppe
steppe*ᶠ*
Steppe*ᶠ*
estepario

desert
désert*ᴹ*
Wüste*ᶠ*
desértico

CONTINENTAL CLIMATES
CLIMATS*ᴹ* CONTINENTAUX
KONTINENTALKLIMATE*ᴺ*
CLIMAS*ᴹ* CONTINENTALES

dry continental - arid
continental aride
kontinental-trocken - trocken
continental seco-árido

dry continental - semiarid
continental semi-aride
kontinental-trocken - halbtrocken
continental seco-semiárido

TEMPERATE CLIMATES
CLIMATS*ᴹ* TEMPÉRÉS
GEMÄSSIGTE KLIMATE*ᴺ*
CLIMAS*ᴹ* TEMPLADOS

humid - long summer
humide, à été*ᴹ* long
feucht - langer Sommer*ᴹ*
húmedo de verano*ᴹ* largo

humid - short summer
humide, à été*ᴹ* court
feucht - kurzer Sommer*ᴹ*
húmedo de verano*ᴹ* corto

marine
océanique
maritim
marítimo

SUBTROPICAL CLIMATES
CLIMATS*ᴹ* SUBTROPICAUX
SUBTROPISCHE KLIMATE*ᴺ*
CLIMAS*ᴹ* SUBTROPICALES

Mediterranean subtropical
méditerranéen
mediterrane Subtropen*ᶠ*
subtropical mediterráneo

humid subtropical
subtropical humide
feuchte Subtropen*ᶠ*
subtropical húmedo

dry subtropical
subtropical sec
trockene Subtropen*ᶠ*
subtropical seco

POLAR CLIMATES
CLIMATS*ᴺ* POLAIRES
POLARKLIMATE*ᴺ*
CLIMAS*ᴹ* POLARES

polar tundra
toundra*ᶠ*
Polartundra*ᶠ*
tundra*ᶠ*

polar ice cap
calotte*ᶠ* glaciaire
Eiskappe*ᶠ*
hielos*ᴹ* perpetuos

HIGHLAND CLIMATES
CLIMATS*ᴹ* DE MONTAGNE*ᶠ*
HOCHLANDKLIMATE*ᴺ*
CLIMAS*ᶠ* DE ALTA MONTAÑA*ᶠ*

highland climates
climats*ᴹ* de montagne*ᶠ*
Hochlandklimate*ᴺ*
climas*ᴹ* de alta montaña*ᶠ*

SUBARCTIC CLIMATES
CLIMATS*ᴹ* SUBARCTIQUES
SUBARKTISCHE KLIMATE*ᴺ*
CLIMAS*ᶠ* SUBÁRTICOS

subarctic climates
climats*ᴹ* subarctiques
subarktische Klimate*ᴺ*
climas*ᴹ* subárticos

45

DESERT
DÉSERT*M*
WÜSTE*F*
DESIERTO*M*

oasis
oasis*r*
Oase*r*
oasis*M*

palm grove
palmeraie*r*
Palmenhain*M*
palmar*M*

mesa
mésa*r*
Tafelberg*M*
otero*M*

butte
butte*r*
Zeugenberg*M*
hamada*r*

rocky desert
désert*M* de pierres*r*
Steinwüste*r*
desierto*M* rocoso

salt lake
lac*M* salé
Salzsee*M*
laguna*r* salada

sandy desert
désert*M* de sable*M*
Sandwüste*r*
desierto*M* arenoso

crescentic dune
dune*r* en croissant*M*
Sicheldüne*r*
barjana*r*

parabolic dune
dune*r* parabolique
Parabeldüne*r*
duna*r* parabólica

transverse dunes
dunes*r* transversales
Querdünen*r*
dunas*r* paralelas

chain of dunes
cordon*M* de dunes*r*
Dünenzug*M*
cadena*r* de dunas*r*

complex dune
dune*r* complexe
komplexe Düne*r*
duna*r* compleja

longitudinal dunes
dunes*r* longitudinales
Längsdünen*r*
dunas*r* longitudinales

46

CARTOGRAPHY
CARTOGRAPHIE*F*
KARTOGRAPHIE*F*
CARTOGRAFÍA*F*

GEOGRAPHY
GÉOGRAPHIE

GEOGRAPHIE
GEOGRAPHY

GEOGRAPHIE
GEOGRAFÍA

HEMISPHERES
HÉMISPHÈRES*M*
HEMISPHÄREN*F*
HEMISFERIOS*M*

Northern hemisphere
hémisphère*M* Nord
nördliche Hemisphäre*F*
hemisferio*M* Norte

Western hemisphere
hémisphère*M* Ouest
westliche Hemisphäre*F*
hemisferio*M* occidental

Eastern hemisphere
hémisphère*M* Est
östliche Hemisphäre*F*
hemisferio*M* oriental

Southern hemisphere
hémisphère*M* Sud
südliche Hemisphäre*F*
hemisferio*M* Sur

GRID SYSTEM
DIVISIONS*F* **CARTOGRAPHIQUES**
GRADNETZ*N*
SISTEMA*M* **DE REJILLA***F*

lines of latitude
latitude*F*
Breitengrade*M*
líneas*F* de latitud*F*

lines of longitude
longitude*F*
Längengrade*M*
líneas*F* de longitud*F*

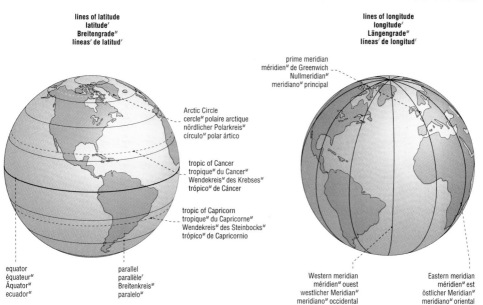

prime meridian
méridien*M* de Greenwich
Nullmeridian*M*
meridiano*M* principal

Arctic Circle
cercle*M* polaire arctique
nördlicher Polarkreis*M*
círculo*M* polar ártico

tropic of Cancer
tropique*M* du Cancer
Wendekreis*M* des Krebses*M*
trópico*M* de Cáncer

tropic of Capricorn
tropique*M* du Capricorne*M*
Wendekreis*M* des Steinbocks*M*
trópico*M* de Capricornio

equator
équateur*M*
Äquator*M*
ecuador*M*

parallel
parallèle*F*
Breitenkreis*M*
paralelo*M*

Western meridian
méridien*M* ouest
westlicher Meridian*M*
meridiano*M* occidental

Eastern meridian
méridien*M* est
östlicher Meridian*M*
meridiano*M* oriental

47

REMOTE DETECTION SATELLITE
SATELLITE^M DE TÉLÉDÉTECTION^F
ERDERKENNUNGSGEODÄTISCHER SATELLIT^M
SATÉLITE^M DE DETECCIÓN^F A LARGA DISTANCIA^F

solar array
panneau^M solaire
Sonnenzellenausleger^M
panel^M solar

stowed configuration
position^F repliée
zusammengefaltete Konfiguration^F
configuración^F de almacenamiento^M

radar antenna
antenne^F radar^M
Radarantenne^F
antena^F del radar^M

launching orbit
orbite^F de lancement^M
Startumlaufbahn^F
órbita^F de lanzamiento^M

support structure
structure^F du support^M
stützende Struktur^F
estructura^F de soporte^M

designated orbit
orbite^F présélectionnée
anvisierte Umlaufbahn^F
órbita^F designada

solar array deployment
déploiement^M des panneaux^M solaires
Entfaltung^F der Sonnenzellenausleger^M
despliegue^M del panel^M solar

solar array extended
panneaux^M solaires déployés
entfalteter Sonnenzellenausleger^M
panel^M solar extendido

GEOGRAPHIE
GEOGRAFÍA

GEOGRAPHY
GÉOGRAPHIE

48

payload module
module^M de charge^F utile
Nutzlastmodul^N
módulo^M del equipo^M

bus module
plate-forme^F
Busmodul^N
módulo^M de la barra^F colectora

RADARSAT SATELLITE
SATELLITE^M RADARSAT
RADARSAT^M
SATÉLITE^M RADARSAT

battery radiator
radiateur^M de batterie^F
Batterie-Radiator^M
radiador^M de la batería^F

zenith S-band antenna
antenne^F de bande^F S au zénith^M
Zenith S-Band-Antenne^F
antena^F cenit^M de banda S^F

thruster
propulseur^M
Korrekturtriebwerk^N
propulsor^M

Earth sensor
détecteur^M d'horizon^M terrestre
Erdsensor^M
sensor^M terrestre

deployment mechanism
mécanisme^M de déploiement^M
Entfaltungsmechanismus^M
mecanismo^M de despliegue^M

X-band antenna
antenne^F en bande^F X
X-Band-Antenne^F
antena^F de banda X^F

remote command antenna
antenne^F de télécommande^F
ferngesteuerte Kommandoantenne^F
antena^F de control^M a larga distancia^F

Sun sensor
détecteur^M solaire
Sonnensensor^M
sensor^M solar

radar antenna deployment
déploiement^M de l'antenne^F radar^M
Entfaltung^F der Radarantenne^F
despliegue^M de la antena^F del radar^M

CARTOGRAPHY
CARTOGRAPHIE*F*
KARTOGRAPHIE*F*
CARTOGRAFÍA*F*

MAP PROJECTIONS
PROJECTIONS*F* CARTOGRAPHIQUES
KARTENNETZENTWÜRFE*M*
PROYECCIONES*F* DEL MAPA*M*

cylindrical projection
projection*F* cylindrique
Zylinderprojektion*F*
proyección*F* cilíndrica

conic projection
projection*F* conique
Kegelprojektion*F*
proyección*F* cónica

interrupted projection
projection*F* interrompue
zerlappte Projektion*F*
proyección*F* interrumpida

plane projection
projection*F* horizontale
Azimutalprojektion*F*
proyección*F* plana

POLITICAL MAP
CARTE^F POLITIQUE
POLITISCHE KARTE^F
MAPA^M POLÍTICO

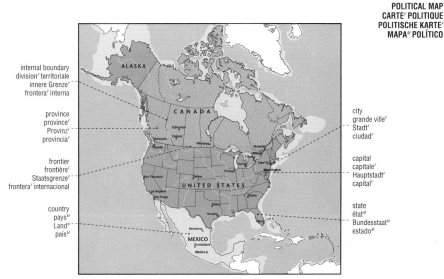

internal boundary
division^F territoriale
innere Grenze^F
frontera^F interna

province
province^F
Provinz^F
provincia^F

frontier
frontière^F
Staatsgrenze^F
frontera^F internacional

country
pays^M
Land^N
país^M

city
grande ville^F
Stadt^F
ciudad^F

capital
capitale^F
Hauptstadt^F
capital^F

state
état^M
Bundesstaat^M
estado^M

PHYSICAL MAP
CARTE^F PHYSIQUE
LANDSCHAFTSKARTE^F
MAPA^M FÍSICO

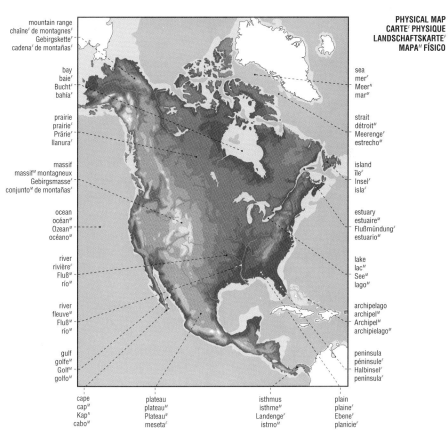

mountain range
chaîne^F de montagnes^F
Gebirgskette^F
cadena^F de montañas^F

bay
baie^F
Bucht^F
bahía^F

prairie
prairie^F
Prärie^F
llanura^F

massif
massif^M montagneux
Gebirgsmasse^F
conjunto^M de montañas^F

ocean
océan^M
Ozean^M
océano^M

river
rivière^F
Fluß^M
río^M

river
fleuve^M
Fluß^M
río^M

gulf
golfe^M
Golf^M
golfo^M

sea
mer^F
Meer^N
mar^M

strait
détroit^M
Meerenge^F
estrecho^M

island
île^F
Insel^F
isla^F

estuary
estuaire^M
Flußmündung^F
estuario^M

lake
lac^M
See^M
lago^M

archipelago
archipel^M
Archipel^M
archipielago^M

peninsula
péninsule^F
Halbinsel^F
península^F

cape
cap^M
Kap^N
cabo^M

plateau
plateau^M
Plateau^N
meseta^F

isthmus
isthme^M
Landenge^F
istmo^M

plain
plaine^F
Ebene^F
planicie^F

CARTOGRAPHY
CARTOGRAPHIE*F*
KARTOGRAPHIE*F*
CARTOGRAFÍA*F*

URBAN MAP
PLAN*M* URBAIN
STADTPLAN*M*
MAPA*M* URBANO

suburbs
banlieue*F*
Vororte*M*
suburbios*M*

ring road
boulevard*M* périphérique
Ringstraße*F*
ruta*F* circular

avenue
avenue*F*
Allee*F*
avenida*F*

city boundary
limite*F* de la ville*F*
Stadtgrenze*F*
límite*M* de la ciudad*F*

park
parc*M*
Park*M*
parque*M*

woods
bois*M*
Wald*M*
bosques*M*

district boundary
limite*F* d'arrondissement*M*
Stadtteilgrenze*F*
límite*M* de distrito*M*

roundabout
rond-point*M*
Kreisverkehr*M*
rotonda*F*

district
arrondissement*M*
Stadtteil*M*
distrito*M*

bridge
pont*M*
Brücke*F*
puente*M*

cemetery
cimetière*M*
Friedhof*M*
cementerio*M*

river
fleuve*M*
Fluß*M*
río*M*

monument
monument*M*
Denkmal*N*
monumento*M*

public building
édifice*M* public
öffentliches Gebäude*N*
edificio*M* público

motorway
autoroute*F*
Autobahn*F*
autopista*F*

railway
chemin*M* de fer*M*
Eisenbahn*F*
línea*F* férrea

railway station
gare*F*
Bahnhof*M*
estación*F* del ferrocarril*M*

boulevard
boulevard*M*
Boulevard*M*
bulevar*M*

street
rue*F*
Straße*F*
calle*F*

ROAD MAP
CARTE*F* ROUTIÈRE
STRASSENKARTE*F*
MAPA*M* DE CARRETERAS*F*

motorway
autoroute*F*
Autobahn*F*
autopista*F*

road
route*F*
Straße*F*
carretera*F*

motorway number
numéro*M* d'autoroute*F*
Autobahnnummer*F*
número*M* de la autopista*F*

road number
numéro*M* de route*F*
Straßennummer*F*
número*M* de la carretera*F*

rest area
aire*F* de repos*M*
Rastplatz*M*
área*F* de descanso*M*

airport
aéroport*M*
Flughafen*M*
aeropuerto*M*

service area
aire*F* de service*M*
Raststätte*F*
área*F* de servicio*M*

point of interest
curiosité*F*
Sehenswürdigkeit*F*
punto*M* de interés

ring motorway
autoroute*F* de ceinture*F*
Umgehungsstraße*F*
carretera*F* de circunvalación*F*

national park
parc*M* national
Nationalpark*M*
parque*M* nacional

secondary road
route*F* secondaire
Nebenstraße*F*
carretera*F* secundaria

scenic route
parcours*M* pittoresque
landschaftlich schöne Strecke*F*
ruta*F* pintoresca

MUSHROOM
CHAMPIGNON^M
PILZ^M
HONGO^M

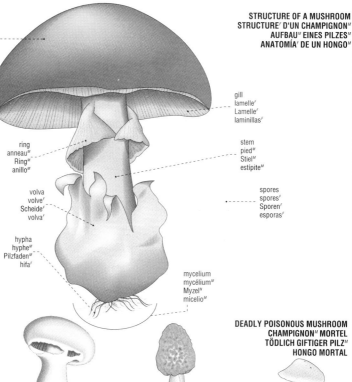

STRUCTURE OF A MUSHROOM
STRUCTURE^F D'UN CHAMPIGNON^M
AUFBAU^M EINES PILZES^M
ANATOMÍA^F DE UN HONGO^M

cap
chapeau^M
Hut^M
sombrero^M

gill
lamelle^F
Lamelle^F
laminillas^F

ring
anneau^M
Ring^M
anillo^M

stem
pied^M
Stiel^M
estípite^M

spores
spores^F
Sporen^F
esporas^F

volva
volve^F
Scheide^F
volva^F

hypha
hyphe^M
Pilzfaden^M
hifa^F

mycelium
mycélium^M
Myzel^N
micelio^M

EDIBLE MUSHROOMS
CHAMPIGNONS^M COMESTIBLES
SPEISEPILZE^M
HONGOS^M COMESTIBLES

truffle
truffe^F
Trüffel^F
trufa^F

cultivated mushroom
champignon^M de couche^F
Zuchtchampignon^M
champiñón^M (Agaricus campestris)

morel
morille^F
Morchel^M
morilla^F (Morchella esculenta)

DEADLY POISONOUS MUSHROOM
CHAMPIGNON^M MORTEL
TÖDLICH GIFTIGER PILZ^M
HONGO MORTAL

destroying angel
amanite^F vireuse
Knollenblätterpilz^M
ángel^M de la muerte^F

royal agaric
oronge^F vraie
Kaiserling^M
amanita^F real

delicious lactarius
lactaire^M délicieux
echter Reizker^M
mízcalo^M (Lactarius deliciosus)

green russula
russule^F verdoyante
grasgrüner Täubling^M
gorroverde^M

POISONOUS MUSHROOM
CHAMPIGNON^M VÉNÉNEUX
GIFTPILZ^M
HONGO^M VENENOSO

chanterelle
chanterelle^F commune
Pfifferling^M
cantarela^F

boletus
cèpe^M
Steinpilz^M
boleto^M

oyster mushroom
pleurote^F en huître^F
Austernseitling^M
sabañón^M

fly agaric
fausse oronge^F
Fliegenpilz^M
amanita^F de las moscas^F

55

TYPES OF LEAF
TYPES^M DE FEUILLES^F
BLATTFORMEN^F
LA HOJA^F SEGÚN SU LIMBO^M

TYPES OF LEAF
TYPES^M DE FEUILLES^F
BLATTFORMEN^F
LA HOJA^F SEGÚN SU LIMBO^M

PFLANZENREICH REINO VEGETAL

PLANT KINGDOM RÈGNE VÉGÉTAL

LEAF MARGIN
BORD^M D'UNE FEUILLE^F
BLATTRAND^M
LA HOJA^F SEGÚN SU BORDE^M

serrate
denté
gesägt
dentada

doubly toothed
doublement denté
doppelt gesägt
bidentada

crenate
crénelé
gekerbt
festoneada

ciliate
cilié
gewimpert
ciliada

entire
entier
ganzrandig
entera

lobate
lobé
gebuchtet
lobulada

LEAF
FEUILLE^F
BLATT^N
HOJA^F

COMPOUND LEAVES
FEUILLES^F COMPOSÉES
ZUSAMMENGESETZTE BLÄTTER^N
HOJAS^F COMPUESTAS

trifoliate
trifoliée
dreizählig
trifoliada

palmate
palmée
handförmig
palmaticompuesta

pinnatifid
pennée
fiederteilig
pinatífida

odd pinnate
imparipennée
unpaarig gefiedert
imparipinada

paripinnate
paripennée
paarig gefiedert
paripinada

SIMPLE LEAVES
FEUILLES^F SIMPLES
EINFACHE BLÄTTER^N
HOJAS^F SIMPLES

orbiculate
arrondie
rund
orbicular

reniform
réniforme
nierenförmig
reniforme

linear
linéaire
lineal
aciculada

peltate
peltée
schildförmig
peltada

hastate
hastée
pfeilförmig
astada

ovate
ovoïde
eiförmig
aovada

cordate
cordée
herzförmig
acorazonada

spatulate
spatulée
spatelförmig
espatulada

lanceolate
lancéolée
lanzettlich
lanceolada

vein
nervure^F secondaire
Blattader^F
nervadura^F secundaria

midrib
nervure^F principale
Mittelrippe^F
nervadura^F principal

stipule
stipule^F
Blattansatz^M
estípula^F

sheath
gaine^F
Blattscheide^F
vaina^F

leaf axil
point^M d'attache^F
Blattachsel^F
axila^F de la hoja^F

petiole
pétiole^M
Blattstiel^M
pecíolo^M

56

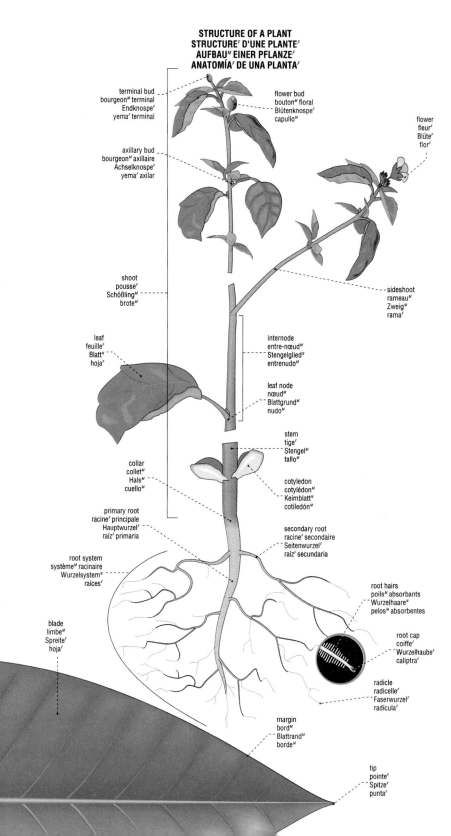

STRUCTURE OF A PLANT
STRUCTURE^F D'UNE PLANTE^F
AUFBAU^M EINER PFLANZE^F
ANATOMÍA^F DE UNA PLANTA^F

terminal bud
bourgeon^M terminal
Endknospe^F
yema^F terminal

flower bud
bouton^M floral
Blütenknospe^F
capullo^M

flower
fleur^F
Blüte^F
flor^F

axillary bud
bourgeon^M axillaire
Achselknospe^F
yema^F axilar

shoot
pousse^F
Schößling^M
brote^M

sideshoot
rameau^M
Zweig^M
rama^F

leaf
feuille^F
Blatt^N
hoja^F

internode
entre-nœud^M
Stengelglied^N
entrenudo^M

leaf node
nœud^M
Blattgrund^M
nudo^M

stem
tige^F
Stengel^M
tallo^M

collar
collet^M
Hals^M
cuello^M

cotyledon
cotylédon^M
Keimblatt^N
cotiledón^M

primary root
racine^F principale
Hauptwurzel^F
raíz^F primaria

secondary root
racine^F secondaire
Seitenwurzel^F
raíz^F secundaria

root system
système^M racinaire
Wurzelsystem^N
raíces^F

root hairs
poils^M absorbants
Wurzelhaare^N
pelos^M absorbentes

blade
limbe^M
Spreite^F
hoja^F

root cap
coiffe^F
Wurzelhaube^F
caliptra^F

radicle
radicelle^F
Faserwurzel^F
radícula^F

margin
bord^M
Blattrand^M
borde^M

tip
pointe^F
Spitze^F
punta^F

PFLANZENREICH
REINO VEGETAL

PLANT KINGDOM
RÈGNE VÉGÉTAL

CONIFER
CONIFÈRE^M
NADELBAUM^M
CONÍFERA^F

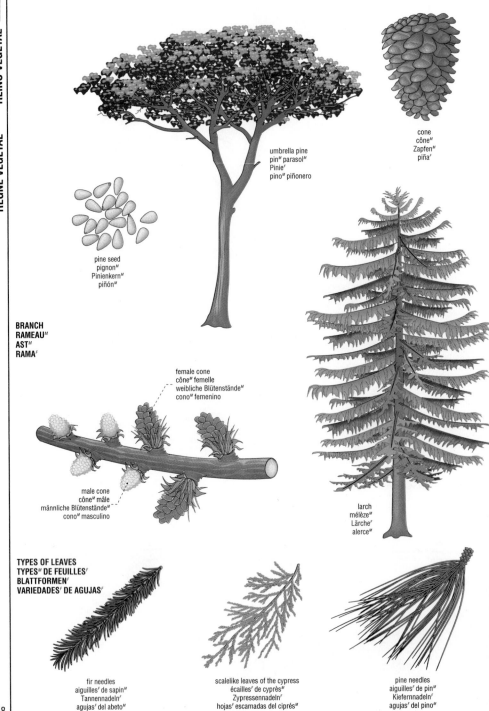

cone
cône^M
Zapfen^M
piña^F

umbrella pine
pin^M parasol^M
Pinie^F
pino^M piñonero

pine seed
pignon^M
Pinienkern^M
piñón^M

BRANCH
RAMEAU^M
AST^M
RAMA^F

female cone
cône^M femelle
weibliche Blütenstände^M
cono^M femenino

male cone
cône^M mâle
männliche Blütenstände^M
cono^M masculino

larch
mélèze^M
Lärche^F
alerce^M

TYPES OF LEAVES
TYPES^M **DE FEUILLES**^F
BLATTFORMEN^F
VARIEDADES^F **DE AGUJAS**^F

fir needles
aiguilles^F de sapin^M
Tannennadeln^F
agujas^F del abeto^M

scalelike leaves of the cypress
écailles^F de cyprès^M
Zypressennadeln^F
hojas^F escamadas del ciprés^M

pine needles
aiguilles^F de pin^M
Kiefernnadeln^F
agujas^F del pino^M

58

STRUCTURE OF A TREE
STRUCTURE^F D'UN ARBRE^M
AUFBAU^M EINES BAUMES^M
ANATOMÍA^F DE UN ÁRBOL^M

TREE
ARBRE^M
BAUM^M
ÁRBOL^M

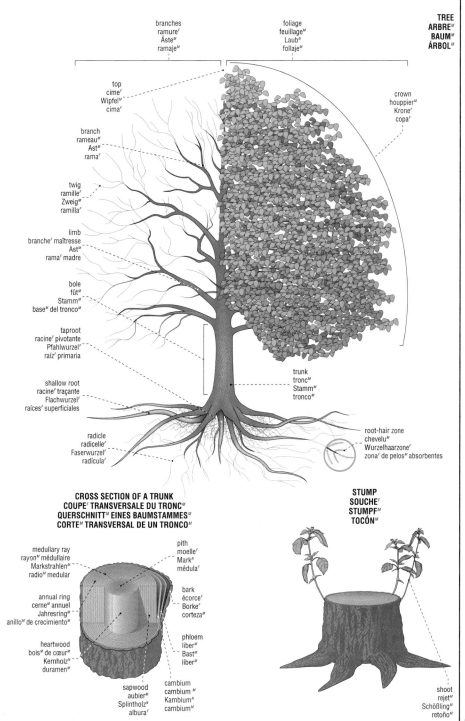

branches
ramure^F
Äste^M
ramaje^M

foliage
feuillage^M
Laub^N
follaje^M

top
cime^F
Wipfel^M
cima^F

crown
houppier^M
Krone^F
copa^F

branch
rameau^M
Ast^M
rama^F

twig
ramille^F
Zweig^M
ramilla^F

limb
branche^F maîtresse
Ast^M
rama^F madre

bole
fût^M
Stamm^M
base^F del tronco^M

taproot
racine^F pivotante
Pfahlwurzel^F
raíz^F primaria

trunk
tronc^M
Stamm^M
tronco^M

shallow root
racine^F traçante
Flachwurzel^F
raíces^F superficiales

radicle
radicelle^F
Faserwurzel^F
radícula^F

root-hair zone
chevelu^M
Wurzelhaarzone^F
zona^F de pelos^M absorbentes

CROSS SECTION OF A TRUNK
COUPE^F TRANSVERSALE DU TRONC^M
QUERSCHNITT^M EINES BAUMSTAMMES^M
CORTE^M TRANSVERSAL DE UN TRONCO^M

STUMP
SOUCHE^F
STUMPF^M
TOCÓN^M

medullary ray
rayon^M médullaire
Markstrahlen^M
radio^M medular

pith
moelle^F
Mark^N
médula^F

annual ring
cerne^M annuel
Jahresring^M
anillo^M de crecimiento^M

bark
écorce^F
Borke^F
corteza^F

heartwood
bois^M de cœur^M
Kernholz^N
duramen^M

phloem
liber^M
Bast^M
líber^M

sapwood
aubier^M
Splintholz^N
albura^F

cambium
cambium^M
Kambium^N
cambium^M

shoot
rejet^M
Schößling^M
retoño^M

STRUCTURE OF A FLOWER
STRUCTURE^F D'UNE FLEUR^F
AUFBAU^M EINER BLÜTE^F
ANATOMÍA^F DE UNA FLOR^F

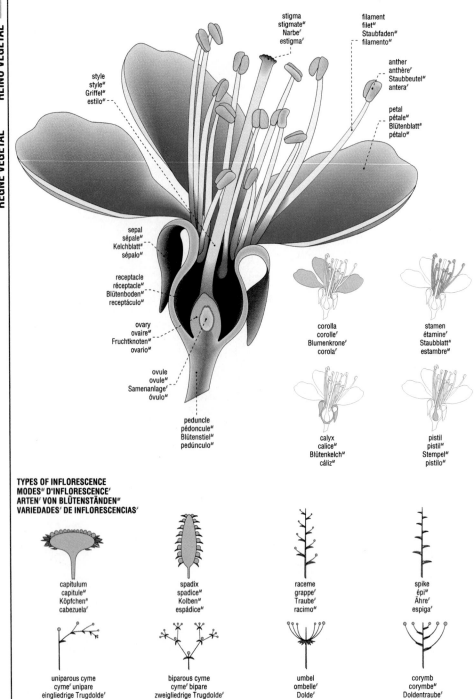

stigma
stigmate^M
Narbe^F
estigma^F

filament
filet^M
Staubfaden^M
filamento^M

anther
anthère^F
Staubbeutel^M
antera^F

style
style^M
Griffel^M
estilo^M

petal
pétale^F
Blütenblatt^N
pétalo^M

sepal
sépale^M
Kelchblatt^N
sépalo^M

receptacle
réceptacle^M
Blütenboden^M
receptáculo^M

ovary
ovaire^M
Fruchtknoten^M
ovario^M

ovule
ovule^M
Samenanlage^F
óvulo^M

peduncle
pédoncule^M
Blütenstiel^M
pedúnculo^M

corolla
corolle^F
Blumenkrone^F
corola^F

stamen
étamine^F
Staubblatt^N
estambre^M

calyx
calice^M
Blütenkelch^M
cáliz^M

pistil
pistil^M
Stempel^M
pistilo^M

TYPES OF INFLORESCENCE
MODES^M D'INFLORESCENCE^F
ARTEN^F VON BLÜTENSTÄNDEN^M
VARIEDADES^F DE INFLORESCENCIAS^F

capitulum
capitule^M
Köpfchen^N
cabezuela^F

spadix
spadice^M
Kolben^M
espádice^M

raceme
grappe^F
Traube^F
racimo^M

spike
épi^M
Ähre^F
espiga^F

uniparous cyme
cyme^F unipare
eingliedrige Trugdolde^F
cima^F unípara

biparous cyme
cyme^F bipare
zweigliedrige Trugdolde^F
cima^F bípara

umbel
ombelle^F
Dolde^F
umbela^F

corymb
corymbe^M
Doldentraube^F
corimbo^M

GRAPE
VIGNE^F
REBE^F
UVA^F

STEPS TO RIPENESS
ÉTAPES^F DE MATURATION^F
STUFEN^F DER REIFE^F
ETAPAS^F DE LA MADURACIÓN^F

flowering
floraison^F
Blüte^F
en flor^F

fruiting
nouaison^F
Fruchtbildung^F
fructificación^F

ripening
véraison^F
Reifeprozeß^M
proceso^M de maduración^F

ripeness
maturité^F
Vollreife^F
maduración^F completa

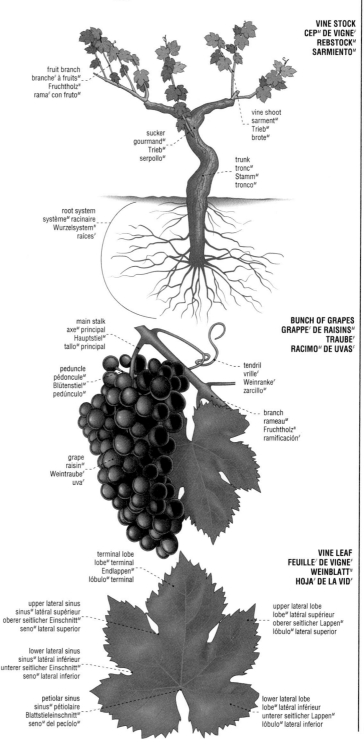

VINE STOCK
CEP^M DE VIGNE^F
REBSTOCK^M
SARMIENTO^M

fruit branch
branche^F à fruits^M
Fruchtholz^N
rama^F con fruto^M

vine shoot
sarment^M
Trieb^M
brote^M

sucker
gourmand^M
Trieb^M
serpollo^M

trunk
tronc^M
Stamm^M
tronco^M

root system
système^F racinaire
Wurzelsystem^N
raíces^F

BUNCH OF GRAPES
GRAPPE^F DE RAISINS^M
TRAUBE^F
RACIMO^M DE UVAS^F

main stalk
axe^M principal
Hauptstiel^M
tallo^M principal

peduncle
pédoncule^M
Blütenstiel^M
pedúnculo^M

tendril
vrille^F
Weinranke^F
zarcillo^M

branch
rameau^M
Fruchtholz^N
ramificación^F

grape
raisin^M
Weintraube^F
uva^F

VINE LEAF
FEUILLE^F DE VIGNE^F
WEINBLATT^N
HOJA^F DE LA VID^F

terminal lobe
lobe^M terminal
Endlappen^M
lóbulo^M terminal

upper lateral sinus
sinus^M latéral supérieur
oberer seitlicher Einschnitt^M
seno^M lateral superior

upper lateral lobe
lobe^M latéral supérieur
oberer seitlicher Lappen^M
lóbulo^M lateral superior

lower lateral sinus
sinus^M latéral inférieur
unterer seitlicher Einschnitt^M
seno^M lateral inferior

petiolar sinus
sinus^M pétiolaire
Blattstieleinschnitt^M
seno^M del pecíolo^M

lower lateral lobe
lobe^M latéral inférieur
unterer seitlicher Lappen^M
lóbulo^M lateral inferior

FLESHY FRUITS: BERRY FRUITS
FRUITS*ᴹ* CHARNUS: BAIES*ᶠ*
FLEISCHIGE FRÜCHTE*ᶠ*: BEERENOBST*ᴺ*
FRUTOS*ᴹ* CARNOSOS: BAYAS*ᶠ*

SECTION OF A BERRY
COUPE*ᶠ* D'UNE BAIE*ᶠ*
QUERSCHNITT*ᴹ* EINER BEERE*ᶠ*
CORTE*ᴹ* DE UNA BAYA*ᶠ*

GRAPE
RAISIN*ᴹ*
WEINTRAUBE*ᶠ*
UVA*ᶠ*

popular terms
termes*ᴹ* familiers
gebräuchliche Bezeichnungen*ᶠ*
términos familiares

scientific terms
termes*ᴹ* techniques
wissenschaftliche Bezeichnungen*ᶠ*
términos técnicos

style
style*ᴹ*
Stylus*ᴹ*
estilo*ᴹ*

skin
peau*ᶠ*
Haut*ᶠ*
piel*ᶠ*

exocarp
épicarpe*ᴹ*
Exokarp*ᴺ*
epicarpio*ᴹ*

pip
pépin*ᴹ*
Kern*ᴹ*
pepita*ᶠ*

seed
graine*ᶠ*
Samen*ᴹ*
semilla*ᶠ*

flesh
pulpe*ᶠ*
Fruchtfleisch*ᴺ*
pulpa*ᶠ*

mesocarp
mésocarpe*ᴹ*
Mesokarp*ᴹ*
mesocarpio*ᴹ*

funiculus
funicule*ᴹ*
Funiculus*ᴹ*
funículo*ᴹ*

stalk
queue*ᶠ*
Stiel*ᴹ*
rabillo*ᴹ*

peduncle
pédoncule*ᴹ*
Stiel*ᴹ*
pedúnculo*ᴹ*

SECTION OF A RASPBERRY
COUPE*ᶠ* D'UNE FRAMBOISE*ᶠ*
QUERSCHNITT*ᴹ* EINER HIMBEERE*ᶠ*
CORTE*ᴹ* DE UNA FRAMBUESA*ᶠ*

seed
graine*ᶠ*
Samen*ᴹ*
semilla*ᶠ*

receptacle
réceptacle*ᴹ*
Blütenboden*ᴹ*
receptáculo*ᴹ*

drupelet
drupéole*ᶠ*
Steinfrüchtchen*ᴺ*
drupéolo*ᴹ*

sepal
sépale*ᴹ*
Kelchblatt*ᴺ*
sépalo*ᴹ*

peduncle
pédoncule*ᴹ*
Stiel*ᴹ*
pedúnculo*ᴹ*

SECTION OF A STRAWBERRY
COUPE*ᶠ* D'UNE FRAISE*ᶠ*
QUERSCHNITT*ᴹ* EINER ERDBEERE*ᶠ*
CORTE*ᴹ* DE UNA FRESA*ᶠ*

receptacle
réceptacle*ᴹ*
Blütenboden*ᴹ*
receptáculo*ᴹ*

peduncle
pédoncule*ᴹ*
Stiel*ᴹ*
pedúnculo*ᴹ*

achene
akène*ᴹ*
Samen*ᴹ*
aquenio*ᴹ*

flesh
pulpe*ᶠ*
Fruchtfleisch*ᴺ*
pulpa*ᶠ*

epicalyx
calicule*ᴹ*
Außenkelch*ᴹ*
calículo*ᴹ*

calyx
calice*ᴹ*
Kelch*ᴹ*
cáliz*ᴹ*

PRINCIPAL TYPES OF BERRY
PRINCIPALES VARIÉTÉS*ᶠ* DE BAIES*ᶠ*
DIE WICHTIGSTEN BEERENARTEN*ᶠ*
PRINCIPALES VARIEDADES*ᶠ* DE BAYAS*ᶠ*

blackcurrant
cassis*ᴹ*
schwarze Johannisbeere*ᶠ*
grosella*ᶠ* negra

redcurrant
groseille*ᶠ* à grappes*ᶠ*
Johannisbeere*ᶠ*
grosella*ᶠ*

grape
raisin*ᴹ*
Weintraube*ᶠ*
uva*ᶠ*

gooseberry
groseille*ᶠ* à maquereau*ᴹ*
Stachelbeere*ᶠ*
grosella*ᶠ* espinosa

blueberry
myrtille*ᶠ*
Heidelbeere*ᶠ*
arándano*ᴹ*

huckleberry
airelle*ᶠ*
amerikanische Heidelbeere*ᶠ*
ráspano*ᴹ*

cranberry
canneberge*ᶠ*
Preiselbeere*ᶠ*
arándano*ᴹ* agrio

FLESHY STONE FRUITS
FRUITS^M CHARNUS À NOYAU^M
STEINOBST^N
FRUTOS^M CARNOSOS CON HUESO^M

PEACH
PÊCHE^F
PFIRSICH^M
MELOCOTÓN^M

SECTION OF A STONE FRUIT
COUPE^F D'UN FRUIT^M À NOYAU^M
QUERSCHNITT^M EINER STEINFRUCHT^F
CORTE^M DE UN FRUTO^M CARNOSO CON HUESO^M

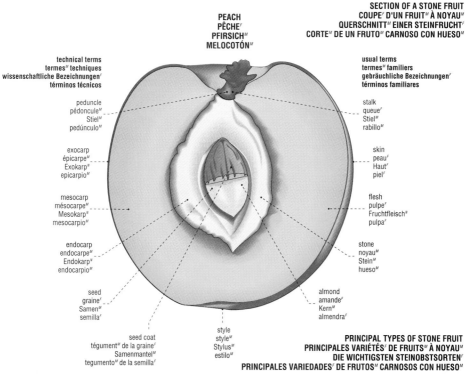

technical terms
termes^M techniques
wissenschaftliche Bezeichnungen^F
términos técnicos

usual terms
termes^M familiers
gebräuchliche Bezeichnungen^F
términos familiares

peduncle
pédoncule^M
Stiel^M
pedúnculo^M

stalk
queue^F
Stiel^M
rabillo^M

exocarp
épicarpe^M
Exokarp^N
epicarpio^M

skin
peau^F
Haut^F
piel^F

mesocarp
mésocarpe^M
Mesokarp^N
mesocarpio^M

flesh
pulpe^F
Fruchtfleisch^N
pulpa^F

endocarp
endocarpe^M
Endokarp^N
endocarpio^M

stone
noyau^M
Stein^M
hueso^M

seed
graine^F
Samen^M
semilla^F

almond
amande^F
Kern^M
almendra^F

seed coat
tégument^M de la graine^F
Samenmantel^M
tegumento^M de la semilla^F

style
style^M
Stylus^M
estilo^M

PRINCIPAL TYPES OF STONE FRUIT
PRINCIPALES VARIÉTÉS^F DE FRUITS^M À NOYAU^M
DIE WICHTIGSTEN STEINOBSTSORTEN^F
PRINCIPALES VARIEDADES^F DE FRUTOS^M CARNOSOS CON HUESO^M

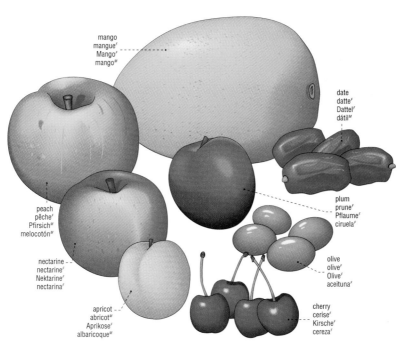

mango
mangue^F
Mango^F
mango^M

date
datte^F
Dattel^F
dátil^M

plum
prune^F
Pflaume^F
ciruela^F

peach
pêche^F
Pfirsich^M
melocotón^M

olive
olive^F
Olive^F
aceituna^F

nectarine
nectarine^F
Nektarine^F
nectarina^F

apricot
abricot^M
Aprikose^F
albaricoque^M

cherry
cerise^F
Kirsche^F
cereza^F

FLESHY POMES
FRUITS*M* CHARNUS À PÉPINS*M*
KERNOBST*N*
FRUTOS*M* CARNOSOS CON SEMILLAS*F*

SECTION OF A POME
COUPE*F* D'UN FRUIT*M* À PÉPINS*M*
QUERSCHNITT*M* EINER KERNFRUCHT*F*
CORTE*M* DE UN FRUTO*M* CARNOSO CON SEMILLAS*F*

APPLE
POMME*F*
APFEL*M*
MANZANA*F*

scientific terms
termes*M* techniques
wissenschaftliche Bezeichnungen*F*
términos técnicos

popular terms
termes*M* familiers
gebräuchliche Bezeichnungen*F*
términos familiares

loculus
loge*F*
Fruchtknotenfach*F*
lóculo*M*

peduncle
pédoncule*M*
Stiel*M*
pedúnculo*M*

stalk
queue*F*
Stiel*M*
rabillo*M*

mesocarp
mésocarpe*M*
Mesokarp*M*
mesocarpio*M*

flesh
pulpe*F*
Fruchtfleisch*N*
pulpa*F*

seed
graine*F*
Samen*M*
semilla*F*

pip
pépin*M*
Kern*M*
pepita*F*

endocarp
endocarpe*M*
Endokarp*N*
endocarpio*M*

core
cœur*M*
Kerngehäuse*N*
corazón*M*

exocarp
épicarpe*M*
Exokarp*N*
epicarpio*M*

skin
peau*F*
Schale*F*
piel*F*

style
style*M*
Stylus*M*
estilo*M*

stamen
étamine*F*
Stamen*N*
estambre*M*

sepal
sépale*M*
Sepalum*N*
sépalo*M*

PRINCIPAL TYPES OF POME
PRINCIPALES VARIÉTÉS*F* DE FRUITS*M* À PÉPINS*M*
DIE WICHTIGSTEN KERNOBSTSORTEN*F*
PRINCIPALES VARIEDADES*F* DE FRUTOS*M*
CARNOSOS CON SEMILLAS*F*

pear
poire*F*
Birne*F*
pera*F*

quince
coing*M*
Quitte*F*
membrillo*M*

apple
pomme*F*
Apfel*M*
manzana*F*

medlar
nèfle*F* du Japon*M*
Mispel*M*
níspero*M*

FLESHY FRUITS: CITRUS FRUITS
FRUITS^M CHARNUS: AGRUMES^M
FLEISCHIGE FRÜCHTE^F: ZITRUSFRÜCHTE^F
FRUTOS^M CARNOSOS: CÍTRICOS^M

ORANGE
ORANGE^F
ORANGE^F
NARANJA^F

SECTION OF A CITRUS FRUIT
COUPE^F D'UN AGRUME^M
QUERSCHNITT^M EINER ZITRUSFRUCHT^F
CORTE^M DE UN CÍTRICO^M

scientific terms
termes^M techniques
wissenschaftliche Bezeichnungen^F
términos técnicos

popular terms
termes^M familiers
gebräuchliche Bezeichnungen^F
términos familiares

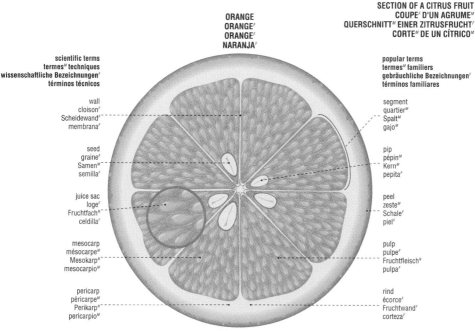

wall
cloison^F
Scheidewand^F
membrana^F

segment
quartier^M
Spalt^M
gajo^M

seed
graine^F
Samen^M
semilla^F

pip
pépin^M
Kern^M
pepita^F

juice sac
loge^F
Fruchtfach^N
celdilla^F

peel
zeste^M
Schale^F
piel^F

mesocarp
mésocarpe^M
Mesokarp^N
mesocarpio^M

pulp
pulpe^F
Fruchtfleisch^N
pulpa^F

pericarp
péricarpe^M
Perikarp^N
pericarpio^M

rind
écorce^F
Fruchtwand^F
corteza^F

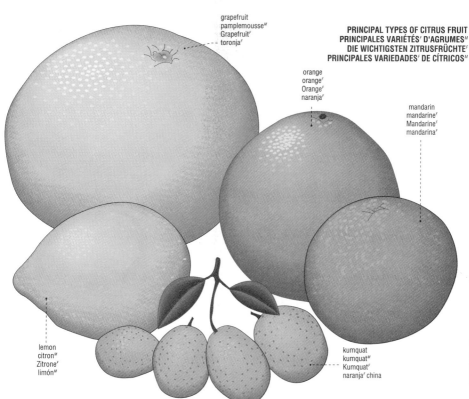

grapefruit
pamplemousse^M
Grapefruit^F
toronja^F

PRINCIPAL TYPES OF CITRUS FRUIT
PRINCIPALES VARIÉTÉS^F D'AGRUMES^M
DIE WICHTIGSTEN ZITRUSFRÜCHTE^F
PRINCIPALES VARIEDADES^F DE CÍTRICOS^M

orange
orange^F
Orange^F
naranja^F

mandarin
mandarine^F
Mandarine^F
mandarina^F

lemon
citron^M
Zitrone^F
limón^M

kumquat
kumquat^M
Kumquat^F
naranja^F china

65

DRY FRUITS: NUTS
FRUITS^M SECS: NOIX^F
TROCKENFRÜCHTE^F: NÜSS^F
FRUTOS^M SECOS: OLEAGINOSOS

SECTION OF A HAZELNUT
COUPE^F D'UNE NOISETTE^F
LÄNGSSCHNITT^M EINER HASELNUSS^F
CORTE^M DE UNA AVELLANA^F

cupule
cupule^F
Fruchtbecher^M
cúpula^F

bract
bractée^F
Deckblatt^W
bráctea^F

seed
graine^M
Samen^M
semilla^F

pericarp
péricarpe^M
Fruchtwand^F
pericarpio^M

achene
akène^M
Schließfrucht^F
aquenio^M

stigma
stigmate^M
Narbe^F
estigma^M

SECTION OF A WALNUT
COUPE^F D'UNE NOIX^F
LÄNGSSCHNITT^M EINER WALNUSS^F
CORTE^M DE UNA NUEZ^F

shell
coque^F
Schale^F
cáscara^F

green walnut
cerneau^M
Samen^M
nuez^F verde

partition
zeste^M
Scheidewand^F
bizna^F

HUSK
BROU^M
HÜLLE^F
CÁSCARA^F

PRINCIPAL TYPES OF NUT
PRINCIPALES VARIÉTÉS^F DE NOIX^F
DIE WICHTIGSTEN NUSSARTEN^F
PRINCIPALES VARIEDADES^F DE FRUTOS^M SECOS

coconut
noix^F de coco^M
Kokosnuß^F
coco^M

walnut
noix^F
Walnuß^F
nuez^F

pistachio nut
pistache^F
Pistazie^F
pistacho^M

pecan nut
noix^F de pacane^F
Pecannuß^F
pacana^F

almond
amande^F
Mandel^F
almendra^F

peanut
arachide^F
Erdnuß^F
cacahuete^M

Brazil nut
noix^F du Brésil^M
Paranuß^F
nuez^F del Brasil^M

hazelnut
noisette^F
Haselnuß^F
avellana^F

chestnut
marron^M
Eßkastanie^F
castaña^M

pine nut
pignon^M
Pinienkern^M
piñón^M

cashew
noix^F de cajou^M
Cashewkern^M
nuez^F de la India^M

VARIOUS DRY FRUITS
FRUITS^M SECS DIVERS
VERSCHIEDENE TROCKENFRÜCHTE^F
FRUTOS^M SECOS: DEHISCENTES

SECTION OF A FOLLICLE
COUPE^F D'UN FOLLICULE^M
QUERSCHNITT^M EINER FRUCHTKAPSEL^F
CORTE^M DE UN FOLÍCULO^M

star anise
anis^M étoilé
Sternanis^M
anís^M estrellado

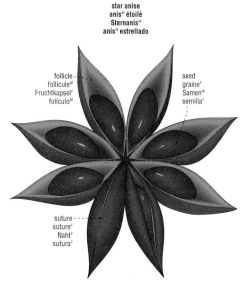

follicle
follicule^M
Fruchtkapsel^F
folículo^M

seed
graine^F
Samen^M
semilla^F

suture
suture^F
Naht^F
sutura^F

SECTION OF A LEGUME
COUPE^F D'UNE GOUSSE^F
LÄNGSSCHNITT^M EINER HÜLSENFRUCHT^F
CORTE^M DE UNA LEGUMBRE^F

pea
pois^M
Erbsenschote^F
guisante^M

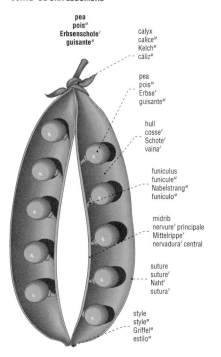

calyx
calice^M
Kelch^M
cáliz^M

pea
pois^M
Erbse^F
guisante^M

hull
cosse^F
Schote^F
vaina^F

funiculus
funicule^M
Nabelstrang^M
funículo^M

midrib
nervure^F principale
Mittelrippe^F
nervadura^F central

suture
suture^F
Naht^F
sutura^F

style
style^M
Griffel^M
estilo^M

SECTION OF A SILIQUE
COUPE^F D'UNE SILIQUE^F
LÄNGSSCHNITT^M EINER FRUCHTSCHOTE^F
CORTE^M DE UNA SILICUA^F

mustard
moutarde^F
Senf^M
mostaza^F

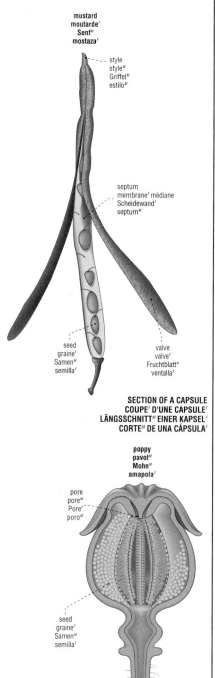

style
style^M
Griffel^M
estilo^M

septum
membrane^F médiane
Scheidewand^F
septum^M

seed
graine^F
Samen^M
semilla^F

valve
valve^F
Fruchtblatt^N
ventalla^F

SECTION OF A CAPSULE
COUPE^F D'UNE CAPSULE^F
LÄNGSSCHNITT^M EINER KAPSEL^F
CORTE^M DE UNA CÁPSULA^F

poppy
pavot^M
Mohn^M
amapola^F

pore
pore^M
Pore^F
poro^M

seed
graine^F
Samen^M
semilla^F

TROPICAL FRUITS
FRUITS*M* TROPICAUX
SÜDFRÜCHTE*F*
FRUTAS*F* TROPICALES

PRINCIPAL TYPES OF TROPICAL FRUIT
PRINCIPAUX FRUITS*M* TROPICAUX
DIE WICHTIGSTEN SÜDFRÜCHTE*F*
PRINCIPALES VARIEDADES*F* DE FRUTAS*F* TROPICALES

litchi; lychee
litchi*M*
Litschi*F*
litchi*M*

Japanese persimmon
kaki*M*
Kaki*F*
caqui*M*

papaya
papaye*F*
Papaya*F*
papaya*F*

kiwi
kiwi*M*
Kiwi*F*
kiwi*M*

banana
banane*F*
Banane*F*
plátano*M*

pomegranate
grenade*F*
Granatapfel*M*
granada*F*

cherimoya
chérimole*F*
Chirimoya*F*
chirimoya*F*

Indian fig
figue*F* de Barbarie
Kaktusfeige*F*
higo chumbo*M*

avocado
avocat*M*
Avocado*F*
aguacate*M*

guava
goyave*F*
Guave*F*
guayaba*F*

pineapple
ananas*M*
Ananas*M*
piña*F*

VEGETABLES / LÉGUMES^M / GEMÜSE^N / HORTALIZAS^F

FRUIT VEGETABLES / LÉGUMES^M FRUITS^M / FRUCHTGEMÜSE^N / FRUTOS^M

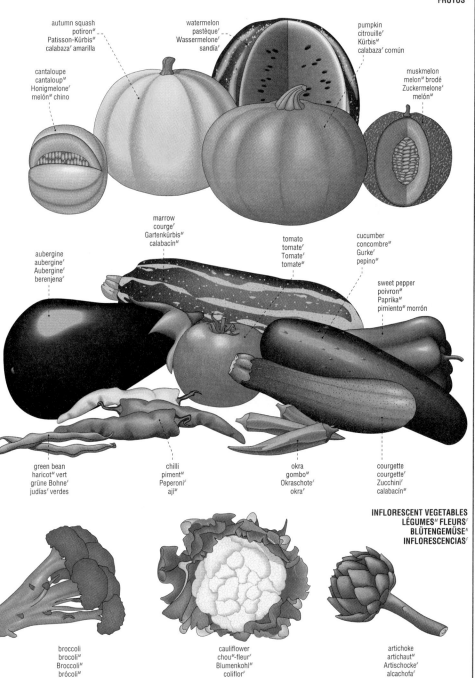

Labels:

autumn squash / potiron^M / Patisson-Kürbis^M / calabaza^F amarilla

watermelon / pastèque^F / Wassermelone^F / sandía^F

pumpkin / citrouille^F / Kürbis^M / calabaza^F común

cantaloupe / cantaloup^M / Honigmelone^F / melón^M chino

muskmelon / melon^M brodé / Zuckermelone^F / melón^M

marrow / courge^F / Gartenkürbis^M / calabacín^M

tomato / tomate^F / Tomate^F / tomate^M

cucumber / concombre^M / Gurke^F / pepino^M

aubergine / aubergine^F / Aubergine^F / berenjena^F

sweet pepper / poivron^M / Paprika^M / pimiento^M morrón

green bean / haricot^M vert / grüne Bohne^F / judías^F verdes

chilli / piment^M / Peperoni^F / ají^M

okra / gombo^M / Okraschote^F / okra^F

courgette / courgette^F / Zucchini^F / calabacín^M

INFLORESCENT VEGETABLES / LÉGUMES^M FLEURS^F / BLÜTENGEMÜSE^N / INFLORESCENCIAS^F

broccoli / brocoli^M / Broccoli^M / brócoli^M

cauliflower / chou^M-fleur^F / Blumenkohl^M / coliflor^F

artichoke / artichaut^M / Artischocke^F / alcachofa^F

PLANT KINGDOM / RÈGNE VÉGÉTAL / PFLANZENREICH / REINO VEGETAL

69

VEGETABLES
LÉGUMES*M*
GEMÜSE*N*
HORTALIZAS*F*

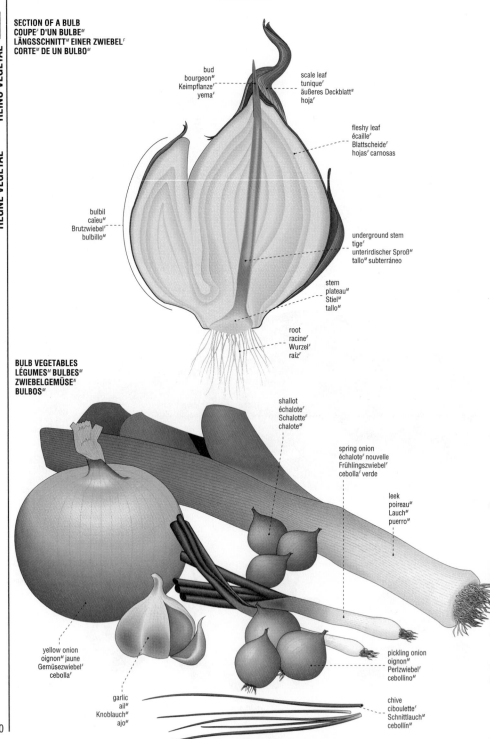

SECTION OF A BULB
COUPE*F* D'UN BULBE*M*
LÄNGSSCHNITT*M* EINER ZWIEBEL*F*
CORTE*M* DE UN BULBO*M*

bud
bourgeon*M*
Keimpflanze*F*
yema*F*

scale leaf
tunique*F*
äußeres Deckblatt*N*
hoja*F*

fleshy leaf
écaille*F*
Blattscheide*F*
hojas*F* carnosas

bulbil
caïeu*M*
Brutzwiebel*F*
bulbillo*M*

underground stem
tige*F*
unterirdischer Sproß*M*
tallo*M* subterráneo

stem
plateau*M*
Stiel*M*
tallo*M*

root
racine*F*
Wurzel*F*
raíz*F*

BULB VEGETABLES
LÉGUMES*M* BULBES*M*
ZWIEBELGEMÜSE*N*
BULBOS*M*

shallot
échalote*F*
Schalotte*F*
chalote*M*

spring onion
échalote*F* nouvelle
Frühlingszwiebel*F*
cebolla*F* verde

leek
poireau*M*
Lauch*M*
puerro*M*

yellow onion
oignon*M* jaune
Gemüsezwiebel*F*
cebolla*F*

pickling onion
oignon*M*
Perlzwiebel*F*
cebollino*M*

garlic
ail*M*
Knoblauch*M*
ajo*M*

chive
ciboulette*F*
Schnittlauch*M*
cebollín*M*

VEGETABLES
LÉGUMES^M
GEMÜSE^N
HORTALIZAS^F

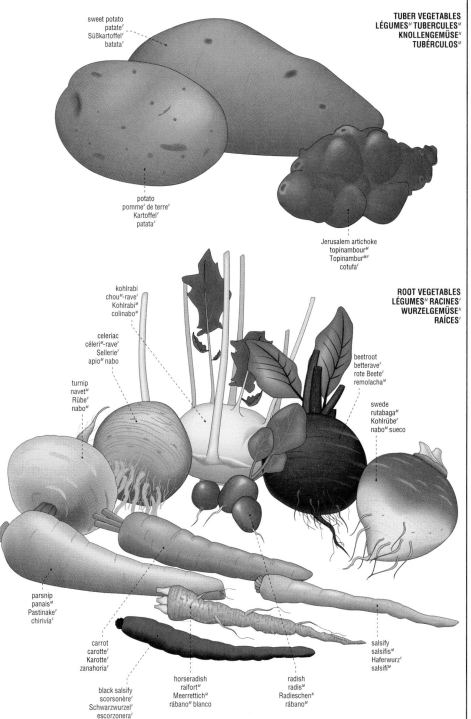

sweet potato
patate^F
Süßkartoffel^F
batata^F

TUBER VEGETABLES
LÉGUMES^M TUBERCULES^M
KNOLLENGEMÜSE^N
TUBÉRCULOS^M

potato
pomme^F de terre^F
Kartoffel^F
patata^F

Jerusalem artichoke
topinambour^M
Topinambur^{M,F}
cotufa^F

kohlrabi
chou^M-rave^F
Kohlrabi^M
colinabo^M

ROOT VEGETABLES
LÉGUMES^M RACINES^F
WURZELGEMÜSE^N
RAÍCES^F

celeriac
céleri^M-rave^F
Sellerie^F
apio^M nabo

beetroot
betterave^F
rote Beete^F
remolacha^M

turnip
navet^M
Rübe^F
nabo^M

swede
rutabaga^M
Kohlrübe^F
nabo^M sueco

parsnip
panais^M
Pastinake^F
chirivía^F

carrot
carotte^F
Karotte^F
zanahoria^F

salsify
salsifis^M
Haferwurz^F
salsifí^M

black salsify
scorsonère^F
Schwarzwurzel^F
escorzonera^F

horseradish
raifort^M
Meerrettich^M
rábano^M blanco

radish
radis^M
Radieschen^N
rábano^M

**PFLANZENREICH
REINO VEGETAL**

**PLANT KINGDOM
RÈGNE VÉGÉTAL**

**STALK VEGETABLES
LÉGUMES**^M **TIGES**^F
STENGEL- UND SPROSSENGEMÜSE^N
TALLOS^M

rhubarb
rhubarbe^F
Rhabarber^M
ruíbarbo^M

**asparagus
asperge**^F
Spargel^M
espárrago^M

spear
turion^M
Stange^F
turión^M

bundle
botte^F
Bund^N
manojo^M

**celery
céleri**^M
Stangensellerie^{M/F}
apio^M

cardoon
cardon^M
Kardone^F
cardo^M

tip
pointe^F
Spitze^F
punta^F

**Swiss chard
bette**^F **à carde**^F
Mangold^M
acelga^F

branch
branche^F
Stange^F
tallo^M

leaf
feuille^F
Blatt^N
hoja^F

**fennel
fenouil**^M
Fenchel^M
hinojo^M

stalk
tige^F
Stiel^M
tallo^M

head
pied^M
Stielgrund^M
base^F

bulb
bulbe^M
Knolle^F
bulbo^M

rib
carde^F
Rippe^F
tallo^M

**PULSES
LÉGUMES**^M **GRAINES**^F
HÜLSENFRÜCHTE^F
LEGUMBRES^F

**SWEETCORN
MAÏS**^M
ZUCKERMAIS^M
MAÍZ^M

broad beans
fèves^F
dicke Bohnen^F
habas^F

mangetout
pois^M mange-tout^M
Zuckererbsen^F
guisantes^M

green peas
petits pois^M
grüne Erbsen^F
guisantes^M

silk
barbe^F
Bart^M
pelusa^F de maíz^M

cob
épi^M
Kolben^M
mazorca^M

lentils
lentilles^F
Linsen^F
lentejas^F

chick peas
pois^M chiches
Kichererbsen^F
garbanzos^M

husk
feuille^F
Hülse^F
hoja^F

soybeans
graines^F de soja^M
Sojabohnen^F
semillas^F de soja^F

bean sprouts
germes^M de soja^M
Sojasprossen^M
brotes^M de soja^F

kernel
grain^M
Kern^M
grano^M

VEGETABLES
LÉGUMES^M
GEMÜSE^N
HORTALIZAS^F

LEAF VEGETABLES
LÉGUMES^M FEUILLES^F
BLATTGEMÜSE^N
VERDURAS^F DE HOJAS^F

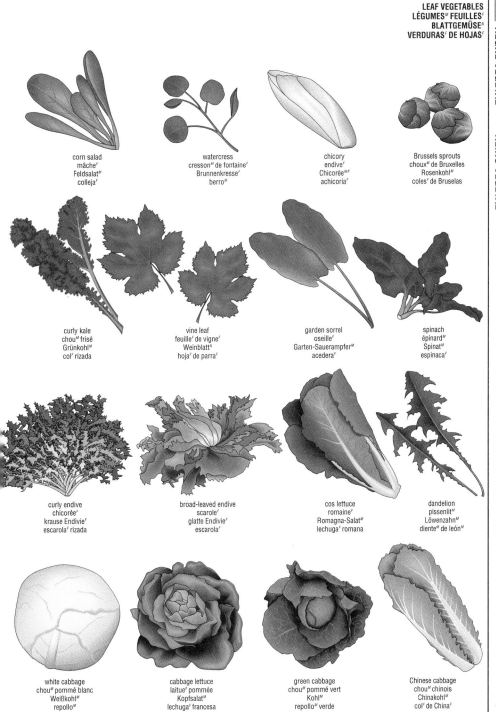

corn salad
mâche^F
Feldsalat^M
colleja^F

watercress
cresson^M de fontaine^F
Brunnenkresse^F
berro^M

chicory
endive^F
Chicorée^{M/F}
achicoria^F

Brussels sprouts
choux^M de Bruxelles
Rosenkohl^M
coles^F de Bruselas

curly kale
chou^M frisé
Grünkohl^M
col^F rizada

vine leaf
feuille^F de vigne^F
Weinblatt^N
hoja^F de parra^F

garden sorrel
oseille^F
Garten-Sauerampfer^M
acedera^F

spinach
épinard^M
Spinat^M
espinaca^F

curly endive
chicorée^F
krause Endivie^F
escarola^F rizada

broad-leaved endive
scarole^F
glatte Endivie^F
escarola^F

cos lettuce
romaine^F
Romagna-Salat^M
lechuga^F romana

dandelion
pissenlit^M
Löwenzahn^M
diente^M de león^M

white cabbage
chou^M pommé blanc
Weißkohl^M
repollo^M

cabbage lettuce
laitue^F pommée
Kopfsalat^M
lechuga^F francesa

green cabbage
chou^M pommé vert
Kohl^M
repollo^M verde

Chinese cabbage
chou^M chinois
Chinakohl^M
col^F de China^F

HERBS
FINES HERBES[F]
KRÄUTER[N]
HIERBAS[F] AROMÁTICAS

dill
aneth[M]
Dill[M]
eneldo[M]

basil
basilic[M]
Basilikum[N]
albahaca[F]

borage
bourrache[F]
Boretsch[M]
borraja[F]

chervil
cerfeuil[M]
Kerbel[M]
perifollo[M]

coriander
coriandre[F]
Koriander[M]
cilantro[M]

tarragon
estragon[M]
Estragon[M]
estragón[M]

hyssop
hysope[F]
Ysop[M]
hisopo[M]

bay
laurier[M]
Lorbeer[M]
laurel[M]

lovage
livèche[F]
Liebstöckel[MN]
ligústico[M]

mint
menthe[F]
Minze[F]
hierbabuena[F]

oregano
origan[M]
Oregano[M]
orégano[M]

parsley
persil[M]
Petersilie[F]
perejil[M]

rosemary
romarin[M]
Rosmarin[M]
romero[M]

savory
sarriette[F]
Bohnenkraut[N]
ajedrea[F]

sage
sauge[F]
Salbei[M]
salvia[F]

thyme
thym[M]
Thymian[M]
tomillo[M]

ANIMAL KINGDOM
RÈGNE ANIMAL

TIERREICH
REINO ANIMAL

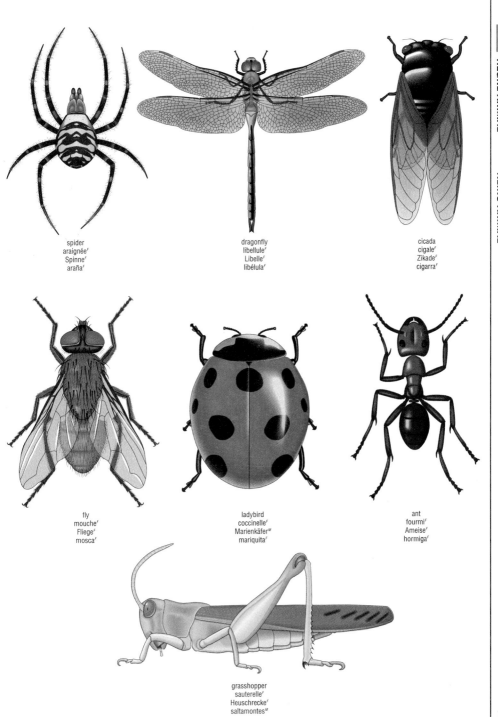

spider
araignée^F
Spinne^F
araña^F

dragonfly
libellule^F
Libelle^F
libélula^F

cicada
cigale^F
Zikade^F
cigarra^F

fly
mouche^F
Fliege^F
mosca^F

ladybird
coccinelle^F
Marienkäfer^M
mariquita^F

ant
fourmi^F
Ameise^F
hormiga^F

grasshopper
sauterelle^F
Heuschrecke^F
saltamontes^M

BUTTERFLY
PAPILLON*M*
SCHMETTERLING*M*
MARIPOSA*F*

CATERPILLAR
CHENILLE*F*
RAUPE*F*
ORUGA*F*

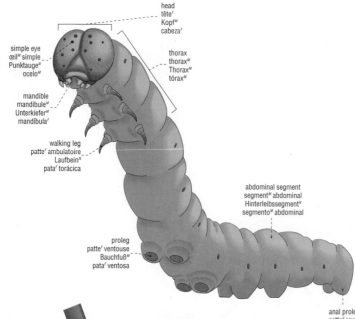

head
tête*F*
Kopf*M*
cabeza*F*

simple eye
œil*M* simple
Punktauge*N*
ocelo*M*

thorax
thorax*M*
Thorax*M*
tórax*M*

mandible
mandibule*F*
Unterkiefer*M*
mandíbula*F*

walking leg
patte*F* ambulatoire
Laufbein*N*
pata*F* torácica

abdominal segment
segment*M* abdominal
Hinterleibssegment*N*
segmento*M* abdominal

proleg
patte*F* ventouse
Bauchfuß*M*
pata*F* ventosa

anal proleg
patte*F* anale
Analfuß*M*
pata*F* anal

CHRYSALIS
CHRYSALIDE*F*
PUPPE*F*
CRISÁLIDA*F*

cremaster
crémaster*M*
Kremaster*M*
cremáster*M*

abdomen
abdomen*M*
Hinterleib*M*
abdomen*M*

spiracle
stigmate*M*
Stigma*N*
estigma*M*

wing
aile*F*
Flügel*M*
ala*F*

metathorax
métathorax*M*
Metathorax*M*
metatórax*M*

antenna
antenne*F*
Antenne*F*
antena*F*

mesothorax
mésothorax*M*
Mesothorax*M*
mesotórax*M*

prothorax
prothorax*M*
Prothorax*M*
protórax*M*

HIND LEG
PATTE*F* **POSTÉRIEURE**
HINTERBEIN*N*
PATA*F* **POSTERIOR**

coxa
hanche*F*
Hüfte*F*
coxa*F*

trochanter
trochanter*M*
Schenkelring*M*
trocánter*M*

tibia
tibia*M*
Schiene*F*
tibia*F*

femur
fémur*M*
Schenkel*M*
fémur*M*

tarsus
tarse*M*
Fuß*M*
tarso*M*

claw
griffe*F*
Klaue*F*
tenacilla*F*

78

BUTTERFLY
PAPILLON^M
SCHMETTERLING^M
MARIPOSA^F

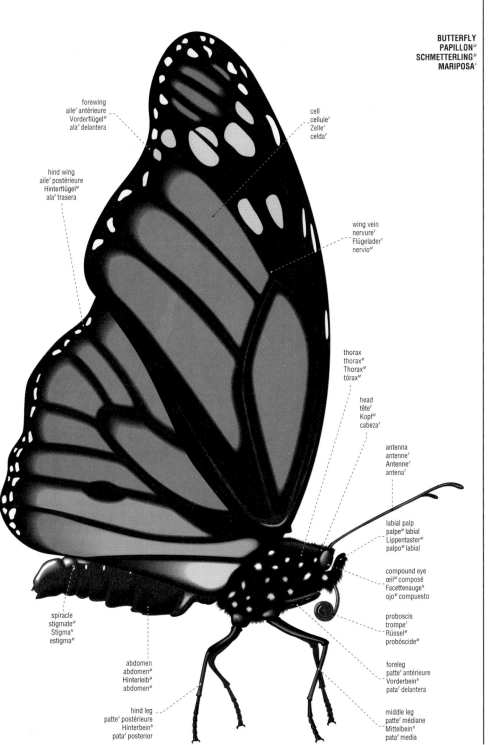

forewing
aile^F antérieure
Vorderflügel^M
ala^F delantera

hind wing
aile^F postérieure
Hinterflügel^M
ala^F trasera

cell
cellule^F
Zelle^F
celda^F

wing vein
nervure^F
Flügelader^F
nervio^M

thorax
thorax^M
Thorax^M
tórax^M

head
tête^F
Kopf^M
cabeza^F

antenna
antenne^F
Antenne^F
antena^F

labial palp
palpe^M labial
Lippentaster^M
palpo^M labial

compound eye
œil^M composé
Facettenauge^N
ojo^M compuesto

proboscis
trompe^F
Rüssel^M
probóscide^M

spiracle
stigmate^M
Stigma^N
estigma^M

abdomen
abdomen^M
Hinterleib^M
abdomen^M

hind leg
patte^F postérieure
Hinterbein^N
pata^F posterior

foreleg
patte^F antérieure
Vorderbein^N
pata^F delantera

middle leg
patte^F médiane
Mittelbein^N
pata^F media

HONEYBEE
ABEILLE^F
HONIGBIENE^F
ABEJA^F

WORKER
OUVRIÈRE^F
ARBEITERIN^F
OBRERA^F

head
tête^F
Kopf^M
cabeza^F

thorax
thorax^M
Thorax^M
tórax^M

simple eye
œil^M simple
Punktauge^N
ocelo^M

compound eye
œil^M composé
Facettenauge^N
ojo^M compuesto

antenna
antenne^F
Antenne^F
antena^F

mandible
mandibule^F
Unterkiefer^M
mandíbula^F

foreleg
patte^F antérieure
Vorderbein^N
pata^F delantera

middle leg
patte^F médiane
Mittelbein^N
pata^F media

FORELEG (OUTER SURFACE)
PATTE^F ANTÉRIEURE (FACE^F EXTERNE)
VORDERBEIN^N (AUSSENSEITE^F)
PATA^F DELANTERA (SUPERFICIE^F EXTERIOR)

MIDDLE LEG (OUTER SURFACE)
PATTE^F MÉDIANE (FACE^F EXTERNE)
MITTELBEIN^N (AUSSENSEITE^F)
PATA^F MEDIA (SUPERFICIE^F EXTERIOR)

coxa
hanche^F
Hüfte^F
coxa^F

trochanter
trochanter^M
Schenkelring^M
trocánter^M

femur
fémur^M
Schenkel^M
fémur^M

tibia
tibia^M
Schiene^F
tibia^M

spur
éperon^M
Sporn^M
espolón^M

velum
vélum^M
Putzsporn^M
velo^M

antennae cleaner
brosse^F d'antennes^F
Fühlerputzer^M
limpiador^M de antenas^F

pollen brush
brosse^F à pollen^M
Pollenbürste^F
cepillo^M

metatarsus
métatarse^M
Mittelfuß^M
metatarso^M

tarsus
tarse^M
Fuß^M
tarso^M

claw
griffe^F
Klaue^F
uña^F

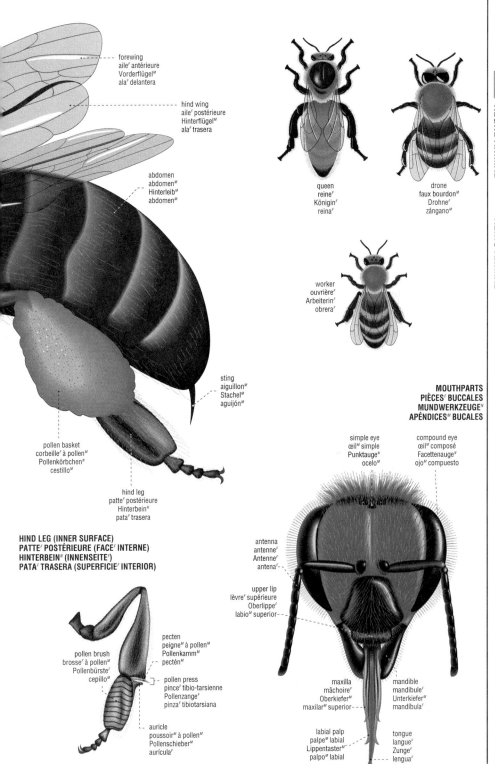

forewing
aile^f antérieure
Vorderflügel^M
ala^f delantera

hind wing
aile^f postérieure
Hinterflügel^M
ala^f trasera

abdomen
abdomen^M
Hinterleib^M
abdomen^M

sting
aiguillon^M
Stachel^M
aguijón^M

pollen basket
corbeille^f à pollen^M
Pollenkörbchen^N
cestillo^M

hind leg
patte^f postérieure
Hinterbein^N
pata^f trasera

queen
reine^f
Königin^f
reina^f

drone
faux bourdon^M
Drohne^f
zángano^M

worker
ouvrière^f
Arbeiterin^f
obrera^f

MOUTHPARTS
PIÈCES^f BUCCALES
MUNDWERKZEUGE^N
APÉNDICES^M BUCALES

simple eye
œil^M simple
Punktauge^N
ocelo^M

compound eye
œil^M composé
Facettenauge^N
ojo^M compuesto

HIND LEG (INNER SURFACE)
PATTE^f POSTÉRIEURE (FACE^f INTERNE)
HINTERBEIN^N (INNENSEITE^f)
PATA^f TRASERA (SUPERFICIE^f INTERIOR)

antenna
antenne^f
Antenne^f
antena^f

upper lip
lèvre^f supérieure
Oberlippe^f
labio^M superior

pecten
peigne^M à pollen^M
Pollenkamm^M
pectén^M

pollen brush
brosse^f à pollen^M
Pollenbürste^f
cepillo^M

pollen press
pince^f tibio-tarsienne
Pollenzange^f
pinza^f tibiotarsiana

auricle
poussoir^M à pollen^M
Pollenschieber^M
aurícula^f

maxilla
mâchoire^f
Oberkiefer^M
maxilar^M superior

mandible
mandibule^f
Unterkiefer^M
mandíbula^f

labial palp
palpe^M labial
Lippentaster^M
palpo^M labial

tongue
langue^f
Zunge^f
lengua^f

HONEYBEE
ABEILLE^F
HONIGBIENE^F
ABEJA^F DE COLMENA^F

HONEYCOMB SECTION
COUPE^F D'UN RAYON^M DE MIEL^M
WABENAUSSCHNITT^M
CORTE^M DE UN PANAL^M

chrysalis
nymphe^F
Puppe^F
crisálida^F

larva
larve^F
Larve^F
larva^F

honey cell
alvéole^M à miel^M
Honigzelle^F
celdilla^F de la miel^F

pollen cell
alvéole^M à pollen^M
Pollenzelle^F
celdilla^F del polen^M

sealed cell
alvéole^M operculé
verdeckelte Zelle^F
celdilla^F sellada

egg
œuf^M
Ei^N
huevo^M

queen cell
cellule^F royale
Weiselwiege^F
celdilla^F operculada

HIVE
RUCHE^F
BIENENSTOCK^M
COLMENA^F

roof
toit^M
Dach^N
techo^M

honeycomb
rayon^M de miel^M
Wabe^F
panal^M

exit cone
sortie^F
Ausflugloch^N
respiradero^M

roof section
toiture^F
Dach^N
techo^M

cell
alvéole^F
Zelle^F
celdilla^F

super
hausse^F
Honigraum^M
alza^F

frame
cadre^M
Rähmchen^N
compartimentos^M

queen excluder
grille^F à reine^F
Absperrgitter^N
separador^M de reinas^F

brood chamber
nid^M à couvain^M
Brutraum^M
cámara^F de incubación^F

alighting board
planche^F de vol^M
Flugbrettchen^N
estribo^M

hive body
corps^M de ruche^F
Gehäuse^N
conjunto^M de la colmena^F

entrance
entrée^F
Einflugloch^N
entrada^F

entrance slide
coulisse^F d'entrée^F
Fluglochschieber^M
reductor^M de entrada^F

GASTROPOD
GASTÉROPODE[M]
SCHNECKE[F]
MOLUSCO[M] GASTERÓPODO

SNAIL
ESCARGOT[M]
SCHNECKE[F]
CARACOL[M] TERRESTRE

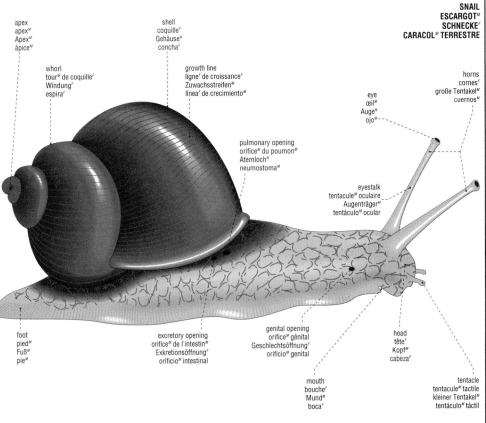

apex
apex[M]
Apex[M]
ápice[M]

shell
coquille[F]
Gehäuse[M]
concha[F]

whorl
tour[M] de coquille[F]
Windung[F]
espira[F]

growth line
ligne[F] de croissance[F]
Zuwachsstreifen[M]
línea[F] de crecimiento[M]

horns
cornes[F]
große Tentakel[M]
cuernos[M]

eye
œil[M]
Auge[N]
ojo[M]

pulmonary opening
orifice[M] du poumon[M]
Atemloch[N]
neumostoma[M]

eyestalk
tentacule[M] oculaire
Augenträger[M]
tentáculo[M] ocular

foot
pied[M]
Fuß[M]
pie[M]

excretory opening
orifice[M] de l'intestin[M]
Exkretionsöffnung[F]
orificio[M] intestinal

genital opening
orifice[M] génital
Geschlechtsöffnung[F]
orificio[M] genital

head
tête[F]
Kopf[M]
cabeza[F]

mouth
bouche[F]
Mund[M]
boca[F]

tentacle
tentacule[M] tactile
kleiner Tentakel[M]
tentáculo[M] táctil

PRINCIPAL EDIBLE GASTROPODS
PRINCIPAUX GASTÉROPODES[M] COMESTIBLES
WICHTIGSTE ESSBARE SCHNECKEN[F]
GASTERÓPODOS[M] COMESTIBLES

limpet
patelle[F]
Napfschnecke[F]
lapa[F]

common periwinkle
bigorneau[M]
Strandschnecke[F]
caracol[M] marino común

whelk
buccin[M]
Wellhornschnecke[F]
buccino[M]

83

AMPHIBIANS
AMPHIBIENS*M*
AMPHIBIEN*F*
ANFIBIOS*M*

FROG
GRENOUILLE*F*
FROSCH*M*
RANA*F*

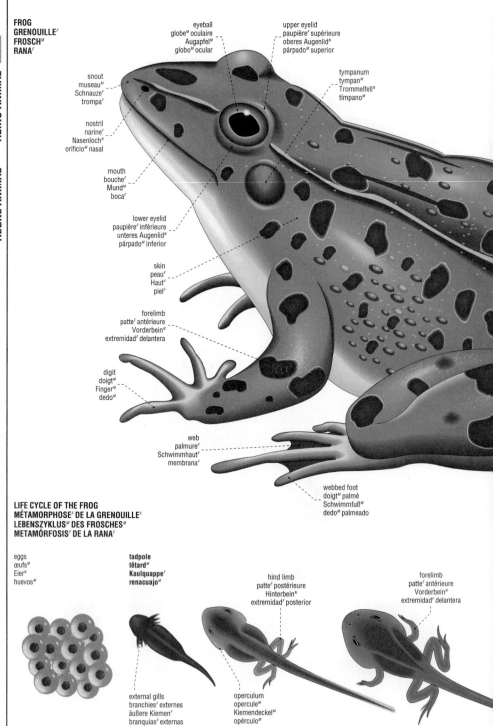

eyeball
globe*M* oculaire
Augapfel*M*
globo*M* ocular

upper eyelid
paupière*F* supérieure
oberes Augenlid*N*
párpado*M* superior

tympanum
tympan*M*
Trommelfell*N*
tímpano*M*

snout
museau*M*
Schnauze*F*
trompa*F*

nostril
narine*F*
Nasenloch*N*
orificio*M* nasal

mouth
bouche*F*
Mund*M*
boca*F*

lower eyelid
paupière*F* inférieure
unteres Augenlid*N*
párpado*M* inferior

skin
peau*F*
Haut*F*
piel*F*

forelimb
patte*F* antérieure
Vorderbein*N*
extremidad*F* delantera

digit
doigt*M*
Finger*M*
dedo*M*

web
palmure*F*
Schwimmhaut*F*
membrana*F*

webbed foot
doigt*M* palmé
Schwimmfuß*M*
dedo*M* palmeado

LIFE CYCLE OF THE FROG
MÉTAMORPHOSE*F* **DE LA GRENOUILLE***F*
LEBENSZYKLUS*M* **DES FROSCHES***M*
METAMÓRFOSIS*F* **DE LA RANA***F*

eggs
œufs*M*
Eier*N*
huevos*M*

tadpole
têtard*M*
Kaulquappe*F*
renacuajo*M*

hind limb
patte*F* postérieure
Hinterbein*N*
extremidad*F* posterior

forelimb
patte*F* antérieure
Vorderbein*N*
extremidad*F* delantera

external gills
branchies*F* externes
äußere Kiemen*F*
branquias*F* externas

operculum
opercule*M*
Kiemendeckel*M*
opérculo*M*

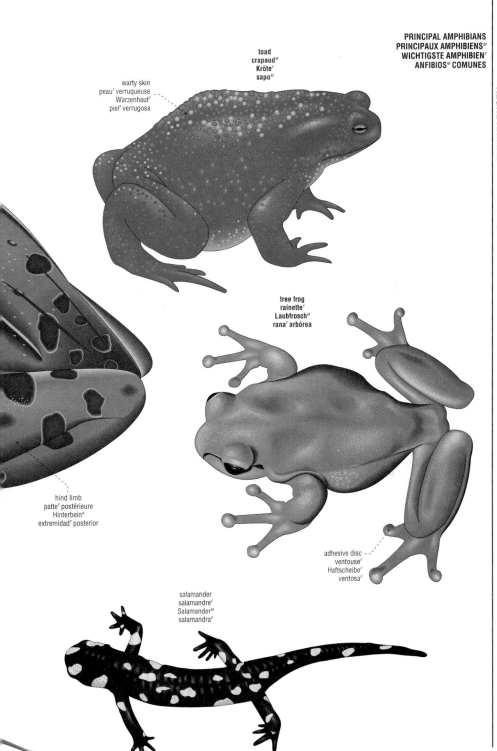

PRINCIPAL AMPHIBIANS
PRINCIPAUX AMPHIBIENS^M
WICHTIGSTE AMPHIBIEN^F
ANFIBIOS^M COMUNES

ANIMAL KINGDOM
RÈGNE ANIMAL

TIERREICH
REINO ANIMAL

toad
crapaud^M
Kröte^F
sapo^M

warty skin
peau^F verruqueuse
Warzenhaut^F
piel^F verrugosa

tree frog
rainette^F
Laubfrosch^M
rana^F arbórea

hind limb
patte^F postérieure
Hinterbein^N
extremidad^F posterior

adhesive disc
ventouse^F
Haftscheibe^F
ventosa^F

salamander
salamandre^F
Salamander^M
salamandra^F

85

FISH
POISSON^M
FISCH^M
PEZ^M

MORPHOLOGY
MORPHOLOGIE^F
MORPHOLOGIE^F
MORFOLOGÍA^F

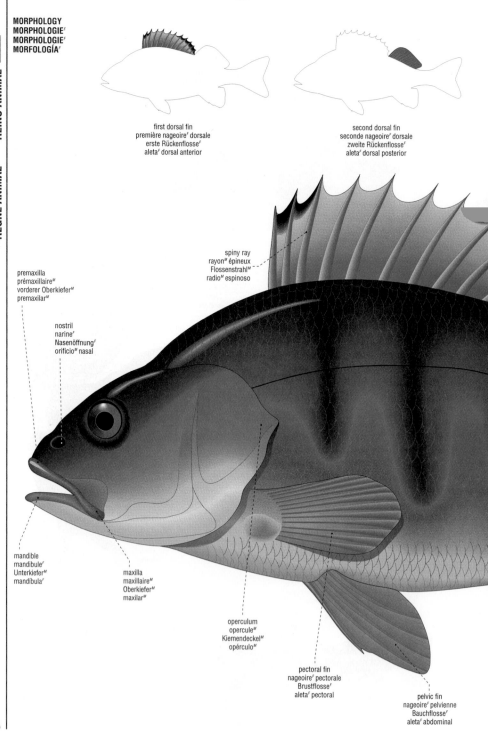

first dorsal fin
première nageoire^F dorsale
erste Rückenflosse^F
aleta^F dorsal anterior

second dorsal fin
seconde nageoire^F dorsale
zweite Rückenflosse^F
aleta^F dorsal posterior

spiny ray
rayon^M épineux
Flossenstrahl^M
radio^M espinoso

premaxilla
prémaxillaire^M
vorderer Oberkiefer^M
premaxilar^M

nostril
narine^F
Nasenöffnung^F
orificio^M nasal

mandible
mandibule^F
Unterkiefer^M
mandíbula^F

maxilla
maxillaire^M
Oberkiefer^M
maxilar^M

operculum
opercule^M
Kiemendeckel^M
opérculo^M

pectoral fin
nageoire^F pectorale
Brustflosse^F
aleta^F pectoral

pelvic fin
nageoire^F pelvienne
Bauchflosse^F
aleta^F abdominal

GILLS
BRANCHIES^F
KIEMEN^F
BRANQUIAS^F

upper gill arch
arc^M branchial supérieur
oberer Kiemenbogen^M
arco^M branquial superior

gill raker
branchicténie^F
Kiemenreuse^F
branquiespinas^F

lower gill arch
arc^M branchial inférieur
unterer Kiemenbogen^M
arco^M branquial inferior

gill filament
filament^M branchial
Kiemenfaden^M
filamento^M branquial

soft ray
rayon^M mou
Weichstrahl^M
radio^M blando

lateral line
ligne^F latérale
Seitenlinie^F
línea^F lateral

caudal fin
nageoire^F caudale
Schwanzflosse^F
aleta^F caudal

scale
écaille^F
Schuppe^F
escama^F

anal fin
nageoire^F anale
Afterflosse^F
aleta^F anal

87

FISH
POISSON^M
FISCH^M
PEZ^M

ANATOMY
ANATOMIE^F
ANATOMIE^F
ANATOMÍA^F

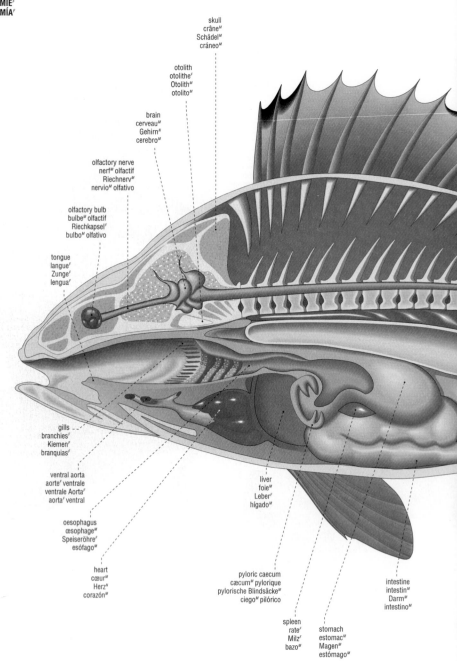

skull
crâne^M
Schädel^M
cráneo^M

otolith
otolithe^F
Otolith^M
otolito^M

brain
cerveau^M
Gehirn^N
cerebro^M

olfactory nerve
nerf^M olfactif
Riechnerv^M
nervio^M olfativo

olfactory bulb
bulbe^M olfactif
Riechkapsel^F
bulbo^M olfativo

tongue
langue^F
Zunge^F
lengua^F

gills
branchies^F
Kiemen^F
branquias^F

ventral aorta
aorte^F ventrale
ventrale Aorta^F
aorta^F ventral

liver
foie^M
Leber^F
hígado^M

oesophagus
œsophage^M
Speiseröhre^F
esófago^M

heart
cœur^M
Herz^N
corazón^M

pyloric caecum
cæcum^M pylorique
pylorische Blindsäcke^M
ciego^M pilórico

intestine
intestin^M
Darm^M
intestino^M

spleen
rate^F
Milz^F
bazo^M

stomach
estomac^M
Magen^M
estómago^M

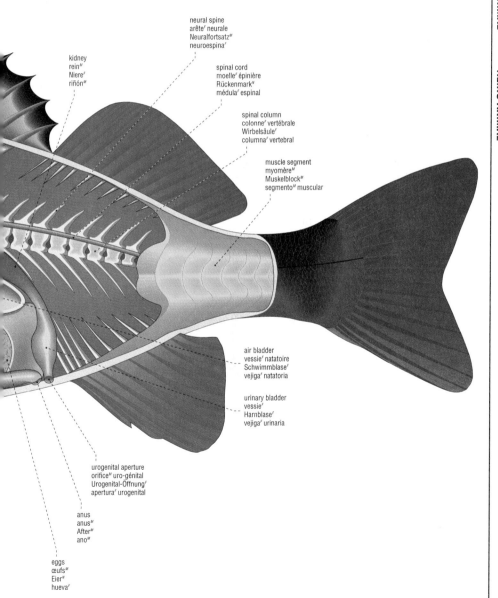

neural spine
arête^f neurale
Neuralfortsatz^M
neuroespina^F

kidney
rein^M
Niere^F
riñón^M

spinal cord
moelle^f épinière
Rückenmark^N
médula^F espinal

spinal column
colonne^f vertébrale
Wirbelsäule^F
columna^F vertebral

muscle segment
myomère^M
Muskelblock^M
segmento^M muscular

air bladder
vessie^f natatoire
Schwimmblase^F
vejiga^F natatoria

urinary bladder
vessie^f
Harnblase^F
vejiga^F urinaria

urogenital aperture
orifice^M uro-génital
Urogenital-Öffnung^F
apertura^F urogenital

anus
anus^M
After^M
ano^M

eggs
œufs^M
Eier^N
hueva^F

CRUSTACEAN
CRUSTACÉ[M]
KREBSTIERE[N]
CRUSTÁCEO[M]

LOBSTER
HOMARD[M]
HUMMER[M]
LANGOSTA[F]

rostrum
rostre[M]
Rostrum[N]
rostro[M]

eye
œil[M]
Auge[N]
ojo[M]

antennule
antennule[F]
Antennula[F]
anténula[F]

maxilla
maxille[F]
Oberkiefer[M]
maxilar[M]

maxillipeds
pattes[F]-mâchoires[F]
Kieferfüße[M]
maxilípedos[M]

claw
pince[F]
Schere[F]
pinza[F]

cephalothorax
céphalothorax[M]
Kopfbruststück[N]
cefalotórax[M]

thoracic legs
pattes[F] thoraciques
Brustbeine[N]
apéndices[M] torácicos

MAJOR EDIBLE CRUSTACEANS
PRINCIPAUX CRUSTACÉS[M] COMESTIBLES
WICHTIGSTE ESSBARE KREBSE[M]
CRUSTÁCEOS[M] COMESTIBLES COMUNES

prawn
crevette[F]
Garnele[F]
gamba[F]

crayfish
écrevisse[F]
Flußkrebs[M]
cigala[F]

crab
crabe[M]
Krabbe[F]
cangrejo[M]

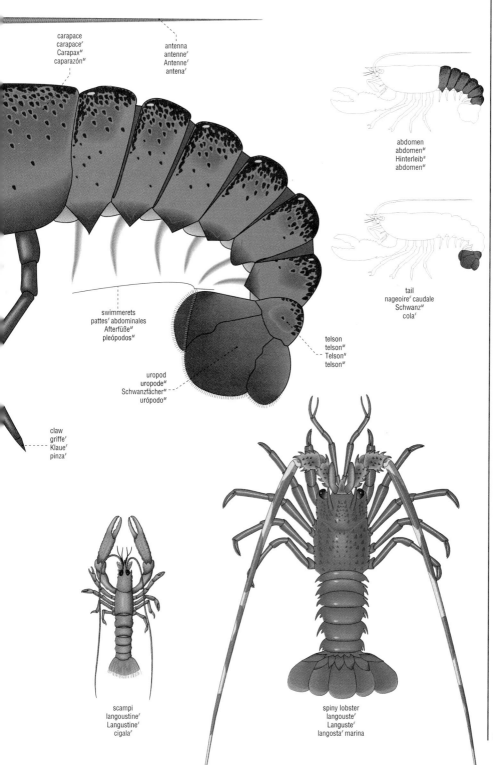

carapace
carapace^f
Carapax^M
caparazón^M

antenna
antenne^f
Antenne^f
antena^f

abdomen
abdomen^M
Hinterleib^N
abdomen^M

tail
nageoire^f caudale
Schwanz^M
cola^f

swimmerets
pattes^f abdominales
Afterfüße^M
pleópodos^M

telson
telson^M
Telson^N
telson^M

uropod
uropode^M
Schwanzfächer^M
urópodo^M

claw
griffe^f
Klaue^f
pinza^f

scampi
langoustine^f
Langustine^f
cigala^f

spiny lobster
langouste^f
Languste^f
langosta^f marina

91

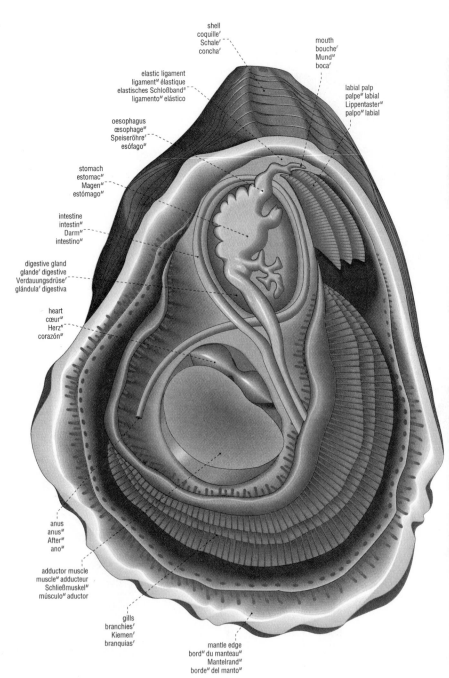

OYSTER
HUÎTRE^F
AUSTER^F
OSTRA^F

TIERREICH
REINO ANIMAL

ANIMAL KINGDOM
RÈGNE ANIMAL

shell
coquille^F
Schale^F
concha^F

mouth
bouche^F
Mund^M
boca^F

elastic ligament
ligament^M élastique
elastisches Schloßband^N
ligamento^M elástico

labial palp
palpe^M labial
Lippentaster^M
palpo^M labial

oesophagus
œsophage^M
Speiseröhre^F
esófago^M

stomach
estomac^M
Magen^M
estómago^M

intestine
intestin^M
Darm^M
intestino^M

digestive gland
glande^F digestive
Verdauungsdrüse^F
glándula^F digestiva

heart
cœur^M
Herz^N
corazón^M

anus
anus^M
After^M
ano^M

adductor muscle
muscle^M adducteur
Schließmuskel^M
músculo^M aductor

gills
branchies^F
Kiemen^F
branquias^F

mantle edge
bord^M du manteau^M
Mantelrand^M
borde^M del manto^M

PRINCIPAL EDIBLE MOLLUSCS
PRINCIPAUX MOLLUSQUES*M* COMESTIBLES
WICHTIGSTE ESSBARE WEICHTIERE*N*
MOLUSCOS*M* COMESTIBLES

ANIMAL KINGDOM
RÈGNE ANIMAL

TIERREICH
REINO ANIMAL

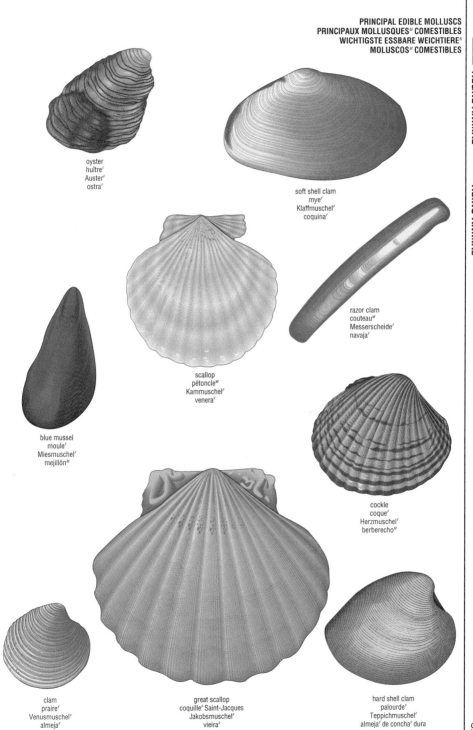

oyster
huître*F*
Auster*F*
ostra*F*

soft shell clam
mye*F*
Klaffmuschel*F*
coquina*F*

razor clam
couteau*M*
Messerscheide*F*
navaja*F*

scallop
pétoncle*M*
Kammuschel*F*
venera*F*

blue mussel
moule*F*
Miesmuschel*F*
mejillón*M*

cockle
coque*F*
Herzmuschel*F*
berberecho*M*

clam
praire*F*
Venusmuschel*F*
almeja*F*

great scallop
coquille*F* Saint-Jacques
Jakobsmuschel*F*
vieira*F*

hard shell clam
palourde*F*
Teppichmuschel*F*
almeja*F* de concha*F* dura

UNIVALVE SHELL
COQUILLE*F* UNIVALVE
EINKLAPPIGE SCHALE*F*
CONCHA*F* UNIVALVA

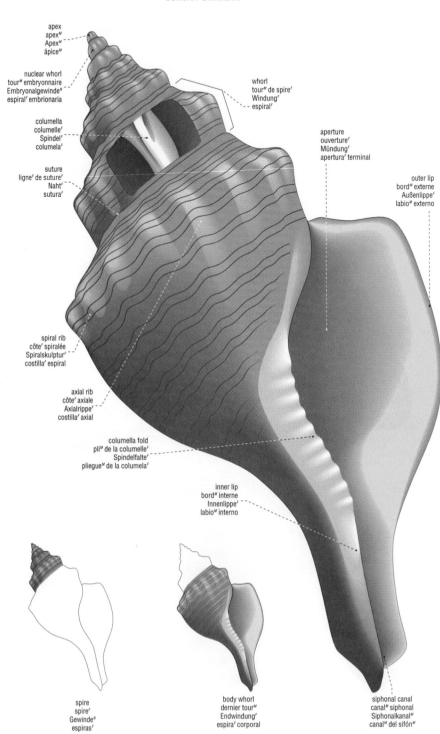

apex
apex*M*
Apex*M*
ápice*M*

nuclear whorl
tour*M* embryonnaire
Embryonalgewinde*N*
espiral*F* embrionaria

columella
columelle*F*
Spindel*F*
columela*F*

suture
ligne*F* de suture*F*
Naht*F*
sutura*F*

whorl
tour*M* de spire*F*
Windung*F*
espiral*F*

aperture
ouverture*F*
Mündung*F*
apertura*F* terminal

outer lip
bord*M* externe
Außenlippe*F*
labio*M* externo

spiral rib
côte*F* spiralée
Spiralskulptur*F*
costilla*F* espiral

axial rib
côte*F* axiale
Axialrippe*F*
costilla*F* axial

columella fold
pli*M* de la columelle*F*
Spindelfalte*F*
pliegue*M* de la columela*F*

inner lip
bord*M* interne
Innenlippe*F*
labio*M* interno

spire
spire*F*
Gewinde*N*
espiras*F*

body whorl
dernier tour*M*
Endwindung*F*
espira*F* corporal

siphonal canal
canal*M* siphonal
Siphonalkanal*M*
canal*M* del sifón*M*

94

BIVALVE SHELL
COQUILLE^F BIVALVE
ZWEIKLAPPIGE SCHALE^F
CONCHA^F BIVALVA

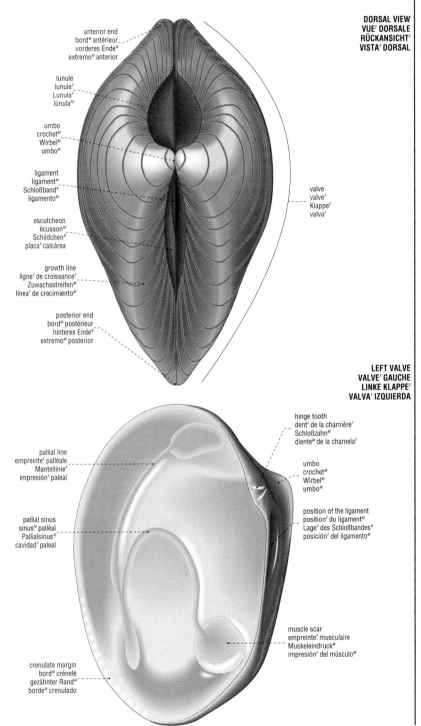

DORSAL VIEW
VUE^F DORSALE
RÜCKANSICHT^F
VISTA^F DORSAL

anterior end
bord^M antérieur
vorderes Ende^N
extremo^M anterior

lunule
lunule^F
Lunula^F
lúnula^M

umbo
crochet^M
Wirbel^M
umbo^M

ligament
ligament^M
Schloßband^N
ligamento^M

escutcheon
écusson^M
Schildchen^N
placa^F calcárea

growth line
ligne^F de croissance^F
Zuwachsstreifen^M
línea^F de crecimiento^M

posterior end
bord^M postérieur
hinteres Ende^N
extremo^M posterior

valve
valve^F
Klappe^F
valva^F

LEFT VALVE
VALVE^F GAUCHE
LINKE KLAPPE^F
VALVA^F IZQUIERDA

hinge tooth
dent^F de la charnière^F
Schloßzahn^M
diente^M de la charnela^F

pallial line
empreinte^F palléale
Mantellinie^F
impresión^F paleal

umbo
crochet^M
Wirbel^M
umbo^M

position of the ligament
position^F du ligament^M
Lage^F des Schloßbandes^N
posición^F del ligamento^M

pallial sinus
sinus^M palléal
Pallialsinus^M
cavidad^F paleal

muscle scar
empreinte^F musculaire
Muskeleindruck^M
impresión^F del músculo^M

crenulate margin
bord^M crénelé
gezähnter Rand^M
borde^M crenulado

ANIMAL KINGDOM
RÈGNE ANIMAL

TIERREICH
REINO ANIMAL

VENOMOUS SNAKE'S HEAD
TÊTE^F DE SERPENT^M VENIMEUX
KOPF^M EINER GIFTSCHLANGE^F
CABEZA^F DE SERPIENTE^F VENENOSA

movable maxillary
maxillaire^M basculant
beweglicher Oberkiefer^M
maxilar^M separable

pit
fossette^F
Grubenorgan^N
cavidad^F nasal

venom-conducting tube
conduit^M de la glande^F
Gift-Leitfurche^F
conducto^M del veneno^M

venom canal
canal^M à venin^M
Giftkanal^M
canal^M del veneno^M

fang
crochet^M à venin^M
Giftzahn^M
colmillo^M

venom gland
glande^F à venin^M
Giftdrüse^F
glándula^F de veneno^M

glottis
glotte^F
Glottis^F
glotis^F

tooth
dent^F
Zahn^M
diente^M

forked tongue
langue^F bifide
gespaltene Zunge^F
lengua^F bífida

nostril
narine^F
Nasenloch^N
orificio^M nasal

vertical pupil
pupille^F verticale
senkrechte Pupille^F
pupila^F vertical

eye
œil^M
Auge^N
ojo^M

scale
écaille^F
Schuppe^F
escama^F

tongue sheath
fourreau^M de la langue^F
Zungenscheide^F
forro^M de la lengua^F

SHELL
CARAPACE^F
PANZER^M
CAPARAZÓN^M

carapace
dossière^F
Rückenpanzer^M
espaldar^M

pygal shield
plaque^F supra-caudale
Pygalschild^M
placa^F supracaudal

tail
queue^F
Schwanz^M
cola^F

marginal shield
plaque^F marginale
Marginalschild^M
placa^F marginal

plastron
plastron^M
Bauchpanzer^M
plastrón^M

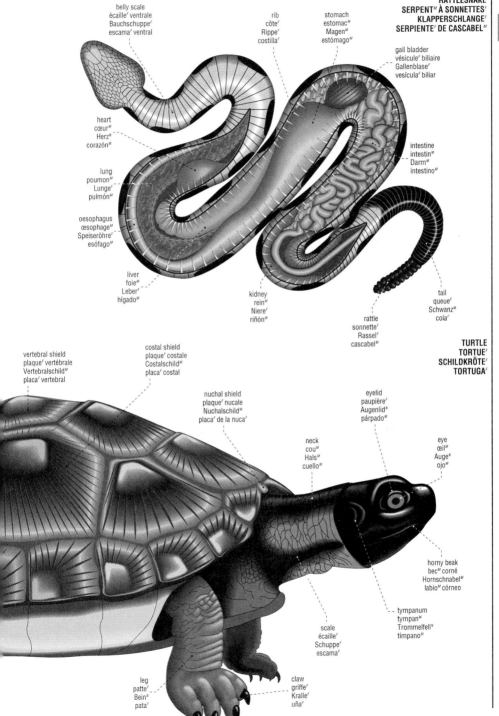

RATTLESNAKE
SERPENT[M] **À SONNETTES**[F]
KLAPPERSCHLANGE[F]
SERPIENTE[F] **DE CASCABEL**[M]

belly scale
écaille[F] ventrale
Bauchschuppe[F]
escama[F] ventral

rib
côte[F]
Rippe[F]
costilla[F]

stomach
estomac[M]
Magen[M]
estómago[M]

gall bladder
vésicule[F] biliaire
Gallenblase[F]
vesícula[F] biliar

heart
cœur[M]
Herz[N]
corazón[M]

intestine
intestin[M]
Darm[M]
intestino[M]

lung
poumon[M]
Lunge[F]
pulmón[M]

oesophagus
œsophage[M]
Speiseröhre[F]
esófago[M]

liver
foie[M]
Leber[F]
hígado[M]

kidney
rein[M]
Niere[F]
riñón[M]

tail
queue[F]
Schwanz[M]
cola[F]

rattle
sonnette[F]
Rassel[F]
cascabel[M]

TURTLE
TORTUE[F]
SCHILDKRÖTE[F]
TORTUGA[F]

vertebral shield
plaque[F] vertébrale
Vertebralschild[M]
placa[F] vertebral

costal shield
plaque[F] costale
Costalschild[M]
placa[F] costal

nuchal shield
plaque[F] nucale
Nuchalschild[M]
placa[F] de la nuca[F]

eyelid
paupière[F]
Augenlid[N]
párpado[M]

neck
cou[M]
Hals[M]
cuello[M]

eye
œil[M]
Auge[N]
ojo[M]

horny beak
bec[M] corné
Hornschnabel[M]
labio[M] córneo

tympanum
tympan[M]
Trommelfell[N]
tímpano[M]

scale
écaille[F]
Schuppe[F]
escama[F]

leg
patte[F]
Bein[N]
pata[F]

claw
griffe[F]
Kralle[F]
uña[F]

97

TYPES OF JAW
TYPES*M* DE MÂCHOIRES*F*
GEBISSARTEN*F*
TIPOS*M* DE MANDÍBULAS*F*

BEAVER
CASTOR*M*
BIBER*M*
CASTOR*M*

RODENT'S JAW
MÂCHOIRE*F* DE RONGEUR*M*
NAGETIERGEBISS*N*
MANDÍBULA*F* DE ROEDOR*M*

molar
molaire*F*
Molar*M*
molar*M*

premolar
prémolaire*F*
Prämolar*M*
premolar*M*

incisor
incisive*F*
Schneidezahn*M*
incisivo*M*

diastema
barre*F*
Laden*M*
diastema*F*

LION
LION*M*
LÖWE*M*
LEÓN*M*

CARNIVORE'S JAW
MÂCHOIRE*F* DE CARNIVORE*M*
FLEISCHFRESSERGEBISS*N*
MANDÍBULA*F* DE CARNÍVORO*M*

incisor
incisive*F*
Schneidezahn*M*
incisivo*M*

canine
canine*F*
Eckzahn*M*
colmillo*M*

premolar
prémolaire*F*
Prämolar*M*
premolar*M*

molar
molaire*F*
Molar*M*
molar*M*

carnassial
carnassière*F*
Reißzahn*M*
carnicero*M*

HORSE
CHEVAL*M*
PFERD*N*
CABALLO*M*

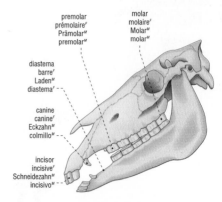

HERBIVORE'S JAW
MÂCHOIRE*F* D'HERBIVORE*M*
PFLANZENFRESSERGEBISS*N*
MANDÍBULA*F* DE HERBÍVORO*M*

premolar
prémolaire*F*
Prämolar*M*
premolar*M*

molar
molaire*F*
Molar*M*
molar*M*

diastema
barre*F*
Laden*M*
diastema*F*

canine
canine*F*
Eckzahn*M*
colmillo*M*

incisor
incisive*F*
Schneidezahn*M*
incisivo*M*

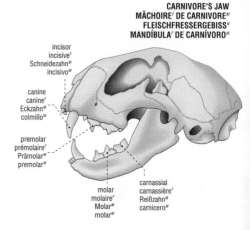

PRINCIPAL TYPES OF HORN
PRINCIPAUX TYPES^M DE CORNES^F
WICHTIGSTE HORNARTEN^F
CUERNOS^M: TIPOS^M MÁS COMUNES

horns of a mouflon
cornes^f de mouflon^M
Hörnerⁿ eines Mufflons^M
cuernos^M de carnero^M

horns of a giraffe
cornes^f de girafe^f
Hörnerⁿ einer Giraffe^f
cuernos^M de jirafa^f

horns of a rhinoceros
cornes^f de rhinocéros^M
Hörnerⁿ eines Nashornsⁿ
cuernos^M de rinoceronte^M

PRINCIPAL TYPES OF TUSK
PRINCIPAUX TYPES^M DE DÉFENSES^F
WICHTIGSTE STOSSZÄHNE^M
COLMILOS^M: TIPOS^M MÁS COMUNES

tusks of an elephant
défenses^f d'éléphant^M
Stoßzähne^M eines Elefanten^M
colmillos^M de elefante^M

tusks of a walrus
défenses^f de morse^M
Eckzähne^M eines Walrossesⁿ
colmillos^M de morsa^f

tusks of a wart hog
défenses^f de phacochère^M
Hauer^M eines Warzenschweinsⁿ
colmillos^M de jabalí^M verrugoso

TYPES OF HOOF
TYPES^M DE SABOTS^M
HUFARTEN^F
PATAS^F DE UNGULADOS^M: TIPOS^M MÁS COMUNES

one-toe hoof
sabot^M à 1 doigt^M
Ein-Zehenhuf^M
de una pezuña^f

two-toed hoof
sabot^M à 2 doigts^M
Zwei-Zehenhuf^M
de dos pezuñas^f

three-toed hoof
sabot^M à 3 doigts^M
Drei-Zehenhuf^M
de tres pezuñas^f

four-toed hoof
sabot^M à 4 doigts^M
Vier-Zehenhuf^M
de cuatro pezuñas^f

HORSE
CHEVAL^M
PFERD^N
CABALLO^M

MORPHOLOGY
MORPHOLOGIE^F
MORPHOLOGIE^F
MORFOLOGÍA^F

cheek
ganache^F
Ganasche^F
quijada^F

forelock
toupet^M
Stirnschopf^F
copete^M

mane
crinière^F
Mähne^F
crin^F

nose
chanfrein^M
Nase^F
testuz^M

withers
garrot^M
Widerrist^M
cruz^F

muzzle
bout^M du nez^M
Maul^N
belfo^M

nostril
naseau^M
Nüster^F
orificio^M nasal

lip
lèvre^F
Lippe^F
labio^M

neck
encolure^F
Hals^M
cuello^M

shoulder
épaule^F
Schulter^F
paletilla^F

chest
poitrail^M
Brust^F
pecho^M

arm
bras^M
Arm^M
brazo^M

elbow
coude^M
Ellbogen^M
codillo^M

knee
genou^M
Knie^N
rodilla^F

chestnut
châtaigne^F
Kastanie^F
espejuelo^M

100

amble
amble^M
Paßgang^M
el paso^M de andadura^F

walk
pas^M
Schritt^M
el paso^M

trot
trot^M
Trab^M
el trote^M

gallop
galop^M
Galopp^M
el galope^M

back
dos^M
Rücken^M
lomo^M

loin
rein^M
Lende^F
riñones^M

croup
croupe^F
Kruppe^F
grupa^F

flank
flanc^M
Flanke^F
ijar^M

tail
queue^F
Schwanz^M
cola^F

thigh
cuisse^F
Schenkel^M
muslo^M

stifle
grasset^M
Kniescheibe^F
babilla^F

belly
ventre^M
Bauch^M
vientre^M

gaskin
jambe^F
Hose^F
pierna^F

sheath
fourreau^M
Präputialtasche^F
prepucio^M

hock
jarret^M
Sprunggelenk^N
corvejón^M

fetlock joint
boulet^M
Kötengelenk^N
menudillo^M

cannon
canon^M
Mittelfuß^M
caña^F

fetlock
fanon^M
Köte^F
espolón^M

pastern
paturon^M
Fessel^F
cuartilla^F

coronet
couronne^F
Krone^F
corona^F

hoof
sabot^M
Huf^M
casco^M

HORSE
CHEVAL[M]
PFERD[N]
CABALLO[M]

SKELETON
SQUELETTE[M]
SKELETT[N]
ESQUELETO[M]

atlas
atlas[M]
Atlas[M]
atlas[M]

rib
côte[F]
Rippe[F]
costilla[F]

skull
crâne[M]
Schädel[M]
cráneo[M]

scapula
omoplate[F]
Schulterblatt[N]
omoplato[M]

mandible
mandibule[F]
Unterkiefer[M]
mandíbula[F] inferior

skull
crâne[M]
Schädel[M]
cráneo[M]

humerus
humérus[M]
Oberarmbein[N]
húmero[M]

olecranon
olécrane[M]
Ellbogenhöcker[M]
olécrano[M]

sternum
sternum[M]
Brustbein[N]
esternón[M]

radius
radius[M]
Speiche[F]
radio[M]

ulna
cubitus[M]
Elle[F]
cúbito[M]

cervical vertebrae
vertèbres[F] cervicales
Halswirbel[M]
vértebras[F] cervicales

carpus
carpe[M]
Vorderfußwurzel[F]
carpo[M]

metacarpus
métacarpe[M]
Röhrbein[N]
metacarpo[M]

proximal sesamoid
grand sésamoïde[M]
Sesambein[N]
sesamoideo[M] mayor

thoracic vertebrae
vertèbres[F] dorsales
Brustwirbel[M]
vértebras[F] torácicas

distal sesamoid
petit sésamoïde[M]
Strahlbein[N]
sesamoideo[M] menor

lumbar vertebrae
vertèbres^f lombaires
Lendenwirbel^M
vértebras^f lumbares

sacral vertebrae
vertèbres^f sacrées
Kreuzbeinwirbel^M
vértebras^f sacras

caudal vertebrae
vertèbres^f coccygiennes
Schwanzwirbel^M
vértebras^f caudales

pelvis
bassin^M
Darmbein^N
pelvis^f

femur
fémur^M
Oberschenkel^M
fémur^M

fibula
péroné^M
Griffelbein^N
peroné^M

tibia
tibia^M
Unterschenkel^M
tibia^f

patella
rotule^f
Kniescheibe^f
rótula^f

calcaneus
calcanéum^M
Fersenbeinhöcker^M
calcáneo^M

phalanx prima
première phalange^f
Fesselbein^N
primera falange^f

tarsus
tarse^M
Fußwurzel^f
tarso^M

phalanx secunda
deuxième phalange^f
Kronbein^N
falangina^f

metatarsus
métatarse^M
Mittelfußknochen^M
metatarso^M

phalanx tertia
troisième phalange^f
Hufbein^N
falangeta^f

103

PLANTAR SURFACE OF THE HOOF
FACE*F* PLANTAIRE DU SABOT*M*
UNTERSEITE*F* DES HUFS*M*
SUPERFICIE*F* PLANTAR DEL CASCO*M*

bulb
glome*M*
Ballen*M*
pulpejo*M*

heel
talon*M*
Trachte*F*
talón*M*

median groove
lacune*F* médiane
mittlere Strahlgrube*F*
lámina*F* medial

frog
fourchette*F*
Hornstrahl*M*
ranilla*F*

lateral groove
lacune*F* latérale
seitliche Strahlgrube*F*
lámina*F* lateral

bar
barre*F*
Eckstrebe*F*
barra*F*

sole
sole*F*
Hornsohle*F*
palma*F*

quarter
quartier*M*
Trachtenwand*F*
cuarto*M*

wall
paroi*F*
Hornwand*F*
pared*F*

side wall
mamelle*F*
Seitenwand*F*
pared*F* lateral

white line
ligne*F* blanche
weiße Linie*F*
limbo*M* de la palma*F*

toe
pince*F*
Zehenwand*F*
uña*F*

HORSESHOE
FER*M* À CHEVAL*M*
HUFEISEN*N*
HERRADURA*F*

heel
éponge*F*
Trachte*F*
talón*M*

HOOF
SABOT*M*
HUF*M*
CASCO*M*

quarter
quartier*M*
Trachtenwand*F*
cuarto*M*

nail hole
étampure*F*
Nagelloch*N*
clavera*F*

nail
clou*M*
Nagel*M*
clavo*M*

branch
branche*F*
Schenkel*M*
rama*F*

side wall
mamelle*F*
Seitenwand*F*
pared*F* lateral

outer edge
rive*F* externe
äußerer Rand*M*
borde*M* externo

inner edge
rive*F* interne
innerer Rand*M*
borde*M* interno

toe
pince*F*
Zeh*M*
uña*F*

coronet
bourrelet*M*
Saumrand*M*
perioplo*M*

bulb
glome*M*
Ballen*M*
pulpejo*M*

toe
pince*F*
Zehenwand*F*
uña*F*

heel
talon*M*
Trachte*F*
talón*M*

toe clip
pinçon*M*
Zehenaufzug*M*
pestaña*F*

horseshoe
fer*M*
Hufeisen*N*
herradura*F*

side wall
mamelle*F*
Seitenwand*F*
pared*F* lateral

quarter
quartier*M*
Trachtenwand*F*
cuarto*M*

TIERREICH
REINO ANIMAL

ANIMAL KINGDOM
RÈGNE ANIMAL

DEER FAMILY
CERVIDÉS^M
FAMILIE^F DER HIRSCHE^M
CÉRVIDOS^M

DEER ANTLERS
BOIS^M DE CERF^M
HIRSCHGEWEIH^N
CORNAMENTA^F

fork
enfourchure^F
Gabel^F
horquilla^F

palm
empaumure^F
Krone^F
palma^F

crown tine
époi^M
Kronenende^N
candil^M coronal

pearl
perlure^F
Perle^F
capa^F córnea

royal antler
chevillure^F
Mittelsproß^M
tercera^F

gutter
gouttière^F
Furche^F
canalón^M

surroyal antler
trochure^F
Wolfssproß^M
cuarta^F

bay antler
surandouiller^M
Eissproß^M
baya^F

beam
merrain^M
Stange^F
asta^F

brow tine
andouiller^M de massacre^M
Augsproß^M
candil^M frontal

burr
meule^F
Rose^F
rodete^M

pearls
pierrures^F
Perlen^F
perlas^F

pedicle
pivot^M
Rosenstock^M
muñón^M

PRINCIPAL KINDS OF DEER
PRINCIPAUX CERVIDÉS^M
HIRSCHARTEN^F
PRINCIPALES CÉRVIDOS^M

reindeer
renne^M
Rentier^N
caribú^M

white-tailed deer
cerf^M de Virginie
Reh^N
ciervo^M de Virginia

elk
élan^M
Elch^M
alce^M

Canadian elk
cerf^M du Canada
Wapitihirsch^M
uapití^M

**MORPHOLOGY
MORPHOLOGIE**^F
MORPHOLOGIE^F
MORFOLOGÍA^F

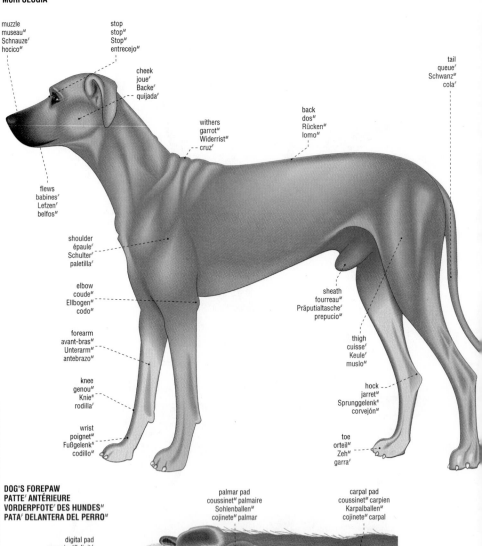

muzzle
museau^M
Schnauze^F
hocico^M

stop
stop^M
Stop^M
entrecejo^M

cheek
joue^F
Backe^F
quijada^F

tail
queue^F
Schwanz^M
cola^F

withers
garrot^M
Widerrist^M
cruz^F

back
dos^M
Rücken^M
lomo^M

flews
babines^F
Lefzen^F
belfos^M

shoulder
épaule^F
Schulter^F
paletilla^F

sheath
fourreau^M
Präputialtasche^F
prepucio^M

elbow
coude^M
Ellbogen^M
codo^M

thigh
cuisse^F
Keule^F
muslo^M

forearm
avant-bras^M
Unterarm^M
antebrazo^M

hock
jarret^M
Sprunggelenk^N
corvejón^M

knee
genou^M
Knie^N
rodilla^F

wrist
poignet^M
Fußgelenk^N
codillo^M

toe
orteil^M
Zeh^M
garra^F

**DOG'S FOREPAW
PATTE**^F **ANTÉRIEURE
VORDERPFOTE**^F **DES HUNDES**^M
PATA^F **DELANTERA DEL PERRO**^M

palmar pad
coussinet^M palmaire
Sohlenballen^M
cojinete^M palmar

carpal pad
coussinet^M carpien
Karpalballen^M
cojinete^M carpal

digital pad
coussinet^M digité
Zehenballen^M
cojinete^M digital

claw
griffe^F
Kralle^F
uña^F

toe
orteil^M
Zeh^M
garra^F

dew pad
coussinet^M de l'ergot^M
Afterkrallenballen^M
cojinete^M

dewclaw
ergot^M
Afterkralle^F
espolón^M

CAT
CHAT^M
KATZE^F
GATO^M DOMÉSTICO

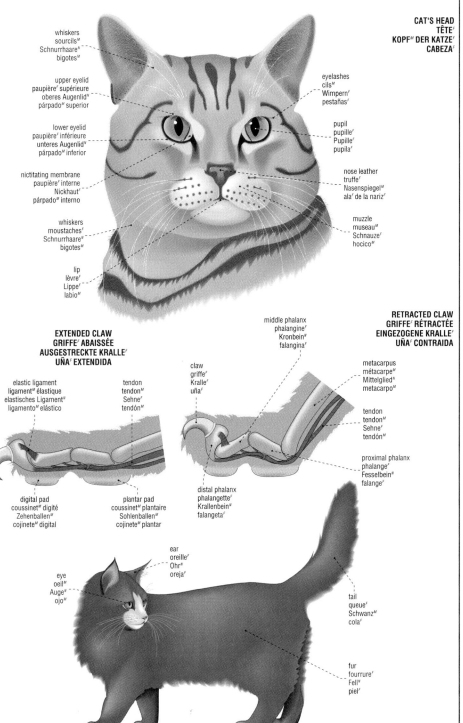

**CAT'S HEAD
TÊTE^F
KOPF^M DER KATZE^F
CABEZA^F**

whiskers
sourcils^M
Schnurrhaare^N
bigotes^M

upper eyelid
paupière^F supérieure
oberes Augenlid^N
párpado^M superior

lower eyelid
paupière^F inférieure
unteres Augenlid^N
párpado^M inferior

nictitating membrane
paupière^F interne
Nickhaut^F
párpado^M interno

whiskers
moustaches^F
Schnurrhaare^N
bigotes^M

lip
lèvre^F
Lippe^F
labio^M

eyelashes
cils^M
Wimpern^F
pestañas^F

pupil
pupille^F
Pupille^F
pupila^F

nose leather
truffe^F
Nasenspiegel^M
ala^F de la nariz^F

muzzle
museau^M
Schnauze^F
hocico^M

**EXTENDED CLAW
GRIFFE^F ABAISSÉE
AUSGESTRECKTE KRALLE^F
UÑA^F EXTENDIDA**

elastic ligament
ligament^M élastique
elastisches Ligament^N
ligamento^M elástico

tendon
tendon^M
Sehne^F
tendón^M

digital pad
coussinet^M digité
Zehenballen^M
cojinete^M digital

plantar pad
coussinet^M plantaire
Sohlenballen^M
cojinete^M plantar

middle phalanx
phalangine^F
Kronbein^N
falangina^F

claw
griffe^F
Kralle^F
uña^F

distal phalanx
phalangette^F
Krallenbein^N
falangeta^F

**RETRACTED CLAW
GRIFFE^F RÉTRACTÉE
EINGEZOGENE KRALLE^F
UÑA^F CONTRAIDA**

metacarpus
métacarpe^M
Mittelglied^N
metacarpo^M

tendon
tendon^M
Sehne^F
tendón^M

proximal phalanx
phalange^F
Fesselbein^N
falange^F

ear
oreille^F
Ohr^N
oreja^F

eye
oeil^M
Auge^N
ojo^M

tail
queue^F
Schwanz^M
cola^F

fur
fourrure^F
Fell^N
piel^F

MORPHOLOGY
MORPHOLOGIE[F]
MORPHOLOGIE[F]
MORFOLOGÍA[F]

nape
nuque[F]
Nacken[M]
cerviz[F]

back
dos[M]
Rücken[M]
lomo[M]

bill
bec[M]
Schnabel[M]
pico[M]

chin
menton[M]
Kinn[N]
mentón[M]

throat
gorge[F]
Kehle[F]
garganta[F]

wing covert
tectrice[F] sus-alaire
Deckfeder[F]
coberteras[F]

breast
poitrine[F]
Brust[F]
pechuga[F]

wing
aile[F]
Flügel[M]
ala[F]

abdomen
abdomen[M]
Bauch[M]
abdomen

tarsus
tarse[M]
Lauf[M]
tarso[M]

flank
flanc[M]
Flanke[F]
flanco[M]

inner toe
doigt[M] interne
zweite Zehe[F]
dedo[M] interno

thigh
tibia[M]
Schenkel[M]
muslo[M]

middle toe
doigt[M] médian
dritte Zehe[F]
dedo[M] medio

hind toe
doigt[M] postérieur
Hinterzehe[F]
dedo[M] posterior

outer toe
doigt[M] externe
vierte Zehe[F]
dedo[M] externo

claw
griffe[F]
Kralle[F]
uña[F]

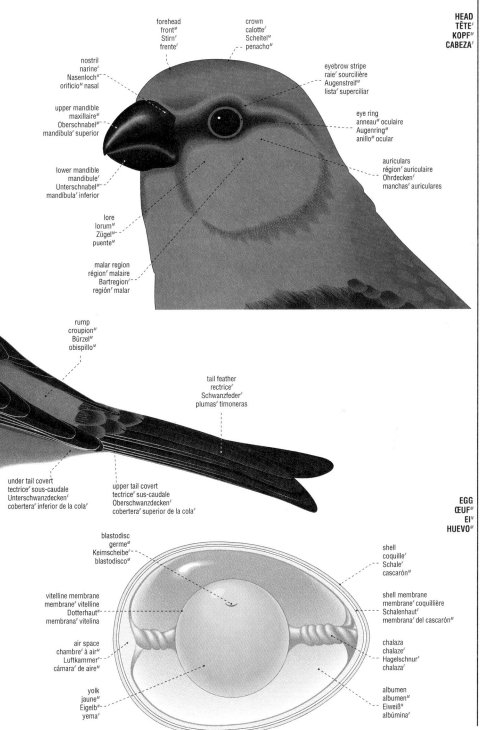

HEAD
TÊTE[F]
KOPF[M]
CABEZA[F]

forehead
front[M]
Stirn[F]
frente[F]

crown
calotte[F]
Scheitel[M]
penacho[M]

nostril
narine[F]
Nasenloch[N]
orificio[M] nasal

eyebrow stripe
raie[F] sourcilière
Augenstreif[M]
lista[F] superciliar

upper mandible
maxillaire[M]
Oberschnabel[M]
mandíbula[F] superior

eye ring
anneau[M] oculaire
Augenring[M]
anillo[M] ocular

auriculars
région[F] auriculaire
Ohrdecken[F]
manchas[F] auriculares

lower mandible
mandibule[F]
Unterschnabel[M]
mandíbula[F] inferior

lore
lorum[M]
Zügel[M]
puente[M]

malar region
région[F] malaire
Bartregion[F]
región[F] malar

rump
croupion[M]
Bürzel[M]
obispillo[M]

tail feather
rectrice[F]
Schwanzfeder[F]
plumas[F] timoneras

under tail covert
tectrice[F] sous-caudale
Unterschwanzdecken[F]
cobertera[F] inferior de la cola[F]

upper tail covert
tectrice[F] sus-caudale
Oberschwanzdecken[F]
cobertera[F] superior de la cola[F]

EGG
ŒUF[M]
EI[N]
HUEVO[M]

blastodisc
germe[M]
Keimscheibe[F]
blastodisco[M]

shell
coquille[F]
Schale[F]
cascarón[M]

vitelline membrane
membrane[F] vitelline
Dotterhaut[F]
membrana[F] vitelina

shell membrane
membrane[F] coquillière
Schalenhaut[F]
membrana[F] del cascarón[M]

air space
chambre[F] à air[M]
Luftkammer[F]
cámara[F] de aire[M]

chalaza
chalaze[F]
Hagelschnur[F]
chalaza[F]

yolk
jaune[M]
Eigelb[N]
yema[F]

albumen
albumen[M]
Eiweiß[N]
albúmina[F]

BIRD
OISEAU^M
VOGEL^M
AVE^F

WING
AILE^F
FLÜGEL^M
ALA^F

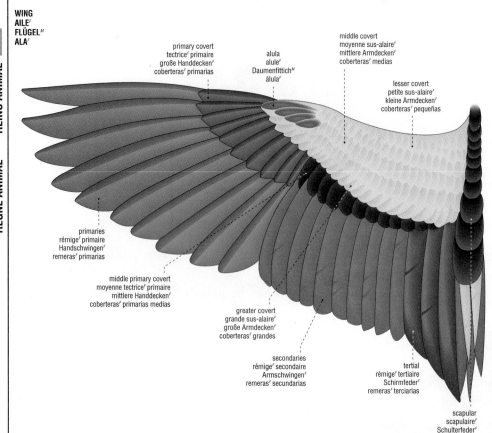

primary covert
tectrice^F primaire
große Handdecken^F
coberteras^F primarias

alula^F
alule^F
Daumenfittich^M
álula^F

middle covert
moyenne sus-alaire^F
mittlere Armdecken^F
coberteras^F medias

lesser covert
petite sus-alaire^F
kleine Armdecken^F
coberteras^F pequeñas

primaries
rémige^F primaire
Handschwingen^F
remeras^F primarias

middle primary covert
moyenne tectrice^F primaire
mittlere Handdecken^F
coberteras^F primarias medias

greater covert
grande sus-alaire^F
große Armdecken^F
coberteras^F grandes

secondaries
rémige^F secondaire
Armschwingen^F
remeras^F secundarias

tertial
rémige^F tertiaire
Schirmfeder^F
remeras^F terciarias

scapular
scapulaire^F
Schulterfeder^F
escapulares^M

CONTOUR FEATHER
PENNE^F
KONTURFEDER^F
PLUMA^F

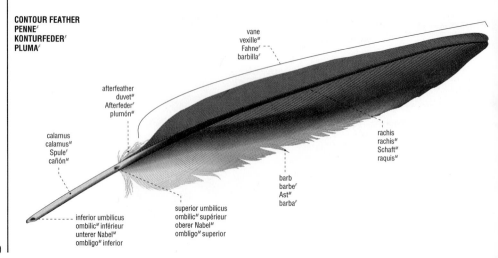

vane
vexille^M
Fahne^F
barbilla^F

afterfeather
duvet^M
Afterfeder^F
plumón^M

calamus
calamus^M
Spule^F
cañón^M

rachis
rachis^M
Schaft^M
raquis^M

barb
barbe^F
Ast^M
barba^F

inferior umbilicus
ombilic^M inférieur
unterer Nabel^M
ombligo^M inferior

superior umbilicus
ombilic^M supérieur
oberer Nabel^M
ombligo^M superior

PRINCIPAL TYPES OF BILL
PRINCIPAUX TYPES^M DE BECS^M
WICHTIGSTE SCHNABELARTEN^F
PRINCIPALES TIPOS^M DE PICOS^M

bird of prey
oiseau^M de proie^F
Raubvogel^M
ave^F de rapiña

aquatic bird
oiseau^M aquatique
Wasservogel^M
ave^F acuática

wading bird
oiseau^M échassier
Watvogel^M
ave^F zancuda

granivorous bird
oiseau^M granivore
Körnerfresser^M
ave^F granívora

insectivorous bird
oiseau^M insectivore
Insektenfresser^M
ave^F insectívora

PRINCIPAL TYPES OF FOOT
PRINCIPAUX TYPES^M DE PATTES^F
WICHTIGSTE FUSSARTEN^F
PRINCIPALES TIPOS^M DE PATAS^F

perching bird
oiseau^M percheur
Baumvogel^M
aves^F trepadoras

bird of prey
oiseau^M de proie^F
Raubvogel^M
aves^F de rapiña

toe
doigt^M
Zehe^F
dedo^M

hind toe
pouce^M
Hinterzehe^F
dedo^M posterior

talon
serre^F
Kralle^F
garra^F

scale
écaille^F
Hornschuppe^F
escama^F

aquatic bird
oiseau^M aquatique
Wasservogel^M
aves^F acuáticas

aquatic bird
oiseau^M aquatique
Wasservogel^M
aves^F acuáticas

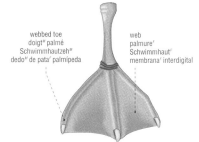

webbed toe
doigt^M palmé
Schwimmhautzeh^M
dedo^M de pata^F palmípeda

web
palmure^F
Schwimmhaut^F
membrana^F interdigital

lobe
lobe^M
Lappen^M
lóbulo^M

lobate toe
doigt^M lobé
Schwimmlappenzeh^M
dedo^M de pata^F lobulada

BAT
CHAUVE-SOURIS^F
FLEDERMAUS^F
MURCIÉLAGO^M

BAT'S HEAD
TÊTE^F
KOPF^M DER FLEDERMAUS^F
CABEZA^F DEL MURCIÉLAGO^M

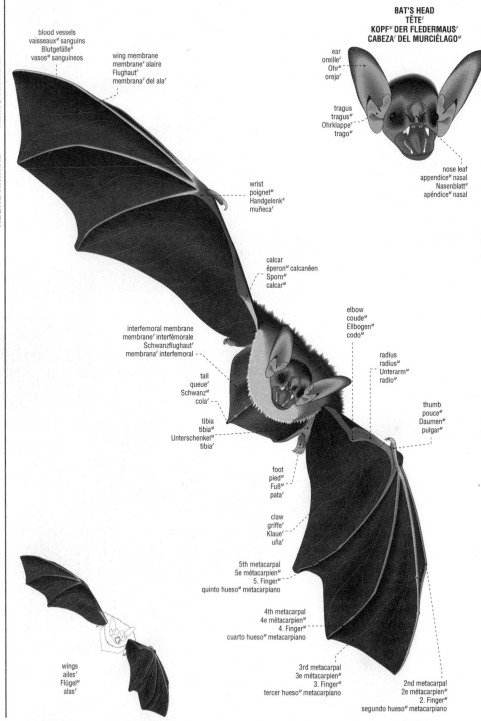

blood vessels
vaisseaux^M sanguins
Blutgefäße^N
vasos^M sanguíneos

wing membrane
membrane^F alaire
Flughaut^F
membrana^F del ala^F

ear
oreille^F
Ohr^N
oreja^F

tragus
tragus^M
Ohrklappe^F
trago^M

nose leaf
appendice^M nasal
Nasenblatt^N
apéndice^M nasal

wrist
poignet^M
Handgelenk^N
muñeca^F

calcar
éperon^M calcanéen
Sporn^M
calcar^M

elbow
coude^M
Ellbogen^M
codo^M

interfemoral membrane
membrane^F interfémorale
Schwanzflughaut^F
membrana^F interfemoral

radius
radius^M
Unterarm^M
radio^M

tail
queue^F
Schwanz^M
cola^F

thumb
pouce^M
Daumen^M
pulgar^M

tibia
tibia^M
Unterschenkel^M
tibia^F

foot
pied^M
Fuß^M
pata^F

claw
griffe^F
Klaue^F
uña^F

5th metacarpal
5e métacarpien^M
5. Finger^M
quinto hueso^M metacarpiano

4th metacarpal
4e métacarpien^M
4. Finger^M
cuarto hueso^M metacarpiano

wings
ailes^F
Flügel^M
alas^F

3rd metacarpal
3e métacarpien^M
3. Finger^M
tercer hueso^M metacarpiano

2nd metacarpal
2e métacarpien^M
2. Finger^M
segundo hueso^M metacarpiano

SUMMARY

PLANT CELL
CELLULE^F VÉGÉTALE
PFLANZENZELLE^F
CÉLULA^F VEGETAL

cytoplasm
cytoplasme^M
Zytoplasma^N
citoplasma^M

cell wall
membrane^F squelettique
Zellwand^F
pared^F celulósica

ribosome
ribosome^M
Ribosom^M
ribosoma^M

lipid droplet
gouttelette^F lipidique
Fett-Tröpfchen^N
glóbulo^M de grasa^F

chloroplast
chloroplaste^M
Chloroplast^M
cloroplasto^M

starch granule
grain^M d'amidon^M
Stärkekörnchen^N
glóbulo^M de almidón^M

plasmodesma
plasmodesme^M
Plasmabrücke^F
plasmodesma^M

cell membrane
membrane^F cytoplasmique
Zytoplasmamembran^F
membrana^F celulósica

endoplasmic reticulum
réticulum^M endoplasmique
endoplasmatisches Retikulum^N
retículo^M endoplasmático

vacuole
vacuole^F
Vakuole^F
vacuola^F

pore
pore^M
Pore^F
poro^M

Golgi apparatus
appareil^M de Golgi
Golgi-Apparat^M
aparato^M de Golgi

nucleus
noyau^M
Zellkern^M
núcleo^M

leucoplast
leucoplaste^M
Leukoplast^M
leucoplasto^M

nuclear membrane
membrane^F nucléaire
Kernmembran^F
membrana^F nuclear

mitochondrion
mitochondrie^F
Mitochondrium^N
mitocondrio^M

nucleolus
nucléole^M
Nukleolus^M
nucléolo^M

ANIMAL CELL
CELLULE^F ANIMALE
TIERISCHE ZELLE^F
CÉLULA^F ANIMAL

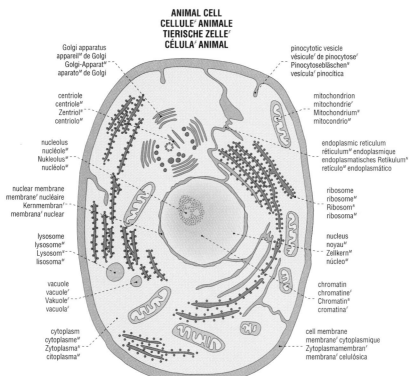

Golgi apparatus
appareil^M de Golgi
Golgi-Apparat^M
aparato^M de Golgi

pinocytotic vesicle
vésicule^F de pinocytose^F
Pinocytosebläschen^N
vesícula^F pinocítica

centriole
centriole^M
Zentriol^N
centriolo^M

mitochondrion
mitochondrie^F
Mitochondrium^N
mitocondrio^M

nucleolus
nucléole^M
Nukleolus^M
nucléolo^M

endoplasmic reticulum
réticulum^M endoplasmique
endoplasmatisches Retikulum^N
retículo^M endoplasmático

nuclear membrane
membrane^F nucléaire
Kernmembran^F
membrana^F nuclear

ribosome
ribosome^M
Ribosom^N
ribosoma^M

lysosome
lysosome^M
Lysosom^N
lisosoma^M

nucleus
noyau^M
Zellkern^M
núcleo^M

vacuole
vacuole^F
Vakuole^F
vacuola^F

chromatin
chromatine^F
Chromatin^N
cromatina^F

cytoplasm
cytoplasme^M
Zytoplasma^N
citoplasma^M

cell membrane
membrane^F cytoplasmique
Zytoplasmamembran^F
membrana^F celulósica

115

HUMAN BODY
CORPS^M HUMAIN
MENSCHLICHER KÖRPER^M
CUERPO^M HUMANO

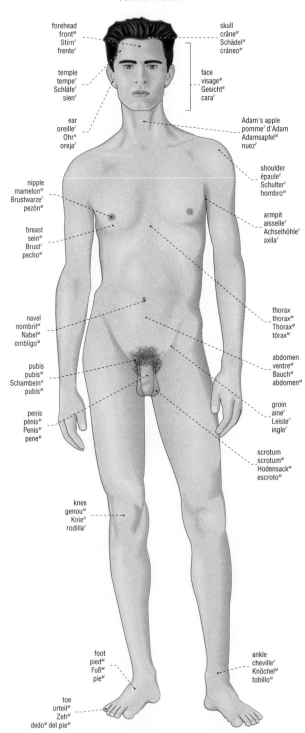

forehead
front^M
Stirn^F
frente^F

temple
tempe^F
Schläfe^F
sien^F

ear
oreille^F
Ohr^N
oreja^F

nipple
mamelon^M
Brustwarze^F
pezón^M

breast
sein^M
Brust^F
pecho^M

navel
nombril^M
Nabel^M
ombligo^M

pubis
pubis^M
Schambein^N
pubis^M

penis
pénis^M
Penis^M
pene^M

knee
genou^M
Knie^N
rodilla^F

foot
pied^M
Fuß^M
pie^M

toe
orteil^M
Zeh^M
dedo^M del pie^M

skull
crâne^M
Schädel^M
cráneo^M

face
visage^M
Gesicht^N
cara^F

Adam's apple
pomme^F d'Adam
Adamsapfel^M
nuez^F

shoulder
épaule^F
Schulter^F
hombro^M

armpit
aisselle^F
Achselhöhle^F
axila^F

thorax
thorax^M
Thorax^M
tórax^M

abdomen
ventre^M
Bauch^M
abdomen^M

groin
aine^F
Leiste^F
ingle^F

scrotum
scrotum^M
Hodensack^M
escroto^M

ankle
cheville^F
Knöchel^M
tobillo^M

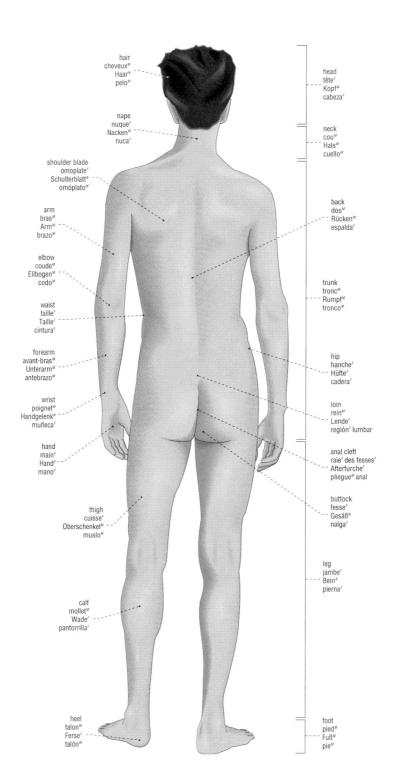

hair
cheveux^M
Haar^N
pelo^M

nape
nuque^F
Nacken^M
nuca^F

shoulder blade
omoplate^F
Schulterblatt^N
omóplato^M

arm
bras^M
Arm^M
brazo^M

elbow
coude^M
Ellbogen^M
codo^M

waist
taille^F
Taille^F
cintura^F

forearm
avant-bras^M
Unterarm^M
antebrazo^M

wrist
poignet^M
Handgelenk^N
muñeca^F

hand
main^F
Hand^F
mano^F

thigh
cuisse^F
Oberschenkel^M
muslo^M

calf
mollet^M
Wade^F
pantorrilla^F

heel
talon^M
Ferse^F
talón^M

head
tête^F
Kopf^M
cabeza^F

neck
cou^M
Hals^M
cuello^M

back
dos^M
Rücken^M
espalda^F

trunk
tronc^M
Rumpf^M
tronco^M

hip
hanche^F
Hüfte^F
cadera^F

loin
rein^M
Lende^F
región^F lumbar

anal cleft
raie^F des fesses^F
Afterfurche^F
pliegue^M anal

buttock
fesse^F
Gesäß^N
nalga^F

leg
jambe^F
Bein^N
pierna^F

foot
pied^M
Fuß^M
pie^M

HUMAN BODY
CORPS^M HUMAIN
MENSCHLICHER KÖRPER^M
CUERPO^M HUMANO

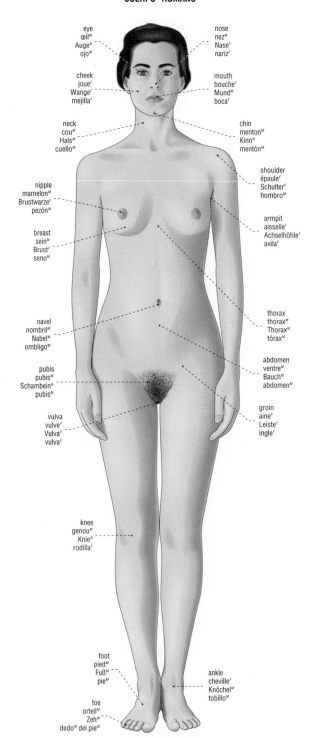

eye
œil^M
Auge^N
ojo^M

nose
nez^M
Nase^F
nariz^F

cheek
joue^F
Wange^F
mejilla^F

mouth
bouche^F
Mund^M
boca^F

neck
cou^M
Hals^M
cuello^M

chin
menton^M
Kinn^N
mentón^M

shoulder
épaule^F
Schulter^F
hombro^M

nipple
mamelon^M
Brustwarze^F
pezón^M

armpit
aisselle^F
Achselhöhle^F
axila^F

breast
sein^M
Brust^F
seno^M

thorax
thorax^M
Thorax^M
tórax^M

navel
nombril^M
Nabel^M
ombligo^M

abdomen
ventre^M
Bauch^M
abdomen^M

pubis
pubis^M
Schambein^N
pubis^M

groin
aine^F
Leiste^F
ingle^F

vulva
vulve^F
Vulva^F
vulva^F

knee
genou^M
Knie^N
rodilla^F

foot
pied^M
Fuß^M
pie^M

ankle
cheville^F
Knöchel^M
tobillo^M

toe
orteil^M
Zeh^M
dedo^M del pie^M

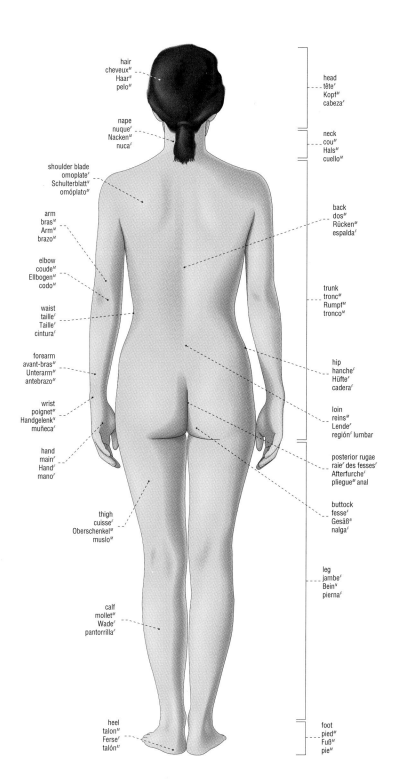

hair
cheveux^M
Haar^N
pelo^M

nape
nuque^F
Nacken^M
nuca^F

shoulder blade
omoplate^F
Schulterblatt^N
omóplato^M

arm
bras^M
Arm^M
brazo^M

elbow
coude^M
Ellbogen^M
codo^M

waist
taille^F
Taille^F
cintura^F

forearm
avant-bras^M
Unterarm^M
antebrazo^M

wrist
poignet^M
Handgelenk^N
muñeca^F

hand
main^F
Hand^F
mano^F

thigh
cuisse^F
Oberschenkel^M
muslo^M

calf
mollet^M
Wade^F
pantorrilla^F

heel
talon^M
Ferse^F
talón^M

head
tête^F
Kopf^M
cabeza^F

neck
cou^M
Hals^M
cuello^M

back
dos^M
Rücken^M
espalda^F

trunk
tronc^M
Rumpf^M
tronco^M

hip
hanche^F
Hüfte^F
cadera^F

loin
reins^M
Lende^F
región^F lumbar

posterior rugae
raie^F des fesses^F
Afterfurche^F
pliegue^M anal

buttock
fesse^F
Gesäß^N
nalga^F

leg
jambe^F
Bein^N
pierna^F

foot
pied^M
Fuß^M
pie^M

119

MUSCLES
MUSCLES^M
MUSKELN^M
MÚSCULOS^M

ANTERIOR VIEW
FACE^F ANTÉRIEURE
VORDERANSICHT^F
VISTA^F ANTERIOR

frontal
frontal^M
Stirn^F
frontal^F

orbicularis oculi
orbiculaire^M des paupières^F
Augenringmuskel^M
orbicular^M

sternocleidomastoid
sterno-cléido-mastoïdien^M
Kopfnicker^M
esternocleidomastoideo^M

masseter
masséter^M
Kaumuskel^M
masetero^M

trapezius
trapèze^M
Kapuzenmuskel^M
trapecio^M

deltoid
deltoïde^M
Deltamuskel^M
deltoides^M

greater pectoral
grand pectoral^M
großer Brustmuskel^M
pectoral^M mayor

external oblique
grand oblique^M de l'abdomen^M
äußerer schräger Bauchmuskel^M
oblicuo^M mayor

biceps of arm
biceps^M brachial
zweiköpfiger Armstrecker^M
bíceps^M braquial

abdominal rectus
grand droit^M de l'abdomen^M
gerader Bauchmuskel^M
recto^M del abdomen^M

brachial
brachial^M antérieur
Armbeuger^M
braquial^M anterior

brachioradialis
huméro-stylo-radial^M
Oberarmspeichenmuskel^M
supinador^M largo

round pronator
rond pronateur^M
runder Einwärtsdreher^M
pronador^M redondo

tensor of fascia lata
tenseur^M du fascia lata^M
Schenkelbindenspanner^M
tensor^M de la fascia lata^F

long palmar
grand palmaire^M
langer Hohlhandmuskel^M
palmar^M mayor

long adductor
moyen adducteur^M
langer
Oberschenkelanzieher^M
aductor^M del muslo^M

short palmar
petit palmaire^M
kurzer Hohlhandmuskel^M
palmar^M menor

sartorius
couturier^M
Schneidermuskel^M
sartorio^M

ulnar flexor of wrist
cubital^M antérieur
Handbeuger^M der Ellenseite^F
cubital^M anterior

rectus femoris
droit^M antérieur de la cuisse^F
gerader Schenkelmuskel^M
recto^M anterior

vastus lateralis
vaste^M externe du membre^M inférieur
äußerer Schenkelmuskel^M
vasto^M interno

vastus medialis
vaste^M interne du membre^M inférieur
innerer Schenkelmuskel^M
vasto^M externo

gastrocnemius
jumeau^M
Zwillingswadenmuskel^M
gemelos^M

long peroneal
long péronier^M latéral
langer Wadenbeinmuskel^M
peroneo^M lateral largo

soleus
soléaire^M
Schollenmuskel^M
sóleo^M

anterior tibial
jambier^M antérieur
vorderer Schienbeinmuskel^M
tibial^M anterior

long extensor of toes
extenseur^M commun des orteils^M
langer Zehenstrecker^M
extensor^M común de los dedos^M del pie^M

short extensor of toes
pédieux^M
kurzer Zehenstrecker^M
pedio^M

plantar interosseous
interosseux^M
Zwischenknochenmuskel^M
interóseos^M del pie^M

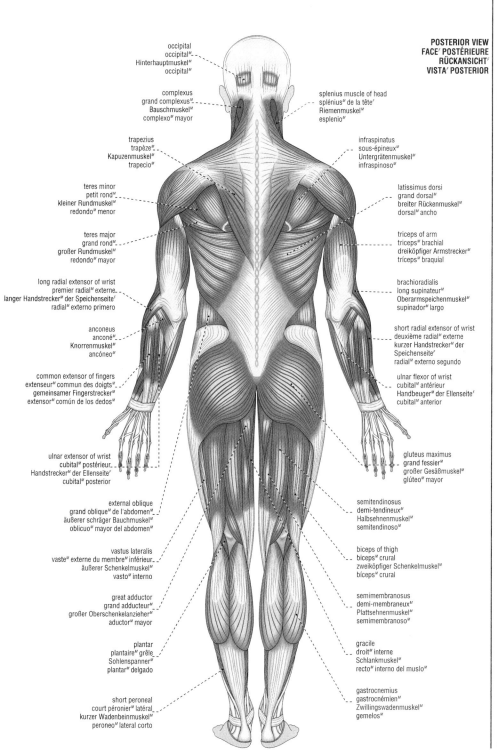

occipital
occipital^M
Hinterhauptmuskel^M
occipital^M

complexus
grand complexus^M
Bauschmuskel^M
complexo^M mayor

trapezius
trapèze^M
Kapuzenmuskel^M
trapecio^M

teres minor
petit rond^M
kleiner Rundmuskel^M
redondo^M menor

teres major
grand rond^M
großer Rundmuskel^M
redondo^M mayor

long radial extensor of wrist
premier radial^M externe
langer Handstrecker^M der Speichenseite^F
radial^M externo primero

anconeus
anconé^M
Knorrenmuskel^M
ancóneo^M

common extensor of fingers
extenseur^M commun des doigts^M
gemeinsamer Fingerstrecker^M
extensor^M común de los dedos^M

ulnar extensor of wrist
cubital^M postérieur
Handstrecker^M der Ellenseite^F
cubital^M posterior

external oblique
grand oblique^M de l'abdomen^M
äußerer schräger Bauchmuskel^M
oblicuo^M mayor del abdomen^M

vastus lateralis
vaste^M externe du membre^M inférieur
äußerer Schenkelmuskel^M
vasto^M interno

great adductor
grand adducteur^M
großer Oberschenkelanzieher^M
aductor^M mayor

plantar
plantaire^M grêle
Sohlenspanner^M
plantar^M delgado

short peroneal
court péronier^M latéral
kurzer Wadenbeinmuskel^M
peroneo^M lateral corto

splenius muscle of head
splénius^M de la tête^F
Riemenmuskel^M
esplenio^M

infraspinatus
sous-épineux^M
Untergrätenmuskel^M
infraspinoso^M

latissimus dorsi
grand dorsal^M
breiter Rückenmuskel^M
dorsal^M ancho

triceps of arm
triceps^M brachial
dreiköpfiger Armstrecker^M
tríceps^M braquial

brachioradialis
long supinateur^M
Oberarmspeichenmuskel^M
supinador^M largo

short radial extensor of wrist
deuxième radial^M externe
kurzer Handstrecker^M der
Speichenseite^F
radial^M externo segundo

ulnar flexor of wrist
cubital^M antérieur
Handbeuger^M der Ellenseite^F
cubital^M anterior

gluteus maximus
grand fessier^M
großer Gesäßmuskel^M
glúteo^M mayor

semitendinosus
demi-tendineux^M
Halbsehnenmuskel^M
semitendinoso^M

biceps of thigh
biceps^M crural
zweiköpfiger Schenkelmuskel^M
bíceps^M crural

semimembranosus
demi-membraneux^M
Plattsehnenmuskel^M
semimembranoso^M

gracile
droit^M interne
Schlankmuskel^M
recto^M interno del muslo^M

gastrocnemius
gastrocnémien^M
Zwillingswadenmuskel^M
gemelos^M

SKELETON
SQUELETTE^M
SKELETT^N
ESQUELETO^M

ANTERIOR VIEW
VUE^F ANTÉRIEURE
VORDERANSICHT^F
VISTA^F ANTERIOR

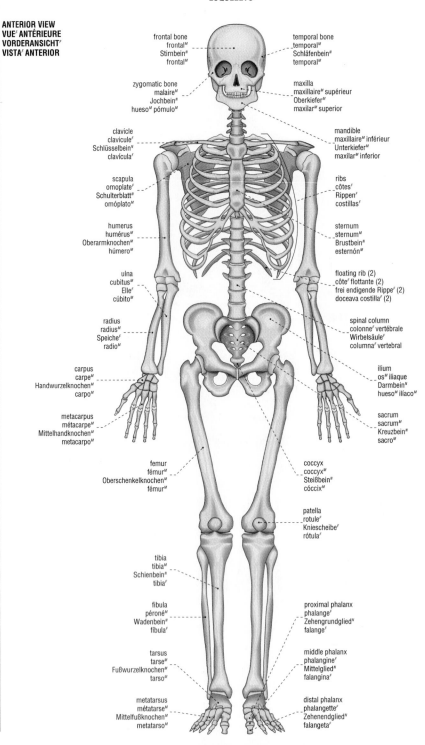

frontal bone
frontal^M
Stirnbein^N
frontal^M

temporal bone
temporal^M
Schläfenbein^N
temporal^M

zygomatic bone
malaire^M
Jochbein^N
hueso^M pómulo^M

maxilla
maxillaire^M supérieur
Oberkiefer^M
maxilar^M superior

clavicle
clavicule^F
Schlüsselbein^N
clavícula^F

mandible
maxillaire^M inférieur
Unterkiefer^M
maxilar^M inferior

scapula
omoplate^F
Schulterblatt^N
omóplato^M

ribs
côtes^F
Rippen^F
costillas^F

humerus
humérus^M
Oberarmknochen^M
húmero^M

sternum
sternum^M
Brustbein^N
esternón^M

ulna
cubitus^M
Elle^F
cúbito^M

floating rib (2)
côte^F flottante (2)
frei endigende Rippe^F (2)
doceava costilla^F (2)

radius
radius^M
Speiche^F
radio^M

spinal column
colonne^F vertébrale
Wirbelsäule^F
columna^F vertebral

carpus
carpe^M
Handwurzelknochen^M
carpo^M

ilium
os^M iliaque
Darmbein^N
hueso^M ilíaco^M

metacarpus
métacarpe^F
Mittelhandknochen^M
metacarpo^M

sacrum
sacrum^M
Kreuzbein^N
sacro^M

femur
fémur^M
Oberschenkelknochen^M
fémur^M

coccyx
coccyx^M
Steißbein^N
cóccix^M

patella
rotule^F
Kniescheibe^F
rótula^F

tibia
tibia^M
Schienbein^N
tibia^F

fibula
péroné^M
Wadenbein^N
fíbula^F

proximal phalanx
phalange^F
Zehengrundglied^N
falange^F

tarsus
tarse^M
Fußwurzelknochen^M
tarso^M

middle phalanx
phalangine^F
Mittelglied^N
falangina^F

metatarsus
métatarse^M
Mittelfußknochen^M
metatarso^M

distal phalanx
phalangette^F
Zehenendglied^N
falangeta^F

POSTERIOR VIEW
VUE^F POSTÉRIEURE
RÜCKANSICHT^F
VISTA POSTERIOR

HUMAN BEING
ÊTRE HUMAIN

MENSCH
SER HUMANO

occipital bone
occipital^M
Hinterhauptbein^N
occipital^M

parietal bone
pariétal^M
Scheitelbein^N
parietal^M

atlas
atlas^M
Atlas^M
atlas^M

axis
axis^M
Axis^F
axis^M

acromion
acromion^M
Schulterhöhe^F
acromión^M

cervical vertebra (7)
vertèbre^F cervicale (7)
Halswirbel^M (7)
vértebras^F cervicales (7)

spine of scapula
épine^F de l'omoplate^F
Schulterblattgräte^F
espina^F del omóplato^M

head of humerus
tête^F de l'humérus^M
Humeruskopf^M
cabeza^F del húmero^M

scapula
omoplate^F
Schulterblatt^N
omóplato^M

thoracic vertebra (12)
vertèbre^F dorsale (12)
Brustwirbel^M (12)
vértebras^F dorsales (12)

epicondyle
épicondyle^M
Gelenkhöcker^M
epicóndilo^M

false rib (3)
fausse côte^F (3)
freie Rippe^F (3)
costilla^F falsa (3)

olecranon
olécrâne^M
Olekranon^N
olécrano^M

lumbar vertebra (5)
vertèbre^F lombaire (5)
Lendenwirbel^M (5)
vértebras^F lumbares (5)

epitrochlea
épitrochlée^F
gekehlte Rolle^F
epitroclea^F

sacrum
sacrum^M
Kreuzbein^N
sacro^M

greater trochanter
grand trochanter^M
Schenkelbein^N
trocánter^M mayor

proximal phalanx
phalange^F
Grundglied^N
falange^F

neck of femur
col^M du fémur^M
Schenkelhals^M
cuello^M del fémur^M

middle phalanx
phalangine^F
Mittelglied^N
falangina^F

distal phalanx
phalangette^F
Endglied^N
falangeta^F

head of femur
tête^F du fémur^M
Femurkopf^M
cabeza^F del fémur^M

lateral condyle of femur
condyle^M externe
Condylus^M femoris lateralis
cóndilo^M externo

ischium
ischion^M
Sitzbein^N
isquión^M

medial condyle of femur
condyle^M interne
Condylus^M femoris medialis
cóndilo^M interno

talus
astragale^M
Sprungbein^N
astrágalo^M

calcaneus
calcanéum^M
Fersenbein^N
calcáneo^M

BLOOD CIRCULATION
CIRCULATION^F SANGUINE
BLUTKREISLAUF^M
CIRCULACIÓN^F SANGUÍNEA

CIRCULATION DIAGRAM
SCHÉMA^M DE LA CIRCULATION^F
SCHEMA^N DES BLUTKREISLAUFS^M
DIAGRAMA^M DE LA CIRCULACIÓN^F

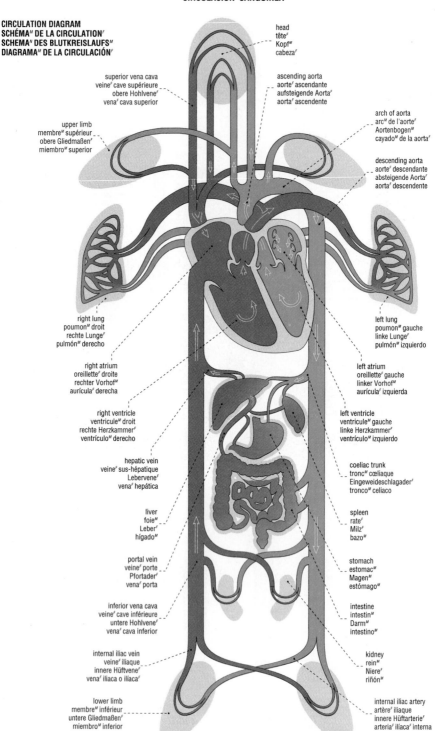

head
tête^F
Kopf^M
cabeza^F

superior vena cava
veine^F cave supérieure
obere Hohlvene^F
vena^F cava superior

ascending aorta
aorte^F ascendante
aufsteigende Aorta^F
aorta^F ascendente

arch of aorta
arc^M de l'aorte^F
Aortenbogen^M
cayado^M de la aorta^F

upper limb
membre^M supérieur
obere Gliedmaßen^F
miembro^M superior

descending aorta
aorte^F descendante
absteigende Aorta^F
aorta^F descendente

right lung
poumon^M droit
rechte Lunge^F
pulmón^M derecho

left lung
poumon^M gauche
linke Lunge^F
pulmón^M izquierdo

right atrium
oreillette^F droite
rechter Vorhof^M
aurícula^F derecha

left atrium
oreillette^F gauche
linker Vorhof^M
aurícula^F izquierda

right ventricle
ventricule^M droit
rechte Herzkammer^F
ventrículo^M derecho

left ventricle
ventricule^M gauche
linke Herzkammer^F
ventrículo^M izquierdo

hepatic vein
veine^F sus-hépatique
Lebervene^F
vena^F hepática

coeliac trunk
tronc^M cœliaque
Eingeweideschlagader^F
tronco^M celíaco

liver
foie^M
Leber^F
hígado^M

spleen
rate^F
Milz^F
bazo^M

portal vein
veine^F porte
Pfortader^F
vena^F porta

stomach
estomac^M
Magen^M
estómago^M

inferior vena cava
veine^F cave inférieure
untere Hohlvene^F
vena^F cava inferior

intestine
intestin^M
Darm^M
intestino^M

internal iliac vein
veine^F iliaque
innere Hüftvene^F
vena^F ilíaca o ilíaca^F

kidney
rein^M
Niere^F
riñón^M

lower limb
membre^M inférieur
untere Gliedmaßen^F
miembro^M inferior

internal iliac artery
artère^F iliaque
innere Hüftarterie^F
arteria^F ilíaca^F interna

superior vena cava
veine^F cave supérieure
obere Hohlvene^F
vena^F cava superior

arch of aorta
arc^M de l'aorte^F
Aortenbogen^M
cayado^M de la aorta^F

right pulmonary vein
veine^F pulmonaire droite
rechte Lungenvene^F
vena^F pulmonar derecha

right atrium
oreillette^F droite
rechter Vorhof^M
aurícula^F derecha

pulmonary trunk
artère^F pulmonaire
Lungenarterienstamm^M
arteria^F pulmonar

pulmonary valve
valve^F du tronc^M pulmonaire
Pulmonalklappe^F
válvula^F pulmonar

left atrium
oreillette^F gauche
linker Vorhof^M
aurícula^F izquierda

left pulmonary vein
veine^F pulmonaire gauche
linke Lungenvene^F
vena^F pulmonar izquierda

aortic valve
valve^F de l'aorte^F
Aortenklappe^F
válvula^F aórtica

mitral valve
valvule^F mitrale
Mitralklappe^F
válvula^F mitral

left ventricle
ventricule^M gauche
linke Herzkammer^F
ventrículo^M izquierdo

interventricular septum
septum^M interventriculaire
Kammerscheidewand^F
tabique^M interventricular

papillary muscle
muscle^M papillaire
Papillarmuskel^M
músculo^M papilar

right ventricle
ventricule^M droit
rechte Herzkammer^F
ventrículo^M derecho

inferior vena cava
veine^F cave inférieure
untere Hohlvene^F
vena^F cava inferior

tricuspid valve
valvule^F tricuspide
Trikuspidalklappe^F
válvula^F tricúspide

aorta
aorte^F
Aorta^F
aorta^F

BLOOD CIRCULATION
CIRCULATION^F SANGUINE
BLUTKREISLAUF^M
CIRCULACIÓN^F SANGUÍNEA

PRINCIPAL VEINS AND ARTERIES
PRINCIPALES VEINES^F ET ARTÈRES^F
DIE WICHTIGSTEN VENEN^F UND ARTERIEN^F
PRINCIPALES VENAS^F Y ARTERIAS^F

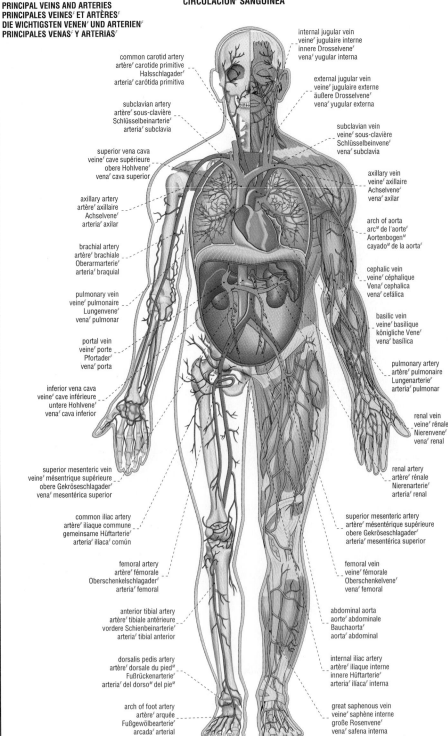

common carotid artery
artère^F carotide primitive
Halsschlagader^F
arteria^F carótida primitiva

subclavian artery
artère^F sous-clavière
Schlüsselbeinarterie^F
arteria^F subclavia

superior vena cava
veine^F cave supérieure
obere Hohlvene^F
vena^F cava superior

axillary artery
artère^F axillaire
Achselvene^F
arteria^F axilar

brachial artery
artère^F brachiale
Oberarmarterie^F
arteria^F braquial

pulmonary vein
veine^F pulmonaire
Lungenvene^F
vena^F pulmonar

portal vein
veine^F porte
Pfortader^F
vena^F porta

inferior vena cava
veine^F cave inférieure
untere Hohlvene^F
vena^F cava inferior

superior mesenteric vein
veine^F mésentrique supérieure
obere Gekröseschlagader^F
vena^F mesentérica superior

common iliac artery
artère^F iliaque commune
gemeinsame Hüftarterie^F
arteria^F ilíaca común

femoral artery
artère^F fémorale
Oberschenkelschlagader^F
arteria^F femoral

anterior tibial artery
artère^F tibiale antérieure
vordere Schienbeinarterie^F
arteria^F tibial anterior

dorsalis pedis artery
artère^F dorsale du pied^M
Fußrückenarterie^F
arteria^F del dorso^M del pie^M

arch of foot artery
artère^F arquée
Fußgewölbearterie^F
arcada^F arterial

internal jugular vein
veine^F jugulaire interne
innere Drosselvene^F
vena^F yugular interna

external jugular vein
veine^F jugulaire externe
äußere Drosselvene^F
vena^F yugular externa

subclavian vein
veine^F sous-clavière
Schlüsselbeinvene^F
vena^F subclavia

axillary vein
veine^F axillaire
Achselvene^F
vena^F axilar

arch of aorta
arc^M de l'aorte^F
Aortenbogen^M
cayado^M de la aorta^F

cephalic vein
veine^F céphalique
Vena^F cephalica
vena^F cefálica

basilic vein
veine^F basilique
königliche Vene^F
vena^F basílica

pulmonary artery
artère^F pulmonaire
Lungenarterie^F
arteria^F pulmonar

renal vein
veine^F rénale
Nierenvene^F
vena^F renal

renal artery
artère^F rénale
Nierenarterie^F
arteria^F renal

superior mesenteric artery
artère^F mésentérique supérieure
obere Gekröseschlagader^F
arteria^F mesentérica superior

femoral vein
veine^F fémorale
Oberschenkelvene^F
vena^F femoral

abdominal aorta
aorte^F abdominale
Bauchaorta^F
aorta^F abdominal

internal iliac artery
artère^F iliaque interne
innere Hüftarterie^F
arteria^F ilíaca^F interna

great saphenous vein
veine^F saphène interne
große Rosenvene^F
vena^F safena interna

MALE GENITAL ORGANS
ORGANES^M GÉNITAUX MASCULINS
MÄNNLICHE GESCHLECHTSORGANE^N
ÓRGANOS^M GENITALES MASCULINOS

SAGITTAL SECTION
COUPE^F SAGITTALE
SAGITTALSCHNITT^M
CORTE^M SAGITAL

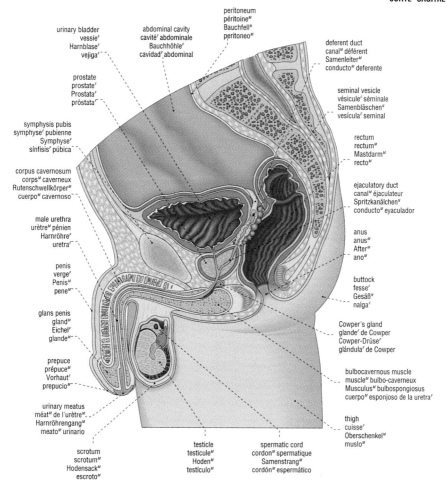

urinary bladder
vessie^F
Harnblase^F
vejiga^F

abdominal cavity
cavité^F abdominale
Bauchhöhle^F
cavidad^F abdominal

peritoneum
péritoine^M
Bauchfell^N
peritoneo^M

deferent duct
canal^M déférent
Samenleiter^M
conducto^M deferente

prostate
prostate^F
Prostata^F
próstata^F

seminal vesicle
vésicule^F séminale
Samenbläschen^N
vesícula^F seminal

symphysis pubis
symphyse^F pubienne
Symphyse^F
sínfisis^F púbica

rectum
rectum^M
Mastdarm^M
recto^M

corpus cavernosum
corps^M caverneux
Rutenschwellkörper^M
cuerpo^M cavernoso

ejaculatory duct
canal^M éjaculateur
Spritzkanälchen^N
conducto^M eyaculador

male urethra
urètre^M pénien
Harnröhre^F
uretra^F

anus
anus^M
After^M
ano^M

penis
verge^F
Penis^M
pene^M

buttock
fesse^F
Gesäß^N
nalga^F

glans penis
gland^M
Eichel^F
glande^F

Cowper's gland
glande^F de Cowper
Cowper-Drüse^F
glándula^F de Cowper

prepuce
prépuce^M
Vorhaut^F
prepucio^M

bulbocavernous muscle
muscle^M bulbo-caverneux
Musculus^M bulbospongiosus
cuerpo^M esponjoso de la uretra^F

urinary meatus
méat^M de l'urètre^M
Harnröhrengang^M
meato^M urinario

thigh
cuisse^F
Oberschenkel^M
muslo^M

scrotum
scrotum^M
Hodensack^M
escroto^M

testicle
testicule^M
Hoden^M
testículo^M

spermatic cord
cordon^M spermatique
Samenstrang^M
cordón^M espermático

SPERMATOZOON
SPERMATOZOÏDE^M
SPERMA^N
ESPERMATOZOIDE^M

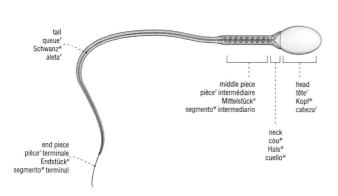

tail
queue^F
Schwanz^M
aleta^F

middle piece
pièce^F intermédiaire
Mittelstück^N
segmento^M intermediario

head
tête^F
Kopf^M
cabeza^F

neck
cou^M
Hals^M
cuello^M

end piece
pièce^F terminale
Endstück^N
segmento^M terminal

FEMALE GENITAL ORGANS
ORGANES^M GÉNITAUX FÉMININS
WEIBLICHE GESCHLECHTSORGANE^N
ÓRGANOS^M GENITALES FEMENINOS

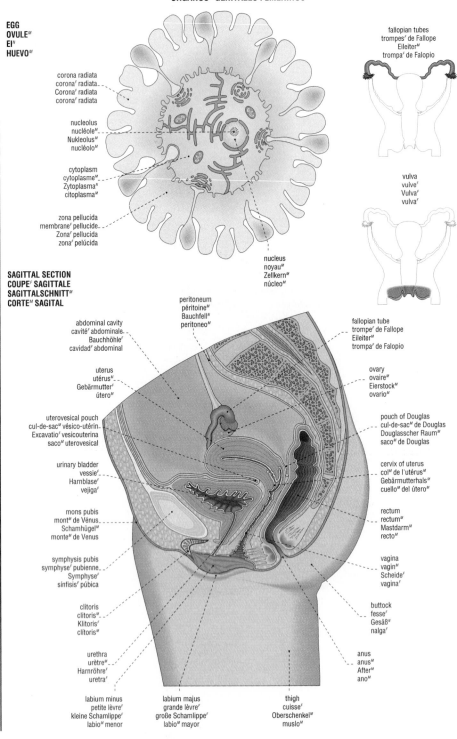

EGG
OVULE^M
EI^N
HUEVO^M

corona radiata
corona^f radiata
Corona^f radiata
corona^f radiata

nucleolus
nucléole^M
Nukleolus^M
nucléolo^M

cytoplasm
cytoplasme^M
Zytoplasma^N
citoplasma^M

zona pellucida
membrane^f pellucide
Zona^f pellucida
zona^f pelúcida

nucleus
noyau^M
Zellkern^M
núcleo^M

fallopian tubes
trompes^f de Fallope
Eileiter^M
trompa^f de Falopio

vulva
vulve^f
Vulva^f
vulva^f

SAGITTAL SECTION
COUPE^f SAGITTALE
SAGITTALSCHNITT^M
CORTE^M SAGITAL

peritoneum
péritoine^M
Bauchfell^N
peritoneo^M

abdominal cavity
cavité^f abdominale
Bauchhöhle^f
cavidad^f abdominal

uterus
utérus^M
Gebärmutter^f
útero^M

uterovesical pouch
cul-de-sac^M vésico-utérin
Excavatio^f vesicouterina
saco^M uterovesical

urinary bladder
vessie^f
Harnblase^f
vejiga^f

mons pubis
mont^M de Vénus
Schamhügel^M
monte^M de Venus

symphysis pubis
symphyse^f pubienne
Symphyse^f
sínfisis^f púbica

clitoris
clitoris^M
Klitoris^f
clítoris^M

urethra
urètre^M
Harnröhre^f
uretra^f

labium minus
petite lèvre^f
kleine Schamlippe^f
labio^M menor

labium majus
grande lèvre^f
große Schamlippe^f
labio^M mayor

thigh
cuisse^f
Oberschenkel^M
muslo^M

fallopian tube
trompe^f de Fallope
Eileiter^M
trompa^f de Falopio

ovary
ovaire^M
Eierstock^M
ovario^M

pouch of Douglas
cul-de-sac^M de Douglas
Douglasscher Raum^M
saco^M de Douglas

cervix of uterus
col^M de l'utérus^M
Gebärmutterhals^M
cuello^M del útero^M

rectum
rectum^M
Mastdarm^M
recto^M

vagina
vagin^M
Scheide^f
vagina^f

buttock
fesse^f
Gesäß^N
nalga^f

anus
anus^M
After^M
ano^M

FEMALE GENITAL ORGANS
ORGANES^M GÉNITAUX FÉMININS
WEIBLICHE GESCHLECHTSORGANE^N
ÓRGANOS^M GENITALES FEMENINOS

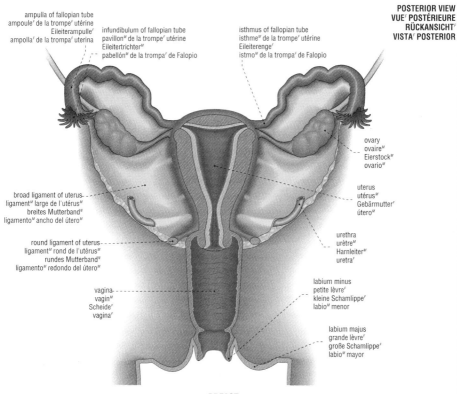

POSTERIOR VIEW
VUE^F POSTÉRIEURE
RÜCKANSICHT^F
VISTA^F POSTERIOR

ampulla of fallopian tube
ampoule^F de la trompe^F utérine
ampolla^F de la trompa^F uterina

Eileiterampulle^F

infundibulum of fallopian tube
pavillon^M de la trompe^F utérine
Eileitertrichter^M
pabellón^M de la trompa^F de Falopio

isthmus of fallopian tube
isthme^M de la trompe^F utérine
Eileiterenge^F
istmo^M de la trompa^F de Falopio

ovary
ovaire^M
Eierstock^M
ovario^M

uterus
utérus^M
Gebärmutter^F
útero^M

broad ligament of uterus
ligament^M large de l'utérus^M
breites Mutterband^N
ligamento^M ancho del útero^M

urethra
urètre^M
Harnleiter^M
uretra^F

round ligament of uterus
ligament^M rond de l'utérus^M
rundes Mutterband^N
ligamento^M redondo del útero^M

labium minus
petite lèvre^F
kleine Schamlippe^F
labio^M menor

vagina
vagin^M
Scheide^F
vagina^F

labium majus
grande lèvre^F
große Schamlippe^F
labio^M mayor

BREAST
SEIN^M
BRUST^F
SENO^M

SAGITTAL SECTION
COUPE^F SAGITTALE
SAGITTALSCHNITT^M
CORTE^M SAGITAL

rib
côte^F
Rippe^F
costilla^F

adipose tissue
tissu^M adipeux
Fettgewebe^N
tejido^M adiposo

mammary gland
glande^F mammaire
Brustdrüse^F
glándula^F mamaria

areola
aréole^F
Warzenhof^M
areola^F

nipple
mamelon^M
Brustwarze^F
pezón^M

lactiferous duct
conduit^M lactifère
Milchgang^M
conducto^M galactófero

RESPIRATORY SYSTEM
APPAREIL^M RESPIRATOIRE
LUFTWEGE^M
APARATO^M RESPIRATORIO

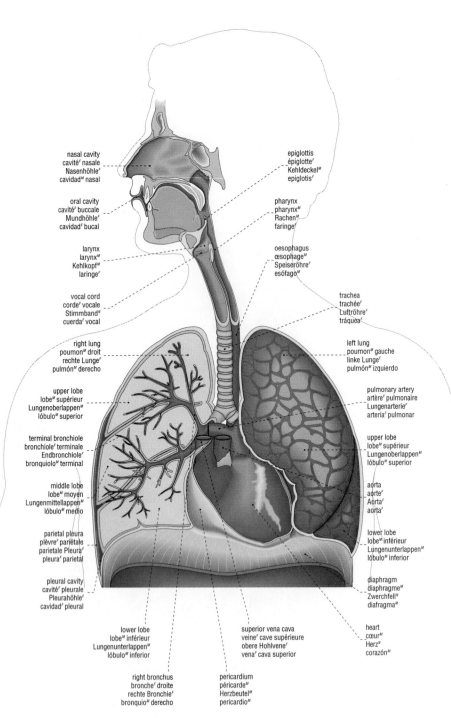

nasal cavity
cavité^F nasale
Nasenhöhle^F
cavidad^M nasal

oral cavity
cavité^F buccale
Mundhöhle^F
cavidad^F bucal

larynx
larynx^M
Kehlkopf^M
laringe^F

vocal cord
corde^F vocale
Stimmband^N
cuerda^F vocal

right lung
poumon^M droit
rechte Lunge^F
pulmón^M derecho

upper lobe
lobe^M supérieur
Lungenoberlappen^M
lóbulo^M superior

terminal bronchiole
bronchiole^F terminale
Endbronchiole^F
bronquiolo^M terminal

middle lobe
lobe^M moyen
Lungenmittellappen^M
lóbulo^M medio

parietal pleura
plèvre^F pariétale
parietale Pleura^F
pleura^F parietal

pleural cavity
cavité^F pleurale
Pleurahöhle^F
cavidad^F pleural

epiglottis
épiglotte^F
Kehldeckel^M
epiglotis^F

pharynx
pharynx^M
Rachen^M
faringe^F

oesophagus
œsophage^M
Speiseröhre^F
esófago^M

trachea
trachée^F
Luftröhre^F
tráquèa^F

left lung
poumon^M gauche
linke Lunge^F
pulmón^M izquierdo

pulmonary artery
artère^F pulmonaire
Lungenarterie^F
arteria^F pulmonar

upper lobe
lobe^M supérieur
Lungenoberlappen^M
lóbulo^M superior

aorta
aorte^F
Aorta^F
aorta^F

lower lobe
lobe^M inférieur
Lungenunterlappen^M
lóbulo^M inferior

diaphragm
diaphragme^M
Zwerchfell^N
diafragma^M

heart
cœur^M
Herz^N
corazón^M

lower lobe
lobe^M inférieur
Lungenunterlappen^M
lóbulo^M inferior

superior vena cava
veine^F cave supérieure
obere Hohlvene^F
vena^F cava superior

right bronchus
bronche^F droite
rechte Bronchie^F
bronquio^M derecho

pericardium
péricarde^M
Herzbeutel^M
pericardio^M

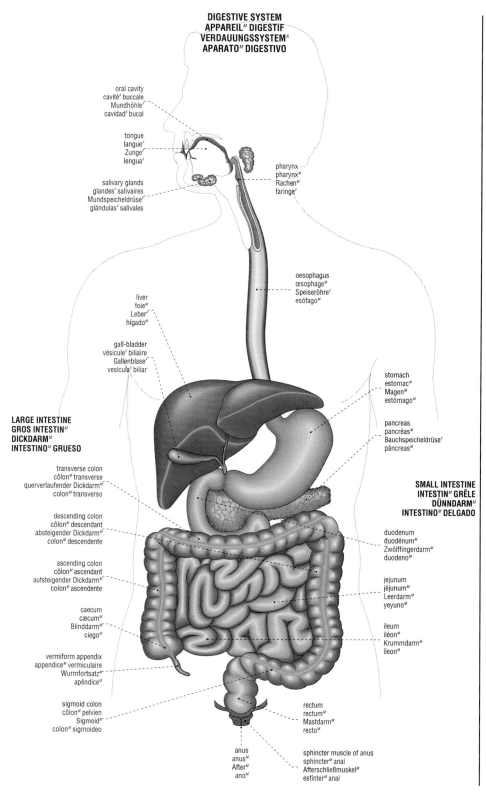

DIGESTIVE SYSTEM
APPAREIL *M* **DIGESTIF**
VERDAUUNGSSYSTEM *N*
APARATO *M* **DIGESTIVO**

oral cavity
cavité *F* buccale
Mundhöhle *F*
cavidad *F* bucal

tongue
langue *F*
Zunge *F*
lengua *F*

salivary glands
glandes *F* salivaires
Mundspeicheldrüse *F*
glándulas *F* salivales

pharynx
pharynx *M*
Rachen *M*
faringe *F*

oesophagus
œsophage *M*
Speiseröhre *F*
esófago *M*

liver
foie *M*
Leber *F*
hígado *M*

gall-bladder
vésicule *F* biliaire
Gallenblase *F*
vesícula *F* biliar

stomach
estomac *M*
Magen *M*
estómago *M*

pancreas
pancréas *M*
Bauchspeicheldrüse *F*
páncreas *M*

LARGE INTESTINE
GROS INTESTIN *M*
DICKDARM *M*
INTESTINO *M* **GRUESO**

transverse colon
côlon *M* transverse
querverlaufender Dickdarm *M*
colon *M* transverso

descending colon
côlon *M* descendant
absteigender Dickdarm *M*
colon *M* descendente

ascending colon
côlon *M* ascendant
aufsteigender Dickdarm *M*
colon *M* ascendente

caecum
cæcum *M*
Blinddarm *M*
ciego *M*

vermiform appendix
appendice *M* vermiculaire
Wurmfortsatz *M*
apéndice *M*

sigmoid colon
côlon *M* pelvien
Sigmoid *M*
colon *M* sigmoideo

SMALL INTESTINE
INTESTIN *M* **GRÊLE**
DÜNNDARM *M*
INTESTINO *M* **DELGADO**

duodenum
duodénum *M*
Zwölffingerdarm *M*
duodeno *M*

jejunum
jéjunum *M*
Leerdarm *M*
yeyuno *M*

ileum
iléon *M*
Krummdarm *M*
íleon *M*

rectum
rectum *M*
Mastdarm *M*
recto *M*

anus
anus *M*
After *M*
ano *M*

sphincter muscle of anus
sphincter *M* anal
Afterschließmuskel *M*
esfínter *M* anal

URINARY SYSTEM
APPAREIL^M URINAIRE
HARNSYSTEM^N
APARATO^M URINARIO

inferior vena cava
veine^f cave inférieure
untere Hohlvene^f
vena^f cava inferior

coeliac trunk
tronc^M cœliaque
Eingeweideschlagader^f
tronco^M celiaco

adrenal gland
glande^f surrénale
Nebenniere^f
glándula^f suprarrenal

left kidney
rein^M gauche
linke Niere^f
riñón^M izquierdo

renal hilus
hile^M du rein^M
Nierenhilus^M
hilio^M renal

cortex
substance^f corticale
Rinde^f
capa^f cortical

right kidney
rein^M droit
rechte Niere^f
riñón^M derecho

medulla
substance^f médullaire
Mark^M
médula^f

renal papilla
papille^f rénale
Nierenpapille^f
papila^f renal

calyx
calice^M
Nierenkelch^M
cáliz^M renal

renal pelvis
bassinet^M
Nierenbecken^N
pelvis^f renal

abdominal aorta
aorte^f abdominale
Bauchaorta^f
aorta^f abdominal

renal vein
veine^f rénale
Nierenvene^f
vena^f renal

ureter
uretère^M
Harnleiter^M
uréter^M

renal artery
artère^f rénale
Nierenarterie^f
arteria^f renal

common iliac artery
artère^f iliaque commune
gemeinsame Hüftarterie^f
arteria^f ilíaca^f común

superior mesenteric artery
artère^f mésentérique supérieure
obere Gekrösearterie^f
arteria^f mesentérica superior

common iliac vein
veine^f iliaque commune
gemeinsame Hüftvene^f
vena^f ilíaca^f común

inferior mesenteric artery
artère^f mésentérique inférieure
untere Gekrösearterie^f
arteria^f mesentérica inferior

internal iliac artery
artère^f iliaque interne
innere Hüftarterie^f
arteria^f ilíaca^f interna

urinary bladder
vessie^f
Harnblase^f
vejiga^f

urethra
urètre^M
Harnröhre^f
uretra^f

PERIPHERAL NERVOUS SYSTEM
SYSTÈME^M NERVEUX PÉRIPHÉRIQUE
PERIPHERES NERVENSYSTEM^N
SISTEMA^M NERVIOSO PERIFÉRICO

brachial plexus
plexus^M brachial
Armgeflecht^N
plexo^M braquial

cranial nerves
nerfs^M crâniens
Hirnnerven^M
nervios^M craneales

median nerve
nerf^M médian
Mittelarmnerv^M
nervio^M mediano

axillary nerve
nerf^M circonflexe
Achselnerv^M
nervio^M circunflejo

ulnar nerve
nerf^M cubital
Ellennerv^M
nervio^M cubital

radial nerve
nerf^M radial
Speichennerv^M
nervio^M radial

obturator nerve
nerf^M obturateur
Hüftlochnerv^M
nervio^M obturador

intercostal nerve
nerf^M intercostal
Interkostalnerv^M
nervio^M intercostal

iliohypogastric nerve
nerf^M grand abdomino-génital
Hüft-Becken-Nerv^M
nervio^M abdominogenital mayor

lumbar plexus
plexus^M lombaire
Lendengeflecht^N
plexo^M lumbar

ilioinguinal nerve
nerf^M petit abdomino-génital
Hüft-Leisten-Nerv^M
nervio^M abdominogenital menor

sacral plexus
plexus^M sacré
Kreuzgeflecht^N
plexo^M sacro

lateral cutaneous femoral nerve
nerf^M fémoro-cutané
Nervus^M cutaneus femoris lateralis
nervio^M femorocutáneo

femoral nerve
nerf^M crural
Oberschenkelnerv^M
nervio^M crural

digital nerve
nerf^M digital
Fingernerv^M
nervio^M digital

sciatic nerve
nerf^M grand sciatique
Hüftnerv^M
nervio^M ciático mayor

gluteal nerve
nerf^M fessier
Gesäßnerv^M
nervio^M glúteo

saphenous nerve
nerf^M saphène interne
großer Rosennerv^M
nervio^M safeno interno

minor sciatic nerve
nerf^M petit sciatique
kleiner Hüftnerv^M
nervio^M ciático menor

common peroneal nerve
nerf^M sciatique poplité externe
gemeinsamer Wadenbeinnerv^M
nervio^M ciático poplíteo externo

tibial nerve
nerf^M sciatique poplité interne
Schienbeinnerv^M
nervio^M ciático poplíteo interno

superficial peroneal nerve
nerf^M musculo-cutané
oberflächlicher Wadenbeinnerv^M
nervio^M musculocutáneo de la pierna^F

sural nerve
nerf^M saphène externe
Wadennerv^M
nervio^M safeno externo

deep peroneal nerve
nerf^M tibial antérieur
tiefer Wadenbeinnerv^M
nervio^M tibial anterior

HUMAN BEING
ÊTRE HUMAIN

MENSCH
SER HUMANO

133

CENTRAL NERVOUS SYSTEM
SYSTÈME^M NERVEUX CENTRAL
ZENTRALES NERVENSYSTEM^N
SISTEMA^M NERVIOSO CENTRAL

body of fornix
corps^M du fornix^M
Gewölbekörper^M
cuerpo^M del fórnix^M

cerebrum
cerveau^M
Großhirn^N
cerebro^M

septum pellucidum
septum^M lucidum
Septum^N pellucidum
septum^M lucidum

skull
boîte^F crânienne
Schädel^M
cráneo^M

corpus callosum
corps^M calleux
Balken^M
cuerpo^M calloso

pineal body
épiphyse^F
Zirbeldrüse^F
glándula^F pineal

cerebellum
cervelet^M
Kleinhirn^N
cerebelo^M

pons Varolii
pont^M de Varole
Brücke^F
puente^M de Varolio

medulla oblongata
bulbe^M rachidien
verlängertes Mark^N
bulbo^M raquídeo

optic chiasm
chiasma^M optique
Sehnervkreuzung^F
quiasma^M óptico

pituitary gland
hypophyse^F
Hirnanhangsdrüse^F
hipófisis^F

spinal column
colonne^F vertébrale
Wirbelsäule^F
columna^F vertebral

skin
peau^F
Haut^F
piel^F

motor end plate
plaque^F motrice
motorische Endplatte^F
placa^F motriz

sensory receptor
récepteur^M sensoriel
Sinnesrezeptor^M
receptor^M sensorial

spinal cord
moelle^F épinière
Rückenmark^N
médula^F espinal

internal filum terminale
cul-de-sac^M dural
filum^M terminale
filum^M terminal interno

dura mater
dure-mère^F
harte Rückenmarkshaut^F
duramadre^F

terminal filament
filum^M terminal
Endfaden^M
filum^M terminal

sensory neuron
neurone^M sensoriel
sensibles Neuron^N
neurona^F sensorial

muscle fibre
fibre^F musculaire
Muskelfaser^F
fibra^F muscular

LUMBAR VERTEBRA
VERTÈBRE^F LOMBAIRE
LENDENWIRBEL^M
VÉRTEBRA^F LUMBAR

sympathetic ganglion
ganglion^M du tronc^M sympathique
symphatisches Ganglion^N
ganglio^M simpático

communicating ramus
rameau^M communicant
Verbindungsast^M
rama^F comunicante

anterior root
racine^F antérieure
vordere Wurzel^F
raíz^F anterior

posterior root
racine^F postérieure
hintere Wurzel^F
raíz^F posterior

spinal cord
moelle^F épinière
Rückenmark^N
médula^F espinal

spinous process
apophyse^F épineuse
Dornfortsatz^M
apófosis^F espinosa

vertebral body
corps^M vertébral
Wirbelkörper^M
cuerpo^M vertebral

spinal nerve
nerf^M rachidien
Spinalnerv^M
nervio^M raquídeo

transverse process
apophyse^F transverse
Querfortsatz^M
apófosis^F transversa

dura mater
dure-mère^F
harte Rückenmarkshaut^F
duramadre^F

CHAIN OF NEURONS
CHAÎNE^F DE NEURONES^M
NEURONENKETTE^F
ENCADENAMIENTO^M DE NEURONAS^F

synapse
synapse^F
Synapse^F
sinapsis^F

myelin sheath
gaine^F de myéline^F
Markscheide^F
vaina^F de mielina^F

axon hillock
collet^M de l'axone^M
Ursprungskegel^M
cuerpos^M de Nissl

axon
axone^M
Axon^N
axón^M

spinal cord
moelle^F épinière
Rückenmark^N
médula^F espinal

nucleus
noyau^M
Zellkern^M
núcleo^M

cell body
corps^M cellulaire
Zellkörper^M
cuerpo^M celular

terminal arborization
arborisation^F terminale
Endaufzweigung^F
arborización^F terminal

node of Ranvier
nœud^M de Ranvier
Ranvierscher Schnürring^M
nódulo^M de Ranvier

collateral
collatérale^F
Kollaterale^F
ramificación^F colateral

sheath of Schwann
gaine^F de Schwann
Schwannsche Scheide^F
célula^F de Schwann

dendrite
dendrite^F
Dendrit^M
dendrita^F

SENSORY IMPULSE
INFLUX^M NERVEUX
SINNESIMPULS^M
IMPULSO^M NERVIOSO

protoneuron
protoneurone^F sensitif
peripher-sensorisches Neuron^N
protoneurona^F

spinal nerve
nerf^M rachidien
Spinalnerv^M
nervio^M raquídeo

spinal ganglion
ganglion^M spinal
Spinalganglion^N
ganglio^M espinal

sensory root
racine^F sensitive
sensorische Wurzel^F
raíz^F sensorial

white matter
substance^F blanche
weiße Substanz^F
substancia^F blanca

grey matter
substance^F grise
graue Substanz^F
materia^F gris

motor neuron
neurone^M moteur
motorisches Neuron^N
neurona^F motriz

motor root
racine^F motrice
motorische Wurzel^F
raíz^F motriz

synapse
synapse^M
Synapse^F
sinápsis^F

spinal cord
moelle^F épinière
Rückenmark^N
médula^F espinal

SENSE ORGANS: TOUCH
ORGANES^M DES SENS^M: TOUCHER^M
SINNESORGANE^N: TASTSINN^M
TACTO^M

SKIN
PEAU^F
HAUT^F
PIEL^F

hair shaft
tige^F du poil^M
Haarschaft^M
tallo^M

hair
poil^M
Haar^N
pelo^M

pore
pore^M sudoripare
Pore^F
poro^M

stratum corneum
couche^F cornée
Hornschicht^F
capa^F córnea

Ruffini's corpuscle
corpuscule^M de Ruffini
Ruffinisches Körperchen^N
corpúsculo^M de Ruffini

Meissner's corpuscle
corpuscule^M de Meissner
Meissnersches Tastkörperchen^N
corpúsculo^M de Meissner

stratum lucidum
couche^F claire
Glanzschicht^F
estrato^M lúcido

stratum granulosum
couche^F granuleuse
Körnerschicht^F
capa^F granular

stratum spinosum
couche^F de Malpighi
Stachelzellenschicht^F
estrato^M de Malpighi

stratum basale
couche^F basale
Basalschicht^F
capa^F basilar

nerve termination
terminaison^F nerveuse
Nervenendigung^F
terminación^F nerviosa

arrector pili muscle
muscle^M arrecteur
Haaraufrichter^M
músculo^M erector del pelo

sebaceous gland
glande^F sébacée
Talgdrüse^F
glándula^F sebácea

hair follicle
follicule^M
Haarbalg^M
folículo^M piloso

hair bulb
bulbe^M
Haarzwiebel^F
bulbo^M piloso

nerve fibre
fibre^F nerveuse
Nervenfaser^F
fibra^F nerviosa

papilla
papille^F
Papille^F
papila^F

nerve
nerf^M
Nerv^M
nervio^M

blood vessel
vaisseau^M sanguin
Blutgefäß^N
vaso^M sanguíneo

apocrine sweat gland
glande^F sudoripare apocrine
apokrine Schweißdrüse^F
glándula^F sudorípara apocrina

sudoriferous duct
canal^M sudoripare
Ausführungsgang^M der Schweißdrüse^F
conducto^M sudorífero

Pacinian corpuscle
corpuscule^M de Pacini
Vater-Pacinische Körperchen^N
corpúscula^F de Pacini

eccrine sweat gland
glande^F sudoripare eccrine
ekkrine Schweißdrüse^F
glándula^F sudorípara ecrina

adipose tissue
tissu^M adipeux
Fettgewebe^N
tejido^M adiposo

FINGER
DOIGT^M
FINGER^M
DEDO^M

HUMAN BEING
ÊTRE HUMAIN
MENSCH
SER HUMANO

dermis
derme^M
Lederhaut^F
dermis^F

epidermis
épiderme^M
Oberhaut^F
epidermis^F

root of nail
racine^F de l'ongle^M
Nagelwurzel^F
raíz^F de la uña

lunula
lunule^F
Nagelmöndchen^N
lúnula^F

skin surface
surface^F de la peau^F
Hautoberfläche^F
superficie^F de la piel^F

body of nail
corps^M de l'ongle^M
Nagelkörper^M
cuerpo^M de la uña^F

free margin
bord^M libre
freier Rand^M
extremo^M libre

epidermis
épiderme^M
Oberhaut^F
epidermis^F

nail bed
lit^M de l'ongle^M
Nagelbett^N
lecho^M ungular

connective tissue
tissu^M conjonctif
Bindegewebe^N
tejido^M conjuntivo

nail matrix
matrice^F de l'ongle^M
Nageltasche^F
matriz^F ungular

digital pulp
pulpe^F
Fingerbeere^F
yema^F

dermis
derme^M
Lederhaut^F
dermis^F

middle phalanx
phalangine^F
Mittelglied^N
falangina^F

distal phalanx
phalangette^F
Fingerendglied^N
falangeta^F

capillary blood vessel
vaisseau^M capillaire
Kapillargefäß^N
vaso^M capilar

subcutaneous tissue
hypoderme^M
Unterhaut^F
tejido^M subcutáneo

HAND
MAIN^F
HAND^F
MANO^F

thumb
pouce^M
Daumen^M
pulgar^M

fingernail
ongle^M
Fingernagel^M
uña^F

palm
paume^F
Handfläche^F
palma^F

lunula
lunule^F
Nagelmöndchen^N
lúnula^F

index finger
index^M
Zeigefinger^M
dedo^M índice

wrist
poignet^M
Handgelenk^N
muñeca^F

middle finger
majeur^M
Mittelfinger^M
dedo^M del corazón^M

third finger
annulaire^M
Ringfinger^M
dedo^M anular

little finger
auriculaire^M
kleiner Finger^M
dedo^M meñique

SENSE ORGANS: HEARING
ORGANES*M* DES SENS*M*: OUÏE*F*
SINNESORGANE*N*: GEHÖR*N*
EL OÍDO*M*

PARTS OF THE EAR
PARTIES*F* DE L'OREILLE*F*
TEILE*N* DES OHRS*N*
PARTES*F* DEL OÍDO*M*

AUDITORY OSSICLES
OSSELETS*M*
GEHÖRKNÖCHELCHEN*N*
HUESECILLOS*M* AUDITIVOS

incus
enclume*F*
Amboß*M*
yunque*M*

malleus
marteau*M*
Hammer*M*
martillo*M*

stapes
étrier*M*
Steigbügel*M*
estribo*M*

MENSCH
SER HUMANO

HUMAN BEING
ÊTRE HUMAIN

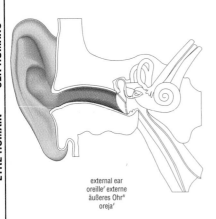

external ear
oreille*F* externe
äußeres Ohr*N*
oreja*F*

middle ear
oreille*F* moyenne
Mittelohr*N*
oído*M* medio

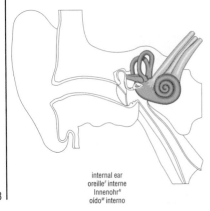

internal ear
oreille*F* interne
Innenohr*N*
oído*M* interno

auricle
pavillon*M*
Ohrmuschel*F*
pabellón*M* de la oreja*F*

acoustic meatus
conduit*M* auditif
Gehörgang*M*
meato*M* auditivo

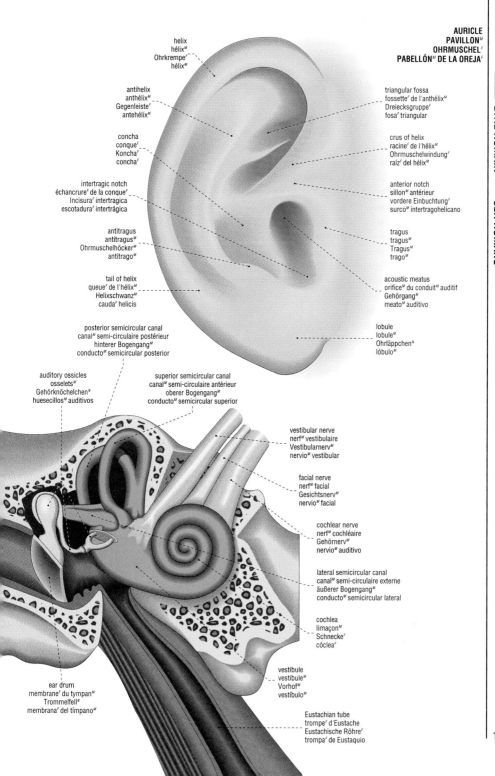

AURICLE
PAVILLON^M
OHRMUSCHEL^F
PABELLÓN^M DE LA OREJA^F

HUMAN BEING
ÊTRE HUMAIN

MENSCH
SER HUMANO

helix
hélix^M
Ohrkrempe^F
hélix^M

antihelix
anthélix^M
Gegenleiste^F
antehélix^M

concha
conque^F
Koncha^F
concha^F

intertragic notch
échancrure^F de la conque^F
Incisura^F intertragica
escotadura^F intertrágica

antitragus
antitragus^M
Ohrmuschelhöcker^M
antitrago^M

tail of helix
queue^F de l'hélix^M
Helixschwanz^M
cauda^F helicis

posterior semicircular canal
canal^M semi-circulaire postérieur
hinterer Bogengang^M
conducto^M semicircular posterior

auditory ossicles
osselets^M
Gehörknöchelchen^N
huesecillos^M auditivos

superior semicircular canal
canal^M semi-circulaire antérieur
oberer Bogengang^M
conducto^M semicircular superior

ear drum
membrane^F du tympan^M
Trommelfell^N
membrana^F del tímpano^M

triangular fossa
fossette^F de l'anthélix^M
Dreiecksgruppe^F
fosa^F triangular

crus of helix
racine^F de l'hélix^M
Ohrmuschelwindung^F
raíz^F del hélix^M

anterior notch
sillon^M antérieur
vordere Einbuchtung^F
surco^M intertragohelicano

tragus
tragus^M
Tragus^M
trago^M

acoustic meatus
orifice^F du conduit^M auditif
Gehörgang^M
meato^M auditivo

lobule
lobule^M
Ohrläppchen^N
lóbulo^M

vestibular nerve
nerf^M vestibulaire
Vestibularnerv^M
nervio^M vestibular

facial nerve
nerf^M facial
Gesichtsnerv^M
nervio^M facial

cochlear nerve
nerf^M cochléaire
Gehörnerv^M
nervio^M auditivo

lateral semicircular canal
canal^M semi-circulaire externe
äußerer Bogengang^M
conducto^M semicircular lateral

cochlea
limaçon^M
Schnecke^F
cóclea^F

vestibule
vestibule^M
Vorhof^M
vestíbulo^M

Eustachian tube
trompe^F d'Eustache
Eustachische Röhre^F
trompa^F de Eustaquio

**MENSCH
SER HUMANO**

**HUMAN BEING
ÊTRE HUMAIN**

**EYE
ŒIL*M*
AUGE*N*
OJO*M***

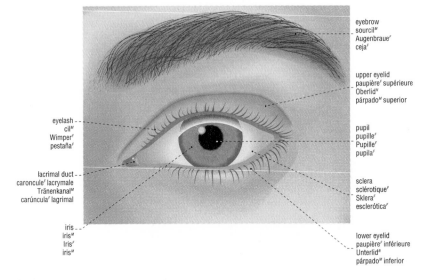

eyebrow
sourcil*M*
Augenbraue*F*
ceja*F*

upper eyelid
paupière*F* supérieure
Oberlid*N*
párpado*M* superior

eyelash
cil*M*
Wimper*F*
pestaña*F*

pupil
pupille*F*
Pupille*F*
pupila*F*

lacrimal duct
caroncule*F* lacrymale
Tränenkanal*M*
carúncula*F* lagrimal

sclera
sclérotique*F*
Sklera*F*
esclerótica*F*

iris
iris*M*
Iris*F*
iris*M*

lower eyelid
paupière*F* inférieure
Unterlid*N*
párpado*M* inferior

**EYEBALL
GLOBE*M* OCULAIRE
AUGAPFEL*M*
GLOBO*N* OCULAR**

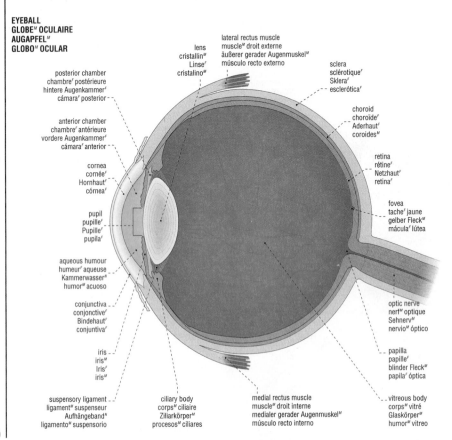

posterior chamber
chambre*F* postérieure
hintere Augenkammer*F*
cámara*F* posterior

lens
cristallin*M*
Linse*F*
cristalino*M*

lateral rectus muscle
muscle*M* droit externe
äußerer gerader Augenmuskel*M*
músculo recto externo

sclera
sclérotique*F*
Sklera*F*
esclerótica*F*

anterior chamber
chambre*F* antérieure
vordere Augenkammer*F*
cámara*F* anterior

choroid
choroïde*F*
Aderhaut*F*
coroides*M*

cornea
cornée*F*
Hornhaut*F*
córnea*F*

retina
rétine*F*
Netzhaut*F*
retina*F*

pupil
pupille*F*
Pupille*F*
pupila*F*

fovea
tache*F* jaune
gelber Fleck*M*
mácula*F* lútea

aqueous humour
humeur*F* aqueuse
Kammerwasser*N*
humor*M* acuoso

conjunctiva
conjonctive*F*
Bindehaut*F*
conjuntiva*F*

optic nerve
nerf*M* optique
Sehnerv*M*
nervio*M* óptico

iris
iris*M*
Iris*F*
iris*M*

papilla
papille*F*
blinder Fleck*M*
papila*F* óptica

suspensory ligament
ligament*M* suspenseur
Aufhängeband*N*
ligamento*M* suspensorio

ciliary body
corps*M* ciliaire
Ziliarkörper*M*
procesos*M* ciliares

medial rectus muscle
muscle*M* droit interne
medialer gerader Augenmuskel*M*
músculo recto interno

vitreous body
corps*M* vitré
Glaskörper*M*
humor*M* vitreo

SENSE ORGANS: SMELL
ORGANES^M DES SENS^M: ODORAT^M
SINNESORGANE^N: GERUCHSSINN^M
EL OLFATO^M

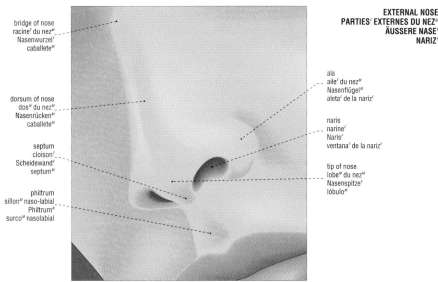

EXTERNAL NOSE
PARTIES^F EXTERNES DU NEZ^M
ÄUSSERE NASE^F
NARIZ^F

bridge of nose
racine^F du nez^M
Nasenwurzel^F
caballete^M

dorsum of nose
dos^M du nez^M
Nasenrücken^M
caballete^M

septum
cloison^F
Scheidewand^F
septum^M

philtrum
sillon^M naso-labial
Philtrum^N
surco^M nasolabial

ala
aile^F du nez^M
Nasenflügel^M
aleta^F de la nariz^F

naris
narine^F
Naris^F
ventana^F de la nariz^F

tip of nose
lobe^M du nez^M
Nasenspitze^F
lóbulo^M

NASAL FOSSAE
FOSSES^F NASALES
NASENHÖHLE^F
FOSAS^F NASALES

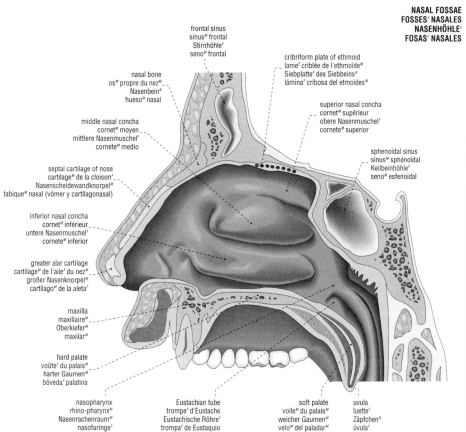

frontal sinus
sinus^M frontal
Stirnhöhle^F
seno^M frontal

nasal bone
os^M propre du nez^M
Nasenbein^N
hueso^M nasal

middle nasal concha
cornet^M moyen
mittlere Nasenmuschel^F
cornete^M medio

septal cartilage of nose
cartilage^M de la cloison^F
Nasenscheidewandknorpel^M
tabique^M nasal (vómer y cartilagonasal)

inferior nasal concha
cornet^M inférieur
untere Nasenmuschel^F
cornete^M inferior

greater alar cartilage
cartilage^M de l'aile^F du nez^M
großer Nasenknorpel^M
cartílago^M de la aleta^F

maxilla
maxillaire^M
Oberkiefer^M
maxilar^M

hard palate
voûte^F du palais^M
harter Gaumen^M
bóveda^F palatina

cribriform plate of ethmoid
lame^F criblée de l'ethmoïde^M
Siebplatte^F des Siebbeins^N
lámina^F cribosa del etmoides^M

superior nasal concha
cornet^M supérieur
obere Nasenmuschel^F
cornete^M superior

sphenoidal sinus
sinus^M sphénoïdal
Keilbeinhöhle^F
seno^M esfenoidal

nasopharynx
rhino-pharynx^M
Nasenrachenraum^M
nasofaringe^F

Eustachian tube
trompe^F d'Eustache
Eustachische Röhre^F
trompa^F de Eustaquio

soft palate
voile^M du palais^M
weicher Gaumen^M
velo^M del paladar^M

uvula
luette^F
Zäpfchen^N
úvula^F

SENSES OF SMELL AND TASTE
SENS^M DE L'ODORAT^M ET DU GOÛT^M
GERUCHS- UND GESCHMACKSSINN^M
EL OLFATO^M Y EL GUSTO^M

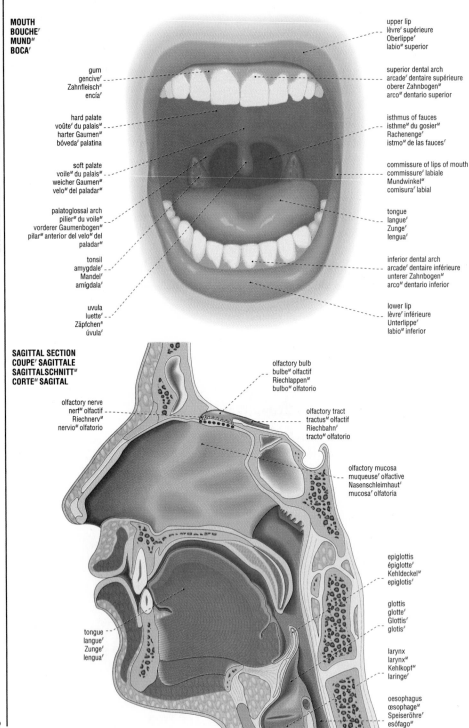

MOUTH
BOUCHE^F
MUND^M
BOCA^F

gum
gencive^F
Zahnfleisch^N
encía^F

hard palate
voûte^F du palais^M
harter Gaumen^M
bóveda^F palatina

soft palate
voile^M du palais^M
weicher Gaumen^M
velo^M del paladar^M

palatoglossal arch
pilier^M du voile^M
vorderer Gaumenbogen^M
pilar^M anterior del velo^M del
paladar^M

tonsil
amygdale^F
Mandel^F
amígdala^F

uvula
luette^F
Zäpfchen^N
úvula^F

upper lip
lèvre^F supérieure
Oberlippe^F
labio^M superior

superior dental arch
arcade^F dentaire supérieure
oberer Zahnbogen^M
arco^M dentario superior

isthmus of fauces
isthme^M du gosier^M
Rachenenge^F
istmo^M de las fauces^F

commissure of lips of mouth
commissure^F labiale
Mundwinkel^M
comisura^F labial

tongue
langue^F
Zunge^F
lengua^F

inferior dental arch
arcade^F dentaire inférieure
unterer Zahnbogen^M
arco^M dentario inferior

lower lip
lèvre^F inférieure
Unterlippe^F
labio^M inferior

SAGITTAL SECTION
COUPE^F SAGITTALE
SAGITTALSCHNITT^M
CORTE^M SAGITAL

olfactory nerve
nerf^M olfactif
Riechnerv^M
nervio^M olfatorio

olfactory bulb
bulbe^M olfactif
Riechlappen^M
bulbo^M olfatorio

olfactory tract
tractus^M olfactif
Riechbahn^F
tracto^M olfatorio

olfactory mucosa
muqueuse^F olfactive
Nasenschleimhaut^F
mucosa^F olfatoria

epiglottis
épiglotte^F
Kehldeckel^M
epiglotis^F

glottis
glotte^F
Glottis^F
glotis^F

tongue
langue^F
Zunge^F
lengua^F

larynx
larynx^M
Kehlkopf^M
laringe^F

oesophagus
œsophage^M
Speiseröhre^F
esófago^M

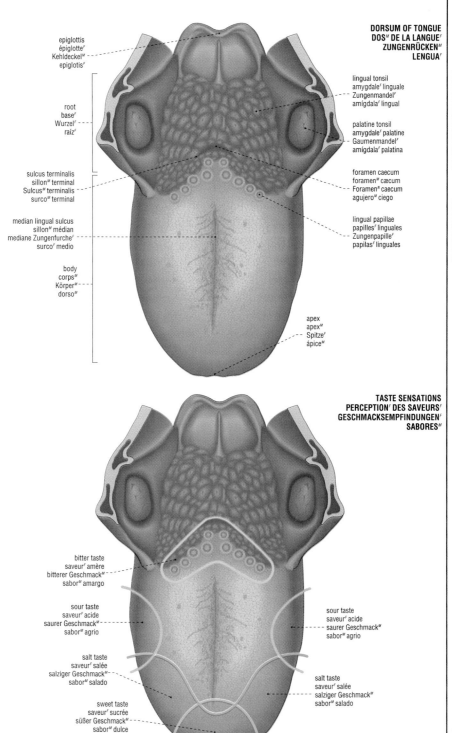

DORSUM OF TONGUE
DOS^M DE LA LANGUE^F
ZUNGENRÜCKEN^M
LENGUA^F

epiglottis
épiglotte^F
Kehldeckel^M
epiglotis^F

lingual tonsil
amygdale^F linguale
Zungenmandel^F
amígdala^F lingual

root
base^F
Wurzel^F
raíz^F

palatine tonsil
amygdale^F palatine
Gaumenmandel^F
amígdala^F palatina

sulcus terminalis
sillon^M terminal
Sulcus^M terminalis
surco^M terminal

foramen caecum
foramen^M cæcum
Foramen^N caecum
agujero^M ciego

median lingual sulcus
sillon^M médian
mediane Zungenfurche^F
surco^F medio

lingual papillae
papilles^F linguales
Zungenpapille^F
papilas^F linguales

body
corps^M
Körper^M
dorso^M

apex
apex^M
Spitze^F
ápice^M

TASTE SENSATIONS
PERCEPTION^F DES SAVEURS^F
GESCHMACKSEMPFINDUNGEN^F
SABORES^M

bitter taste
saveur^F amère
bitterer Geschmack^M
sabor^M amargo

sour taste
saveur^F acide
saurer Geschmack^M
sabor^M agrio

sour taste
saveur^F acide
saurer Geschmack^M
sabor^M agrio

salt taste
saveur^F salée
salziger Geschmack^M
sabor^M salado

salt taste
saveur^F salée
salziger Geschmack^M
sabor^M salado

sweet taste
saveur^F sucrée
süßer Geschmack^M
sabor^M dulce

143

TEETH
DENTS^F
ZÄHNE^M
DIENTES^M

HUMAN DENTURE
DENTURE^F HUMAINE
MENSCHLICHES GEBISS^N
DENTADURA^F HUMANA

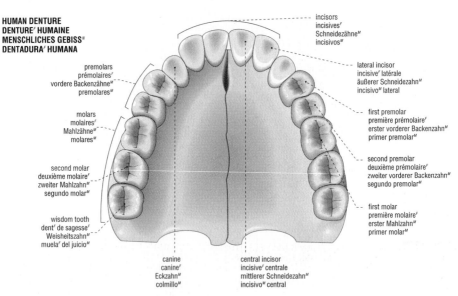

premolars
prémolaires^F
vordere Backenzähne^M
premolares^M

molars
molaires^F
Mahlzähne^M
molares^M

second molar
deuxième molaire^F
zweiter Mahlzahn^M
segundo molar^M

wisdom tooth
dent^F de sagesse^F
Weisheitszahn^M
muela^F del juicio^M

incisors
incisives^F
Schneidezähne^M
incisivos^M

lateral incisor
incisive^F latérale
äußerer Schneidezahn^M
incisivo^M lateral

first premolar
première prémolaire^F
erster vorderer Backenzahn^M
primer premolar^M

second premolar
deuxième prémolaire^F
zweiter vorderer Backenzahn^M
segundo premolar^M

first molar
première molaire^F
erster Mahlzahn^M
primer molar^M

canine
canine^F
Eckzahn^M
colmillo^M

central incisor
incisive^F centrale
mittlerer Schneidezahn^M
incisivo^M central

CROSS SECTION OF A MOLAR
COUPE^F D'UNE MOLAIRE^F
LÄNGSSCHNITT^M DURCH EINEN MAHLZAHN^M
CORTE^M TRANSVERSAL DE UN MOLAR^M

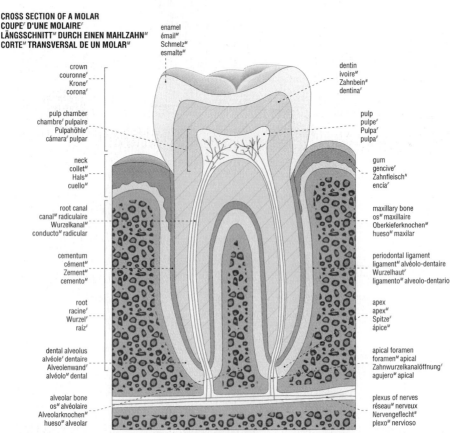

crown
couronne^F
Krone^F
corona^F

pulp chamber
chambre^F pulpaire
Pulpahöhle^F
cámara^F pulpar

neck
collet^M
Hals^M
cuello^M

root canal
canal^M radiculaire
Wurzelkanal^M
conducto^M radicular

cementum
cément^M
Zement^M
cemento^M

root
racine^F
Wurzel^F
raíz^F

dental alveolus
alvéole^F dentaire
Alveolenwand^F
alvéolo^M dental

alveolar bone
os^M alvéolaire
Alveolarknochen^M
hueso^M alveolar

enamel
émail^M
Schmelz^M
esmalte^M

dentin
ivoire^M
Zahnbein^N
dentina^F

pulp
pulpe^F
Pulpa^F
pulpa^F

gum
gencive^F
Zahnfleisch^N
encía^F

maxillary bone
os^M maxillaire
Oberkieferknochen^M
hueso^M maxilar

periodontal ligament
ligament^M alvéolo-dentaire
Wurzelhaut^F
ligamento^M alveolo-dentario

apex
apex^M
Spitze^F
ápice^M

apical foramen
foramen^M apical
Zahnwurzelkanalöffnung^F
agujero^M apical

plexus of nerves
réseau^M nerveux
Nervengeflecht^N
plexo^M nervioso

SUMMARY

LANDWIRTSCHAFT
AGRICULTURA

FARMING
FERME

TRACTOR
TRACTEUR*M* AGRICOLE
TRAKTOR*M*
TRACTOR*M*

REAR VIEW
VUE*F* ARRIÈRE
HINTERANSICHT*F*
VISTA*F* TRASERA

compression link
bielle*F* de compression*F*
Oberlenker*M*
eslabón*M* de compresión*F*

taillight
phare*M* arrière
Schlußleuchte*F*
faros*M* traseros

hydraulic coupling
coupleur*M* hydraulique
Hydraulikkupplung*F*
empalme*M* hidráulico

hydraulic ram
vérin*M* hydraulique
Hydraulikzylinder*M*
cilindro*M* hidráulico

coupler head
tête*F* d'attelage*M*
Kupplungskopf*M*
cabeza*F* de empalme*M*

spotlight
phare*M*
Scheinwerfer*M*
luces*F* traseras

lifting lever
levier*M* de relevage*M*
Hubstreben*M*
palanca*F* de elevación*F*

power takeoff
prise*F* de force*F*
Zapfwellenstummel*M*
toma*F* de fuerza*F*

lifting link
bras*M* de relevage*M*
Unterlenker*M*
eslabón*M* de levantamiento*M*

towing hitch
crochet*M* d'attelage*M*
Zugpendel*N*
gancho*M* del remolque*M*

steering wheel
volant*M*
Lenkrad*N*
volante*M*

cab
cabine*F* de conduite*F*
Kabine*F*
cabina*F*

mudguard
garde-boue*M*
Kotflügel*M*
guardabarros*M*

FRONT VIEW
VUE*F* AVANT
VORDERANSICHT*F*
VISTA*F* FRONTAL

exhaust stack
cheminée*F* d'échappement*M*
Auspuff*M*
tubo*M* de escape*M*

headlight
phare*M*
Scheinwerfer*M*
faro*M* delantero

rim
jante*F*
Felge*F*
llanta*F*

step
marchepied*M*
Aufstieg*M*
peldaño*M*

counterweight
contrepoids*M*
Frontgewicht*N*
contrapeso*M*

driving wheel
roue*F* motrice
Antriebsrad*N*
rueda*F* motriz

front wheel
roue*F* avant
Vorderrad*N*
rueda*F* delantera

tread bar
sculpture*F*
Stollen*M*
banda*F* de rodamiento*M*

engine
moteur*M*
Motor*M*
motor*M*

FARMSTEAD
FERME^F
BAUERNHOF^M
GRANJA^F

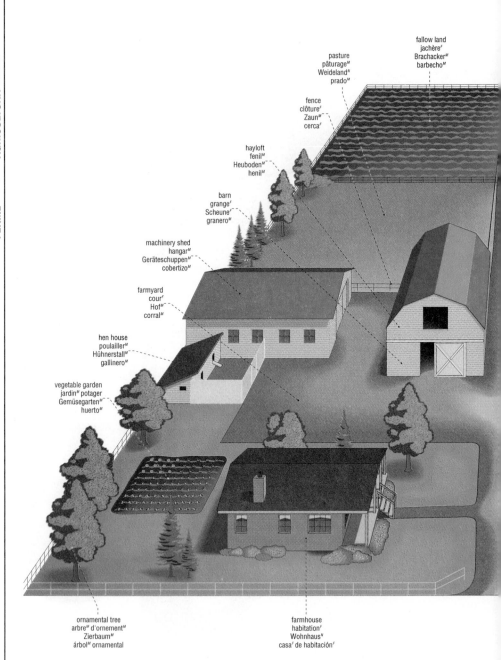

fallow land
jachère^F
Brachacker^M
barbecho^M

pasture
pâturage^M
Weideland^N
prado^M

fence
clôture^F
Zaun^M
cerca^F

hayloft
fenil^M
Heuboden^M
henil^M

barn
grange^F
Scheune^F
granero^M

machinery shed
hangar^M
Geräteschuppen^M
cobertizo^M

farmyard
cour^F
Hof^M
corral^M

hen house
poulailler^M
Hühnerstall^M
gallinero^M

vegetable garden
jardin^M potager
Gemüsegarten^M
huerto^M

ornamental tree
arbre^M d'ornement^M
Zierbaum^M
árbol^M ornamental

farmhouse
habitation^F
Wohnhaus^N
casa^F de habitación^F

fodder corn
maïs^M fourrager
Futtergetreide^N
maíz^M forrajero

meadow
prairie^F
Wiese^F
pradera^F

dairy
laiterie^F
Milchkammer^F
vaquería^F

cowshed
étable^F
Kuhstall^M
establo^M

tower silo
silo^M-tour^F
Hochsilo^M
silo^M

bunker silo
silo^M-couloir^M
Flachsilo^M
troje^M

pigsty
porcherie^F
Schweinestall^M
pocilga^F

enclosure
enclos^M
Auslauf^M
cercado^M

orchard
verger^M
Obstgarten^M
huerta^F

greenhouse
serre^F
Treibhaus^N
invernadero^M

sheep shelter
bergerie^F
Schafstall^M
cobertizo^M para ovejas^F

fruit tree
arbre^M fruitier
Obstbaum^M
árbol^M frutal

beehive
ruche^F
Bienenstock^M
colmena^F

FARM ANIMALS
ANIMAUX*ᴹ* DE LA FERME*ᶠ*
NUTZVIEH*ᴺ*
ANIMALES*ᴹ* DE LA GRANJA*ᶠ*

hen
poule*ᶠ*
Henne*ᶠ*
gallina*ᶠ*

chick
poussin*ᴹ*
Küken*ᴺ*
pollito*ᴹ*

rooster
coq*ᴹ*
Hahn*ᴹ*
gallo*ᴹ*

duck
canard*ᴹ*
Ente*ᶠ*
pato*ᴹ*

goose
oie*ᶠ*
Gans*ᶠ*
ganso*ᴹ*

turkey
dindon*ᴹ*
Truthahn*ᴹ*
pavo*ᴹ*

goat
chèvre*ᶠ*
Ziege*ᶠ*
cabra*ᶠ*

lamb
agneau*ᴹ*
Lamm*ᴺ*
cordero*ᴹ*

sheep
mouton*ᴹ*
Schaf*ᴺ*
oveja*ᶠ*

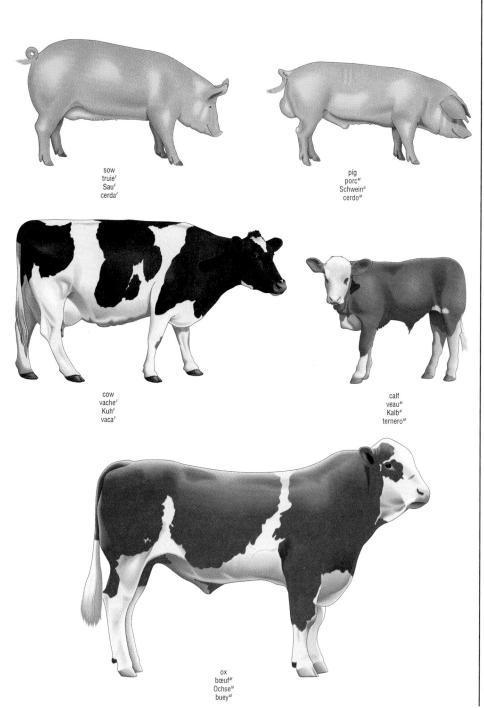

sow
truie^F
Sau^F
cerda^F

pig
porc^M
Schwein^N
cerdo^M

cow
vache^F
Kuh^F
vaca^F

calf
veau^M
Kalb^N
ternero^M

ox
bœuf^M
Ochse^M
buey^M

PRINCIPAL TYPES OF CEREAL
PRINCIPALES VARIÉTÉS^F DE CÉRÉALES^F
DIE WICHTIGSTEN GETREIDESORTEN^F
PRINCIPALES TIPOS^M DE CEREALES^M

SECTION OF A GRAIN OF WHEAT
COUPE^F D'UN GRAIN^M DE BLÉ^M
LÄNGSSCHNITT^M EINES WEIZENKORNS^N
CORTE^M DE UN GRANO^M DE TRIGO^M

brush
brosse^F
Granne^F
brocha^F

starch
albumen^M farineux
Stärke^F
almidón^M

seed coat
tégument^M
Samenschale^F
cáscara^F

germ
germe^M
Keim^M
germen^M

wheat
blé^M
Weizen^M
trigo^M

sweetcorn
maïs^M
Mais^M
maíz^M

barley
orge^F
Gerste^F
cebada^F

rye
seigle^M
Roggen^M
centeno^M

rice
riz^M
Reis^M
arroz^M

sorghum
sorgho^M
Sorghum^N
sorgo^M

oats
avoine^F
Hafer^M
avena^F

millet
millet^M
Hirse^F
mijo^M

buckwheat
sarrazin^M
Buchweizen^M
trigo^M sarraceno

BREAD
PAIN^M
BROT^N
PAN^M

French bread
pain^M parisien
Baguette^N
pan^M francés

French loaf
baguette^F parisienne
französisches Weißbrot^N
barra^F de pan^M

ear loaf
baguette^F épi^M
Ährenbrot^N
pan^M espiga^F

Vienna loaf
pain^M bâtard
Wiener Brot^N
pan^M vienés

Danish rye bread
pain^M de seigle^M danois
dänisches Roggenbrot^N
pan^M danés de centeno^M

German rye bread
pain^M de seigle^M allemand
deutsches Roggenbrot^N
pan^M alemán de centeno^M

Greek bread
pain^M grec
griechisches Brot^N
pan^M griego

Jewish challah
pain^M tchallah juif
jüdisches Weißbrot^N
pan^M judío hallah

wholemeal bread
pain^M complet
Vollkornbrot^N
pan^M integral

American corn bread
pain^M de maïs^M américain
amerikanisches Maisbrot^N
pan^M americano de maíz^M

English loaf
pain^M de mie^F
englisches Weißbrot^N
pan^M de flor^F

pumpernickel bread
pain^M pumpernickel^M
Pumpernickel^M
pan^M negro

milk bread
pain^M au lait^M
Milchbrot^N
panecillo^M

Indian chapati bread
pain^M chapati indien
indisches Fladenbrot^N
pan^M indio chapatí

pitta bread
pain^M pita
Pittabrot^N
pan^M de pita^F

farmhouse loaf
pain^M de campagne^F
Bauernbrot^N
pan^M campesino

Indian naan bread
pain^M naan indien
indisches Naanbrot^N
pan^M indio naan

black bread
pain^M de seigle^M noir
dunkles Roggenbrot^N
pan^M de centeno^M negro

Russian black bread
pain^M noir russe
russischer Pumpernickel^M
pan^M negro ruso

Irish soda bread
pain^M irlandais
irisches Brot^N
pan^M irlandés

caraway seeded rye bread
pain^M de seigle^M/ graines^F de carvi^M
Roggenbrot^M mit Kümmel^M
pan^M de centeno^M con semillas^F de
alcaravea^F

American white bread
pain^M blanc
amerikanisches Weißbrot^N
pan^M blanco americano de molde^M

unleavened bread
pain^M azyme
ungesäuertes Brot^N
pan^M ázimo

whole wheat bread
pain^M de blé^M entier
Grahambrot^N
pan^M integral de molde^M

croissant
croissant^M
Croissant^N
croissant^M

sesame seeded pitta
pain^M pita/ graines^F de sésame^M
Pittabrot^M mit Sesam^M
pan^M de pita^F con semillas^F de ajonjolí^M

rye crispbread
cracker^M de seigle^M
Roggenknäckebrot^N
galleta^F de centeno^M

Scandinavian crispbread
cracker^M scandinave
skandinavisches Knäckebrot^N
galleta^F escandinava

153

STEPS IN SOIL CULTIVATION
ÉTAPES*F* DE LA CULTURE*F* DU SOL*M*
ARBEITSVERFAHREN*N* DER BODENBEARBEITUNG*F*
PASOS*M* PARA EL CULTIVO*M* DEL SUELO*M*

PLOUGHING
RETOURNER LA TERRE*F*
PFLÜGEN*N* DES BODENS*M*
ARADO*M*

ribbing plough
charrue*F* à soc*M*
Beetpflug*N*
arado*M* de vertedera*F*

FERTILIZING
FERTILISER LA TERRE*F*
DÜNGEN*N* DES BODENS*M*
ABONADO*M*

manure spreader
épandeur*M* de fumier*M*
Dungstreuer*M*
esparcidora*F* de estiércol*M*

PULVERIZING
AMEUBLIR LA TERRE*F*
EGGEN*N* DES BODENS*M*
PULVERIZACIÓN*F*

tandem disc harrow
pulvérisateur*M* tandem*M*
Scheibenegge*F*
pulverizador*M* de discos*M*

cultivator
cultivateur*M*
Hackrahmen*M*
cultivador*M*

PLANTING
SEMER
SÄEN*N*
SIEMBRA*F*

seed drill
semoir*M* en lignes*F*
Drillmaschine*F*
sembradora*F* a chorrillo*M*

MOWING
FAUCHER
MÄHEN*N*
SIEGA*F*

flail mower
faucheuse*F*-conditionneuse*F*
Anhängemähwerk*N*
segadora*F*

TEDDING
FANER
ZETTEN[N] **UND WENDEN**[N]
HENIFICACIÓN[F]

rake
râteau[M]
Schubrechwender[M]
rastrillo[M]

HARVESTING
RÉCOLTER
ERNTEN[N]
COSECHA[F]

hay baler
ramasseuse[F]-presse[F]
Hochdruckpresse[F]
empacadora[F] de heno[M]

HARVESTING
RÉCOLTER
ERNTEN[N]
COSECHA[F]

combine harvester
moissonneuse[F]-batteuse[F]
Mähdrescher[M]
cosechadora[F] trilladora[F]

forage harvester
fourragère[F]
Feldhäckseler[M]
cosechadora[F] de forraje[M]

ENSILING
ENSILER
SILIEREN[N]
ENSILAJE[M]

forage blower
souffleuse[F] de fourrage[M]
Abladegebläse[N]
aventador[M] de frorraje[M]

155

PLOUGHING
RETOURNER LA TERRE^F
PFLÜGEN^N
ARADO^M

RIBBING PLOUGH
CHARRUE^F À SOC^M
BEETPFLUG^N
ARADO^M DE VERTEDERA^F

beam
age^M
Pflugrahmen^M
barra^F

coupler head
tête^F d'attelage^M
Dreipunktbock^M
cabeza^F de empalme^M

leg
étançon^M
Grindel^M
espolón^M

frog
sep^M
Griessäule^F
montante^M

mouldboard
versoir^M
Streichblech^N
vertedera^F

coulter
coutre^M
Scheibensech^M
cuchilla^F de disco^M

heel
talon^M
Anlage^F
reja^F

share
soc^M
Schar^N
reja^F

coulter shaft
bras^M de coutre^M
Scheibensechhalter^M
eje^M de cuchillas^F

FERTILIZING
FERTILISER LA TERRE^F
DÜNGEN^N
ABONADO^M

MANURE SPREADER
ÉPANDEUR^M DE FUMIER^M
DUNGSTREUER^M
ESPARCIDORA^M DE ESTIÉRCOL^M

beater
éparpilleur^M
Streuwerk^N
batidor^M

box
remorque^F
Ladefläche^F
cajón^M

coupler head
tête^F d'attelage^M
Kupplungsmaul^N
cabeza^F de empalme^M

chain drive
entraînement^M de la chaîne^F
Kettenantrieb^M
cadena^F de transmisión^F

power-takeoff shaft
cardan^M
Zapfwelle^F
eje^M de toma^F de fuerza^F

frame
châssis^M
Rahmen^M
chasis^M

hydraulic hose
conduit^M hydraulique
Hydraulikschlauch^M
manguera^F hidráulica

support leg
béquille^F d'appui^M
Abstellstütze^F
pata^F de soporte^M

PULVERIZING
AMEUBLIR LA TERRE^F
EGGEN^N DES BODENS^M
PULVERIZACIÓN^F

TANDEM DISC HARROW
PULVÉRISEUR^M TANDEM^M
SCHEIBENEGGE^F
PULVERIZADOR^M DE DISCOS^M

arm
bras^M
Arm^M
brazo^M

frame
châssis^M
Rahmen^M
chasis^M

height adjustment
ajustement^M de la hauteur^F
Hubwerk^N
palanca^F para graduar la altura^F

FARMING
FERME

LANDWIRTSCHAFT
AGRICULTURA

disc
disque^M
Scheibe^F
disco^M

hydraulic hose
conduit^M hydraulique
Hydraulikschlauch^M
manguera^F hidráulica

coupler head
tête^F d'attelage^M
Kupplungsmaul^N
cabeza^F de emplame^M

CULTIVATOR
CULTIVATEUR^M
GRUBBER^M
CULTIVADOR^M

frame
châssis^M
Rahmen^M
armazón^M

rotary hoe
houe^F rotative
Sternscheibe^F
azadón^M rotatorio

tine
dent^M
Zinke^F
púa^F de muelle^M

PLANTING
SEMER
SÄEN[N]
SIEMBRA[F]

SEED DRILL
SEMOIR[M] EN LIGNES[F]
DRILLMASCHINE[F]
SEMBRADORA[F] A CHORRILLO[M]

hopper
trémie[F]
Saatgutbehälter[M]
tolva[F]

grain tube
tube[M] d'ensemencement[M]
Fallrohr[N]
tubo[M] para el grano[M]

disc spacing lever
levier[M] d'écartement[M]
Einstellhebel[M]
palanca[F] de espaciamiento[M] de los discos

chain drive
chaîne[F] d'entraînement[M]
Antrieb[M]
cadena[F] de transmisión[F]

coulter
coutre[M]
Sech[M]
cuchilla[F]

press wheel
roue[F] de pression[F]
Druckrolle[F]
rueda[F] compresora

covering disc
disque[M] d'enterrage[M]
Zustreicher[M]
disco[M] tapador

MOWING
FAUCHER
MÄHEN[N]
SIEGA[F]

FLAIL MOWER
FAUCHEUSE[F]-CONDITIONNEUSE[F]
ANHÄNGEMÄHWERK[N]
SEGADORA[F]

tooth
dent[F]
Zinke[F]
diente[M]

crushing roll
rouleau[M] conditionneur
Konditionierer[M]
rodillo[M] triturador

pickup reel
rabatteur[M]
Haspel[F]
carrete[M] recogedor

tow bar
timon[M]
Zugrohr[N]
barra[F] de remolque[M]

hydraulic hose
conduit[M] hydraulique
Hydraulikanschluß[M]
manguera[F] hidráulica

cutter bar
barre[F] de coupe[F]
Messerbalken[M]
plataforma[F] de corte[M]

coupler head
tête[F] d'attelage[M]
Anhängemaul[N]
cabeza[F] de empalme[M]

TEDDING
FANER
ZETTEN^N UND WENDEN^N
HENIFICACIÓN^M

RAKE
RÂTEAU^M
SCHUBRECHWENDER^M
RASTRILLO^M

height adjustment
ajustement^M de la hauteur^F
Verstellspindel^F
palanca^F para graduar la altura^F

frame
châssis^M
Rahmen^M
chasis^M

rake bar
peigne^M
Rechenbalken^M
barra^F de rastrillos^M

tooth
dent^F
Zinke^F
diente^M

HARVESTING
RÉCOLTER
ERNTEN^N
COSECHA^F

HAY BALER
RAMASSEUSE^F-PRESSE^F
HOCHDRUCKPRESSE^F
EMPACADORA^F DE HENO^M

binder
lieuse^F
Knoter^M
agavilladora^F

press chamber
presse^F
Presskammer^F
caja^F de compresión^F

plungerhead
foulon^M
Kolbenantrieb^M
émbolo^M

power-takeoff shaft
cardan^M
Zapfwelle^F
eje^M de toma^F de fuerza^F

tow bar
timon^M
Zugrohr^N
barra^F de remolque^M

pickup cylinder
ramasseur^M
Pickup^M
cilindro^M recogedor

coupler head
tête^F d'attelage^M
Anhängemaul^N
cabeza^F de empalme^M

159

COMBINE HARVESTER
MOISSONNEUSE^F-BATTEUSE^F
MÄHDRESCHER^M
COSECHADORA^F TRILLADORA^F

LANDWIRTSCHAFT AGRICULTURA

FARMING FERME

grain tank
réservoir^M à grain^M
Korntank^M
depósito^M del grano^M

cab
cabine^F de conduite^F
Kabine^F
cabina^F

concave
contre-batteur^M
Dreschtrommel^F
reja^F trilladora

propeller
hélice^F
Propeller^M
propulsor^M

rotating auger
vis^F d'alimentation^F
Einzugsschnecke^F
rodillo^M de entrada^F

feeding tube
engreneur^M
Schrägförderer^M
tubo^M de alimentación^F

crop elevator
convoyeur^M
Schrägfördererkette^F
elevador^M

tooth
dent^F
Zinke^F
diente^M

bat
batte^F
Haspelrohr^N
garrote^M

pickup reel
rabatteur^M
Haspel^F
molinete^M

cutter bar
barre^F de coupe^F
Messerbalken^M
barra^F de cuchillas^F

divider
diviseur^M
Halmteiler^M
separador^M

grain elevator
élévateur[F] à grain[M]
Kornelevator[M]
elevador[M]

engine
moteur[M]
Motor[M]
motor[M]

unloading tube
tube[M] de déchargement[M]
Auslaufrohr[N]
tubo[M] de descarga[F]

rotor
rotor[M]
Rotor[M]
rotor[M]

threshing area
cage[F] de battage[M]
Dreschwerk[N]
área[F] de trilla[F]

screen
grille[F]
Dreschkorb[M]
criba[M]

straw spreader
éparpilleur[M] de paille[F]
Strohverteiler[M]
esparcidor[M] de paja[F]

sieve
crible[M]
Sieb[N]
criba[M]

tailing auger
vis[F] à otons[M]
Überkehr[F]
entrega[F] del grano[M]

grain pan
récepteur[M] de grain[M]
Rücklaufboden[M]
depósito[M] de grano[M]

grain auger
vis[F] à grain[M]
Kornschnecke[F]
sinfín[M] para el grano[M]

fan
ventilateur[M]
Gebläse[N]
ventilador[M]

header
tablier[M]
Schneidwerk[N]
conductor[M] transversal

FARMING
FERME

LANDWIRTSCHAFT
AGRICULTURA

FORAGE HARVESTER
FOURRAGÈRE^F
FELDHÄCKSELER^M
COSECHERA^F **DE FORRAJE**^M

wagon
remorque^F
Wagen^M
vagón^M

spout
souffleuse^F
Auswurfrohr^N
surtidor^M

rotating auger
vis^F d'alimentation^F
Einzugswalze^F
rodillo^M de entrada^F

tow bar
timon^M
Zugrohr^N
barra^F de remolque^M

power-takeoff shaft
cardan^M
Zapfwelle^F
eje^M de toma^F de fuerza^F

coupler head
tête^F d'attelage^M
Anhängemaul^N
cabeza^F de empalme^M

pickup cylinder
ramasseur^M
Pickup^M
cilindro^M recogedor

tooth
dent^F
Zinke^F
diente^M

FORAGE BLOWER
SOUFFLEUSE^F **DE FOURRAGE**^M
ABLADEGEBLÄSE^N
AVENTADOR^M **DE FORRAJE**^M

ensiling tube
tuyau^M d'ensilage^M
Sammelrohr^N
tubo^M de ensilaje^M

fan
ventilateur^M
Gebläse^N
ventilador^M

fan duct
tuyau^M du ventilateur^M
Gebläserohr^N
tubo^M de ventilación^F

manœuvring bar
barre^F de manœuvre^F
Bedienungshebel^M
barra^F de maniobra^F

hopper
trémie^F
Behälter^M
tolva^F

feed table
table^F d'alimentation^F
Dosierteller^M
mesa^F alimentadora

ARCHITEKTUR
ARQUITECTURA

ARCHITECTURE
ARCHITECTURE

TRADITIONAL DWELLINGS
MAISONS^F TRADITIONNELLES
TRADITIONELLE WOHNHÄUSER^N
VIVIENDAS^F TRADICIONALES

igloo
igloo^M
Iglu^M
iglú^M

wigwam
wigwam^M
Wigwam^M
wigwam^M

yurt
yourte^F
Jurte^F
yurta^F

isba
isba^F
Isba^F
isba^F

(mud) hut
case^F
Hütte^F
chabola^F

(straw) hut
hutte^F
Hütte^F
choza^F indígena

tepee
tipi^M
Tipi^N
tipi^M

pile dwelling
maison^F sur pilotis^M
Pfahlbau^M
habitación^F lacustre

IONIC ORDER
ORDRE^M IONIQUE
IONISCHE SÄULENORDNUNG^F
ORDEN^M JÓNICO

pediment
fronton^M
Giebeldreieck^N
frontón^F

entablature
entablement^M
Gebälk^N
entablamento^M

architrave
architrave^F
Architrav^M
arquitrabe^M

abacus
abaque^M
Abakus^M
ábaco^M

capital
chapiteau^M
Kapitell^N
capitel^M

volute
volute^F
Volute^F
voluta^F

shaft
fût^M
Schaft^M
fuste^M

column
colonne^F
Säule^F
columna^F

torus
tore^M
Torus^M
bocel^M

base
base^F
Basis^F
base^F

crepidoma
crépis^F
Krepis^F
crépida^F

euthynteria
euthynterie^F
Euthynterie^F
basamento^M

tympanum
tympan^M
Tympanon^N
tímpano^M

sima
cimaise^F
Sima^F
cimacio^M

cornice
corniche^F
Kranzgesims^N
cornisa^F

frieze
frise^F
Fries^M
friso^M

dentil
denticule^M
Zahnschnitt^M
dentículo^M

fascia
fasce^F
Faszie^F
banda^F de arquitrabe^M

flute
cannelure^F
Kannelüre^F
estría^F

fillet
arête^F plate
Steg^M
listel^M

scotia
scotie^F
Trochilus^M
escocia^F

stylobate
stylobate^M
Stylobat^M
estilóbato^M

DORIC ORDER
ORDRE^M **DORIQUE**
DORISCHE SÄULENORDNUNG^F
ORDEN^M **DÓRICO**

acroterion
acrotère^M
Akroterion^N
acrotera^F

mutule
mutule^F
Mutulus^M
modillón^M

gutta
goutte^F
Gutta^F
gota^F

triglyph
triglyphe^M
Triglyphe^F
triglifo^M

metope
métope^F
Metope^F
metopa^F

abacus
abaque^M
Abakus^M
ábaco^M

echinus
échine^F
Echinus^M
equino^M

annulet
annelet^M
Halsring^M
collarino^M

flute
cannelure^F
Kannelüre^F
estría^F

arris
arête^F vive
Grat^M
arista^F

drum
tambour^M
Tambour^M
tambor^M

CORINTHIAN ORDER
ORDRE^M **CORINTHIEN**
KORINTHISCHE SÄULENORDNUNG^F
ORDEN^M **CORINTIO**

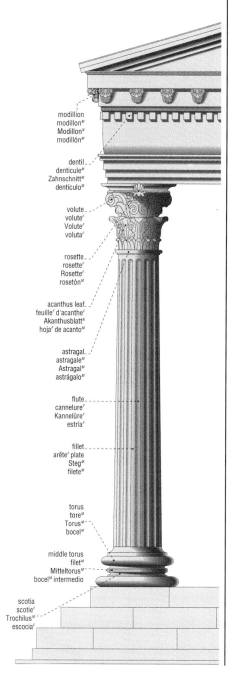

modillion
modillon^M
Modillon^N
modillón^M

dentil
denticule^F
Zahnschnitt^M
dentículo^M

volute
volute^F
Volute^F
voluta^F

rosette
rosette^F
Rosette^F
rosetón^M

acanthus leaf
feuille^F d'acanthe^F
Akanthusblatt^N
hoja^F de acanto^M

astragal
astragale^M
Astragal^M
astrágalo^M

flute
cannelure^F
Kannelüre^F
estría^F

fillet
arête^F plate
Steg^M
filete^M

torus
tore^M
Torus^M
bocel^M

middle torus
filet^M
Mitteltorus^M
bocel^M intermedio

scotia
scotie^F
Trochilus^M
escocia^F

GREEK TEMPLE
TEMPLE^M GREC
GRIECHISCHER TEMPEL^M
TEMPLO^M GRIEGO

tympanum
tympan^M
Tympanon^N
tímpano^M

acroterion
acrotère^M
Akroterion^N
acrotera^F

roof timber
charpente^F
Balken^M
maderamen^M que soporta el tejado^M

pediment
fronton^M
Giebeldreieck^N
frontón^M

sloping cornice
rampant^M
Schräggeison^M
cornisa^F inclinada

cornice
corniche^F
Kranzgesims^N
cornisa^F

frieze
frise^F
Fries^M
friso^M

architrave
architrave^F
Architrav^M
arquitrabe^M

entablature
entablement^M
Gebälk^N
entablamento^M

column
colonne^F
Säule^F
columna^F

crepidoma
crépis^F
Krepis^F
crépida^F

peristyle
péristyle^M
Peristyl^N
peristilo^M

stylobate
stylobate^M
Stylobat^M
estilóbato^M

euthynteria
euthynterie^F
Euthynterie^F
basamento^M

grille
grille^F
Gitter^N
reja^F de entrada^F al pronaos^M

ramp
rampe^F
Rampe^F
rampa^F de acceso^M

pronaos
pronaos^M
Pronaos^M
pronaos^M

naos
naos^M
Naos^M
naos^M

tile
tuile^F
Ziegel^M
cubierta^F de tejas^F

antefix
antéfixe^F
Stirnziegel^M
antefijas^F de la cumbrera^F

PLAN
PLAN^M
GRUNDRISS^M
PLANO^M

crepidoma
crépis^F
Krepis^F
crépida^F

opisthodomos
opisthodome^M
Opisthodomos^M
opistodemo^M

location of the statue
emplacement^M de la statue^F
Standort^M des Kultbildes^N
ubicación^F de la estatua^F

naos
naos^M
Naos^M
naos^M

pronaos
pronaos^M
Pronaos^M
pronaos^M

column
colonne^F
Säule^F
columna^F

peristyle
péristyle^M
Peristyl^N
peristilo^M

169

ROMAN HOUSE
MAISON^F ROMAINE
RÖMISCHES WOHNHAUS^N
CASA^F ROMANA

tablinum
tablinum^M
Tablinum^N
tablino^M

timber
charpente^F
Balken^M
viga^F

compluvium
compluvium^M
Compluvium^N
compluvio^M

fresco
fresque^F
Fresko^N
fresco^M

tile
tuile^F
Ziegel^M
teja^F

vestibule
vestibule^M
äußerer Hausflur^M
vestíbulo^M

atrium
atrium^M
Atrium^M
atrio^M

impluvium
impluvium^M
Impluvium^N
impluvio^M

shop
boutique^F
Laden^M
almacén^M

bed chamber
cubiculum^M
Cubiculum^N
cubículo^M

peristyle
péristyle^M
Peristyl^N
peristilo^M

garden
jardin^M
Garten^M
jardín^M

mosaic
mosaïque^F
Mosaik^N
mosaico^M

dining room
triclinium^M
Küche^F
cocina^F

kitchen
cuisine^F
Triclinium^N
triclinio^M

latrines
latrines^F
Latrinen^F
letrinas^F

VIEW FROM ABOVE
VUE^F PLONGEANTE
DRAUFSICHT^F
VISTA^F POR ENCIMA

garden
jardin^M
Garten^M
jardín^M

roof
toit^M
Dach^N
techo^M

compluvium
compluvium^M
Compluvium^N
compluvio^M

impluvium
impluvium^M
Impluvium^N
impluvio^M

171

MOSQUE
MOSQUÉE*F*
MOSCHEE*F*
MEZQUITA*F*

porch dome
coupole*F* du porche*M*
Portalkuppel*F*
cúpula*F* del pórtico*M*

prayer hall
salle*F* de prière*F*
Gebetshalle*F*
sala*F* de oración*F*

porch
porche*M*
Portal*N*
pórtico*M*

service room
locaux*M* de service*M*
Betriebsraum*M*
cuarto*M* de servicio*M*

minaret
minaret*M*
Minarett*N*
minarete*M*

arcades
portique*M*
Arkaden*F*
arcadas*F* sombreadas

reception hall
salle*F* de réception*F*
Empfangshalle*F*
vestíbulo*M* de recibo*M*

fountain for ritual ablutions
fontaine*F* des ablutions*F*
Brunnen*M* für rituelle Waschungen*F*
fuente*F* para abluciones*F*

courtyard
cour*F*
Innenhof*M*
patio*M*

fortified wall
mur*M* fortifié
befestigte Umfassungsmauer*F*
muro*M* fortificado

direction of Mecca
direction^f de la Mecque^f
Richtung^f Mekka
dirección^f de la Meca^f

Mihrab dome
coupole^f du mihrab^м
Kuppel^f des Mihrab^м
cúpula^f del Mihrab^м

central nave
nef^f centrale
Mittelschiffⁿ
nave^f central

Qibla wall
mur^м de la qibla^f
Kibla^f
muro^м de la Qibla^f

door
porte^f
Eingang^м
puerta^f

PLAN
PLAN^м
GRUNDRISS^м
PLANO^м

Mihrab
mihrab^м
Mihrab^м
Mihrab^м

Minbar
minbar^м
Minbar^м
Minbar^м

Mihrab dome
coupole^f du mihrab^м
Kuppel^f des Mihrab^м
cúpula^f del Mihrab^м

prayer hall
salle^f de prière^f
Gebetshalle^f
sala^f de oración^f

central nave
nef^f centrale
Mittelschiffⁿ
nave^f central

porch dome
coupole^f du porche^м
Portalkuppel^f
cúpula^f del pórtico^м

door
porte^f
Eingang^м
puerta^f

shady arcades
portique^м
Arkaden^f
arcadas^f sombreadas

courtyard
cour^f
Innenhof^м
patio^м

fountain for ritual ablutions
fontaine^f des ablutions^f
Brunnen^м für rituelle Waschungen^f
fuente^f para abluciones^f

minaret
minaret^м
Minarettⁿ
minarete^м

service room
locaux^м de service^м
Betriebsraum^м
cuarto^м de servicio^м

reception hall
salle^f de réception^f
Empfangshalle^f
vestíbulo^м de recibo^м

TYPES OF ARCH
ARC^M
BOGEN^M
ARCO^M

SEMICIRCULAR ARCH
ARC^M EN PLEIN CINTRE^M
RUNDBOGEN^M
ARCO^M DE MEDIO PUNTO^M

keystone
clé^F de voûte^F
Schlußstein^M
clave^F

spandrel
écoinçon^M
Zwickel^M
albanega^F

voussoir
claveau^M
Keilstein^M
dovela^F

springer
sommier^M
Anfänger^M
imposta^F

impost
imposte^F
Kämpfer^M
imposta^F

extrados
extrados^M
Rücken^M
trasdós^M

intrados
intrados^M
Laibung^F
intradós^M

pier
piédroit^M
Widerlager^M
pilar^M

TYPES OF ARCHES
TYPES^M D'ARCS^M
BOGENFORMEN^F
TIPOS^M DE ARCOS^M

pointed
en ogive^F
Spitzbogen^M
ojival^M

lancet
en lancette^F
Lanzettbogen^M
de ojiva^F lanceolada

ogee
en accolade^F
Kielbogen^M
conopial^M

horseshoe
en fer^M à cheval^M
Hufeisenbogen^M
de herradura^F

basket handle
surbaissé
Flachbogen^M
adintelado^M

stilted
surhaussé
gestelzter Bogen^M
peraltado^M

Tudor
Tudor
Tudorbogen^M
Tudor

trefoil
trilobé
Kleeblattbogen^M
trebolado^M

GOTHIC CATHEDRAL
CATHÉDRALE^F GOTHIQUE
GOTHISCHER DOM^M
CATEDRAL^F GÓTICA

FAÇADE
FAÇADE^F
FASSADE^F
FACHADA^F

ARCHITECTURE
ARCHITECTURE
ARCHITEKTUR
ARQUITECTURA

louvre-board
abat-son^M
Schallbrett^N
lucernas^F del campanario^M

bell tower
clocher^M
Glockenturm^M
campanario^M

rose window
rose^F
Rosette^F
rosetón^M

tracery
remplage^M
Maßwerk^N
tracería^F

stained glass
vitrail^M
Glasmalerei^F
vitrales^M

gallery
galerie^F
Galerie^F
galería^F

spire
flèche^F
Turmspitze^F
aguja^F

pinnacle
clocheton^M
Glockenstube^F
campanario^M

flying buttress
arc^M-boutant
Strebebogen^M
arbotante^M

gable
gâble^M
Wimperg^M
gablete^M

trefoil
trèfle^M
Dreipaß^M
trifolio^M

order
voussure^F
Archivolte^F
dovelaje^M

lintel
linteau^M
Türsturz^M
dintel^M

splay
ébrasement^M
Gewände^N
alféizar^M

tympanum
tympan^M
Bogenfeld^N
tímpano^M

portal
portail^M
Portal^N
portal^M

pier
trumeau^M
Pfeiler^M
parteluz^M

pier
piedroit^M
Pfeiler^M
pilar^M

CATHEDRAL
CATHÉDRALE[F]
DOM[M]
CATEDRAL[F]

GOTHIC CATHEDRAL
CATHÉDRALE[F] GOTHIQUE
GOTISCHER DOM[M]
CATEDRAL[F] GÓTICA

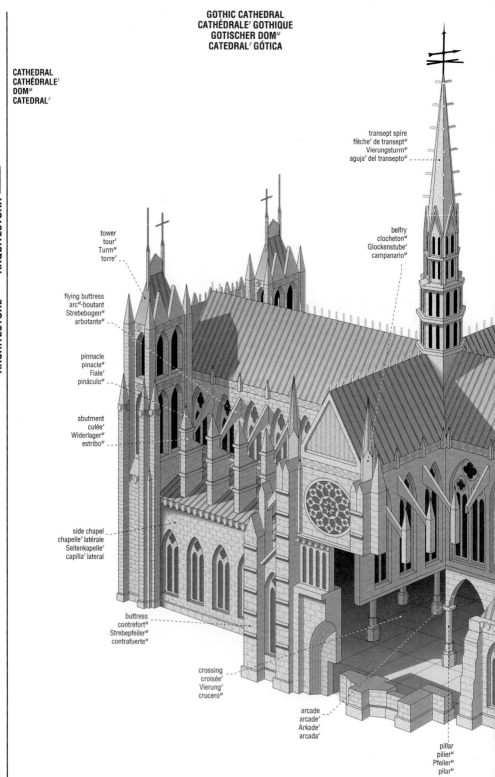

transept spire
flèche[F] de transept[M]
Vierungsturm[M]
aguja[F] del transepto[M]

tower
tour[F]
Turm[M]
torre[F]

belfry
clocheton[M]
Glockenstube[F]
campanario[M]

flying buttress
arc[M]-boutant
Strebebogen[M]
arbotante[M]

pinnacle
pinacle[M]
Fiale[F]
pináculo[M]

abutment
culée[F]
Widerlager[M]
estribo[M]

side chapel
chapelle[F] latérale
Seitenkapelle[F]
capilla[F] lateral

buttress
contrefort[M]
Strebepfeiler[M]
contrafuerte[M]

crossing
croisée[F]
Vierung[F]
crucero[M]

arcade
arcade[F]
Arkade[F]
arcada[F]

pillar
pilier[M]
Pfeiler[M]
pilar[M]

PLAN
PLAN^M
GRUNDRISS^M
PLANO^M

Lady chapel
chapelle^F axiale
Chorscheitelkapelle^F
capilla^F axial

apsidiole
absidiole^F
Radialkapelle^F
capilla^F radial

ambulatory
déambulatoire^M
Chorumgang^M
deambulatorio^M

transept
transept^M
Querschiff^N
crucero^M del transepto^M

aisle
collatéral^M
Seitenschiff^N
nave^F lateral

porch
porche^M
Portal^N
pórtico^M

chevet
chevet^M
Chorhaupt^N
ábside^M

apse
abside^F
Hauptapsis^F
ábside^M

choir
chœur^M
Chor^M
coro^M

crossing
croisée^F du transept^M
Vierung^F
crucero^M

nave
nef^F
Mittelschiff^N
nave^F

VAULT
VOÛTE^F
GEWÖLBE^N
BÓVEDA^F

traverse arch
arc^M-doubleau^M
Schildbogen^M
nervio^M transversal

formeret
arc^M-formeret^M
Gurtbogen^M
imposta^F principal

keystone
clé^F de voûte^F
Schlußstein^M
clave^F

lierne
lierne^F
Scheitelrippe^F
nervio^M secundario

tierceron
tierceron^M
Tierceron^M
tercelete^M

diagonal buttress
arc^M diagonal
Kreuzrippe^F
nervio^M diagonal

Lady chapel
chapelle^F axiale
Chorscheitelkapelle^F
capilla^F axial

choir
chœur^M
Chor^M
coro^M

apsidiole
absidiole^F
Radialkapelle^F
capilla^F radial

VAUBAN FORTIFICATION
FORTIFICATION^F À LA VAUBAN
VAUBAN-FESTUNG^F
FORTIFICACIÓN^F DE VAUBAN

retrenchment
cavalier^M
Katze^F
trinchera^F

curtain
courtine^F
Kurtine^F
cortina^F

parade ground
place^F d'armes^F
Übungsplatz^M
patio^M de armas^F

scarp
escarpe^F
innere Grabenböschung^F
escarpa^F

bartizan
échauguette^F
Scharwachturm^M
garita^F

counterscarp
contrescarpe^F
Kontreskarpe^F
contraescarpa^F

ground sill
traverse^F
Traverse^F
traversa^F

salient angle
saillant^M
aufspringender Winkel^M
ángulo^M saliente

guardhouse
corps^M de garde^F
Wachhäuschen^N
cuartel^M de la guardia^F

rampart
rempart^M
Festungswall^M
muralla^F

moat
fossé^M
Graben^M
foso^M

covered way
chemin^M couvert
gedeckter Weg^M
camino^M de ronda^F cubierto

glacis
glacis^M
Glacis^N
explanada^F

barrack buildings
casernement^M
Kaserne^F
cuarteles^M

battlement
parapet^M
Brustwehr^F
almena^F

embrasure
embrasure^F
Schießscharte^F
cañonera^F

bastion
bastion^M
Bollwerk^N
bastión^M

face
face^F
Vorderseite^F
frente^F

flank
flanc^M
Flanke^F
flanco^M

tenaille
tenaille^F
Zangenwerk^N
tenaza^F

demilune
demi-lune^F
Halbmond^M
medialuna^F

postern
poterne^F
Ausfallpforte^F
poterna^F

caponiere
caponnière^F
Schießgrube^F
caponera^F

terreplein
terre-plein^M
Binnenraum^M
terraplén^M

counterguard
contre-garde^F
Kontergarde^F
contraguardia^F

179

CASTLE
CHÂTEAU^M FORT
BURG^F
CASTILLO^M

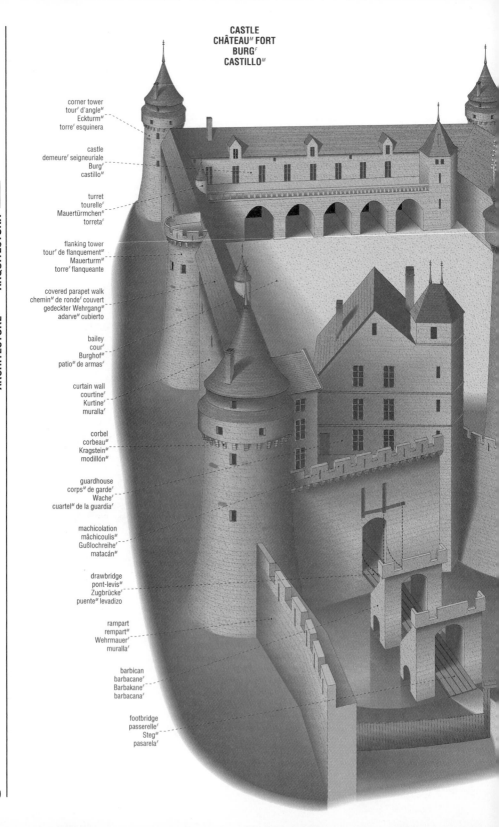

corner tower
tour^F d'angle^M
Eckturm^M
torre^F esquinera

castle
demeure^F seigneuriale
Burg^F
castillo^M

turret
tourelle^F
Mauertürmchen^N
torreta^F

flanking tower
tour^F de flanquement^M
Mauerturm^M
torre^F flanqueante

covered parapet walk
chemin^M de ronde^F couvert
gedeckter Wehrgang^M
adarve^M cubierto

bailey
cour^F
Burghof^M
patio^M de armas^F

curtain wall
courtine^F
Kurtine^F
muralla^F

corbel
corbeau^M
Kragstein^M
modillón^M

guardhouse
corps^M de garde^F
Wache^F
cuartel^M de la guardia^F

machicolation
mâchicoulis^M
Gußlochreihe^F
matacán^M

drawbridge
pont-levis^M
Zugbrücke^F
puente^M levadizo

rampart
rempart^M
Wehrmauer^F
muralla^F

barbican
barbacane^F
Barbakane^F
barbacana^F

footbridge
passerelle^F
Steg^M
pasarela^F

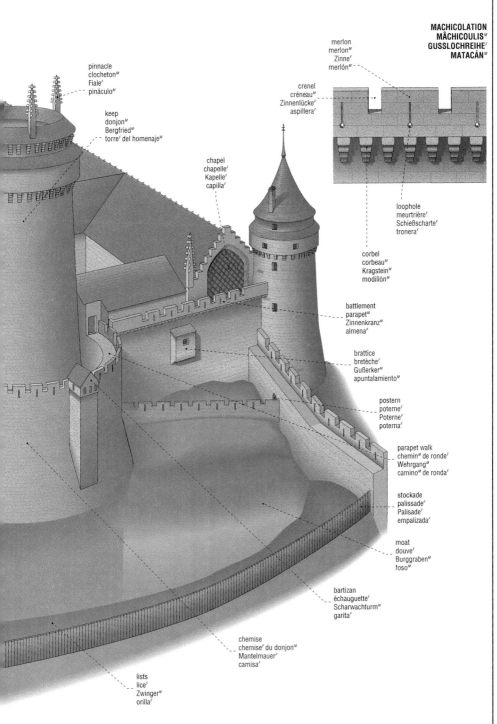

pinnacle
clocheton*M*
Fiale*F*
pináculo*M*

keep
donjon*M*
Bergfried*M*
torre*F* del homenaje*M*

chapel
chapelle*F*
Kapelle*F*
capilla*F*

MACHICOLATION
MÂCHICOULIS*M*
GUSSLOCHREIHE*F*
MATACÁN*M*

merlon
merlon*M*
Zinne*F*
merlón*M*

crenel
créneau*M*
Zinnenlücke*F*
aspillera*F*

loophole
meurtrière*F*
Schießscharte*F*
tronera*F*

corbel
corbeau*M*
Kragstein*M*
modillón*M*

battlement
parapet*M*
Zinnenkranz*M*
almena*F*

brattice
bretèche*F*
Gußerker*M*
apuntalamiento*M*

postern
poterne*F*
Poterne*F*
poterna*F*

parapet walk
chemin*M* de ronde*F*
Wehrgang*M*
camino*M* de ronda*F*

stockade
palissade*F*
Palisade*F*
empalizada*F*

moat
douve*F*
Burggraben*M*
foso*M*

bartizan
échauguette*F*
Scharwachturm*M*
garita*F*

chemise
chemise*F* du donjon*M*
Mantelmauer*F*
camisa*F*

lists
lice*F*
Zwinger*M*
orilla*F*

181

pitched roof
toit^M en pente^F
Satteldach^N
en pendiente^F

gable roof
toit^M à pignon^M
steiles Satteldach^N
de dos aguas^F

hip roof
toit^M à deux croupes^F
Walmdach^N
de cuatro aguas^F

lean-to roof
toit^M en appentis^M
Pultdach^N
de vertiente^F simple

flat roof
toit^M plat
Flachdach^N
plano^M

sawtooth roof
toit^M en shed^M
Sheddach^N
tejado^M en diente^M de sierra^F

monitor roof
toit^M avec lanterneau^M
Dach^N mit Firstlaterne^F
de linternilla^F

ogee roof
toit^M en carène^F
Kieldach^N
de arco^M conopial

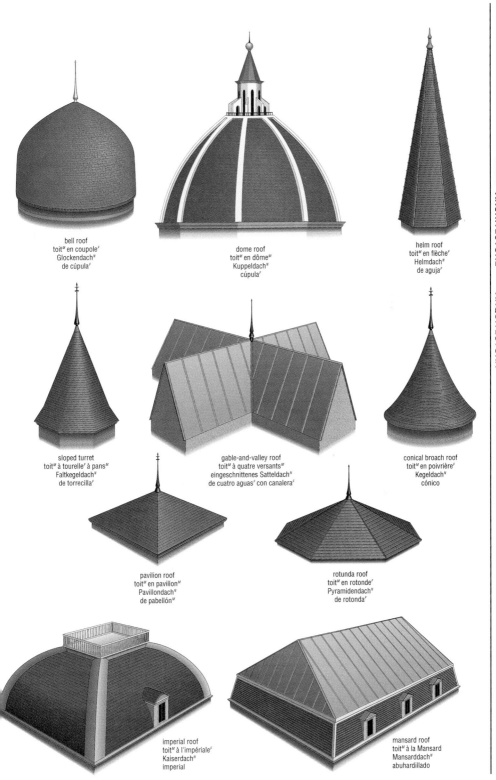

bell roof
toit^M en coupole^F
Glockendach^N
de cúpula^F

dome roof
toit^M en dôme^M
Kuppeldach^N
cúpula^F

helm roof
toit^M en flèche^F
Helmdach^N
de aguja^F

sloped turret
toit^M à tourelle^F à pans^M
Faltkegeldach^N
de torrecilla^F

gable-and-valley roof
toit^M à quatre versants^M
eingeschnittenes Satteldach^N
de cuatro aguas^F con canalera^F

conical broach roof
toit^M en poivrière^F
Kegeldach^N
cónico

pavilion roof
toit^M en pavillon^M
Pavillondach^N
de pabellón^M

rotunda roof
toit^M en rotonde^F
Pyramidendach^N
de rotonda^F

imperial roof
toit^M à l'impériale^F
Kaiserdach^N
imperial

mansard roof
toit^M à la Mansard
Mansarddach^N
abuhardillado

CITY CENTRE
CENTRE^M-VILLE^F
CITY^F
CENTRO^M DE UNA CIUDAD^F

park
parc^M
Park^M
parque^M

conference centre
palais^M des congrès^M
Kongreßzentrum^N
centro^M de congresos^M

office tower
tour^F à bureaux^M
Bürohochhaus^N
edificio^M de oficinas^F

green space
espace^M vert
Grünanlage^F
zona^F verde

cathedral
cathédrale^F
Kathedrale^F
catedral^F

train station
gare^F
Bahnhof^M
estación^M de ferrocarril^M

central reservation
terre-plein^M
Mittelstreifen^M
separador^M

planetarium
planétarium^M
Planetarium^N
planetario^M

railway
voie^F ferrée
Eisenbahn^F
vía^F férrea

traffic island
îlot^M refuge^M
Verkehrsinsel^F
separador^M

boulevard
boulevard^M
Boulevard^M
avenida^F

street
rue^F
Straße^F
calle^F

delivery ramp
rampe^F de livraison^F
Auffahrt^F
rampa^F para mercancías^F

motorway
autoroute^F
Autobahn^F
autopista^F

hotel
hôtel^M
Hotel^N
hotel^M

restaurant
restaurant^M
Dachrestaurant^N
restaurante^M

skyscraper
gratte-ciel^M
Wolkenkratzer^M
rascacielos^M

church
église^F
Kirche^F
iglesia^F

high-rise block
tour^F d'habitation^F
Hochhaus^N
edificio^M de apartamentos^M

street light
lampadaire^M
Straßenlaterne^F
farol^M

parking lot
aire^F de stationnement^M
Parkplatz^M
estacionamiento^M

commercial premises
immeuble^M commercial
Geschäftshaus^N
edificio^M comercial

office building
immeuble^M à bureaux^M
Bürogebäude^N
edificio^M de oficinas^F

museum
musée^M
Museum^N
museo^M

stadium
stade^M
Stadion^N
estadio^M

CROSS SECTION OF A STREET
COUPE^F D'UNE RUE^F
QUERSCHNITT^M EINER STRASSE^F
VISTA^F TRANSVERSAL DE UNA CALLE^F

street light
réverbère^M
Straßenlaterne^F
farol^M

pavement
trottoir^M
Bürgersteig^M
acera^F

roadway
chaussée^F
Fahrbahn^F
calzada^F

traffic lights
feux^M de circulation^F
Verkehrsampel^F
semáforo^M

manhole
regard^M de visite^F
Kabelschacht^M
boca^F de acceso^M

central reservation
terre-plein^M
Mittelstreifen^M
mediana^F

kerb
bordure^F de trottoir^M
Bordstein^M
guarnición^F

fire hydrant
borne^F d'incendie^M
Hydrant^M
boca^F de agua^F para incendios^M

pedestrian crossing
passage^M pour piétons^M
Fußgängerüberweg^M
paso^M de peatones^M

surface water drain
branchement^M pluvial
Regenwasserabfluß^M
tubo^M drenaje^M de tormenta^F

bus stop
arrêt^M d'autobus^M
Bushaltestelle^F
parada^F de autobús^M

barrier
barrière^F
Sperre^F
valla^F

bus shelter
abribus^M
Wartehäuschen^N
cobertizo^M de la parada^F

sewer
égout^M
Abwasserkanal^M
alcantarilla^F

electricity cable
câble^M électrique
Stromversorgungskabel^N
cable^M eléctrico

water main
conduite^F d'eau^F potable
Trinkwasserleitung^F
toma^F de agua^F potable

telephone cable
câble^M téléphonique
Telefonkabel^N
red^F de cables^M telefónicos

gas main
conduite^F de gaz^M
Gasleitung^F
conducto^M principal de gas^M

water main
conduite^F d'eau^F potable
Trinkwasserleitung^F
toma^F de agua^F potable

main sewer
égout^M collecteur
Mischwasserkanal^M
alcantarilla^F principal

TOWN HOUSES
MAISONS^F DE VILLE^F
HÄUSERFORMEN^F IN DER STADT
VIVIENDAS^F URBANAS

small detached house
villa^F
Cottage^N
casa^F de campo^M

large detached house
maison^F individuelle
Einfamilienhaus^N
casas^F independientes

freehold flats
appartements^M en copropriété^F
Eigentumswohnungen^F
condominios^M

semi-detached houses
maison^F individuelle jumelée
Doppelhaus^N
casas^F gemelas

terraced houses
maisons^F en rangée^F
Reihenhaus^N
casas^F en serie^F

high-rise block
tour^F d'habitation^F
Wohnblock^N
edificio^M de apartamentos^M

THEATRE
SALLE*F* DE SPECTACLE*M*
THEATER*N*
TEATRO*M*

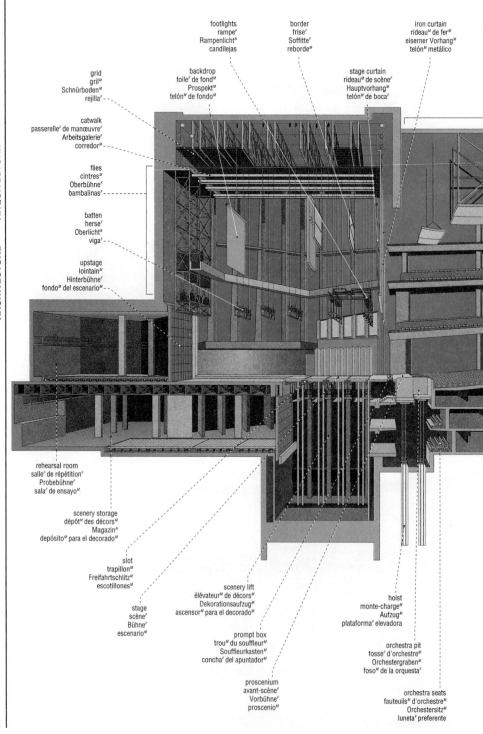

footlights
rampe*F*
Rampenlicht*N*
candilejas

border
frise*F*
Soffitte*F*
reborde*M*

iron curtain
rideau*M* de fer*M*
eiserner Vorhang*M*
telón*M* metálico

grid
gril*M*
Schnürboden*M*
rejilla*F*

backdrop
toile*F* de fond*M*
Prospekt*M*
telón*M* de fondo*M*

stage curtain
rideau*M* de scène*F*
Hauptvorhang*M*
telón*M* de boca*F*

catwalk
passerelle*F* de manœuvre*F*
Arbeitsgalerie*F*
corredor*M*

flies
cintres*M*
Oberbühne*F*
bambalinas*F*

batten
herse*F*
Oberlicht*N*
viga*F*

upstage
lointain*M*
Hinterbühne*F*
fondo*M* del escenario*M*

rehearsal room
salle*F* de répétition*F*
Probebühne*F*
sala*F* de ensayo*M*

scenery storage
dépôt*M* des décors*M*
Magazin*N*
depósito*M* para el decorado*M*

slot
trapillon*M*
Freifahrtschlitz*M*
escotillones*M*

stage
scène*F*
Bühne*F*
escenario*M*

scenery lift
élévateur*M* de décors*M*
Dekorationsaufzug*M*
ascensor*M* para el decorado*M*

prompt box
trou*M* du souffleur*M*
Souffleurkasten*M*
concha*F* del apuntador*M*

proscenium
avant-scène*F*
Vorbühne*F*
proscenio*M*

hoist
monte-charge*M*
Aufzug*M*
plataforma*F* elevadora

orchestra pit
fosse*F* d'orchestre*M*
Orchestergraben*M*
foso*M* de la orquesta*F*

orchestra seats
fauteuils*M* d'orchestre*M*
Orchestersitz*M*
luneta*F* preferente

front lights
projecteurs[M]
Beleuchtung[F]
luces[F] de frente

auditorium
salle[F]
Zuschauerraum[M]
sala[F] para el público[M]

acoustic ceiling
plafond[M] acoustique
Akustik-Decke[F]
techo[M] acústico

dress circle
balcon[M]
erster Rang[M]
balcón[M]

gallery
galerie[F]
dritter Rang[M]
galería[F]

escalator
escalier[M] mobile
Rolltreppe[F]
escalera[F] eléctrica

box
loge[F]
Loge[F]
palco[M]

control room
régie[F]
Stellwarte[F]
sala[F] de control[M]

foyer
foyer[M]
Foyer[N]
vestíbulo[M]

dressing room
loge[F] d'artiste[M]
Garderobe[F]
camarín[M]

stalls
parterre[M]
Parterre[N]
luneta[F]

STAGE
SCÈNE[F]
BÜHNE[F]
ESCENA[F]

border
frise[F]
Soffitte[F]
reborde[M]

stage curtain
rideau[M] de scène[F]
Hauptvorhang[M]
telón[M] de boca[F]

wings
coulisses[F]
Kulissen[F]
bastidores[M]

prompt side
côté[M] jardin[M]
rechts
derecha[F] del actor[M]

opposite prompt side
côté[M] cour[F]
links
derecha[F] del espectador[M]

upstage
lointain[M]
Hinterbühne[F]
fondo[M] del escenario[M]

OFFICE BUILDING
ÉDIFICE^M À BUREAUX^M
BÜROGEBÄUDE^N
EDIFICIO^M DE OFICINAS^F

panoramic window
fenêtre^F panoramique
Panoramafenster^N
ventana^F panorámica

office tower
tour^F à bureaux^M
Büroturm^M
torre^F de oficinas^F

main entrance
entrée^F principale
Haupteingang^M
entrada^F principal

**PODIUM AND BASEMENTS
BASILAIRE^M ET SOUS-SOL^M
SOCKEL^M UND UNTERGESCHOSS^N
PODIO^M Y BASAMENTO^M**

commercial area
galerie^F marchande
Ladenpassage^F
zona^F comercial

public garden
jardin^M public
Grünanlage^F
jardín^M público

street
rue^F
Straße^F
calle^F

podium
basilaire^M
Sockel^M
podio^M

rotunda
rotonde^F
Rotunde^F
rotonda^F

lift
ascenseur^M
Aufzug^M
ascensor^M

glassed roof
verrière^F
Glasdach^N
techo^M de vidrio^M

restaurant
restaurant^M
Restaurant^N
restaurante^M

bus
autobus^M
Bus^M
autobús^M

escalator
escalier^M mobile
Rolltreppe^F
escalera^F eléctrica

loading dock
quai^M de chargement^M
Laderampe^F
muelle^M para cargar mercancía^F

delivery entrance
entrée^F des marchandises^F
Lieferanteneinfahrt^F
entrada^F para mercancía^F

underground
métro^M
U-Bahn^F
metro^M

lobby
hall^M
Eingangshalle^F
vestíbulo^M

parking
stationnement^M
Parkdeck^N
entrada^F para entregas^F

SUMMARY

HAUS
CASA

HOUSE
MAISON

READING PLANS
LECTURE^F DE PLANS^M

READING PLANS
LECTURE^F **DE PLANS**^{M}
GEBÄUDEPLANUNG^F
PLANO^M **DE UNA CASA**

ELEVATION
ÉLÉVATION^F
ANSICHT^F
ELEVACIÓN^F

SITE PLAN
PLAN^M **DU TERRAIN**^{M}
LAGEPLAN^M
PLANO^M **DEL TERRENO**

shed
remise^F
Schuppen^M
cobertizo^M

vegetable garden
jardin^M potager
Nutzgarten^M
huerto^M

ornamental garden
jardin^M d'agrément^M
Ziergarten^M
jardín^M

patio
terrasse^F
Terrasse^F
terraza^F

bank
déclivité^F du terrain^M
Böschung^F
desnivel^M

property line
limite^F du terrain^M
Grundstücksgrenze^F
lindero^M

house
maison^F
Haus^N
casa^F

parking
stationnement^M
Abstellplatz^M
estacionamiento^M

driveway
allée^F
Zufahrt^F
entrada^F del coche^M

lawn
pelouse^F
Rasen^M
césped^M

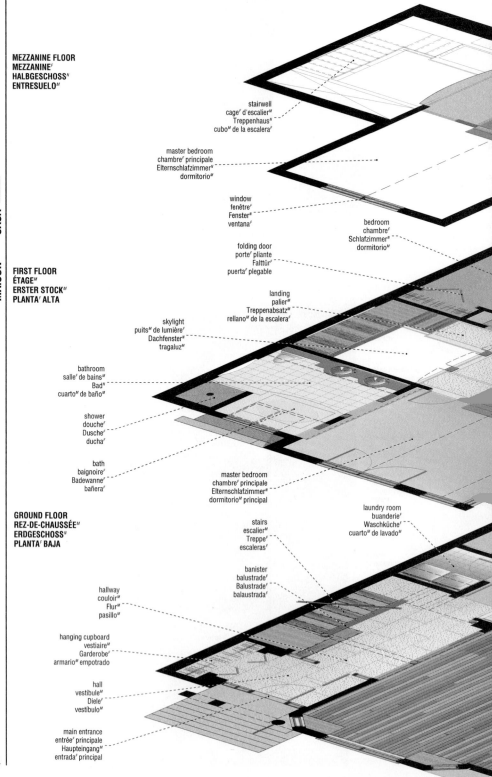

HOUSE
MAISON

HAUS
CASA

MEZZANINE FLOOR
MEZZANINE^F
HALBGESCHOSS^N
ENTRESUELO^M

stairwell
cage^F d'escalier^M
Treppenhaus^N
cubo^M de la escalera^F

master bedroom
chambre^F principale
Elternschlafzimmer^N
dormitorio^M

window
fenêtre^F
Fenster^N
ventana^F

bedroom
chambre^F
Schlafzimmer^N
dormitorio^M

folding door
porte^F pliante
Falttür^F
puerta^F plegable

FIRST FLOOR
ÉTAGE^M
ERSTER STOCK^M
PLANTA^F **ALTA**

landing
palier^M
Treppenabsatz^M
rellano^M de la escalera^F

skylight
puits^M de lumière^F
Dachfenster^N
tragaluz^M

bathroom
salle^F de bains^M
Bad^N
cuarto^M de baño^M

shower
douche^F
Dusche^F
ducha^F

bath
baignoire^F
Badewanne^F
bañera^F

master bedroom
chambre^F principale
Elternschlafzimmer^N
dormitorio^M principal

laundry room
buanderie^F
Waschküche^F
cuarto^M de lavado^M

GROUND FLOOR
REZ-DE-CHAUSSÉE^M
ERDGESCHOSS^N
PLANTA^F **BAJA**

stairs
escalier^M
Treppe^F
escaleras^F

banister
balustrade^F
Balustrade^F
balaustrada^F

hallway
couloir^M
Flur^M
pasillo^M

hanging cupboard
vestiaire^M
Garderobe^F
armario^M empotrado

hall
vestibule^M
Diele^F
vestíbulo^M

main entrance
entrée^F principale
Haupteingang^M
entrada^F principal

194

READING PLANS
LECTURE^F DE PLANS^M
GEBÄUDEPLANUNG^F
ELEMENTOS^M BÁSICOS DE UN PLANO^M

mezzanine
mezzanine^F
Halbgeschoß^N
entresuelo^M

mezzanine stairs
escalier^M de la mezzanine^F
Treppe^F zum Halbgeschoß^N
escalera^F del entresuelo^M

glass roof
verrière^F
Glasdach^N
techo^M de vidrio

bathroom
salle^F de bains^M
Bad^N
cuarto^M de baño^M

window
fenêtre^F
Fenster^N
ventana^F

bedroom
chambre^F
Schlafzimmer^N
dormitorio^M

wardrobe
garde-robe^F
Kleiderschrank^M
guardarropa^M

walk-in wardrobe
garde-robe^F
Kleiderschrank^M
entrada^F

hinged door
porte^F à charnière^F
Drehflügeltür^F
puerta^F abatible

patio door
porte^F-fenêtre^F
Terrassentür^F
puerta^F trasera

sitting room
salle^F de séjour^M
Wohnzimmer^N
sala^F

kitchen-diner
dînette^F
Wohnküche^F
cocina^F pequeña

kitchen
cuisine^F
Küche^F
cocina^F

toilet
w.c.^{M}
Toilette^F
baño^M

pantry
garde-manger^M
Speisekammer^F
despensa^F

dining room
salle^F à manger
Eßzimmer^N
comedor^M

living room
salon^M
Wohnzimmer^N
cuarto^M de estar

fireplace
cheminée^F
Kamin^M
chimenea^F

EXTERIOR OF A HOUSE
EXTÉRIEUR*M* D'UNE MAISON*F*
AUSSENANSICHT*F* EINES HAUSES*N*
EXTERIOR*M* DE UNA CASA*F*

roof vent
chatière*F*
Lüftungsziegel*M*
respiradero*M*

cornice
corniche*F*
Gesims*N*
cornisa*F*

first floor
étage*M*
erster Stock*M*
planta*F* alta

garage
garage*M*
Garage*F*
garaje*M*

driveway
accès*M* au garage*M*
Garagenzufahrt*F*
entrada*F* del coche*M*

stone steps
perron*M*
Treppenvorbau*M*
escalinata*F*

outdoor light
applique*F* d'extérieur*M*
Außenleuchte*F*
luz*F* exterior

chimney pot
mitron^M
Kaminaufsatz^M
capuchón^M de la chimenea^F

chimney stack
souche^F
Kamin^M
cañón^M de chimenea^F

chimney
cheminée^F
Schornstein^M
chimenea^F

roof
toit^M
Dach^N
tejado^M

lightning conductor
paratonnerre^M
Blitzableiter^M
pararrayos^M

skylight
tabatière^F
Dachfenster^N
tragaluz^M

gable
pignon^M
Giebelseite^F
buhardilla^F

gable vent
évent^M de pignon^M
Belüftungsgitter^N
respiradero^M

gutter
gouttière^F
Dachrinne^F
canalón^M

bay window
fenêtre^F en baie^F
Erkerfenster^N
mirador^M

downpipe
descente^F de gouttière^F
Regenrohr^N
bajada^F de aguas^F

bow window
fenêtre^F en saillie^F
Erkerfenster^N
ventanal^M

ground floor
rez-de-chaussée^M
Erdgeschoß^N
planta^F baja

basement window
fenêtre^F de sous-sol^M
Kellerfenster^N
respiradero^M

basement
sous-sol^M
Keller^M
sótano^M

STRUCTURE OF A HOUSE
STRUCTURE*F* D'UNE MAISON*F*
KONSTRUKTION*F* EINES HAUSES*N*
ESTRUCTURA*F* DE UNA CASA*F*

TIMBER FRAME
CHARPENTE*F*
RAHMEN*M*
ARMAZÓN*M*

ceiling joist
solive*F* de plafond*M*
Deckenbalken*M*
vigueta*F* del techo*M*

sheathing
revêtement*M*
Verkleidung*F*
entablado*M*

double plate
sablière*F* double
Zange*F*
sofera*F* doble

rafter
chevron*M*
Sparren*M*
cabrio*M*

subfloor
sous-plancher*M*
Unterboden*M*
contrapiso*M*

gable stud
montant*M*
Giebelständer*M*
montante*M*

tie beam
faîtage*M*
Firstpfette*F*
caballete*M*

fireproofing
coupe-feu*M*
feuerhemmendes Element*N*
cortafuego*M*

lintel
linteau*M*
Wechsel*M*
cabezal*M*

sill rail
appui*M* de fenêtre*F*
Brüstungsriegel*M*
alféizar*M*

sill plate
lisse*F* d'assise*F*
Schwelle*F*
solera*F* inferior

stud
poteau*M*
Pfosten*M*
pie*M* derecho

foundation
mur*M* de fondation*F*
Fundament*N*
muro*M* de cimentación*F*

girder
poutre*F*
Träger*M*
viga*F* maestra

footing
semelle*F*
Fundamentstreifen*M*
zarpa*F*

ledger board
lambourde*F*
Längsriegel*M*
travesaño*M*

corner stud
poteau*M* cornier
Eckpfosten*M*
montante*M* esquinero

brace
étai*M*
Strebe*F*
tirante*M*

bridging
croix*F* de Saint-André
Kreuzaussteifung*F*
puntales*M* de refuerzo*M*

floor joist
solive*F* de plancher*M*
Deckenbalken*M*
vigueta*F* del piso*M*

end joist
solive*F* de rive*F*
Fußbalken*M*
vigueta*F* esquinera

ROOF TRUSS
FERME^F DE TOIT^M
DACHSTUHL^M
ARMADURA^F DEL TECHO^M

king post
poinçon^M
Hängesäule^F
pendolón^M

side post
jambette^F
Ständer^M
virotillo^M

principal rafter
arbalétrier^M
Hauptsparren^M
par^M

tie beam
entrait^M
Bundbalken^M
tirante^M

strut
contre-fiche^F
Strebe^F
puntal^M

FOUNDATIONS
FONDATIONS^F
FUNDAMENT^N
CIMIENTOS^M

sheathing
revêtement^M
Innenputz^M
entablado^M

subfloor
sous-plancher^M
Unterboden^M
contrapiso^M

skirting board
plinthe^F
Sockelleiste^F
zócalo^M

wall stud
poteau^M mural
Wandpfosten^M
montante^M del muro^M

moulding
quart-de-rond^M
Viertelstab^M
moldura^F

brick wall
mur^M de briques^F
Mauerwerk^N
muro^M de ladrillos^M

wood flooring
parquet^M
Parkettboden^M
piso^M de madera^F

insulating material
isolant^M
Isolierstoff^M
material^M aislante

sill
lisse^F
Schwelle^F
solera^F

foundation
mur^M de fondation^F
Fundament^N
cimentación^F

floor joist
solive^F de plancher^M
Deckenbalken^M
vigueta^F del piso^M

end joist
solive^F de rive^F
Fußbalken^M
vigueta^F esquinera

sill plate
lisse^F d'assise^F
Schwelle^F
solera^F interior

footing
semelle^F
Fundamentstreifen^M
zarpa^F

gravel
gravier^M
Kies^M
grava^F

drain tile
drain^M
Sickerrohr^N
tubo^M de drenaje^M

WOOD FLOORING
PARQUET[M]
PARKETTBODEN[M]
PISOS[M] DE MADERA[F]

WOOD FLOORING ON CEMENT SCREED
PARQUET[M] SUR CHAPE[F] DE CIMENT[M]
PARKETTBODEN[M] AUF ZEMENTESTRICH[M]
PARQUÉ[M] SOBRE BASE[F] DE CEMENTO[M]

WOOD FLOORING ON WOODEN BASE
PARQUET[M] SUR OSSATURE[F] DE BOIS[M]
PARKETTBODEN[M] AUF HOLZUNTERBAU[M]
ENTARIMADO[M] SOBRE ESTRUCTURA[F] DE MADERA[F]

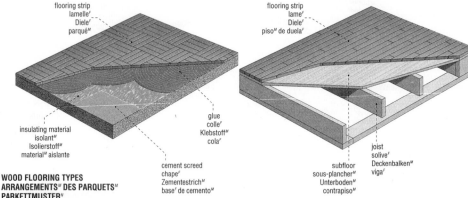

flooring strip
lamelle[F]
Diele[F]
parqué[M]

flooring strip
lame[F]
Diele[F]
piso[M] de duela[F]

insulating material
isolant[M]
Isolierstoff[M]
material[M] aislante

glue
colle[F]
Klebstoff[M]
cola[F]

cement screed
chape[F]
Zementestrich[M]
base[F] de cemento[M]

subfloor
sous-plancher[M]
Unterboden[M]
contrapiso[M]

joist
solive[F]
Deckenbalken[M]
viga[F]

WOOD FLOORING TYPES
ARRANGEMENTS[M] DES PARQUETS[M]
PARKETTMUSTER[N]
TIPOS[M] DE PARQUÉ[M]

woodstrip flooring
parquet[M] à coupe[F] perdue
Stabparkett[N] im verlorenen Verband[M]
parqué[M] sobrepuesto

brick-bond woodstrip flooring
parquet[M] à coupe[F] de pierre[F]
Stabparkett[N]
parqué[M] alternado a la inglesa

herringbone parquet
parquet[M] à bâtons[M] rompus
Fischgrätenparkett[N]
parqué[M] espinapez[M]

herringbone pattern
parquet[M] en chevrons[M]
Fischgrätenmuster[N]
espinapez[M]

inlaid parquet
parquet[M] mosaïque[F]
Mosaikparkett[N]
parqué[M] entretejido

basket weave pattern
parquet[M] en vannerie[F]
Würfelmusterparkett[N]
parqué[M] de cestería[F]

Arenberg parquet
parquet[M] d'Arenberg
Arenberg-Parkett[N]
parqué[M] Arenberg

Chantilly parquet
parquet[M] Chantilly
Chantilly-Parkett[N]
parqué[M] Chantilly

Versailles parquet
parquet[M] Versailles
Versailles-Parkett[N]
parqué[M] Versailles

banister
rampe^F
Geländer^N
barandilla^F

cap
couronnement^M
Kopfteil^M
remate^M

goose-neck
col^M-de-cygne^M
Krümmling^M
cuello^M de cisne^M

handrail
main^F courante
Handlauf^M
pasamanos^M

landing
palier^M
Podest^N
rellano^M

inner string
limon^M
Wandwange^F
gualdera^F de contén^M

tread
marche^F
Trittstufe^F
escalón^M

nosing
nez^M-de-marche^F
Überstand^M
vuelo^M del escalón^M

rise
hauteur^F de marche^F
Steigung^F
altura^F del escalón^M

riser
contremarche^F
Setzstufe^F
contraescalón^M

flight of stairs
volée^F
Treppenlauf^M
tramo^M

bottom stair
marche^F de départ^M
Antrittsstufe^F
primer escalón^M

outer string
crémaillère^F
Freiwange^F
gualdera^F

run
giron^M
Stufe^F
huella^F

baluster
barreau^M
Geländerstab^M
balaustre^M

newel post
pilastre^M
Antrittspfosten^M
poste^M

step groove
emmarchement^M
Nut^F
rebajo^M de escalón^M

skirting board
plinthe^F
Sockelleiste^F
zócalo^M

HOUSE
MAISON

HAUS
CASA

201

DOOR
PORTE^F
TÜR^F
PUERTA^F

EXTERIOR DOOR
PORTE^F EXTÉRIEURE
HAUSTÜR^F
PUERTA^F DE ENTRADA^F

cornice
corniche^F
Gesims^N
cornisa^F

lintel
linteau^M
Oberschwelle^F
dintel^M

jamb
chambranle^M
Türpfosten^M
jamba^F

central stile
petit montant^M
Sprosse^F
larguero^F central

lock rail
traverse^F intermédiaire
Querriegel^M
peinazo^M de la cerradura^F

middle panel
frise^F
Mittelfüllung^F
entrepaño^M horizontal

hanging stile
montant^M de ferrage^M
Türzapfen^M
larguero^M de la bisagra^F

hinge
gond^M
Scharnier
bisagra^F

entablature
entablement^M
Gebälk^N
entablamento^M

top rail
traverse^F supérieure
Kopfriegel^M
peinazo^M superior

panel
panneau^M
Füllung^F
entrepaño^M vertical

shutting stile
montant^M de la serrure^F
Schloßbrett^N
larguero^M de la cerradura^F

lock
serrure^F
Türschloß^N
cerradura^F

door handle
poignée^F de porte^F
Türknopf^M
perilla^F

bottom rail
traverse^F inférieure
Fußholz^N
peinazo^M inferior

weatherboard
jet^M d'eau^F
Wetterschenkel^M
botaguas^F

threshold
seuil^M
Schwelle^F
umbral^M

TYPES OF DOOR
TYPES^M DE PORTES^F
TÜRFORMEN^F
TIPOS^M DE PUERTAS^F

conventional door
porte^F classique
Drehflügeltür^F
puerta^F convencional

concertina-type folding door
porte^F accordéon^M
Harmonikatür^F
puerta^F de acordeón^M

folding door
porte^F pliante
Falttür^F
puerta^F plegable

sliding door
porte^F coulissante
Schiebetür^F
puerta^F corrediza

STRUCTURE
STRUCTURE^F
KONSTRUKTION^F
ESTRUCTURA^F

muntin
petit bois^M
Sprosse^F
parteluz^M

head of frame
tête^F de dormant^M
Blendrahmen^M oben
travesaño^M

pane
carreau^M
Scheibe^F
vidrio^M

top rail of sash
traverse^F supérieure d'ouvrant^M
Oberschenkel^M
travesaño^M superior de la vidriera^F

casing
chambranle^M
Holzleibung^F
chambrana^F

jalousie
persienne^F
Jalousie^F
celosía^F veneciana

casement
battant^M
Flügel^M
batiente^F

hanging stile
montant^M de rive^F
Flügelrahmen^M
larguero^M

sash frame
dormant^M
Blendrahmen^M
montante^M vertical

hook
crochet^M
Hakenverriegelung^F
pestillo^M

shutter
contrevent^M
Fensterladen^M
contraventana^F

stile tongue of sash
montant^M mouton^M
Deckleiste^F
montante^M central

sill of frame
base^F de dormant^M
Fensterbrett^N
alféizar^M

hinge
paumelle^F
Scharnier^N
bisagra^F

weatherboard
jet^M d'eau^F
Wetterschenkel^M
botaguas^F

stile groove of sash
montant^M embrevé
Falz^F
ranura^F del larguero^M de la vidriera^F

TYPES OF WINDOW
TYPES^M DE FENÊTRES^F
FENSTERTYPEN^M
TIPOS^M DE VENTANA^F

casement window opening inwards
fenêtre^F à la française^F
Drehflügel^M nach innen
ventana^F francesa

casement window
fenêtre^F à l'anglaise^F
Drehflügel^M nach außen
ventana^F de dos hojas^F

horizontal pivoting window
fenêtre^F basculante
Schwingflügel^M
ventana^F basculante

sliding window
fenêtre^F coulissante
horizontales Schiebefenster^N
ventana^F corrediza

sliding folding window
fenêtre^F en accordéon^M
Faltfenster^N
ventana^F de acordeón^M

vertical pivoting window
fenêtre^F pivotante
Wendeflügel^M
ventana^F giratoria

sash window
fenêtre^F à guillotine^F
vertikales Schiebefenster^N
ventana^F de guillotina^F

louvred window
fenêtre^F à jalousies^F
Jalousiefenster^N
ventana^F de celosía^F

HOUSE
MAISON
HAUS
CASA

HEATING
CHAUFFAGE^M
HEIZUNG^F
CALEFACCIÓN^F

FIREPLACE
CHEMINÉE^F À FOYER^M OUVERT
KAMIN^M
CHIMENEA^F

corbel piece
corbeau^M
Kragstein^M
ménsula^F

firebrick back
cœur^M
Schamotteplatte^F
ladrillos^M refractarios

jamb
jambage^M
seitliche Einfassung^F
jamba^F

fireplace
âtre^M
Feuerstätte^F
hogar^M

hood
hotte^F
Rauchmantel^M
campana^F

mantlepiece
tablette^F
Kaminsims^M
repisa^F

mantle
manteau^M
Kamineinfassung^F
manto^M

lintel
linteau^M
Sturz^M
dintel^M

frame
encadrement^M
Rahmen^M
armazón^M

base
socle^M
Sockel^M
base^F del hogar^M

wood storage space
bûcher^M
Brennholzstauraum^M
lugar^M para la leña^F

SLOW-BURNING STOVE
POÊLE^M À COMBUSTION^F LENTE
LANGSAM BRENNENDER OFEN^M
ESTUFA^F DE LEÑA^F A FUEGO^M LENTO

warm-air baffle
déflecteur^M d'air^M chaud
Warmluftklappe^F
tiro^M de aire^M caliente

hot-air outlet
sortie^F d'air^M chaud
Heißluftaustritt^M
salida^F de aire^M caliente

box
caisson^M
Blechverkleidung^F
caja^F para la ceniza^F

chimney connection
conduit^M de raccordement^M
Kaminanschluß^M
conexión^F de la chimenea^F

smoke baffle
déflecteur^M de fumée^F
Rauchklappe^F
salida^F de humo^M

loading door
porte^F-foyer^M
Fülltür^F
puerta^F del fogón^M

handle
poignée^F
Griff^M
asa^F

firebrick
brique^F réfractaire
Schamottestein^M
ladrillo^M refractario

combustion space
chambre^F de combustion^F
Brennraum^M
fogón^M

air inlet control
manette^F d'admission^F d'air^M
Luftzufuhrregler^M
control^M de la entrada^F de aire^M

CHIMNEY
CHEMINÉE^F
KAMIN^M
CHIMENEA^F

roof
toit^M
Dach^N
tejado^M

rain cap
mitre^F
Kaminabdeckung^F
capuchón^M

storm collar
collet^M
Kaminabdichtung^F
collarín^M

flashing
solin^M
Kamineinfassung^F
botaguas^F

ceiling
plafond^M
Decke^F
techo^M

ceiling collar
collier^M coupe-feu^M
Deckendurchführung^F
collar^M cortafuego

pipe section
section^F de conduit^M
Rohrabschnitt^M
sección^F del cañón^M

floor
plancher^M
Fußboden^M
piso^M

ceiling collar
collier^M coupe-feu^M
Deckendurchführung^F
collar^M cortafuego

capped tee
té^M de base^F
Revisionsöffnung^F
remate^M en T

FIRE IRONS
ACCESSOIRES^M **DE FOYER**^M
KAMINBESTECK^N
UTENSILIOS^M **PARA LA**

tongs
pince^F
Feuerzange^F
tenazas^F

poker
tisonnier^M
Schürhaken^M
atizador^M

broom
balai^M
Besen^M
escobilla^F

shovel
pelle^F
Kohlenschaufel^F
pala^F

log carrier
porte-bûches^M
Holzträger^M
portaleños^M

andirons
chenêts^M
Feuerbock^M
morillos^M

HEATING
CHAUFFAGE*M*
HEIZUNG*F*
CALEFACCIÓN*F*

FORCED WARM-AIR SYSTEM
INSTALLATION*F* À AIR*M* CHAUD PULSÉ
WARMLUFTSYSTEM*N* MIT ZWANGSUMLAUF*M*
SISTEMA*M* DE AIRE*M* CALIENTE A PRESIÓN*F*

warm-air outlet
bouche*F* de soufflage*M*
Warmluftaustritt*M*
registro*M* de aire*M* caliente

branch duct
gaine*F* de dérivation*F*
Abzweigkanal*M*
conducto*M* secundario

main duct
gaine*F* principale
Hauptverteilleitung*F*
conducto*M* principal

return air
reprise*F* d'air*M*
Umluft*F*
recuperación*F* de aire*M*

damper
registre*M* de réglage*M*
Regulierklappe*F*
regulador*M*

furnace
générateur*M* d'air*M* chaud
Kessel*M*
generador*M* de aire*M* caliente

wall stack section
conduit*M* de distribution*F* vertical
Kanalabschnitt*M*
conducto*M* de distribución*F* vertical

plenum
plénum*M*
Mischkammer*F*
pleno*M*

elbow
coude*M*
Bogen*M*
codo*M*

return air
reprise^f d'air^M
Umluft^f
recuperación^f de aire^M

warm-air outflow
sortie^f d'air^M chaud
Warmluftaustritt^M
salida^f de aire^M caliente

ELECTRIC FURNACE
GÉNÉRATEUR^M D'AIR^M CHAUD ÉLECTRIQUE
ELEKTRISCHER KESSEL^M
CALEFACCIÓN^f ELÉCTRICA

plenum
plénum^M
Mischkammer^f
pleno^M

heating element
élément^M de chauffe^f
Heizelement^N
elemento^M calorífero

mains connection
entrée^f électrique
Stromanschluß^M
conexión^f eléctrica

blower motor
moteur^M
Gebläsemotor^M
motor^M del ventilador^M

blower
ventilateur^M
Gebläse^N
ventilador^M

access panel
panneau^M d'accès^M
Revisionstür^f
panel^M de acceso^M

filter
filtre^M à air^M
Filter^M
filtro^M

HOUSE
MAISON

HAUS
CASA

TYPES OF OUTLET
TYPES^M DE BOUCHES^f
LUFTDURCHLÄSSE^M
REJILLAS^f

skirting outlet
bouche^f de soufflage^M
Leistendurchlaß^M
rejilla^f de piso^M

ceiling outlet
bouche^f à induction^f
Deckendurchlaß^M
rejilla^f de techo^M

wall grille
bouche^f d'extraction^f
Wanddurchlaß^M
rejilla^f de pared^f

207

**HAUS
CASA**

**HOUSE
MAISON**

PUMPED HOT-WATER SYSTEM
INSTALLATION[F] À EAU[F] CHAUDE
WARMWASSERHEIZUNG[F] MIT ZWANGSUMLAUF[M]
SISTEMA[M] DE AGUA[F] CALIENTE A PRESIÓN[F]

branch supply pipe
colonne[F] ascendante
Steigleitung[F] Vorlauf[M]
tubería[F] ascendente

radiator
radiateur[M]
Heizkörper[M]
radiador[M]

branch return pipe
colonne[F] descendante
Steigleitung[F] Rücklauf[M]
tubería[F] descendente

main return pipe
canalisation[F] de retour[M]
Rücklauf[M]
tubería[F] de retorno[M]

main supply pipe
canalisation[F] d'alimentation[F]
Vorlauf[M]
surtidor[M] principal

boiler
chaudière[F]
Kessel[M]
caldera[F]

expansion tank
vase[M] d'expansion[F]
Ausdehnungsgefäß[N]
tanque[M] de expansión[F]

circulating pump
pompe[F] de circulation[F]
Umwälzpumpe[F]
bomba[F] de circulación[F]

GILLED-TUBE RADIATOR
RADIATEUR[M] À COLONNES[F]
PLATTENHEIZKÖRPER[M]
RADIADOR[M] TUBULAR

bleeder valve
purgeur[M]
Entlüftungsventil[N]
válvula[F] de purga[F]

gill
colonne[F] de radiateur[M]
Konvektor[M]
tubo[M]

hot-water outlet
sortie[F] d'eau[F] chaude
Rücklaufverschraubung[F]
salida[F] de agua[F] caliente

regulating valve
valve[F] de réglage[M]
Regulierventil[N]
válvula[F] de regulación[F]

covering grille
grille[F] d'habillage[M]
Abdeckung[F]
rejilla[F]

BOILER
CHAUDIÈRE*F*
KESSEL*M*
CALDERA*F*

HOUSE
MAISON

HAUS
CASA

chimney
cheminée*F*
Abgasrohr*N*
chimenea*F*

pressure relief valve
soupape*F* de sureté*F*
Sicherheitsventil*N*
válvula*F* de escape*M*

casing
caisson*M*
Verkleidung*F*
armazón*M*

aquastat
aquastat*M*
Thermometer*N*
manómetro*M*

insulation
isolant*M*
Wärmedämmung*F*
aislamiento*M*

heating element
élément*M* de chauffe*F*
Heizflächen*F*
elemento*M* calorífero

draught hole
regard*M*
Durchzugsöffnung*F*
aspirador*M* de aire*M*

heat exchanger
échangeur*M* de chaleur*F*
Wärmetauscher*M*
distribuidor*M* de calor*M*

combustion space
chambre*F* de combustion*F*
Brennraum*M*
cámara*F* de combustión*F*

air tube
manchon*M*
Zuluft*F*
tubo*M* de aire*M*

burner
brûleur*M*
Brenner*M*
quemador*M*

nozzle
gicleur*M*
Düse*F*
boquilla*F*

ignition transformer
transformateur*M*
Zündtransformator*M*
transformador*M* de ignición*F*

igniting electrode
électrode*F* d'allumage*M*
Zündelektroden*F*
electrodos*M* de encendido*M*

heat control
contrôle*M* thermique
Temperaturregler*M*
control*M* de temperatura*F*

air tube
manchon*M*
Zuluft*F*
tubo*M* de aire*M*

oil feed pipe
canalisation*F* d'alimentation*F*
Ölzufuhr*F*
tubo*M* de suministro*M* de petróleo*M*

oil pump
pompe*F*
Ölpumpe*F*
bomba*F* de petróleo*M*

electric motor
moteur*M* électrique
Elektromotor*M*
motor*M* eléctrico

oil supply
arrivée*F* du mazout*M*
Ölzufuhr*F*
tubo*M* de suministro*M* de petróleo*M*

fan
ventilateur*M*
Gebläse*N*
ventilador*M*

HEATING
CHAUFFAGE[M]
HEIZUNG[F]
CALEFACCIÓN[F]

HUMIDIFIER
HUMIDIFICATEUR[M]
LUFTBEFEUCHTER[M]
HUMIDIFICADOR[M]

vaporizing grille
grille[F] de vaporisation[F]
Verdampfungsgitter[N]
rejilla[F] de vaporización[F]

air filter
filtre[M] à air[M]
Luftfilter[M]
filtro[M] de aire[M]

water tank
réservoir[M] d'eau[F]
Wasserbehälter[M]
recipiente[M] de agua[F]

vaporizer
vaporiseur[M]
Verdampfer[M]
vaporizador[M]

control panel
panneau[M] de commande[F]
Schalttafel[F]
tablero[M] de control[M]

water level
niveau[M] d'eau[F]
Wasserstand[M]
nivel[M] de agua[F]

tray
plateau[M]
Kondenssammler[M]
bandeja[F]

HYGROMETER
HYGROMÈTRE[M]
HYGROMETER[N]
HIGRÓMETRO[M]

45 %   23.0°C

humidity
humidité[F]
Luftfeuchtigkeit[F]
humedad[F] del aire[M]

temperature
température[F]
Temperatur[F]
temperatura[F]

air purifier
purificateur[M] d'air[M]
Luftreiniger[M]
purificador[M] de aire[M]

FLOOR-LEVEL ELECTRIC CONVECTOR
PLINTHE[F] CHAUFFANTE ÉLECTRIQUE
ELEKTROKONVEKTOR[M]
RADIADOR[M] ELÉCTRICO

thermostat
thermostat[M]
Thermostat[M]
termostato[M]

fin
ailette[F]
Rippe[F]
aleta[F]

deflector
déflecteur[M]
Deflektor[M]
deflector[M]

CONVECTOR HEATER
CONVECTEUR^M
KONVEKTOR^M
RADIADOR^M DE CONVEXIÓN^F

outlet grille
grillage^M
Luftaustrittsöffnung^F
rejilla^F de salida^F

casing
carter^M
Gehäuse^N
cubierta^F

AUXILIARY HEATING
CHAUFFAGE^M D'APPOINT^M
ZUSATZHEIZUNG^F
CALEFACCIÓN^F AUXILIAR

radiant heater
radiateur^M rayonnant
Heizstrahler^M
calentador^M eléctrico

oil-filled radiator
radiateur^M bain^M d'huile^F
ölgefüllter Heizkörper^M
calentador^M de aceite^M

fan heater
radiateur^M soufflant
Heizlüfter^M
ventilador^M de aire^M caliente

211

HEATING
CHAUFFAGE^M
HEIZUNG^F
CALEFACCIÓN^F

HEAT PUMP
POMPE^F À CHALEUR^F
WÄRMEPUMPE^F
SISTEMA^M DE BOMBA^F DE CALOR^M

HAUS
CASA

HOUSE
MAISON

OUTDOOR UNIT
MODULE^M EXTÉRIEUR
ANLAGE^F FÜR
AUSSENAUFSTELLUNG^F
UNIDAD^F EXTERIOR

fan
ventilateur^M hélicoïde
Ventilator^M
ventilador^M

outdoor condensing unit
échangeur^M extérieur
Kondensator^M für Außenaufstellung^F
unidad^F exterior condensadora

compressor
compresseur^M
Kompressor^M
compresor^M

refrigerant tank
réservoir^M de fluide^M
Kältemittelbehälter^M
tanque^M de refrigeración^F

reversing device
inverseur^M
Umschaltvorrichtung^F
mecanismo^M de reversión^F

circuit breaker
disjoncteur^M
Leistungsschalter^M
interruptor^M automático

INDOOR UNIT
MODULE^M INTÉRIEUR
ANLAGE^F FÜR INNENAUFSTELLUNG^F
UNIDAD^F INTERIOR

supply duct
gaine^F de distribution^F
Zuluftkanal^M
manga^F de distribución^F

blower
ventilateur^M
Ventilator^M
ventilador^M centrífugo

cooling/heating coils
échangeur^M intérieur
Kühl- und Heizbatterie^F
serpentines^M de enfriamiento^M y calefacción^F

refrigerant tubing
liaison^F frigorifique
Kältemittelleitung^F
tubería^F de refrigeración

mains connection
liaison^F électrique
Stromanschluß^M
conexión^F eléctrica

cover
couvercle^M
Abdeckung^F
tapa^F

ROOM THERMOSTAT
THERMOSTAT^M D'AMBIANCE^F
RAUMTHERMOSTAT^M
TERMOSTATO^M

refrigerant tubing
liaison^F frigorifique
Kältemittelleitung^F
tubería^F de refrigeración

temperature control
réglage^M de la température^F
Temperaturregler^M
control^M de temperatura

desired temperature
température^F désirée
Solltemperatur^F
temperatura^F deseada

pointer
aiguille^F
Zeiger^M
aguja^F indicadora

actual temperature
température^F ambiante
tatsächliche Temperatur^F
temperatura^F real

AIR CONDITIONING
CLIMATISATION*F*
KLIMAANLAGE*F*
AIRE*M* ACONDICIONADO

CEILING FAN
VENTILATEUR*M* DE PLAFOND*M*
DECKENVENTILATOR*M*
VENTILADOR*M* DE TECHO*M*

rod
tige*F*
Stange*F*
flecha*F*

motor*M*
moteur*M*
Motor*M*
motor*M*

blade
pale*F*
Blatt*N*
aspa*F*

ROOM AIR CONDITIONER
CLIMATISEUR*M* DE FENÊTRE*F*
RAUMKLIMAANLAGE*F*
ACONDICIONADOR*M* DE AIRE*M*

condenser fan
ventilateur*M* du condenseur*M*
Ventilator*M*
ventilador*M* del condensador*M*

condenser coil
serpentin*M* du condenseur*M*
Wärmetauscher*M*
serpentín*M* del condensador*M*

casing
boîtier*M*
Gehäuse*N*
cubierta*F*

fan motor
moteur*M* du ventilateur*M*
Ventilatormotor*M*
motor*M* del ventilador*M*

evaporator blower
ventilateur*M* de l'évaporateur*M*
Gebläse*N*
ventilador*M* del evaporador*M*

louvre
déflecteur*M*
Jalousie*F*
rejilla*F* de ventilación*F*

thermostat
thermostat*M*
Thermostat*M*
termostato*M*

fan control
commande*F* de ventilateur*M*
Ventilatorregler*M*
control*M* del ventilador*M*

function selector
sélecteur*M*
Funktionswähler*M*
selector*M*

control panel
tableau*M* de commande*F*
Schalttafel*F*
tablero*M* de control*M*

grille
grillage*M*
Gitter*N*
rejilla*F*

evaporator coils
serpentin*M* de l'évaporateur*M*
Verdampferschlangen*F*
serpentines*M* del evaporador*M*

blower motor
moteur*M* du ventilateur*M*
Ventilatormotor*M*
motor*M* del ventilador*M*

vent
évent*M* latéral
Entlüfter*M*
respiradero*M*

PLUMBING SYSTEM
CIRCUIT^M DE PLOMBERIE^F
SANITÄRINSTALLATIONSSYSTEM^N
CAÑERÍAS^F

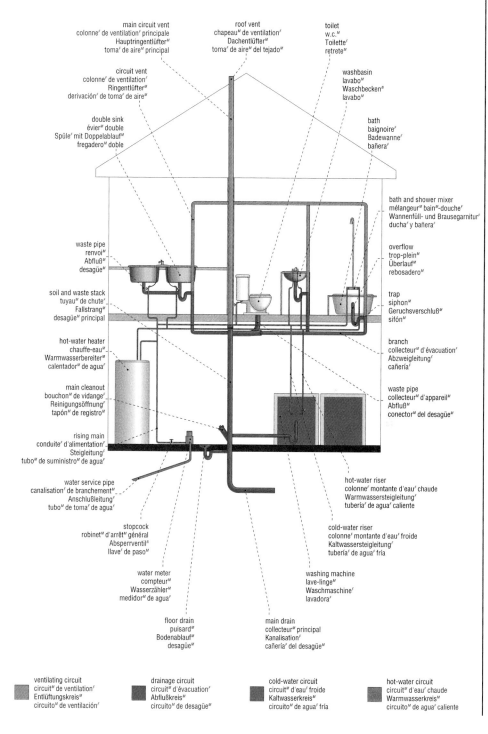

main circuit vent
colonne^F de ventilation^F principale
Hauptringentlüfter^M
toma^F de aire^M principal

roof vent
chapeau^M de ventilation^F
Dachentlüfter^M
toma^F de aire^M del tejado^M

toilet
w.c.^M
Toilette^F
retrete^M

circuit vent
colonne^F de ventilation^F
Ringentlüfter^M
derivación^F de toma^F de aire^M

washbasin
lavabo^M
Waschbecken^N
lavabo^M

double sink
évier^M double
Spüle^F mit Doppelablauf^M
fregadero^M doble

bath
baignoire^F
Badewanne^F
bañera^F

bath and shower mixer
mélangeur^M bain^M-douche^F
Wannenfüll- und Brausegarnitur^F
ducha^F y bañera^F

waste pipe
renvoi^M
Abfluß^M
desagüe^M

overflow
trop-plein^M
Überlauf^M
rebosadero^M

soil and waste stack
tuyau^M de chute^F
Fallstrang^M
desagüe^M principal

trap
siphon^M
Geruchsverschluß^M
sifón^M

hot-water heater
chauffe-eau^M
Warmwasserbereiter^M
calentador^M de agua^M

branch
collecteur^M d'évacuation^F
Abzweigleitung^F
cañería^F

main cleanout
bouchon^M de vidange^F
Reinigungsöffnung^F
tapón^M de registro^M

waste pipe
collecteur^M d'appareil^M
Abfluß^M
conector^M del desagüe^M

rising main
conduite^F d'alimentation^F
Steigleitung^F
tubo^M de suministro^M de agua^F

water service pipe
canalisation^F de branchement^M
Anschlußleitung^F
tubo^M de toma^F de agua^F

hot-water riser
colonne^F montante d'eau^F chaude
Warmwassersteigleitung^F
tubería^F de agua^F caliente

stopcock
robinet^M d'arrêt^M général
Absperrventil^N
llave^F de paso^M

cold-water riser
colonne^F montante d'eau^F froide
Kaltwassersteigleitung^F
tubería^F de agua^F fría

water meter
compteur^M
Wasserzähler^M
medidor^M de agua^F

washing machine
lave-linge^M
Waschmaschine^F
lavadora^F

floor drain
puisard^M
Bodenablauf^M
desagüe^M

main drain
collecteur^M principal
Kanalisation^F
cañería^F del desagüe^M

ventilating circuit
circuit^M de ventilation^F
Entlüftungskreis^M
circuito^M de ventilación^F

drainage circuit
circuit^M d'évacuation^F
Abflußkreis^M
circuito^M de desagüe^M

cold-water circuit
circuit^M d'eau^F froide
Kaltwasserkreis^M
circuito^M de agua^F fría

hot-water circuit
circuit^M d'eau^F chaude
Warmwasserkreis^M
circuito^M de agua^F caliente

PEDESTAL-TYPE CESSPIT PUMP
POMPE^F DE PUISARD^M
SCHMUTZWASSERHEBEANLAGE^F
BOMBA^F TIPO^M PEDESTAL^M PARA SUMIDERO^M

on-off switch
contacteur^M
Ein-/Ausschalter^M
interruptor^M de arranque^M
automático

pump motor
moteur^M électrique
Pumpenmotor^M
motor^M de la bomba^F

check valve
clapet^F de retenue^F
Rückschlagventil^M
válvula^F de control^M

waterproofed electricity supply
prise^F avec borne^F de terre^F
wasserbeständiger Stromanschluß^M
contacto^M con conexión^F a tierra^F

discharge pipe
canalisation^F de refoulement^M
Auslaufleitung^F
tubo^M de salida^F

float clamp
étrier^M du flotteur^M
Rohrschelle^F
anillo^M de retención^F

float
flotteur^M
Schwimmer^M
flotador^M

cesspit
puisard^M
Pumpensumpf^M
sumidero^M

gravel
gravier^M
Kies^M
grava^F

pump suction head
tête^F d'aspiration^F
Ansaugstutzen^M
culata^F de succión^F

SEPTIC TANK
FOSSE^F SEPTIQUE
VERSITZGRUBE^F
FOSA^F SÉPTICA

main drain
collecteur^M principal
Kanalisation^F
cañería^F de desagüe^M

tank
réservoir^M
Becken^N
tanque^M

gravel
gravier^M
Kies^M
grava^F

distribution box
distributeur^M
Zulaufverteiler^M
caja^F de distribución^F

leach field
champ^M d'épandage^M
Sickeranlage^F
área^F de lixiviación^F

perforated pipe
drain^M
Lochrohr^N
cañería^F perforada

inspection plug
regard^M de prélèvement^M
Revisionsöffnung^F
tapón^M de registro^M

surface scum
mousse^F graisseuse
Schwimmschlamm^M
espuma^F

baffle
séparateur^M
Trennwand^F
deflector^M

sludge
boue^F
Sinkschlamm^M
sedimento^M

effluent
liquide^F
Abwasser^N
efluvio^M

SUMMARY

TABLE
TABLE^F
TISCH^M
MESA^F

GATE-LEG TABLE
TABLE^F À ABATTANTS^M
KLAPPTISCH^M
MESA^F DE HOJAS^F ABATIBLES

drop-leaf
abattant^M
Klappe^F
extensión^F plegable

top
plateau^M
Tischplatte^F
tablero^M

drawer
tiroir^M
Schublade^F
cajón^M

apron
ceinture^F
Zarge^F
guarnición^F

stretcher
traverse^F
Traverse^F
travesaño^M

gate-leg
tréteau^M
Ausziehbein^N
pata^F móvil

knob
bouton^M
Knauf^M
pomo^M

leg
pied^M
Bein^N
pata^F

crosspiece
entrejambe^M
Querstück^N
travesaño^M

PRINCIPAL TYPES OF TABLE
PRINCIPAUX TYPES^M DE TABLES^F
DIE WICHTIGSTEN TISCHTYPEN^M
TIPOS^M DE MESAS^F

top
plateau^M
Tischplatte^F
tablero^M

extending table
table^F à rallonges^F
Ausziehtisch^M
mesa^F plegable

extension
rallonge^F
Auszug^M
extensión^F

serving trolley
desserte^F
Servierwagen^M
mesita^F de servicio^M

nest of tables
tables^F gigognes
Satztische^M
juego^M de mesas^F

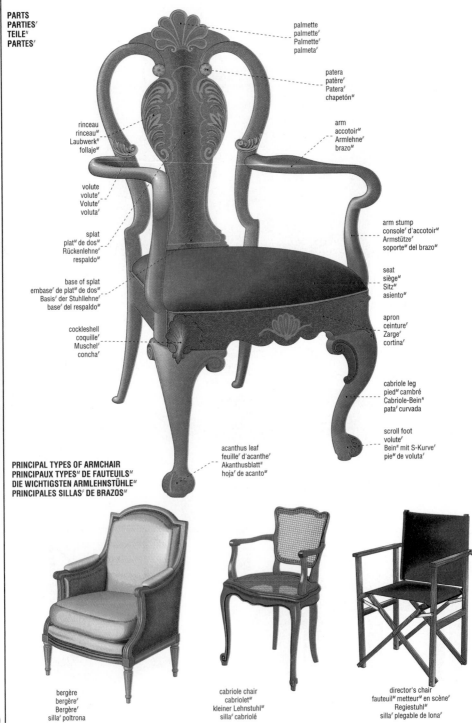

ARMCHAIR
FAUTEUIL[M]
ARMLEHNSTUHL[M]
SILLA[F] **DE BRAZOS**[M]

PARTS
PARTIES[F]
TEILE[N]
PARTES[F]

palmette
palmette[F]
Palmette[F]
palmeta[F]

patera
patère[F]
Patera[F]
chapetón[M]

rinceau
rinceau[M]
Laubwerk[N]
follaje[M]

arm
accotoir[M]
Armlehne[F]
brazo[M]

volute
volute[F]
Volute[F]
voluta[F]

arm stump
console[F] d'accotoir[M]
Armstütze[F]
soporte[M] del brazo[M]

splat
plat[M] de dos[M]
Rückenlehne[F]
respaldo[M]

seat
siège[M]
Sitz[M]
asiento[M]

base of splat
embase[F] de plat[M] de dos[M]
Basis[F] der Stuhllehne[F]
base[F] del respaldo[M]

apron
ceinture[F]
Zarge[F]
cortina[F]

cockleshell
coquille[F]
Muschel[F]
concha[F]

cabriole leg
pied[M] cambré
Cabriole-Bein[N]
pata[F] curvada

scroll foot
volute[F]
Bein[N] mit S-Kurve[F]
pie[M] de voluta[F]

acanthus leaf
feuille[F] d'acanthe[F]
Akanthusblatt[N]
hoja[F] de acanto[M]

PRINCIPAL TYPES OF ARMCHAIR
PRINCIPAUX TYPES[M] DE FAUTEUILS[M]
DIE WICHTIGSTEN ARMLEHNSTÜHLE[M]
PRINCIPALES SILLAS[F] DE BRAZOS[M]

bergère
bergère[F]
Bergère[F]
silla[F] poltrona

cabriole chair
cabriolet[M]
kleiner Lehnstuhl[M]
silla[F] cabriolé

director's chair
fauteuil[M] metteur[M] en scène[F]
Regiestuhl[M]
silla[F] plegable de lona[F]

sofa
canapé^M
Sofa^N
sofá^F

two-seater settee
causeuse^F
Zweisitzer^M
confidente^M

chaise longue
récamier^M
Récamiere^F
sofá^M tipo^M imperio

chesterfield
canapé^M capitonné
Polstersofa^N
chesterfield^M

méridienne
méridienne^F
Kanapee^N
meridiana^F

Wassily chair
fauteuil^M Wassily
Wassily-Stuhl^M
silla^F Wassily

rocking chair
berceuse^F
Schaukelstuhl^M
mecedora^F

club chair
fauteuil^M club^M
Clubsessel^M
butaca^F

HAUSEINRICHTUNG
ENSERES DOMÉSTICOS

HOUSE FURNITURE
AMEUBLEMENT DE LA MAISON

banquette
banquette*F*
Sitzbank*F*
banco*M*

ottoman
pouf*M*
Puff*M*
taburete*M*

bean bag chair
fauteuil*M*-sac*M*
Sitzsack*M*
silla*F* cojín*M*

bench
banc*M*
Bank*F*
banco*F*

bar stool
tabouret*M*-bar*M*
Barhocker*M*
taburete*M*

footstool
tabouret*M*
Hocker*M*
escabel*M*

step chair
chaise*F*-escabeau*M*
Tritthocker*M*
banco*M* escalera*F*

222

SIDE CHAIR
CHAISE^F
STUHL^M
SILLA^F SIN BRAZOS^M

ear
oreille^F
Ohr^N
oreja^F

top rail
traverse^F supérieure
obere Sprosse^F
peinazo^M superior

cross rail
traverse^F médiane
Querholz^N
peinazo^M inferior

stile
montant^M
Seitenstück^N
larguero^M

apron
ceinture^F
Zarge^F
guarnición^F

spindle
barreau^M
Steg^M
travesaño^M

rear leg
pied^M arrière
Hinterbein^N
pata^F trasera

front leg
pied^M avant
Vorderbein^N
pata^F delantera

back
dossier^M
Rückenlehne^F
respaldo^M

seat
siège^M
Sitz^M
asiento^M

support
piètement^M
Fußgestell^N
pata^F

PARTS
PARTIES^F
TEILE^N
PARTES^F

TYPES OF CHAIR
TYPES^M **DE CHAISES**^F
STUHLTYPEN^M
TIPOS^M **DE SILLAS**^F

recliner
chaise^F longue
Liegestuhl^M
tumbona^F

stacking chairs
chaises^F empilables
Stapelstühle^M
sillas^F apilables

rocking chair
chaise^F berçante
Schaukelstuhl^M
mecedora^F

folding chair
chaise^F pliante
Klappstuhl^M
silla^F plegable

HOUSE FURNITURE
AMEUBLEMENT DE LA MAISON
HAUSEINRICHTUNG
ENSERES DOMÉSTICOS

223

BED
LIT^M
BETT^N
CAMA^F

PARTS
PARTIES^F
TEILE^N
PARTES^F

headboard
tête^F de lit^M
Kopfende^N
cabecera^F

bolster
traversin^M
große Nackenrolle^F
cabezal^M

footboard
pied^M de lit^M
Fußende^N
pie^M de la cama^F

mattress cover
protège-matelas^M
Matratzenauflage^F
funda^F de colchón^M

pillow cover
housse^F d'oreiller^M
Kopfkissenschonbezug^M
funda^F de almohada^F

handle
poignée^F
Griff^M
asa^F

mattress
matelas^M
Matratze^F
colchón^M de muelles^M

elastic
élastique^M
Gummiband^N
elástico^M

sprung base
sommier^M tapissier^M
Sprungfederrahmen^M
somier^M

pillow
oreiller^M
Kopfkissen^N
almohada^F

leg
pied^M
Fuß^M
pata^F

sham
couvre-oreiller^M
Schutzbezug^M
falso almohadón^M

pillowcase
taie^F d'oreiller^M
Kopfkissenbezug^M
funda^F de la almohada^F

BED LINEN
LITERIE^F
BETTWÄSCHE^F
ROPA^F **DE CAMA**^F

scatter cushion
coussin^M carré
kleines Kissen^N
cojín^M

eiderdown
édredon^M
Daunendecke^F
edredón^M

neckroll
polochon^M
Nackenrolle^F
cojín^M

flat sheet
drap^M
Bettuch^N
sábana^F

blanket
couverture^F
Decke^F
manta^F

valance
volant^M
Volant^N
faldón^M

fitted sheet
drap^M-housse^F
Spannbettuch^N
sábana^F ajustable

STORAGE FURNITURE
MEUBLES*M* DE RANGEMENT*M*
AUFBEWAHRUNGSMÖBEL*N*
ARMARIOS*M* Y GABINETES*M*

ARMOIRE
ARMOIRE*F*
KLEIDERSCHRANK*M*
ARMARIO*M*

frieze
frise*F*
Fries*M*
friso*M*

centre post
dormant*M*
Setzholz*N*
montante*M* central

cornice
corniche*F*
Kranzprofil*N*
cornisa*F*

top rail
traverse*F* supérieure
obere Querleiste*F*
peinazo*M* superior

door panel
panneau*M* de vantail*M*
Türfüllung*F*
entrepaño*M*

diamond point
pointe*F* de diamant*M*
Rautenspitze*F*
punta*F* de diamante*M*

lock
serrure*F*
Schloß*N*
cerradura*F*

hanging stile
montant*M* de ferrage*M*
Hängesäule*F*
larguero*M* de la bisagra*F*

rail
traverse*F*
Querleiste*F*
peinazo*M*

frame stile
montant*M* de bâti*M*
Rahmenleiste*F*
larguero*M* del marco*M*

hinge
gond*M*
Scharnier*N*
bisagra*F*

peg
cheville*F*
Zapfen*M*
espiga*F*

bottom rail
traverse*F* inférieure
untere Querleiste*F*
peinazo*M* inferior

foot
pied*M*
Fuß*M*
pata*F*

bracket base
soubassement*M*
Sockelprofil*N*
rodapié*M*

frame
bâti*M*
Rahmen*M*
armazón*M*

door
vantail*M*
Tür*F*
puerta*F*

225

linen chest
coffre^M
Truhe^F
baúl^M

dressing table
commode^F
Kommode^F
tocador^M

drawer
tiroir^M
Schublade^F
cajón^M

chiffonier
chiffonnier^M
Chiffoniere^F
chifonier^M

tray
casier^M
Zugschublade^F
batea^F

fall front
abattant^M
herausklappbare Schreibplatte^F
escritorio^M

bureau
secrétaire^M
Sekretär^M
bufete^M

shelf
tablette^F
Fach^N
anaquel^M

hanging cupboard
penderie^F
Schrankteil^N
guardarropa^M

wardrobe
armoire^F-penderie^F
Kleiderschrank^M
ropero^M

display cabinet
vitrine^f
Vitrine^f
vitrina^f

cocktail cabinet
bar^M
Cocktailbar^f
mueble^M bar^M

glass-fronted display cabinet
buffet^M-vaisselier^M
Vitrinenschrank^M
armario^M de vajilla^f

corner cupboard
encoignure^f
Eckschrank^M
rinconera^f

sideboard
buffet^M
Büfett^N
aparador^M

WINDOW ACCESSORIES
PARURES^F DE FENÊTRE^F
DEKORATIONEN^F
ACCESORIOS^M PARA LAS VENTANAS^F

TYPES OF CURTAIN
TYPES^M DE RIDEAUX^M
GARDINENTYPEN^M
TIPOS^M DE CORTINAS^F

WINDOW CURTAIN
RIDEAU^M DE VITRAGE^M
SCHEIBENGARDINE^F
CORTINA^F DE VENTANA^F

valance
cantonnière^F
Querbehang^M
doselera^F

frilled curtain
rideau^M bonne femme^F
Landhausgardine^F
visillos^M recogidos

tieback
embrasse^F
Zurückhalter^M
lazo^M

café curtain
rideau^M brise-bise^M
Kaffeehausgardine^F
visillo^M

frill
volant^M
Volant^M
volante^M

ATTACHED CURTAIN
RIDEAU^M COULISSÉ
SPANNER^M
CORTINA^F SUJETA DE DOBLE BARRA^F

LOOSE CURTAIN
RIDEAU^M FLOTTANT
LOSER VORHANG^M
CORTINA^F SUELTA CORREDIZA

TYPES OF PLEAT
TYPES^M DE PLIS^M
FALTENARTEN^F
TIPOS^M DE CENEFAS^F

box pleat
pli^M creux
Schachtelfalte^F
pliegue^M de cajón^M

pinch pleat
pli^M pincé
Kirsorfalte^F
pliegue^M de pinza^F

inverted pleat
pli^M rond
eingelegte Falte^F
pliegue^M de cajón^M invertido

CURTAIN
RIDEAU^M
VORHANG^M
CORTINA^F

pelmet
bandeau^M
Schabracke^F
dosel^M

over curtain
double rideau^M
Überbehang^M
sobrecortina^F

draw curtain
rideau^M
Zugvorhang^M
cortinas^F corredizas

tieback knob
patère^F à embrasse^F
Zurückhalter^M
anilla^F del cordón^M

cord tieback
cordelière^F
Kordel^F
cordón^M

sheer curtain
voilage^M
Untervorhang^M
visillos^M sencillos

tassel
gland^M
Troddel^F
borla^F

BALLOON CURTAIN
RIDEAU^M BALLON^M
BALLONVORHANG^M
CORTINA^F ABOMBADA

CRISSCROSS CURTAINS
RIDEAUX^M CROISÉS
RAFFGARDINE^F
CORTINAS^F CRUZADAS

fringe trimming
frange^F de passementerie^F
Fransen^F
cenefa^F con flecos^M

panel
panneau^M
Panel^N
cortina^F

TYPES OF HEADING
TYPES^M DE TÊTES^F
KÖPFCHENTYPEN^M
TIPOS^M DE DOSELES^M

draped swag
cantonnière^F drapée
Freihand-Dekoration^F
festón^M colgado

pencil-pleated heading
fronçage^M tuyauté
Bleistiftband^N
dosel^M plisado de canotillo^M

pinch-pleated heading
tête^F plissée
Kirschband^N
dosel^M plisado

shirred heading
tête^F froncée
Durchzug^M
dosel^M fruncido

WINDOW ACCESSORIES
PARURES^F DE FENÊTRE^F
FENSTERZUBEHÖR^N
ACCESORIOS^M PARA LAS VENTANAS^F

HAUSEINRICHTUNG
ENSERES DOMÉSTICOS

HOUSE FURNITURE
AMEUBLEMENT DE LA MAISON

CURTAIN POLE
TRINGLE^F-BARRE^F
GARDINENSTANGE^F
BARRA^F DE CORTINA^F

ring
anneau^M
Ring^M
anillo^M

pole
barre^F
Stange^F
barra^F

plain pole
barre^F lisse
einfache Stange^F
barra^F lisa

fluted pole
barre^F cannelée
Vollmessingstange^F
barra^F acanalada

finial
embout^M
Endknopf^M
tope^M

support bracket
support^M de fixation^F
runder Träger^M
abrazadera^F

eyelet
œillet^M
Haken^M
ojete^M

single curtain rail
tringle^F simple
einläufige Gardinenstange^F
barra^F de varilla^F simple

double curtain rail
tringle^F double
zweiläufige Gardinenstange^F
barra^F de varilla^F doble

CURTAIN TRACK
TRINGLE^F-RAIL^M
GARDINENSCHIENE^F
RIEL^M

roller
galet^M
Rolle^F
corredera^F

ceiling bracket
support^M de plafond^M
Deckenträger^M
soporte^M de techo^M

wall bracket
support^M mural
Wandträger^M
soporte^M de pared^F

bridge
bride^F de raccord^M
Brücke^F
puente^M

end stop
butoir^M
Feststeller^M
tope^M

track
rail^M
Schiene^F
riel^M

hook
agrafe^F
Haken^M
gancho^M

clip
pince^F
Klammer^F
clip^M

ring
anneau^M
Ring^M
anilla^F

glider
chariot^M
Laufwagen^M
carro^M

TRAVERSE ROD
TRINGLE^F EXTENSIBLE
KOPFSCHIENE^F
CORTINA^F DE RIEL^M

support
support^M
Aufhängung^F
soporte^M

end bracket
support^M d'extrémité^F
Endträger^M
tope^M

operating cord
cordon^M de tirage^M
Bedienungsschnur^F
cordón^M

yoke
chape^F
Anschluß^M
balancín^M

main glider
chariot^M d'entraînement^M
Laufwagen^M
corredera^F

tension pulley wheel
roue^F de poulie^F
Schnurspanner^M
polea^F tensora

pulley
poulie^F
Schnurwelle^F
polea^F

sliding overlap arm
chariot^M de croisement^M
Zugwagen^M
corredera^F con enganches^M

spring housing
gaine^F du ressort^M
Federgehäuse^N
resorte^M

fastening device
fixation^F
Feststellvorrichtung^F
sujeción^F

ROLLER BLIND
STORE^M À ENROULEMENT^M AUTOMATIQUE
ROLLO^N
PERSIANA^F ENROLLABLE AUTOMÁTICA

round end pin
pointe^F ronde
Stift^M mit rundem Ende^N
espiga^F de punta^F redonda

roller
rouleau^M
Welle^F
rodillo^M

winding mechanism
mécanisme^M d'enroulement^M
Rollmechanismus^M
mecanismo^M de enrollado^M

bracket
support^M
Träger^M
soporte^M

flat end pin
pointe^F plate
Vierkantstift^M
espiga^F de punta^F cuadrada

lath
latte^F
Rollo-Fallstab^M
listón^M

blind cloth
toile^F
Rollostoff^M
visillo^M

hem
ourlet^M
Saum^M
jareta^F

coil spring
ressort^M en spirale^F
Sprungfeder^F
resorte^M espiral

VENETIAN BLIND
STORE^M VÉNITIEN
JALOUSIE^F
PERSIANA^F VENECIANA

tilt tube
tube^M d'orientation^F des lames^F
Wenderohr^N
pértiga^F de inclinación^F

drum
tambour^M
Trommel^F
tambor^M

lift cord lock
blocage^M du cordon^M de tirage^M
Schnurfeststeller^M
seguro^M del cordón^M

headrail
boîtier^M
Kopfprofil^N
caja^F superior

lift cord
cordon^M de tirage^M
Zugschnur^F
cordón^M

slat tilt device
manivelle^F d'orientation^F des lames^F
Wendestab^M
regulador^M de luminosidad^F

slat
lame^F
Lamelle^F
listón^M

cord
cordon^M
Leiterkordel^F
cordones^M de listones^M

equalizing buckle
boucle^F de réglage^M
Schnurversteller^M
hebilla^F niveladora

bottom rail
barre^F inférieure
Abschlußprofil^N
barra^F inferior

knob
gland^M
Knopf^M
borla^F

roll-up blind
store^M à enroulement^M manuel
Stäbchenrollo^N
persiana^F enrollable

Roman blind
store^M bateau^M
Raffrollo^N
persianas^F romana

indoor shutters
volets^M d'intérieur^M
Innenläden^M
postigos^M interiores

231

LIGHTS
LUMINAIRES*M*
LAMPEN*F*
LÁMPARAS*F*

INCANDESCENT LIGHT BULB
LAMPE*F* À INCANDESCENCE*F*
GLÜHLAMPE*F*
BOMBILLA*F* INCANDESCENTE

inert gas
gaz*M* inerte
Edelgas*N*
gas*M* inerte

filament
filament*M*
Glühfaden*M*
filamento*M*

tube
ampoule*F*
Kolben*M*
ampolla*F* de vidrio*M*

support
support*M*
Halter*M*
soporte*M*

button
bouton*M*
Knopf*M*
botón*M*

stem
pied*M*
Stab*M*
vástago*M* de vidrio*M*

input wire
entrée*F* de courant*M*
Zuleitungsdraht*M*
alambre*M* de corriente*F*

heat deflecting disc
déflecteur*M* de chaleur*F*
Wärmedeflektorscheibe*F*
disco*M* desviador de calor*M*

pinch
pincement*M*
Quetschfuß*M*
pie*M*

discharge tube
queusot*M*
Entladungsröhre*F*
tubo de escape*M*

cap
culot*M*
Sockel*M*
casquillo*M*

screw cap
culot*M* à vis*F*
Schraubfassung*F*
bombilla*F* de rosca*F*

bayonet cap
culot*M* à baïonnette*F*
Bajonettfassung*F*
bombilla*F* de bayoneta*F*

FLUORESCENT TUBE
TUBE*M* FLUORESCENT
LEUCHTSTOFFRÖHRE*F*
TUBO*M* FLUORESCENTE

pin base
culot*M* à broches*F*
Stiftsockel*M*
base*F* del tubo*M*

phosphorescent coating
couche*F* fluorescente
Phosphorschicht*F*
revestimiento*M* de fósforo*M*

electrode
électrode*F*
Elektrode*F*
electrodo*M*

input wire
entrée*F* de courant*M*
Zuleitungsdraht*M*
alambre*M* de corriente*F*

discharge tube
queusot*M*
Entladungsröhre*F*
tubo*M* de escape*M*

pinch
pincement*M*
Quetschfuß*M*
pie*M* del electrodo*M*

pin
broche*F*
Stift*M*
pata*F*

bulb
tube*M*
Kolben*M*
tubo*M*

gas
gaz*M*
Gas*N*
gas*M* inerte

mercury
mercure*M*
Quecksilber*N*
mercurio*M*

TUNGSTEN-HALOGEN BULB
LAMPE^F À HALOGÈNE^M
WOLFRAM-HALOGENLAMPE^F
LÁMPARA^F HALÓGENA

bulb
ampoule^F
Kolben^M
lámpara^F

filament support
support^M du filament^M
Wendelhalter^M
filamento^M

tungsten filament
filament^M de tungstène^M
Wolframwendel^F
filamento^M de tungsteno^M

inert gas
gaz^M inerte
Edelgas^N
gas^M inerte

electric circuit
circuit^M électrique
elektrischer Kreislauf^M
circuito^M eléctrico

cap
culot^M
Sockel^M
casquillo^M

contact
plot^M
Kontakt^M
contacto^M

TUNGSTEN-HALOGEN BULB
LAMPE^F À HALOGÈNE^M
WOLFRAM-HALOGENLAMPE^F
LÁMPARA^F HALÓGENA

tungsten filament
filament^M de tungstène^M
Wolframwendel^F
filamento^M de tungsteno^M

pin
broche^F
Stift^M
pata^F

ENERGY SAVING BULB
LAMPE^F À ÉCONOMIE^F D'ÉNERGIE^F
ENERGIESPARLAMPE^F
BOMBILLA^F ECONÓMICA

bulb
ampoule^F
Kolben^M
bombilla^F

fluorescent tube
tube^M fluorescent
Leuchtstoffröhre^F
tubo^M fluorescente

tube retention clip
attache^F du tube^M
Ionisationsclip^M
clip^M de ajuste^M

mounting plate
plaque^F de montage^M
Röhrenfassung^F
placa^F de instalación^F

electronic ballast
ballast^M électronique
elektronische Schaltung^F
electrodos^M

housing
boîtier^M
Gehäuse^N
pantalla^F

cap
culot^M
Sockel^M
casquillo^M

LIGHTS
LUMINAIRES^M
LAMPEN^F
LÁMPARAS^F

wall light
applique^F
Wandleuchte^F
aplique^M

swivel wall lamp
applique^F orientable
Scherenleuchte^F
lámpara^F orientable de pared^F

ADJUSTABLE LAMP
LAMPE^F D'ARCHITECTE^M
ARBEITSLEUCHTE^F
LÁMPARA^F AJUSTABLE

on-off switch
interrupteur^M
Ein-/Ausschalter^M
interruptor^M

arm
bras^M
Arm^M
brazo^M

shade
abat-jour^M
Schirm^M
pantalla^F

spring
ressort^M
Feder^F
resorte^M

adjustable clamp
support^M de fixation^F
verstellbare Klemme^F
tornillo^M de ajuste^M

desk lamp
lampe^F de bureau^M
Schreibtischleuchte^F
lámpara^F de escritorio^M

bed lamp
lampe^F liseuse
Leseleuchte^F
lámpara^F de cabecera^F

TRACK LIGHTING
RAIL^M D'ÉCLAIRAGE^M
STROMSCHIENENLEUCHTE^F
RIEL^M DE ILUMINACIÓN^F

post lantern
lanterne^F de pied^M
Straßenlaterne^F
farola^F

track frame
gouttière^F
Schiene^F
armazón^M

transformer
transformateur^M
Transformator^M
transformador^M

contact lever
manette^F de contact^M
Befestigungshebel^M
interruptor^M

spot
spot^M
Spot^M
foco^M

clamp spotlight
spot^M à pince^F
Klemmspot^M
lámpara de pinza^F

wall lantern
lanterne^F murale
Wandlaterne^F
farol^M

multiple light fitting
rampe^F d'éclairage^M
Lampenreihe^F
lámparas^F en serie^F

CHANDELIER
LUSTRE*M*
KRONLEUCHTER*M*
ARAÑA*F* DE LUCES*F*

sconce
coupelle*F*
Teller*M*
arandela*F*

crystal drop
pendeloque*F*
Kristalltropfen*M*
colgante*M*

crystal button
pampille*F*
Koppen*M*
gota*F*

column
fût*M*
Mittelsäule*F*
columna*F*

standard lamp
lampadaire*M*
Standleuchte*F*
lámpara*F* de pie*M*

ceiling fitting
plafonnier*M*
Deckenleuchte*F*
plafón*M*

hanging pendant
suspension*F*
Hängeleuchte*F*
lámpara*F* de techo*M*

table lamp
lampe*F* de table*F*
Tischleuchte*F*
lámpara*F* de mesa*F*

shade
abat-jour*M*
Schirm*M*
pantalla*F*

stand
pied*M*
Fuß*M*
pedestal*M*

base
socle*M*
Sockel*M*
base*F*

HAUSEINRICHTUNG
ENSERES DOMÉSTICOS

HOUSE FURNITURE
AMEUBLEMENT DE LA MAISON

236

port glass
verre^M à porto^M
Süßweinglas^N
copa^F para oporto^M

champagne glass
coupe^F à mousseux^M
Sektschale^F
copa^F de cava^F

brandy glass
verre^M à cognac^M
Kognakschwenker^M
copa^F de coñac^M

liqueur glass
verre^M à liqueur^F
Likörglas^N
copa^F para licores^M

white wine glass
verre^M à vin^M blanc
Weißweinglas^N
copa^F de vino^M blanco

bordeaux glass
verre^M à bordeaux^M
Bordeauxglas^N
copa^F para vinos^M de Burdeos

burgundy glass
verre^M à bourgogne^M
Burgunderglas^N
copa^F para vinos^M de Borgoña

hock glass
verre^M à vin^M d'Alsace
Elsaßglas^N
copa^F para vino^M de Alsacia

whisky tumbler
verre^M à whisky^M
Whiskybecher^M
vaso^M corto

tall tumbler
verre^M à gin^M
Longdrinkglas^N
vaso^M largo

cocktail glass
verre^M à cocktail^M
Cocktailglas^N
copa^F de cóctel^M

water goblet
verre^M à eau^F
Wasserglas^N
copa^F para agua^F

decanter
carafe^F
Karaffe^F
garrafa^F

carafe
carafon^M
kleine Karaffe^F
garrafita^F

champagne flute
flûte^F à champagne^M
Sektkelch^M
copa^F de champaña^M

beer glass
chope^F à bière^F
Bierkrug^M
jarra^M para cerveza^F

CROCKERY
VAISSELLE*F*
GESCHIRR*N*
VAJILLA*F* Y SERVICIO*M* DE MESA*F*

demitasse
tasse*F* à café*M*
Mokkatasse*F*
tacita*F* de café*M*

tea cup
tasse*F* à thé*M*
Tasse*F*
taza*F*

coffee mug
chope*F* à café*M*
Becher*M*
jarra*F* para café*M*

cream jug
crémier*M*
Milchkännchen*N*
jarrita*F* de la leche*F*

sugar bowl
sucrier*M*
Zuckerdose*F*
azucarero*M*

pepperpot
poivrière*F*
Pfefferstreuer*M*
pimentera*F*

saltcellar
salière*F*
Salzstreuer*M*
salero*M*

gravy boat
saucière*F*
Sauciere*F*
salsera*F*

butter dish
beurrier*M*
Butterdose*F*
mantequera*F*

ramekin
ramequin*M*
Auflaufförmchen*N*
cuenco*M* de queso*M* blando

soup bowl
bol*M*
Suppenschale*F*
bol*M* para sopa*F*

rim soup bowl
assiette*F* creuse
Suppenteller*M*
plato*M* sopero

dinner plate
assiette*F* plate
flacher Teller*M*
plato*M* llano

salad plate
assiette*F* à salade*F*
Salatteller*M*
plato*M* para ensalada*F*

side plate
assiette*F* à dessert*M*
kleiner Teller*M*
plato*M* para pan*M* y mantequilla*F*

teapot
théière*F*
Teekanne*F*
tetera*F*

serving dish
plat*M* ovale
Platte*F*
fuente*F* de servir

vegetable dish
légumier*M*
Kartoffelschüssel*F*
fuente*F* de verdura*F*

fish dish
plat*M* à poisson*M*
Fischplatte*F*
fuente*F* para pescado*M*

hors d'oeuvre dish
ravier*M*
Horsd'oeuvre-Schale*F*
bandeja*F* para canapés*M*

water jug
pichet*M*
Wasserkrug*M*
jarra*F* para agua*F*

salad bowl
saladier*M*
Salatschüssel*F*
ensaladera*F*

salad dish
bol*M* à salade*F*
Salatschale*F*
bol*M* para ensalada*F*

soup tureen
soupière*F*
Suppenterrine*F*
sopera*F*

CUTLERY
COUVERT^M
SILBERBESTECK^N
CUBERTERÍA^F

KNIFE
COUTEAU^M
MESSER^N
CUCHILLO^M

blade
lame^F
Klinge^F
hoja^F

handle
manche^M
Griff^M
mango^M

bolster
mitre^F
Krone^F
cabezal^M

back
dos^M
Rücken^M
lomo^M

tip
bout^M
Spitze^F
punta^F

tang
soie^F
Angel^F
espiga^F

side
face^F
Seite^F
cara^F

cutting edge
tranchant^M
Schneide^F
filo^M

PRINCIPAL TYPES OF KNIFE
PRINCIPAUX TYPES^M DE COUTEAUX^M
DIE WICHTIGSTEN MESSERTYPEN^M
TIPOS^M DE CUCHILLOS^M

butter knife
couteau^M à beurre^M
Buttermesser^N
cuchillo^M para mantequilla^F

dessert knife
couteau^M à dessert^M
Dessertmesser^N
cuchillo^M para postre^M

fish knife
couteau^M à poisson^M
Fischmesser^N
cuchillo^M para pescado^M

cheese knife
couteau^M à fromage^M
Käsemesser^N
cuchillo^M para queso^M

dinner knife
couteau^M de table^F
Menümesser^N
cuchillo^M de mesa^F

steak knife
couteau^M à bifteck^M
Steakmesser^N
cuchillo^M para carne^F

CUTLERY
COUVERT[M]
SILBERBESTECK[N]
CUBERTERÍA[F]

FORK
FOURCHETTE[F]
GABEL[F]
TENEDOR[M]

slot
entredent[M]
Schlitz[M]
entrediente[M]

tine
dent[F]
Zinke[F]
diente[M]

neck
collet[M]
Hals[M]
cuello[M]

point
pointe[F]
Spitze[F]
punta[F]

root
fond[M] d'yeux[M]
Wurzel[F]
raíz[F]

handle
manche[M]
Griff[M]
mango[M]

back
dos[M]
Rücken[M]
lomo[M]

PRINCIPAL TYPES OF FORK
PRINCIPAUX TYPES[M] **DE FOURCHETTES**[F]
DIE WICHTIGSTEN GABELTYPEN[M]
TIPOS[M] **DE TENEDORES**[M]

oyster fork
fourchette[F] à huîtres[F]
Austerngabel[F]
tenedor[M] para ostras[F]

dessert fork
fourchette[F] à dessert[M]
Dessertgabel[F]
tenedor[M] para postre[M]

salad fork
fourchette[F] à salade[F]
Salatgabel[F]
tenedor[M] para ensalada[F]

fish fork
fourchette[F] à poisson[M]
Fischgabel[F]
tenedor[M] para pescado[M]

dinner fork
fourchette[F] de table[F]
Menügabel[F]
tenedor[M] de mesa[F]

fondue fork
fourchette[F] à fondue[F]
Fonduegabel[F]
tenedor[M] para fondue[F]

SPOON
CUILLER[f]
LÖFFEL[M]
CUCHARA[f]

bowl
creux[M]
Laffe[f]
cuenco[M]

handle
manche[M]
Stiel[M]
mango[M]

neck
collet[M]
Hals[M]
cuello[M]

bowl
cuilleron[M]
Schöpfteil[M]
cuchara[f]

back
dos[M]
Rücken[M]
lomo[M]

tip
bec[M]
Spitze[f]
punta[f]

PRINCIPAL TYPES OF SPOON
PRINCIPAUX TYPES[M] DE CUILLERS[f]
DIE WICHTIGSTEN LÖFFELTYPEN[M]
TIPOS[M] DE CUCHARAS[f]

coffee spoon
cuiller[f] à café[M]
Kaffeelöffel[M]
cuchara[f] para café[M]

teaspoon
cuiller[f] à thé[M]
Teelöffel[M]
cuchara[f] para té[M]

soup spoon
cuiller[f] à soupe[f]
Suppenlöffel[M]
cuchara[f] para sopa[f]

dessert spoon
cuiller[f] à dessert[M]
Dessertlöffel[M]
cuchara[f] para postre[M]

sundae spoon
cuiller[f] à soda[M]
Limonadenlöffel[M]
cuchara[f] para helado[M]

tablespoon
cuiller[f] de table[f]
Eßlöffel[M]
cuchara[f] de mesa[f]

KITCHEN UTENSILS
USTENSILES^M DE CUISINE^F
KÜCHENUTENSILIEN^N
UTENSILIOS^M DE COCINA^F

KITCHEN KNIFE
COUTEAU^M DE CUISINE^F
KÜCHENMESSER^N
CUCHILLO^M DE COCINA^F

half handle
demi-manche^F
halbes Heft^N
mango^M

tang
soie^F
Angel^F
espiga^F

bolster
mitre^F
Krone^F
cabeza^F

back
dos^M
Rücken^M
lomo^M

point
pointe^F
Spitze^F
punta^F

cutting edge
tranchant^M
Schneide^F
filo^M

blade
lame^F
Klinge^F
hoja^F

guard
épaulement^M
Schild^N
guarda^F

heel
talon^M
Angelwurzel^F
talón^F de la hoja^F

rivet
rivet^M
Niet^M
remache^M

TYPES OF KITCHEN KNIFE
TYPES^M DE COUTEAUX^M DE CUISINE^F
MESSERTYPEN^M
TIPOS^M DE CUCHILLOS^M DE COCINA^F

filleting knife
couteau^M à filets^M de sole^F
Filiermesser^N
filetero^M

cleaver
couperet^M
Küchenspalter^M
hacha^F de cocinero^M

boning knife
couteau^M à désosser
Ausbeinmesser^N
para deshuesar

bread knife
couteau^M à pain^M
Brotmesser^N
para pan^M

ham knife
couteau^M à jambon^M
Schinkenmesser^N
para jamón^M

cook's knife
couteau^M de chef^M
Kochmesser^N
de carnicero^M

carving knife
couteau^M à découper
Tranchiermesser^N
cuchillo^M de trinchar

carving fork
fourchette^F à découper
Tranchiergabel^F
tenedor^M de trinchar

sharpening steel
fusil^M
Wetzstahl^M
afilador^M

grapefruit knife
couteau^M à pamplemousse^M
Grapefruitmesser^N
para pomelos^M

butter curler
coquilleur^M à beurre^M
Butterroller^M
rizador^M de mantequilla^F

oyster knife
couteau^M à huîtres^F
Austernmesser^N
para ostras^F

peeler
éplucheur^M
Schäler^M
pelapatatas^M

paring knife
couteau^M d'office^M
Officemesser^N
montado

zester
couteau^M à zester
Zitronenschaber^M
rallador^M

HAUSEINRICHTUNG
ENSERES DOMÉSTICOS

HOUSE FURNITURE
AMEUBLEMENT DE LA MAISON

242

funnel
entonnoir^M
Trichter^M
embudo^M

colander
passoire^F
Durchschlag^M
escurridor^M

strainer
passoire^F
Sieb^N
cedazo^M

salad spinner
essoreuse^F à salade^F
Salatschleuder^F
secadora^F de ensalada^F

pestle
pilon^M
Stößel^M
mano^M

mortar
mortier^M
Mörser^M
mortero^M

nutcracker
casse-noix^M
Nußknacker^M
cascanueces^M

garlic press
presse-ail^M
Knoblauchpresse^F
triturador^M de ajos^M

lemon squeezer
presse-agrumes^M
Zitronenpresse^F
exprimelimones^M

mincer
hachoir^M
Fleischwolf^M
máquina^F de picar carne^F

grater
râpe^F
Reibe^F
rallador^M

pasta maker
machine^F à faire les pâtes^F
Nudelmaschine^F
máquina^F para hacer pasta^F italiana

243

SET OF UTENSILS
JEU^M D'USTENSILES^M
KÜCHENSET^N
JUEGO^M DE UTENSILIOS^M

potato masher
pilon^M
Kartoffelstampfer^M
pasapuré^M

spatula
spatule^F
Palette^F
espátula^F

skimmer
écumoire^F
Abseihkelle^F
espumadera^F

ladle
louche^F
Schöpflöffel^M
cucharón^M

slice
pelle^F
Pfannenwender^M
paleta^F

draining spoon
cuiller^F à égoutter
Abseihlöffel^M
escurridera^F

FOR OPENING
POUR OUVRIR
ZUM ÖFFNEN^N
UTENSILIOS^M PARA ABRIR Y DESCORCHAR

bottle opener
décapsuleur^M
Flaschenöffner^M
abrebotellas^M

wine waiter corkscrew
tire-bouchon^M de sommelier^M
Kellnerbesteck^N
sacacorchos^M

lever corkscrew
tire-bouchon^M à levier^M
Hebel-Korkenzieher^M
sacacorchos^M con brazos^M

tin opener
ouvre-boîtes^M
Büchsenöffner^M
abrelatas^M

FOR MEASURING
POUR MESURER
ZUM MESSEN^N
UTENSILIOS^M PARA MEDIR

kitchen timer
minuteur^M
Küchenuhr^F
reloj^M de cocina^F

egg timer
sablier^M
Eieruhr^F
minutero^M para huevos^M pasados por agua^F

meat thermometer
thermomètre^M à viande^F
Fleischthermometer^N
termómetro^M para carne^F

measuring spoons
cuillers^F doseuses
Meßlöffel^M
cucharas^F para medir

kitchen scale
balance^F de cuisine^F
Küchenwaage^F
báscula^F de cocina^F

measuring cups
mesures^F
Meßbecher^M
tazas^F para medir

pastry brush
pinceau[M] à pâtisserie[F]
Kuchenpinsel[M]
pincel[M] de repostería[F]

icing syringe
piston[M] à décorer
Garnierspritze[F]
tubito[M] de decoración[F]

whisk
fouet[M]
Schneebesen[M]
batidor[M]

egg beater
batteur[M] à œufs[M]
Rad-Schneeschläger[M]
batidor[M] mecánico

pastry cutting wheel
roulette[F] de pâtissier[M]
Kuchenrad[N]
cortapastas[M]

sifter
tamis[M] à farine[F]
Mehlsieb[N]
tamiz[M]

bun tin
moule[M] à muffins[M]
Mohrenkopfform[F]
molde[M] para magdalenas[F]

pastry bag and nozzles
poche[F] à douilles[F]
Spritzbeutel[M] mit Düsen[F]
manga[F] y boquillas[F]

biscuit sheet
plaque[F] à biscuits[M]
Backblech[N]
bandeja[F] para hornear galletas[F]

rolling pin
rouleau[M] à pâtisserie[F]
Nudelholz[N]
rodillo[M]

mixing bowls
bols[M] à mélanger
Rührschüsseln[F]
boles[M] para batir

biscuit cutters
emporte-pièces[M]
Ausstechformen[F]
moldes[M] de pastas[F]

removable-bottomed tin
moule[M] à fond[M] amovible
Springform[F]
molde[M] redondo con muelles[M]

pie tin
moule[M] à tarte[F]
flache Kuchenform[F]
molde[M] para tartas[F]

quiche tin
moule[M] à quiche[F]
Quicheform[F]
molde[M] acanalado

cake tin
moule[M] à gâteau[M]
Kuchenform[F]
molde[M] para bizcocho[M]

245

MISCELLANEOUS UTENSILS
USTENSILES DIVERS
VERSCHIEDENERLEI UTENSILIEN
UTENSILIOS DIVERSOS

stoner
dénoyauteur^M
Entsteiner^M
deshuesador^M de frutas^F

ice cream scoop
cuiller^F à glace^F
Eisportionierer^M
cuchara^F para servir helado^M

poultry shears
cisaille^F à volaille^F
Geflügelschere^F
tijeras^F para aves^F

spaghetti tongs
pince^F à spaghettis^M
Spaghettizange^F
tenacillas^F para espagueti^M

baster
poire^F à jus^M
Fettgießer^M
engrasador^M

tongs
pince^F
Zange^F
tenacillas^F

vegetable brush
brosse^F à légumes^M
Gemüsebürste^F
cepillo^M para verduras^F

tea infuser
boule^F à thé^M
Tee-Ei^N
esfera^F de té^M

snail tongs
pince^F à escargots^M
Schneckenzange^F
tenacillas^F para caracoles^M

dredger
saupoudreuse^F
Streuer^M
espolvoreador^M

egg slicer
coupe-œuf^M
Eierschneider^M
cortador^M de huevos^M duros

snail dish
plat^M à escargots^M
Schneckenpfännchen^N
plato^M para caracoles^M

COFFEE MAKERS
CAFETIÈRES^F
KAFFEEMASCHINEN^F
CAFETERAS^F

AUTOMATIC FILTER COFFEE MAKER
CAFETIÈRE^F FILTRE^M
KAFFEEMASCHINE^F
CAFETERA^F DE FILTRO^M AUTOMÁTICA

reservoir
réservoir^M
Wasserbehälter^M
depósito^M de agua^F

water level
niveau^M d'eau^F
Wasserstand^M
nivel^M de agua^F

pilot light
voyant^M lumineux
Kontrolleuchte^F
piloto^M

on-off switch
interrupteur^M
Ein-/Ausschalter^M
interruptor^M

lid
couvercle^M
Deckel^M
tapa^F

filter
panier^M
Filter^M
filtro^M

jug
verseuse^F
Kanne^F
cafetera^F

warming plate
plaque^F chauffante
Warmhalteplatte^F
placa^F térmica

PERCOLATOR
PERCOLATEUR^M
PERKULATOR^M
PERCOLADOR^M

spout
bec^M verseur^M
Tülle^F
pitorro^M

pilot light
voyant^M lumineux
Kontrolleuchte^F
piloto^M

VACUUM COFFEE MAKER
CAFETIÈRE^F À INFUSION^F
VAKUUM-KAFFEEMASCHINE^F
CAFETERA^F DE INFUSIÓN^F

upper bowl
tulipe^F
oberer Glaskolben^M
recipiente^M superior

stem
tige^F
Röhre^F
tubo^M de subida^F del agua^F

lower bowl
ballon^M
unterer Glaskolben^M
recipiente^M inferior

CAFETIÈRE WITH PLUNGER
CAFETIÈRE^F À PISTON^M
PRESSFILTERKANNE^F
CAFETERA^F DE ÉMBOLO^M

NEAPOLITAN COFFEE MAKER
CAFETIÈRE^F NAPOLITAINE
NEAPOLITANISCHE TROPFKANNE^F
CAFETERA^F NAPOLITANA

ESPRESSO COFFEE MAKER
CAFETIÈRE^F ESPRESSO^M
ESPRESSO-MASCHINE^F
CAFETERA^F ITALIANA

WOK SET
WOK*M*
WOK-SET*N*
WOK*M*

lid
couvercle*M*
Deckel*M*
tapa*F*

rack
grille*F*
Gittereinsatz*M*
rejilla*F*

wok
wok*M*
Wok*M*
wok*M*

burner ring
collier*M*
Aufsatz*M*
quemador*M*

FISH KETTLE
POISSONNIÈRE*F*
FISCHKOCHTOPF*M*
BESUGERA*F*

strainer
grille*F*
Gittereinsatz*M*
rejilla*F* desmontable

lid
couvercle*M*
Deckel*M*
tapa*F*

FONDUE SET
SERVICE*M* À FONDUE*F*
FONDUE-SET*N*
JUEGO*M* PARA FONDUE*F*

fondue pot
caquelon*M*
Fonduetopf*M*
cacerola*F* para fondue*F*

stand
support*M*
Ständer*M*
soporte*M*

burner
réchaud*M*
Brenner*M*
quemador*M*

roasting pans
plats*M* à four*M*
Bräter*M*
asadores*M*

PRESSURE COOKER
AUTOCUISEUR*M*
DAMPFKOCHTOPF*M*
OLLA*F* A PRESIÓN*F*

pressure regulator
régulateur*M* de pression*F*
Überdruckventil*N*
regulador*M* de presión*F*

safety valve
soupape*F*
Sicherheitsventil*N*
válvula*F* de seguridad*F*

Dutch oven
faitout^M
flacher Bratentopf^M
cacerola^F refractaria

stock pot
marmite^F
Suppentopf^M
olla^F

frying pan
poêle^F à frire
Bratpfanne^F
sartén^F

pancake pan
poêle^F à crêpes^F
Crêpe-Pfanne^F
sartén^F para crepes^F

couscous kettle
couscoussier^M
Kuskustopf^M
olla^F para alcuzcuz^M

egg poacher
pocheuse^F
Eipochierer^M
escalfador^M de huevos^M

sauté pan
sauteuse^F
Schmorpfanne^F
sartén^F honda

vegetable steamer
étuveuse^F
Gemüsedünster^M
alcachofa^F para verduras^F

double boiler
bain-marie^M
Wasserbadtopf^M
cacerola^F para baño^M de María

saucepan
casserole^F
Stielkasserolle^F
cacerola^F

BLENDER
MÉLANGEUR*M*
MIXER*M*
BATIDORA*F*

cap
bouchon*M*
Deckelknopf*M*
tapa*F* de medida*F*

container
récipient*M*
Behälter*M*
recipiente*M* con asa*F*

cutting blade
couteau*M*
Schneidmesser*M*
cuchilla*F*

motor unit
bloc*M*-moteur*M*
Motorblock*M*
motor*M*

push button
bouton*M*-poussoir*M*
Drucktaste
botón*M* de velocidades*F*

HAND MIXER
BATTEUR*M* À MAIN*F*
HANDRÜHRGERÄT*N*
BATIDORA*F* DE MANO*F*

beater ejector
éjecteur*M* de fouets*M*
Auswurftaste*F*
eyector*M* de las varillas*F*

beater
fouet*M*
Rührbesen*M*
varilla*F* de batir

speed control
commande*F* de vitesse*F*
Geschwindigkeitsregelung*F*
selector*M* de velocidades*F*

handle
poignée*F*
Handgriff*M*
asa*F*

heel rest
talon*M* d'appui*M*
Heck*N*
talón*M* de apoyo*M*

HAND BLENDER
MÉLANGEUR*M* À MAIN*F*
STABMIXER*M*
BATIDORA*F* DE BRAZO*M*

motor unit
bloc*M*-moteur*M*
Motorblock*M*
motor*M*

blending attachment
pied*M*-mélangeur*M*
Messerschutz*M*
cuchillas*F* para batir

TABLE MIXER
BATTEUR*M* SUR SOCLE*M*
TISCHRÜHRGERÄT*N*
BATIDORA*F* DE MESA*F*

beater ejector
éjecteur*M* de fouets*M*
Auswurftaste*F*
eyector*M* de las varillas*F*

beater
fouet*M*
Rührbesen*M*
varilla*F* de batir

tilt-back head
tête*F* basculante
Schwenkarm*M*
cabeza*F* móvil

mixing bowl
bol*M*
Rührschüssel*F*
bol*M* mezclador

turntable
plateau*M* tournant
Drehscheibe*F*
disco*M* giratorio

stand
socle*M*
Ständer*M*
pie*M*

speed control
commande*F* de vitesse*F*
Geschwindigkeitsregelung*F*
selector*M* de velocidades*F*

BEATERS
FOUETS*M*
RÜHRBESEN*M*
TIPOS*M* DE VARILLAS*F*

four blade beater
fouet*M* quatre pales*F*
Rührbesen*M*
de aspas*F*

spiral beater
fouet*M* en spirale*F*
Spiralkneter*M*
en espiral*F*

wire beater
fouet*M* à fil*M*
Drahtbesen*M*
circular

dough hook
crochet*M* pétrisseur
Knethaken*M*
de gancho*M*

FOOD PROCESSOR
ROBOT^M **DE CUISINE**^F
KÜCHENMASCHINE^F
ROBOT^M **DE COCINA**^F

DISCS
DISQUES^M
SCHEIBEN^F
DISCO^M

pusher
poussoir^M
Stopfer^M
embutidor^M

feed tube
entonnoir^M
Einfüllschacht^M
tubo^M de entrada^F

lid
couvercle^M
Deckel^M
tapa^F

blade
couteau^M
Schneidmesser^N
cuchilla^F

handle
poignée^F
Handgriff^M
asa^F

bowl
bol^M
Schüssel^F
bol^M

speed selector
sélecteur^M de vitesse^F
Geschwindigkeitsregelung^F
selector^M de velocidades^F

spindle
arbre^M
Antriebswelle^F
eje^M

motor unit
bloc^M-moteur^M
Motorblock^M
motor^M

LEMON SQUEEZER
PRESSE-AGRUMES^M
ZITRUSPRESSE^F
EXPRIMIDOR^M **DE CÍTRICOS**^M

strainer
passoire^F
Sieb^N
colador^M

dome
toupie^F
Kegel^M
exprimidor^M

bowl with serving spout
bol^M verseur
Behälter^M mit Gießer^M
recipiente^M con vertedor^M

motor unit
bloc^M-moteur^M
Motorblock^M
motor^M

JUICE EXTRACTOR
CENTRIFUGEUSE^F
ENTSAFTER^M
LICUADORA^F

pusher
poussoir^M
Stopfer^M
embutidor^M

feed tube
entonnoir^M
Einfüllschlacht^M
tubo^M alimentador

lid
couvercle^M
Deckel^M
tapa^F

strainer
passoire^F
Sieb^N
colador^M

motor unit
bloc^M-moteur^M
Motorblock^M
motor^M

bowl
pichet^M
Schüssel^F
recipiente^M

ICE CREAM MAKER
SORBETIÈRE^F
EISMASCHINE^F
HELADERA^F

motor unit
bloc^M-moteur^M
Motorblock^M
motor^M

cover
couvercle^M
Deckel^M
cubierta^F

handle
poignée^F
Handgriff^M
asa^F

ice cream container
seau^M isotherme
Eisbehälter^M
cubeta^F congeladora

251

DOMESTIC APPLIANCES
APPAREILS^M **ÉLECTROMÉNAGERS**
HAUSHALTSGERÄTE^N
APARATOS^M **ELECTRODOMÉSTICOS**

HAUSEINRICHTUNG
ENSERES DOMÉSTICOS

HOUSE FURNITURE
AMEUBLEMENT DE LA MAISON

KETTLE
BOUILLOIRE^F
WASSERKESSEL^M
HERVIDOR^M **DE SILBATO**^{M}

handle
poignée^F
Handgriff^M
asa^F

whistle
sifflet^M
Pfeife^F
silbato^M

pilot light
voyant^M lumineux
Kontrolleuchte^F
piloto^M

spout
bec^M verseur
Tülle^F
vertedor^M

base
socle^M
Boden^M
base^F

body
corps^M
Gehäuse^N
cuerpo^M

TOASTER
GRILLE-PAIN^M
TOASTER^M
TOSTADOR^M

slot
fente^F
Schlitz^M
ranura^F para el pan^M

bread guide
guide^M
Brothalter^M
rejilla^F

lever
manette^F
Hebel^M
palanca^F

handle
poignée^F
Handgriff^M
asa^F

temperature control
thermostat^M
Temperaturregler^M
selector^M de tostado^M

DEEP FRYER
FRITEUSE^F
FRITEUSE^F
FREIDORA^F

basket
panier^M
Fritierkorb^M
canastilla^F

rack
crémaillère^F
Regler^M
selector^M

lid
couvercle^M
Deckel^M
tapa^F

timer
minuterie^F
Zeituhr^F
reloj^M

filter
filtre^M
Filter^M
filtro^M

thermostat
thermostat^M
Thermostat^M
termostato^M

pilot light
voyant^M lumineux
Kontrolleuchte^F
piloto^M

252

WAFFLE IRON
GAUFRIER^M-GRIL^M
WAFFELEISEN^N
BARQUILLERO^M ELÉCTRICO

handle
poignée^F
Handgriff^M
asa^F

lid
couvercle^M
Deckel^M
plancha^F superior

plate
plaque^F
Platte^F
parrilla^F

hinge
charnière^F
Scharnier^N
bisagra^F

plate
plaque^F
Platte^F
parrilla^F

temperature selector
sélecteur^M de température^F
Temperaturwähler^M
selector^M de temperatura^F

MICROWAVE OVEN
FOUR^M À MICRO-ONDES^F
MIKROWELLENGERÄT^N
HORNO^M DE MICROONDAS^F

door
porte^F
Tür^F
puerta^F

latch
loquet^M
Riegel^M
seguro^M

clock timer
horloge^F programmatrice
Zeitschalter^M
reloj^M programador

handle
poignée^F
Handgriff^M
asa^F

control panel
tableau^M de commande^F
Bedienblende^F
panel^M de controles^M

probe socket
prise^F de la sonde^F thermique
Sensorhülse^F
enchufe^M del termómetro^M

sensor probe
sonde^F thermique
Sensor^M
termómetro^M para carnes^F

window
hublot^M
Sichtfenster^N
ventana^F

GRIDDLE
GRIL^M ÉLECTRIQUE
GRILL^M
PLANCHA^F

handle
poignée^F
Handgriff^M
asa^F

cooking surface
surface^F de cuisson^F
Grillfläche^F
plancha^F

detachable control
commande^F amovible
abziehbarer Temperaturregler^M
enchufe^M y selector^M desmontables

grease well
collecteur^M de graisse^F
Fettauffangschale^F
colector^M de grasa^F

DOMESTIC APPLIANCES
APPAREILS^M ÉLECTROMÉNAGERS
HAUSHALTSGERÄTE^N
APARATOS^M ELECTRODOMÉSTICOS

REFRIGERATOR
RÉFRIGÉRATEUR^M
KÜHLSCHRANK^M
FRIGORÍFICO^M

ice cube tray
bac^M à glaçons^M
Eiswürfelschale^F
bandeja^F para cubitos^M de hielo^M

freezer door
porte^F
Tür^F
puerta^F del congelador^M

freezer compartment
congélateur^M
Gefrierfach^N
congelador^M incorporado

door stop
butée^F de porte^F
Türstopper^M
tope^M de la puerta^F

thermostat control
commande^F de température^F
Temperaturregler^M
termostato^M

magnetic gasket
joint^M magnétique
magnetische Dichtung^F
imán^M

handle
poignée^F
Handgriff^M
asa^F

switch
interrupteur^M
Schalter^M
interruptor^M

egg tray
œufrier^M
Eierfach^N
huevera^F

butter compartment
casier^M à beurre^M
Butterfach^N
compartimiento^M para mantequilla^F

dairy compartment
casier^M laitier
Fach^N für Molkereiprodukte^N
compartimiento^M para queso^M y crema^F

storage door
porte^F étagère^F
Innentür^F
puerta^F del refrigerador^M

door shelf
balconnet^M
Türfach^N
anaquel^M

guard rail
barre^F de retenue^F
Sicherheitsleiste^F
pasamanos^M

meat keeper
bac^M à viande^F
Fleisch- und Wurstfach^N
cajón^M para carnes^F

shelf
clayette^F
Abstellrost^N
parrilla^F

shelf channel
crémaillère^F
Rasterleiste^F
riel^M para las parrillas^F

refrigerator compartment
réfrigérateur^M
Kühlfach^N
espacio^M interior

glass cover
tablette^F de verre^M
Glasplatte^F
cubierta^F de vidrio^M

salad crisper
bac^M à légumes^M
Obst- und Gemüseschale^F
cubeta^F para verdura^F

EXTRACTOR HOOD
HOTTE*
DUNSTABZUGSHAUBE*
CAMPANA*

filter
filtre*
Filter*
filtro*

ELECTRIC COOKER
CUISINIÈRE* ÉLECTRIQUE
ELEKTROHERD*
COCINA* ELÉCTRICA

clock timer
horloge* programmatrice
Schaltuhr*
reloj*

oven control knob
réglage* du four*
Backofenschalter*
botón* del horno*

pilot light
voyant* lumineux
Kontrolleuchte*
piloto*

back panel
dosseret*
Blende*
panel* de mandos*

control knob
bouton* de commande*
Schalter*
botón* de control*

timer socket
prise* chronométrée
Zusatzstecker*
enchufe* con control* de tiempo*

control panel
tableau* de commande*
Bedienblende*
tablero* de controles*

cooker ring
serpentin*
Kochplatte*
placa*

hob edge
rebord*
Herdkante*
borde*

oven
four*
Backofen*
horno*

shelf
grille*
Rost*
rejilla*

hob
surface* de cuisson*
Kochstelle*
cubierta*

window
hublot*
Sichtfenster*
ventana*

handle
poignée*
Griff*
asa*

drawer
tiroir*
Geschirrwagen*
cajón*

trim ring
anneau*
Schutzring*
arandela*

drip bowl
cuvette*
Auffangschüssel*
protector*

terminal
borne*
Anschluß*
enchufe*

tubular element
élément* tubulaire
Heizspirale*
resistencia*

HOUSE FURNITURE / AMEUBLEMENT DE LA MAISON
HAUSEINRICHTUNG / ENSERES DOMÉSTICOS

STEAM IRON
FER*ᴹ* À VAPEUR*ᶠ*
DAMPFBÜGELEISEN*ᴺ*
PLANCHA*ᶠ* DE VAPOR*ᴹ*

front tip
pointe*ᶠ* avant
Spitze*ᶠ*
punta*ᶠ* de la plancha*ᶠ*

body
capot*ᴹ*
Gehäuse*ᴺ*
armazón*ᴹ*

filler hole
orifice*ᶠ* de remplissage*ᴹ*
Einfüllöffnung*ᶠ*
boquilla*ᶠ* de llenado*ᴹ*

water-level tube
repère*ᴹ* de niveau*ᴹ* d'eau*ᶠ*
Wasserstandsanzeiger*ᴹ*
nivel*ᴹ* del agua*ᶠ*

spray
vaporisateur*ᴹ*
Spray*ᴹ*
vaporizador*ᴹ*

spray control
contrôle*ᴹ* de la vapeur*ᶠ*
Sprayregler*ᴹ*
control*ᴹ* del vaporizador*ᴹ*

spray button
bouton*ᴹ* de vaporisation*ᶠ*
Sprühknopf*ᴹ*
botón*ᴹ* del vaporizador*ᴹ*

fabric guide
guide*ᴹ* des températures*ᶠ*
Gewebe-Einstellskala*ᶠ*
cuadro*ᴹ* de temperaturas*ᶠ*

soleplate
semelle*ᶠ*
Bügelsohle*ᶠ*
plancha*ᶠ*

handle
poignée*ᶠ*
Handgriff*ᴹ*
asa*ᶠ*

temperature control
réglage*ᴹ* des températures*ᶠ*
Temperaturregler*ᴹ*
control*ᴹ* de temperatura*ᶠ*

flex support
lève-fil*ᴹ*
Kabelversteifung*ᶠ*
embocadura*ᶠ* del cable*ᴹ*

heel rest
talon*ᴹ* d'appui*ᴹ*
Bügelheck*ᴺ*
talón*ᴹ* de apoyo*ᴹ*

flex
cordon*ᴹ*
Netzkabel*ᴺ*
cordón*ᴹ*

pilot light
voyant*ᴹ* lumineux
Kontrolleuchte*ᶠ*
piloto*ᴹ*

COFFEE MILL
MOULIN*ᴹ* À CAFÉ*ᴹ*
KAFFEEMÜHLE*ᶠ*
MOLINILLO*ᴹ* DE CAFÉ*ᴹ*

lid
couvercle*ᴹ*
Deckel*ᴹ*
tapa*ᶠ*

pierce lever
levier*ᴹ* de perçage*ᴹ*
Einstechhebel*ᴹ*
palanca*ᶠ* de perforación*ᶠ*

TIN OPENER
OUVRE-BOÎTES*ᴹ*
DOSENÖFFNER*ᴹ*
ABRELATAS*ᴹ*

magnetic lid holder
aimant*ᴹ* de retenue*ᶠ*
magnetischer Deckelhalter*ᴹ*
retén*ᴹ* imantado

blade
couteau*ᴹ*
Messer*ᴺ*
cuchilla*ᶠ*

cutting blade
lame*ᶠ* de coupe*ᶠ*
Schneidklinge*ᶠ*
cuchilla*ᶠ*

on-off button
bouton*ᴹ* marche*ᶠ*/arrêt*ᴹ*
Ein-/Ausschalter*ᴹ*
interruptor*ᴹ*

drive wheel
molette*ᶠ* d'entraînement*ᴹ*
Druckzahnrädchen*ᴺ*
engranaje*ᴹ* de avance*ᴹ*

motor unit
bloc*ᴹ*-moteur*ᴹ*
Motorblock*ᴹ*
motor*ᴹ*

256

DOMESTIC APPLIANCES
APPAREILS[M] ÉLECTROMÉNAGERS
HAUSHALTSGERÄTE[N]
APARATOS[M] ELECTRODOMÉSTICOS

CONTROL PANEL
TABLEAU[M] DE COMMANDE[F]
BEDIENBLENDE[F]
PANEL[M] DE MANDOS[M]

latch
loquet[M]
Riegel[M]
palanca[F] de cierre[M]

program selector
programmateur[M]
Programmwähler[M]
programador[M]

pilot light
voyant[M] lumineux
Kontrolleuchte[F]
piloto[M]

push button
bouton[M]-poussoir[M]
Drucktaste[F]
botón[M] selector

air vent
grille[F] d'aération[F]
Belüftungsschlitz[M]
rejilla[F] de ventilación[F]

DISHWASHER
LAVE-VAISSELLE[M]
GESCHIRRSPÜLMASCHINE[F]
LAVAVAJILLAS[M]

spray arm
bras[M] gicleur[M]
Sprüharm[M]
pulverizador[M]

wash tower
tourelle[F]
Wascherarm[M]
torrecilla[F] de lavado[M]

rack
panier[M]
Korb[M]
canastilla[F]

insulating material
isolant[M]
Isoliermaterial[N]
aislante[M]

overflow protection switch
dispositif[M] antidébordement[M]
Überlaufschutz[M]
regulador[M] de entrada[F] de agua[F]

tub
cuve[F]
Bottich[M]
cubeta[F] de lavado[M]

hinge
charnière[F]
Scharnier[N]
bisagra[F]

slide
glissière[F]
Schiene[F]
riel[M] corredizo

detergent dispenser
distributeur[M] de détergent[M]
Reinigungsmittelgeber[M]
recipiente[M] del detergente[M]

water hose
conduite[F] d'eau[F]
Wasserschlauch[M]
manguera[F] de alimentación[F]

rinse-aid dispenser
distributeur[M] de produit[M] de rinçage[M]
Klarspülmittelgeber[M]
recipiente[M] de enjuague[M]

heating element
élément[M] chauffant
Heizelement[N]
resistencia[F]

drain hose
tuyau[M] de vidange[F]
Ablaufschlauch[M]
manguera[F] de desagüe[M]

pump
pompe[F]
Pumpe[F]
bomba[F]

motor
moteur[M]
Motor[M]
motor[M]

gasket
joint[M]
Dichtungsring[M]
junta[F]

cutlery basket
panier[M] à couverts[M]
Besteckkorb[M]
canastilla[F] para cubiertos[M]

levelling foot
pied[M] de nivellement[M]
Nivellierfuß[M]
pie[M] ajustable

HOUSE FURNITURE
AMEUBLEMENT DE LA MAISON

HAUSEINRICHTUNG
ENSERES DOMÉSTICOS

257

WASHING MACHINE
LAVE-LINGE^M
WASCHMASCHINE^F
LAVADORA^F

water-level selector
sélecteur^M de niveau^M d'eau^F
Wasserstandsregler^M
selector^M de nivel^M de agua^F

temperature selector
sélecteur^M de température^F
Temperaturwähler^M
selector^M de temperatura^F

control panel
tableau^M de commande^F
Bedienblende^F
panel^M de mandos^M

control knob
programmateur^M
Programmwähler^M
programador^M

backguard
dosseret^M
Blende^F
panel^M de mandos^M

lid
couvercle^M
Deckel^M
tapa^F

tub rim
rebord^M de cuve^F
Bottichrand^M
borde^M de la cubeta^F

agitator
agitateur^M
Rührwerk^N
agitador^M de aspas^F

drum
panier^M de lavage^M
Trommel^F
tambor^M

cabinet
carrosserie^F
Gehäuse^N
armazón^M

tub
cuve^F
Laugenbehälter^M
cubeta^F

lint filter
filtre^M à charpie^F
Flusensieb^N
filtro^M de pelusa^F

transmission
transmission^F
Getriebe^N
transmisión^F

suspension arm
bras^M de suspension^F
Schwingungsdämpfer^M
brazo^M de suspensión^F

motor
moteur^M
Motor^M
motor^M

drain hose
tuyau^M d'évacuation^F
Ablaufschlauch^M
manguera^F de desagüe^M

emptying hose
tuyau^M de vidange^F
Entleerungsschlauch^M
manguera^F de vaciado^M

pump
pompe^F
Pumpe^F
bomba^F

torque converter
convertisseur^M de couple^M
Drehmomentwandler^M
convertidor^M de tensión^F

levelling foot
pied^M de nivellement^M
Nivellierfuß^M
pie^M ajustable

drive belt
courroie^F d'entraînement^M
Keilriemen^M
correa^F del tambor^M

spring
ressort^M de suspension^F
Feder^F
resorte^M

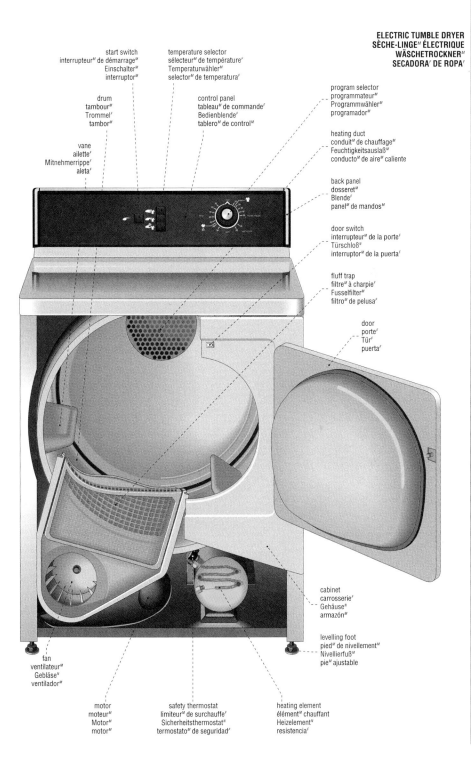

ELECTRIC TUMBLE DRYER
SÈCHE-LINGE^M ÉLECTRIQUE
WÄSCHETROCKNER^M
SECADORA^F DE ROPA^F

start switch
interrupteur^M de démarrage^M
Einschalter^M
interruptor^M

temperature selector
sélecteur^M de température^F
Temperaturwähler^M
selector^M de temperatura^F

program selector
programmateur^M
Programmwähler^M
programador^M

drum
tambour^M
Trommel^F
tambor^M

control panel
tableau^M de commande^F
Bedienblende^F
tablero^M de control^M

heating duct
conduit^M de chauffage^M
Feuchtigkeitsauslaß^M
conducto^M de aire^M caliente

vane
ailette^F
Mitnehmerrippe^F
aleta^F

back panel
dosseret^M
Blende^F
panel^M de mandos^M

door switch
interrupteur^M de la porte^F
Türschloß^N
interruptor^M de la puerta^F

fluff trap
filtre^M à charpie^F
Fusselfilter^M
filtro^M de pelusa^F

door
porte^F
Tür^F
puerta^F

cabinet
carrosserie^F
Gehäuse^N
armazón^M

levelling foot
pied^M de nivellement^M
Nivellierfuß^M
pie^M ajustable

fan
ventilateur^M
Gebläse^N
ventilador^M

motor
moteur^M
Motor^M
motor^M

safety thermostat
limiteur^M de surchauffe^F
Sicherheitsthermostat^N
termostato^M de seguridad^F

heating element
élément^M chauffant
Heizelement^N
resistencia^F

DOMESTIC APPLIANCES
APPAREILS^M ÉLECTROMÉNAGERS
HAUSHALTSGERÄTE^N
APARATOS^M ELECTRODOMÉSTICOS

HAND VACUUM CLEANER
ASPIRATEUR^M À MAIN^F
AKKU-MINI-STAUBSAUGER^M
ASPIRADOR^M MANUAL

locking button
verrouillage^M
Entriegelungstaste^F
botón^M de cierre^M

dust receiver
godet^M à poussière^F
Staubbehälter^M
depósito de polvo^M

on-off switch
interrupteur^M
Ein-/Ausschalter^M
interruptor^M

motor unit
bloc^M-moteur^M
Motorblock^M
motor^M

recharging base
socle^M-chargeur^M
Lade-Anschlußbuchse^F
cargador^M

CYLINDER VACUUM CLEANER
ASPIRATEUR^M-TRAÎNEAU^M
KESSELSTAUBSAUGER^M
ASPIRADOR^M

locking device
système^M de verrouillage^M
Verschluß^M
seguro^M

on-off switch
interrupteur^M
Ein-/Ausschalter^M
interruptor^M

rigid tube
tube^M droit
Saugrohr^M
tubo^M rígido

hood
capot^M
Haube^F
tapa^F

handle
poignée^F
Handgriff^M
asa^F

ventilating grille
grille^F de ventilation^F
Luftaustrittsschlitz^M
rejilla^F del ventilador^M

flexible hose
tuyau^M flexible
beweglicher Schlauch^M
manguera^F

bumper
pare-chocs^M
Stoßleiste^F
tope^M amortiguador

extension tube
rallonge^F
Ansatzrohr^N
tubo^M de extensión^F

caster
roulette^F
Lenkrolle^F
ruedecilla^F

flex
cordon^M
Kabel^N
cordón^M

carpet and floor brush
suceur^M à tapis^M et planchers^M
Bodendüse^F
boquilla^F para pisos^M y alfombras^F

CLEANING TOOLS
ACCESSOIRES^M
SAUGZUBEHÖR^N
ACCESORIOS^M

upholstery nozzle
suceur^M triangulaire à tissus^M
Polsterdüse^F
boquilla^F para tapicería^F

crevice tool
suceur^M plat
Fugendüse^F
boquilla^F rinconera

floor brush
brosse^F à planchers^M
Bürste^F
cepillo^M para pisos^M

dusting brush
brosse^F à épousseter
Saugpinsel^M
cepillo^M-plumero^M

SUMMARY

GARTENARBEIT
JARDINERÍA

GARDENING
JARDINAGE

PLEASURE GARDEN
JARDIN^M D'AGRÉMENT^M
ZIERGARTEN^M
JARDÍN^M

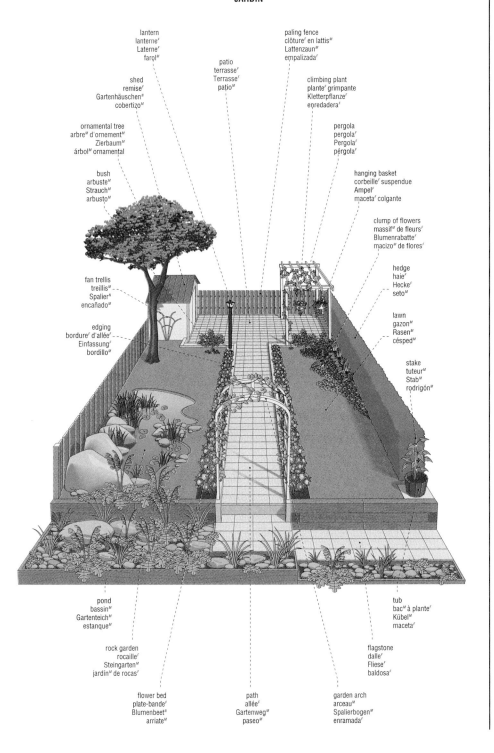

lantern
lanterne^F
Laterne^F
farol^M

patio
terrasse^F
Terrasse^F
patio^M

paling fence
clôture^F en lattis^M
Lattenzaun^M
empalizada^F

shed
remise^F
Gartenhäuschen^N
cobertizo^M

climbing plant
plante^F grimpante
Kletterpflanze^F
enredadera^F

ornamental tree
arbre^M d'ornement^M
Zierbaum^M
árbol^M ornamental

pergola
pergola^F
Pergola^F
pérgola^F

bush
arbuste^M
Strauch^M
arbusto^M

hanging basket
corbeille^F suspendue
Ampel^F
maceta^F colgante

clump of flowers
massif^M de fleurs^F
Blumenrabatte^F
macizo^M de flores^F

fan trellis
treillis^M
Spalier^N
encañado^M

hedge
haie^F
Hecke^F
seto^M

lawn
gazon^M
Rasen^M
césped^M

edging
bordure^F d'allée^F
Einfassung^F
bordillo^M

stake
tuteur^M
Stab^M
rodrigón^M

pond
bassin^M
Gartenteich^M
estanque^M

tub
bac^M à plante^F
Kübel^M
maceta^F

rock garden
rocaille^F
Steingarten^M
jardín^M de rocas^F

flagstone
dalle^F
Fliese^F
baldosa^F

flower bed
plate-bande^F
Blumenbeet^N
arriate^M

path
allée^F
Gartenweg^M
paseo^M

garden arch
arceau^M
Spalierbogen^M
enramada^F

TOOLS AND EQUIPMENT
OUTILLAGE^M
GARTENGERÄT^N
HERRAMIENTAS^F Y MÁQUINAS^F

pistol nozzle
pistolet^M d'arrosage^M
Gießpistole^F
pistola^F pulverizadora

spray nozzle
pistolet^M arrosoir^M
Gießbrause^F
boquilla^F pulverizadora

sprayer
vaporisateur^M
Sprühflasche^F
pulverizador^M

arm
bras^M
Drehdüse^F
brazo^M

oscillating sprinkler
arroseur^M oscillant
Viereckregner^M
irrigador^M oscilante

**REVOLVING SPRINKLER
ARROSEUR^M ROTATIF
KREISREGNER^M
IRRIGADOR^M GIRATORIO**

IMPULSE SPRINKLER
ARROSEUR^M CANON^M
IMPULSREGNER^M
IRRIGADOR^M DE IMPULSO^M

metal arm
balancier^M
Hammer^M
brazo^M metálico

diffuser pin
brise-jet^M
Zerstäuberstift^M
perno^M difusor

nozzle
buse^F
Düse^F
boquilla^F

deflector
déflecteur^M
Strahlstörer^M
deflector^M

hose connector
raccord^M de tuyau^M
Schlauchkupplung^F
boca^F para la manguera^F

adjusting ring
bague^F de réglage^M
Stellring^M
disparador^M

sled
traîneau^M
Fuß^M
soporte^M

HOSE TROLLEY
DÉVIDOIR*ᴹ* SUR ROUES*ᶠ*
SCHLAUCHWAGEN*ᴹ*
CARRETILLA*ᶠ* PARA MANGUERA*ᶠ*

sprinkler hose
tuyau*ᴹ* perforé
Regnerschlauch*ᴹ*
manguera*ᶠ* de riego*ᴹ*

hose connector
raccord*ᴹ* de robinet*ᴹ*
Schlauchkupplung*ᶠ*
toma*ᶠ*

reel
dévidoir*ᴹ*
Trommel*ᶠ*
carrete*ᴹ*

garden hose
tuyau*ᴹ* d'arrosage*ᴹ*
Gartenschlauch*ᴹ*
manguera*ᶠ*

reel crank
manivelle*ᶠ*
Kurbel*ᶠ*
manivela*ᶠ* del carrete*ᴹ*

hose nozzle
lance*ᶠ* d'arrosage*ᴹ*
Schlauchdüse*ᶠ*
boquilla*ᶠ*

pump sprayer
pulvérisateur*ᴹ*
Gartenspritze*ᶠ*
pulverizador*ᴹ*

WATERING CAN
ARROSOIR*ᴹ*
GIESSKANNE*ᶠ*
REGADERA*ᶠ*

handle
anse*ᶠ*
Griff*ᴹ*
asa*ᶠ*

rose
pomme*ᶠ*
Brause*ᶠ*
roseta*ᶠ*

TOOLS AND EQUIPMENT
OUTILLAGE^M
GARTENGERÄT^N
HERRAMIENTAS^F Y MÁQUINAS^F

shovel
pelle^F
Grabschaufel^F
pala^F

spade
bêche^F
Spaten^M
laya^F

digging fork
fourche^F à bêcher
Grabgabel^F
horca^F

lawn edger
coupe-bordures^M
Kantenstecher^M
cuchilla^F para delimitar el césped^M

lawn aerator
aérateur^M à gazon^M
Vertikulator^M
ventilador^M de césped^M

hoe-fork
serfouette^F
Kombihacke^F
almocafre^M

scuffle hoe
ratissoire^F
Ziehhacke^F
azada^F de doble filo^M

draw hoe
binette^F
Rübenhacke^F
azada^F

weeding hoe
sarcloir^M
Handkultivator^M
escardillo^M

hook
croc*ᴹ* à défricher
Krail*ᴹ*
garabato*ᴹ*

rake
râteau*ᴹ*
Rechen*ᴹ*
rastrillo*ᴹ*

scythe
faux*ᶠ*
Sense*ᶠ*
guadaña*ᶠ*

lawn rake
balai*ᴹ* à feuilles*ᶠ*
Rasenbesen*ᴹ*
rastrillo*ᴹ*

hoe
houe*ᶠ*
Rodehacke*ᶠ*
azadón*ᴹ*

pick
pioche*ᶠ*
Kreuzhacke*ᶠ*
pico*ᴹ*

267

TOOLS AND EQUIPMENT
OUTILLAGE^M
GARTENGERÄT^N
HERRAMIENTAS^F Y MÁQUINAS^F

GARTENARBEIT
JARDINERÍA

GARDENING
JARDINAGE

hand fork
fourche^F à fleurs^F
Handgabel^F
horquilla^F de mano^F

weeder
tire-racine^M
Unkrautstecher^M
desyerbador^M

trowel
transplantoir^M
Blumenkelle^F
desplantador^M

small hand cultivator
griffe^F à fleurs^F
Kralle^F
cultivador^M de mano^F

seeder
semoir^M à main^F
Sähkelle^F
sembradora^F de mano^F

garden line
cordeau^M
Pflanzschnur^F
instrumento^M para alinear el jardín^M

dibber
plantoir^M
Pflanzholz^N
plantador^M

HEDGE TRIMMER
TAILLE-HAIES^M
ELEKTRISCHE HECKENSCHERE^F
CORTASETOS^M ELÉCTRICO

flex
cordon^M
Kabel^N
cable^M

bulb dibber
plantoir^M à bulbes^M
Pflanzlochstecher^M
plantador^M de bulbos^M

hand protector
bouclier^M
Handschutz^M
protector^M

trigger
gâchette^F
Drückerschalter^M
gatillo^M

blade
lame^F
Messer^N
cuchilla^F

tooth
dent^F
Zahn^M
diente^M

electric motor
moteur^M électrique
Elektromotor^M
motor^M eléctrico

lopping shears
ébrancheur^M
Astschere^F
podadera^F

garden shears
cisaille^F à haies^F
Heckenschere^F
tijeras^F para podar setos^M

grafting knife
greffoir^M
Veredelungsmesser^N
navaja^F de injertar

secateurs
sécateur^M
Baumschere^F
tijeras^F de podar

pruning saw
scie^F d'élagage^M
Baumsäge^F
sierra^F de podar

sickle
faucille^F
Sichel^F
hoz^F

pruning knife
serpette^F
Baumhippe^F
podón^M

tree pruner
échenilloir^M-élagueur^M
Raupenschere^F mit Teleskopstiel^M
podadera^F de árboles^M

billhook
serpe^F
Hippe^F
navaja^F jardinera

TOOLS AND EQUIPMENT
OUTILLAGE^M
GARTENGERÄT^N
HERRAMIENTAS^F Y MÁQUINAS^F

spreader
épandeur^M
Düngerstreuer^M
esparcidora^F de abono^M

MOTORIZED GROUND AUGER
TARIÈRE^F MOTORISÉE
ERDBOHRER^M
TALADRO^M DE MOTOR^M

handle
mancheron^M
Lenkholm^M
manillar^M

control cable
câble^M de commande^F
Gaszug^M
cable^M de control^M

auger bit
mèche^F de tarière^F
Bohrschnecke^F
taladro^M

starting cable
câble^M du démarreur^M
Starterzug^M
cable^M de arranque^M

motor
moteur^M
Motor^M
motor^M

WHEELBARROW
BROUETTE^F
SCHUBKARRE^F
CARRETILLA^F

container
caisse^F
Mulde^F
caja^F

roller
rouleau^M
Walze^F
rodillo^M

handle
brancard^M
Griff^M
brazo^M

leg
pied^M
Stütze^F
pata^F

wheel
roue^F
Rad^N
rueda^F

270

HAND MOWER
TONDEUSE^F MÉCANIQUE
HANDRASENMÄHER^M
CORTACÉSPED^M

TRIMMER
TAILLE-BORDURES^M
RASENTRIMMER^M
PODADORA^F DE BORDES^M

flex
cordon^M
Kabel^N
cable^M

blade
lame^F
Messer^N
cuchilla^F

electric motor
moteur^M électrique
Elektromotor^M
motor^M eléctrico

protective casing
carter^M de sécurité^F
Schutzgehäuse^N
cubierta^F de seguridad^F

nylon line
fil^M de nylon^M
Nylonschnur^F
hilo^M de nilón^M

cutting cylinder
cylindre^M de coupe^F
Schneidzylinder^M
cilindro^M de corte^M

POWER MOWER
TONDEUSE^F À MOTEUR^M
MOTORRASENMÄHER^M
CORTACÉSPED^M **ELÉCTRICO**

handle
guidon^M
Griff^M
barra^F

throttle
sélecteur^M de régime^M
Geschwindigkeitsregler^M
control^M de velocidad^F

safety handle
poignée^F de sécurité^F
Sicherheitsgriff^M
palanca^F de seguridad^F

ignition key
clé^F de contact^M
Zündschlüssel^M
encendido^M

grassbox
bac^M de ramassage^M
Grasfang^M
caja^F para el césped^M

motor
moteur^M
Motor^M
motor^M

starter
démarreur^M manuel
Anlasser^M
motor^M de arranque^M

throttle cable
câble^M d'accélération^F
Gaszug^M
cable^M del acelerador^M

filler cap
bouchon^M de remplissage^M
Einfüllstutzen^M
boca^F del tanque^M de combustible^M

sparking plug
bougie^F
Zündkerze^F
bujía^F

deflector
déflecteur^M
Leitblech^N
deflector^M

casing
carter^M
Gehäuse^N
caja^F

TOOLS AND EQUIPMENT
OUTILLAGE^M
GARTENGERÄT^N
HERRAMIENTAS^F Y MÁQUINAS^F

CHAINSAW
SCIE^F À CHAÎNE^F
KETTENSÄGE^F
SIERRA^F DE CADENA^F

air filter
filtre^M à air^M
Luftfilter^M
filtro^M de aire^M

anti-vibration handle
poignée^F antivibrations^F
schwingungsdämpfender
Bügelgriff^M
barra^F antivibración

stop button
bouton^M d'arrêt^M
Ausschalter^M
botón^M de apagado^M

bar nose
nez^M du guide^M
Umlenkstern^M
extremo^M del brazo^M

chain brake
frein^M de chaîne^F
Kettenbremse^F
freno^M de la cadena^F

security trigger
gâchette^F de sécurité^F
Rasthebel^M
gatillo^M de seguridad^F

guide bar
guide-chaîne^M
Schwert^M
brazo^M de la sierra^F

cutter link
maillon^M-gouge^F
Hobelzahn^M
eslabón^M de corte^M

chainsaw chain
chaîne^F coupante
Sägekette^F
cadena^F

handle
poignée^F
Griff^M
mango^M

engine housing
boîtier^M du moteur^M
Motorgehäuse^N
caja^F del motor^M

starter handle
poignée^F du démarreur^M
Startergriff^M
palanca^F de arranque^M

throttle control
commande^F d'accélération^F
Gashebel^M
acelerador^M

oil tank
réservoir^M d'huile^F
Ölsumpf^M
depósito^M de aceite^M

fuel tank
réservoir^M d'essence^F
Kraftstofftank^M
tanque^M del combustible^M

ROTAVATOR
MOTOCULTEUR^M
GARTENFRÄSE^F
CULTIVADORA^F

handlebar
mancheron^M
Lenkholm^M
barra^F guía^F

frame
châssis^M
Rahmen^M
chasis^M

starter
démarreur^M manuel
Anlasser^M
arranque^M

clutch lever
levier^M d'embrayage^M
Kupplungshebel^M
palanca^F del embrague^M

forward/reverse
marche^F avant/marche^F arrière
vorwärts/rückwärts
palanca^F de avance^M/marcha^F atrás

tine
dent^F
Messer^N
púa^F de muelle^M

motor
moteur^M
Motor^M
motor^M

SUMMARY

CARPENTRY: TOOLS
MENUISERIE^F: OUTILS^M
SCHREINEREI^F: WERKZEUGE^N
CARPINTERÍA^F: HERRAMIENTAS^F

CLAW HAMMER
MARTEAU^M DE CHARPENTIER^M
ZIMMERMANNSHAMMER^M
MARTILLO^M DE UÑA^F

claw
arrache-clou^M
Klaue^F
uña^F

cheek
joue^F
Wange^F
cotillo^M

handle
manche^M
Stiel^M
mango^M

wood chisel
ciseau^M à bois^M
Stemmeisen^N
escoplo^M

face
tête^F de frappe^F
Bahn^F
cara^F

eye
œil^M
Auge^N
ojo^M

carpenter's hammer
marteau^M de menuisier^M
Hammer^M
martillo^M de carpintero^M

MALLET
MAILLET^M
HOLZHAMMER^M
MAZO^M

head
tête^F
Kopf^M
cabeza^F

BALL-PEEN HAMMER
MARTEAU^M À PANNE^F RONDE
HAMMER^M MIT RUNDER BAHN^F
MARTILLO^M DE BOLA^F

ball peen
panne^F ronde
runde Bahn^F
bola^F

NAIL
CLOU^M
NAGEL^M
CLAVO^M

head
tête^F
Kopf^M
cabeza^F

shank
tige^F
Schaft^M
vástago^M

tip
pointe^F
Spitze^F
punta^F

setsquare
équerre^F
Metallwinkel^M
escuadra^F

SCREWDRIVER
TOURNEVIS*M*
SCHRAUBENZIEHER*M*
DESTORNILLADOR*M*

shank
tige*F*
Schaft*M*
vástago*M*

tip
pointe*F*
Schneide*F*
punta*F*

handle
manche*M*
Heft*N*
mango*M*

blade
lame*F*
Klinge*F*
hoja*F*

SPIRAL SCREWDRIVER
TOURNEVIS*M* À SPIRALE*F*
DRILLSCHRAUBENZIEHER*M*
DESTORNILLADOR*M* DE TRINQUETE*M*

ratchet
cliquet*M*
Ratsche*F*
trinquete*M*

spiral
spirale*F*
Spiralspindel*F*
espiral*M*

jaw
mors*M*
Backen*F*
mordaza*F*

handle
poignée*F*
Heft*N*
mango*M*

locking ring
bague*F* de blocage*M*
Feststellring*M*
anillo*M* de ajuste*M*

chuck
mandrin*M*
Backenfutter*N*
mandril*M*

blade
lame*F*
Klinge*F*
hoja*F*

square-headed tip
pointe*F* carrée
Schneide*F* für Imbusschrauben*F*
punta*F* de caja*F* cuadrada (Robertson)

cross-headed tip
pointe*F* cruciforme
Schneide*F* für Kreuzschlitzschrauben*F*
punta*F* de cruz*F* (Phillips)

flat tip
pointe*F* plate
Schneide*F* für Schlitzschrauben*F*
punta*F* de hoja*F* plana

expansion bolt
boulon*M* à gaine*F* d'expansion*F*
Spreizdübel*M*
perno*M* de expansión*F*

TOGGLE BOLT
BOULON*M* À AILETTES*F*
KNEBELBOLZEN*M*
PERNO*M* PARA FALSO PLAFÓN*M*

spring toggle
ailette*F* à ressort*M*
Federflügel*M*
mariposa*F* de resorte*M*

SCREW
VIS*F*
SCHRAUBE*F*
TORNILLO*M*

head
tête*F*
Kopf*M*
cabeza*F*

slot
fente*F*
Schlitz*M*
ranura*F*

shank
fût*M*
Schaft*M*
vástago*M*

thread
filet*M*
Gewinde*N*
rosca*F*

TYPES OF HEAD
TYPES*M* DE TÊTES*F*
KOPFARTEN*F*
TIPOS*M* DE CABEZA*F*

countersunk head
tête*F* plate
Senkkopf*M* mit Schlitz*M*
tornillo*M* de cabeza*F* plana

socket head
tête*F* creuse
Senkkopf*M* mit Imbus*M*
tornillo*M* de caja*F* cuadrada (Robertson)

cross head
tête*F* cruciforme
Senkkopf*M* mit Kreuzschlitz*M*
tornillo*M* de cruz*F* (Phillips)

one way head
tête*F* à sens*M* unique
Sicherungskopf*M*
tornillo*M* de un solo sentido*M*

round head
tête*F* ronde
Rundkopf*M* mit Schlitz*M*
tornillo*M* de cabeza*F* redonda

raised head
tête*F* bombée
Linsenkopf*M* mit Schlitz*M*
tornillo*M* de cabeza*F* achaflanada

PLANE
RABOT^M
HOBEL^M
CEPILLO^M

lateral-adjustment lever
levier^M de réglage^M latéral
Seitenverstellhebel^M
nivelador^M

wedge lever
levier^M du bloc^M
Keilhebel^M
palanca^F de la cuña^F

handle
poignée^F
Griff^M
mango^M

wedge iron
bloc^M d'arrêt^M
Keil^M
cuña^F

front knob
pommeau^M
Nase^F
perilla^F

depth-adjustment mechanism
réglage^M de la profondeur^F
Tiefenverstellschraube^F
tornillo^M elevador

heel
talon^M
hinteres Ende^N
talón^M

face
semelle^F
Sohle^F
base^F

blade
fer^M
Hobeleisen^N
hoja^F

toe
nez^M
Stirn^F
puntera^F

frog-adjustment screw
réglage^M de l'angle^M
Spannschraube^F
ajustador^M de ranilla^F

cap iron
contre-fer^M
Klappe^F
contrahoja^F

HACKSAW
SCIE^F À MÉTAUX^M
BÜGELSÄGE^F
SIERRA^F PARA METALES^M

adjustable frame
monture^F réglable
verstellbarer Bügel^M
marco^M ajustable

grip handle
poignée^F
Griff^M
asa^F

file
lime^F
Flachfeile^F
lima^F

blade
lame^F
Blatt^N
hoja^F

HANDSAW
SCIE^F ÉGOÏNE
FUCHSSCHWANZ^M
SERRUCHO^M

handle
poignée^F
Griff^M
asa^F

blade
lame^F
Sägeblatt^N
segueta^F

back
dos^M
Rücken^M
canto^M

toe
pointe^F
Spitze^F
punta^F

heel
talon^M
hinteres Ende^N
talón^M

tooth
dent^F
Zahn^M
diente^M

SLIP JOINT PLIERS
PINCE^F MOTORISTE
KOMBIZANGE^F
ALICATES^M DE PIVOTE^M MÓVIL

slip joint
joint^M à coulisse^F
Gleitfuge^F
pivote^M móvil

curved jaw
mâchoire^F incurvée
gekrümmte Backe^F
mordaza^F curva

handle
branche^F
Griff^M
mango^M

WATER PUMP PLIERS
PINCE^F MULTIPRISE
ECKROHRZANGE^F
ALICATES^M DE EXTENSIÓN^F

adjustable channel
cran^M de réglage^M
Verstellnut^F
canal^M de ajuste^M

straight jaw
mâchoire^F droite
gerade Backe^F
mordaza^F recta

nut
écrou^M
Mutter^F
tuerca^F

handle
branche^F
Griff^M
mango^M

bolt
boulon^M
Schraube^F
perno^M

MOLE WRENCH
PINCE^F-ÉTAU^M
WASSERPUMPENZANGE^F
ALICATES^M DE PRESIÓN^F

spring
ressort^M
Feder^F
resorte^M

lever
levier^M
Hebel^M
seguro^M

adjusting screw
vis^F de réglage^M
Stellschraube^F
tornillo^M de ajuste^M

toothed jaw
mâchoire^F dentée
Zahnbacke^F
mordaza^F

rivet
rivet^M
Niet^M
remache^M

release lever
levier^M de dégagement^M
Entspannhebel^M
liberador^M del seguro^M

WASHERS
RONDELLES^F
BEILAGSCHEIBEN^F
ARANDELAS^F

flat washer
rondelle^F plate
Beilagscheibe^F
arandela^F simple

spring washer
rondelle^F à ressort^M
Federring^M
arandela^F de presión^F común

internal tooth lock washer
rondelle^F à denture^F intérieure
Sicherungsscheibe^F
arandela^F de presión^F con dientes^M internos

external tooth lock washer
rondelle^F à denture^F extérieure
Zahnscheibe^F
arandela^F de presión^F con dientes^M externo

DO-IT-YOURSELF
REPARACIONES CASERAS

DO-IT-YOURSELF
BRICOLAGE

ADJUSTABLE SPANNER
CLÉ^F À MOLETTE^F
ENGLÄNDER^M
LLAVE^F INGLESA

fixed jaw
mâchoire^F fixe
feste Backe^F
mordaza^F fija

handle
manche^M
Griff^M
mango^M

movable jaw
mâchoire^F mobile
bewegliche Backe^F
mordaza^F móvil

thumbscrew
molette^F
Stellschraube^F
tornillo^M

open-ended spanner
clé^F à fourches^F
Gabelschlüssel^M
llave^F de tuercas^F española

combination spanner
clé^F mixte
Gabel-Ringschlüssel^M
llave^F combinada

flare nut spanner
clé^F polygonale à têtes^F fendues
offener Doppelringschlüssel^M
llave^F de estrías^F abierta

ratchet ring spanner
clé^F à cliquet^M
Ratschenringschlüssel^M
llave^F de estrías^F hexagonal

ring spanner
clé^F polygonale
Ringschlüssel^M
llave^F de estrías^F común

nut
écrou^M
Mutter^F
tuerca^F

cap nut
écrou^M borgne
Hutmutter^F
tuerca^F cerrada

wing nut
écrou^M à oreilles^F
Flügelmutter^F
tuerca^F de mariposa^F

shoulder
épaulement^M
Ansatz^M
collarín^M

SHOULDER BOLT
BOULON^M À ÉPAULEMENT^M
SCHRAUBENBOLZEN^M MIT ANSATZ^M
PERNO^M CON COLLARÍN^M

BOLT
BOULON^M
SCHRAUBENBOLZEN^M
PERNO^M

head
tête^F
Kopf^M
cabeza^F

nut
écrou^M
Mutter^F
tuerca^F

threaded rod
tige^F filetée
Gewindeschaft^M
rosca^F

CARPENTRY: TOOLS
MENUISERIE^F: OUTILS^M
SCHREINEREI^F: WERKZEUGE^N
CARPINTERÍA^F: HERRAMIENTAS^F

ELECTRIC DRILL
PERCEUSE^F **ÉLECTRIQUE**
ELEKTRISCHE BOHRMASCHINE^F
TALADRO^M **ELÉCTRICO**

specification plate
plaque^F signalétique
Typenschild^N
placa^F de especificaciones^F

warning plate
plaque^F d'instructions^F
Sicherheitshinweisschild^N
placa^F de advertencias^F

switch lock
blocage^M de l'interrupteur^M
Feststellknopf^M
seguro^M del interruptor^M

housing
boîtier^M
Gehäuse^N
caja^F

switch
interrupteur^M
Schalter^M
interruptor^M

chuck
mandrin^M
Backenfutter^N
mandril^M

auxiliary handle
poignée^F auxiliaire
zusätzlicher Griff^M
mango^M auxiliar

jaw
mors^M
Backen^F
mordaza^F

pistol grip handle
poignée^F-pistolet^M
Pistolengriff^M
mango^M

cable sleeve
manchon^M de câble^M
Kabelmantel^M
protector^M del cable^M

cable
câble^M
Kabel^N
cable^M de corriente^F

plug
fiche^F
Stecker^M
enchufe^M

HAND DRILL
CHIGNOLE^F
HANDBOHRER^M
TALADRO^M **DE MANO**^F

turning handle
manivelle^F
Kurbel^F
manivela^F

side handle
poignée^F latérale
Seitengriff^M
perilla^F

main handle
poignée^F supérieure
Hauptgriff^M
mango^M

jaw
mors^M
Backe^F
mordaza^F

drive wheel
roue^F d'engrenage^M
Stirnzahnrad^N
cremallera^F

pinion
pignon^M
Kegelzahnrad^N
piñón^M

chuck
mandrin^M
Backenfutter^N
mandril^M

drill bit
foret^M
Bohrer^F
broca^F

BRACE
VILEBREQUIN^M
BOHRWINDE^F
BERBIQUÍ^M

crank
manivelle^F
Bügel^M
arco^M

handle
poignée^F
Drehgriff^M
mango^M

cam ring
anneau^M du cliquet^M
Nockenring^M
leva^F

front knob
pommeau^M
Brustkopf^M
empuñadura^F

jaw
mors^M
Backen^M
mordaza^F

pawl
cliquet^M
Sperrklinke^F
seguro^M

ratchet
rochet^M
Ratsche^F
matraca^F

quill
fourreau^M
Scheide^F
casquillo^M de la empuñadura^F

chuck
mandrin^M
Backenfutter^N
mandril^M

countersink
fraise^F
Versenker^M
broca^F avellanadora

AUGER BIT
MÈCHE^F **HÉLICOÏDALE**
AMERIKANISCHER SCHLANGENBOHRER^M
BROCA^F **SALOMÓNICA DE CANAL**^M **ANCHO**

chuck key
clé^F de mandrin^M
Backenfutterschlüssel^F
llave^F del mandril^M

shank
queue^F
Schaft^M
talón^M

double-twist auger bit
mèche^F double torsade^F
doppelschneckiger Schlangenbohrer^M
broca^F salomónica de canal^M angosto

TWIST DRILL BIT
FORET^M **HÉLICOÏDAL**
SPIRALBOHRER^M
BROCA^F **COMÚN**

shank
queue^F
Schaft^M
talón^M

flute
goujure^F
Spangang^M
canal^M

land
listel^M
Flanke^F
borde^M del lomo^M

single twist
simple torsade^F
einfache Schnecke^F
espiral^F de corte^M

body
corps^M
Bohrkörper^M
cuerpo^M

fluted land
lèvre^F
Kante^F
lomo^M con canal^M

spur
traçoir^M
Vorschneider^M
espolón^M

centring point
pointe^F de centrage^M
Zentrierspitze^F
borde^M de la punta^F

centring point
pointe^F de centrage^M
Zentrierspitze^F
tornillo^M guía

CARPENTRY: TOOLS
MENUISERIE*ᶠ*: OUTILS*ᴹ*
SCHREINEREI*ᶠ*: WERKZEUGE*ᴺ*
CARPINTERÍA*ᶠ*: HERRAMIENTAS*ᶠ*

G-CLAMP
SERRE-JOINTᴹ
ZWINGEᶠ
PRENSAᶠ **EN C**

fixed jaw
mors*ᴹ* fixe
feste Backe*ᶠ*
mordaza*ᶠ* fija

movable jaw
mors*ᴹ* mobile
bewegliche Backe*ᶠ*
mordaza*ᶠ* móvil

swivel head
rotule*ᶠ*
Schwenkkopf*ᴹ*
plato*ᴹ* giratorio

clamping screw
vis*ᶠ* de serrage*ᴹ*
Stellschraube*ᶠ*
tornillo*ᴹ* de ajuste*ᴹ*

throat
gorge*ᶠ*
Öffnung*ᶠ*
boca*ᶠ*

frame
monture*ᶠ*
Rahmen*ᴹ*
bastidor*ᴹ*

handle
levier*ᴹ* de serrage*ᴹ*
Spanngriff*ᴹ*
mango*ᴹ*

VICE
ÉTAUᴹ
SCHRAUBSTOCKᴹ
TORNOᴹ **DE BANCO**ᴹ

movable jaw
mors*ᴹ* mobile
bewegliche Backe*ᶠ*
mordaza*ᶠ* móvil

fixed jaw
mors*ᴹ* fixe
feste Backe*ᶠ*
mordaza*ᶠ* fija

clamping screw
vis*ᶠ* de serrage*ᴹ*
Stellschraube*ᶠ*
tornillo*ᴹ* de ajuste*ᴹ*

swivel lock
blocage*ᴹ* du pivot*ᴹ*
Schwenkverschluß*ᴹ*
seguro*ᴹ* de la base*ᶠ*

handle
levier*ᴹ* de serrage*ᴹ*
Spanngriff*ᴹ*
brazo*ᴹ* de presión*ᶠ*

bolt
boulon*ᴹ*
Bolzen*ᴹ*
perno*ᴹ*

swivel base
semelle*ᶠ* pivotante
Schwenksockel*ᴹ*
base*ᶠ* giratoria

fixed base
socle*ᴹ* fixe
fester Sockel*ᴹ*
base*ᶠ* fija

ROUTER
TOUPIE^F
OBERFRÄSER^M
ACANALADOR^M

head
tête^F
Kopf^M
parche^M

flex sleeve
manchon^M du cordon^M
Kabelmantel^M
protector^M del cable^M

guide handle
poignée^F de guidage^M
Führungsgriff^M
asa^F

collet
collet^M
Anlaufhülse^F
collarín^M

base
base^F
Fuß^M
base^F

motor
moteur^M
Motor^M
motor^M

switch
interrupteur^M
Schalter^M
interruptor^M

depth adjustment
réglage^M de profondeur^F
Tiefeneinstellung^F
ajuste^M de profundidad^F

tool holder
porte-outil^M
Werkzeugfutter^N
mordaza^F

PILLAR DRILL
PERCEUSE^F **À COLONNE**^F
STÄNDERBOHRMASCHINE^F
TALADRO^M **VERTICAL**

drivebelt safety guard
protège-poulie^M
Riementriebabdeckung^F
protector^M de la correa^F

switch
interrupteur^M
Schalter^M
interruptor^M

depth stop
blocage^M de profondeur^F
Tiefenanschlag^M
tope^M de profundidad^F

quill
fourreau^M
Scheide^F
funda^F telescópica

chuck
mandrin^M
Bohrfutter^N
mandril^M

table
plateau^M
Bohrtisch^M
mesa^F

base
socle^M
Fuß^M
base^F

motor
moteur^M
Motor^M
motor^M

feed lever
levier^M de commande^F
Führungshebel^M
brazo^M elevador

table-locking clamp
manette^F de blocage^M du plateau^M
Tischfeststellschraube^F
seguro^M de la mesa^F

column
colonne^F
Ständer^M
pedestal^M

CIRCULAR SAW BLADE
LAME*F* DE SCIE*F* CIRCULAIRE
KREISSÄGEBLATT*N*
DISCO*M*

tooth
dent*F*
Zahn*M*
diente*M*

tip
pointe*F*
Bestückung*F*
punta*F*

CIRCULAR SAW
SCIE*F* CIRCULAIRE
HANDKREISSÄGE*F*
SIERRA*F* CIRCULAR DE MANO*F*

handle
poignée*F*
Griff*M*
asa*F*

trigger switch
interrupteur*M* à gâchette*F*
Druckschalter*M*
interruptor*M* de gatillo*M*

blade
lame*F*
Blatt*N*
disco*M*

height adjustment scale
échelle*F* de profondeur*F*
Höhenverstellskala*F*
escala*F* de altura*F*

upper blade guard
protège-lame*M* supérieur
obere Abdeckhaube*F*
guarda*F* fija del disco*M*

motor
moteur*M*
Motor*M*
motor*M*

blade tilting mechanism
inclinaison*F* de la lame*F*
Schrägstellungsvorrichtung*F*
escala*F* de inclinación*F*

blade tilting lock
blocage*M* de l'inclinaison*F*
Feststellschraube*F* für Schrägstellung*F*
seguro*M* de inclinación*F* del disco*M*

lower guard retracting lever
levier*M* du protège-lame*M* inférieur
Hebel*M* für die untere Abdeckhaube*F*
palanca*F* retractora de la guarda*F*
móvil

lower blade guard
protège-lame*M* inférieur
untere Abdeckhaube*F*
guarda*F* móvil del disco*M*

blade locking bolt
écrou*M* de la lame*F*
Feststellschraube*F* für das Blatt*N*
tornillo*M* de sujeción*F*

knob handle
bouton*M*-guide*M*
Führungsgriff*M*
perilla*F*

rip fence
guide*M* de refend*M*
Parallelanschlag*M*
guía*F* de corte*M*

base plate
semelle*F*
Gleitschuh*M*
soporte*M*

TABLE SAW
PLATEAU^M DE SCIAGE^M
TISCHKREISSÄGE^F
SIERRA^F CIRCULAR DE MESA^F

blade guard
protège-lame^M
Schutzhaube^F
guarda^F del disco^M

table
plateau^M
Arbeitstisch^M
mesa^F

blade
lame^F
Sägeblatt^N
disco^M

mitre gauge slot
rainure^F du guide^M à onglet^M
Führungsnut^F für den Gehrungsanschlag^M
carril^M para el tope^M de ingletes^M

rip fence
guide^M de refend^M
Parallelanschlag^M
guía^F de corte^M

table extension
rallonge^F du plateau^M
Tischverlängerung^F
extensión^F de la mesa^F

rip fence guide
glissière^F du guide^M
Anschlagführung^F
corredera^F de la guía^F

rip fence lock
blocage^M du guide^M
Spannhebel^M
seguro^M de la guía^F

rip fence slot
rainure^F du guide^M de refend^M
Führungsnut^F
ranura^F de corte^M

rip fence rule
règle^F du guide^M de refend^M
Skala^F
regla^F de corte^M

mitre gauge
guide^M à onglet^M
Gehrungsanschlag^M
tope^M de ingletes^M

blade tilting mechanism
inclinaison^F de la lame^F
Schwenkverstellung^F für das Sägeblatt^N
mecanismo^M de indicación del disco^M

switch
interrupteur^M
Schalter^M
interruptor^M

blade height adjustment
relèvement^M de la lame^F
Sägeblatthöhenverstellung^F
mecanismo^M elevador del disco^M

BASIC BUILDING MATERIALS
MATÉRIAUX*M* DE BASE*F*
DIE WICHTIGSTEN BAUMATERIALIEN*N*
MATERIALES*M* BÁSICOS

brick
brique*F*
Ziegelstein*M*
ladrillo*M*

steel
acier*M*
Stahl*M*
acero*M*

stone
pierre*F*
Bruchstein*M*
piedra*F*

prestressed concrete
béton*M* précontraint
Spannbeton*M*
hormigón*M* precomprimido

reinforced concrete
béton*M* armé
Stahlbeton*M*
hormigón*M* armado

concrete block
bloc*M* de béton*M*
Betonblock*M*
bloque*M* de hormigón*M*

COVERING MATERIALS
MATÉRIAUX*M* DE REVÊTEMENT*M*
VERKLEIDUNGSMATERIALIEN*N*
MATERIALES*M* DE REVESTIMIENTO*M*

expanded metal lath
lattis*M* métallique à losanges*M*
metallenes Lattengitter*N*
hoja*F* de lámina*F* diamantada

tile
tuile*F*
Dachziegel*M*
teja*F*

roofing felt
papier*M* goudronné
Teerpappe*F*
papel*M* de brea*F*

shingle
bardeau*M*
Schindel*F*
ripia*F*

gypsum tile
carreau*M* de plâtre*M*
Rigipsplatte*F*
tablero*M* de yeso*M*

plain gypsum lath
lattis*M* de plâtre*M* lisse
ebene Rigipsplatte*F*
hoja*F* de yeso*M* liso

floor tile
carreau*M*
Fliese*F*
baldosa*F*

asphalt shingle
bardeau*M* d'asphalte*M*
Asphaltschindel*F*
teja*F* de asfalto*M*

sprung strip metal insulation
isolant^M de ruban^M métallique
Metallverbindung^F
aislante^M metálico

foam insulation
isolant^M moussé
Bauschaumisolierung^F
aislante^M de espuma^F

moulded insulation
isolant^M en coquille^F
geformte Rohrummantelung^F
aislante^M premoldeado

foam-rubber insulation
isolant^M en caoutchouc^M-mousse^F
Schaumgummiisolierung^F
aislante^M de esponja^F

vinyl insulation
isolant^M en vinyle^M
Vinylisolierung^F
aislante^M vinílico

board insulation
isolant^M en panneau^M
Plattenisolierung^F
tablero^M rígido aislante

pipe-wrapping insulation
isolant^M en ruban^M
Rohrummantelung^F
cinta^F aislante para tubería^F

loose fill insulation
isolant^M en vrac^M
Schüttungsisolierung^F
aislante^M a granel

blanket insulation
isolant^M en rouleau^M
Mattenisolierung^F
rollo^M para recubrimiento^M impermeabilizante

BUILDING MATERIALS
MATÉRIAUX^M DE CONSTRUCTION^F
BAUMATERIALIEN^N
MATERIALES^M DE CONSTRUCCIÓN^F

WOOD
BOIS^M
HOLZ^N
MADERA^F

SECTION OF A LOG
COUPE^F D'UNE BILLE^F
SCHNITT^M DURCH EINEN BAUMSTAMM^M
CORTE^F DE UN TRONCO^M

slab
dosse^F
Schwarte^F
costero^M

log
bille^F
Baumstamm^M
tronco^M

board
planche^F
Brett^N
tabla^F

BOARD
PLANCHE^F
BRETT^N
TABLA^F

face side
parement^M
rechte Seite^F
cara^F

grain
fil^M
Maserung^F
veta^F

end grain
bois^M de bout^M
Hirnholzende^N
cabeza^F

back
contreparement^M
linke Seite^F
dorso^M

edge
rive^F
Kantenfläche^F
canto^M

WOOD-BASED MATERIALS
DÉRIVÉS^M **DU BOIS**^{M}
HOLZWERKSTOFFE^M
LÁMINAS^F **Y TABLEROS**^{M}

ply
pli^M
Sperrholzschichten^F
contrachapado^M

blockboard
panneau^M à âme^F lattée
Stabplatte^F
panel^M de listones^M

multi-ply plywood
contre-plaqué^M multiplis
Mehrschichtsperrholz^N
contrachapado^M múltiple

laminboard
panneau^M à âme^F lamellée
Stäbchenplatte^F
panel^M laminado

waferboard
panneau^M de copeaux^F
Grobspanplatte^F
aglomerado^M

peeled veneer
placage^M déroulé
Schälfurnier^N
chapa^F de madera^F

WOOD-BASED MATERIALS
DÉRIVÉS^M DU BOIS^M
HOLZWERKSTOFFE^M
LÁMINAS^F Y TABLEROS^M

hardboard
panneau^M de fibres^F
Hartfaserplatte^F
tablero^M de fibra^F de madera^F

perforated hardboard
panneau^M de fibres^F perforé
gelochte Hartfaserplatte^F
tablero^M de fibra^F de madera^F perforada

plastic-coated chipboard
panneau^M de particules^F lamifié
kunststoffbeschichtete Hartfaserplatte^F
tablero^M de aglomerado^M con laminado^M
de plástico^M

chipboard
panneau^M de particules^F
Spanplatte^F
tablero^M de aglomerado^M

LOCK
SERRURE^F
SCHLOSS^N
CERRAJERÍA^F

GENERAL VIEW
VUE^F D'ENSEMBLE^M
ÜBERSICHT^F
VISTA^F GENERAL

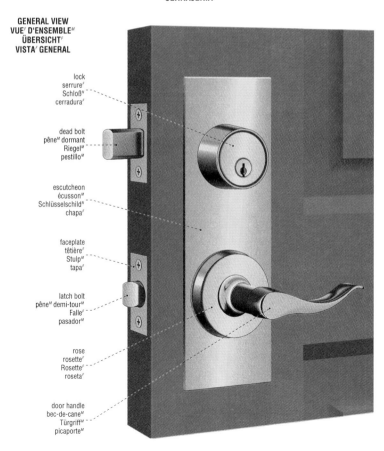

lock
serrure^F
Schloß^N
cerradura^F

dead bolt
pêne^M dormant
Riegel^M
pestillo^M

escutcheon
écusson^M
Schlüsselschild^N
chapa^F

faceplate
têtière^F
Stulp^M
tapa^F

latch bolt
pêne^M demi-tour^M
Falle^F
pasador^M

rose
rosette^F
Rosette^F
roseta^F

door handle
bec-de-cane^M
Türgriff^M
picaporte^M

MORTISE LOCK
SERRURE[F] À MORTAISER
ZYLINDERSCHLOSS[N]
CERRADURA[F] EMBUTIDA

cylinder
barillet[M]
Schließzylinder[M]
cilindro[M]

stator
stator[M]
Stator[M]
estator[M]

key
clé[F]
Schlüssel[M]
llave[F]

spring
ressort[M]
Feder[F]
muelle[M]

rotor
rotor[M]
Rotor[M]
rotor[M]

cotter pin
clavette[F]
Splint[M]
clavija[F] hendida

cylinder case
logement[M] du barillet[M]
Zylindergehäuse[N]
caja[F] del cilindro[M]

keyway
entrée[F] de clé[M]
Schlüsselloch[N]
ojo[M]

dead bolt
pêne[M] dormant
Riegel[M]
pestillo[M]

ring
anneau[M]
Rosette[F]
anillo[M]

faceplate
têtière[F]
Stulp[M]
tapa[F]

strike plate
gâche[F]
Schließblech[N]
cajetín[M]

TUBULAR LOCK
SERRURE[F] TUBULAIRE
EINSTECKSCHLOSS[N] MIT DREH- UND
VERRIEGELUNGSMECHANIK[F]
CERRADURA[F] DE POMO[M] CON SEGURO[M]

outside knob
bouton[M] extérieur
Außenknauf[M]
pomo[M] exterior

threaded sleeve
écrou[M]
Hülsenschraube[F]
tuerca[F]

bolt
boulon[M]
Schraube[F]
perno[M]

spindle
axe[M]
Spindel[F]
eje[M]

rose
rosette[F]
Rosette[F]
roseta[F]

faceplate
têtière[F]
Stulp[M]
tapa[F]

latch bolt
pêne[M] demi-tour[M]
Falle[F]
pasador[M]

inside knob
bouton[M] intérieur
Innenknauf[M]
pomo[M] interior

push-button
poussoir[M]
Druckknopf[M]
seguro[M]

MASONRY
MAÇONNERIE^F
MAUREREI^F
HERRAMIENTAS^F DE ALBAÑIL^M

MASON'S TROWEL
TRUELLE^F DE MAÇON^M
MAURERKELLE^F
PALETA^F DE ALBAÑIL^M

square trowel
truelle^F de plâtrier^M
Putzkelle^F
llana^F

tang
soie^F
Angel^F
espiga^F

handle
manche^M
Griff^M
mango^M

blade
lame^F
Blatt^N
hoja^F

bricklayer's hammer
marteau^M de maçon^M
Maurerhammer^M
martillo^M de albañil^M

hawk
taloche^F
Reibebrett^F
esparavel^M

joint filler
tire-joint^M
Fugenkelle^F
paleta^F de relleno^M

spirit level
niveau^M à bulle^F
Wasserwaage^F
nivel^M de aire^M

CAULKING GUN
PISTOLET^M À CALFEUTRER
KARTUSCHENPISTOLE^F
PISTOLA^F PARA CALAFATEO^M

cartridge
cartouche^F
Kartusche^F
cartucho^M

piston release
dégagement^M du piston^M
Druckstab^M
desenganchador^M

tip
bec^M
Spitze^F
punta^F

piston lever
levier^M du piston^M
Pumpengriff^M
gatillo^M

gun
pistolet^M
Zylinder^M
pistola^F

nozzle
buse^F
Düse^F
boquilla^F

PLUMBING: BATHROOM
PLOMBERIE^F: SALLE^F DE BAINS^M
SANITÄRINSTALLATION^F: BADEZIMMER^N
FONTANERÍA: CUARTO^M DE BAÑO^M

sliding door
porte^F coulissante
Schiebetür^F
puerta^F plegable

shower cubicle
cabine^F de douche^F
Duschkabine^F
cubículo^M de la ducha^F

shower hose
flexible^M
Brauseschlauch^M
manguera^F

portable shower head
douchette^F
Handbrause^F
ducha^F de teléfono^M

overflow
trop-plein^M
Überlauf^M
desagüe^M

shower head
pomme^F de douche^F
Brausenkopf^M
alcachofa^F de la ducha^F

tap
robinet^M
Wasserhahn^M
grifo^M

mirror
miroir^M
Spiegel^M
espejo^M

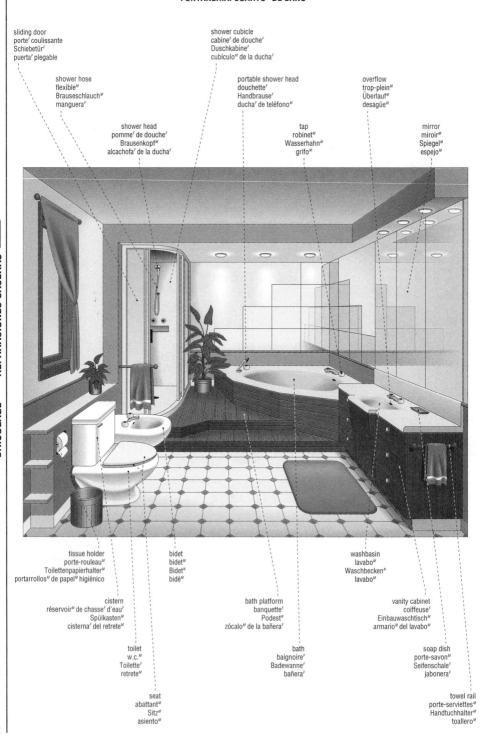

tissue holder
porte-rouleau^M
Toilettenpapierhalter^M
portarrollos^M de papel^M higiénico

bidet
bidet^M
Bidet^N
bidé^M

washbasin
lavabo^M
Waschbecken^N
lavabo^M

cistern
réservoir^M de chasse^F d'eau^F
Spülkasten^M
cisterna^F del retrete^M

bath platform
banquette^F
Podest^N
zócalo^M de la bañera^F

vanity cabinet
coiffeuse^F
Einbauwaschtisch^M
armario^M del lavabo^M

toilet
w.c.^M
Toilette^F
retrete^M

bath
baignoire^F
Badewanne^F
bañera^F

soap dish
porte-savon^M
Seifenschale^F
jabonera^F

seat
abattant^M
Sitz^M
asiento^M

towel rail
porte-serviettes^M
Handtuchhalter^M
toallero^M

flush handle
manette*F* de chasse*F* d'eau*F*
Spülhebel*M*
palanca*F* de la cisterna*F*

overflow pipe
trop-plein*M*
Überlauf*M*
rebosadero*M*

refill pipe
tube*M* de remplissage*M* de la cuvette*F*
Nachfüllrohr*N*
manguera*F* del rebosadero*M*

trip lever
levier*M* de déclenchement*M*
Spülarm*M*
palanca*F* del tapón*M*

float ball
flotteur*M*
Schwimmer*M*
flotador*M*

cistern lid
couvercle*M* de réservoir*M*
Spülkastendeckel*M*
tapa*F* de la cisterna*F*

lift chain
chaînette*F* de levage*M*
Kette*F*
cadenita*F* del tapón*M*

seat cover
couvercle*M*
Klosettdeckel*M*
tapa*F* del retrete*M*

ball-cock supply valve
robinet*M* flotteur à clapet*M*
Schwimmerventil*N*
válvula*F* de entrada*F*

seat
siège*M*
Klosettbrille*F*
asiento*M*

filler pipe
tube*M* de remplissage*M* du réservoir*M*
Füllrohr*N*
tubo*M* de llenado*M*

cistern ball
clapet*M*
Ventil*N*
tapón*M*

valve seat
siège*M*
Ventilsitz*M*
asiento*M* del tapón*M*

conical washer
rondelle*F* conique
Glockendichtung*F*
zapata*F*

cold-water supply
conduite*F* principale
Kaltwasserzulauf*M*
tubería*F* de agua*F* fría

shutoff valve
robinet*M* d'arrêt*M*
Absperrventil*N*
llave*F* de paso*M*

trap
siphon*M*
Geruchsverschluß*M*
sifón*M* inodoro

wax seal
anneau*M* d'étanchéité*F* en cire*F*
Rollring*M*
aislante*M* de cera*F*

toilet bowl
cuvette*F*
Klosettbecken*N*
taza*F*

waste pipe
tuyau*M* de chute*F*
Ablaufrohr*N*
tubo*M* de desagüe*M*

293

PLUMBING
PLOMBERIE^F
SANITÄRINSTALLATION^F
FONTANERÍA^F

BIB TAP
ROBINET^M
WANDAUSLAUFVENTIL^N
GRIFO^M

handle
poignée^F
Handgriff^M
llave^F

packing
presse-étoupe^M
Packung^F
empaquetadura^F

gland nut
écrou^M du presse-étoupe^M
Dichtungsmutter^F
tuerca^F de la empaquetadura^F

spindle
tige^F
Spindel^F
huso^M

washer
rondelle^F
Beilagscheibe^F
arandela^F

jumper valve plate
cuvette^F porte-clapet^M
Ventilteller^M
base^F de la espiga^F

spout
bec^M
Auslauf^M
surtidor^M

washer
clapet^M
Dichtung^F
zapata^F

thread
filetage^M
Gewinde^N
rosca^F

valve seat
siège^F
Ventilsitz^M
asiento^M de la válvula^F

handle
levier^M
Handgriff^M
palanca^F

BALL-TYPE MIXER TAP
MITIGEUR^M **À BILLE**^F **CREUSE**
MISCHBATTERIE^F **MIT KUGELDICHTUNG**^F
GRIFO^M **DE BOLA**^F

spout
bec^M
Auslauf^M
surtidor^M

bonnet
enjoliveur^M
Rosette^F
casquete^M

aerator
aérateur^M
Luftsprudler^M
filtro^M

body
corps^M
Messingkörper^M
cuerpo^M

packing retainer ring
bague^F de fond^M
Dichtungsmutter^F
anillo^M sujetador de la empaquetadura^F

washer
rondelle^F
Dichtung^F
arandela^F

ball assembly
bille^F creuse
Kugelaggregat^N
bola^F

valve seat
siège^M
Ventilsitz^M
asiento^M de la válvula^F

spring
ressort^M
Feder^F
resorte^M

o-ring
joint^M torique
O-Ring^M
junta^F del anillo^M

DISC MIXER
MITIGEUR^M À DISQUE^M
MISCHBATTERIE^F MIT KERAMIKDICHTUNG^F
GRIFO^M DE DISCO^M

handle
levier^M
Handgriff^M
palanca^F

bonnet
enjoliveur^M
Rosette^F
casquete^M

cylinder
cylindre^M
Zylinder^M
cilindro^M

seal
anneau^M d'étanchéité^F
Dichtung^F
zapata^F

spout
bec^M
Auslauf^M
surtidor^M

water inlet
entrée^F d'eau^F
Wasserzulauf^M
entrada^F de agua^F

aerator
aérateur^M
Luftsprudler^M
filtro^M

escutcheon
applique^F du robinet^M
Messingkörper^M
placa^F

CARTRIDGE MIXER
MITIGEUR^M À CARTOUCHE^F
MISCHBATTERIE^F MIT KARTUSCHENDICHTUNG^F
GRIFO^M DE CARTUCHO^M

lever cover
capuchon^M du levier^M
Deckel^M
casquete^M de la palanca^F

lever
levier^M
Handgriff^M
palanca^F

cartridge stem
tige^F
Kartuschenkolben^M
espiga^F del cartucho^M

cartridge
cartouche^F
Kartusche^F
cartucho^M

spout
bec^M
Auslauf^M
surtidor^M

retaining ring
bague^F de serrage^M
Dichtung^F
anillo^M de retención^F

aerator
aérateur^M
Luftsprudler^M
filtro^M

body
corps^M
Messingkörper^M
cuerpo^M

o-ring
joint^M torique
O-Ring^M
junta^F del anillo^M

SINK WITH WASTE DISPOSAL UNIT
ÉVIER[M]-BROYEUR[M]
SPÜLE[F] MIT MÜLLSCHLUCKER[M]
FREGADERO[M] CON TRITURADOR[M] DE BASURA[F]

lever
levier[M]
Hebel[M]
palanca[F]

lever kitchen-tap
mitigeur[M] d'évier[M]
Einhand-Mischbatterie[F]
grifo[M] de cocina[F] de tres vías[F]

spout assembly
bec[M]
Auslaufgarnitur[F]
surtidor[M]

shower head
douchette[F]
Brausenkopf[M]
rociador[M]

escutcheon
applique[F] du robinet[M]
Messingkörper[M]
placa[F]

sink
évier[M]
Spüle[F]
fregadero[M]

compression coupling
raccord[M] à compression[F]
Quetschverschraubung[F]
tuerca[F] de ajuste[M]

strainer body
bonde[F]
Filter[M]
colador[M]

rubber gasket
joint[M] d'étanchéité[F]
Gummiring[M]
junta[F] de goma[F]

locknut
écrou[M] de fixation[F]
Kontermutter[F]
tuerca[F] plana de seguridad[F]

strainer coupling
écrou[M] de bonde[F]
Überwurfmutter[F]
tuerca[F] de ajuste[F]

waste disposal unit
broyeur[M]
Müllschlucker[M]
triturador[M] de basura[F]

supply pipe
tube[M] d'arrivée[F]
Zulauf[M]
tubo[M] de suministro[M] de agua[F]

tailpiece
about[M]
Rohr[N]
cañería[F]

shower hose
flexible[M]
Brauseschlauch[M]
manguera[F]

cleaning eye
bouchon[M] de dégorgement[M]
Reinigungsöffnung[F]
tapón[M] del sifón[M]

cold-water supply
conduite[F] d'eau[F] froide
Kaltwasserzulauf[M]
salida[F] de agua[F] fría

hot-water supply
conduite[F] d'eau[F] chaude
Warmwasserzulauf[M]
salida[F] de agua[F] caliente

trap
siphon[M]
Geruchsverschluß[M]
sifón[M]

trap coupling
écrou[M] à collet[M]
Quetschverschraubung[F]
tuerca[F] de ajuste[F]

shutoff valve
robinet[M] d'arrêt[M]
Absperrventil[N]
llave[F] de paso[M]

GEYSER
CHAUFFE-EAU*M* AU GAZ*M*
GASWARMWASSERBEREITER*M*
CALENTADOR*M* DE GAS*M*

flue hat
dériveur*M* de tirage*M*
Strömungssicherung*F*
caperuza*F*

hot-water outlet
tuyau*M* d'eau*F* chaude
Warmwasseraustritt*M*
salida*F* de agua*F* caliente

insulation
isolant*M*
Isolierung*F*
aislante*M*

anode rod
anode*F*
Opferanode*F*
ánodo*M*

flue
cheminée*F*
Abgas*N*
tubo*M*

outer jacket
enveloppe*F* extérieure
Verkleidung*F*
envoltura*F* metálica

glass-lined tank
cuve*F* vitrifiée
Emaillierung*F*
revestimiento*M* de fibra*F* de vidrio*M*

gas burner
brûleur*M*
Gasbrenner*M*
quemador*M* de gas*M*

drain cock
robinet*M* de vidange*F*
Entleerungsventil*N*
válvula*F* de desagüe*M*

pressure-relief valve
soupape*F* de sûreté*F*
Sicherheitsventil*N*
válvula*F* de presión*F*

overflow pipe
trop-plein*M*
Überlauf*M*
tubo*M* de desagüe*M*

cold-water supply
tuyau*M* d'eau*F* froide
Kaltwasserzulauf*M*
entrada*F* de agua*F* fría

thermostat
thermostat*M*
Thermostat*M*
termostato*M*

reset button
allumage*M* manuel
Zündknopf*M*
botón*M* de seguridad*F*

gas tap
régulateur*M*
Gasventil*N*
llave*F* de gas*M*

control box
boîte*F* de contrôle*M*
Regelgerät*N*
cajita*F* reguladora

temperature control
contrôle*M* de la température*F*
Temperaturregler*M*
control*M* de temperatura*F*

pilot gas tube
canalisation*F* de la veilleuse*F*
Zündgasleitung*F*
tubería*F* para la llama*F* piloto*M*

thermocouple tube
conducteur*M* du thermocouple*M*
Thermoelementkabel*N*
tubo*M* de par*M* térmico

thermocouple
thermocouple*M*
Thermoelement*N*
par*M* térmico

burner gas tube
canalisation*F* du brûleur*M*
Gasrohr*N*
tubo*M* de suministro*M* de gas*M*

WASHING MACHINE
LAVE-LINGE^M
WASCHMASCHINE^F
LAVADORA^F

air chamber
colonne^F d'air^M
Entlüfter^M
cámara^F de aire^M

shutoff valve
robinet^M d'arrêt^M
Absperrventil^N
llave^F de paso^M

flexible rubber hose
tuyau^M souple d'arrivée^F
Gummischlauch^M
manguera^F

cold-water supply
conduite^F d'eau^F froide
Kaltwasserzulauf^M
tubería^F de agua^F fría

tee connector
raccord^M té^M
T-Stück^N
connector^M en T

hot-water supply
conduite^F d'eau^F chaude
Warmwasserzulauf^M
tubería^F de agua^F caliente

washing machine
lave-linge^M
Waschmaschine^F
lavadora^F

standpipe
tuyau^M de chute^F
Standrohr^N
toma^F de aire^M

drain hose
tuyau^M d'évacuation^F
Ablaufschlauch^M
manguera^F de desagüe^M

waste pipe
renvoi^M
Ablaufrohr^N
sifón^M de desagüe^M

DISHWASHER
LAVE-VAISSELLE^M
GESCHIRRSPÜLMASCHINE^F
MÁQUINA^F **LAVAPLATOS**^M

drain hose
tuyau^M de vidange^F
Ablaufschlauch^M
manguera^F de desagüe^M

dishwasher
lave-vaisselle^M
Geschirrspülmaschine^F
máquina^F lavaplatos^M

air chamber
colonne^F d'air^M
Entlüfter^M
cámara^F de aire^M

waste tee connector
raccord^M té^M d'égout^M
Abwasser-T-Stück^N
conector^M en T del desagüe^M

hot-water supply
conduite^F d'eau^F chaude
Warmwasserzulauf^M
tubería^F de agua^F caliente

shutoff valve
robinet^M d'arrêt^M
Absperrventil^N
llave^F de paso^M

hot-water supply
arrivée^F d'eau^F chaude
Warmwasserzulauf^M
tubo^M de suministro^M de agua^F caliente

PLUMBING
PLOMBERIE^F
SANITÄRINSTALLATION^F
FONTANERÍA^F

blowtorch
lampe^F à souder
Lötlampe^F
soplete^M

PLUMBING TOOLS
OUTILS^M POUR PLOMBERIE^F
INSTALLATIONSWERKZEUGE^N
HERRAMIENTAS^F DE FONTANERO^M

pencil point tip
brûleur^M flamme^F crayon^M
Punktbrenner^M
boquilla^F del soplete^M

pipe cutter
coupe-tube^M
Rohrabschneider^M
cortatubos^M

pipe wrench
clé^F à tuyau^M
Einhand-Rohrzange^F
llave^F inglesa

strap wrench
clé^F à sangle^F
Gurtrohrzange^F
llave^F de cincho^M

square-jawed adjustable spanner
clé^F à crémaillère^F
Rollgabelschlüssel^M
llave^F ajustable

chain pipe wrench
clé^F à chaîne^F
Kettenrohrzange^F
llave^F de cadena^F

disposable gas cylinder
cartouche^F jetable
Einwegbrennstoffflasche^F
bombona^F de gas^M

pipe threader
filière^F
Gewindeschneider^M
terraja^F

plumber's snake
furet^M de dégorgement^M
Spirale^F
sonda^F destapacaños^M

tube flaring tool
évaseur^M
Bördelgerät^N
avellanadora^F de tubos^M

plumbing wrench
clé^F coudée à tuyau^M
Standhahnzange^F
llave^F pico^M de ganso^M

plunger
ventouse^F
Ausgußreiniger^M
desatrancador^M

hacksaw
scie^F à métaux^M
Bügelsäge^F
sierra^F para metales^M

valve seat wrench
lève-soupape^M
Ventilsitzzange^F
llave^F de asientos^M de válvula^F

PLUMBING
PLOMBERIE*F*
SANITÄRINSTALLATION*F*
FONTANERÍA*F*

MECHANICAL CONNECTIONS
RACCORDS*M* MÉCANIQUES
MECHANISCHE VERBINDUNGEN*F*
CONEXIONES*F* MECÁNICAS

compression fitting
raccord*M* à compression*F*
Quetschverschraubung*F*
ensamblaje*M* por compresión*F*

pipe A
tube*M* A
Rohr*N* A
tubo*M* A

pipe B
tube*M* B
Rohr*N* B
tubo*M* B

nut
écrou*M*
Mutter*F*
tuerca*F*

connector
raccord*M*
Verschraubung*F*
conector*M*

gasket
garniture*F*
Schneidring*M*
junta*F*

flare joint
raccord*M* à collet*M* repoussé
Bördelverbindung*F*
ensamblaje*M* abocinado

pipe A
tube*M* A
Rohr*N* A
tubo*M* A

pipe B
tube*M* B
Rohr*N* B
tubo*M* B

nut
écrou*M*
Mutter*F*
tuerca*F*

connector
raccord*M*
Verschraubung*F*
conector*M*

pipe end
collet*M* repoussé
Rohrende*N*
extremo*M* abocinado

union
raccord*M* union*F*
Verschraubung*F*
unión*F*

ring nut
écrou*M* de serrage*M*
Ringmutter*F*
anilla*F* de la tuerca*F*

female union nut
raccord*M* femelle
Verschraubungsmutter*F*
tuerca*F* de ajuste*M*

pipe A
tube*M* A
Rohr*N* A
tubo*M* A

male union nut
raccord*M* mâle
Verschraubungsmutter*F*
tuerca*F* de ajuste*M*

gasket
rondelle*F* de fibre*F*
Dichtung*F*
junta*F*

pipe B
tube*M* B
Rohr*N* B
tubo*M* B

TRANSITION FITTINGS
ADAPTEURS^M
ÜBERGÄNGE^M
CONEXIONES^F **DE TRANSICIÓN**^F

steel to plastic
plastique^M et acier^M
Stahl^M auf Kunststoff^M
de acero^M a plástico^M

copper to plastic
plastique^M et cuivre^M
Kupfer^N auf Kunststoff^M
de cobre^M a plástico^M

copper to steel
cuivre^M et acier^M
Kupfer^N auf Stahl^M
de cobre^M a acero^M

FITTINGS
RACCORDS^M
FITTINGS^N
CONEXIONES^F

45° elbow
coude^M à 45°
Winkel^M 45°
codo^M de 45 grados^M

elbow
coude^M
Winkel^M
codo^M de 90 grados^M

U-bend
coude^M à 180°
Doppelbogen^M
conexión^F en U

tee connector
té^M
Strömungs-T^N
conexión^F en T

Y-branch
culotte^F
Abzweig^M 45°
conexión^F en Y

offset
coude^M de renvoi^M
Etagenbogen^M
desviación^F

trap
siphon^M
Siphonwinkel^M
sifón^M

square head plug
bouchon^M mâle sans bourrelet^M
Vierkantstopfen^M
tapón^M macho^M

cap
bouchon^M femelle
Kappe^F
tapón^M

flush bushing
réduction^F mâle-femelle
Muffe^F
boquilla^F de reducir

nipple
mamelon^M double
Nippel^M
boquilla^F

reducing coupling
raccord^M de réduction^F
Reduziermuffennippel^M
reductor^M de calibre^M

threaded cap
bouchon^M femelle à visser
Gewindekappe^F
tapón^M hembra^F

pipe coupling
manchon^M
Rohrverschraubung^F
unión^F

hexagon bushing
réduction^F mâle-femelle hexagonale
Sechskantstopfen^M
boquilla^F de reducir con cabeza^F hexagonal

STEPLADDER
ESCABEAU^M
STEHLEITER^F
ESCALERA^F **DE TIJERA**^F

EXTENSION LADDER
ÉCHELLE^F **COULISSANTE**
AUSZIEHLEITER^F
ESCALERA^F **DE EXTENSIÓN**^F

tool shelf
tablette^F porte-outil^M
Arbeitsbrett^N
bandeja^F para herramientas^F

top
plateau^M
Ablage^F
parte^F superior

step
marche^F
Tritt^M
peldaño^M

rung
échelon^M
Sprosse^F
travesaño^M

side rail
montant^M
Holm^M
larguero^M

step stool
tabouret^M-escabeau^M
Tritthocker^M
escalerilla^F

brace
entretoise^F
Ausklapparretierung^F
tirante^M

pulley
poulie^F
Seilzug^M
polea^F

locking device
dispositif^M de blocage^M
Sprossenarretierung^F
broche^M

PLATFORM LADDER
MARCHEPIED^M
TRITTLEITER^F
ESCALERA^F **DE PLATAFORMA**^F

shelf
tablette^F
Ablagebrett^N
entrepaño^M

safety rail
garde-corps^M
Sicherheitsholm^M
barandilla^F

frame
piètement^M
Gestell^N
armazón^M

platform
plate-forme^F
Plattform^F
plataforma^F

step
marche^F
Stufe^F
peldaño^M

hoisting rope
corde^F de tirage^M
Seil^N
cuerda^F de elevación^F

rubber stopper
embout^M
Gummistöpsel^M
zapata^F de goma^F

anti-slip foot
patin^M antidérapant
Anti-Rutschfuß^M
zapata^F antideslizante

DO-IT-YOURSELF
REPARACIONES CASERAS

DO-IT-YOURSELF
BRICOLAGE

straight ladder
échelle*f* droite
Anlegeleiter*f*
escalera*f* común

loft ladder
échelle*f* escamotable
Dachbodenklappleiter*f*
escalera*f* de guardilla*f*

hook ladder
échelle*f* à crochets*M*
Einhängeleiter*f*
escalera*f* de gancho*M*

rope ladder
échelle*f* de corde*f*
Strickleiter*f*
escalera*f* de cuerda*f*

multi-purpose ladder
échelle*f* transformable
Mehrzweckleiter*f*
escalera*f* para usos*M* múltiples

ladder scaffold
échelle*f* d'échafaudage*M*
Leitergerüst*V*
andamio*M* sobre ruedas*f*

fruit-picking ladder
échelle*f* fruitière
landwirtschaftliche Nutzleiter*f*
escalera*f* de recolección*f* de fruta*f*

rolling ladder
échelle*f* roulante
Rollenleiter*f*
escalera*f* rodante

PAINTING ACCESSORIES
PEINTURE^F D'ENTRETIEN^M
MALERBEDARF^M
HERRAMIENTAS^F PARA PINTAR

SPRAY GUN
PISTOLET^M À PEINTURE^F
SPRITZPISTOLE^F
PISTOLA^F DE PINTAR

spreader adjustment screw
soupape^F de réglage^M du fluide^M
Einstellventil^N für die Strahlbreite^F
válvula^F de ajuste^M

fluid adjustment screw
réglage^M du pointeau^M du fluide^M
Einstellventil^N für die Flüssigkeitsmenge^F
regulador^M de fluidos^M

nozzle
buse^F à fluide^M
Düse^F
boquilla^F

air valve
soupape^F à air^M
Luftventil^N
válvula^F de aire^M

air cap
bouchon^M d'air^M
Lufteinlaß^M
anillo^M de ajuste^M

gun handle
corps^M du pistolet^M
Pistolengriff^M
mango^M

trigger
gâchette^F
Druckabzug^M
gatillo^M

air hose connection
raccord^M d'arrivée^F d'air^M
Luftdruckanschluß^M
conexión^F para la manguera^F de aire^M

vent hole
orifice^F d'aération^F
Entlüftung^F
orificio^M de entrada^F de aire^M

SCRAPER
GRATTOIR^M
SPACHTEL^M
RASPADOR^M

blade
lame^F
Blatt^N
hoja^F

container
godet^M
Behälter^M
depósito^M de pintura^F

knurled bolt
bouton^M moleté
Niet^M
tornillo^M

PAINTBRUSH
PINCEAU^M
STREICHBÜRSTE^F
BROCHA^F

handle
manche^M
Griff^M
mango^M

PAINT ROLLER
ROULEAU^M
FARBROLLER^M
RODILLO^M DE PINTOR^M

tray
bac^M
Wanne^F
bandeja^F de pintura^F

handle
manche^M
Griff^M
mango^M

handle
poignée^F
Griff^M
mango^M

ferrule
virole^F
Stock^M
collar^M

roller frame
armature^F
Walzenbefestigung^F
armazón^M

bristles
soies^F
Borsten^F
cerdas^F

roller sleeve
manchon^M
Walze^F
rodillo^M

SOLDERING AND WELDING
SOUDAGE^M
LÖTEN^N UND SCHWEISSEN^N
SOLDADURA^F

soldering iron
fer^M à souder
Lötkolben^M
hierro^M para soldar

SOLDERING GUN
PISTOLET^M À SOUDER
LÖTPISTOLE^F
PISTOLA^F PARA SOLDAR

tip
panne^F
Lötspitze^F
punta^F

heating element
élément^M chauffant
Heizelement^N
resistencia^F

housing
boîtier^M
Gehäuse^N
caja^F

on-off switch
interrupteur^M
Ein-/Ausschalter^M
interruptor^M

pistol grip handle
poignée^F pistolet^M
Pistolengriff^M
mango^M

flex sleeve
manchon^M du cordon^M
Kabelmantel^M
protector^M del cable^M

ARC WELDING
SOUDAGE^M À L'ARC^M
ELEKTROSCHWEISSEN^N
EQUIPO^M DE SOLDADURA^F ELÉCTRICA

electrode holder
porte-électrode^M
Elektrodenhalter^M
pinza^F del electrodo^M

electrode
électrode^F
Elektrode^F
electrodo^M

electrode lead
câble^M d'alimentation^F de l'électrode^F
Elektrodenkabel^N
cable^M de corriente^F

arc welder
poste^M de soudage^M
Schweißtransformator^M
máquina^F de soldar eléctrica

earth lead
câble^M de masse^F
Massekabel^N
cable^M de tierra^F

earth clamp
prise^F de masse^F
Polzwinge^F
pinza^F de conexión^F a tierra^F

305

SOLDERING AND WELDING
SOUDAGE[M]
LÖTEN[N] UND SCHWEISSEN[N]
SOLDADURA[F]

CUTTING TORCH
CHALUMEAU[M] COUPEUR
SCHWEISSBRENNER[M] MIT SCHNEIDEEINSATZ[M]
SOPLETE[M] DE CORTE[M]

cutting nozzle
tête[F] de coupe[F]
Schneiddüse[F]
boquilla[F] de corte[M]

oxygen control handle
poignée[F]-oxygène[M] de coupe[F]
Brennerhebel[M]
control[M] de oxígeno[M]

oxygen valve
robinet[M] d'oxygène[M]
Sauerstoffventil[N]
válvula[F] de oxígeno[M]

WELDING TORCH
CHALUMEAU[M] SOUDEUR
SCHWEISSBRENNER[M]
SOPLETE[M] DE SOLDADURA[F]
AUTÓGENA

head tube
lance[F]
Schweißeinsatz[M]
cuello[M]

handle
manche[M]
Griff[M]
mango[M]

nozzle
buse[F]
Düse[F]
boquilla[F]

acetylene valve
robinet[M] d'acétylène[M]
Acetylenventil[N]
válvula[F] de acetileno[M]

mixing chamber
chambre[F] de mélange[M]
Mischkammer[F]
cámara[F] de mezcla[F]

OXYACETYLENE WELDING
SOUDAGE[M] OXYACÉTYLÉNIQUE
AUTOGENSCHWEISSEN[N]
EQUIPO[M] DE SOLDADURA[F] AUTÓGENA

trolley
chariot[M]
Flaschenwagen[M]
diablo[M]

pressure regulator
régulateur[M] de pression[F]
Druckregler[M]
regulador[M] de presión[F]

acetylene cylinder
bouteille[F] d'acétylène[M]
Acetylenflasche[F]
tanque[M] de acetileno[M]

oxygen cylinder
bouteille[F] d'oxygène[M]
Sauerstoffflasche[F]
tanque[M] de oxígeno[M]

hose
tuyau[M]
Schlauch[M]
manguera[F]

welding torch
chalumeau[M]
Schweißbrenner[M]
soplete[M]

PRESSURE REGULATOR
RÉGULATEUR[M] DE PRESSION[F]
DRUCKREGLER[M]
REGULADOR[M] DE PRESIÓN[F]

working pressure gauge
manomètre[M] de chalumeau[M]
Arbeitsdruckmesser[M]
manómetro[M] del soplete[M]

cylinder pressure gauge
manomètre[M] de bouteille[F]
Flaschendruckmesser[M]
manómetro[M] del tanque[M]

adjusting screw
vis[F] de réglage[M]
Stellschraube[F]
tornillo[M] de ajuste[M]

check valve
clapet[M] de non-retour[M]
Absperrventil[N]
válvula[F] de freno[M]

DO-IT-YOURSELF
REPARACIONES CASERAS

DO-IT-YOURSELF
BRICOLAGE

DANGER

welding rod
baguette' d'apport"
Schweißstab"
varilla' de relleno"

BUTT WELDING
SOUDAGE" BOUT" À BOUT"
SCHMELZSCHWEISSEN"
SOLDADURA' A TOPE"

metal B
métal" B
Metall" B
placa' metálica B

welding torch
chalumeau" soudeur
Schweißbrenner"
boquilla' del soplete"

weld bead
cordon" de soudure'
Schweißfuge'
soldadura'

metal A
métal" A
Metall" A
placa' metálica A

BLOWTORCH
LAMPE' À SOUDER
LÖTLAMPE'
SOPLETE"

nozzle cleaners
aiguilles' de nettoyage"
Düsenreiniger"
limpiador" de boquillas'

pencil point tip
brûleur" flamme' crayon"
Punktbrenner"
boquilla' para concentrar la llama'

flame spreader
brûleur" bec" plat
Farbabbrennervorsatz"
boquilla' para expandir la llama'

STRIKER
BRIQUET"
ANZÜNDER"
ENCENDEDOR"

disposable gas cylinder
cartouche' jetable
Einweg-Brennstoffflasche'
bombona' de gas"

friction strip
frottoir"
Reibefläche'
frotador"

flint
pierre'
Feuerstein"
pedernal"

solder
soudure'
Lot"
soldadura'

WELDING: PROTECTIVE EQUIPMENT
SOUDAGE*M*: ÉQUIPEMENT*M* DE PROTECTION*F*
LÖTEN*N* UND SCHWEISSEN*N*: SCHUTZKLEIDUNG*F*
SOLDADURA*F*: ACCESORIOS*M* DE PROTECCIÓN*F*

goggles
lunettes*F*
Schutzbrille*F*
anteojos*M* protectores

hand shield
écran*M* à main*F*
Handschild*N*
careta*F* de mano*F*

helmet
casque*M*
Gesichtsschutz*M*
careta*F*

gauntlet
gant*M* à crispin*M*
fünffingriger Schweißerhandschuh*M*
guantes*M*

welding curtain
écran*M* de soudeur*M*
Schutzschirm*M*
biombo*M* para soldar

mitten
moufle*F*
Fausthandschuh*M*
manoplas*F*

ELECTRICITY
ÉLECTRICITÉ^F
ELEKTRIZITÄT^F
ELECTRICIDAD^F

dimmer switch
rhéostat^M
Dimmerschalter^M
conmutador^M de intensidad^F

escutcheon plate
plaque^F de commutateur^M
Schalterabdeckplatte^F
placa^F del interruptor^M

LAMPHOLDER
DOUILLE^F DE LAMPE^F
LAMPENFASSUNG^F
PORTALÁMPARAS^M

cap
capuchon^M
Kappe^F
tapa^F

socket
douille^F
Fassung^F
casquillo^M

electrical box
boîte^F électrique
Buchsenhalter^M
caja^F de conexiones^F

switch
interrupteur^M
Schalter^M
interruptor^M

insulating sleeve
gaine^F isolante
Isolierhülse^F
manga^F de aislamiento^M

three-pin socket
prise^F de courant^M
dreipolige Steckdose^F
enchufe^M

outer shell
enveloppe^F
äußere Hülse^F
cubierta^F

AMERICAN PLUG
FICHE^F AMÉRICAINE
AMERIKANISCHER DREIPOLIGER STECKER^M
ENCHUFE^M DE TIPO^M AMERICANO

pin
lame^F
Spannungsstift^M
pata^F

earthing pin
prise^F de terre^F
Erdungsstift^M
pata^F de conexión^F a tierra^F

terminal
borne^F
Anschlußklemme^F
terminal^M

EUROPEAN PLUG
FICHE^F EUROPÉENNE
STECKER^M
ENCHUFE^M DE TIPO^M EUROPEO

earth terminal
prise^F de terre^F
Erdungsklemme^F
terminal^M de tierra^F

clamp
étrier^M
Zugentlastungsklemme^F
abrazadera^F

pin
broche^F
Stift^M
pata^F

cover
couvercle^M
Kappe^F
tapa^F

ELECTRICIAN'S TOOLS
OUTILS[M] D'ÉLECTRICIEN[M]
ELEKTROINSTALLATEURWERKZEUGE[N]
HERRAMIENTAS[F] DE ELECTRICISTA[M]

tester screwdriver
vérificateur[M] de tension[F]
Spannungsprüfer[M]
detector[M] de tensión[F]

multimeter
multimètre[M]
Multimeter[N]
voltímetro[M]

housing
boîtier[M]
Gehäuse[N]
caja[F]

digital display
afficheur[M] numérique
Digitalanzeige[F]
registro[M] digital

probe
fiche[F]
Meßspitze[F]
varilla[F] de contacto[M]

data hold
mémorisation[F] des données[F]
Meßspeicher[M]
retención[F] de datos[M]

flex
cordon[M]
Meßkabel[N]
cable[M]

auto/manual selector
lecture[F] automatique/manuelle
Auto-Manualumschalter[M]
selección auto/manual

function selection switch
commutateur[M]
Bereichsumschalter[M]
selector[M]

input terminal
borne[F] d'entrée[F]
Eingangsbuchse[F]
terminal[M] de entrada[F]

insulated blade
lame[F] isolée
isolierte Klinge[F]
vástago[M] aislado

insulated handle
manche[M] isolé
isolierter Griff[M]
mango[M] aislado

neon lamp
lampe[F] au néon[M]
Glimmlampe[F]
lámpara[F] de neón[M]

continuity tester
vérificateur[M] de continuité[F]
Durchgangsprüfer[M]
detector[M] de continuidad[F]

inspection light
baladeuse[F]
Handlampe[F]
linterna[F] movible

hook
crochet[M]
Haken[N]
gancho[M]

reflector
réflecteur[M]
Reflektor[M]
reflector[M]

bulb
lampe[F]
Glühbirne[F]
bombilla[F]

guard
grillage[M] de protection[F]
Schutzgitter[N]
reja[F]

convenience outlet
prise[F] de courant[M]
Zusatzsteckdose[F]
enchufe[M]

handle
manche[M]
Griff[M]
mango[M]

flex
cordon[M]
Kabel[N]
cable[M]

socket tester
vérificateur[M] de prise[F] de courant[M]
Steckdosenprüfer[M]
probador[M] de contactos[M] con tierra[F]

test-lamp
vérificateur[M] de circuit[M]
Prüflampe[F]
lámpara[F] de prueba[F] de neón[M]

high-voltage tester
vérificateur[M] de haute tension[F]
Hochspannungsprüfer[M]
detector[M] de alta tensión[F]

multipurpose tool
pince' universelle
Mehrzweckzange'
pinzas' multiuso

pivot
pivot^M
Drehzapfen^M
pivote^M

wire cutter
coupe-fil^M
Drahtschneider^M
cortador^M de alambre^M

wire stripper
dénude-fil^M
Abisolierer^M
pinzas' pelacables

insulated handle
manche^M isolant
isolierter Griff^M
mango^M aislante

hammer
marteau^M d'électricien^M
Hammer^M
martillo^M

fuse puller
pince' à fusible^M
Sicherungszieher^M
extractor^M de fusibles^M

wire stripper
dénudeur^M de fil^M
Kabelabisolierer^M
pelacables^M

combination pliers
pince' d'électricien^M
Kombizange'
alicates^M de electricista'

jaw
mâchoire'
Backen'
mordaza'

wire cutter
coupe-fil^M
Drahtschneider^M
cortador^M de alambre^M

pivot
pivot^M
Drehzapfen^M
pivote^M

insulated handle
manche^M isolant
isolierter Griff^M
mango^M aislante

wire nut
marette'
Kabeltülle'
capuchón^M de plástico^M

cutter
couteau^M d'électricien^M
Messer^N
cuchilla'

adjustment wheel
molette' de réglage^M
Stellschraube'
tornillo^M de ajuste^M

fish wire
câble^M de traction'
Einziehdraht^M
alambre^M en tubo^M

needle-nose pliers
pince' à long bec^M
Spitzzange'
alicates^M

wire stripper
pince' à dénuder
Abisolierzange'
pinzas' pelacables

FUSE BOX
TABLEAU^M DE DISTRIBUTION^F
SICHERUNGSKASTEN^M
CAJETÍN^M DE FUSIBLES^M

240-volt feeder cable
câble^M d'alimentation^F de 240 V
240 V Speisekabel^N
cable^M de alimentación^F de 240 voltios

knockout cable entry
débouchure^F
ausbrechbare Kabeldurchführung^F
agujero^M ciego

bonding terminal
connecteur^M de liaison^F
Verbindungsdraht^M
borne^M de enlace^M

connector
connecteur^M
Durchgangstülle^F
conector^M

main circuit breaker
disjoncteur^M principal
Hauptschalter^M
interruptor^M automático principal

main power cable
fil^M thermique
Leistungskabel^N
cable^M principal

double pole circuit breaker
disjoncteur^M bipolaire
zweipoliger Schalter^M
interruptor^M automático bipolar

single pole circuit breaker
disjoncteur^M unipolaire
einpoliger Schalter^M
interruptor^M automático unipolar

earthing bond
fil^M de liaison^F
Erdungsdraht^M
cable^M de enlace^M

earth fault circuit breaker
disjoncteur^M de fuite^F de terre^F
Stromunterbrecher^M bei
spannungsführendem Nulleiter^M
fusible^M de seguridad^F a tierra^F

240-volt circuit
circuit^M de 240 V
240 V Stromkreis^M
circuito^M de 240 voltios

120-volt circuit
circuit^M de 120 V
120 V Stromkreis^M
circuito^M de 120 voltios

neutral wire
fil^M neutre
Nulleiter^M
cable^M neutro

neutral service wire
fil^M de service^M neutre
Nulleiterverbinder^M
cable^M principal neutro

earth block
barre^F collectrice neutre
Nulleitersammelschiene^F
barra^F ómnibus neutra/a tierra^F

hot bus bar
barre^F collectrice thermique
Spannungssammelschiene^F
barra^F ómnibus de carga^F

terminal
borne^F
Schraubklemme^F
terminal^M

plastic insulator
isolant^M en plastique^M
Kunststoffisolator^M
aislante^M plástico

earth
prise^F de terre^F
Masse^F
cable^M a tierra^F

earth connection
prise^F de terre^F
Erdanschluß^M
cañería^F metálica para agua^F

earth wire
fil^M de terre^F
Erdleitung^F
cable^M a tierra^F

FUSES
FUSIBLES^M
SICHERUNGEN^F
FUSIBLES^M

cartridge fuse
fusible^M-cartouche^F
Patronensicherung^F
fusible^M de cartucho^M

plug fuse
fusible^M à culot^M
Stöpselsicherung^F
fusible^M de rosca^F

knife-blade cartridge fuse
fusible^M-cartouche^F à lames^F
Hauptsicherung^F
fusible^M de bayoneta^F

SUMMARY

**KLEIDUNG
VESTIDO**

**CLOTHING
VÊTEMENTS**

PEPLOS
PÉPLOS*M*
PEPLOS*M*
PEPLO*M*

fibula
fibule*F*
Fibel*F*
fibula*F*

fold
repli*M*
Umschlag*M*
pliegue*M*

TOGA
TOGE*F*
TOGA*F*
TOGA*F*

sinus
sinus*M*
Sinus*M*
seno*M*

purple border
bande*F* de pourpre*F*
Purpursaum*M*
orla*F* de púrpura*F*

justaucorps
justaucorps*M*
Justaucorps*M*
casaca*F*

waistcoat
veste*F*
Weste*F*
chaleco*M*

cuff
parement*M*
Aufschlag*M*
puño*M*

breeches
culotte*F*
Kniehose*F*
calzas*F*

FEATURES OF HISTORICAL COSTUME
ÉLÉMENTS^M DU COSTUME^M ANCIEN
ELEMENTE^N HISTORISCHER KOSTÜME^N
VESTIDURAS^F ANTIGUAS

doublet
pourpoint^M
Wams^N
jubón^M

wing
aileron^M
Achselstück^N
hombrera^F

hanging sleeve
manche^F pendante
Hängeärmel^M
manga^F colgante

trunk hose
haut-de-chausse^M
Pluderhose^F
gregüescos^M

COTEHARDIE
COTARDIE^F
COTARDIE^F
TÚNICA^F DE MANGA^F LARGA

DRESS WITH BUSTLE
ROBE^F À TOURNURE^F
KLEID^N MIT TURNÜRE^F
VESTIDO^M CON POLISÓN^M

floating sleeve
manche^F flottante
Hängeärmel^M
manga^F flotante

vertical pocket
poche^F verticale
senkrechte Tasche^F
bolsillo^M vertical

caraco jacket
caraco^M
Caraco^M
blusa^F caracó

bustle
tournure^F
Turnüre^F
polisón^M

HOUPPELANDE
HOUPPELANDE^F
HOUPPELANDE^F
TOGA^F

frock coat
frac^M
Schoßrock^M
levita^F

waistcoat
gilet^M
Weste^F
chaleco^M

breeches
culotte^F
Kniehose^F
calzas^F

DRESS WITH PANNIERS
ROBE^F **À PANIERS**^M
KLEID^N **MIT FLACHEM REIFROCK**^M
GUARDAINFANTE^M

ruffle
engageante^F
Spitzenvolant^N
manga^F de volante^M

stomacker
pièce^F d'estomac^M
Mieder^N
peto^M

FEATURES OF HISTORICAL COSTUME
ÉLÉMENTS^M DU COSTUME^M ANCIEN
ELEMENTE^N HISTORISCHER KOSTÜME^N
VESTIDURAS^F ANTIGUAS

DRESS WITH CRINOLINE
ROBE^F À CRINOLINE^F
KLEID^N MIT KRINOLINENROCK^M
VESTIDO^M CON MIRIÑAQUE^M

short sleeve
mancheron^M
Ärmelpuff^M
manga^F corta

sleeve
manche^F
Ärmel^M
manga^F

fringe
frange^F
Franse^F
orla^F

hennin
hennin^M
Hennin^M
cofia^F cónica

bicorne
bicorne^M
Zweispitz^M
bicornio^M

tricorne
tricorne^M
Dreispitz^M
tricornio^M

fraise
fraise^F
Halskrause^F
gorguera^F

collaret
collerette^F
kleiner Kragen^M
cuello^M de Holanda

heeled shoe
soulier^M à talon^M
Absatzschuh^M
zapato^M de tacón^M

crakow
soulier^M à la poulaine^F
Schnabelschuh^M
zapato^M a la polaca

MEN'S CLOTHING
VÊTEMENTS^M D'HOMME^M
HERRENKLEIDUNG^F
ROPA^F DE HOMBRE^M

RAINCOAT
IMPERMÉABLE^M
REGENMANTEL^M
IMPERMEABLE^M

collar
col^M
Kragen^M
cuello^M

notched lapel
revers^M cranté
abfallendes Revers^N
solapa^F con ojal^M

raglan sleeve
manche^F raglan
Raglanärmel^M
manga^F ranglán

broad welt side pocket
poche^F raglan
Raglantasche^F
bolsillo^M de ribete^M ancho

tab
patte^F
Spange^F
lengüeta^F

buttonhole
boutonnière^F
Knopfloch^N
ojal^M

side panel
pan^M
Seitenteil^N
paño^M lateral

TRENCH COAT
TRENCH^M
TRENCHCOAT^M
TRINCHERA^F

two-way collar
col^M transformable
transformabler Kragen^M
cuello^M de doble vista^F

epaulet
patte^F d'épaule^F
Schulterklappe^F
hombrera^F

gun flap
bavolet^M
Koller^M
protector^M

raglan sleeve
manche^F raglan
Raglanärmel^M
manga^F ranglán

double-breasted buttoning
double boutonnage^M
zweireihig
botonadura^F cruzada

belt
ceinture^F
Gürtel^M
cinturón^M

sleeve strap
patte^F de serrage^M
Ärmellasche^F
correa^F de la manga^F

sleeve strap loop
passant^M
Riegel^M
presilla^F de la manga^F

belt loop
passant^M
Gürtelschlaufe^F
presilla^F del cinturón^M

broad welt side pocket
poche^F raglan
Raglantasche^F
bolsillo^M de ribete^M ancho

buckle
boucle^F de ceinture^F
Schnalle^F
hebilla^F

DUFFLE COAT
DUFFLE-COAT^M
DUFFLECOAT^M
TRENCA^F

hood
capuchon^M
Kapuze^F
capucha^F

yoke
empiècement^M
Sattel^M
hombrillo^M

frog
brandebourg^M
Lasche^F
alamar^M

OVERCOAT
PARDESSUS^M
MANTEL^M
ABRIGO^M

notched lapel
revers^M cranté
abfallendes Revers^N
solapa^F con ojal^M

breast pocket
poche^F poitrine^F
Brusttasche^F
bolsillo^M superior

breast dart
pince^F de taille^F
Taillenabnäher^M
pinza^F

patch pocket
poche^F plaquée
aufgesetzte Tasche^F
bolsillo^M de parche^M

toggle
bûchette^F
Knebelverschluß^M
botón^M de madera^F

WINDCHEATER
BLOUSON^M LONG
WINDJACKE^F
CAZADORA^F

waistband
ceinture^F montée
Bund^M
pretina^F

drawstring
cordon^M coulissant
Durchziehschnur^F
cordón^M

flap pocket
poche^F à rabat^M
Klappentasche^F
bolsillo^M con cartera^F

three-quarter coat
paletot^M
dreiviertellanger Mantel^M
abrigo^M de tres cuartos

PARKA
PARKA^F
PARKA^M
PARKA^M

zip fastener
fermeture^F à glissière^F
Reißverschluß^M
cremallera^F

snap-fastening tab
patte^F à boutons^M-pression^F
Druckknopfleiste^F
corchete^M de presión^F

WINDCHEATER
BLOUSON^M **COURT**
WINDJACKE^F
CAZADORA^F

snap fastener
bouton^M-pression^F
Druckknopf^M
broche^F de presión^F

sheepskin jacket
canadienne^F
Lammfelljacke^F
zamarra^F

hand-warmer pocket
poche^F repose-bras^M
Mufftasche^F
bolsillo^M de ojal^M

elastic waistband
ceinture^F élastique
elastischer Bund^M
pretina^F elástica

DOUBLE-BREASTED JACKET
VESTON^M CROISÉ
ZWEIREIHER^M
CHAQUETA^F CRUZADA

lining
doublure^F
Futter^N
forro^M

peaked lapel
revers^M à cran^M aigu
steigendes Revers^N
solapa^F puntiaguda

collar
col^M
Kragen^M
cuello^M

breast welt pocket
pochette^F
Brustleistentasche^F
bolsillo^M de ojal^M

sleeve
manche^F
Ärmel^M
manga^F

flap
rabat^M
Klappe^F
solapa^F

outside ticket pocket
poche^F-ticket^M
Billettasche^F
bolsillo^M del cambio^M

V-neck
encolure^F en V
V-Ausschnitt^M
cuello^M en V

patch pocket
poche^F plaquée
aufgesetzte Tasche^F
bolsillo^M de parche^M

side back vent
fente^F latérale
seitlicher Rückenschlitz^M
abertura^F trasera lateral

WAISTCOAT
GILET^M
WESTE^F
CHALECO^M

lining
doublure^F
Futter^N
forro^M

welt
patte^F
Patte^F
ribete^M

front
devant^M
Vorderseite^F
delantero^M

seaming
découpe^F
Teilungsnaht^F
costura^F

welt pocket
poche^F gilet^M
Leistentasche^F
bolsillo^M de ribete^M

adjustable waist tab
tirant^M de réglage^M
Rückenspange^F
lengüeta^F ajustable del talle^M

SINGLE-BREASTED JACKET
VESTE^F DROITE
EINREIHER^M
CHAQUETA^F

lining
doublure^F
Futter^N
forro^M

notch
cran^M
Crochetwinkel^M
muesca^F

pocket handkerchief
pochette^F
Einstecktuch^N
pañuelo^M de bolsillo^M

lapel
revers^M
Revers^N
solapa^F

back
dos^M
Rücken^M
espalda^F

sleeve
manche^F
Ärmel^M
manga^F

front
devant^M
Vorderseite^F
delantero^M

flap pocket
poche^F tiroir^M
Klappentasche^F
bolsillo^M con cartera^F

centre back vent
fente^F médiane
Rückenmittelschlitz^M
abertura^F trasera central

BELT
CEINTUREᶠ
GÜRTELᴹ
CINTURÓNᴹ

top stitching
surpiqûreᶠ
Zier-Steppnahtᶠ
sobrepespunteᴹ

buckle
boucleᶠ de ceintureᶠ
Schnalleᶠ
montura de la hebillaᶠ

tip
capucinᴹ
Gürtelspitzeᶠ
puntaᶠ

punch hole
cranᴹ
gestanztes Lochᴺ
ojeteᴹ

panel
croûteᶠ de cuirᴹ
Gürtelbandᴺ
cueroᴹ

tongue
ardillonᴹ
Dornᴹ
pasadorᴹ

belt loop
passantᴹ
Gürtelschlaufeᶠ
presillaᶠ

buckle
boucleᶠ
Gürtelschnalleᶠ
hebillaᶠ

BRACES
BRETELLESᶠ
HOSENTRÄGERᴹ
TIRANTESᴹ

TROUSERS
PANTALONᴹ
HOSEᶠ
PANTALONESᴹ

waistband
ceintureᶠ montée
Hosenbundᴹ
pretinaᶠ

belt loop
passantᴹ tunnelᴹ
Gürtelschlaufeᶠ
trabilla

elastic webbing
bandeᶠ élastique
Gummibandᴺ
bandaᶠ elástica

front top pocket
pocheᶠ cavalière
Flügeltascheᶠ
bolsilloᴹ delantero

adjustment slide
coulisseᶠ
Verstellerᴹ
corredera de ajusteᴹ

waistband extension
patteᶠ boutonnée
Bundverlängerungᶠ
traslapeᴹ de la pretinaᶠ

fly
braguetteᶠ
Hosenschlitzᴹ
braguetaᶠ

knife pleat
pliᴹ plat
einfache Falteᶠ
pinzaᶠ

leather end
patteᶠ
Lederstrippeᶠ
lengüeta de cueroᴹ

brace clip
pinceᶠ
Klipsᴹ
pinzaᶠ

button loop
boutonnièreᶠ
Knopflascheᶠ
presillaᶠ

crease
pliᴹ
Bügelfalteᶠ
rayaᶠ

back pocket
pocheᶠ-revolverᴹ
Gesäßtascheᶠ
bolsilloᴹ trasero

turn-up
reversᴹ
Aufschlagᴹ
vueltaᶠ

323

MEN'S CLOTHING
VÊTEMENTS^M D'HOMME^M
HERRENKLEIDUNG^F
ROPA^F DE HOMBRE^M

SHIRT
CHEMISE^F
HEMD^N
CAMISA^F

yoke
empiècement^M
Sattel^M
canesú^M

set-in sleeve
manche^F montée
eingesetzter Ärmel^M
manga^F empotrada

collar
col^M
Kragen^M
cuello^M

breast pocket
poche^F poitrine^F
Brusttasche^F
bolsillo^M superior

collar point
pointe^F de col^M
Kragenspitze^F
punta^F del cuello^M

button facing
patte^F de boutonnage^M
Knopfleiste^F
aletilla^F

front^M
devant^M
Vorderseite^F
delantero^M

pointed tab end
patte^F capucin^M
Ärmelschlitz^M
abertura^F con aletilla^F

button
bouton^M
Knopf^M
botón^M

cuff
poignet^M
Manschette^F
puño^M

shirttail
pan^M
Schoß^M
faldón^M de la camisa^F

buttondown collar
col^M pointes^F boutonnées
Button-down-Kragen^M
cuello^M con botones^M

cravat
lavallière^F
Krawattenschal^M
corbata^F inglesa

spread collar
col^M italien
gespreizter Kragen^M
cuello^M italiano

collar stiffener
baleine^F de col^M
Kragenstäbchen^N
ballena^F

bow tie
nœud^M papillon^M
Fliege^F
pajarita^F

NECKTIE
CRAVATE^F
KRAWATTE^F
CORBATA^F

front apron
pan^M avant
Vorderteil^N
faldón^M delantero

neck end
tour^M de cou^M
Bindeteil^N
contorno^M del cuello^M

rear apron
pan^M arrière
Endteil^N
faldón^M trasero

lining
doublure^F
Futter^N
forro^M

loop
passant^M
Schlaufe^F
presilla^F

slip-stitched seam
couture^F médiane
Verziehnaht^F
costura^F invisible

KLEIDUNG VESTIDO

CLOTHING VÊTEMENTS

vest
gilet*ᴹ* athlétique
Trägerhemd*ᴺ*
camiseta*ᶠ*

neckhole
encolure*ᶠ*
Halsausschnitt*ᴹ*
cuello*ᴹ*

armhole
emmanchure*ᶠ*
Armausschnitt*ᴹ*
sisa*ᶠ*

combinations
combinaison*ᶠ*
Hemdhose*ᶠ*
pijama*ᶠ* de una pieza*ᶠ*

briefs
slip*ᴹ* ouvert
Slip*ᴹ*
calzoncillos*ᴹ*

waistband
ceinture*ᶠ* élastique
Bündchen*ᴺ*
pretina*ᶠ* elástica

fly
braguette*ᶠ*
Schlitz*ᴹ*
bragueta*ᶠ*

elasticized leg opening
jambe*ᶠ* élastique
elastischer Beinausschnitt*ᴹ*
pierna*ᶠ* elástica

crotch
enfourchure*ᶠ*
Schritt*ᴹ*
entrepierna*ᶠ*

long johns
caleçon*ᴹ* long
lange Unterhose*ᶠ*
calzoncillos*ᴹ* largos

mini briefs
mini-slip*ᴹ*
Minislip*ᴹ*
calzoncillos*ᴹ*

boxer shorts
caleçon*ᴹ*
Boxershorts*ᶠ*
calzoncillos*ᴹ*

SOCKS
CHAUSSETTESᶠ
SOCKENᶠ
CALCETINESᴹ

knee-length sock
mi-bas*ᴹ*
Kniestrumpf*ᴹ*
largo*ᴹ* ejecutivo

straight-up ribbed top
bord*ᴹ*-côte*ᶠ*
gerades Rippenbündchen*ᴺ*
tirilla*ᶠ* elástica

mid-calf length sock
chaussette*ᶠ*
Wadenstrumpf*ᴹ*
largo*ᴹ* a media pantorrilla*ᶠ*

leg
jambe*ᶠ*
Bein*ᴺ*
pierna*ᶠ*

ankle sock
mi-chaussette*ᶠ*
Knöchelsocke*ᶠ*
largo*ᴹ* al tobillo*ᴹ*

heel
talon*ᴹ*
Ferse*ᶠ*
talón*ᴹ*

foot
pied*ᴹ*
Fuß*ᴹ*
empeine*ᴹ*

sole
semelle*ᶠ*
Sohle*ᶠ*
planta*ᶠ*

toe
pointe*ᶠ*
Spitze*ᶠ*
punta*ᶠ*

V-NECK CARDIGAN
GILET^M **DE LAINE**^F
STRICKJACKE^F **MIT V-AUSSCHNITT**^M
JERSEY^M **DE CUELLO**^M **EN V**

hanger loop
bride^F de suspension^F
Aufhänger^M
trabilla^F de suspensión^F

set-in sleeve
manche^F montée
eingesetzter Ärmel^M
manga^F empotrada

V-neck
encolure^F en V
V-Ausschnitt^M
cuello^M de pico^M

button
bouton^M
Knopf^M
botón^M

ribbing
bord^M-côte^F
Patentrand^M
tirilla^F elástica

welt pocket
poche^F passepoilée
Paspeltasche^F
bolsillo^M

polo-neck sweater
col^M roulé
Rollkragenpullover^M
jersey^M de cuello^M de tortuga^F

KNIT SHIRT
POLO^M
STRICKHEMD^N
POLO^M

button facing
patte^F polo^M
Knopfleiste^F
aletilla^F

crew neck sweater
ras-de-cou^M
kragenloser Pullover^M
jersey^M de cuello^M redondo

slipover
débardeur^M
Pullunder^M
chaleco^M de punto^M

cardigan
cardigan^M
Strickjacke^F
chaqueta^F de punto^M

GLOVES
GANTS*M*
HANDSCHUHE*M*
GUANTES*M*

thumb
pouce*M*
Daumen*M*
pulgar*M*

fourchette
fourchette*F*
Keil*M*
horquilla*F*

glove finger
doigt*M*
Finger*M*
dedo*M*

palm
paume*F*
Innenfläche*F*
palma*F*

snap fastener
bouton*M*-pression*F*
Druckknopf*M*
broche*M* de presión*F*

stitching
baguette*F*
Ziernaht*F*
sobrepespunte*M*

seam
couture*F* d'assemblage*M*
Naht*F*
costura*F*

DRIVING GLOVE
GANT*M* DE CONDUITE*F*
AUTOHANDSCHUH*M*
GUANTE*M* PARA CONDUCIR

perforation
perforation*M*
Perforierung*F*
perforaciones*F*

opening
fenêtre*F*
Öffnung*F*
aberturas*F* para los nudillos*M*

FINGERLESS MITT
MITAINE*F*
FINGERLOSER SPITZENHANDSCHUH*M*
MITÓN*M* SIN DEDOS*M*

gauntlet
rebras*M*
Stulpe*F*
brazo*M*

mitten
moufle*F*
Fäustling*M*
manopla*F*

evening glove
gant*M* long
langer Abendhandschuh*M*
guante*M* de brazo*M* largo

wrist-length glove
gant*M* saxe
Langhandschuh*M*
guante*M* a la muñeca*F*

gauntlet
gant*M* à crispin*M*
Stulpenhandschuh*M*
manopla*F*

short glove
gant*M* court
Kurzhandschuh*M*
guante*M* corto

TRILBY
CHAPEAU^M DE FEUTRE^M
FILZHUT^M
SOMBRERO^M DE FIELTRO^M

crown
calotte^F
Kopfteil^M
copa^F

hatband
bourdalou^M
Hutband^N
cinta^F

brim
bord^M
Krempe^F
ala^F

binding
galon^M
Einfaßband^N
ribete^M

bow
nœud^M plat
Schleife^F
lazo^M

boater
canotier^M
Strohhut^M
canotier^M

top hat
haut-de-forme^M
Zylinder^M
chistera^F

bowler
melon^M
Melone^F
sombrero^M de hongo^M

KLEIDUNG
VESTIDO

CLOTHING
VÊTEMENTS

HUNTING CAP
CASQUETTE^F NORVÉGIENNE
JAGDKAPPE^F
GORRA^F NORUEGA

ear flap
cache-oreilles^M abattant
Ohrschützer^M
orejera^F

shapka
chapka^M
Kosakenmütze^F
chapka^F

CAP
CASQUETTE^F
SCHIRMMÜTZE^F
GORRA^F

crown
calotte^F
Kopfteil^M
copa^F

peak
visière^F
Mützenschirm^M
visera^F

panama
panama^M
Panamahut^M
panamá^M

astrakhan cap
calot^M
Fellmütze^F
gorra^F de cuartel^M

skullcap
calotte^F
Käppchen^N
casquete^M

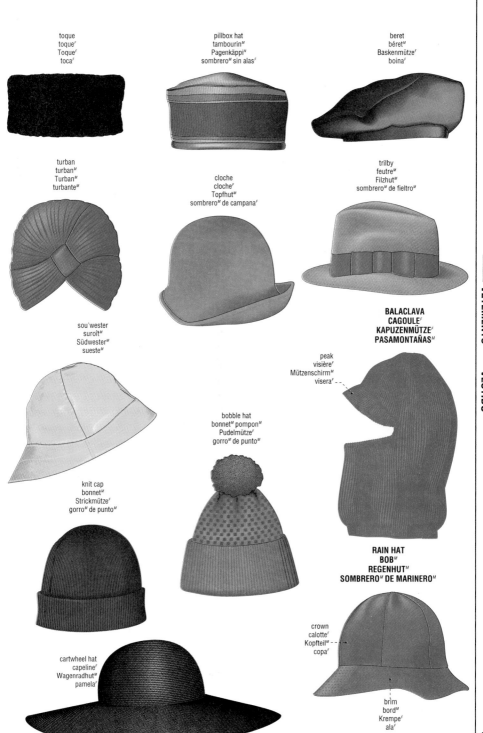

toque
toque^F
Toque^F
toca^F

pillbox hat
tambourin^M
Pagenkäppi^N
sombrero^M sin alas^F

beret
béret^M
Baskenmütze^F
boina^F

turban
turban^M
Turban^M
turbante^M

cloche
cloche^F
Topfhut^M
sombrero^M de campana^F

trilby
feutre^M
Filzhut^M
sombrero^M de fieltro^M

sou'wester
suroît^M
Südwester^M
sueste^M

**BALACLAVA
CAGOULE^F
KAPUZENMÜTZE^F
PASAMONTAÑAS^M**

peak
visière^F
Mützenschirm^M
visera^F

bobble hat
bonnet^M pompon^M
Pudelmütze^F
gorro^M de punto^M

knit cap
bonnet^M
Strickmütze^F
gorro^M de punto^M

**RAIN HAT
BOB^M
REGENHUT^M
SOMBRERO^M DE MARINERO^M**

crown
calotte^F
Kopfteil^M
copa^F

cartwheel hat
capeline^F
Wagenradhut^M
pamela^F

brim
bord^M
Krempe^F
ala^F

TYPES OF COAT
TYPES^M DE MANTEAUX^M
MANTELARTEN^F
ABRIGOS^M Y CHAQUETAS^F

car coat
paletot^M
Autocoat^M
chaquetón^M

pea jacket
caban^M
Caban^M
chaquetón^M marinero

tailored collar
col^M tailleur^M
Schneiderkragen^M
cuello^M hechura^F sastre^M

hand warmer pocket
poche^F repose-bras^M
Mufftasche^F
bolsillo^M de ojal^M

mock pocket
fausse poche^F
falsche Tasche^F
bolsillo^M simulado

raglan
raglan^M
Raglanmantel^M
abrigo^M corto

back belt
martingale^F
Rückengürtel^M
cinturón^M trasero^M

pelerine
pèlerine^F
Pelerine^F
abrigo^M con esclavina^F

raglan sleeve
manche^F raglan
Raglanärmel^M
manga^F ranglán

pelerine
pèlerine^F
Pelerine^F
esclavina^F

fly front closing
boutonnage^M sous patte^F
verdeckte Knopfleiste^F
pestaña^F

broad welt side pocket
poche^F raglan
schräge Pattentasche^F
bolsillo^M de ribete^M ancho

seam pocket
poche^F prise dans une couture^F
Nahttasche^F
bolsillo^M disimulado

KLEIDUNG
VESTIDO

CLOTHING
VÊTEMENTS

cape
cape^F
Cape^N
capa^F

overcoat
manteau^M
Mantel^M
abrigo^M

riding coat
redingote^F
Redingote^F
abrigo^M cruzado

arm slit
passe-bras^M
Durchgrifftasche^F
abertura^F para el brazo^M

poncho
poncho^M
Poncho^M
poncho^M

suit
tailleur^M
Kostüm^N
traje^M

jacket
veste^F
Jacke^F
chaqueta^F

jacket
veste^F
Blazer^M
chaquetón^M

skirt
jupe^F
Rock^M
falda^F

TYPES OF DRESS
TYPES^M DE ROBES^F
KLEIDERARTEN^F
TIPOS^M DE VESTIDO^M

sheath dress
robe^F fourreau^M
Schlauchkleid^N
recto entallado

princess dress
robe^F princesse^F
Prinzeßkleid^N
corte^M princesa^F

coat dress
robe^F-manteau^M
Mantelkleid^N
vestido^M abrigo

drop waist dress
robe^F taille^F basse
Kleid^N mit angesetztem Schoß^M
de talle^M largo

trapeze dress
robe^F trapèze^M
Trapez-Form^F
de campana^F

sundress
robe^F bain^M-de-soleil^M
Trägerkleid^N
de verano^M

KLEIDUNG
VESTIDO

CLOTHING
VÊTEMENTS

332

polo dress
robe*-polo*
Polokleid*
de camiseta*

house dress
robe* de maison*
Hauskleid*
casero

shirtwaist dress
robe* chemisier*
Hemdblusenkleid*
camisero*

pinafore
chasuble*
Kleiderrock*
pichi*

wrapover dress
robe* enveloppe*
Wickelkleid*
cruzado

tunic dress
robe* tunique*
Tunikakleid*
túnica*

TYPES OF SKIRT
TYPES^M **DE JUPES**^F
ROCKARTEN^F
TIPOS^M **DE FALDA**^F

yoke skirt
jupe^F à empiècement^M
Sattelrock^M
de campana^F

gored skirt
jupe^F à lés^M
Bahnenrock^M
de piezas^F

sheath skirt
jupe^F fourreau^M
Etuirock^M
falda^F de tubo^M

ruffled skirt
jupe^F à volants^M étagés
Stufenrock^M
de volantes^M

sarong
paréo^M
Sarong^M
sarong^M malayo

wrapover skirt
jupe^F portefeuille^M
Wickelrock^M
cruzada

straight skirt
jupe^F droite
gerader Rock^M
recta

culottes
jupe^F-culotte^F
Hosenrock^M
falda^F pantalón^M

KLEIDUNG
VESTIDO

CLOTHING
VÊTEMENTS

kilt
kilt^M
Schottenrock^M
escocesa

gather skirt
jupe^F froncée
Kräuselrock^M
fruncida

inverted pleat
pli^M creux
Kellerfalte^F
tablón^M delantero

kick pleat
pli^M d'aisance^F
Gehfalte^F
tabla^F abierta

TYPES OF PLEAT
TYPES^M DE PLIS^M
FALTENARTEN^F
TIPOS^M DE PLIEGUE^M

accordion pleat
plissé^M accordéon^M
Bahnenplissee^N
plisada

knife pleat
pli^M plat
einfache Falte^F
tablas^F

top stitched pleat
pli^M surpiqué
abgesteppte Falte^F
sobrepespunteada^F

WOMEN'S CLOTHING
VÊTEMENTS^M DE FEMME^F
DAMENKLEIDUNG^F
ROPA^F DE MUJER^F

TYPES OF TROUSERS
TYPES^M DE PANTALONS^M
HOSENARTEN^F
PANTALONES^M

jeans
jean^M
Jeans^F
vaqueros^M

Bermuda shorts
bermuda^M
Bermudashorts^F
bermudas^M

shorts
short^M
Shorts^F
pantalón^M corto

ski pants
fuseau^M
Steghose^F
pantalones^M de tubo^M

knickerbockers
knicker^M
Kniebundhose^F
bombachos^M

pedal pushers
corsaire^M
Caprihose^F
pescadores^M

footstrap
sous-pied^M
Steg^M
trabilla^F

jumpsuit
combinaison^F-pantalon^M
Overall^M
traje^M pantalón^M

dungarees
salopette^F
Latzhose^F
mono^M

bell bottoms
pantalon^M pattes^F d'éléphant^M
Schlaghose^F
acampanado

CLOTHING
VÊTEMENTS

336

classic blouse
chemisier^M classique
klassische Bluse^F
camisera clásica

sailor tunic
marinière^F
Matrosenbluse^F
marinera

polo shirt
polo^M
Polohemd^N
camiseta^F

button-through smock
tablier^M-blouse^F
Kittelbluse^F
blusón^M

yoke
empiècement^M
Sattel^M
canesú^M

gather
fronce^F
Kräuselfalte^F
fruncido^M

smock
tunique^F
Arbeitskittel^M
blusón^M con aletilla^F

wrapover top
cache-cœur^M
Wickelbluse^F
blusa^F cruzada

overshirt
liquette^F
Hosenbluse^F
camisa^F

body shirt
corsage^M-culotte^F
Bodyshirt^N
pantiblusa^F

tunic
casaque^F
Tunika^F
túnica^F

shirttail
pan^M
Schoß^M
faldón^M

crotch piece
patte^F d'entrejambe^M
Schritt^M
entrepierna^F

WAISTCOATS AND JACKETS
VESTES^F ET PULLS^M
WESTEN^F UND JACKEN^F
CHALECOS^M, JERSEYS^M Y CHAQUETAS^F

safari jacket
saharienne^F
Safarijacke^F
cazadora^F

gusset pocket
poche^F soufflet^M
Blasebalgtasche^F
bolsillo^M de fuelle^M

blazer
blazer^M
Blazer^M
americana^F

spencer
spencer^M
Spenzer^M
bolero^M con botones^M

bolero
boléro^M
Bolero^M
bolero^M

waistcoat
gilet^M
Weste^F
chaleco^M

twin-set
tandem^M
Twinset^N
jerseys^M combinados

polo neck
col^M roulé
Rollkragen^M
de tortuga^F

V-neck cardigan
gilet^M de laine^F
Strickjacke^F mit V-Ausschnitt^M
jersey^M abierto de cuello^M en V

inset pocket
poche^F prise dans une découpe^F
eingesetzte Tasche^F
simulado

seam pocket
poche^F prise dans une couture^F
Nahttasche^F
bolsillo^M disimulado

broad welt side pocket
poche^F raglan
Raglantasche^F
de ojal^M con ribete^M

hand warmer pouch
poche^F manchon^M
Mufftasche^F
de manguito^M

gusset pocket
poche^F soufflet^M
Blasebalgtasche^F
de fuelle^M

flap pocket
poche^F à rabat^M
Klappentasche^F
bolsa^F de parche^M con cartera^F

patch pocket
poche^F plaquée
aufgesetzte Tasche^F
de parche^M

welt pocket
poche^F passepoilée
Paspeltasche^F
de ojal^M de sastre^M

French cuff
poignet^M mousquetaire^M
Doppelmanschette^F
puño^M para gemelos^M

pointed tab end
patte^F capucin^M
Ärmelschlitz^M
aletilla^F

cuff link
bouton^M de manchette^F
Manschettenknopf^M
gemelos^M

three-quarter sleeve
manche^F trois-quarts
Dreiviertelarm^M
recta de tres cuartos^M

batwing sleeve
manche^F chauve-souris^F
Fledermausärmel^M
de murciélago^M

cap sleeve
mancheron^M
angeschnittener Ärmel^M
corta sencilla

TYPES OF SLEEVES
TYPES^M DE MANCHES^F
ÄRMELARTEN^F
TIPOS^M DE MANGA^F

bishop sleeve
manche^F bouffante
Bauschärmel^M
común fruncida

leg-of-mutton sleeve
manche^F gigot^M
Keulenärmel^M
de jamón^M

puff sleeve
manche^F ballon^M
Puffärmel^M
de globo^M

tailored sleeve
manche^F tailleur^M
Schneiderärmel^M
hechura^F sastre^M

epaulet sleeve
manche^F marteau^M
Zungenraglan^M
con hombrera^F

kimono sleeve
manche^F kimono^M
Kimonoärmel^M
kimono^M

shirt sleeve
manche^F chemisier^M
Hemdblusenärmel^M
camisera^F

raglan sleeve
manche^F raglan
Raglanärmel^M
manga^F ranglán

pagoda sleeve
manche^F pagode^F
Pagodenärmel^M
de pagoda^F

stand
montant^M
Stand^M
doblez^M

fall
tombant^M
Fall^M
caída^F

collar point
pointe^F
Kragenecke^F
punta^F del cuello^M

notch
cran^M
Crochetwinkel^M
muesca^F

leading edge
bord^M de pli^M
Fassonübertritt^M
escote^M

roll
chute^F
Kragensteg^M
alzada^F

break line
cassure^F
Umschlag^M
línea de caída^F

lapel
revers^M
Revers^N
solapa^F

TYPES OF COLLARS
TYPES^M **DE COLS**^M
KRAGENARTEN^F
CUELLOS^M

CLOTHING
VÊTEMENTS
KLEIDUNG
VESTIDO

shirt collar
col^M chemisier^M
Hemdblusenkragen^M
camisero

tailored collar
col^M tailleur^M
Schneiderkragen^M
hechura^F de sastre^M

dog ear collar
col^M banane^F
Dackelohrkragen^M
plano con orejas^F

Peter Pan collar
col^M Claudine
Bubikragen^M
plano tipo^M Peter Pan

shawl collar
col^M châle^M
Schalkragen^M
de chal^M

collaret
collerette^F
Halskrause^F
de volantes^M

TYPES OF COLLARS
TYPES^M DE COLS^M
KRAGENARTEN^F
CUELLOS^M

bertha collar
col^M berthe^F
Berthe^F
Berta

bow collar
col^M cravate^F
Schleifenkragen^M
de lazo^M

sailor collar
col^M marin^M
Matrosenkragen^M
marinero

mandarin collar
col^M chinois
Chinesenkragen^M
chino

jabot
jabot^M
Jabot^N
con chorrera^F

stand-up collar
col^M officier^M
Stehbordkragen^M
Mao

polo collar
col^M polo^M
Polokragen^M
con aletilla^F

cowl neck
col^M cagoule^F
Kuttenkragen^M
tipo^M cogulla^F

turtleneck
col^M roulé
Rollkragen^M
de tortuga^F

CLOTHING
VÊTEMENTS

KLEIDUNG
VESTIDO

plunging neckline
décolleté^M plongeant
spitzes Dekolleté^N
bajo

bateau neck
encolure^F bateau^M
Bateau-Kragen^M
de ojal^M

square neck
décolleté^M carré
viereckiger Ausschnitt^M
cuadrado

draped neck
encolure^F drapée
drapierter Kragen^M
drapeado

round neck
encolure^F ras-de-cou^M
runder Ausschnitt^M
redondo

sweetheart neckline
décolleté^M en cœur^M
Coeur-Dekolleté^N
de corazón^M

draped neckline
décolleté^M drapé
drapierter Ausschnitt^M
drapeado

V-shaped neck
décolleté^M en V
V-Ausschnitt^M
de pico^M

HOSE
BAS*M*
STRÜMPFE*M*
MEDIAS*F*

short sock
socquette*F*
Kurzsocke*F*
calcetín*M*

ankle sock
mi-chaussette*F*
Söckchen*N*
tobillera*F*

sock
chaussette*F*
Socke*F*
calcetín*M* largo

knee sock
mi-bas*M*
Kniestrumpf*M*
calceta*F*

KLEIDUNG
VESTIDO

CLOTHING
VÊTEMENTS

tights
collant*M*
Strumpfhose*F*
pantimedias*F*

stocking
bas*M*
Strumpf*M*
medias*F*

thigh stocking
bas*M*-cuissarde*F*
Overknee-Strumpf*M*
media*F* tres-cuartos

fishnet stocking
bas*M* résille*F*
Netzstrumpf*M*
medias*F* de malla*F*

344

body suit
body^M
Bodysuit^M
corpiño^M

teddy
teddy^M
Teddy^M
canesú^M

camisole
caraco^M
Camisol^N
camisola^F

foundation slip
fond^M de robe^F
Vollachsel-Unterkleid^N
combinación^F

slip
combinaison^F-jupon^M
Unterkleid^N
combinación^F con sostén^M

princess seaming
découpe^F princesse^F
Prinzeßnaht^F
costura^F de corte^M princesa^F

half-slip
jupon^M
Unterrock^M
media combinación^F

345

UNDERWEAR
SOUS-VÊTEMENTS^M
UNTERWÄSCHE^F
ROPA^F INTERIOR

décolleté bra
soutien-gorge^M corbeille^F
Halbschale^F
sostén^M de escote^M bajo

strapless brassiere
bustier^M
trägerloser Büstenhalter^M
sostén^M sin tirantes^M

steel
baleine^F
Stab^M
varilla^F

bra
soutien-gorge^M
BH^M
sostén^M

shoulder strap
bretelle^F
Träger^M
tirante^M

briefs
culotte^F
Slip^M
bragas^F

brassiere cup
bonnet^M
Büstenschale^F
copa^F

midriff band
basque^F
Mittelsteg^M
talle^M corto

girdle
gaine^F
Mieder^N
faja^F

panty girdle
gaine^F-culotte^F
Miederhose^F
pantifaja^F

corset
corset^M
Korsett^N
faja^F con liguero^M

panel
plastron^M
Magenstütze^F
refuerzo^M

corselette
combiné^M
Korselett^N
faja^F con sostén^M

push-up bra
soutien-gorge^M balconnet^M
Dirndl-BH^M
sostén^M con talle^M reforzado

underwiring
armature^F
Unterbruststäbchen^N
varilla^F

suspender belt
porte-jarretelles^M
Strumpfhaltergürtel^M
liguero^M

bikini
slip^M
Slip^M
slip^M

suspender
jarretelle^F
Strumpfhalter^M
liga^F

stocking
bas^M
Strumpf^M
medias^F

panty corselette
combiné^M-culotte^F
Panty-Korselett^N
faja^F corsé^M

wasp-waisted corset
guêpière^F
Torselett^N
corsé^M de cintura^F de avispa^F

NIGHTWEAR
VÊTEMENTS^M **DE NUIT**^F
NACHTWÄSCHE^F
LENCERÍA^F

nightgown
chemise^F de nuit^F
Nachthemd^N
camisón^M

baby doll
nuisette^F
Baby-Doll^N
camisón^M corto

kimono
kimono^M
Kimono^M
kimono^M

pyjamas
pyjama^M
Schlafanzug^M
pijama^M

negligee
déshabillé^M
Negligé^N
salto^M de cama^F

bathrobe
peignoir^M
Bademantel^M
albornoz^M

KLEIDUNG VESTIDO

CLOTHING
VÊTEMENTS

348

CHILDREN'S CLOTHING
VÊTEMENTS^M D'ENFANT^M
KINDERKLEIDUNG^F
ROPA^F DE NIÑOS^M

HOODED TOWELLING ROBE
CAPE^F DE BAIN^M
BADETUCH^N MIT KAPUZE^F
TOALLA^F CON CAPUCHÓN^M

decorative braid
galon^M d'ornement^M
Zierborte^F
orla^F decorativa

hood
capuche^F
Kapuze^F
capuchón^M

false tuck
biais^M
Paspel^F
falso doblez^M

bib
bavoir^M
Lätzchen^N
babero^M

snuggle suit
nid^M d'ange^M
Schneesack^M
bolsa^F portabebé^M

PLASTIC PANTS
CULOTTE^F PLASTIQUE
GUMMIHÖSCHEN^N
BRAGAS^F DE HULE^M

Velcro® closure
fermeture^F Velcro®
Haftgurtband^N
tirita^F Velcro®

waterproof pants
poche^F intérieure isolante
dichtes Windelhöschen^N
material^M impermeable

frilly nylon tights
collant^M fantaisie^F
Rüschenstrumpfhose^F
mallas^F con volantes^M

nappy
couche^F
Windel^F
pañal^M

rompers
grenouillère^F
Strampelhöschen^N
pantalón^M de peto^M

shirt
brassière^F
Hemdchen^N
camiseta^F

FRILLY PANTS
CULOTTE^F À RUCHÉS^M
RÜSCHENHÖSCHEN^N
CALZÓN^M DE VOLANTES^M

ruching
ruché^M
Rüschen^F
volantes^M

349

CHILDREN'S CLOTHING
VÊTEMENTS*ᴹ* D'ENFANT*ᴹ*
KINDERKLEIDUNG*ᶠ*
ROPA*ᶠ* DE NIÑOS*ᴹ*

BLANKET SLEEPSUIT
DORMEUSE*ᶠ*-COUVERTURE*ᶠ*
WAGENANZUG*ᴹ*
MAMELUCO*ᴹ*

ribbing
bord*ᴹ*-côte*ᶠ*
Rippenbündchen*ᴺ*
tirilla*ᶠ* elástica

SLEEPSUIT
COMBINAISON*ᶠ* DE NUIT*ᶠ*
SCHLAFANZUG*ᴹ*
MAMELUCOS*ᴹ*

raglan sleeve
manche*ᶠ* raglan
Raglanärmel*ᴹ*
manga*ᶠ* ranglán

ribbing
bord*ᴹ*-côte*ᶠ*
Rippenbündchen*ᴺ*
tirilla*ᶠ* elástica

screen print
motif*ᴹ*
Druckmotiv*ᴺ*
dibujo*ᴹ*

snap-fastening front
pression*ᶠ* devant
vordere Druckknopfleiste*ᶠ*
broches*ᴹ* delanteros

inside-leg snap-fastening
entrejambe*ᴹ* pressionné
Druckknopfleiste*ᶠ* an der Beininnenseite*ᶠ*
broches*ᴹ* de la pierna*ᶠ*

zip
fermeture*ᶠ* à glissière*ᶠ*
Reißverschluß*ᴹ*
cremallera*ᶠ*

vinyl grip sole
semelle*ᶠ* antidérapante
Vinyl-Laufsohle*ᶠ*
suela*ᶠ* de hule*ᴹ*

HIGH-BACK DUNGAREES
SALOPETTE*ᶠ* À DOS*ᴹ* MONTANT
LATZHOSE*ᶠ* MIT HOHEM RÜCKENTEIL*ᴹ*
PANTALÓN*ᴹ* CON TIRANTES*ᴹ*

adjustable strap
bretelle*ᶠ* réglable
verstellbarer Träger*ᴹ*
tirante*ᴹ* ajustable

patch pocket
poche*ᶠ* plaquée
aufgesetzte Tasche*ᶠ*
bolsillo*ᴹ* de parche*ᴹ*

bib
bavette*ᶠ*
Lätzchen*ᴺ*
peto*ᴹ*

top stitching
surpiqûre*ᶠ*
Zier-Steppnaht*ᶠ*
sobrepespunte*ᴹ*

BABYGRO
DORMEUSE*ᶠ* DE CROISSANCE*ᶠ*
ZWEITEILIGER SCHLAFANZUG*ᴹ*
MAMELUCOS*ᴹ* DE DOS PIEZAS*ᶠ*

screen print
motif*ᴹ*
Aufdruck*ᴹ*
dibujo*ᴹ*

crew neck
encolure*ᶠ* ras-de-cou*ᴹ*
halsnaher Ausschnitt*ᴹ*
cuello*ᴹ* redondo

snap-fastening waist
pression*ᶠ* à la taille*ᶠ*
Bund*ᴹ* mit Druckknöpfen*ᴹ*
pretina*ᶠ* con broches*ᴹ*

fly
braguette*ᶠ*
Schlitz*ᴹ*
bragueta*ᶠ*

inside-leg snap-fastening
entrejambe*ᴹ* pressionné
Druckknopfleiste*ᶠ* an der Beininnenseite*ᶠ*
broches*ᴹ* de presión*ᶠ*

foot
pied*ᴹ*
Fuß*ᴹ*
pie*ᴹ*

TRAINING SET
TENUE^F D'EXERCICE^M
SPORTSET^N
CONJUNTO^M DEPORTIVO

tank top
débardeur^M
Trägerhemdchen^N
camiseta^F

shorts
short^M
kurze Hose^F
pantalón^M corto

SNOWSUIT
ESQUIMAU^M
SCHNEEANZUG^M
TRAJE^M DE INVIERNO^M CON CAPUCHÓN^M

drawstring hood
capuche^F coulissée
Kapuze^F mit Zugband^N
capuchón^M con cordón^M

fly front closing
fermeture^F sous patte^F
Verschluß^M mit verdeckter
Knopfleiste^F
cremallera^F

DUNGAREES WITH CROSSOVER BACK STRAPS
SALOPETTE^F À BRETELLES^F CROISÉES
LATZHOSE^F MIT GEKREUZTEN RÜCKENTRÄGERN^M
MONO^M DE TIRANTES CRUZADOS ATRÁS

button strap
bretelle^F boutonnée
Träger^M mit Knopf^F
tirante^M con botones^M

bib
bavette^F
Lätzchen^N
peto^M

rompers
barboteuse^F
Spielanzug^M
pelele^M

T-shirt dress
robe^F tee-shirt^M
T-Shirt Kleid^N
camiseta^F de cuerpo^M entero

slip-on pyjamas
polojama^M
Schlafanzug^M in Schlupfform^F
pijama^M

jumpsuit
combinaison^F
Overall^M
traje^M pantalón^M

RUNNING SHOE
CHAUSSURE^F DE SPORT^M
JOGGINGSCHUH^M
ZAPATO^M DEPORTIVO

tongue
languette^F
Zunge^F
lengüeta^F

nose of the quarter
aile^F de quartier^M
Vorderteil^N
ala^F del cuarto^M

collar
col^M
Fersenrand^M
ribete^M

lining
doublure^F
Futter^N
forro^M

counter
contrefort^M
Hinterkappe^F
contrafuerte^M

quarter
quartier^M
Quartier^M
cuarto^M

stitch
surpiqûre^F
Naht^F
pespunteado^M

heel
talon^M
Absatz^M
talón^M

middle sole
semelle^F intercalaire
Zwischensohle^F
cambrillón^M

air cushion
coussin^M d'air^M
Luftpolster^N
cámara^F de aire^M

tag
ferret^M
Schnürsenkelende^N
herrete^M

shoelace
lacet^M
Schnürsenkel^M
cordón^M

TRAINING SUIT
SURVÊTEMENT^M
TRAININGSANZUG^M
TRAJE^M DE ENTRENAMIENTO^M

hooded sweat shirt
pull^M à capuche^F
Sweatshirt^N mit Kapuze^F
camiseta^F de chándal^M con capucha^F

jogging pants
pantalon^M molleton^M
Trainingshose^F
pantalones^M de chándal^M

sweat shirt
pull^M d'entraînement^M
Sweatshirt^N
camiseta^F de chándal^M

swimming trunks
slip^M de bain^M
Badehose^F
traje^M de baño^M

swimsuit
maillot^M de bain^M
Badeanzug^M
traje^M de baño^M

eyelet
œillet^M
Öse^F
ojillo^M

vamp
claque^F
Vorderblatt^N
empella^F

punch hole
perforation^F
gestanztes Loch^N
perforación^F

leotard
justaucorps^M
Trikot^N
body^M

footless tights
collant^M sans pied^M
Gymnastikhose^F ohne Fuß^M
traje^M de malla^F

stud
crampon^M
Stollen^M
montante^M

outsole
semelle^F d'usure^F
Laufsohle^F
suela^F

boxer shorts
short^M boxeur^M
Shorts^F
pantalón^M de boxeo^M

leg-warmer
jambière^F
Legwarmer^M
calentador^M de pierna^F

trousers
pantalon^M
Hose^F
pantalones^M

anorak
anorak^M
Anorak^M
anorak^M

tank top
débardeur^M
Trägerhemd^N
camiseta^F

SHOES
CHAUSSURES[F]
SCHUHE[M]
ZAPATOS[M]

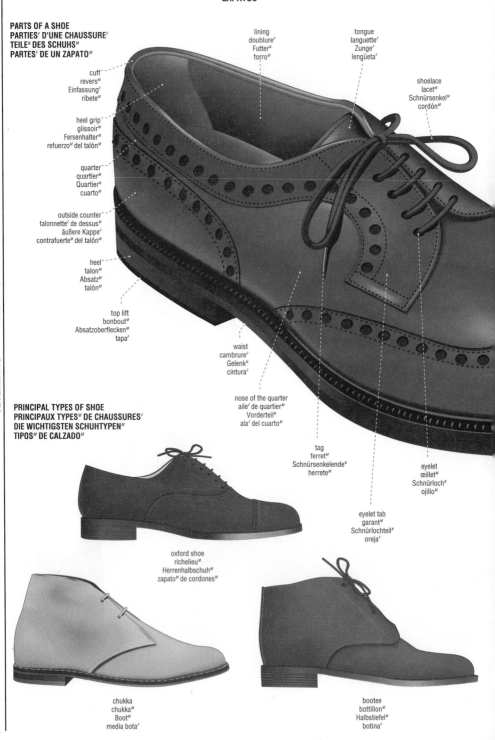

PARTS OF A SHOE
PARTIES[F] D'UNE CHAUSSURE[F]
TEILE[N] DES SCHUHS[M]
PARTES[F] DE UN ZAPATO[M]

lining
doublure[F]
Futter[N]
forro[M]

tongue
languette[F]
Zunge[F]
lengüeta[F]

cuff
revers[M]
Einfassung[F]
ribete[M]

shoelace
lacet[M]
Schnürsenkel[M]
cordón[M]

heel grip
glissoir[M]
Fersenhalter[M]
refuerzo[M] del talón[M]

quarter
quartier[M]
Quartier[M]
cuarto[M]

outside counter
talonnette[F] de dessus[M]
äußere Kappe[F]
contrafuerte[M] del talón[M]

heel
talon[M]
Absatz[M]
talón[M]

top lift
bonbout[M]
Absatzoberflecken[M]
tapa[F]

waist
cambrure[F]
Gelenk[N]
cintura[F]

nose of the quarter
aile[F] de quartier[M]
Vorderteil[N]
ala[F] del cuarto[M]

tag
ferret[M]
Schnürsenkelende[N]
herrete[M]

eyelet
œillet[M]
Schnürloch[N]
ojillo[M]

eyelet tab
garant[M]
Schnürlochteil[N]
oreja[F]

PRINCIPAL TYPES OF SHOE
PRINCIPAUX TYPES[M] DE CHAUSSURES[F]
DIE WICHTIGSTEN SCHUHTYPEN[M]
TIPOS[M] DE CALZADO[M]

oxford shoe
richelieu[M]
Herrenhalbschuh[M]
zapato[M] de cordones[M]

chukka
chukka[M]
Boot[M]
media bota[F]

bootee
bottillon[M]
Halbstiefel[M]
botina[F]

CLOTHING
VÊTEMENTS

KLEIDUNG
VESTIDO

354

plimsoll
tennis
Tennisschuh
zapato de tenis

lace-up
derby
Schnürschuh
zapato de vestir

vamp
claque
Vorderblatt
empella

stitch
surpiqûre
Naht
costura

moccasin
mocassin
Mokassin
mocasín

punch hole
perforation
gestanztes Loch
perforaciones

perforated toe cap
bout fleuri
perforierte Vorderkappe
puntera

welt
trépointe
Rahmen
vira

slip-on
loafer
Slipper
zapato de calle

outsole
semelle d'usure
Laufsohle
suela

mule
mule
Pantoffel
pantufla

heavy duty boot
brodequin
Arbeitsstiefel
bota de trabajo

galosh
claque
Überziehschuh
chanclo de goma

MAJOR TYPES OF SHOES
PRINCIPAUX TYPES^M **DE CHAUSSURES**^F
DIE WICHTIGSTEN SCHUHTYPEN^M
TIPOS^M **DE CALZADO**^M

court
escarpin^M
Pumps^M
zapato^M de tacón^M alto

sling back shoe
escarpin^M-sandale^F
Slingpumps^M
zapato^M de tacón^M alto con presillas^F

ankle-strap
sandale^F
Sandalette^F mit Fersenriemen^M
sandalia^F

T-strap shoe
salomé^M
Stegspangenschuh^M
zapato^M de correa^F

one-bar shoe
Charles IX^M
Einspangenschuh^M
escarpín^M con correa^F

pump
ballerine^F
Ballerinaschuh^M
zapatilla^F de ballet^M

casual shoe
trotteur^M
Straßenschuh^M
zapato^M de calle^F

boot
botte^F
Stiefel^M
bota^F

toe-strap
nu-pied^M
Sandale^F mit Zehenriemchen^N
sandalia^F

flip-flop
tong^M
Römerpantolette^F
chancleta^F

ankle boot
bottine^F
knöchelhohe Stiefelette^F
botín^M

clog
socque^M
Pantolette^F
chanclo^M

espadrille
espadrille^F
Espadrille^F
alpargata^F

thigh-boot
cuissarde^F
Schaftstiefel^M
bota^F de medio muslo^M

sandal
sandalette^F
Sandale^F
sandalia^F

ACCESSORIES
ACCESSOIRES[M]
ZUBEHÖR[N]
ACCESORIOS[M]

shoeshine kit
nécessaire[M] à chaussures[F]
Schuhputzzeug[N]
juego[M] limpiabotas[M]

chamois leather
peau[F] de chamois[M]
Ledertuch[N]
gamuza[F]

case
étui[M]
Tasche[F]
estuche[M]

shoe polisher
cireur[M]
Schuhbürste[F]
enceradora[F]

shoehorn
chausse-pied[M]
Schuhlöffel[M]
calzador[M]

shoe polish
boîte[F] de cirage[M]
Schuhcreme[F]
betún[M]

shoebrush
brosse[F] à chaussure[F]
Schuhbürste[F]
cepillo[M]

climbing iron
crampon[M]
Steigeisen[N]
trepadora[F]

insole
semelle[F]
Einlegesohle[F]
plantilla[F]

CLOTHING
VÊTEMENTS

KLEIDUNG
VESTIDO

boot jack
arrache-bottes[M]
Stiefelknecht[M]
sacabotas[M]

shoetree
embauchoir[M]
Schuhspanner[M]
horma[F]

shoe rack
porte-chaussures[M]
Schuhständer[M]
zapatera[F] de alambre[M]

358

SUMMARY

SCHMUCK UND SCHÖNHEITSPFLEGE
ADORNOS PERSONALES

PERSONAL ADORNMENT
PARURE

JEWELLERY
BIJOUTERIE*F*
SCHMUCK*M*
JOYERÍA*F*

EARRINGS
BOUCLES*F* D'OREILLE*F*
OHRRINGE*M*
PENDIENTES*M*

hoop earrings
anneaux*M*
Kreolen*F*
pendientes*M* de aro*M*

clip earrings
boucles*F* d'oreille*F* à pince*F*
Klips*M*
pendientes*M* de clip*M*

drop earrings
pendants*M* d'oreille*F*
Ohrgehänge*N*
pendientes*M*

ear studs
boucles*F* d'oreille*F* à tige*F*
Ohrstecker*M*
pendientes*M* de espiga*F*

screw earrings
boucles*F* d'oreille*F* à vis*F*
Ohrringe*M* mit Schraubverschluß*M*
pendientes*M* de tornillo*M*

NECKLACES
COLLIERS*M*
HALSKETTEN*F*
COLLARES*M*

pendant
pendentif*M*
Anhänger*M*
pendiente*M*

locket
médaillon*M*
Medaillon*N*
relicario*M*

matinee-length necklace
collier*M* de perles*F*, longueur*F* matinée*F*
Halskette*F* in Matineelänge*F*
collar*M* de una vuelta*F*

velvet-band choker
collier*M*-de-chien*M*
Samtkropfband*N*
garagantilla*F* de terciopelo*M*

opera-length necklace
sautoir*M*, longueur*F* opéra*M*
Halskette*F* in Opernlänge*F*
collar*M* de una vuelta*F*

rope
sautoir*M*
Endlosperlenkette*F*
sarta*F*

choker
ras-de-cou*M*
Chokerkette*F*
gargantilla*F*

bib necklace
collier*M* de soirée*F*
mehrreihige Halskette*F*
collar*M* de 5 hilos*M*

361

JEWELLERY
BIJOUTERIE*F*
SCHMUCK*M*
JOYERÍA*F*

CUT FOR GEMSTONES
TAILLE*F* DES PIERRES*F*
SCHLIFFORMEN*F* FÜR EDELSTEINE*M*
TALLAS*F* DE PIEDRAS*F* PRECIOSAS

SCHMUCK UND SCHÖNHEITSPFLEGE
ADORNOS PERSONALES

PERSONAL ADORNMENT
PARURE

navette cut
taille*F* marquise*F*
Navette*F*
marquesa*F*

baguette cut
taille*F* baguette*F*
Baguetteform*F*
baguette*F*

oval cut
taille*F* ovale
ovale Form*F*
oval

French cut
taille*F* française
French-cut*M*
francés

pear-shaped cut
taille*F* en poire*F*
Birnkernform*F*
pera*F*

briolette cut
taille*F* en goutte*F*
Briolettform*F*
gota*F*

table cut
taille*F* en table*F*
Tafelschliff*M*
tabla*F*

rose cut
taille*F* en rose*F*
Rosenschliff*M*
rosa*F* holandesa

cabochon cut
taille*F* cabochon*M*
Cabochonschliff*M*
cabujón*M*

step cut
taille*F* en escalier*M*
Treppenschliff*M*
en escalera*F*

brilliant full cut
taille*F* brillant*M*
Vollbrillantschliff*M*
brillante*M*

eight cut
taille*F* huit facettes*F*
Achtkant*M*
ocho facetas*F*

scissors cut
taille*F* en ciseaux*M*
Scherenschliff*M*
en tijera*F*

emerald cut
taille*F* émeraude*F*
Smaragdschliff*M*
esmeralda*F*

BOTTOM FACE
FACE[F] INFÉRIEURE
RÜCKSEITE[F]
CARA[F] INFERIOR

pavilion facet (8)
pavillon[M] (8)
Unterteilhauptfacette[F] (8)
faceta[F] de pabellón[M]

culet
colette[F]
Kulette[F]
culata[F]

lower girdle facet (16)
halefis[M] de culasse[F] (16)
untere Rondistenfacette[F] (16)
faceta[F] inferior del contorno[M]

BRILLIANT CUT FACETS
TAILLE[F] D'UN DIAMANT[M]
FACETTEN[F] DES BRILLANTSCHLIFFS[M]
CORTE[M] DE UN DIAMANTE[M]

TOP FACE
FACE[F] SUPÉRIEURE
VORDERSEITE[F]
CARA[F] SUPERIOR

star facet (8)
étoile[F] (8)
Tafelfacette[F] (8)
faceta[F] de estrella[F] (8)

table
table[F]
Tafel[F]
tabla[F]

bezel facet (8)
bezel[M] (8)
Oberteilhauptfacette[F] (8)
faceta[F] bisel (8)

upper girdle facet (16)
halefis[M] de table[F] (16)
obere Rondistenfacette[F] (16)
faceta[F] superior del contorno[M]

SIDE FACE
PROFIL[M]
SEITENANSICHT[F]
PERFIL[M]

table
table[F]
Tafel[F]
tabla[F]

girdle
rondiste[M]
Rondiste[F]
corona[F]

culet
colette[F]
Kulette[F]
culata[F]

crown
couronne[F] de table[F]
Krone[F]
corona[F]

pavilion
culasse[F]
Unterteil[N]
pabellón[M]

PRECIOUS STONES
PIERRES[F] PRÉCIEUSES
EDELSTEINE[M]
PIEDRAS[F] PRECIOSAS

emerald
émeraude[F]
Smaragd[M]
esmeralda[F]

ruby
rubis[M]
Rubin[M]
rubí[M]

sapphire
saphir[M]
Saphir[M]
zafiro[M]

diamond
diamant[M]
Diamant[M]
diamante[M]

SEMIPRECIOUS STONES
PIERRES[F] FINES
HALBEDELSTEINE[M]
PIEDRAS[F] SEMIPRECIOSAS

amethyst
améthyste[F]
Amethyst[M]
amatista[F]

garnet
grenat[M]
Granat[M]
granate[M]

topaz
topaze[F]
Topas[M]
topacio[M]

aquamarine
aigue-marine[F]
Aquamarin[M]
aguamarina[F]

tourmaline
tourmaline[F]
Turmalin[M]
turmalina[F]

opal
opale[F]
Opal[M]
ópalo[M]

turquoise
turquoise[F]
Türkis[M]
turquesa[F]

lapis lazuli
lapis-lazuli[M]
Lapislazuli[M]
lapislázuli[M]

JEWELLERY
BIJOUTERIE^F
SCHMUCK^M
JOYERÍA^F

RINGS
BAGUES^F
RINGE^M
ANILLOS^M

signet ring
chevalière^F
Herrenring^M
sortija^F de sello^M

setting
sertissure^F
Fassung^F
montadura^F

claw
griffe^F
Krappe^F
uña^F

stone
pierre^F
Stein^M
piedra^F

bezel
chaton^M
Chaton^M
engaste^M

class ring
bague^F de finissant^M
Collegering^M
anillo^M de graduación^F

band ring
jonc^M
Bandring^M
alianza^F

wedding ring
alliance^F
Ehering^M
alianza^F

engagement ring
bague^F de fiançailles^F
Verlobungsring^M
anillo^M de compromiso^M

solitaire ring
bague^F solitaire^M
Solitärring^M
solitario^M

BRACELETS
BRACELETS^M
ARMBÄNDER^N
BRAZALETES^M

bangle
bracelet^M tubulaire
Armreif^M
brazalete^M tubular

identity bracelet
gourmette^F d'identité^F
Identitätsband^N
brazalete^M de identificación^F

charm bracelet
gourmette^F
Armband^N
pulsera^F de dijes^M

CHARMS
BRELOQUES^F
ANHÄNGER^M
DIJES^M

PINS
ÉPINGLES^F
ANSTECKNADELN^F
ALFILERES^M

brooch
broche^F
Brosche^F
broche^M

stickpin
broche^F épingle^F
Sticker^M
alfiler^M de corbata^F

nameplate
plaque^F d'identité^F
Gravurplatte^F
placa^F de identificación^F

horseshoe
fer^F à cheval^M
Hufeisen^N
herradura^F

tiepin
épingle^F à cravate^F
Krawattennadel^F
alfiler^M de corbata^F

tiepin
tige^F pour col^M
Kragenklammer^F
yugo^M

tieclip
pince^F à cravate^F
Krawattenklemme^F
pisacorbatas^M

horn
corne^F
Horn^N
cuerno^M

MANICURE
MANUCURE*F*
MANIKÜRE*F*
MANICURA*F*

MANICURE SET
TROUSSE*F* DE MANUCURE*F*
NAGELNECESSAIRE*N*
ESTUCHE*M* DE MANICURA*F*

cuticle pusher
repousse-chair*F*
Nagelhautschieber*M*
empujacutículas*M*

cuticle trimmer
coupe-cuticules*M*
Nagelhautentferner*M*
desbastador*M* de cutícula*F*

nail shaper
gratte-ongles*M*
Nagelhautschaber*M*
cuchilla*F* para moldear

nail file
lime*F* à ongles*M*
Nagelfeile*F*
lima*F* de uñas*F*

nail scissors
ciseaux*M* à ongles*M*
Nagelschere*F*
tijeras*F*

cuticle nippers
pince*F* à cuticules*M*
Nagelzange*F*
alicates*M* para cutícula*F*

eyebrow tweezers
pince*F* à épiler
Augenbrauenpinzette*F*
pinzas*F* para depilar cejas*F*

case
étui*M*
Etui*N*
estuche*M*

zip
fermeture*F* à glissière*F*
Reißverschluß*M*
cremallera*F*

cuticle scissors
ciseaux*M* à cuticules*M*
Nagelhautschere*F*
tijeras*F* para cutícula*F*

strap
bride*F*
Schlaufe*F*
correa*F*

NAIL CLIPPERS
COUPE-ONGLES*M*
NAGELKNIPSER*M*
CORTAÚÑAS*M*

jaw
mors*M*
Klemmbacke*F*
mordaza*F*

lever
levier*M*
Hebel*M*
palanca*F*

folding nail file
lime*F*
klappbare Nagelfeile*F*
lima*F* de uñas*F*

nail cleaner
cure-ongles*M*
Nagelreiniger*M*
limpiador*M* de uñas*F*

emery boards
limes*F*-émeri*M*
Sandblattfeilen*F*
lima*F* de uñas*F*

nail whitener pencil
crayon*M* blanchisseur d'ongles*M*
Nagelweißstift*M*
lápiz*M* blanco para uñas*F*

MANICURING IMPLEMENTS
ACCESSOIRES*M* DE MANUCURE*F*
NAGELPFLEGEZUBEHÖR*N*
INSTRUMENTOS*M* DE MANICURA*F*

safety scissors
ciseaux*M* de sûreté*F*
Nasen-Bartschere*F*
tijeras*F* de punta*F* roma

toenail scissors
ciseaux*M* de pédicure*M*
Fußnagelschere*F*
tijeras*F* de pedicura*F*

MAKE-UP
MAQUILLAGE^M
MAKE-UP^N
MAQUILLAJE^M FACIAL

fan brush
pinceau^M éventail^M
Fächerpinsel^M
brocha^F en forma^F de abanico^M

loose powder
poudre^F libre
loser Puder^M
polvos^M sueltos

liquid foundation
fond^M de teint^M liquide
flüssige Grundierung^F
base^F líquida

loose powder brush
pinceau^M pour poudre^F libre
Puderpinsel^M
brocha^F

powder puff
houpette^F
Puderkissen^N
borla^F

blusher brush
pinceau^M pour fard^M à joues^F
Rougepinsel^M
brocha^F aplicadora de rubor^M

compact
poudrier^M
Puderdose^F
polvera^F

pressed powder
poudre^F pressée
gepreßter Puder^M
polvo^M compacto

powder blusher
fard^M à joues^F en poudre^F
Puderrouge^N
rubor^M en polvo^M

LIP MAKE-UP
MAQUILLAGE^M DES LÈVRES^F
LIPPEN-MAKE-UP^N
MAQUILLAJE^M LABIAL

lipbrush
pinceau^M à lèvres^F
Lippenpinsel^M
pincel^M para labios^M

lipstick
rouge^M à lèvres^F
Lippenstift^M
lápiz^M labial

lipliner
crayon^M contour^M des lèvres^F
Lippenkonturenstift^M
delineador^M de labios^M

eyebrow pencil
crayon^M à sourcils^M
Augenbrauenstift^M
lápiz^M de cejas^F

brow brush and lash comb
brosse^F-peigne^M pour cils^M et sourcils^M
Brauenbürstchen^N und Wimpernkämmchen^N
cepillo^M para cejas^F y pestañas^F

liquid eyeliner
eye-liner^M liquide
flüssiger Eyeliner^M
delineador^M

liquid mascara
mascara^M liquide
flüssige Mascara^F
rímel^M líquido

eyelash curler
recourbe-cils^M
Wimpernzange^F
rizador^M de pestañas^F

mascara brush
brosse^F à mascara^M
Mascarabürstchen^N
cepillo^M aplicador de rímel^M

sponge-tipped applicator
applicateur^M-mousse^F
Schwammstäbchen^N
aplicador^M de esponja^F

**cake mascara
mascara^M en pain^M
Mascarastein^M
rímel^M en pasta^F**

**eyeshadow
ombre^F à paupières^F
Lidschatten^M
sombra^F de ojos^M**

**SPONGES^F
ÉPONGES^F
SCHWÄMME^M
ESPONJAS^F**

vegetable sponge
éponge^F végétale
Luffaschwamm^M
esponja^F vegetal

natural sponge
éponge^F de mer^F
Naturschwamm^M
esponja^F natural

synthetic sponge
éponge^F synthétique
Kunstschwamm^M
esponja^F sintética

HAIRDRESSING
COIFFURE^F
HAARPFLEGE^F
PEINADO^M

ILLUMINATED MIRROR
MIROIR^M LUMINEUX
BELEUCHTETER SPIEGEL^M
ESPEJO^M LUMINOSO

side mirror
miroir^M latéral
Seitenspiegel^M
espejo^M lateral

dual swivel mirror
miroir^M double pivotant
Drehspiegel^M
espejo^M doble giratorio

lighting
éclairage^M
Beleuchtung^F
iluminación^F

base
base^F
Sockel^M
base^F

on-off switch
interrupteur^M d'éclairage^M
Ein-/Ausschalter^M
interruptor^M

HAIRBRUSHES
BROSSES^F À CHEVEUX^M
HAARBÜRSTEN^F
CEPILLOS^M

flat-back brush
brosse^F pneumatique
flache Frisierbürste^F
cepillo^M con base^F de goma^F

round brush
brosse^F ronde
Rundbürste^F
cepillo^M redondo

vent brush
brosse^F-araignée^F
Skelettbürste^F
cepillo^M metálico

quill brush
brosse^F anglaise
Drahtbürste^F
cepillo^M de púas^F

COMBS
PEIGNES^M
KÄMME^M
PEINES^M

teaser comb
peigne^M à crêper
Toupierkamm^M
peine^M metálico

rake comb
démêloir^M
Griffkamm^M
peine^M para desenredar

tail comb
peigne^M à tige^F
Stielkamm^M
peine^M de mango^M

pitchfork comb
combiné 2 dans 1
Haarliftkamm^M
peine^M combinado^M

Afro pick
peigne^M afro
Strähnenkamm^M
peine^M tenedor^M

barber comb
peigne^M de coiffeur^M
Haarschneidekamm^M
peine^M de peluquero^M

HAIRCUTTING SCISSORS
CISEAUX^M DE COIFFEUR^M
HAARSCHNEIDESCHERE^F
TIJERAS^F DE PELUQUERO^M

cutting edge
tranchant^M
Schneide^F
filo^M

blade
lame^F
Blatt^N
hoja^F

ringhandle
anneau^M
Auge^N
ojo^M

pivot
pivot^M
Schloß^N
pivote^M

shank
branche^F
Halm^M
brazo^M

blade close stop
amortisseur^M
Klingenstopper
tope^M

clippers
tondeuse^F
Haarschneider^M
maquinilla^F para cortar el cabello^M

NOTCHED DOUBLE-EDGED THINNING SCISSORS
CISEAUX^M À EFFILER
ZWEISEITIG GEZAHNTE EFFILIERSCHERE^F
TIJERAS^F CON DOBLE FILO^M PARA ENTRESACAR

thinning razor
rasoir^M effileur
Effiliermesser^N
navaja^F para entresacar

NOTCHED SINGLE-EDGED THINNING SCISSORS
CISEAUX^M SCULPTEURS
EINSEITIG GEZAHNTE MODELLIERSCHERE^F
TIJERAS^F CON FILO^M SIMPLE PARA ENTRESACAR

tooth
dents^F
Zahn^M
diente^M

blade
lame^F droite
Blatt^N
cuchilla^F

notched edge
lame^F dentée
gekerbtes Scherenblatt^N
desbastador^M

HAIRSTYLING ACCESSORIES
ACCESSOIRES^M DE COIFFURE^F
HAARZUBEHÖR^N
ACCESORIOS^M PARA EL PEINADO^M

hair grip
pince^F à cheveux^M
Haarklemme^F
horquilla^F

hairpin
épingle^F à cheveux^M
Lockennadel^F
horquilla^F

wave clip
pince^F à boucles^F de cheveux^M
Abteilklammer^F
pinza^F para rizar

HAIR ROLLER
BIGOUDI^M
LOCKENWICKLER^M
RULO^M PARA EL CABELLO^M

roller
rouleau^M
Wickler^M
tubo^M

hair roller pin
épingle^F à bigoudi^M
Haarstecker^M
alfiler^M

hair clip
pince^F de mise^F en plis^M
Haarclip^M
pinza^F para el cabello^M

hair slide
barrette^F
Haarspange^F
pasador^M

CURLING IRON
FER*M* À FRISER
LOCKENSTAB*M*
PINZA*F* RIZADORA

shaped handle
poignée*F* profilée
Griff*M*
mango*M*

clamp lever
levier*F*
Hebel*M* für den Klemmbügel*M*
palanca*F*

on-off indicator
voyant*M* lumineux
Kontrollampe*F*
luz*F* piloto*M*

swivel flex
cordon*M* d'alimentation*F* pivotant
Drehanschlußleitung*F*
cable*M* giratorio

heat ready indicator
point*M* indicateur*M* de température*F*
Bereitschaftsanzeige*F*
indicador*M* de temperatura*F*

clamp
pince*F*
Klemmbügel*M*
pinza*F*

on-off switch
interrupteur*F*
Ein-/Ausschalter*M*
interruptor*M*

STYLING BRUSH
BROSSE*F* À COIFFER
LOCKENBÜRSTE*F*
CEPILLO*M* ELÉCTRICO

stand
support*M*
Ständer*M*
soporte*F*

cool tip
embout*M* isolant
Cool tip*M*
punta*F* de plástico*M*

barrel
tube*M*
Zylinder*M*
varilla*F* rizadora

curling brush
brosse*F* à peignes*M*
Lockenbürste*F*
cepillo*M* rizador

HAIR DRYER
SÈCHE-CHEVEUX*M*
FÖN*M*
SECADOR*F* MANUAL

fan housing
boîtier*M* du ventilateur*M*
Föngehäuse*N*
caja*F* del ventilador*M*

air-inlet grille
grille*F* d'aspiration*F*
Ansauggitter*N*
rejilla*F* de entrada*F* de aire*M*

barrel
corps*M*
Heizfläche*F*
tubo*M* de aire*M*

speed selector switch
sélecteur*M* de vitesse*F*
Luftstromschalter*M*
botón*M* seleccionador de velocidad*F*

heat air
0 1 2 3
0 1 2
chad air

on-off switch
interrupteur*M*
Ein-/Ausschalter*M*
interruptor*M*

hang-up ring
anneau*M* de suspension*F*
Aufhängeöse*F*
trabilla*F*

heat selector switch
sélecteur*M* de température*F*
Temperaturschalter*M*
botón*M* seleccionador de temperatura*F*

handle
poignée*F*
Griff*M*
mango*M*

air-outlet grille
grille*F* de sortie*F* d'air*M*
Luftaustrittsöffnung*F*
rejilla*F* de salida*F* de aire*M*

air concentrator
buse*F*
Luftstromrichtdüse*F*
concentrador*M* de aire*M*

flex
cordon*M* d'alimentation*F*
Netzkabel*N*
cable*M* de corriente*F*

SUMMARY

PERSÖNLICHE ARTIKEL
ARTÍCULOS PERSONALES

PERSONAL ARTICLES
OBJETS PERSONNELS

DENTAL CARE
HYGIÈNE^F DENTAIRE
ZAHNPFLEGE^F
HIGIENE^F DENTAL

TOOTHBRUSH
BROSSE^F À DENTS^F
ZAHNBÜRSTE^F
CEPILLO^M DE DIENTES^M

gum massager
stimulateur^M de gencives^F
Massagespitze^F
estimulador^M de encias^F

handle
manche^M
Griff^M
mango^M

bristle
poil^M
Borste^F
cerda^F

row
rang^M
Reihe^F
hilera^F

head
tête^F
Kopf^M
cabeza^F hexagonal

toothpaste
dentifrice^M
Zahnpasta^F
dentífrico^M

dental floss
soie^F dentaire
Zahnseide^F
seda^F dental

ELECTRIC TOOTHBRUSH
COMBINÉ^M BUCCO-DENTAIRE
ELEKTRISCHE ZAHNBÜRSTE^F
CEPILLO^M DE DIENTES^M ELÉCTRICO

brush
brosse^F
Bürste^F
cepillo^M

toothbrush shaft
tige^F
Achse^F für die Aufsteckbürste^F
eje^M del cepillo^M

on-off switch
interrupteur^M
Ein-/Ausschalter^M
interruptor^M

handle
manche^M
Griff^M
mango^M

jet tip
buse^F
Aufsteckdüse^F
surtidor^M de agua^F

toothbrush
brosse^F à dents^F
Zahnbürste^F
cepillo^M de dientes^M

water tank
réserve^F d'eau^F
Wasserbehälter^M
depósito^M del agua^F

oral irrigator
jet^M dentaire
Munddusche^F
irrigador^M bucal

motor unit
bloc^M-moteur^M
Motorblock^M
motor^M

pressure control
réglage^M de la pression^F
Druckregler^M
control^M de presión^F

toothbrush well
réceptacle^M de brosses^F
Box^F für die Aufsteckbürsten^F
receptáculo^M del cepillo^M

RAZORS
RASOIRS^M
RASIERER^M
RASURADORAS^F

ELECTRIC RAZOR
RASOIR^M ÉLECTRIQUE
ELEKTRORASIERER^M
MAQUINILLA^F DE AFEITAR ELÉCTRICA

floating head
tête^F flottante
Scherkopf^M
cabeza^F flotante

screen
grille^F
Scherkopfhalter^M
peine^M y cuchilla^F

cleaning brush
brosse^F de nettoyage^M
Reinigungsbürste^F
escobilla^F limpiadora

charge indicator
indicateur^M de charge^F
Kapazitätsanzeige^F
indicador^M de recarga^F

charging socket
prise^F de charge^F
Geräteanschluß^M
enchufe^M de recarga^F

trimmer
tondeuse^F
Langhaarschneider^M
recortador^M de patillas^F

closeness setting
sélecteur^M de coupe^F
Justierring^M
selector^M de corte^M

housing
boîtier^M
Gehäuse^N
caja^F

charging light
voyant^M de charge^F
Ladekontrollampe^F
luz^F de encendido^M

on-off switch
interrupteur^M
Ein-/Ausschalter^M
interruptor^M

flex
cordon^M d'alimentation^F
Netzkabel^N
cable^F de corriente^F

CUT-THROAT RAZOR
RASOIR^M À MANCHE^M
RASIERMESSER^N
NAVAJA^F DE BARBERO^M

blade
lame^F
Klinge^F
hoja^F

pivot
pivot^M
Schloß^N
eje^M

handle
manche^M
Griff^M
mango^M

bristle
soie^F
Borste^F
cerdas^F

SHAVING BRUSH
BLAIREAU^M
RASIERPINSEL^M
BROCHA^F DE AFEITAR

shaving mug
bol^M à raser
Seifenbecher^M
jabonera^F

plug adapter
adaptateur^M de fiche^F
Adapter^M
adaptador^M de enchufes^M

DOUBLE-EDGED RAZOR
RASOIR^M À DOUBLE TRANCHANT^M
ZWEISCHNEIDIGER RASIERER^M
MAQUINILLA^F DE AFEITAR

head
tête^F
Kopf^M
cabeza^F

collar
anneau^M
Ring^M
anillo^M

disposable razor
rasoir^M jetable
Einwegrasierer^M
maquinilla^F desechable

double-edged razor blade
lame^F à double tranchant^M
zweischneidige Klinge^F
hoja^F de afeitar

handle
manche^M
Griff^M
mango^M

5   5

blade dispenser
distributeur^M de lames^F
Klingenkassette^F
despachador^M de hojas^F de afeitar

UMBRELLA AND STICK
PARAPLUIE^M ET CANNE^F
SCHIRM^M UND STOCK^M
PARAGUAS^M Y BASTONES^M

UMBRELLA
PARAPLUIE^M
SCHIRM^M
PARAGUAS^M

spreader
rayon^M
Gabel^F
extensor^M

ring
coulant^M
Schieber^M
anillo^M

tie
attache^F
Litze^F
tope^M

rib
baleine^F
Stange^F
varilla^F

tip
embout^M de baleine^F
Spitze^F
punta^F

stick
manche^M
Unterstock^M
bastón^M

canopy
toile^F
Bahne^F
tela^F impermeable

catch
ferret^M
Feder^F
pestillo^M de resorte^M

handle
poignée^F
Griff^M
empuñadura^F

TELESCOPIC UMBRELLA
PARAPLUIE^M TÉLESCOPIQUE
TASCHENSCHIRM^M
PARAGUAS^M PLEGABLE

push button
poussoir^M d'ouverture^F
Auslöseknopf^M
botón^M de presión^F

STICK UMBRELLA
PARAPLUIE^M-CANNE^F
STOCKSCHIRM^M
PARAGUAS^M DE BASTÓN^M

cover
fourreau^M
Futteral^M
funda^F

ferrule
embout^M
Stahlspitze^F
contera^F

swagger stick
badine^F
Spazierstock^M
bastón^M ligero

tie closure
courroie^F d'attache^F
Litze^F
correa^F con broche^M

umbrella stand
porte-parapluies^M
Schirmständer^M
paragüero^M

walking stick
canne^F
Spazierstock^M
bastón^M

shoulder strap
bandoulière^F
Schulterriemen^M
bandolera^F

SPECTACLES
LUNETTES^F
BRILLE^F
GAFAS^F

PARTS OF SPECTACLES
PARTIES^F DES LUNETTES^F
TEILE^N DER BRILLE^F
GAFAS^F: PARTES^F

bridge
pont^M
Brücke^W
puente^M

endpiece
tenon^M
Backe^F
espiga^F

bar
barre^F
Steg^M
barra^F

lens
verre^M
Glas^N
lente^F

sidepiece
branche^F
Bügel^M
patilla^F

butt-strap
talon^M
Bügelanschlag^M
extremo^M

pad plate
support^M de plaquette^F
Stegplättchen^N
placa^F del cojinete^M

nose pad
plaquette^F
Seitensteg^M
cojinete^M

earpiece
cambre^F
Bügelende^N
gafa^F

rim
cercle^M
Rand^M
aro^M

pad arm
bras^M de plaquette^F
Stegstütze^F
brazo^M del cojinete^M

bend
coude^M
Bügelbug^M
codo^M

BIFOCAL LENS
VERRE^M BIFOCAL
BIFOKALGLAS^N
LENTE^F BIFOCAL

distance lens
segment^M de loin
Fernteil^N
enfoque^M de lejos

rim
cercle^M
Rand^M
aro^M

reading lens
segment^M de près
Nahteil^N
enfoque^M de cerca

FRAMES
MONTURE^F
FASSUNGEN^F
MONTURA^F

half-glasses
demi-lune^F
Halbbrille^F
media luna^F

scissors-glasses
binocle^M
Scherenbrille^F
binóculos^M de tijera^F

sunglasses
lunettes^F de soleil^M
Sonnenbrille^F
gafas^F de sol^M

pince-nez
bésicles^F à pont^M élastique
Kneifer^M
quevedos^M

lorgnette
face-à-main^M
Lorgnette^F
impertinentes^M

monocle
monocle^M
Monokel^N
monóculo^M

opera glasses
lorgnette^F
Opernglas^N
gemelos^M de teatro^M

377

LEATHER GOODS
ARTICLES^M DE MAROQUINERIE^F
LEDERWAREN^F
ARTÍCULOS^M DE PIEL^F

ATTACHÉ CASE
MALLETTE^F PORTE-DOCUMENTS^M
AKTENKOFFER^M
MALETÍN^M

divider
séparation^F-classeur^M
Einteilung^F
separador^M

pocket
pochette^F
Tasche^F
bolsillo^M

hinge
charnière^F
Scharnier^N
bisagra^F

lining
doublure^F
Futter^N
forro^M

clasp
fermoir^M
Schnappschloß^N
broche^F

expandable file pouch
classeur^M à soufflets^M
Ziehharmonikafach^F
clasificador^M de fuelle^M

pen holder
porte-stylo^M
Stifthalter^M
portaplumas^M

frame
cadre^M
Rahmen^M
bastidor^M

handle
poignée^F
Griff^M
asa^F

combination lock
serrure^F à combinaison^F
Zahlenschloß^N
cerradura^F de combinación^F

BRIEFCASE
SERVIETTE^F
AKTENTASCHE^F
CARTERA^F

BOTTOM-FOLD DOCUMENT CASE
PORTE-DOCUMENTS^M À SOUFFLET^M
KOLLEGMAPPE^F MIT GRIFF^M
CARTERA^F DE FONDO^M PLEGABLE

retractable handle
poignée^F rentrante
ausziehbarer Griff^M
asa^F extensible

exterior pocket
poche^F extérieure
Außentasche^F
bolsillo^M delantero

tab
patte^F
Lasche^F
lengüeta^F

gusset
soufflet^M
Keil^M
fuelle^M

key lock
serrure^F à clé^F
Schlüsselschloß^N
cerradura^F

underarm briefcase
porte-documents^M plat
Unterarmmappe^F
cartera^F portadocumentos^M

writing case
écritoire^F
Schreibmappe^F
agenda^F

spectacles case
étui^F à lunettes^F
Brillenetui^N
funda^F para gafas^F

CALCULATOR/CHEQUE BOOK HOLDER
PORTEFEUILLE^M CHÉQUIER^M
ETUI^N FÜR RECHNER^M UND SCHECKHEFT^N
PORTACHEQUERA^F CON CALCULADORA^F

snap fastener
grébiche^F
Druckverschluß^M
broche^M automático

credit card wallet
porte-cartes^M
Kreditkartenfach^N
tarjetero^M

calculator
calculette^F
Taschenrechner^M
calculadora^F

pen holder
porte-stylo^M
Stifthalter^M
portaplumas^M

hidden pocket
poche^F secrète
Unterfach^N
bolsillo^M secreto

cheque book
chéquier^M
Scheckheft^N
talonario^M de cheques^M

CREDIT CARD WALLET
PORTE-CARTES^M
KREDITKARTENETUI^N
TARJETERO^M

wallet section
poche^F américaine
Scheinfach^N
billetera^F

transparent pockets
feuillets^M
Klarsichtfenster^N
plásticos^M transparentes

tab
patte^F
Lasche^F
lengüeta^F

key case
porte-clés^M
Schlüsseletui^N
llavero^M

slot
fente^F
Fach^N
ranura^F

window
volet^M transparent
Klarsichtfenster^N
plástico^M transparente

wallet
porte-coupures^M
Scheintasche^F
billetera^F

purse
bourse^F à monnaie^F
Knipsbörse^F
monedero^M

wallet
portefeuille^M
Scheintasche^F
billetera^F

cheque book cover
porte-chéquier^M
Scheckhülle^F
talonario^M de cheques^M

passport case
porte-passeport^M
Brieftasche^F
portapasaportes^M

coin purse
porte-monnaie^M
Schüttelbörse^F
portamonedas^M

HANDBAGS
SACS^M À MAIN^F
HANDTASCHEN^F
BOLSAS^F DE MANO^F

men's bag
pochette^F d'homme^M
Herrentasche^F
mariconera^F

SATCHEL BAG
SAC^M CARTABLE^M
AKTENTASCHE^F
BOLSO^M CLÁSICO

handle
poignée^F
Griff^M
asa^F

flap
rabat^M
Überschlag^M
ala^F

clasp
fermoir^M
Schnappschloß^M
broche^M

lock
serrure^F
Schloß^M
cierre^M

pouch
aumônière^F
Beutel^M
bolsita^F de cordones^M

SHOULDER BAG
SAC^M À BANDOULIÈRE^F
SCHULTERTASCHE^F
BOLSO^M

buckle
boucle^F
Schnalle^F
hebilla^F

shoulder strap
bandoulière^F
Schulterriemen^M
bandolera^F

ACCORDION BAG
SAC^M ACCORDÉON^M
UMHÄNGETASCHE^F MIT DEHNFALTE^F
BOLSO^M DE ACORDEÓN^M

gusset
soufflet^M
Keil^M
fuelle^M

tote bag
sac^M fourre-tout^M
Stadttasche^F
bolsa^F de paja^F

small drawstring bag
balluchon^M
kleine Beuteltasche^F
saco^M de viaje^M

shoulder bag with zip
sac^M besace^F
Umhängetasche^F mit Reißverschluß^M
morral^M

duffle bag
sac^M marin^M
Matchbeutel^M
saco^M de marinero^M

box bag
sac^M boîte^F
Boxtasche^F
bolso^M de vestir

clutch bag
pochette^F
Klemmtasche^F
monedero^M

DRAWSTRING BAG
SAC^M SEAU^M
BEUTELTASCHE^F
BOLSA^F DE CORDONES^M

eyelet
œillet^M
Öse^F
ojal^M

drawstring
lacet^M de serrage^M
Zugschnur^F
cordón^M

front pocket
poche^F frontale
Vortasche^F
bolsillo^M exterior

holdall
sac^M polochon^M
Dreivierteltasche^F
bolso^M de viaje^M

muff
manchon^M
Mufftasche^F
bolso^M manguito^M

shopping bag
cabas^M
Einkaufstasche^F
bolso^M de la compra^F

shopping bag
sac^M à provisions^F
Tragetasche^F
bolso^M de la compra^F

PERSONAL ARTICLES
OBJETS PERSONNELS

PERSÖNLICHE ARTIKEL
ARTÍCULOS PERSONALES

TRAVEL BAG
SAC^M DE VOL^M
REISETASCHE^F
BOLSO^M DE VIAJE^M

handle
poignée^F
Griff^M
asa^F

exterior pocket
poche^F extérieure
Außentasche^F
bolsillo^M exterior

shoulder strap
bandoulière^F
Schulterriemen^M
bandolera^F

flight bag
sac^M fourre-tout^M
Flugtasche^F
maletín^M

VANITY CASE
MALLETTE^F DE TOILETTE^F
KOSMETIKKOFFER^M
NECESER^M

mirror
miroir^M
Spiegel^M
espejo^M

hinge
charnière^F
Scharnier^N
bisagra^F

SUIT CARRIER
HOUSSE^F À VÊTEMENTS^M
KLEIDERSACK^M
BOLSA^F PARA TRAJES^M

cosmetic tray
plateau^M
Einsatz^M
bandeja^F para cosméticos^M

toilet bag
trousse^F de toilette^F
Kulturbeutel^M
estuche^M de tocador^M

LUGGAGE TROLLEY
PORTE-BAGAGES^M
GEPÄCKROLLER^M
CARRITO^M PORTAMALETAS^M

frame
armature^F
Rahmen^M
armazón^M

luggage elastic
sangle^F élastique
Gepäckgummi^M
elástico^M

zip
fermeture^F à glissière^F
Reißverschluß^M
cremallera^F

stand
béquille^F
Ständer^M
soporte^M

SUITCASE
VALISE^F PULLMAN^M
KOFFER^M
MALETA^F CLÁSICA

handle
poignée^F
Griff^M
asa^F

frame
cadre^M
Rahmen^M
chasis^M

pull strap
dragonne^F
Zugriemen^M
correa^F

WEEKEND CASE
VALISE^F FIN^F DE SEMAINE^F
WOCHENENDKOFFER^M
MALETA^F DE FIN^M DE SEMANA^F

divider
panneau^M de séparation^F
Packplatte^F
panel^M de separación^F

interior pocket
poche^F intérieure
Innentasche^F
bolso^M interior

retaining strap
sangle^F serre-vêtements^M
Packriemen^M
correa^F de retención^F

lock
serrure^F
Schloß^N
cerradura^F

wheel
roulette^F
Rolle^F
ruedecilla^F

trim
garniture^F
Blende^F
guarnición^F

identity tag
porte-adresse^M
Gepäckanhänger^M
etiqueta^F

shell
coque^F
Schale^F
tapa^F

TRUNK
MALLE^F
ÜBERSEEKOFFER^M
BAÚL^M

hasp
moraillon^M
Haspe^F
aldaba^F

latch
crampon^M de fermeture^F
Monomatic-Schloß^N
abrazadera^F

tray
plateau^M
Einsatz^M
bandeja^F

handle
poignée^F
Griff^M
asa^F

reinforced edging
ferrure^F
Schutzkante^F
herraje^M

cornerpiece
cantonnière^F
Eckstück^N
contera^F

PERSONAL ARTICLES
OBJETS PERSONNELS

PERSÖNLICHE ARTIKEL
ARTÍCULOS PERSONALES

383

SMOKING ACCESSORIES
ARTICLES^M DE FUMEUR^M
RAUCHERBEDARF^M
ACCESORIOS^M PARA FUMAR

CIGAR
CIGARE^M
ZIGARRE^F
PURO^M

cigar band
bague^F
Banderole^F
vitola^F

wrapper
cape^F
Deckblatt^N
envoltura^F de tabaco^M de hoja^F

tobacco
tabac^M
Tabak^M
tabaco^M

filler
tripe^F
Einlage^F
tripa^F

head
tête^F
Spitze^F
cabeza^F

bunch
corps^M
Mittelstück^N
cuerpo^M

tuck
pied^M
Endstück^N
punta^F

CIGARETTE
CIGARETTE^F
ZIGARETTE^F
CIGARRILLO^M

cigarette holder
fume-cigarettes^M
Zigarettenspitze^F
boquilla^F

filter tip
bout^M-filtre^M
Filterspitze^F
filtro^M

paper
papier^M
Papier^N
papel^M

seam
couture^F
Naht^F
costura^F

tobacco
tabac^M
Tabak^M
tabaco^M

cigarette papers
papier^M à cigarettes^F
Zigarettenpapier^N
papel^M de fumar

CIGARETTE PACKET
PAQUET^M **DE CIGARETTES**^F
ZIGARETTENPACKUNG^F
PAQUETE^M **DE CIGARRILLOS**^M

stamp
timbre^M
Steuermarke^F
timbre^M

tear tape
bandelette^F d'arrachage^M
Aufreißband^N
tira^F para rasgar la envoltura^F

trade name
marque^F déposée
Markenname^M
marca^F registrada

carton
cartouche^F
Stange^F
cartón^M de cigarrillos^M

384

PIPE
PIPE^F
PFEIFE^F
PIPA^F

bowl
talon^M
Pfeifenkopf^M
cazoleta^F

shank
tige^F
Holm^M
asta^F

bit
lentille^F
Biß^M
boquilla^F

stummel
tête^F
Pfeifenkopf^M
barba^F

stem
tuyau^M
Pfeifenmundstück^N
cañon^M

tobacco hole
fourneau^M
Tabakkammer^F
cazoleta^F

CROSS SECTION OF A PIPE
COUPE^F D'UNE PIPE^F
QUERSCHNITT^M EINER PFEIFE^F
CORTE^M TRANSVERSAL DE UNA PIPA^F

peg
tenon^M
Zapfen^M
estaca^F

air hole
trou^M de l'embout^M
Luftloch^N
respiradero^M

mortise
mortaise^F
Zapfenloch^N
caja^F

filter
système^M filtre^M
Filter^M
filtro^M

pipe rack
porte-pipes^M
Pfeifenständer^M
portapipas^M

pipe cleaners
nettoie-pipes^M
Pfeifenputzer^M
escobillas^F

PIPE TOOLS
BOURRE-PIPE^M
PFEIFENBESTECK^N
ACCESORIOS^M PARA LA PIPA^F

tamper
bourre-pipe^M
Stopfer^M
pisón^M

scoop
curette^F
Auskratzer^M
raspador^M

pick
pointe^F
Dorn^M
palillo^M

tobacco pouch
blague^F à tabac^M
Tabaksbeutel^M
tabaquera^F

BOOK OF MATCHES
POCHETTE^F D'ALLUMETTES^F
STREICHHOLZHEFTCHEN^N
CARTERITA^F DE CERILLAS^F

cover
grand rabat^M
Deckel^M
tapa^F

back
dos^M
Rücken^M
respaldo^M

front flap
petit rabat^M
Vorderfläche^F
solapa^F

friction strip
frottoir^M
Reibefläche^F
frotador^M de fósforo^M

head
tête^F
Kopf^M
cabeza^F

matchstick
tige^F
Streichholz^N
cerilla^F

MATCHBOX
BOÎTE^F D'ALLUMETTES^F
STREICHHOLZSCHACHTEL^F
CAJA^F DE CERILLAS^F

safety match
allumette^F de sûreté^F
Sicherheitsstreichholz^N
cerillas^F de seguridad^F

GAS LIGHTER
BRIQUET^M À GAZ^M
GASFEUERZEUG^N
ENCENDEDOR^M

cover
couvercle^M
Abdeckkappe^F
tapa^F

striker wheel
molette^F
Zahnrädchen^N
esmeril^M

flame adjustment wheel
molette^F de réglage^M de la flamme^F
Flammenregulierung^F
ajuste^M de la llama^F

ASHTRAY
CENDRIER^M
ASCHENBECHER^M
CENICERO^M

butt
mégot^M
Stummel^M
colilla^F

gas tank
réservoir^M
Butangastank^M
depósito^M de gas^M

ash
cendre^F
Asche^F
ceniza^F

SUMMARY

KOMMUNIKATION
COMUNICACIONES

COMMUNICATIONS
COMUNICATIONS

WRITING INSTRUMENTS
INSTRUMENTS^M D'ÉCRITURE^F
SCHREIBGERÄTE^N
INSTRUMENTOS^M PARA ESCRIBIR

quill
plume^F d'oie^F
Kielfeder^F
pluma^F de ave^F

Roman metal pen
plume^F métallique romaine
römische Metallfeder^F
pluma^F metálica romana

cane pen
plume^F creuse de roseau^M
Rohrfeder^F
pluma^F de caña^F

Egyptian reed pen
calame^M
Binsenstengel^M
cálamo^M egipcio

writing brush
pinceau^M
Schreibpinsel^M
pincel^M

stylus
stylet^M
Stilus^M
estilo^M

lead pencil
crayon^M en plomb^M
Graphitstift^M
lápiz^M de grafito^M

steel pen
plume^F métallique
Stahlschreibfeder^F
pluma^F metálica

pencil
crayon^M
Bleistift^M
lápiz^M

marker
marqueur^M
Marker^M
marcador^M

FOUNTAIN PEN
STYLO^M-PLUME^F
FÜLLFEDERHALTER^M
ESTILOGRÁFICA^F

nib
plume^F
Feder^F
punta^F

propelling pencil
porte-mine^M
Druckbleistift^M
portaminas^M

cap
capuchon^M
Kappe^F
tapa^F

barrel
corps^M
Tintenraum^M
caña^F

air hole
évent^M
Luftloch^N
orificio^M

BALLPOINT PEN
STYLO^M-BILLE^F
KUGELSCHREIBER^M
BOLÍGRAFO^M

thrust tube
tube^M de poussée^F
Druckrohr^N
tubo^M de empuje^M

clip
agrafe^F
Clip^M
pinza^F

joint
joint^M
Verbindung^F
unión^F

point
pointe^F
Spitze^F
punta^F

push-button
bouton^M-poussoir^M
Druckknopf^M
botón^M de presión^F

thrust device
dispositif^M de poussée^F
Druckmechanik^F
mecanismo^M de empuje^M

cartridge
cartouche^F
Mine^F
carga^F

spring
ressort^M
Feder^F
resorte^M

refill
recharge^F
Nachfüllmine^F
repuesto^M

ink
encre^F
Farbmasse^F
tinta^F

ball
bille^F
Kugelmechanik^F
bola^F de rodamiento^M

CROSS SECTION OF A REFLEX CAMERA
COUPE^F D'UN APPAREIL^M REFLEX
QUERSCHNITT^M DURCH EINE SPIEGELREFLEXKAMERA^F
CORTE^M TRANSVERSAL DE UNA CÁMARA^F REFLEX

lens
lentille^F
Linse^F
objetivo^M

pentaprism
prisme^M pentagonal
Pentaprisma^N
prisma^M

eyepiece
oculaire^M
Okular^N
ocular^M

focusing screen
verre^M de visée^F
Mattscheibe^F
filtro^M de focalización^F

main reflex mirror
miroir^M principal
Hauptreflexspiegel^M
espejo^M reflector central

focal plane shutter
rideau^M d'obturateur^M
Schlitzverschluß^M
obturador^M de cortina^F

film
film^M
Film^M
película^F

secondary mirror
miroir^M secondaire
Sekundärspiegel^M
espejo^M secundario

light sensor
photodiode^F
Lichtsensor^M
sensor^M de luz^F

lens mount
monture^F d'objectif^M
Objektivanschluß^M
montura^F del objetivo^M

diaphragm
diaphragme^M
Blende^F
diafragma^M de iris^M

CAMERA BACK
DOS^M DE L'APPAREIL^M
RÜCKSEITE^F DER KAMERA^F
PARTE^F TRASERA DE UNA CÁMARA^F

viewfinder
viseur^M
Bildsucher^M
visor^M

take-up spool
bobine^F réceptrice
Filmaufrollspule^F
carrete^M de rebobinado^M

neckstrap eyelet
œillet^M d'attache^F
Öse^F für Schulterriemen^M
ojete^M para la correa^F del cuello^M

film rewind system
mécanisme^M de rebobinage^M
Filmrückspulung^F
sistema^M de rebobinado^M de la
película^F

focal plane shutter
rideau^M d'obturateur^M
Schlitzverschluß^M
obturador^M de cortina^F

film sprocket
tambour^M d'entraînement^M
Transporträdchen^N
piñón^M de la rueda^F de la película^F

pressure plate
presseur^M
Andruckplatte^F
lámina^F de presión^F

film cassette chamber
logement^M de la bobine^F
Patronenkammer^F
cámara^F para el cartucho^M de la película^F

film guide roller
cylindre^M guide^M-film^M
Transportwalze^F
rodillo^M guía^F de la película^F

film guide rail
rail^M guide^M-film^M
Transportschiene^F
carril^M guía^F de la película^F

film leader indicator
témoin^M de l'amorce^F du film^M
Markierung^F für Filmanfang^M
indicador^M principal de la película^F

SINGLE-LENS REFLEX (SLR) CAMERA
APPAREIL^{u} À VISÉE^{f} REFLEX MONO-OBJECTIF^{u}
EINÄUGIGE SPIEGELREFLEXKAMERA^{f}
CÁMARA^{f} RÉFLEX DE UN OBJETIVO^{u}

film rewind knob
rebobinage^{f}
Rückspulknopf^{u}
tornillo^{u} de rebobinado^{u} de la película^{f}

data panel
écran^{u} de contrôle^{u}
Datenmonitor^{u}
panel^{u} de controles^{u}

exposure adjustment knob
correction^{f} d'exposition^{f}
Belichtungskorrekturknopf^{u}
tornillo^{u} de ajuste^{u} de la exposición^{f}

on/off switch
commutateur^{u} marche^{f}/arrêt^{u}
Ein-/Ausschalter^{u}
interruptor^{u} de encendido^{u}/apagado^{u}

program selector
sélecteur^{u} de fonctions^{f}
Programmwählscheibe^{f}
esfera^{f} de control^{u} de la modalidad^{f}

hot-shoe contact
contact^{u} électrique
Blitzkontakt^{u}
contacto^{u} del patín^{u}

accessory shoe
griffe^{f} porte-accessoires^{u}
Zubehörschuh^{u}
patín^{u} para accesorios^{u}

film advance mode
mode^{u} d'entraînement^{u} du film^{u}
Filmtransporteinstellung^{f}
modalidad^{f} de avance^{u} de la película^{f}

film speed
sensibilité^{f} du film^{u}
Filmempfindlichkeit^{f}
indicador^{u} de velocidad^{f}

multiple exposure mode
surimpression^{f}
Belichtungsmesser^{u}
modalidad^{f} de exposición^{f} múltiple

exposure mode
mode^{u} d'exposition^{f}
Belichtungseinstellung^{f}
modalidad^{f} de exposición^{f}

self-timer indicator
témoin^{u} du retardateur^{u}
Selbstauslöser-Lichtsignal^{u}
indicador^{u} de tiempo^{u}

shutter release button
déclencheur^{u}
Auslöser^{u}
botón^{u} liberador de la película^{f}

camera body
boîtier^{u}
Kameragehäuse^{u}
caja^{f}

lens release button
déverrouillage^{u} de l'objectif^{u}
Objektivauswurf^{u}
botón^{u} liberador^{u} del objetivo^{u}

remote control terminal
prise^{f} de télécommande^{f}
Diode^{f} des Selbstauslösers^{u}
terminal^{u} del control^{u} a larga distancia^{f}

focus mode selector
mode^{u} de mise^{f} au point^{u}
Autofocus-Umschalter^{u}
selector^{u} de focalización^{f}

depth-of-field preview button
vérification^{f} de la profondeur^{f} de champ^{u}
Schärfentiefenknopf^{u}
botón^{u} de visionamiento^{u} preliminar de profundidad^{f} de campo^{u}

lens
objectif^{u}
Objektiv^{u}
objetivo^{u}

PHOTOGRAPHY
PHOTOGRAPHIE*F*
FOTOGRAFIE*F*
FOTOGRAFÍA*F*

LENSES
OBJECTIFS*M*
OBJEKTIVE*N*
OBJETIVOS*M*

standard lens
objectif*M* normal
Standardobjektiv*N*
objetivo*M* normal

lens
lentille*F*
Linse*F*
objetivo*M*

distance scale
échelle*F* des distances*F*
Entfernungsskala*F*
escala*F* de distancia*F*

focussing ring
bague*F* de mise*F* au point*M*
Blendenring*M*
anillo*M* de ajuste*M* del enfoque*M*

depth-of-field scale
échelle*F* de profondeur*F* de champ*M*
Schärfentiefenskala*F*
escala*F* de profundidad*F* de campo*M* de visión*F*

lens aperture scale
échelle*F* d'ouverture*F* de diaphragme*M*
Blendenskala*F*
escala*F* de abertura*F* del diafragma*M*

wide-angle lens
objectif*M* grand-angulaire
Weitwinkelobjektiv*N*
gran angular*M*

bayonet mount
monture*F* baïonnette*F*
Bayonettanschluß*M*
montura*F* de bayoneta*F*

LENS ACCESSORIES
ACCESSOIRES*M* DE L'OBJECTIF*M*
OBJEKTIVZUBEHÖR*N*
OBJETIVOS*M* Y ACCESORIOS*M*

lens cap
capuchon*M* d'objectif*M*
Objektivschutzdeckel*M*
tapa*F* del objetivo*M*

lens hood
parasoleil*M*
Gegenlichtblende*F*
capuchón*M*

zoom lens
objectif*M* zoom*M*
Zoomobjektiv*N*
zoom*M*

semi-fisheye lens
objectif*M* super-grand-angle*M*
Super-Weitwinkelobjektiv*N*
ojo*M* de pez*M*

colour filter
filtre*M* de couleur*F*
Farbfilter*M*
filtro*M* de color*M*

close-up lens
lentille*F* de macrophotographie*F*
Nahlinse*F*
lente*M* de acercamiento*M*

polarizing filter
filtre*M* de polarisation*F*
Polarisationsfilter*M*
filtro*M* de polarización*F*

lens
objectif*M*
Objektiv*N*
objetivo*M* normal

telephoto lens
téléobjectif*M*
Teleobjektiv*N*
teleobjetivo*M*

fisheye lens
hypergone*M*
Fischaugenobjektiv*N*
lente*F* de 180 grados*M*

tele-converter
multiplicateur*M* de focale*F*
Telekonverter*M*
teleconvertidor*M*

electronic flash
flash^M électronique
Elektronenblitz^M
flash^M electrónico

air bulb shutter release
déclencheur^M pneumatique
pneumatischer Auslöser^M
disparador^M neumático

flashtube
réflecteur^M
Blitzröhre^F
tubo^M de flash^M

photoelectric cell
cellule^F photoélectrique
Fotozelle^F
celda^F fotoeléctrica

flash bulb
lampe^F-éclair^M
Blitzbirne^F
bombilla^F de flash^M

mounting foot
pied^M de fixation^F
Aufsteckschuh^M
pie^M de montura^F

flashcube
flash^M-cube^M
Blitzwürfel^M
cubo^M de flash^M

battery
pile^F
Batterie^F
pila^F

cable shutter release
déclencheur^M souple
Drahtauslöser^M
disparador^M de cable^M

TRIPOD
TRÉPIED^M
STATIV^N
TRÍPODE^M

camera screw
vis^F de fixation^F
Kameraschraube^F
tornillo^M de fijación^F

plate
embase^F
Platte^F
placa^F

quick release system
déblocage^M instantané
Schnellkupplungssystem^N
sistema^M de disparo^M rápido

side-tilt lock
blocage^M vertical
Feststellgriff^M für Hochkantstellung^F
seguro^M de inclinación^F lateral

horizontal motion lock
blocage^M horizontal
Feststellgriff^M für Panoramadrehung^F
seguro^M de movimiento^M horizontal

column
colonne^F
Säule^F
columna^F central

camera platform
plate-forme^F
Kameraplattform^F
plataforma^F

panoramic head
tête^F panoramique
Panoramakopf^M
cabeza^F panorámica

camera platform lock
blocage^M de la plate-forme^F
Feststellgriff^M für Kameraplattform^F
seguro^M de la plataforma^F

column lock
blocage^M de la colonne^F
Feststeller^M für Säule^F
seguro^M de la columna^F

column crank
manivelle^F de la colonne^F
Kurbel^F für Säule^F
manivela^F

collet
bague^F de serrage^M
Beinklemme^F
anillo^M

telescoping leg
branche^F télescopique
Teleskopbein^N
pata^F telescópica

STILL CAMERAS
APPAREILS*M* PHOTOGRAPHIQUES
FOTOAPPARATE*M*
CÁMARAS*M* FIJAS

rangefinder camera
appareil*M* à télémètre*M* couplé
Sucherkamera*F*
telémetro*M*

Polaroid® Land camera
Polaroid®*M*
Sofortbildkamera*F*
cámara*F* Polaroid Land

underwater camera
appareil*M* de plongée*F*
Unterwasserkamera*F*
cámara*F* submarina

single-lens reflex camera
appareil*M* à visée*F* reflex mono-objectif*M*
einäugige Spiegelreflexkamera*F*
cámara*F* reflex con objetivo*M* simple

disposable camera
appareil*M* jetable
Einwegkamera*F*
cámara*F* desechable

twin-lens reflex camera
appareil*M* reflex à deux objectifs*M*
zweiäugige Spiegelreflexkamera*F*
cámara*F* tipo*M* réflex con dos objetivos*M*

view camera
chambre*F* photographique
Großformatkamera*F*
cámara*F* de enfoque*M*

medium format SLR (6 x 6)
appareil^M reflex 6 X 6 mono-objectif^M
Mittelformatkamera^F SLR(6 x 6)
formato^M mediano SLR (6x6)

STILL CAMERAS
APPAREILS^M PHOTOGRAPHIQUES
FOTOAPPARATE^M
DIFERENTES TIPOS^M DE CÁMARAS^F FOTOGRÁFICAS

pocket camera
appareil^M petit-format^M
Pocket-Instamatic Kamera^F
cámara^F de bolsillo^M

disc camera
appareil^M pour photodisque^M
Disc-Kamera^F
cámara^F de disco^M

still video camera
appareil^M de videophoto^F
Videokamera^F
cámara^F de video^M fijo

stereoscopic camera
appareil^M stéréoscopique
Stereokamera^F
cámara^F estereofotogramétrica

film leader
amorce^F
Filmlasche^F
principio^M de la película^F

perforation
perforation^F
Perforierung^F
perforación^F

FILMS
PELLICULES^F
FILME^M
PELÍCULAS^F

still video film disc
disque^M videophoto^F
Videofilmdiskette^F
película^F de disco^M para video^M fijo

cassette film
cartouche^F de pellicule^F
Patronenfilm^M
cartucho^M de la película^F

film disc
film^M-disque^M
Filmdiskette^F
película^F de disco^M

cartridge film
cassette^F de pellicule^F
Kassettenfilm^M
cartucho^M de la película^F

sheet film
pellicule^F en feuille^F
Planfilm^M
hoja^F de la película^F

roll film
rouleau^M de pellicule^F
Rollfilm^M
rollo^M de la película^F

film pack
film^M-pack^M
Filmkassette^F
paquete^M de placas^F fotográficas

PHOTOGRAPHY
PHOTOGRAPHIE[F]
FOTOGRAFIE[F]
FOTOGRAFÍA[F]

EXPOSURE METER
POSEMÈTRE[M] PHOTO-ÉLECTRIQUE
BELICHTUNGSMESSER[M]
FOTÓMETRO[M]

diffuser
tête[F] diffusante
Diffusionskalotte[F]
difusor[M]

indicator needle
aiguille[F]
Anzeigenadel[F]
aguja[F] indicadora

light-reading scale
échelle[F] de lecture[F] de la luminosité[F]
Lichtwertskala[F]
escala[F] de lectura[F]

exposure value
indice[F] d'exposition[F]
Belichtungswert[M]
índices[M] de exposición[F]

cine scale
cadence[F] images[F]/seconde[F]
Cine-Skala[F]
escala[F] de imágenes[F] por segundo[M]

exposure-time scale
échelle[F] des temps[M] d'exposition[F]
Belichtungszeitskala[F]
escala[F] de duración[F] de la exposición[F]

aperture scale
échelle[F] d'ouverture[F]
Blendenskala[F]
escala[F] de abertura[F]

film speed
sensibilité[F] du film[M]
Filmempfindlichkeit[F]
velocidad[F] de la película[F]

calculator dial
disque[M] de réglage[M]
Rechenscheibe[F]
cuadrante[M] calculador

transfer scale
report[M] de lecture[F]
Umrechnungsskala[F]
escala[F] de transferencia[F]

SPOTMETER
POSEMÈTRE[M] À VISÉE[F] REFLEX
SPOTMETER[M]
FOTÓMETRO[M] ELECTRÓNICO

average key
réglage[M] sur demi-teinte[F]
Taste[F] für Mittelwerte[M]
botón[M] de luminosidad[F] media

highlight key
réglage[M] sur haute lumière[F]
Hi.-Taste[F]
botón[M] de fuerte luminosidad[F]

shadow key
réglage[M] sur ombre[F]
Shadow-Taste[F]
botón[M] de sombra[F]

eyepiece
oculaire[M]
Okular[N]
ocular[M]

lock switch
fixe-lecture[M]
Ein-/Ausschalter[M]
seguro[M]

data display
écran[M] d'affichage[M]
Display[N]
visualización[F] de la información[F]

lens
objectif[M]
Objektiv[N]
objetivo[M]

memory cancel
effacement[M] de mémoire[F]
Speicherlöschtaste[F]
botón[M] para cancelar la memoria[F]

shutter speed setting
réglage[M] de la vitesse[F] d'obturation[F]
Tasten[F] für Erhöhen[N]/Absenken[N]
ajuste[F] de la velocidad[F] del obturador[M]

measuring button
bouton[M] de mise[F] en circuit[M]
Meßtaste[F]
botón[M] de medición[F]

aperture/exposure value display
affichage[M] ouverture[F]/temps[M] d'exposition[F]
Anzeige[F] für Blende[F]/Belichtungswert[M]
visualización[F] de valores[M] de abertura[F] y de exposición[F]

film speed
sensibilité[F] du film[M]
Filmempfindlichkeit[F]
sensibilidad[F] de la película[F]

memory recall key
rappel[M] de mémoire[F]
Rückruftaste[F]
botón[M] de llamado[M] de memoria[F]

data display illumination button
éclairage[M] de l'écran[M] d'affichage[M]
Displaybeleuchtungstaste[F]
botón[M] de iluminación[F] de la pantalla[F]

memory key
commande[F] de mémoire[F]
Speichertaste[F]
botón[M] de memoria[F]

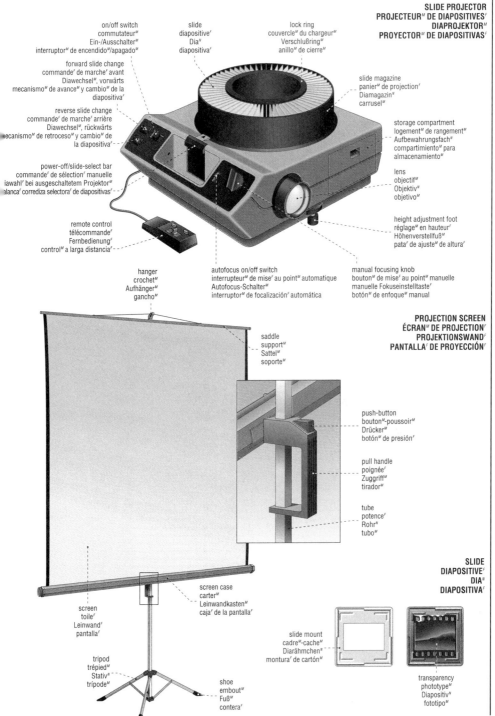

SLIDE PROJECTOR
PROJECTEUR*M* **DE DIAPOSITIVES***F*
DIAPROJEKTOR*M*
PROYECTOR*M* **DE DIAPOSITIVAS***F*

on/off switch
commutateur*M*
Ein-/Ausschalter*M*
interruptor*M* de encendido*M*/apagado*M*

slide
diapositive*F*
Dia*N*
diapositiva*F*

lock ring
couvercle*M* du chargeur*M*
Verschlußring*M*
anillo*M* de cierre*M*

forward slide change
commande*F* de marche*F* avant
Diawechsel*M*, vorwärts
mecanismo*M* de avance*M* y cambio*M* de la
diapositiva*F*

reverse slide change
commande*F* de marche*F* arrière
Diawechsel*M*, rückwärts
mecanismo*M* de retroceso*M* y cambio*M* de
la diapositiva*F*

power-off/slide-select bar
commande*F* de sélection*F* manuelle
Diawahl*F* bei ausgeschaltetem Projektor*M*
palanca*F* corrediza selectora*F* de diapositivas*F*

remote control
télécommande*F*
Fernbedienung*F*
control*M* a larga distancia*F*

hanger
crochet*M*
Aufhänger*M*
gancho*M*

autofocus on/off switch
interrupteur*M* de mise*F* au point*M* automatique
Autofocus-Schalter*M*
interruptor*M* de focalización*F* automática

slide magazine
panier*M* de projection*F*
Diamagazin*N*
carrusel*M*

storage compartment
logement*M* de rangement*M*
Aufbewahrungsfach*N*
compartimiento*M* para
almacenamiento*M*

lens
objectif*M*
Objektiv*N*
objetivo*M*

height adjustment foot
réglage*M* en hauteur*F*
Höhenverstellfuß*M*
pata*F* de ajuste*M* de altura*F*

manual focusing knob
bouton*M* de mise*F* au point*M* manuelle
manuelle Fokuseinstelltaste*F*
botón*M* de enfoque*M* manual

PROJECTION SCREEN
ÉCRAN*M* **DE PROJECTION***F*
PROJEKTIONSWAND*F*
PANTALLA*F* **DE PROYECCIÓN***F*

saddle
support*M*
Sattel*M*
soporte*M*

push-button
bouton*M*-poussoir*M*
Drücker*M*
botón*M* de presión*F*

pull handle
poignée*F*
Zuggriff*M*
tirador*M*

tube
potence*F*
Rohr*N*
tubo*M*

SLIDE
DIAPOSITIVE*F*
DIA*N*
DIAPOSITIVA*F*

screen
toile*F*
Leinwand*F*
pantalla*F*

screen case
carter*M*
Leinwandkasten*M*
caja*F* de la pantalla*F*

slide mount
cadre*M*-cache*M*
Diarähmchen*N*
montura*F* de cartón*M*

tripod
trépied*M*
Stativ*N*
trípode*M*

shoe
embout*M*
Fuß*M*
contera*F*

transparency
phototype*M*
Diapositiv*N*
fototipo*M*

DEVELOPING TANK
CUVE^F DE DÉVELOPPEMENT^M
ENTWICKLUNGSTROMMEL^F
TANQUE^M DE REVELADO^M

cap
capuchon^M
Kappe^F
capuchón^M

lid
couvercle^M
Deckel^M
tapa^F

reel
spirale^F
Spirale^F
espiral^F

tank
cuve^F
Dose^F
cubeta^F

lightbox
négatoscope^M
Leuchtpult^N
caja^F luminosa

timer
minuterie^F
Laboruhr^F
reloj^M

guillotine
cisaille^F
Längsschneidemaschine^F
guillotina^F

safelight
éclairage^M inactinique
Laborleuchte^F
luz^F inactínica

film drying cabinet
armoire^F de séchage^M
Trockenschrank^M
armario^M de secado^M de negativos^M

enlarging easel
margeur^M
Vergrößerungsrahmen^M
marginadora^F

contact printer
châssis^M-presse^F
Kontaktkopiergerät^N
prensa^F de contactos^M

NEGATIVE CARRIER
PORTE-NÉGATIF^M
NEGATIVHALTER^M
PORTANEGATIVOS^M

column
colonne^F
Säule^F
columna^F

ENLARGER
AGRANDISSEUR^M
VERGRÖSSERER^M
AMPLIADORA^F

window
fenêtre^F
Sichtfenster^N
ventana^F

lamphouse head
boîte^F à lumière^F
Beleuchtungskopf^M
cabeza^F de la caja^F de iluminación^F

negative carrier
porte-négatif^M
Negativhalter^M
portanegativos^M

lamphouse elevation control
ouverture^F de la boîte^F à lumière^F
Scharfeinsteller^M
control^M de elevación^F de la caja^F de iluminación^F

negative
négatif^M
Negativ^N
negativo^M

height control
réglage^M en hauteur^F
Höhenkontrolle^F
control^M de altura^F

bellows
soufflet^M
Balgen^N
fuelle^M

red safelight filter
filtre^M rouge inactinique
roter Sicherheitsfilter^M
filtro^M rojo^M de la luz^F inactínica

enlarging lens
objectif^M d'agrandissement^M
Vergrößerungsobjektiv^N
lente^F de ampliación^F

height scale
échelle^F de hauteur^F
Höhenskala^F
escala^F de ampliación^F

baseboard
plateau^M
Grundplatte^F
tablero^M de base^F

enlarger timer
compte-pose^M
Belichtungs-Schaltuhr^F
reloj^M de la ampliadora^F

DEVELOPING BATHS
BAINS^M DE DÉVELOPPEMENT^M
ENTWICKLUNGSBÄDER^N
BAÑOS^M DE REVELADO^M

developer bath
bain^M de révélateur^M
Entwickler^M
baño^M de revelado^M

stop bath
bain^M d'arrêt^M
Stoppbad^N
baño^M de pare^M

fixing bath
bain^M de fixation^F
Fixierbad^N
baño^M de fijación^F

focusing magnifier
loupe^F de mise^F au point^M
Scharfsteller^M
lupa^F de focalización^F

PRINT WASHER
LAVEUSE^F POUR ÉPREUVES^F
BILDERWASCHER^M
CUBETA^F PARA LAVAR IMPRESIONES^F

tank
réservoir^M
Wässerungswanne^F
tanque^M

overflow tube
trop-plein^M
Überlaufstutzen^M
tubo^M de drenaje^M

cradle
cadre^M porte-épreuves^M
Fächerkorb^M
soporte^M

inlet hose
flexible^M de branchement^M
Schlauch^M für Wasserzufluß^M
manguera^F de llenado^M

tap connector
raccord^M
Adapter^M
adaptador^M

outlet hose
renvoi^M d'eau^F
Schlauch^M für Wasserablauf^M
manguera^F de vaciado^M

print drying rack
séchoir^M d'épreuves^F
Trockenständer^M
secadora^F de pruebas^F

399

STEREO SOUND SYSTEM
CHAÎNE^F STÉRÉO
TONWIEDERGABESYSTEM^N
EQUIPO^M ESTEREOFÓNICO

SYSTEM COMPONENTS
COMPOSANTES^F D'UN SYSTÈME^M
SYSTEMBAUSTEINE^M
COMPONENTES^M

FM antenna
antenne^F FM
FM-Antenne^F
antena^F FM

AM antenna
antenne^F AM
AM-Antenne^F
antena^F AM

turntable
platine^F tourne-disque^M
Plattenspieler^M
tocadiscos^M

tuner
tuner^M
Rundfunkempfänger^M
sintonizador^M

jack
jack^M
Buchse^F
enchufe^M hembra^F

lead
câble^M de raccordement^M
Verbindungskabel^M
cables^M conectores

BACK OF THE AMPLIFIER
DOS^M DE L'AMPLIFICATEUR^M
VERSTÄRKER-RÜCKSEITE^F
PARTE^F TRASERA DE UN AMPLIFICADOR^M

plug
fiche^F pour jack^M
Stecker^M
enchufe^M

earth connection
prise^F de terre^F
Erdung^F
toma^F a tierra^F

CAUTION
RISK OF ELECTRIC SHOCK
DO NOT OPEN

PHONO   AUX.   TUNER   CD   EQ   TAPE
                                    IN   OUT   IN   OUT

GND

graphic equalizer
égalisateur^M graphique
Equalizer^M
compensador^M gráfico de sintonización^F

compact disc player
lecteur^M de disque^M compact
CD-Spieler^M
tocadiscos^M compacto

cassette deck
platine^F cassette^F
Kassettendeck^N
grabadora^F y tocacintas^M

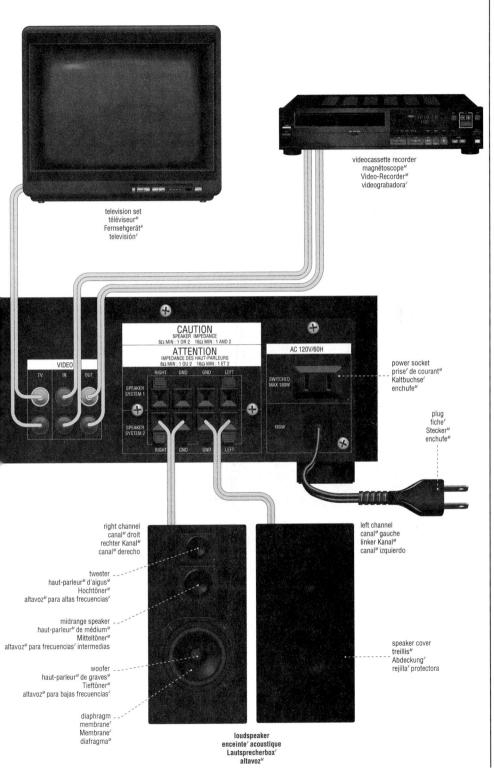

videocassette recorder
magnétoscope^M
Video-Recorder^M
videograbadora^F

television set
téléviseur^M
Fernsehgerät^N
televisión^F

CAUTION
SPEAKER IMPEDANCE
8Ω MIN : 1 OR 2   16Ω MIN : 1 AND 2
ATTENTION
IMPEDANCE DES HAUT-PARLEURS
8Ω MIN : 1 OU 2   16Ω MIN : 1 ET 2

AC 120V/60H

VIDEO

TV   IN   OUT

RIGHT   GND   GND   LEFT

SPEAKER SYSTEM 1

SWITCHED
MAX 180W

SPEAKER SYSTEM 2

RIGHT   GND   GND   LEFT

165W

power socket
prise^F de courant^M
Kaltbuchse^F
enchufe^M

plug
fiche^F
Stecker^M
enchufe^M

right channel
canal^M droit
rechter Kanal^M
canal^M derecho

tweeter
haut-parleur^M d'aigus^M
Hochtöner^M
altavoz^M para altas frecuencias^F

midrange speaker
haut-parleur^M de médium^M
Mitteltöner^M
altavoz^M para frecuencias^F intermedias

woofer
haut-parleur^M de graves^M
Tieftöner^M
altavoz^M para bajas frecuencias^F

diaphragm
membrane^F
Membrane^F
diafragma^M

left channel
canal^M gauche
linker Kanal^M
canal^M izquierdo

speaker cover
treillis^M
Abdeckung^F
rejilla^F protectora

**loudspeaker
enceinte^F acoustique
Lautsprecherbox^F
altavoz^M**

401

STEREO SOUND SYSTEM
CHAÎNE^F STÉRÉO
TONWIEDERGABESYSTEM^N
EQUIPO^M ESTEREOFÓNICO

TUNER
TUNER^M
RUNDFUNKEMPFÄNGER^M
SINTONIZADOR^M

preset tuning button
touche^F de présélection^F
Stationsspeichertaste^F
selector^M de emisoras^F memorizadas

memory button
touche^F mémoire^F
Speichertaste^F
botón^M de memoria^F

mode selector
commutateur^M mono^F/stéréo^F
Mono-Stereo-Taste^F
selector^M mono/estéreo

active tracking
balayage^M automatique des stations^F
automatischer Sendersuchlauf^M
fonolocalización^F activa

power button
interrupteur^M d'alimentation^F
Netzschalter^M
botón^M de encendido^M

band selector
touche^F de modulation^F
Wellenbereichseinstellung^F
selector^M de banda^F

digital frequency display
affichage^M numérique des stations^F
digitale Frequenzanzeige^F
indicador^M digital de frecuencia^F

tuning control
sélecteur^M de stations^F
Sendereinstellung^F
control^M del sintetizador^M

tuning mode
mode^M de sélection^F des stations^F
Modus-Taste^F
modalidad^F sintetizador^M

AMPLIFIER
AMPLIFICATEUR^M
VERSTÄRKER^M
AMPLIFICADOR^M

power button
interrupteur^M d'alimentation^F
Netzschalter^M
botón^M de encendido^M

speaker selector
sélecteur^M d'enceintes^F
Lautsprecherschalter^M
selector^M de altavoz^M

balance control
équilibrage^M des haut-parleurs^M
Balanceregler^M
control^M de balance^M

headphone jack
prise^F casque^M
Kopfhörerbuchse^F
entrada^F para audífonos^M

treble tone control
contrôle^M de tonalité^F des aigus^M
Höhenregler^M
control^M de agudos^M

record control
contrôle^M d'enregistrement^M
Aufnahmeregler^M
control^M de grabación^F

volume control
réglage^M du volume^M
Lautstärkeregler^M
control^M del volumen^M

bass tone control
contrôle^M de tonalité^F des graves^M
Baßregler^M
control^M de graves^M

input selector
commutateur^M d'entrée^F
Eingangsschalter^M
selector^M de entrada^F

function selector
commutateur^M de fonctions^F
Funktionsschalter^M
selector^M de función^F

take-up reel
bobine^F réceptrice
Aufwickelkern^M
carrete^M receptor de la cinta^F

housing
boîtier^M
Gehäuse^N
cubierta^F

recording tape
bande^F magnétique
Kassettenband^N
cinta^F de grabación^F

guide roller
galet^M
Führungsrolle^F
rodillo^Mguía^F

playing window
fenêtre^F de lecture^F
Aussparung^F für Magnetköpfe^M
ventana^F de lectura^F

tape-guide
guide-bande^M
Bandführung^F
guía^F para la cinta^F

CASSETTE TAPE DECK
PLATINE^F CASSETTE^F
KASSETTENDECK^N
GRABADORA^F Y TOCACINTAS^M

counter reset button
bouton^M de remise^F à zéro^M
Rückstelltaste^F
botón^M del contador^M a ceros^M

tape selector
sélecteur^M de bandes^F
Bandsortenschalter^M
selector^M de tipo^M de cinta^F

fast-forward button
avance^F rapide
Schnellvorlauf-Taste^F
botón^M de avance^M rápido

eject button
bouton^M d'éjection^F
Auswurf-Taste^F
botón^M de expulsión^F

tape counter
compteur^M
Zählwerk^N
contador^M

play button
lecture^F
Play-Taste^F
botón^M de reproducción^F

peak level meter
indicateur^M de niveau^M
LED-Pegelanzeige^F
medidor^M de altos niveles^M de frecuencia^F

cassette holder
logement^M de cassette^F
Kassettenfach^N
compartimiento^M del casete^M

stop button
arrêt^M
Stop-Taste^F
botón^M de paro^M

pause button
pause^F
Pause-Taste^F
botón^M de pausa^F

recording level control
réglage^M de niveau^M d'enregistrement^M
manuelle Aussteuerung^F
botón^M de nivel^M de grabación^F

rewind button
rebobinage^M
Rücklauf-Taste^F
botón^M de rebobinado^M

record button
enregistrement^M
Aufnahme-Taste^F
botón^M de inicio^M de grabación^F

record muting button
interrupteur^M d'accord^M
Stummaufnahme-Taste^F
botón^M de grabación^F silenciosa

COMMUNICATIONS
COMMUNICATIONS

KOMMUNIKATION
COMUNICACIONES

COMMUNICATIONS
COMUNICACIONES

STEREO SOUND SYSTEM
CHAÎNE^F STÉRÉO
TONWIEDERGABESYSTEM^N
EQUIPO^M ESTEREOFÓNICO

RECORD
DISQUE^M
SCHALLPLATTE^F
DISCO^M

separating groove
plage^F de séparation^F
Schallrille^F
espiral^M de separación^F

spiral-in groove
sillon^M de départ^M
Einlaufrille^F
surco^M en espiral^M

band
surface^F gravée
Track^F
banda^F grabada

run-off groove
sillon^M de sortie^F
Auslaufrille^F
surco^M de salida^F

repeating groove
sillon^M concentrique
Ausschaltrille^F
surco^M concéntrico

centre hole
trou^M central
Mittelloch^N
orificio^M central

label
étiquette^F
Label^N
etiqueta^F

dust cover
couvercle^M
Abdeckhaube^F
tapa^M guardapolvo

counterweight
contrepoids^M
Balancegewicht^N
contrapeso^M

TURNTABLE UNIT
PLATINE^F **TOURNE-DISQUE**^M
PLATTENSPIELER^M
TOCADISCOS^M

hinge
charnière^F
Scharnier^N
bisagra^F

anti-skating device
compensateur^M de poussée^F latérale
Antiskating-Vorrichtung^F
dispositivo^M antideslizante

arm elevator
relève-bras^M
Tonarmheber^M
elevador^M del brazo^M

arm rest
repose-bras^M
Tonarmstütze^F
soporte^M del brazo^M

rubber mat
couvre-plateau^M
Gummimatte^F
disco^M de caucho^M

turntable
plateau^M
Plattenteller^M
plato^M

base plate
contre-platine^F
Grundplatte^F
base^F del plato^M

speed selector
sélecteur^M de vitesse^F
Drehzahl-Einstellung^F
selector^M de velocidad^F

spindle
axe^M
Plattenstift^M
pivote^M

base
socle^M
Sockel^M
base^F

pick-up arm
bras^M de lecture^F
Tonarm^M
brazo^M fonocaptor

cartridge
cartouche^F
Tonabnehmer^M
cartucho^M

head shell
tête^F de lecture^F
Tonabnehmersystem^N
cubierta^F de la aguja^F

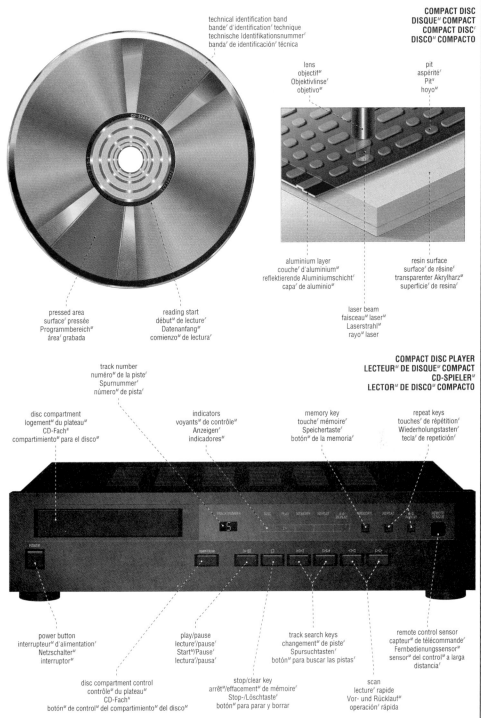

technical identification band
bande f d'identification f technique
technische Identifikationsnummer f
banda f de identificación f técnica

COMPACT DISC
DISQUE M COMPACT
COMPACT DISC f
DISCO M COMPACTO

lens
objectif M
Objektivlinse f
objetivo M

pit
aspérité f
Pit N
hoyo M

aluminium layer
couche f d'aluminium M
reflektierende Aluminiumschicht f
capa f de aluminio M

resin surface
surface f de résine f
transparenter Akrylharz M
superficie f de resina f

pressed area
surface f pressée
Programmbereich M
área f grabada

reading start
début M de lecture f
Datenanfang M
comienzo M de lectura f

laser beam
faisceau M laser M
Laserstrahl M
rayo M laser

COMPACT DISC PLAYER
LECTEUR M DE DISQUE M COMPACT
CD-SPIELER M
LECTOR M DE DISCO M COMPACTO

track number
numéro M de la piste f
Spurnummer f
número M de pista f

disc compartment
logement M du plateau M
CD-Fach N
compartimiento M para el disco M

indicators
voyants M de contrôle M
Anzeigen f
indicadores M

memory key
touche f mémoire f
Speichertaste f
botón M de la memoria f

repeat keys
touches f de répétition f
Wiederholungstasten f
tecla f de repetición f

power button
interrupteur M d'alimentation f
Netzschalter M
interruptor M

play/pause
lecture f/pause f
Start M/Pause f
lectura f/pausa f

track search keys
changement M de piste f
Spursuchtasten f
botón M para buscar las pistas f

remote control sensor
capteur M de télécommande f
Fernbedienungssensor M
sensor M del control M a larga distancia f

disc compartment control
contrôle M du plateau M
CD-Fach N
botón M de control M del compartimiento M del disco M

stop/clear key
arrêt M/effacement M de mémoire f
Stop-/Löschtaste f
botón M para parar y borrar

scan
lecture f rapide
Vor- und Rücklauf M
operación f rápida

COMMUNICATIONS
COMMUNICATIONS

KOMMUNIKATION
COMUNICACIONES

COMUNICACIONES
COMUNICACIONES

DYNAMIC MICROPHONE
MICROPHONE^M DYNAMIQUE
ELEKTRODYNAMISCHES MIKROFON^N
MICRÓFONO^M ELECTRODINÁMICO

acoustic screen
treillis^M de protection^F
Windschutz^M
rejilla^F

diaphragm
membrane^F
Membrane^F
diafragma^M

moving coil
bobine^F mobile
Induktionsspule^F
bobina^F móvil

magnet
aimant^M
Magnet^M
imán^M

on/off switch
interrupteur^M
Ein-/Ausschalter^M
interruptor^M de encendido^M/apagado^M

housing
boîtier^M
Gehäuse^N
caja^F

connector
connecteur^M
Verbindungsstück^N
conector^M

jack plug
fiche^F pour jack^M
Klinkenstecker^M
enchufe^M

cable
cordon^M
Kabel^N
cable^M

HEADPHONES
CASQUE^M D'ÉCOUTE^F
KOPFHÖRER^M
AURICULARES^M

resonator
résonnateur^M
Membrane^F
resonador^M

ear cushion
coussinet^M
Polsterung^F
orejera^F

headband
serre-tête^M
Bügel^M
banda^F acolchada

adjusting band
glissière^F d'ajustement^M
Einstellung^F
banda^F de ajuste^M

connecting cable
cable^M de raccordement^M
Anschlußkabel^N
cable^M de conexión^F

earphone
écouteur^M
Ohrmuschel^F
auricular^M

jack plug
fiche^F pour jack^M
Stecker^M
enchufe^M

studio
studio^M
Sprecherraum^M
estudio^M

microphone
microphone^M
Mikrofon^N
micrófono^M

announcer console
consolette^F de l'annonceur^M
Sprecherpult^N
torre^F del locutor^M

on-air warning light
voyant^M de mise^F en ondes^F
Aufnahmelicht^N
luz^F de advertencia^F de emisión^F

tone leader generator
générateur^M de tonalités^F d'amorces^F
Pegeltongenerator^M
generador^M principal de tono^M

clock
horloge^F
Uhr^F
reloj^M

VU meters
vumètres^M
V.U.-Meter^N
unidad^F de medición^F de volumen^M

monitor speaker
haut-parleur^M de contrôle^M
Abhörlautsprecher^M
monitor^M de sonido^M

cartridge tape recorder
magnétophone^M à cartouches^F
Magnetbandmaschine^F
cartucho^M de la cinta^F grabadora^F

digital audio tape recorder
magnétophone^M à cassette^F numérique
digitales Tonbandgerät^N
cinta^F digital grabadora^F

compact disc player
lecteur^M de disque^M compact
CD-Spieler^M
lector^M de disco^M compacto

cassette deck
platine^F cassette^F
Kassettendeck^N
grabadora^F y tocacintas^M

stop watch
chronomètre^M
Aufnahmezeitanzeige^F
cronómetro^M

producer console
consolette^F du réalisateur^M
Regiepult^N
torre^F del productor^M

jack field
baie^F de jacks^M
Anschlußtafel^F
entrada^F de campo^M

sound console
pupitre^M de son^M
Mischpult^N
consola^F de sonido^M

bargraph type peak meter
crêtemètre^M graphique
digitale Pegelanzeige^F
gráfico^M de líneas^F

control room
régie^F
Regieraum^M
sala^F de control^M

turntable
platine^F tourne-disque^M
Plattenspieler^M
tocadiscos^M

PORTABLE SOUND SYSTEMS
APPAREILS^M DE SON^M PORTATIFS
TRAGBARE TONWIEDERGABESYSTEME^N
SISTEMAS^M DE SONIDO^M PORTÁTILES

PERSONAL RADIO CASSETTE PLAYER
BALADEUR^M
WALKMAN^M ® **MIT RADIOTEIL**^N
RADIO AM \ FM Y LECTOR^M **DE CASETES**^M **PERSONAL**

lead
cordon^M
Kabel^N
cable^M

headphone plug
prise^F casque^M
Kopfhörerstecker^M
enchufe^M para auriculares^M

headband
serre-tête^M
Kopfbügel^M
banda^F de ajuste^M

on/off
marche^F/arrêt^M
Ein/Aus
encendido^M \ apagado

volume control
réglage^M du volume^M
Lautstärkeregler^M
control^M de volumen^M

rewind button
rebobinage^M
Rücklauftaste^F
botón^M de rebobinado^M

tuning knob
sélecteur^M de stations^F
Sendereinstellung^F
botón^M de sintonización^F

play button
avance^F
Wiedergabetaste^F
botón^M de funcionamiento^M

headphones
casque^M d'écoute^F
Kopfhörer^M
auriculares^M

fast-forward button
avance^F rapide
Schnellvorlauftaste^F
botón^M de rebobinado^M rápido

cassette
cassette^F
Kassette^F
casete^M

auto reverse button
auto-inversion^F
Autoreverse-Taste^F
botón^M de rebobinado^M automático

cassette player
lecteur^M de cassette^F
Kassettenteil^N
lector^M de casetes^M

radio section
radio^F
Empfangsteil^N
sintonizador^M

PORTABLE CD RADIO CASSETTE RECORDER
RADIOCASSETTE^F
RADIORECORDER^M **MIT CD-SPIELER**^M
RADIOCASETE^M **CON LECTOR**^M **DE DISCO**^M **COMPACTO**

stereo control
contrôle^M de la stéréophonie^F
Stereotaste^F
control^M estereo

carrying handle
poignée^F
Tragebügel^M
asa^F

mode selectors
sélecteurs^M de mode^M
Betriebseinstellung^F
selectores^M de modalidad^F

aerial
antenne^F
Antenne^F
antena^F

on/off/volume
marche^F/arrêt^M/volume^M
Ein/Aus/Lautstärke^F
encendido^M \ apagado^M \ volumen^M

compact disc player
lecteur^M de disque^M compact
CD-Spieler^M
lector^M de discos^M compactos

headphone jack
prise^F casque^M
Kopfhörerbuchse^F
toma^F para auriculares^M

compact disc
disque^M compact
Compact Disc^F
disco^M compacto

compact disc player controls
contrôles^M du lecteur^M laser^M
CD-Tasten^F
controles^M del lector^M de discos^M compacto

speaker
haut-parleur^M
Lautsprecher^M
altavoz^M

radio section
radio^F
Empfangsteil^N
sintonizador^M

tuning control
sélecteur^M de stations^F
Sendereinstellung^F
control^M de sintonización^F

power socket
alimentation^F sur secteur^M
Netzanschluß^M
enchufe^M

cassette
cassette^F
Kassette^F
casete^M

cassette player
lecteur^M de cassette^F
Kassettenteil^N
lector^M de casetes^M

cassette player controls
contrôles^M du lecteur^M de cassette^F
Kassettendecktasten^F
controles^M del lector^M de casetes^M

VIDEO CAMERA
CAMÉRA^M VIDÉO
VIDEOKAMERA^F
CÁMARA^F DE VÍDEO^M

eyepiece
oculaire^M
Okular^N
adaptador^M al ojo^M

power zoom button
commande^F électrique du zoom^M
Telezoom-Taste^F
botón^M de funcionamiento^M del zoom^M

electronic viewfinder
viseur^M électronique
elektronischer Bildsucher^M
visor^M electrónico

white balance sensor
senseur^M d'équilibrage^M des blancs^M
Weißabgleichsensor^M
captador^M de luz^F

accessory shoe
griffe^F porte-accessoires^M
Zubehörschuh^M
patín^M para accesorios^M

cassette eject switch
commande^F d'éjection^F de la cassette^F
Kassettenauswurfschalter^M
botón^M de eyección^F de la casete^F

videotape operation controls
commandes^F de la bande^F vidéo
Videobedientasten^F
controles^M de la casete^F de vídeo^M

viewfinder adjustment keys
réglage^M du viseur^M
Scharfeinstellung^F des Bildsuchers^M
botones^M de ajuste^M del visor^M

built-in microphone
microphone^M incorporé
eingebautes Mikrofon^N
micrófono^M integrado

macro set button
commande^F de réglage^M macro^F
Makro-Einstelltaste^F
botón^M de acercamiento^M

cassette compartment
logement^M de la cassette^F
Kassettenlift^M
compartimento^M para la casete^F

zoom lens
objectif^M zoom^M
Zoomobjektiv^N
lente^F zoom^M

data display
affichage^M des données^F
Display^N
visualización^F de la información^F

battery eject switch
commande^F d'éjection^F de la pile^F
Batterieauswurfschalter^M
botón^M para sacar la pila^F

lens hood
pare-soleil^M
Gegenlichtblende^F
capuchón^M

shooting adjustment keys
commandes^F de prise^F de vue^F
Aufnahmeeinstellungstasten^F
botones^M de ajuste^M del rodaje^M

battery
pile^F
Batterie^F
pila^F

edit/search buttons
commandes^F de montage^M
Editsearch-Tasten^F
botones de montaje^M y búsqueda^F

TELEVISION
TÉLÉVISION^F
FERNSEHEN^N
TELEVISIÓN^F

TELEVISION SET
TÉLÉVISEUR^M
FERNSEHAPPARAT^M
TELEVISOR^M

cabinet
coffret^M
Gehäuse^N
caja^F

screen
écran^M
Bildschirm^M
pantalla^F

remote control sensor
capteur^M de télécommande^F
Empfangsauge^N
sensor^M de control^M a larga distancia^F

power button
interrupteur^M d'alimentation^F
Netzschalter^M
botón^M de encendido^M

indicators
lampes^F témoins^M
Betriebsanzeigen^F
indicadores^M

tuning controls
boutons^M de réglage^M
Abstimmtasten^F
controles^M de sintonización^F

PICTURE TUBE
TUBE^M-IMAGE^F
BILDRÖHRE^F
TUBO^M DE PANTALLA^F

funnel
cône^M
Trichter^M
cono^M

electron gun
canon^M à électrons^M
Elektronenkanone^F
cañón^M de electrones^M

base
culot^M
Basis^F
base^F

neck
col^M
Hals^M
cuello^M

electron beam
faisceau^M d'électrons^M
Elektronenstrahl^M
haz^M de electrones^M

protective window
vitre^F protectrice
Schutzglas^N
ventana^F protectora

colour selection filter
masque^M de sélection^F des couleurs^F
Farbfilter^M
filtro^M selector del color^M

screen
écran^M
Bildschirm^M
pantalla^F

electron gun
canon^M à électrons^M
Elektronenkanone^F
cañón^M de electrones^M

red beam
faisceau^M rouge
Rotstrahl^M
haz^M rojo

green beam
faisceau^M vert
Grünstrahl^M
haz^M verde

blue beam
faisceau^M bleu
Blaustrahl^M
haz^M azul

grid
grille^F
Gitter^N
rejilla^F

magnetic field
champ^M magnétique
magnetisches Feld^N
campo^M magnético

KOMMUNIKATION
COMUNICACIONES

COMMUNICATIONS
COMMUNICATIONS

410

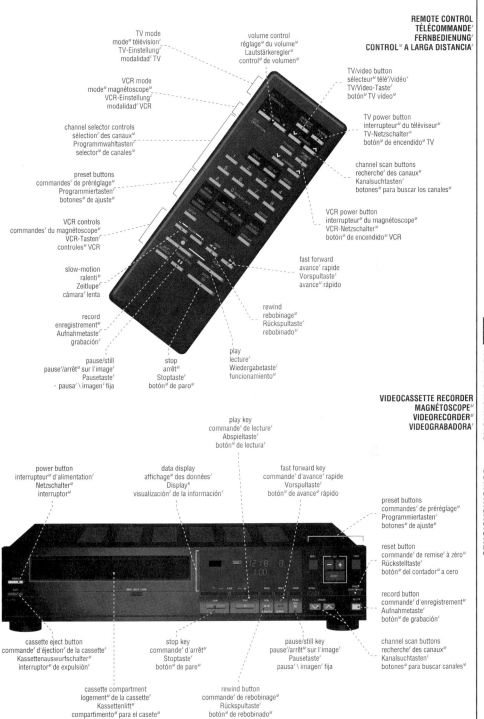

REMOTE CONTROL
TÉLÉCOMMANDE^F
FERNBEDIENUNG^F
CONTROL^M A LARGA DISTANCIA^F

TV mode
mode^M télévision^F
TV-Einstellung^F
modalidad^F TV

VCR mode
mode^M magnétoscope^M
VCR-Einstellung^F
modalidad^F VCR

channel selector controls
sélection^F des canaux^M
Programmwahltasten^F
selector^M de canales^M

preset buttons
commandes^F de préréglage^M
Programmiertasten^F
botones^M de ajuste^M

VCR controls
commandes^F du magnétoscope^M
VCR-Tasten^F
controles^M VCR

slow-motion
ralenti^M
Zeitlupe^F
cámara^F lenta

record
enregistrement^M
Aufnahmetaste^F
grabación^F

pause/still
pause^F/arrêt^M sur l'image^F
Pausetaste^F
pausa^F \ imagen^F fija

stop
arrêt^M
Stoptaste^F
botón^M de paro^M

play
lecture^F
Wiedergabetaste^F
funcionamiento^M

rewind
rebobinage^M
Rückspultaste^F
rebobinado^M

fast forward
avance^F rapide
Vorspultaste^F
avance^M rápido

volume control
réglage^M du volume^M
Lautstärkeregler^M
control^M de volumen^M

TV/video button
sélecteur^M télé^F/vidéo^F
TV/Video-Taste^F
botón^M TV video^M

TV power button
interrupteur^M du téléviseur^M
TV-Netzschalter^M
botón^M de encendido^M TV

channel scan buttons
recherche^F des canaux^M
Kanalsuchtasten^F
botones^M para buscar los canales^M

VCR power button
interrupteur^M du magnétoscope^M
VCR-Netzschalter^M
botón^M de encendido^M VCR

VIDEOCASSETTE RECORDER
MAGNÉTOSCOPE^M
VIDEORECORDER^M
VIDEOGRABADORA^F

play key
commande^F de lecture^F
Abspieltaste^F
botón^M de lectura^F

power button
interrupteur^M d'alimentation^F
Netzschalter^M
interruptor^M

data display
affichage^M des données^F
Display^N
visualización^F de la información^F

fast forward key
commande^F d'avance^F rapide
Vorspultaste^F
botón^M de avance^M rápido

preset buttons
commandes^F de préréglage^M
Programmiertasten^F
botones^M de ajuste^M

reset button
commande^F de remise^F à zéro^M
Rückstelltaste^F
botón^M del contador^M a cero

record button
commande^F d'enregistrement^M
Aufnahmetaste^F
botón^M de grabación^F

cassette eject button
commande^F d'éjection^F de la cassette^F
Kassettenauswurfschalter^M
interruptor^M de expulsión^F

stop key
commande^F d'arrêt^M
Stoptaste^F
botón^M de pare^M

pause/still key
pause^F/arrêt^M sur l'image^F
Pausetaste^F
pausa^F \ imagen^F fija

channel scan buttons
recherche^F des canaux^M
Kanalsuchtasten^F
botones^M para buscar canales^M

cassette compartment
logement^M de la cassette^F
Kassettenlift^M
compartimento^M para el casete^M

rewind button
commande^F de rebobinage^M
Rückspultaste^F
botón^M de rebobinado^M

STUDIO AND CONTROL ROOMS
PLATEAU^M ET RÉGIES^F
SPRECHER- UND REGIERÄUME^M
ESTUDIO^M DE TELEVISIÓN^F Y CABINAS^F DE CONTROL^M

lighting grid access
accès^M à la grille^F d'éclairage^M
Zugang^M zur Beleuchtungsanlage^F
puerta^F de acceso^M a la rejilla^F de las luces^F

additional production personnel
personnel^M additionnel de production^F
zusätzliches Studiopersonal^N
personal^M suplementario de producción^F

lighting technician
éclairagiste^M
Beleuchter(in^F)^M
técnico^M de luces^F

auxiliary facilities room
salle^F polyvalente
allgemeiner Geräteraum^M
sala^F de instalaciones^F auxiliares

connection box
boîte^F de raccordement^M
Kamera-Steckfeld^N
caja^F de conexiones^F

dimmer room
salle^F des gradateurs^M
abgedunkelter Raum^M
sala^F de regulación^F de luces

camera control unit
bloc^M de commande^F des caméras^F
Bildkontrolle^F
unidad^F de control^M de cámaras^F

camera
caméra^F
Kamera^F
cámara^F

lighting board operator
opérateur^M de régie^F d'éclairage^M
Oberbeleuchter(in^F)^M
tablero^M de operación^F de luces^F

camera control technician
contrôleur^M d'images^F
Bildtechniker(in^F)^M
técnico^M de control^M de cámaras^F

microphone boom
perche^F
Mikrofonausleger^M
jirafa^F del micrófono^M

lighting board
pupitre^M d'éclairage^M
Lichtregelanlage^F
tablero^M de luces^F

technical producer
directeur^M technique
Aufsichtsingenieur(in^F)^M
productor^M técnico

video switcher technician
technicien^M aiguilleur^M
Video-Switcher^M
operador^M técnico de video^M

monitor wall
baie^F de contrôle^M
Kontrollmonitore^M
panel^M de monitores^M

producer
réalisateur^M
Sendeleiter(in^F)^M
productor^M

script assistant
assistant^M à la réalisation^F
Skript-Assistent(in^F)^M
asistente^M del guionista^M

production adviser
conseiller^M de production^F
Regieassistent(in^F)^M
consejero^M de producción^F

sound desk
pupitre^M de son^M
Tonregiepult^s
consola^F de sonido^M

sound technician
preneur^M de son^M
Tontechniker(in^F)^M
técnico^M de sonido^M

bass trap
trappe^F acoustique
Baßfalle^F
panel^M retenedor de frecuencias^F bajas

musical advisers
conseillers^M musicaux
Musikregie^F
consejeros^M musicales

equipment rack
bâti^M d'équipement^M
Ausrüstungsspind^M
soporte^M para el equipo^M

sound monitor
haut-parleur^M de contrôle^M
Lautsprecher^M
monitor^M del sonido^M

studio floor
plateau^M
Studioebene^F
estudio^M

lighting/camera control area
régie^F image^F/éclairage^M
Beleuchtung^F/Bildregie^F
sala^F de control^M de luces^F

sound control room
régie^F du son^M
Tonregieraum^M
control^M de sonido^M

production control room
régie^F de production^F
Regieraum^M
sala^F de producción^F y control^M

PRODUCTION CONTROL ROOM
RÉGIE[F] DE PRODUCTION[F]
REGIERAUM[M]
SALA[F] DE CONTROL[M] DE PRODUCCIÓN[F]

sound/video preview unit
poste[M] de contrôle[M] audio/vidéo
Ton-/Bild-Vorschaueinheit[F]
unidad de visualización de imagen[F] \ sonido

stereo phase monitor
oscilloscope[M] de phase[F] audio
Lautsprecher[N] zum Prüfen[N] von Zweikanalton[M]
control[M] del sonido[M] estereofónico

monitor wall
baie[F] de contrôle[M]
Kontrollmonitore[M]
panel[M] de monitores[M]

preview monitors
écrans[M] de précontrôle[M]
Vorschaumonitore[M]
monitores[M] de visualización[F] previa

vector/waveform monitor
oscilloscope[M]/vectoscope[M]
Oszillograph-/Oszilloskopmonitor[M]
control[M] del vector[M] de vibraciones[F]

input monitors
écrans[M] d'entrée[F]
Eingangsmonitore[M]
monitores[M] de entrada[F]

digital video effects monitor
écran[M] du truqueur[M] numérique
Trickmischer[M]
monitor[M] de efectos[M] videodigitales

technical producer monitor
écran[M] du directeur[M] technique
Kontrollmonitor[M] des Aufsichtsingenieurs[M]
monitor[M] de la producción[F] técnica

sound monitor
haut-parleur[M] de contrôle[M]
Lautsprecher[M]
monitor[M] de sonido[M]

clock
horloge[F]
Kontrolluhr[F]
reloj[M]

intercom microphone
microphone[M] d'interphone[M]
Mikrofon[N] zum Studio[N]
micrófono[M] de intercomunicación[F]

auxiliary video switcher
sélecteur[M] vidéo auxiliaire
zusätzlicher Video-Switcher[M]
interruptor[M] para el vídeo[M] auxiliar

video monitoring selector
sélecteur[M] de contrôle[M] vidéo
Video-Kreuzschiene[F]
selector[M] del control[M] de vídeo[M]

intercom station
interphone[M]
Studio-Kommandoanlage[F]
estación[F] de intercomunicación[F]

output monitor
écran[M] de sortie[F]
Ausgangsmonitor[M]
monitor[M] de salida[F]

sound monitoring selector
sélecteur[M] de contrôle[M] audio
Tonvormischung[F]
selector[M] del control[M] de volumen[M]

telephone
poste[M] téléphonique
Telefon[N]
teléfono[M]

main preview monitor
écran[M] principal de précontrôle[M]
Hauptvorschaumonitor[M]
monitor[M] principal de visualización[F] previa

VU meters
vumètres[M] audio
Ton V.U.Meter[M]
compás[M] del volumen[M]

production desk
table[F] de production[F]
Regiepult[N]
mesa[F] de producción[F]

production video switcher
aiguilleur[M] vidéo de production[F]
Video-Switcher[M]
interruptor[M] para la producción[F] de vídeo[M]

digital video special effects
truqueur[M] numérique
Trickmischer[M]
efectos[M] especiales video\digital

413

STUDIO FLOOR
PLATEAU^M
STUDIOEBENE^F
ESTUDIO^M

floodlight on pantograph
projecteur^M d'ambiance^F sur pantographe^M
Flächenleuchte^F an Scherenaufhängung^F
proyector^M sobre el pantógrafo^M

spotlight
projecteur^M à faisceau^M concentré
Spotlight^N
reflector^M orientable

test pattern
mire^F de réglage^M
Testbild^N
patrón^M de prueba^F

lighting grid
grille^F d'éclairage^M
Beleuchtungsanlage^F
rejilla^F de iluminación^F

curtain
rideau^M
Vorhang^M
cortina^F

floodlight
projecteur^M d'ambiance^F
Flächenleuchte^F
proyector^M de luz^F difusa

cables
câbles^M
Kabel^N
cables^M

camera
caméra^F
Kamera^F
cámara^F

cyclorama
cyclorama^M
Zyclorama^N
ciclorama^M

CAMERA
CAMÉRA^F
KAMERA^F
CÁMARA^F

camera viewfinder
viseur^M de caméra^F
Bildsucher^M
visor^M

microphone
microphone^M
Mikrofon^N
micrófono^M

teleprompter
télésouffleur^M
Textablesetafel^F
apuntador^M electrónico

microphone boom
perche^F
Mikrofonausleger^M
jirafa^F

zoom lens
zoom^M
Zoomobjektiv^N
zoom^M

microphone boom tripod
trépied^M de perche^F
Mikrofon-Fahrspinne^F
trípode^M jirafa^F para el micrófono

camera dolly
trépied^M de caméra^F
Kamera-Dolly^M
pedestal^M de la cámara^F

MOBILE UNIT
CAR^M DE REPORTAGE^M
ÜBERTRAGUNGSWAGEN^M
UNIDAD^F MÓBIL

microwave transmitter
émetteur^M micro-ondes^F
Mikrowellensender^M
transmisor^F de microondas^F

wave guide
guide^M d'ondes^F
Wellenleiter^M
guía^F de la onda^F

parabolic antenna
antenne^F parabolique
Parabolantenne^F
antena^F parabólica

microwave dish
réflecteur^M parabolique
Mikrowellenschüssel^F
disco^M microondas^F

equipment rack
bâti^M d'équipement^M
Ausrüstungsspind^M
equipo^M de soporte^M

tripod
trépied^M
Stativ^N
trípode^M

equipment rack
bâti^M d'équipement^M
Ausrüstungsspind^M
equipo^M de soporte

sound control room
régie^F du son^M
Tonregieraum^M
sala^F de control^M de sonido^M

camera control area
régie^F image^F
Bereich^M der Bildkontrolle^F
área^M de control^M de la cámara^F

sound technician
preneur^M de son^M
Tontechniker(in^F)^M
técnico^M de sonido^M

production control room
régie^F de production^F
Regieraum^M
sala^F de control^M de la producción^F

camera control unit
bloc^M de commande^F des caméras^F
Bildkontrolle^F
unidad^F de control^M de la cámara^F

telephone set
poste^M téléphonique
Telefonapparat^M
teléfono^M

monitor wall
baie^F de contrôle^M
Kontrollmonitore^M
panel^M de control^M

camera control technician
contrôleur^M d'images^F
Bildtechniker(in^F)^M
técnico^M de control^M de la cámara^F

sound monitor
haut-parleur^M de contrôle^M
Abhörlautsprecher^M
monitor^M de sonido^M

sound monitor
haut-parleur^M de contrôle^M
Abhörlautsprecher^M
monitor^M de sonido^M

maintenance area
secteur^M maintenance^F
Eingangsbereich^M
área^M de mantenimiento^M

air conditioning unit
système^M de climatisation^F
Klimaanlage^F
unidad^F de aire^M acondicionado

sound console
pupitre^M de son^M
Tonregiepult^N
consola^F de sonido^M

electrical connection panel
panneau^M de raccordement^M électrique
Stromverteiler^M
panel^M de conexiones^F eléctricas

producer
réalisateur^M
Sendeleiter(in^F)^M
productor^M

video connection panel
panneau^M de raccordement^M vidéo
Videoschalttafel^F
panel^M de conexión^F del video^M

technical equipment compartment
soute^F d'équipement^M technique
Fach^N für technische Ausrüstung^F
compartimiento^M del equipo^M técnico

clock
horloge^F
Kontrolluhr^F
reloj^M

preview monitor
écran^M de précontrôle^M
Vorschaumonitor^M
monitor^M de visualización^F previa

technical producer
directeur^M technique
Aufsichtsingenieur(in^F)^M
productor^M técnico

output monitor
écran^M de sortie^F
Ausgangsmonitor^M
monitor^M de producción^F

video switcher technician
technicien^M aiguilleur^M
Video-Switcher^M
operador^M técnico de video^M

cable drum compartment
soute^F des bobines^F de câbles^M
Fach^N für Kabeltrommel^F
compartimiento^M del cable^M de la batería^F

satellite
satellite*M*
Satellit*M*
satélite*M*

local station
station*F* locale
Ortsstation*F*
estación*F* local

cable distributor
câblodistributeur*M*
Kabelverteiler*M*
cable*M* distribuidor

private broadcasting network
réseau*M* privé
privates Rundfunknetz*N*
red*F* de transmisión*F* privada

distribution by cable
transmission*F* par câble*M*
Verteilung*F* durch Kabelnetz*N*
distribución*F* por redes*F* de cable*M*

Hertzian wave transmission
transmission*F* hertzienne
Sendung*F* auf Hertz-Wellen*F*
transmisión*F* de ondas*F* Hertzianas

national broadcasting network
réseau*M* national
öffentliches Übertragungsnetz*N*
red*F* nacional de transmisión*F*

mobile unit
car*M* de reportage*M*
mobile Einheit*F*
unidad*F* móvil

direct home reception
réception*F* directe
Satelliten-Direktempfang*M*
recepción*F* directa en la casa*F*

TELECOMMUNICATIONS BY SATELLITE
TÉLÉCOMMUNICATIONS^F PAR SATELLITE^M
TELEKOMMUNIKATION^F ÜBER NACHRICHTENSATELLIT^M
TELECOMUNICACIONES^F POR SATÉLITE^M

industrial communications
communications^F industrielles
industrielle Telekommunikation^F
comunicaciones^F industriales

teleport
téléport^M
Teleport^M
teleporte^M

in-flight communications
communications^F aériennes
Telekommunikation^F für die Luftfahrt^F
comunicaciones^F aéreas

military communications
communications^F militaires
militärische Telekommunikation^F
comunicaciones^F militares

maritime communications
communications^F maritimes
maritime Telekommunikation^F
comunicaciones^F marítimas

telephone network
réseau^M téléphonique
Telefonnetz^N
red^F telefónica

road communications
communications^F routières
Telekommunikation^F für den Straßenverkehr^M
comunicaciones^F terrestres

personal communications
communications^F individuelles
persönliche Telekommunikation^F
comunicaciones^F personales

consumer
client^M
Konsument^M
consumidor^M

computer communication
téléinformatique^F
Telekommunikation^F über Computer^M
comunicación^F por computador^M

TELECOMMUNICATIONS BY TELEPHONE NETWORK
TÉLÉCOMMUNICATIONS^F PAR LIGNE^F TÉLÉPHONIQUE
TELEKOMMUNIKATIONSTECHNIK^F ÜBER DAS TELEFONNETZ^N
TELECOMUNICACIONES^F POR RED^F TELEFÓNICA

facsimile machine
télécopieur^M
Telefax-Gerät^N
facsímil^M

cellular telephone
téléphone^M cellulaire
Zellfunktelefon^N
teléfono^M celular

telex
télex^M
Telex^M
télex^M

telephone
poste^M téléphonique
Telefonapparat^M
teléfono^M

417

TELECOMMUNICATION SATELLITES
SATELLITES^M DE TÉLÉCOMMUNICATIONS^F
FERNMELDESATELLITEN^M
SATÉLITES^M DE TELECOMUNICACIONES^F

EXAMPLES OF SATELLITES
EXEMPLES^M DE SATELLITES^M
VERSCHIEDENE SATELLITEN^M
EJEMPLOS^M DE SATÉLITES^M

Anik-E
Anik-E
Anik-E^M
Anik-E

EUTELSAT II
EUTELSAT II
EUTELSAT II^M
EUTELSAT II

transceiving dish
antenne^F d'émission^F/réception^F
Sende- und Empfangsantenne^F
antena^F de emisión^F \ recepción^F

communication module
module^M de communication^F
Kommunikationsmodul^M
módulo^M de comunicación^F

solar reflectors
réflecteurs^M solaires
Solarreflektoren^M
reflectores^M solares

solar array
panneau^M solaire
Sonnenzellenausleger^M
panel^M solar

propulsion module
module^M de propulsion^F
Antriebsmodul^M
módulo^M de propulsión^F

service module
module^M de service^M
Versorgungsmodul^M
módulo^M de servicio^M

transmission dish
antenne^F d'émission^F
Sendeantenne^F
antena^F de emisión^F

Intelsat VII
Intelsat VII
Intelsat VII^M
Intelsat VII

KOMMUNIKATION
COMUNICACIONES

COMMUNICATIONS
COMMUNICATIONS

418

Sun mode position
position^F en mode^M solaire
Einstellungsposition^F zur Sonne^F
posición^F respecto al sol^M

preparation for the eclipse
préparation^F avant éclipse^F
Vorbereitung^F auf die Ekliptik^F
preparación^F del eclipse^M

East reflector deployment
déploiement^M du réflecteur^M est
östlich gerichtete Entfaltung des Reflektors^M
despliegue^M del reflector^M del este^M

apogee passage
passage^M en apogée^M
Bahn^F durch das Apogäum^N
apogeo^M de la trayectoria^F

full deployment
stade^M final de déploiement^M
volle Entfaltung^F
despliegue^M completo

passing through the eclipse
passage^M en éclipse^F
Bahn^F durch die Ekliptik^F
cruce^M del eclipse^M

launcher/satellite separation
séparation^F lanceur^M/satellite^M
Abtrennung^F des Satelliten^M von der Trägerrakete^F
separación^F del lanzador^M de satélites^M

solar array deployment
déploiement^M du panneau^M solaire
Entfaltung^F der Sonnenzellenausleger^M
despliegue^M del panel solar

apogee motor firing
manœuvres^F d'apogée^M
Zündung^F des Apogäum-Motors^M
apogeo^M de encendido^M del motor^M

COMMUNICATION BY TELEPHONE
COMMUNICATION*ᶠ* PAR TÉLÉPHONE*ᴹ*
TELEFONISCHE KOMMUNIKATION*ᶠ*
COMUNICACIONES*ᶠ* POR TELÉFONO*ᴹ*

TELEPHONE ANSWERING MACHINE
RÉPONDEUR*ᴹ* TÉLÉPHONIQUE
ANRUFBEANTWORTER*ᴹ*
CONTESTADORA*ᶠ* AUTOMÁTICA

incoming message cassette
cassette*ᶠ* messages*ᴹ*
Aufzeichnungskassette*ᶠ*
cassette*ᶠ* para grabar los mensajes*ᴹ*

calls indicator
voyant*ᴹ* de réception*ᶠ* de messages*ᴹ*
Nachrichtenanzeige*ᶠ*
indicador*ᴹ* de llamadas*ᶠ*

power-on light
voyant*ᴹ* de mise*ᶠ* en circuit*ᴹ*
Netzkontrollampe*ᶠ*
luz*ᶠ* de encendido*ᴹ*

auto answer indicator
voyant*ᴹ* de réponse*ᶠ* automatique
Bereitschaftsanzeige*ᶠ*
indicador*ᴹ* de respuesta*ᶠ* automática

outgoing announcement cassette
cassette*ᶠ* annonce*ᶠ*
Ansagekassette*ᶠ*
cassette*ᶠ* con saludo*ᴹ*

listen button
écoute*ᶠ*
Mithörtaste*ᶠ*
botón*ᴹ* de reproducción*ᶠ*

power-on button
bouton*ᴹ* de mise*ᶠ* en circuit*ᴹ*
Netzschalter*ᴹ*
botón*ᴹ* de encendido*ᴹ*

fast-forward button
avance*ᶠ* rapide
Vorlauftaste*ᶠ*
botón*ᴹ* de avance*ᴹ* rápido

speaker
haut-parleur*ᴹ*
Lautsprecher*ᴹ*
altavoz*ᴹ*

microphone
microphone*ᴹ*
Mikrofon*ᴺ*
micrófono*ᴹ*

record announcement button
enregistrement*ᴹ*
Aufzeichnungstaste*ᶠ*
botón*ᴹ* de grabación*ᶠ*

stop button
arrêt*ᴹ*
Stoptaste*ᶠ*
botón*ᴹ* de paro*ᴹ*

on/play button
mise*ᶠ* en marche*ᶠ*
Einschalt-/Wiedergabetaste*ᶠ*
botón*ᴹ* de encendido*ᴹ*

rewind button
rebobinage*ᴹ*
Rücklauftaste*ᶠ*
botón*ᴹ* de rebobinado*ᴹ*

volume control
commande*ᶠ* de volume*ᴹ*
Lautstärkeregler*ᴹ*
control*ᴹ* del volumen*ᴹ*

erase button
effacement*ᴹ*
Löschtaste*ᶠ*
botón*ᴹ* para borrar

TELEPHONE
POSTE*ᴹ* TÉLÉPHONIQUE
TELEFONAPPARAT*ᴹ*
TELÉFONO*ᴹ*

receiver
récepteur*ᴹ*
Hörer*ᴹ*
receptor*ᴹ*

display
afficheur*ᴹ*
Display*ᴺ*
visualización*ᶠ*

handset
combiné*ᴹ*
Handapparat*ᴹ*
auricular*ᴹ*

on/off light
voyant*ᴹ* de mise*ᶠ* en circuit*ᴹ*
An-/Auskontrollampe*ᶠ*
luz*ᶠ* de encendido*ᴹ* \ apagado*ᴹ*

receiver volume control
commande*ᶠ* de volume*ᴹ* du récepteur*ᴹ*
Lautstärkeregler*ᴹ* für den Hörer*ᴹ*
control*ᴹ* de volumen*ᴹ* del auricular*ᴹ*

transmitter
microphone*ᴹ*
Sprechmuschel*ᶠ*
transmisor*ᴹ*

display setting
réglage*ᴹ* de l'afficheur*ᴹ*
Displayeinstellung*ᶠ*
ajuste*ᴹ* de la visualización*ᶠ*

handset flex
cordon*ᴹ* de combiné*ᴹ*
Leitung*ᶠ*
cable*ᴹ* del auricular*ᴹ*

ringing volume control
commande*ᶠ* de volume*ᴹ* de la sonnerie*ᶠ*
Lautstärkeregler*ᴹ* für den Rufton*ᴹ*
control*ᴹ* de volumen*ᴹ* de la campana*ᶠ*

automatic dialling index
index*ᴹ* de composition*ᶠ* automatique
Rufnummernregister*ᴹ* für automatische Wahl*ᶠ*
marcador*ᴹ* automático

function selectors
sélecteurs*ᴹ* de fonctions*ᶠ*
Funktionswähler*ᴹ*
selectores*ᴹ* de funciones*ᶠ*

push buttons
clavier*ᴹ*
Tasten*ᶠ*
teclado*ᴹ*

telephone list
répertoire*ᴹ* téléphonique
Rufnummernregister*ᴹ*
índice*ᴹ* de teléfonos*ᴹ*

memory button
commande*ᶠ* mémoire*ᶠ*
Speichertaste*ᶠ*
botón*ᴹ* de memoria*ᶠ*

terminal
terminal^M
Terminal^N
terminal^M

printer
imprimante^F
Drucker^M
impresora^F

visual display unit
écran^M d'affichage^M
Datensichtgerät^N
pantalla^F

transmission/reception of messages
expédition^F/réception^F des messages^M
Senden/Empfangen^N von Nachrichten^F
recepción^F y transmisión de mensajes^M

printing of messages
impression^F des messages^M
Ausdrucken^N von Nachrichten^F
impresión^F de mensajes

data display
écran^M d'affichage^M
Datendisplay^N
visualización^F de datos^M

start key
mise^F en marche^F
Starttaste^F
tecla^F de iniciación^M

sent document recovery
sortie^F des originaux^M
Originalrückführung^F
recuperación^F del documento^M enviado

document receiving
réception^F des messages^M
Empfang^M von Dokumenten^N
recepción^F de documentos^M

document-to-be-sent position
entrée^F des originaux^M
Originaleinzug^M
posición^F del documento^M para enviar

paper guide
guide-papier^M
Papierführung^F
guía^F del papel^M

function keys
panneau^M de fonctions^F
Funktionstasten^F
teclas^F de función^F

reset key
touche^F de correction^F
Rückstelltaste^F
tecla^F de reinicialización^F

control keys
panneau^M de commande^F
Bedienungstasten^F
teclas^F de control^M

number key
touche^F de composition^F automatique
Nummerntasten^F
teclas^F de números^M

TYPES OF TELEPHONE
TYPES*M* DE POSTES*M* TÉLÉPHONIQUES
TELEFONARTEN*F*
TELÉFONOS*M*

TELECOMMUNICATION TERMINAL
TERMINAL*M* DE TÉLÉCOMMUNICATION*F*
FERNMELDETERMINAL*N*
TERMINAL*M* DE COMUNICACIONES*F*

cordless telephone
poste*M* sans cordon*M*
drahtloses Telefon*N*
teléfono*M* sin cable*M*

housing
boîtier*M*
Gehäuse*N*
caja*F*

visual display unit
écran*M*
Datensichtgerät*N*
monitor*M*

function keys
touches*F* de fonctions*F*
Funktionstasten*F*
teclas*F* de función*F*

numeric keyboard
clavier*M* numérique
numerische Tastatur*F*
teclado*M* numérico

switchboard operator's set
pupitre*M* dirigeur
Abfrageapparat*M*
teléfono*M* para ejecutivo*M*

operation keys
touches*F* de commande*F*
Bedienungstasten*F*
teclas*F* de operación*F*

alphanumeric keyboard
clavier*M* alphanumérique
alphanumerische Tastatur*F*
teclado*M* alfanumérico

keyboard
clavier*M*
Tastatur*F*
teclado*M*

PAY PHONE
TÉLÉPHONE*M* PUBLIC
ÖFFENTLICHER FERNSPRECHER*M*
TELÉFONO*M* PÚBLICO

portable cellular telephone
téléphone*M* cellulaire portatif
mobiles Zellfunktelefon*N*
teléfono*M* celular portátil

coin slot
fente*F* à monnaie*F*
Münzeinwurf*M*
ranura*F* para monedas*F*

display
écran*M*
Display*N*
visualización*F*

volume control
contrôle*M* du volume*M*
Lautstärkeregler*M*
control*M* de volumen*M*

next call
appel*M* suivant
nächster Ruf*M*
próxima llamada*F*

handset
combiné*M*
Handapparat*M*
auricular*M*

language display button
choix*M* de la langue*F* d'affichage*M*
Sprachanzeigetaste*F*
botón*M* de selección*F* de lengua*F*

armoured flex
cordon*M* à gaine*F* métallique
Panzerschnur*F*
cable*M* con funda*F* metálica

push buttons
clavier*M*
Tasten*F*
teclas*F*

push-button telephone
poste*M* à clavier*M*
Tastentelefon*N*
teléfono*M* de teclado*M*

card reader
lecteur*M* de carte*F*
Kartenschlitz*M*
lector*M* de tarjetas*F*

coin return bucket
sébile*F* de remboursement*M*
Geldrückgabe*F*
devolución*F* de monedas*F*

KOMMUNIKATION
COMUNICACIONES

COMMUNICATIONS
COMMUNICATIONS

422

FORTBEWEGUNG
TRANSPORTE

TRANSPORT
TRANSPORT

CAR
AUTOMOBILE[F]
AUTO[N]
AUTOMÓVIL[M]

sports car
voiture[F] sport[M]
Sportwagen[M]
deportivo[M]

hatchback
trois-portes[F]
Schrägheckmodell[N]
turismo[M] de tres puertas[F]

convertible
cabriolet[M]
Kabriolett[N]
descapotable[M]

four-door saloon
berline[F]
viertürige Limousine[F]
sedán[M] de cuatro puertas[F]

minibus
fourgonnette[F]
Minibus[M]
camioneta[F] cubierta

TYPES OF BODYWORK
TYPES[M] DE CARROSSERIES[F]
WAGENTYPEN[M]
TIPOS[M] DE CARROCERÍAS[F]

coupé
coach[M]
Coupé[N]
turismo[M] de dos puertas[F]

estate car
break[M]
Kombiwagen[M]
coche[M] familiar

pickup truck
camionnette[F]
Pickup[M]
camioneta[F]

all-terrain vehicle
véhicule[M] tout-terrain[M]
Geländewagen[M]
vehículo[M] todo terreno[M]

stretch-limousine
limousine[F]
Pullman-Limousine[F]
pullman[M] de ocho plazas[F]

425

BODY
CARROSSERIE*F*
KAROSSERIE*F*
CARROCERÍA*F*

windscreen
pare-brise*M*
Windschutzscheibe*F*
parabrisas*M*

windscreen wiper
essuie-glace*M*
Scheibenwischer*M*
limpiaparabrisas*M*

scuttle panel
auvent*M*
Stirnwandabdeckung*F*
bóveda*F* del salpicadero*M*

outside mirror
rétroviseur*M* extérieur
Seitenspiegel*M*
espejo*M* lateral

washer nozzle
gicleur*M* de lave-glace*M*
Scheibenwaschdüse*F*
pulverizador*M* de agua*F*

bonnet
capot*M*
Motorhaube*F*
capó*M*

headlight
phare*M*
Scheinwerfer*M*
faro*M* delantero

grille
calandre*F*
Kühlergrill*M*
rejilla*F*

bumper
pare-chocs*M*
Stoßfänger*M*
parachoques*M*

bumper moulding
bouclier*M*
Stoßfängerverkleidung*F*
resguardo*M*

wing
aile*F*
Kotflügel*M*
guardabarros*M*

aerial
antenne^F
Antenne^F
antena^F

roof
pavillon^M
Dach^N
techo^M

sun roof
toit^M ouvrant
Schiebedach^N
techo^M corredizo

door pillar
montant^M latéral
Mittelsäule^F
montante^M central

drip moulding
gouttière^F
Regenleiste^F
canal^M de escurrimiento^M

quarter window
glace^F de custode^F
Dreieckfenster^N
ventanilla^F trasera

boot
coffre^M
Kofferraum^M
maletero^M

fuel tank flap
accès^M au réservoir^M à essence^F
Tankklappe^F
tapa^F del tanque^M de gasolina^F

window
glace^F
Seitenfenster^N
ventanilla^F

mud flap
bavette^F garde-boue^M
Schmutzfänger^M
guardabarros^M

door
portière^F
Tür^F
puerta^F

door lock
serrure^F de porte^F
Türschloß^N
cerradura^F

wheel trim
enjoliveur^M
Radkappe^F
tapacubos^M

body side moulding
baguette^F de flanc^M
Seitenverkleidung^F
moldura^F lateral

door handle
poignée^F de porte^F
Türgriff^M
puño^M de la puerta^F

wheel
roue^F
Rad^N
rueda^F

BUCKET SEAT
SIÈGE*M*-BAQUET*M*
SCHALENSITZ*M*
ASIENTO*N* RECLINABLE

shoulder belt
baudrier*M*
Schultergurt*M*
cinturón*M* de hombros

headrest
appui-tête*M*
Kopfstütze*F*
soporte*M* para la cabeza*F*

seat back
dossier*M*
Rückenlehne*F*
respaldo*M*

seat belt
ceinture*F* de sécurité*F*
Sicherheitsgurt*M*
cinturón*M* de seguridad*F*

seat
siège*M*
Sitz*M*
asiento*M*

seat back adjustment knob
commande*F* de dossier*M*
Einstellrad*N*
rueda*F* para graduar el respaldo*M*

seat adjuster lever
manette*F* de glissement*M*
Entriegelungshebel*M*
palanca*F* del deslizador*M*

sliding rail
rail*M* de glissement*M*
Führungsschiene*F*
riel*M* deslizador

REAR SEAT
BANQUETTE*F* ARRIÈRE
RÜCKSITZBANK*F*
ASIENTO*M* TRASERO

armrest
appui-bras*M*
Armstütze*F*
soporte*M* para el brazo*M*

lap belt
sangle*F*
Beckengurt*M*
correa*F*

buckle
boucle*F*
Gurtschließe*F*
hebilla*F*

bench seat
banquette*F*
Sitzbank*F*
asiento*M*

DOOR
PORTIÈRE^F
WAGENTÜR^F
PUERTA^F

interior door handle
poignée^F intérieure
Türöffnungshebel^M
tirador^M de la puerta^F

window
glace^F
Fenster^N
ventanilla^F

door grip
poignée^F de maintien^M
Seitengriff^M
asidera^F

armrest
appui-bras^M
Armstütze^F
soporte^M para el brazo^M

outside mirror control
commande^F du rétroviseur^M
Seitenspiegelverstellhebel^N
control^M del espejo^M retrovisor exterior

interior door lock button
bouton^M de verrouillage^M
Sicherungsknopf^M
botón^M del seguro^M

window winder handle
manivelle^F de lève-glace^M
Fensterhebel^M
manivela^F de la ventanilla^F

lock
serrure^F
Türschloß^N
cerradura^F

door pocket
vide-poches^M
Türtasche^F
bolsillo^M lateral

trim panel
panneau^M de garnissage^M
Türverkleidung^F
panel^M de la puerta^F

hinge
charnière^F
Scharnier^N
bisagra^F

inner door shell
caisson^M de porte^F
Türinnenschale^F
revestimiento^M interior

LIGHTS
FEUX^M
FAHRZEUGBELEUCHTUNG^F
FAROS^M

front lights
feux^M **avant**
Bugleuchten^F
faros^M **delanteros**

main beam headlight
feux^F de route^F
Fernlicht^N
luz^F larga

indicator
feux^M clignotants
Blinkleuchte^F
intermitente^M

dipped beam headlight
feux^M de croisement^M
Abblendlicht^N
luz^F de cruce^M

side marker light
feux^M de gabarit^M
Begrenzungsleuchte^F
luz^F de posición^F

fog lamp
feux^M de brouillard^M
Nebelleuchte^F
luz^F antiniebla

rear lights
feux^M **arrière**
Heckleuchten^F
luces^F **traseras**

brake light
feu^M stop^M
Bremsleuchte^F
luz^F de freno^M

indicator
feux^M clignotants
Blinkleuchte^F
intermitente^M

number plate light
feu^M de plaque^F
Nummernschildbeleuchtung^F
iluminación^F de la placa^F de matrícula^F

brake light
feux^M stop^M
Bremsleuchte^F
luz^F de freno^M

rear light
feux^M rouges arrière
Schlußleuchte^F
luz^F trasera

reversing light
feux^M de recul^M
Rückfahrscheinwerfer^M
luz^F de marcha^F atrás

side marker light
feux^M de gabarit^M
Begrenzungsleuchte^F
luz^F de posición^F

DASHBOARD
TABLEAU^M DE BORD^M
ARMATURENBRETT^N
SALPICADERO^M

wiper control
commande^F d'essuie-glace^M
Scheibenwischerhebel^M
interruptor^M del limpiaparabrisas^M

vanity mirror
miroir^M de courtoisie^F
Spiegel^M
espejo^M de cortesía^F

clock
montre^F
Zeituhr^F
reloj^M

sun visor
pare-soleil^M
Sonnenblende^F
parasol^M

horn
avertisseur^M
Hupe^F
claxón^M

vent
bouche^F d'air^M
Luftdüse^F
ventilación^F

instrument panel
instruments^M de bord^M
Instrumententafel^F
tablero^M de instrumentos^M

rearview mirror
rétroviseur^M
Rückspiegel^M
espejo^M retrovisor

glove compartment
boîte^F à gants^M
Handschuhkasten^M
guantera^F

climate control
commande^F de chauffage^M
Regulierhebel^M für Heizung^F und Belüftung^F
control^M de la calefacción^F

dipping/indicator stalk
éclairage^M/clignotant^M
Blinker- und Fernlichtanzeige^F
palanca^F de luces^F y de cambio^M
de dirección^F

sound system
système^M audio
Radio-/Kassettengerät^N
sistema^M de audio^M

steering wheel
volant^M
Lenkrad^N
volante^M

gearchange lever
levier^M de vitesse^F
Schalthebel^M
palanca^F de cambio^M de velocidades^F

clutch pedal
pédale^F de débrayage^M
Kupplungspedal^N
pedal^M del embrague^M

accelerator pedal
pédale^F d'accélérateur^M
Gaspedal^N
pedal^M del acelerador^M

handbrake lever
levier^M de frein^M à main^F
Handbremshebel^M
freno^M de mano^F

centre console
console^F centrale
Mittelkonsole^F
consola^F central

ignition switch
démarreur^M électrique
Zündschloß^N
interruptor^M de encendido^M

brake pedal
pédale^F de frein^M
Bremspedal^N
pedal^M de los frenos^M

430

INSTRUMENT PANEL
INSTRUMENTS *M* **DE BORD** *M*
INSTRUMENTENTAFEL *F*
INSTRUMENTOS *M* **DEL SALPICADERO** *M*

battery warning light
témoin *M* de charge *F*
Batterieladekontrolleuchte *F*
luz *F* de advertencia *F* del alternador *M*

main beam indicator light
témoin *M* des feux *M* de route *F*
Fernlichtanzeige *F*
luz *F* indicadora de luz *F* larga

oil warning light
témoin *M* de niveau *M* d'huile *F*
Öldruckwarnleuchte *F*
luz *F* de advertencia *F* del aceite *M*

low fuel warning light
témoin *M* de bas niveau *M* de carburant *M*
Kraftstoffreserveanzeige *F*
luz *F* de advertencia *F* de la gasolina *F*

fuel gauge
indicateur *M* de niveau *M* de carburant *M*
Kraftstoffanzeige *F*
indicador *M* de nivel *M* de gasolina *F*

warning lights
lampes *F* témoins *M*
Warnleuchten *F*
luces *F* de advertencia *F*

indicator telltale
témoin *M* de clignotants *M*
Blinklichtkontrolle *F*
intermitente *M*

temperature gauge
indicateur *M* de température *F*
Temperaturanzeige *F*
indicador *M* de temperatura *F*

tachometer
compte-tours *M*
Drehzahlmesser *M*
tacómetro *M*

mileometer
compteur *M* kilométrique
Kilometerzähler *M*
cuentakilómetros *M*

trip mileometer
totalisateur *M* journalier
Tageskilometerzähler *M*
odómetro *M*

door open warning light
témoin *M* d'ouverture *F* de porte *F*
Warnleuchte *F* "Tür offen"
luz *F* de advertencia *F* de puerta *F*

seat-belt warning light
témoin *M* de ceinture *F* de sécurité *F*
Anzeige *F* "Sicherheitsgurte anlegen"
luz *F* de advertencia *F* del cinturón *M* de seguridad *F*

speedometer
indicateur *M* de vitesse *F*
Tachometer *M*
velocímetro *M*

WINDSCREEN WIPER
ESSUIE-GLACE *M*
SCHEIBENWISCHER *M*
LIMPIAPARABRISAS *M*

windscreen wiper blade
balai *M* d'essuie-glace *M*
Wischblatt *M*
soporte *M*

joint
articulation *F*
Gelenk *N*
articulación *F*

wiper arm
bras *M* d'essuie-glace *M*
Wischerarm *M*
brazo *M*

wiper blade rubber
lame *F*
Wischgummi *M*
limpiador *M*

tension spring
ressort *M* de tension *F*
Zugfeder *F*
resorte *M* tensor

pivot spindle
arbre *M* cannelé
Wischerachse *F*
tubo *M* articulado

431

STRASSENVERKEHR
TRANSPORTE TERRESTRE

ROAD TRANSPORT
TRANSPORT ROUTIER

DISC BRAKE
FREIN^M À DISQUE^M
SCHEIBENBREMSE^F
FRENO^M DE DISCO^M

brake hose
canalisation^F
Bremsschlauch^M
manguera^F de líquido^M para frenos^M

caliper
étrier^M
Bremssattel^M
calibrador^M

piston
piston^M
Kolben^M
pistón^M

brake pad
plaquette^F
Bremsbelag^M
pastilla^F de fricción^F

disc
disque^M
Bremsscheibe^F
disco^M

DRUM BRAKE
FREIN^M À TAMBOUR^M
TROMMELBREMSE^F
FRENO^M DE TAMBOR^M

anchor pin
point^M fixe
Ankerbolzen^M
perno^M de fijación^F

brake shoe
segment^M
Bremsbacke^F
zapata^F

wheel cylinder
cylindre^M de roue^F
Radbremszylinder^M
cilindro^M de freno^M

piston
piston^M
Kolben^M
pistón^M

backplate
plateau^M de frein^M
Bremsträger^M
plato^M de retroceso^M

return spring
ressort^M de rappel^M
Rückholfeder^F
resorte^M de retorno^M

brake lining
garniture^F de frein^M
Bremsbelag^M
revestimiento^M

stud
goujon^M
Radbefestigungsbolzen^M
espiga^F

drum
tambour^M
Bremstrommel^F
tambor^M

BELTED RADIAL TYRE
PNEU^M À CARCASSE^F RADIALE CEINTURÉE
RADIALGÜRTELREIFEN^M
NEUMÁTICO^M RADIAL CON CINTURONES^M

cross-ply tyre
pneu^M à carcasse^F diagonale
Diagonalreifen^M
neumático^M de capas^F al sesgo^M

radial tyre
pneu^M à carcasse^F radiale
Radialreifen^M
neumático^M radial

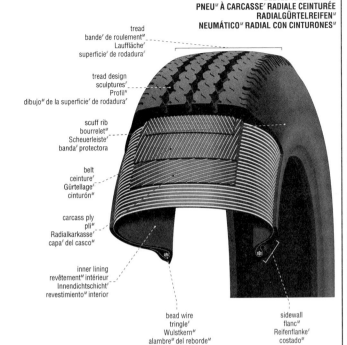

tread
bande^F de roulement^M
Lauffläche^F
superficie^F de rodadura^F

tread design
sculptures^F
Profil^N
dibujo^M de la superficie^F de rodadura^F

scuff rib
bourrelet^M
Scheuerleiste^F
banda^F protectora

belt
ceinture^F
Gürtellage^F
cinturón^M

carcass ply
pli^M
Radialkarkasse^F
capa^F del casco^M

inner lining
revêtement^M intérieur
Innendichtschicht^F
revestimiento^M interior

bead wire
tringle^F
Wulstkern^M
alambre^M del reborde^M

sidewall
flanc^M
Reifenflanke^F
costado^M

TYRE
PNEU^M
REIFEN^M
NEUMÁTICO^M

tread design
sculptures^F
Profil^N
dibujo^M de la superficie^F de rodadura^F

scuff rib
bourrelet^M
Scheuerleiste^F
banda^F protectora

WHEEL
ROUE^F
RAD^N
RUEDA^F

technical specifications
spécifications^F techniques
Kennzeichnung^F
especificaciones^F técnicas^F

disc
voile^M
Radschüssel^F
disco^M

bead
talon^M
Wulst^M
moldura^F

sidewall
flanc^M
Reifenflanke^F
costado^M

rim
jante^F
Felge^F
llanta^F

rim flange
joue^F de jante^F
Felgenhorn^N
pestaña^F de la llanta^F

433

CAR
AUTOMOBILE*F*
AUTO*N*
AUTOMÓVIL*M*

PETROL ENGINE
MOTEUR*M* À ESSENCE*F*
OTTOMOTOR*M*
MOTOR*M* DE GASOLINA*F*

injector
injecteur*M*
Einspritzdüse*F*
inyector*M*

inlet manifold
tubulure*F* d'admission*F*
Saugrohr*N*
múltiple*M* de admisión*F*

valve spring
ressort*M* de soupape*F*
Ventilfeder*F*
resorte*M* de la válvula*F*

timing belt
courroie*F* de distribution*F*
Antriebsriemen*M*
correa*F* de distribución*F*

camshaft
arbre*M* à cames*F*
Nockenwelle*F*
árbol*M* de levas*F*

inlet valve
soupape*F* d'admission*F*
Einlaßventil*N*
válvula*F* de admisión*F*

combustion chamber
chambre*F* de combustion*F*
Verbrennungsraum*M*
cámara*F* de combustión*F*

piston ring
segment*M*
Kolbenring*M*
anillo*M*

piston skirt
jupe*F* de piston*M*
Kolbenschaft*F*
camisa*F* de pistón*M*

alternator
alternateur*M*
Lichtmaschine*F*
alternador*M*

connecting rod
bielle*M*
Pleuelstange*F*
biela*F*

cooling fan
ventilateur*M*
Lüfter*M*
ventilador*M*

pulley
poulie*F*
Riemenscheibe*F*
polea*F*

crankshaft
vilebrequin*M*
Kurbelwelle*F*
cigüeñal*M*

fan belt
courroie*F* de ventilateur*M*
Keilriemen*M*
correa*F* del ventilador*M*

sump gasket
joint*M* de carter*M*
Ölwannendichtung*F*
junta*F* del cárter*M*

oil drain plug
bouchon*M* de vidange*F* d'huile*F*
Ölablaßschraube*F*
tapón*M* de vaciado*M*

sump
carter*M*
Ölwanne*F*
cárter*M*

distributor
allumeur^M
Zündverteiler^M
casquete^M del distribuidor^M

vacuum diaphragm
capsule^F à membrane^F
Zündversteller^M
diafragma^M de vacío^M

valve cover
couvercle^M de culasse^F
Zylinderkopfdeckel^M
culata^F de los cilindros^M

ignition lead
câble^M de bougie^F
Zündkabel^N
cable^M de bujía^F

rocker arm
culbuteur^M
Schwinghebel^M
balancín^M

sparking plug
bougie^F d'allumage^M
Zündkerze^F
bujía^F

exhaust valve
soupape^F d'échappement^M
Auslaßventil^N
válvula^F de escape^M

exhaust manifold
collecteur^M d'échappement^M
Auspuffkrümmer^M
múltiple^M de escape^M

engine block
bloc^M-cylindres^M
Motorblock^M
bloque^M del motor^M

flywheel
volant^M
Schwungrad^N
rueda^F libre

piston
piston^M
Kolben^M
pistón^M

air conditioner compressor
compresseur^M du climatiseur^M
Kompressor^M für Klimaanlage^F
compresor^M del aire^M acondicionado

TYPES OF ENGINE
TYPES^M DE MOTEURS^M
MOTORTYPEN^M
TIPOS^M DE MOTORES^M

FOUR-STROKE ENGINE
MOTEUR^M À QUATRE TEMPS^M
VIERTAKTMOTOR^M
MOTOR^M DE CUATRO TIEMPOS^M

spark
étincelle^F
Funken^M
chispa^F

inlet valve
soupape^F d'admission^F
Einlaßventil^N
válvula^F de admisión^F

connecting rod
bielle^F
Pleuelstange^F
biela^F

air/fuel mixture
mélange^M air^M/carburant^M
Kraftstoff-Luft-Gemisch^N
mezcla^F de aire^M y combustible^M

crankshaft
vilebrequin^M
Kurbelwelle^F
cigüeñal^M

cylinder
cylindre^M
Zylinder^M
cilindro^M

1 **2**

induction
admission^F
Ansaugen^N
admisión^F

compression
compression^F
Verdichten^N
compresión^F

ignition
explosion^F
Verbrennung^F
explosión^F

exhaust valve
soupape^F d'échappement^M
Auslaßventil^N
válvula^F de escape^M

burned gases
gaz^M brûlés
Abgase^N
gases^M quemados

piston
piston^M
Kolben^M
pistón^M

3 **4**

combustion
combustion^F
Zünden^N
combustión^F

exhaust
échappement^M
Ausstoßen^N
escape^M

TWO-STROKE ENGINE
MOTEUR^M À DEUX TEMPS^M
ZWEITAKTMOTOR^M
MOTOR^M DE DOS TIEMPOS^M

exhaust port
canal^M d'échappement^M
Auspuffkanal^M
lumbrera^F de escape^M

transfer port
canal^M de transfert^M
Überströmschlitz^M
lumbrera^F de transferencia^F

inlet port
canal^M d'admission^F
Ansaugkanal^M
lumbrera^F de admisión^F

crankcase
carter^M
Kurbelgehäuse^N
cárter^M

compression/induction
compression^F/admission^F
Verdichten^N/Ansaugen^N
compresión^F/admisión^F

combustion
combustion^F
Verbrennen^N
combustión^F

exhaust
échappement^M
Ausstoßen^N
escape^M

DIESEL ENGINE
MOTEUR^M DIESEL
DIESELMOTOR^M
MOTOR^M DIÉSEL

air
air^M
Luft^F
aire^M

injection/ignition
injection^F/explosion^F
Einspritzung^F/Verbrennung^F
injección^F/explosión^F

fuel injector
injecteur^M
Einspritzdüse^F
injector^M de combustible^M

induction
admission^F
Ansaugen^N
admisión^F

compression
compression^F
Verdichten^N
compresión^F

combustion
combustion^F
Zünden^N
combustión^F

exhaust
échappement^M
Ausstoßen^N
escape^M

ROTARY ENGINE
MOTEUR^M ROTATIF
KREISKOLBENMOTOR^M
MOTOR^M ROTATORIO

inlet manifold
tubulure^F d'admission^F
Einlaßkanal^M
múltiple^M de admisión^F

sparking plug
bougie^F d'allumage^M
Zündkerze^F
bujía^F

exhaust manifold
tubulure^F d'échappement^M
Auslaßkanal^M
múltiple^M de escape^M

induction
admission^F
Ansaugen^N
admisión^F

exhaust
échappement^M
Ausstoßen^N
escape^M

compression
compression^F
Verdichten^N
compresión^F

rotor
rotor^M
Kolben^M
rotor^M

combustion
combustion^F
Zünden^N
combustión^F

437

CAR
AUTOMOBILEF
AUTON
AUTOMÓVILM

RADIATOR
RADIATEURM
KÜHLERM
RADIADORM

filler cap
bouchonM de remplissageM
KühlerverschlußdeckelM
tapaF

radiator core
grilleF
KühlerblockM
rejillaF

cooling fan
ventilateurM
LüfterM
ventiladorM

electric motor
moteurM électrique
ElektromotorM
motorM eléctrico

fan thermostat
thermocontactM
ThermoschalterM
termostatoM del ventiladorM

radiator hose
duriteF de radiateurM
KühlwasserschlauchM
mangueraF

TURBO-CHARGED ENGINE
MOTEURN **À TURBOCOMPRESSION**F
MOTORM **MIT ABGASTURBOLADER**M
MOTORM **TURBO COMPRESOR**

exhaust gas admission
entréeF des gazM d'échappementM
Abgaseintritt M
tomaF de gasesM de combustiónF

cold air inlet
admissionF d'airM refroidi
KaltluftzuleitungF
entradaF de aireM frío

warm air outlet
sortieF d'airM chaud
WarmluftauslaßM
salidaF de aireM caliente

exhaust manifold
collecteurM d'échappementM
AuspuffkrümmerM
múltipleM de escapeM

intercooler
refroidisseurM d'airM
LadeluftkühlerM
enfriadorM

compressor turbine
turbineF du compresseurM
VerdichterradM
turbinaF del compresorM

driving turbine
turbineF d'entraînementM
TurbinenradM
turbinaF de transmisiónF

exhaust pipe
tuyauM d'échappementM
AbgasrohrM
tuboM de escapeM

combustion chamber
chambreF de combustionF
VerbrennungsraumM
cámaraF de combustiónF

piston
pistonM
KolbenM
pistónM

exhaust valve
soupapeF d'échappementM
AuslaßventilN
válvulaF de escapeM

SPARKING PLUG
BOUGIE^F D'ALLUMAGE^M
ZÜNDKERZE^F
BUJÍA^F

sparking plug
borne^F
Anschlußbolzen^M
borne^M

groove
cannelure^F
Kriechstrombarriere^F
ranura^F

centre electrode
électrode^F centrale
Mittelelektrode^F
electrodo^M central

insulator
isolateur^M
Isolator^M
aislador^M

hex nut
écrou^M hexagonal
Sechskantmutter^F
hexagonal^M

sparking plug gasket
joint^M de bougie^F
Zündkerzendichtring^M
junta^F

sparking plug body
culot^M
Zündkerzengehäuse^N
cuerpo^M metálico de la bujía^F

side electrode
électrode^F de masse^F
Masseelektrode^F
electrodo^M de masa^F

sparking plug gap
écartement^M des électrodes^F
Funkenstrecke^F
espacio^M para la chispa^F

EXHAUST SYSTEM
SYSTÈME^M D'ÉCHAPPEMENT^M
AUSPUFFANLAGE^F
SISTEMA^M DE ESCAPE^M

exhaust manifold
collecteur^M d'échappement^M
Auspuffkrümmer^M
múltiple^M de escape^M

front pipe
tuyau^M d'échappement^M
vorderes Auspuffrohr^M
tubo^M de escape^M

catalytic converter
convertisseur^M catalytique
Katalysator^M
convertidor^M catalítico

silencer
pot^M d'échappement^M
Schalldämpfer^M
silenciador^M

tail pipe
tuyau^M arrière
hinteres Auspuffrohr^N
tubo^M de cola^F

tail pipe extension
embout^M
Endrohr^N
extensión^F

BATTERY
BATTERIE^F D'ACCUMULATEURS^M
BATTERIE^F
BATERÍA^F

battery cover
couvercle^M de batterie^F
Blockdeckel^M
tapa^F de la batería^F

positive terminal
borne^F positive
positiver Anschlußpol^M
borne^M positivo

negative terminal
borne^F négative
negativer Anschlußpol^M
borne^M negativo

liquid/gas separator
séparateur^M liquide^M/gaz^M
Entgasungsbohrung^F
separador^M de gas^M y líquido^M

hydrometer
hydromètre^M
Dichtemesser^M
medidor^M de agua^F

positive plate strap
barrette^F positive
Pluspolbrücke^F
banda^F de placa^F positiva

battery case
boîtier^M de batterie^F
Blockkasten^M
caja^F de la batería^F

negative plate strap
barrette^F négative
Minuspolbrücke^F
banda^F de placa^F negativa

positive plate
plaque^F positive
Plusplatte^F
placa^F positiva

negative plate
plaque^F négative
Minusplatte^F
placa^F negativa

plate grid
alvéole^F de plaque^F
Plattengitter^N
rejilla^F

separator
séparateur^M
Plattenscheider^M
separador^M de placas^F

**TRACTOR UNIT
TRACTEUR[M] ROUTIER
SATTELSCHLEPPER[M]
CAMIÓN[M] TRACTOR[M]**

windscreen
pare-brise[M]
Windschutzscheibe[F]
parabrisas[M]

wind deflector
déflecteur[M]
Windabweiser[M]
deflector[M] de viento[M]

air horn
avertisseur[M] pneumatique
Fanfare[F]
bocina[F] de aire[M]

exhaust stack
cheminée[F] d'échappement[M]
Auspuffrohr[N]
tubo[M] de escape[M]

trail-view mirror
rétroviseur[M]
Seitenspiegel[M]
espejo[M] lateral

side marker light
feu[M] de gabarit[M]
Umrißleuchte[F]
luz[F] lateral

sleeper-cab
compartiment[M]-couchette[F]
Schlafkabine[F]
cabina[F] para dormir

bonnet
capot[M]
Haube[F]
capó[M]

grab handle
poignée[F] montoir[M]
Haltestange[F]
asidera[F]

storage compartment
coffre[M] de rangement[M]
Stauraum[M]
espacio[M] para almacenamiento[M]

fifth wheel
sellette[F] d'attelage[M]
Sattelkupplung[F]
disco[M] de articulación[F]

radiator grille
calandre[F]
Kühlergrill[M]
rejilla[F] del radiador[M]

step
marchepied[M]
Trittstufe[F]
escalón[M]

mud flap
bavette[F] garde-boue[F]
Schmutzfänger[M]
guardabarros[M]

headlight
phare[M]
Scheinwerfer[M]
faro[M] delantero

wheel
roue[F]
Gußrad[N]
rueda[F]

tyre
pneu[M]
Reifen[M]
neumático[M]

fog light
phare[M] antibrouillard
Nebelscheinwerfer[M]
luz[F] antiniebla

wing
aile[F]
Kotflügel[M]
guardabarros[M]

filler cap
bouchon[M] du réservoir[M]
Tankdeckel[M]
tapa[F] del tanque[M]

bumper
pare-chocs[M]
Stoßfänger[M]
parachoques[M]

fuel tank
réservoir[M] à carburant[M]
Kraftstofftank[M]
tanque[M] del combustible[M]

**ARTICULATED LORRY WITH TRAILER
TRAIN[M] ROUTIER
SATTELZUG[M]
CAMIÓN[M] TRACTOR[M] CON DOBLE CAJA[F]**

tractor unit
tracteur[M]
Zugmaschine[F]
camión[M] tractor[M]

semitrailer
semi-remorque[F]
Auflieger[M]
caja[F] tipo[M] semirremolque[M]

truck trailer
remorque[F]
Anhänger[M]
caja[F] tipo[M] remolque[M]

SEMITRAILER
SEMI-REMORQUE^F
AUFLIEGER^M
CAJA^F TIPO^M SEMIRREMOLQUE^M

side marker light
feu^M de gabarit^M
Begrenzungsleuchte^F
luz^F lateral

frontwall
paroi^F avant
Stirnwand^F
panel^M frontal

sidewall
paroi^F latérale
Seitenwand^F
panel^M lateral

refrigeration unit
groupe^M frigorifique
Kühlaggregat^N
unidad^F de refrigeración^F

vent door
volet^M d'air^M
Luftklappe^F
ventilador^M

battery box
boîtier^M de batterie^F
Batteriekasten^M
caja^F del acumulador^M

partlow chart
disque^M de papier^M-diagramme^M
Partlow-Diagramm^N
regulador^M de temperatura^F

electrical connection
accouplement^M électrique
Stromanschluß^M
conexiones^F

kingpin
pivot^M d'accouplement^M
Zugsattelzapfen^M
perno^M maestro

support leg crank
manivelle^F
Handkurbel^F
manivela^F de elevación^F de patas^F

support leg
béquille^F
Standbein^N
pata^F soporte

reflector
réflecteur^M
Rückstrahler^M
reflector^M

mud flap
bavette^F garde-boue^M
Schmutzfänger^M
guardabarros^M

auxiliary tank
réservoir^M auxiliaire
Zusatztank^M
tanque^M auxiliar

sand shoe
sabot^M
Stützfuß^M
zapata^F

side rail
longeron^M
Wand-Untergurt^M
banda^F lateral protectora

FLATBED
SEMI-REMORQUE^F PLATE-FORME^F
KOFFER-SATTELANHÄNGER^M
PLATAFORMA^F

stake pocket
gaine^F de rancher^M
Rungentasche^F
ranura^F para toldo^M

bulkhead
paroi^F de bout^M
Stirnwand^F
mampara^F de contención^F

load platform
plate-forme^F
Ladefläche^F
plataforma^F

rear light
feu^M rouge arrière
Rücklicht^N
luz^F trasera

indicator
clignotant^M
Richtungsanzeiger^M
intermitente^M

mud flap
bavette^F garde-boue^M
Spritzlappen^M
guardabarros^M

bumper
pare-chocs^M
Unterfahrschutz^M
parachoques^M

rub rail
rail^M de guidage^M
Rammschutzleiste^F
banda^F protectora

support leg crank
manivelle^F
Handkurbel^F
manivela^F de elevación^F de patas^F

side marker light
feu^M de gabarit^M
Begrenzungsleuchte^F
luz^F lateral

MOTORCYCLE
MOTO*^F*
MOTORRAD*^N*
MOTOCICLETA*^F*

SIDE VIEW
VUE*^F* LATÉRALE
SEITENANSICHT*^F*
VISTA*^F* LATERAL

mirror
rétroviseur*^M*
Rückspiegel*^M*
espejo*^M*

windscreen
pare-brise*^M*
Windschutzscheibe*^F*
parabrisas*^M*

petrol tank
réservoir*^M* à essence*^F*
Kraftstofftank*^M*
tanque*^M* de la gasolina*^F*

clutch lever
levier*^M* d'embrayage*^M*
Kupplungshebel*^M*
palanca*^F* del embrague*^M*

instrument cluster
tableau*^M* de bord*^M*
Instrumententafel*^F*
tablero*^M*

front indicator
feu*^M* clignotant avant
Blinkleuchte*^F*
intermitente*^M*

headlight
phare*^M*
Scheinwerfer*^M*
faro*^M* delantero

handgrip
poignée*^F*
Lenkergriff*^M*
manillar*^M*

front mudguard
garde-boue*^M* avant
vorderes Schutzblech*^N*
guardabarros*^M* delantero

telescopic fork
fourche*^F* télescopique hydraulique
Teleskopgabel*^F*
horquilla*^F* telescópica

fairing
carénage*^M*
Verkleidung*^F*
protector*^M* del motor*^M*

brake caliper
étrier*^M*
Bremssattel*^M*
calibrador*^M* del freno*^M*

rim
jante*^F*
Felge*^F*
llanta*^F*

disc brake
frein*^M* à disque*^M*
Scheibenbremse*^F*
freno*^M* de disco*^M*

carburettor
carburateur*^M*
Vergaser*^M*
carburador*^M*

spoiler
béquet*^M*
Spoiler*^M*
pieza*^F* aerodinámica

engine
moteur*^M*
Motor*^M*
motor*^M*

CRASH HELMET
CASQUE^M DE PROTECTION^F
SCHUTZHELM^M
CASCO^M PROTECTOR

bubble
coque^F
Oberschale^F
casco^M

visor
visière^F
Visier^N
visera^F

air inlet
grille^F d'entrée^F d'air^M
Lufteinlaß^M
respiradero^M

chin protector
mentonnière^F
Kinnschutz^M
protector^M de la barbilla^F

visor hinge
charnière^F de la visière^F
Scharnier^N
visor^M lateral

frame
cadre^M
Rahmen^M
bastidor^M

dual seat
selle^F biplace
Doppelsitz^M
sillín^M doble

rear indicator
clignotant^M arrière
Blinkleuchte^F
intermitente^M

rear light
feu^M arrière
Schlußleuchte^F
luz^F trasera

suspension strut
amortisseur^M arrière
hinterer Stoßdämpfer^M
amortiguador^M

pillion footrest
repose-pied^M du passager^M
Beifahrerfußraste^F
pedal^M trasero

silencer
pot^M d'échappement^M
Auspuffrohr^N
tubo^M de escape^M

kickstand
béquille^F latérale
Seitenständer^M
soporte^M lateral

main stand
béquille^F centrale
Hauptständer^M
soporte^M principal

gearchange pedal
sélecteur^M de vitesses^F
Schaltpedal^N
palanca^F de cambio^M de velocidades^F

front footrest
repose-pied^M du pilote^M
vordere Fußraste^F
pedal^M delantero

443

MOTORCYCLE
MOTO^F
MOTORRAD^N
MOTOCICLETA^F

VIEW FROM ABOVE
VUE^F EN PLONGÉE^F
DRAUFSICHT^F
VISTA^F POR ENCIMA

headlight
phare^M
Scheinwerfer^M
faro^M delantero

front indicator
feu^M clignotant avant
Blinkleuchte^F
intermitente^M

mirror
rétroviseur^M
Seitenspiegel^M
espejo^M

front brake lever
levier^M de frein^M avant
Hebel^M für Vorderbremse^F
palanca^F del freno^M delantero

clutch lever
levier^M d'embrayage^M
Kupplungshebel^M
palanca^F del embrague^M

twist grip throttle
poignée^F des gaz^M
Gashebel^M
acelerador^M

dip switch
inverseur^M route^F-croisement^M
Abblendschalter^M
interruptor^M

emergency switch
coupe-circuit^M d'urgence^F
Notschalter^M
interruptor^M de emergencia^F

horn
avertisseur^M
Hupe^F
claxon^M

starter button
bouton^M de démarreur^M
Zündschalter^M
interruptor^M de encendido^M

petrol tank cap
bouchon^M de remplissage^M
Benzintankverschluß^M
tapa^F del tanque^M de la gasolina^F

clutch housing
carter^M d'embrayage^M
Kupplungsgehäuse^N
cubierta^F del embrague^M

gearchange pedal
sélecteur^M de vitesses^F
Schaltpedal^N
pedal^M de cambio^M de velocidades^F

rear brake pedal
pédale^F de frein^M arrière
Bremspedal^N
pedal^M del freno^M trasero

front footrest
repose-pied^M du pilote^M
vordere Fußraste^F
pedal^M delantero

pillion footrest
repose-pied^M du passager^M
Beifahrer-Fußraste^F
pedal^M trasero

silencer
pot^M d'échappement^M
Auspuffrohr^N
tubo^M de escape^M

rear indicator
feu^M clignotant arrière
Blinkleuchte^F
intermitente^M

rear light
feu^M arrière
Schlußleuchte^F
luz^F trasera

INSTRUMENT CLUSTER
TABLEAU^M DE BORD^M
INSTRUMENTENTAFEL^F
TABLERO^M

speedometer
indicateur^M de vitesse^F
Tachometer^M
velocímetro^M

tachometer
tachymètre^M
Drehzahlmesser^M
tacómetro^M

oil pressure warning indicator
témoin^M de pression^F d'huile^F
Öldruckkontrolleuchte^F
luz^F indicadora de la presión^F del aceite^M

main beam warning light
témoin^M de phare^M
Fernlichtkontrolleuchte^F
indicador^M de luz^F larga

neutral indicator
témoin^M de position^F neutre
Neutralanzeigelicht^N
indicador^M neutro

indicator telltale
témoin^M de clignotants^M
Blinkerkontrolleuchte^F
intermitente^M

ignition switch
démarreur^M électrique
Zündschalter^M
interruptor^M de encendido^M

SNOWMOBILE
MOTONEIGE^F
SCHNEEMOBIL^N
TRINEO^M MOTORIZADO

rear bumper
pare-chocs^M arrière
Stoßstange^F
parachoques^M

seat
selle^F
Sitzbank^F
asiento^M

handlebars
guidon^M
Lenker^M
manillar^M

luggage rack
support^M à bagages^M
Gepäckträger^M
portaequipajes^M

brake handle
manette^F du frein^M
Bremshebel^M
palanca^F del freno^M

windscreen
pare-brise^M
Klarsichtscheibe^F
parabrisas^M

backrest
dossier^M
Rückenlehne^F
respaldo^M

fairing
capot^M
Instrumente^N
cabina^F

headlight
phare^M
Scheinwerfer^M
faro^M delantero

idler wheel
roue^F de support^M
Zwischenrad^N
rueda^F de transmisión^F

track
chenille^F
Kette^F
rueda^F de cadena^F

reflector
catadioptre^M
Rückstrahler^M
reflector^M

body
coque^F
Rumpf^M
carrocería^F

sprocket
roue^F dentée
Antriebsrad^N
diente^M

footboard
marchepied^M
Trittbrett^N
estribo^M

air scoop
prise^F d'air^M
Lufteinlaß^M
entrada^F de aire^M

snow guard
bavette^F garde-neige^F
Schutzblech^N
guardanieve^M

shock absorber
amortisseur^M
Stoßdämpfer^M
amortiguador^M

ski
ski^M
Kufe^F
esquí^M

445

BICYCLE
BICYCLETTE^F
FAHRRAD^N
BICICLETA^F

saddle pillar
tige^F de selle^F
Sattelstütze^F
poste^M del asiento^M

seat stay
hauban^M
hinterer Streben^M
horquilla^F trasera

seat tube
tube^M de selle^F
Sitzrohr^N
tubo^M del asiento^M

rear brake
frein^M arrière
hintere Felgenbremse^F
freno^M trasero

carrier
porte-bagages^M
Gepäckträger^M
portaequipajes^M

dynamo
dynamo^F
Dynamo^M
dínamo^F

rear light
feu^M arrière
Rücklicht^N
luz^F trasera

saddle
selle^F
Sattel^M
sillín^M

crossbar
tube^M horizontal
Oberrohr^N
barra^F

tyre pump
pompe^F
Luftpumpe^F
bomba^F de aire^M

mudguard
garde-boue^M
Schutzblech^N
guardabarros^M

reflector
catadioptre^M
Rückstrahler^M
reflector^M

rear derailleur
dérailleur^M arrière
hinterer Umwerfer^M
cambiador^M de piñones^M

chain stay
base^F
Hinterrohr^N
soporte^M de la cadena^F

drive chain
chaîne^F
Kette^F
cadena^F de transmisión^F

front derailleur
dérailleur^M avant
Kettenblattumwerfer^M
cambiador^M de platos^M

pedal
pédale^F
Pedal^N
pedal^M

toe clip
cale-pied^M
Pedalhaken^M
calapié^M

gear lever
manette^f de dérailleur^M
Schalthebel^M
palanca^f del cambio^M de velocidades^f

brake cable
câble^M de frein^M
Bremszug^M
cable^M del freno^M

handlebars
guidon^M
Lenkstange^f
manillar^M

handlebar stem
potence^f
Lenkerschaft^M
vástago^M

steering tube
tube^M de direction^f
Steuerkopf^M
tubo^M del manillar^M

brake lever
poignée^f de frein^M
Bremsgriff^M
palanca^f del freno^M

front brake
frein^M avant
vordere Felgenbremse^f
freno^M delantero

front lamp
projecteur^M
Scheinwerfer^M
luz^f delantera

fork
fourche^f
Vordergabel^f
horquilla^f

hub
moyeu^M
Nabe^f
eje^M de la rueda^f

water bottle
bidon^M
Wasserflasche^f
botella^f

water bottle clip
porte-bidon^M
Halterung^f der Wasserflasche^f
portabotellas^M

down tube
tube^M oblique
Unterrohr^N
tubo^M inferior del cuadro^M

tyre valve
valve^f
Ventil^N
válvula^f

spoke
rayon^M
Speiche^f
radio^M

rim
jante^f
Felge^f
llanta^f

tyre
pneu^M
Reifen^M
neumático^M

BICYCLE
BICYCLETTE*F*
FAHRRAD*N*
BICICLETA*F*

POWER TRAIN
MÉCANISME*M* DE PROPULSION*F*
KRAFTÜBERTRAGUNG*F*
TRANSMISIÓN*F* DE CADENA*F*

freewheel
roue*F* libre
Freilauf*M*
piñón*M* libre

chain guide
guide-chaîne*M*
Kettenführung*F*
guía*F* de la cadena*F*

chain
chaîne*F*
Kette*F*
cadena*F*

front derailleur
dérailleur*M* avant
Kettenblattumwerfer*M*
cambiador*M* de platos*M*

toe clip
cale-pied*M*
Rennhaken*M*
calapié*M*

gear lever
manette*F* de dérailleur*M*
Schalthebel*M*
palanca*F* del cambio*M* de velocidades*F*

gear cable
câble*M* de commande*F*
Schaltzug*M*
cable*M* del cambio*M*

chain wheel A
plateau*M* A
großes Kettenblatt*N*
corona*F* externa de la cadena*F*

pedal spindle
axe*M* du pédalier*M*
Tretlager*N*
eje*M* del pedal*M*

chain wheel B
plateau*M* B
kleines Kettenblatt*N*
corona*F* interna de la cadena*F*

jockey rollers
galets*M* tendeurs
Abhalter*M*
poleas*F* de tensión*F*

crank
manivelle*F*
Kurbel*F*
manivela*F*

rear derailleur
dérailleur*M* arrière
hinterer Umwerfer*M*
cambiador*M* de piñones*M*

pedal
pédale*F*
Pedal*N*
pedal*M*

ACCESSORIES
ACCESSOIRES*M*
ZUBEHÖR*N*
ACCESORIOS*M*

cycle lock
cadenas*M*
Schloß*N*
candado*M* para bicicleta*F*

cycling helmet
casque*M* de protection*F*
Schutzhelm*M*
casco*M* protector

pannier bag
sacoche*F*
Satteltasche*F*
bolsa*F*

CARAVAN
CARAVANE^F
WOHNWAGEN^M
CARAVANA^F

TRAILER CARAVAN
CARAVANE^F **TRACTÉE**
WOHNWAGEN^M
REMOLQUE^M

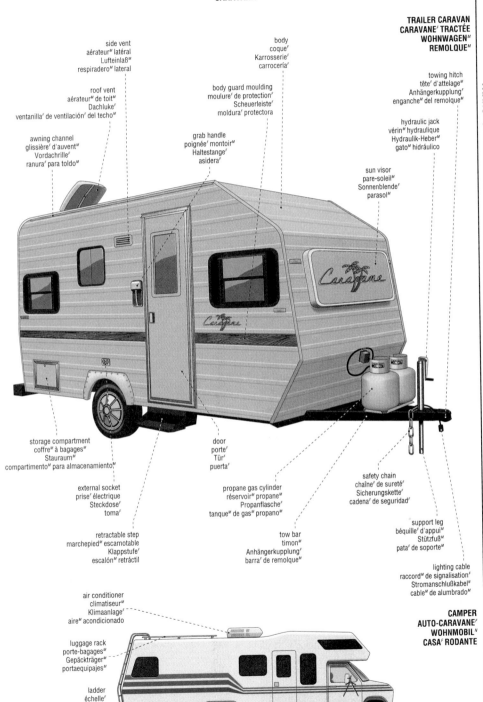

side vent
aérateur^M latéral
Lufteinlaß^M
respiradero^M lateral

roof vent
aérateur^M de toit^M
Dachluke^F
ventanilla^F de ventilación^F del techo^M

awning channel
glissière^F d'auvent^M
Vordachrille^F
ranura^F para toldo^M

body
coque^F
Karrosserie^F
carrocería^F

body guard moulding
moulure^F de protection^F
Scheuerleiste^F
moldura^F protectora

grab handle
poignée^F montoir^M
Haltestange^F
asidera^F

towing hitch
tête^F d'attelage^M
Anhängerkupplung^F
enganche^M del remolque^M

hydraulic jack
vérin^M hydraulique
Hydraulik-Heber^M
gato^M hidráulico

sun visor
pare-soleil^M
Sonnenblende^F
parasol^M

storage compartment
coffre^M à bagages^M
Stauraum^M
compartimento^M para almacenamiento^M

external socket
prise^F électrique
Steckdose^F
toma^F

retractable step
marchepied^M escamotable
Klappstufe^F
escalón^M retráctil

door
porte^F
Tür^F
puerta^F

propane gas cylinder
réservoir^M propane^M
Propanflasche^F
tanque^M de gas^M propano^M

tow bar
timon^M
Anhängerkupplung^F
barra^F de remolque^M

safety chain
chaîne^F de sureté^F
Sicherungskette^F
cadena^F de seguridad^F

support leg
béquille^F d'appui^M
Stützfuß^M
pata^F de soporte^M

lighting cable
raccord^M de signalisation^F
Stromanschlußkabel^N
cable^M de alumbrado^M

air conditioner
climatiseur^M
Klimaanlage^F
aire^M acondicionado

luggage rack
porte-bagages^M
Gepäckträger^M
portaequipajes^M

ladder
échelle^F
Leiter^F
escalerilla^F

CAMPER
AUTO-CARAVANE^F
WOHNMOBIL^N
CASA^F **RODANTE**

449

ROAD SYSTEM
SYSTÈME^M ROUTIER
STRASSENBAU^M
SISTEMA^M DE CARRETERAS^F

CROSS SECTION OF A ROAD
COUPE^F D'UNE ROUTE^F
QUERSCHNITT^M EINER STRASSE^F
VISTA^F TRANSVERSAL DE UNA CARRETERA^F

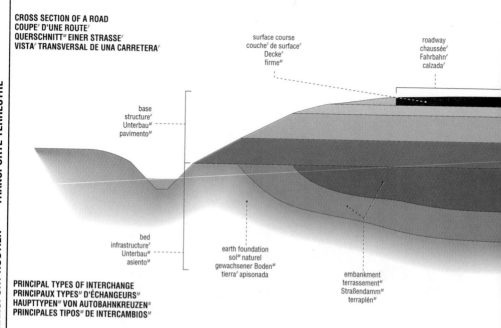

surface course
couche^F de surface^F
Decke^F
firme^M

roadway
chaussée^F
Fahrbahn^F
calzada^F

base
structure^F
Unterbau^M
pavimento^M

bed
infrastructure^F
Unterbau^M
asiento^M

earth foundation
sol^M naturel
gewachsener Boden^M
tierra^F apisonada

embankment
terrassement^M
Straßendamm^M
terraplén^M

PRINCIPAL TYPES OF INTERCHANGE
PRINCIPAUX TYPES^M D'ÉCHANGEURS^M
HAUPTTYPEN^M VON AUTOBAHNKREUZEN^N
PRINCIPALES TIPOS^M DE INTERCAMBIOS^M

cloverleaf
échangeur^M en trèfle^M
Kleeblatt^N
trébol^M

gyratory system
carrefour^M giratoire
Verteiler^M
glorieta^F

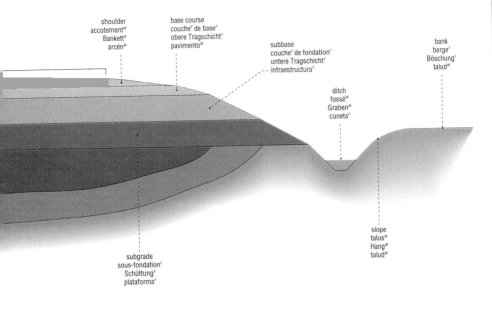

shoulder
accotement^M
Bankett^N
arcén^M

base course
couche^F de base^F
obere Tragschicht^F
pavimento^M

subbase
couche^F de fondation^F
untere Tragschicht^F
infraestructura^F

bank
berge^F
Böschung^F
talud^M

ditch
fossé^M
Graben^M
cuneta^F

slope
talus^M
Hang^M
talud^M

subgrade
sous-fondation^F
Schüttung^F
plataforma^F

diamond interchange
échangeur^M en losange^M
Raute^F
diamante^M

trumpet interchange
échangeur^M en trompette^F
Trompete^F
trompeta^F

ROAD SYSTEM
SYSTÈME^M ROUTIER
AUTOBAHNKREUZ^N
SISTEMA^M DE CARRETERAS^F

CLOVERLEAF
ÉCHANGEUR^M EN TRÈFLE^M
KLEEBLATT^N
TRÉBOL^M

acceleration lane
voie^F d'accélération^F
Beschleunigungsspur^F
línea^F de acceleración^F

deceleration lane
voie^F de décélération^F
Ausfahrtspur^F
carril^M de desaceleración^F

feeder lane
entrée^F
Einfahrt^F
entrada^F

exit
sortie^F
Ausfahrt^F
salida^F

access road
bretelle^F de raccordement^M
Auffahrt^F
rampa^F de transferencia^F

white line
bande^F
Fahrbahnmarkierung^F
línea^F pintada

island
îlot^M
Insel^F
isla^F

central reservation
terre-plein^M central
Mittelstreifen^M
separador^M

side lane
voie^F latérale
Seitenspur^F
línea^F lateral

loop
boucle^F
Schlaufe^F
curva^F

main road
route^F
Schnellstraße^F
carretera^F

flyover
passage^M supérieur
Überführung^F
puente^M

sliproad
bretelle^F
Rampe^F
rampa^F

motorway
autoroute^F
Autobahn^F
autopista^F

slow lane
voie^F pour véhicules^M lents
rechte Spur^F
tránsito^M lento

traffic lanes
voies^F principales
Hauptspuren^F
líneas^F principales

centre lane
voie^F de circulation^F
Mittelspur^F
carril^M de tránsito^M

overtaking lane
voie^F de dépassement^M
Überholspur^F
carril^M de adelantamiento^M

PETROL PUMP
DISTRIBUTEUR*M* D'ESSENCE*F*
ZAPFSÄULE*F*
SURTIDOR*M* DE GASOLINA*F*

cash readout
afficheur*M* totaliseur
Geldbetrag*M*
indicador*M* del importe*M* total*M*

volume readout
afficheur*M* volume*M*
Füllmenge*F*
cuentalitros*M*

price per gallon/litre
afficheur*M* prix*M*
Preis*M* pro Liter*M*/Gallone*F*
indicador*M* del precio*M* por litro*M*/galón*M*

pump nozzle
pistolet*M* de distribution*F*
Zapfhahn*M*
pistola*F* del surtidor*M*

lever
détente*F*
Hebel*M*
palanca*F*

pedestal
socle*M*
Sockel*M*
base*F*

body
châssis*M*
Kopf*M*
caja*F*

type of fuel
type*M* de carburant*M*
Treibstoffart*F*
tipo*M* de combustible*M*

Super   Diesel

1   2

petrol pump hose
flexible*M* de distribution*F*
Zapfschlauch*M*
manguera*F* de servicio*M*

SERVICE STATION
STATION*F*-SERVICE*M*
TANKSTELLE*F*
ESTACIÓN*F* DE SERVICIO*M*

repair shop
atelier*M* de mécanique*F*
Reparaturwerkstatt*F*
taller*M* de mecánica*F*

tyre inflator
borne*F* de gonflage*M*
Druckluft*F*
toma*F* de aire*M*

ice dispenser
distributeur*M* de glaçons*M*
Eisautomat*M*
nevera*F*

soft-drink dispenser
distributeur*M* de boissons*F*
Getränkeautomat*M*
máquina*F* expendedora de bebidas*F*

kiosk
kiosque*M*
Kiosk*M*
kiosco*M*

petrol pump
distributeur*M* d'essence*F*
Zapfsäule*F*
surtidor*M* de gasolina*F*

car wash
lave-auto*M*
Autowaschanlage*F*
lavado*M* de automóviles*M*

service bay
service*M* d'entretien*M*
Service-Bereich*M*
mantenimiento*M*

office
bureau*M*
Kasse*F*
oficina*F*

forecourt
aire*F* de ravitaillement*M*
Vorhof*M*
puesto*M* de bombeo*M*

453

BEAM BRIDGE
PONT^M À POUTRE^F
BALKENBRÜCKE^F
PUENTE^M DE VIGA^F

flyover
passage^M supérieur
Überführung^F
paso^M elevado

continuous beam
poutre^F continue
Durchlaufträger^M
viga^F continua

parapet
garde-corps^M
Geländer^N
parapeto^M

abutment
culée^F
Widerlager^N
contrafuerte^M

deck
tablier^M
Fahrbahn^F
tablero^M

underpass
passage^M inférieur
Unterführung^F
paso^M inferior

pier
pile^F
Pfeiler^M
pilar^M

TYPES OF BEAM BRIDGE
TYPES^M DE PONTS^M À POUTRE^F
BALKENBRÜCKEN^F
TIPOS^M DE PUENTES^M DE VIGA^F

single-span beam bridge
pont^M à poutre^F simple
Einfeldbrücke^F
puente^M de viga^F de un tramo^M

multiple-span beam bridge
pont^M à poutres^F indépendantes
Mehrfeldbrücke^F
puente^M de viga^F de varios tramos^M

suspended span
poutre^F suspendue
Einhängefeld^N
tramo^M suspendido

cantilever span
poutre^F cantilever
Kragträger^M
cantilever^M

cantilever bridge
pont^M cantilever
Auslegerbrücke^F
puente^M voladizo

viaduct
viaduc^M
Viadukt^M
viaducto^M

ARCH BRIDGE
PONT **EN ARC**
BOGENBRÜCKE
PUENTE **DE ARCO**

portal frame
portique
Portalrahmen
portal

upper chord
membrure supérieure
Obergurt
cuerda superior

arch
arche
Bogen
arco

trussed arch
arc métallique à treillis
Fachwerkbogen
arco de entramado

lower chord
membrure inférieure
Untergurt
cuerda inferior

abutment
culée
Widerlager
contrafuerte

column
poteau
Säule
columna

thrust
butée
Schub
empuje

deck
tablier
Fahrbahn
tablero

pier
pile
Pfeiler
pilar

TYPES OF ARCH BRIDGE
TYPES DE PONTS EN ARC
BOGENBRÜCKEN
TIPOS DE PUENTES DE ARCO

deck arch bridge
pont à tablier supérieur
Deckbrücke
puente de tablero superior

through arch bridge
pont à tablier inférieur
Stabbogenbrücke
puente de tablero inferior

portal bridge
pont à béquilles
Portalbrücke
puente de portal

half-through arch bridge
pont à tablier intermédiaire
Hängesprengwerkbrücke
puente de tablero intermedio

TYPES OF ARCH
TYPES D'ARCS
BOGENARTEN
VARIEDADES DE ARCOS

fixed arch
arc encastré
gelenkloser Bogen
arco fijo

two-hinged arch
arc à deux articulations
zweiteiliger Bogen
arco de dos articulaciones

three-hinged arch
arc à trois articulations
dreiteiliger Bogen
arco de tres articulaciones

455

SUSPENSION BRIDGE
PONT^M **SUSPENDU À CÂBLE**^M **PORTEUR**
HÄNGEBRÜCKE^F
PUENTE^M **COLGANTE**

suspension cable
câble^M porteur
Tragkabel^N
cable^M portador

suspender
suspente^F
Hänger^M
tirante^M

approach ramp
rampe^F d'accès^M
Auffahrt^F
rampa^F de acceso^M

anchorage block
massif^M d'ancrage^M des câbles^M
Verankerung^F
anclaje^M

deck
tablier^M
Fahrbahn^F
tablero^M

tower
pylône^M
Pylon^M
pilón^M

abutment
culée^F
Widerlager^N
contrafuerte^M

foundation of tower
fondation^F de pylône^M
Pfeilerfundament^N
cimiento^M del pilón

centre span
travée^F centrale
mittleres Feld^N
tramo^M central

side span
travée^F latérale
Seitenöffnung^F
tramo^M lateral

CABLE-STAYED BRIDGES
PONTS^M **SUSPENDUS À HAUBANS**^M
SCHRÄGSEILBRÜCKE^F
PUENTES^M **DE TIRANTES**^M

fan cable stays
haubans^M **en éventail**^M
Fächerschrägseile^N
tirantes^M **en abanico**^M

cable stay anchorage
ancrage^M des haubans^M
Schrägseilverankerung^F
pilón^M de los tirantes^M

stays
haubans^M
Seile^N
tirantes^M

harp cable stays
haubans^M **en harpe**^F
parallele Schrägseile^N
tirantes^M **en forma**^F **de arpa**^F

MOVABLE BRIDGES
PONTS^M MOBILES
BEWEGLICHE BRÜCKEN^F
PUENTES^M MOVIBLES

turntable
plaque^F tournante
Drehkranz^M
tramo^M giratorio

SWING BRIDGE
PONT^M TOURNANT
DREHBRÜCKE^F
PUENTE^M GIRATORIO

counterweight
contrepoids^M
Gegengewicht^N
contrapeso^M

FLOATING BRIDGE
PONT^M FLOTTANT
PONTONBRÜCKE^F
PUENTE^M DE PONTONES^M

SINGLE-LEAF BASCULE BRIDGE
PONT^M BASCULANT À SIMPLE VOLÉE^F
KLAPPBRÜCKE^F
PUENTE^M LEVADIZO SENCILLO

manrope
garde-corps^M
Seil^N
barandilla^F

pontoon
ponton^M
Ponton^M
pontón^M

LIFT BRIDGE
PONT^M LEVANT
HUBBRÜCKE^F
PUENTE^M ELEVADOR

guiding tower
tour^F de guidage^M
Führungsturm^M
pilón^M guía^M

Bailey bridge
pont^M Bailey
Bailey-Brücke^F
puente^M desmontable tipo^M Bailey

lift span
travée^F levante
Überbau^M
tramo^M de elevación^F

double-leaf bascule bridge
pont^M basculant à double volée^F
Doppelklappbrücke^F
puente^M levadizo doble

TRANSPORTER BRIDGE
PONT^M TRANSBORDEUR
SCHWEBEFÄHRE^F
PUENTE^M TRANSPORTADOR

trolley
chariot^M transbordeur
Laufkatze^F
trole^M

platform
nacelle^F
Fähre^F
plataforma^F

HIGH-SPEED TRAIN
TRAIN*ᴹ* À GRANDE VITESSE*ᶠ* (T.G.V.)
HOCHGESCHWINDIGKEITSZUG*ᴹ*
TREN*ᴹ* DE ALTA VELOCIDAD*ᶠ*

pantograph
pantographe*ᴹ*
Scherenstromabnehmer*ᴹ*
pantógrafo*ᴹ*

passenger car
compartiment*ᴹ* voyageurs*ᴹ*
Mittelwagen*ᴹ*
vagón*ᴹ* de pasajeros*ᴹ*

luggage compartment
compartiment*ᴹ* bagages*ᴹ*
Gepäckraum*ᴹ*
compartimento*ᴹ* para equipaje*ᴹ*

suspension bogie
bogie*ᴹ* porteur
Drehgestell*ᴺ*
suspensión*ᶠ*

air compression unit
bloc*ᴹ* pneumatique
Luftpresser*ᴹ*
unidad*ᶠ* de compresión*ᶠ* de aire*ᴹ*

equipment compartment
coffre*ᴹ* d'appareillage*ᴹ*
Gerätefach*ᴺ*
compartimento*ᴹ* para el equipo*ᴹ*

main transformer
transformateur*ᴹ* principal
Haupttransformator*ᴹ*
transformador*ᴹ* principal

motor unit
bloc*ᴹ*-moteur*ᴹ*
Fahrmotor*ᴹ*
grupo*ᴹ* motor*ᴹ*

overhead wires
caténaire[F]
Oberleitung[F]
moderador[M]

headlight
phare[M] central
Scheinwerfer[M]
faro[M] delantero

driver's cab
cabine[F] de conduite[F]
Führerstand[M]
cabina[F] del maquinista[M]

locomotive
motrice[F]
Lokomotive[F]
locomotora[F]

headlight
projecteur[M]
Scheinwerfer[M]
faro[M] delantero

position light
feu[M] de position[F]
Positionsleuchte[F]
luz[F] de posición[F]

motor bogie
bogie[M] moteur
Triebdrehgestell[N]
carretilla[F] del motor[M]

stone deflector
chasse-pierres[M]
Schienenräumer[M]
quitapiedras[M]

coupling guide device
corne[F] de guidage[M] de l'attelage[M]
Antenne[F] für die Linienzugbeeinflussung[F]
guía[F] de enganche[M]

TYPES OF PASSENGER COACH
TYPES^M DE VOITURES^F
PERSONENZÜGE^M: WAGENTYPEN^M
VAGONES^M DE PASAJEROS^M

OPEN-PLAN COACH
VOITURE^F-COACH^M
GROSSRAUMWAGEN^M
VAGÓN^M DE PASAJEROS^M

centre-aisle
couloir^M central
Mittelgang^M
pasillo^M central

adjustable seat
siège^M réglable
verstellbarer Sitz^M
asiento^M ajustable

SLEEPING CAR
VOITURE^F-LIT^M
SCHLAFWAGEN^M
COCHE^M CAMA^F

berth
couchette^F
Schlafplatz^M
litera^F

linen
lingerie^F
Bettwäsche^F
lencería^F

sleeping compartment
chambre^F
Schlafwagenabteil^N
dormitorio^M

RESTAURANT CAR
VOITURE^F-RESTAURANT^M
SPEISEWAGEN^M
VAGÓN^M COMEDOR^M

dining section
salle^F à manger
Speiseraum^M
comedor^M

kitchen
cuisine^F
Zugküche^F
cocina^F

panoramic window
fenêtre^F panoramique
Panoramafenster^N
ventanilla^F panorámica

luggage compartment
case^F à bagages^M
Gepäckablage^F
red^F para el equipaje^M

vestibule
plate-forme^F
Vorraum^M
vestíbulo^M

entrance door
porte^F d'accès^M de plate-forme^F
Einstiegstür^F
puerta^F del vestíbulo^M

toilet
toilettes^F
Toilette^F
servicios^M sanitarios

wheelchair
fauteuil^M roulant
Rollstuhl^M
silla^F de ruedas^F

coach connection
couloir^M d'intercommunication^F
Wagenübergang^M
corredor^M de enlace^M

steward's desk
desserte^F
Schaffnertisch^M
despacho^M de camareros^M

storage space
rangement^M
Gepäckraum^M
espacio^M de almacenamiento^M

crew's room
vestiaire^M du personnel^M
Personalschließfach^N
armario^M para el personal^M

grab handle
poignée^F montoir^M
Griff^M
asidero^M

PASSENGER STATION
GARE^F DE VOYAGEURS^M
BAHNHOF^M
ESTACIÓN^F DE FERROCARRIL^M

office
locaux^M administratifs
Büro^v
oficina^F

glass roof
verrière^F
Glasüberdachung^F
techo^M de vidiro^M

timetable
panneau^M indicateur
Fahrplan^M
tablero^M de información^F

parcels office
service^M de colis^M
Paketannahme^F
consigna^F

left-luggage office
enregistrement^M des bagages^M
Gepäckaufbewahrung^F
sala^F de equipajes^M

passenger train
train^M
Reisezug^M
tren^M de pasajeros^M

platform edge
bordure^F de quai^M
Bahnsteigkante^F
borde^M del andén^M

passenger platform
quai^M de gare^F
Bahnsteig^M
andén^M de pasajeros^M

gate
barrière^F
Sperre^F
barrera^F

station concourse
salle^F des pas^M perdus
Bahnhofshalle^F
vestíbulo^M

platform number
numéro^M de quai^M
Gleisnummer^F
indicador^M de número^M de andén^M

metal structure
structure^M métallique
Eisenträger^M
estrucutra^F de metal^M

luggage trolley
chariot^M à bagages^M
Förderwagen^M
carro^M portaequipaje

departure time indicator
affichage^M de l'heure^F de départ^M
Abfahrtzeiten^F
indicador^M de hora^F de salida^F

ticket collector
contrôleur^M
Fahrkartenkontrolleur^M
revisor^M de billetes^M

luggage lockers
consigne^F automatique
Gepäckschließfächer^N
casillas^F de consigna^F automática

destination
destination^F
Zielbahnhof^M
destinos^M

platform entrance
accès^M aux quais^M
Zugang^M zum Gleis^N
acceso^M a los andenes^M

track
voie^F ferrée
Gleis^N
vía^F

train indicator
tableau^M horaire
Kursbuchtafeln^F
horarios^M

ticket control
contrôle^M des billets^M
Fahrkartenkontrolle^F
control^M de billetes^M

RAILWAY STATION
GARE^F
BAHNHOF^M
ESTACIÓN^F DE FERROCARRIL^M

station platform
quai^M
Bahnsteig^M
andén^M

footbridge
passerelle^F
Fußgängerbrücke^F
puente^M peatonal

main line
grandes lignes^F
Hauptgleis^N
vía^F principal

passenger station
gare^F de voyageurs^M
Personenbahnhof^M
estación^F de ferrocarril^M

commuter train
train^M de banlieue^F
Pendlerzug^M
tren^M suburbano

level crossing
passage^M à niveau^M
Bahnübergang^M
paso^M a nivel^M

suburban commuter railway
voie^F de banlieue^F
S-Bahn^F
vía^F de tren^M suburbano

siding
voie^F de service^M
Nebengleis^N
vía^F subsidiaria

semaphore signal
sémaphore^M
Formsignal^N
semáforo^M

car park
parking^M
Parkplatz^M
estacionamiento^M

platform shelter
abri^M
Bahnsteigüberdachung^F
cobertizo^M del andén^M

buffers
butoir^M
Prellbock^M
tope^M

signal box
poste^M d'aiguillage^M
Stellwerk^N
torre^F de señales^F

subway
passage^M souterrain
Unterführung^F
pasaje^M subterráneo

crossover
bretelle^F
Gleiskreuzung^F
vía^F de unión^F

signal gantry
portique^M de signalisation^F
Signalbrücke^F
puente^M de señales^F

freight car
wagon^M
Güterwagen^M
vagón^M de carga^F

points
aiguillage^M
Weiche^F
aguja^F de cambio^M

support
pylône^M
Pfeiler^M
poste^M

goods station
gare^F de marchandises^F
Güterbahnhof^M
estación^F de carga^F

diesel engine shed
atelier^M diesel
Lokschuppen^M
taller^M de máquinas^F diésel

MARSHALLING YARD
GARE^F DE TRIAGE^M
RANGIERBAHNHOF^M
TALLERES^M DE FERROCARRIL^M

marshalling yard
zone^F de triage^M
Ordnungsgleise^N
patio^M de clasificación^F

exit track
voie^F de sortie^F
Ausfahrgleis^N
vía^F de salida^F

rolling stock repair shop
atelier^M de réparation^F des wagons^M
Wagenausbesserungshalle^F
taller^M de reparación^F de vagones^M

receiving yard
zone^F de réception^F
Empfangsgleise^N
patio^M de recepción^F

secondary marshalling track
voie^F de tri^M secondaire
Richtungsgleis^N
segunda vía^F de clasificación^F

rolling stock cleaning yard
zone^F de lavage^M des wagons^M
Waschplatte^F
patio^M de lavado^M de vagones^M

water tower
château^M d'eau^F
Wasserturm^M
tanque^M de agua^F

locomotive track
voie^F de circulation^F des locomotives^F
Lokverkehrsgleis^N
vía^F locomotriz

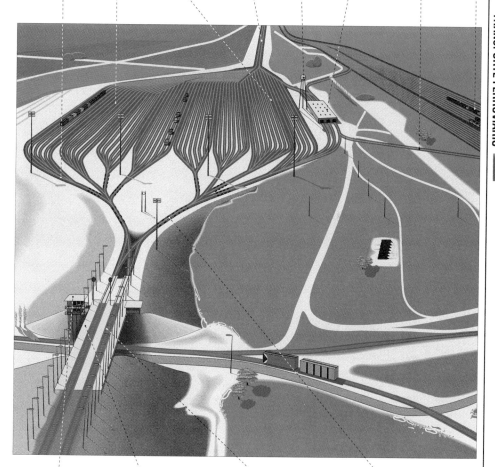

hump control
poste^M de débranchement^M
Ablaufstellwerk^N
oficina^F

hump
butte^F de débranchement^M
Ablaufberg^M
lomo^M de maniobra^F

hump approach
voie^F de butte^F
Auffahrgleis^N
dirección^F

primary marshalling track
voie^F de tri^M primaire
Einfahrgleis^N
primera vía^F de clasificación^F

RAILWAY TRACK
VOIE^F FERRÉE
EISENBAHN-OBERBAU^M
VÍA^F FÉRREA

RAIL JOINT
JOINT^M DE RAIL^M
SCHIENENSTOSS^M
EMPALME^M DE RIELES^M

expansion space
jeu^M de dilatation^F
Dehnungsfuge^F
espacio^M de expansión^F

spike
crampon^M
Schwellenschraube^F
escarpia^F

running surface
table^F de roulement^M
Lauffläche^F
superficie^F de rodamiento^M

soleplate
selle^F de rail^M
Unterlagsplatte^F
placa^F de asiento^M

dating nail
clou^M millésimé
Datierungsnagel^F
clavo^M fechador

fishplate
éclisse^F
Schienenlasche^F
eclisa^F

fishplate bolt
boulon^M d'éclisse^F
Laschenbolzen^M
perno^M de la eclisa^F

nut
écrou^M
Bolzenmutter^F
tuerca^F

RAIL SECTION
PROFIL^M DE RAIL^M
QUERSCHNITT^M EINER SCHIENE^F
CORTE^M DE UN RIEL^M

head
champignon^M
Schienenkopf^M
cabeza^F

web
âme^F
Schienensteg^M
alma^F

base
patin^M
Schienenfuß^M
base^F

RAILWAY TRACK
VOIE^F FERRÉE
OBERBAU^M
VÍA^F FÉRREA

sleeper
traverse^F
Schwelle^F
traviesa^F

rail
rail^M
Schiene^F
riel^M

ballast
ballast^M
Schotter^M
balasto^M

REMOTE-CONTROLLED POINTS
AIGUILLAGE^M **MANŒUVRÉ À DISTANCE**^F
FERNBEDIENTE WEICHE^F
AGUJA^F **DE CONTROL**^M **A LARGA DISTANCIA**^F

switch blade
aiguille^F
Weichenzunge^F
punto^M de cambio^M

pull rod
tringle^F de commande^F
Stellstange^F
varilla^F de empuje^M

gauge rod
tringle^F d'écartement^M
Spurstange^F
varilla^F de cambio^M

closure rail
rail^M de raccord^M
Zwischenschiene^F
riel^M de cierre^M

point wire
transmission^F funiculaire
Drahtzug^M
cable^M de corriente^F de la aguja^F

points motor
moteur^M d'aiguillage^M
Weichenantrieb^M
control^M mecánico de agujas^F

MANUALLY-OPERATED POINTS
AIGUILLAGE^M **MANŒUVRÉ À PIED**^M **D'ŒUVRE**^F
HANDBEDIENTE WEICHE^F
CAMBIADOR^M **MANUAL DE VÍA**^F

frog
cœur^M de croisement^M
Herzstück^N
cruce^M

points signal
signal^M de position^F d'aiguille^F
Weichensignal^N
señal^F de posición^F de la aguja^F

closure rail
rail^M de raccord^M
Zwischenschiene^F
riel^M de cierre^M

check-rail
contre-rail^M
Radlenker^M
riel^M de retención^F

slide chair
coussinet^M de glissement^M
Gleitstuhl^M
patín^M de deslizamiento^M

points lever
levier^M de commande^F manuelle
Stellhebel^M
palanca^F de maniobra^F de la aguja^F

switch blade
aiguille^F
Spurstange^F
aguja^F

pull rod
tringle^F de commande^F
Stellstange^F
varilla^F de empuje^M

467

DIESEL-ELECTRIC LOCOMOTIVE
LOCOMOTIVE^F DIESEL-ÉLECTRIQUE
DIESELELEKTRISCHE LOKOMOTIVE^F
LOCOMOTORA^F DIÉSEL ELÉCTRICA

control stand
pupitre^M de conduite^F
Führerpult^N
tablero^M de mandos^M

driver's cab
cabine^F de conduite^F
Führerstand^M
cabina^F del maquinista^M

horn
avertisseur^M
Signalhorn^N
silbato^M

safety rail
garde-corps^M
Schutzgeländer^N
asidero^M

diesel engine ventilator
ventilateur^M de moteur^M diesel
Dieselmotorlüfter^M
ventilador^M del motor^M diésel

battery
batterie^F
Anlaßbatterie^F
batería^F

dynamic brake
frein^M direct
Betriebsbremse^F
freno^M dinámico

4103

axle
essieu^M
Achsgetriebe^N
eje^M

journal box
boîte^F d'essieu^M
Radsatzgetriebe^N
cojinete^M

bogie
bogie^M
Drehgestell^N
carretilla^F

bogie frame
châssis^M de bogie^M
Drehgestell-Rahmen^M
chasis^M de la carretilla^F

alternator
alternateur^M
Generator^M
alternador^M

fuel tank
réservoir^M à carburant^M
Kraftstoffbehälter^M
depósito^M de combustible^M

468

air compressor
compresseur^m d'air^m
Luftpresser^m
compresor^m de aire^m

ventilating fan
ventilateur^m des radiateurs^m
Kühlwasserventilator^m
ventilador^m

air filter
filtre^m à air^m
Luftfilter^m
filtro^m de aire^m

radiator
radiateur^m
Kühlergruppe^f
radiador^m

diesel engine
moteur^m diesel
Dieselmotor^m
motor^m diésel

water tank
soute^f à eau^f
Speisewasserbehälter^m
depósito^m de agua^f

headlight
phare^m
Scheinwerfer^m
faro^m delantero

sandbox
sablière^f
Sandkasten^m
arenera^f

lubricating system
système^m de lubrification^f
Schmiersystem^x
sistema^m de lubricación^f

compressed air reservoir
réservoir^m d'air^m comprimé
Hauptluftbehälter^m
depósito^m de aire^m comprimido

side footboard
marchepied^m latéral
Laufbrett^N
escalerilla^f lateral

spring
ressort^m de suspension^f
Schraubenfeder^f
resorte^m

stone deflector
chasse-pierres^m
Schienenräumer^m
quitapiedras^m

coupling
tête^f d'attelage^m
Kupplungsbügel^m
cabeza^f de empalme^m

GOODS VAN
WAGON^M
WAGEN^M
VAGÓN^M

BOGIE VAN
WAGON^M **COUVERT**
DREHGESTELLKASTENWAGEN^M
FURGÓN^M

corner cap
chapeau^M d'angle^M
Eckbeschlag^F
esquinera^F

horizontal end handhold
main^F courante
Handstange^F
asidero^M horizontal

hand brake wheel
volant^M de frein^M à main^F
Handbremsrad^N
volante^M del freno^M manual

end ladder
échelle^F de bout^M
Stirnwandleiter^F
escalerilla^F de estribo^M

hand brake gear housing
carter^M d'engrenage^M de frein^M à main^F
Schutzkasten^M für Kegelräder^N
cubierta^F del mecanismo^M del freno^M

hand brake winding lever
levier^M de frein^M à main^F
Handbremsehebel^M
palanca^F de enrrollado^M del freno^M de
mano^F

telescoping uncoupling rod
levier^M télescopique de dételage^M
Abkoppelvorrichtung^F
varilla^F telescópica de desenganche^M

sill step
marchepied^M en étrier^M
Bügeltritt^M
peldaño^M inferior

side ladder
échelle^F latérale
Seitensprossen^F
escalerilla^F lateral

sliding channel
glissière^F
Türführungsschiene^F
guía^F corrediza

CONTAINER
CONTENEUR^M
CONTAINER^M
CONTENEDOR^M

roof
toit^M
Dach^N
techo^M

corner fitting
pièce^F de coin^M
Eckbeschlag^M
herraje^M de la esquina^F

top cross-member
traverse^F d'extrémité^F supérieure
oberer Querträger^M
travesaño^F superior

side wall
paroi^F latérale
Seitenwand^F
panel^M lateral

end door
porte^F d'extrémité^F
Stirntür^F
puerta^F trasera

bottom cross-member
traverse^F d'extrémité^F inférieure
unterer Querträger^M
travesaño^M inferior

corner upright
montant^M d'angle^M
Ecksäule^F
esquina^F

fork pocket
passage^M de fourche^F
Gabelstaplertasche^F
abertura^F para horquilla^F de montacargas^M

bottom side rail
longeron^M latéral inférieur
unterer Längsträger^M
larguero^M inferior

COUPLING
TÊTE'' D'ATTELAGE''
KUPPLUNGSKOPF''
CABEZA'' DE ENGANCHE''

coupling knuckle pin
axe'' d'attelage''
Hauptbolzen''
pivote'' de la rótula'

coupling knuckle
mâchoire' d'attelage''
Herzstück''
rótula' de enganche''

LEVEL CROSSING
PASSAGE'' À NIVEAU''
SCHIENENGLEICHER BAHNÜBERGANG''
PASO'' A NIVEL''

level crossing bell
sonnerie' de passage'' à niveau''
Vorläutewerk''
campana' de aviso'' de cruce''

level crossing sign
croix' de Saint-André
Warnkreuz''
señal' de cruce''

door stop
butée' de porte'
Türsäule'
tope'' de la puerta'

locking lever
levier'' de verrouillage''
Verschlußhebel''
palanca' de cierre''

placard board
porte-étiquette''
Anschriftentafel'
tablero'' de rótulo''

mast
mât''
Mast''
poste''

visor
visière'
Schirm''
visera'

peep hole
œil'' témoin''
Guckloch''
mirilla'

route board
porte-étiquette'' d'acheminement''
Wagenlaufschild''
tarjeta' de ruta'

flashing light
feu'' clignotant
Blinklicht''
luz' intermitente

signal background plate
écran'' de visibilité'
Signalschirm''
fondo'' de la señal'

junction box
boîte' de jonction'
Verteilerdose'
caja' de empalmes''

number of tracks sign
panneau'' nombre'' de voies'
Anzahl' der Gleise''
letrero'' de número'' de vías'

barrier lamp
feu'' de lisse'
Lampe'
luz' de la barrera'

barrier
lisse'
Schranke'
barrera' del paso'' a nivel''

barrier support
support'' de lisse'
Stütze'
soporte'' de la barrera'

counterweight
contrepoids''
Gegengewicht''
contrapeso''

base
base'
Sockel''
base'

crossing barrier mechanism
commande' de barrières'
Antrieb''
mecanismo'' de la barrera'

471

TYPES OF GOODS TRUCK
TYPES^M DE WAGONS^M
GÜTERWAGEN^M
TIPOS^M DE VAGONES^M DE CARGA^F

bogie goods van
wagon^M couvert
Drehgestellkastenwagen^M
vagón^M cerrado

bogie tank wagon
wagon^M-citerne^F
Kesselwagen^M
vagón^M cisterna^F

wood chip wagon
wagon^M à copeaux^M
langer Kastenwagen^M
vagón^M para madera^F

livestock van
wagon^M à bestiaux^M
Verschlagwagen^M
vagón^M para ganado^M

hopper tank wagon
wagon^M-trémie^F
Selbstentladetankwagen^M
vagón^M tolva^F

covered bogie truck
wagon^M-tombereau^M couvert
Planenwagen^M
vagón^M con cubierta^F alquitranada

hopper ore wagon
wagon^M-trémie^F à minerai^M
Schüttgutwagen^M
vagón^M tolva^F para minerales^M

refrigerator van
wagon^M réfrigérant
Kühlwagen^M
vagón^M frigorífico

three-tier car carrier
wagon^M porte-automobiles^M
Autotransportwagen^M
vagón^M para automóviles^M

container truck
wagon^M porte-conteneurs^M
Containerflachwagen^M
vagón^M para contenedores^M

piggyback flat truck
wagon^M rail^M-route^F
Spezialflachwagen^M für den Transport^M von Schwerfahrzeugen^N
plataforma^F para transportar vagones^M

flat truck
wagon^M plat
Drehgestellflachwagen^M
plataforma^F

bulkhead flat truck
wagon^M plat à parois^F de bout^M
Stirnwandflachwagen^M
vagón^M plano con retenedores^M

bogie goods truck
wagon^M-tombereau^M
offener Güterwagen^M
vagón^M de mercancías^F

well wagon
wagon^M plat surbaissé
Tiefladewagen^M
plataforma^F de piso^M bajo

brake van
wagon^M de queue^F
Bremswagen^M
furgón^M de cola^F

473

UNDERGROUND RAILWAY
CHEMIN^M DE FER^M MÉTROPOLITAIN
U-BAHN^F
METRO^M

UNDERGROUND STATION
STATION^F DE MÉTRO^M
U-BAHN-STATION^F
ESTACIÓN^F DE METRO^M

escalator
escalier^M mécanique
Rolltreppe^F
escalera^F mecánica

station entrance
édicule^M
Eingang^M
entrada^F de la estación^F

ticket collector's booth
bureau^M du changeur^M
Fahrkartenkontrolle^F
cabina^F del revisor^M de billetes^M

exterior sign
enseigne^F extérieure
U-Bahn-Schild^N
señal^F exterior

entrance turnstile
tourniquet^M d'accès^M
Eingangssperre^F
torniquete^M de entrada^F

stairs
escalier^M
Treppe^F
escaleras^F

mezzanine
mezzanine^F
Sperrengeschoß^N
entrepiso^M

exit turnstile
tourniquet^M de sortie^F
Ausgangssperre^F
torniquete^M de salida^F

line map
carte^F de ligne^F
Netzplan^M
mapa^M de la ruta^F

station name
nom^M de la station^F
Name^M der Station^F
nombre^M de la estación^F

advertising panel
panneau^M publicitaire
Werbetafel^F
panel^M de publicidad^F

tunnel
tunnel^M
Tunnel^M
túnel^M

underground train
rame^F de métro^M
U-Bahn-Zug^M
tren^M subterráneo

track
voie^F
Gleis^N
vía^F

kiosk
kiosque^M
Verkaufsstand^M
kiosco^M

transfer ticket dispensing machine
distributeur^M de correspondances^F
Automat^M für Umsteigekarten^F
distribuidora^F de billetes^M de transferencia^F

footbridge
passerelle^F
Fußgängerbrücke^F
pasarela^F superior

train direction sign
enseigne^F directionnelle
Fahrtrichtungsanzeige^F
señal^F de dirección^F

bench
banc^M
Sitzbank^F
banco^M

underground map
carte^F de réseau^M
U-Bahn-Netzplan^M
mapa^M de rutas^F

platform
quai^M
Bahnsteig^M
andén^M

platform edge
bordure^F de quai^M
Bahnsteigkante^F
borde^M del andén^M

safety line
ligne^F de sécurité^F
Sicherheitsstreifen^M
línea^F de seguridad^F

475

UNDERGROUND RAILWAY
CHEMIN^M DE FER^M MÉTROPOLITAIN
U-BAHN^F
METRO^M

BOGIE AND TRACK
BOGIE^M ET VOIE^F
DREHGESTELL^N UND GLEIS^N
CARRETILLA^F Y VÍA^F

current-collecting shoe
frotteur^M
Stromabnehmer^M
bloque^M corredizo

pneumatic-tyred running wheel
pneumatique^M porteur
pneubereiftes Laufrad^N
llanta^F neumática de tracción^F

steel safety wheel
roue^F de sécurité^F
Spurkranzrad^N
rueda^F metálica de seguridad^F

pneumatic-tyred guide wheel
pneumatique^M de guidage^M
pneubereiftes Leitrad^N
llanta^F neumática guía^F

guiding and current bar
barre^F de guidage^M et de prise^F de courant^M
Führungs- und Stromschiene^F
riel^M eléctrico

running rail
rail^M et retour^M de courant^M
Notlaufschiene^F
riel^M

runway
piste^F de roulement^M
Fahrbalken^M
carril^M

invert
radier^M
Tunnelsohle^F
invertido^M

UNDERGROUND TRAIN
RAME^F DE MÉTRO^M
U-BAHN-ZUG^M
TREN^M SUBTERRÁNEO

motor car
motrice^F
Triebwagen^M
vagón^M máquina^F

passenger car
remorque^F
Mittelwagen^M
vagón^M de pasajeros^M

PASSENGER CAR
VOITUREᶠ
MITTELWAGENᴹ
VAGÓNᴹ **DE PASAJEROS**ᴹ

communication set
posteᴹ de communicationᶠ
Gegensprechanlageᶠ
altavozᴹ de comunicaciónᶠ

light
éclairageᴹ
Innenbeleuchtungᶠ
lámparaᶠ

side handrail
poignéeᶠ
Einsteigegriffᴹ
asideroᴹ lateral

double seat
siègeᴹ double
Doppelsitzᴹ
asientoᴹ doble

ventilator
grilleᶠ d'aérationᶠ
Lüftungᶠ
ventiladorᴹ

side door
porteᶠ latérale
Einstiegstürᶠ
puertaᶠ lateral

emergency brake
freinᴹ d'urgenceᶠ
Notbremseᶠ
frenoᴹ de emergenciaᶠ

underground map
carteᶠ de réseauᴹ
U-Bahn-Netzplanᴹ
mapaᴹ de rutaᶠ

inflated guiding tyre
pneumatiqueᴹ de guidageᴹ
pneubereiftes Leitradᴺ
llantaᶠ neumática guíaᶠ

window
fenêtreᶠ
Fensterᴺ
ventanillaᶠ

handrail
colonneᶠ
Handstangeᶠ
asideroᴹ vertical

inflated carrying tyre
pneumatiqueᴹ porteur
pneubereiftes Laufradᴺ
llantaᶠ neumática de tracciónᶠ

advertising poster
afficheᶠ publicitaire
Werbetafelᶠ
cartelᴹ comercial

single seat
siègeᴹ simple
Einzelsitzᴹ
asientoᴹ individual

suspension
suspensionᶠ
Federungᶠ
suspensiónᶠ

heating grille
grilleᶠ de chauffageᴹ
Heizungsgitterᴺ
rejillaᶠ de calefacciónᶠ

motor car
motriceᶠ
Triebwagenᴹ
vagónᴹ máquinaᶠ

477

FOUR-MASTED BARK
QUATRE-MÂTS^M BARQUE^F
VIERMASTBARK^F
BARCO^M DE VELA^F DE CUATRO PALOS^M

MASTS AND RIGGING
MÂTURE^F ET GRÉEMENT^M
TAKELAGE^F
ARBOLADURA^F Y APAREJOS^M

footrope
marchepied^M
Fußpferd^N
marchapié^M

mizzenmast
grand mât^M arrière
Kreuzmast^M
palo^M de mesana^F

yard
vergue^F
Rah^F
verga^F

aftermast
mât^M d'artimon^M
Besanmast^M
palo^M popel^M

topping lift
martinet^M
Hanger^M
amantillo^M de botavara^F

gaff
corne^F
Gaffel^F
botavara^F

lift
balancine^F
Toppnant^F
amantillo^M

gaff sail boom
gui^M
Besanbaum^M
botavara^F de cangreja^F

poop
dunette^F
Poop^F
popa^F

bulwark
pavois^M
Schanzkleid^N
amurada^F

lifeboat
canot^M de sauvetage^M
Rettungsboot^N
bote^M salvavidas

davit
bossoir^M
Davit^M
pescante^M

top
hune^F
Saling^F
tope^M

lower mast
bas-mât^M
Untermast^M
palo^M macho

mainmast
grand mât^M avant
Großmast^M
palo^M mayor

foremast
mât^M de misaine^F
Fockmast^M
palo^M de trinquete^M

fore-royal mast
mât^M de cacatois^M
Royalstenge^F
mastelero^M de sobrejuanete^M

pole
fusée^F
Spitze^F
estaca^F

fore-topgallant mast
mât^M de perroquet^M
Bramstenge^F
mastelero^M de juanete^M

masthead
ton^M de mât^M
Vorbramsaling^F
celcés^M

fore-topmast
mât^M de hune^F
Marsstenge^F
mastelero^M

stay
étai^M
Stag^N
estay^M

staysail-stay
draille^F
Stagsegel-Stag^N
nervio^M de vela^F estay^M

backstay
galhauban^M
Pardune^F
burda^F

side
bord^M
Seite^F
banda^F

bowsprit
mât^M de beaupré^M
Bugspriet^M
bauprés^M

shroud
hauban^M
Want^F
obenque^M

stem
étrave^F
Steven^M
roda^F

bobstay
martingale^F
Stampfstag^N
barbiquejo^M

479

FOUR-MASTED BARK
QUATRE-MÂTS^M BARQUE^F
VIERMASTBARK^F
BARCO^M DE VELA^F DE CUATRO PALOS^M

SAILS
VOILURE^F
SEGEL^N
VELAMEN^M

mizzen royal staysail
voile^F d'étai^M de grand perroquet^M arrière
Kreuz-Royalstagsegel^N
sobrejuanete^F de mesana^F de estay^M

mizzen topgallant staysail
voile^F d'étai^M de hune^F arrière
Kreuz-Bramstagsegel^N
juanete^M de mesana^F de estay^M

mizzen topmast staysail
grand-voile^F d'étai^M arrière
Kreuz-Stengestagsegel^N
mastelero^F de mesana^F de estay^M

mizzen royal brace
bras^M de grand cacatois^M arrière
Kreuz-Royalbrasse^F
brazas^F de sobrejuanete^F de mesana^F

jigger topgallant staysail
voile^F d'étai^M de flèche^F
Besan-Bramstagsegel^N
aparejo^M de juanete^M de estay^M

jigger topmast staysail
marquise^F
Besan-Stengestagsegel^N
aparejo^M de mastelero^M de estay^M

gaff topsail
voile^F de flèche^F
Besantoppsegel^N
escandalosa^F

spanker
brigantine^F
Besan^M
cangreja^F de popa^F

brail
cargue^F
Gaitau^N des Besans^M
candaliza^F

mizzen royal staysail — *(duplicate above)*

sheet
écoute^F
Shot^F
escota^M

mizzen sail
grand-voile^F arrière
Kreuzsegel^N
cangreja^F mayor popel

reef band
bande^F de ris^M
Reffband^N
envergue^M de rizo^M

reef point
garcette^F de ris^M
Reffbänsel^N
tomarrizos^M

halyard
drisse^F
Fall^M
driza^F

main royal sail
grand cacatois^M avant
Groß-Royalsegel^N
sobrejuanete^M mayor

main upper topgallant sail
grand perroquet^M volant avant
Groß-Oberbramsegel^N
juanete^M mayor proel alto

main lower topgallant sail
grand perroquet^M fixe avant
Groß-Unterbramsegel^N
juanete^M mayor bajo

main upper topsail
grand hunier^M volant avant
Groß-Obermarsegel^N
gavia^F mayor alta

fore royal sail
petit cacatois^M
Vor-Royalsegel^N
sobrejuanete^M de proa^F

upper fore topgallant sail
petit perroquet^M volant
Vor-Oberbramsegel^N
juanete^M de proa^F alto

lower fore topgallant sail
petit perroquet^M fixe
Vor-Unterbramsegel^N
juanete^M de proa^F bajo

upper fore topsail
petit hunier^M volant
Vor-Obermarsegel^N
gavia^F proel alta

flying jib
clin foc^M
Flieger^M
petifoque^M

main lower topsail
grand hunier^M fixe avant
Groß-Untermarsegel^N
gavia^F mayor baja

clew line
cargue-point^M
Gaitau^N
chafaldete^M

main sail
grand-voile^F avant
Großsegel^N
vela^F mayor proel

lower fore topsail
petit hunier^M fixe
Vor-Untermarsegel^N
gavia^F inferior proel

foresail
misaine^F
Fock^F
trinquete^M

inner jib
petit foc^M
Vorstenge-Stagsegel^N
contrafoque^M

middle jib
faux foc^M
Binnenklüver^M
fofoque^M

outer jib
grand foc^M
Außenklüver^M
foque^M

TYPES OF SAIL
TYPES^M DE VOILES^F
SEGELTYPEN^M
TIPOS^M DE VELAS^F

square sail
voile^F carrée
Rahsegel^N
vela^F cuadrada

lateen sail
voile^F latine
Lateinersegel^N
vela^F latina

gaff sail
voile^F aurique
Gaffelsegel^N
vela^F cangreja

Bermuda sail
voile^F bermudienne
Spitzsegel^N
vela^F Bermuda

TYPES OF RIG
TYPES^M DE GRÉEMENTS^M
ARTEN^F DER TAKELUNG^F
TIPOS^M DE APAREJOS^M

whale boat
baleinière^F
Walboot^N
ballenera^F

brigantine
brigantin^M
Brigantine^F
bergantín^M goleta^F

ketch
ketch^M
Ketsch^F
queche^M

Marconi cutter
cotre^M Marconi
Marconikutter^M
cúter^M Marconi

brig
brick^M
Brigg^F
bergantín^M

schooner
goélette^F
Schoner^M
goleta^F

ANCHOR
ANCRE^F
ANKER^M
ANCLA^F

SHIP'S ANCHOR
ANCRE^F DE MARINE^F
SCHIFFSANKER^M
ANCLA^F DE BUQUE^M

arm
bras^M
Arm^M
brazo^M

crown
diamant^M
Kreuz^N
cruz^F

throat
collet^M
Hals^M
unión^F de caña^F y brazos^M

gravity band
centre^M de gravité^F
Schäkelband^N
anillo^M de gravedad^F

hoisting ring
organeau^M de hissage^F
Heißring^M
argolla^F de izar

ring
organeau^M
Ring^M
arganeo^M

palm
patte^F
Flunke^F
mapa^F

fluke
oreille^F
Ankerhand^F
uña^F

bill
bec^M
Ankerspitze^F
pico^M de loro^M

shank
verge^F
Schaft^M
caña^F

stock
jas^M
Stock^M
cepo^M

TYPES OF ANCHOR
TYPES^M D'ANCRES^F
ANKERARTEN^F
TIPOS^M DE ANCLAS^F

stocked anchor
ancre^F à jas^M
Stockanker^M
ancla^F de cepo^M

stockless anchor
ancre^F sans jas^M
Patentanker^M
ancla^F sin cepo^M

mushroom anchor
ancre^F à champignon^M
Pilzanker^M
ancla^F de hongo^M

sea anchor
ancre^F flottante
Treibanker^M
ancla^F flotante

plow anchor
ancre^F charrue^F
Pfluganker^M
ancla^F de arado^M

grapnel
grappin^M
Draggen^M
anclote^M

MARITIME TRANSPORT
TRANSPORT MARITIME

SCHIFFFAHRT
TRANSPORTE MARÍTIMO

SEXTANT
SEXTANT^M
SEXTANT^M
SEXTANTE^M

index mirror
grand miroir^M
Indexspiegel^M
espejo^M mayor^M

index shade
filtre^M coloré
Blendgläser^N für den Indexspiegel^M
filtro^M

index arm
alidade^F
Alhidade^F
alidada^F

lens hood
pare-soleil^M
Gegenlichtblende^F
capuchón^M

horizon mirror
petit miroir^M
Horizontspiegel^M
espejo^M menor

telescope
lunette^F prismatique
Fernrohr^N
anteojo^M telescópico

frame
bâti^M
Rahmen^M
bastidor^M

graduated arc
limbe^M
Gradbogen^M
limbo^M

vernier scale
vernier^M
Nonius^M
escala^F de nonio

horizon shade
filtre^M coloré
Blendgläser^N für den Horizontspiegel^M
filtro^M

micrometer screw
vis^F micrométrique
Mikrometerschraube^F
tornillo^M micrométrico

drum
tambour^M
Trommel^F
tambor^M

LIQUID COMPASS
COMPAS^M MAGNÉTIQUE LIQUIDE
FLÜSSIGKEITSKOMPASS^M
BRÚJULA^F LÍQUIDA

glass dome
glace^F
Glashaube^F
domo^M de vidrio^M

sliding cover
couvercle^M coulissant
Schiebedeckel^M
cubierta^F deslizable

compass card
rose^F des vents^M
Kompaßrose^F
rosa^F de los vientos^M

pivot
pivot^M
Pinne^F
pivote^M

bowl
cuvette^F
Kessel^M
mortero^M

ECHO SOUNDER
SONDEUR^M À ÉCLATS^M
ECHOLOT^N
SONAR^M

MARITIME TRANSPORT
TRANSPORT MARITIME

SCHIFFAHRT
TRANSPORTE MARÍTIMO

dial-type display
écran^M
Anzeigeskala^F
indicador^M del cuadrante^M

depth scale in metres
échelle^F de profondeur^F en m
Tiefenskala^F in m
escala^F de profundidad^F

housing
boîtier^M
Gehäuse^N
caja^F

sound alarm
alarme^F sonore
Lautsprecher^M
alarma^F sonora

on-off switch
interrupteur^M
Ein-/Ausschalter^M
interruptor^M

alarm threshold setting
réglage^M du seuil^M d'alarme^F
Alarmschwellenwert-Einstellung^F
control^M del nivel^M de alarma^F

alarm threshold display button
visualisation^F du seuil^M d'alarme^F
Knopf^M für Alarmschwellenwert-Anzeige^F
botón^M de visualización^F del nivel^M de alarma^F

gain control
contrôle^M du gain^M
Verstärkerregler^M
control^M de ganancia^F

ECHO SOUNDER PROBE
SONDE^F
SCHWINGER^M
SONDA^F

transducer
émetteur^M/récepteur^M
Überträger^M
transductor^M

transmission cable
câble^M de transmission^F
Übertragungskabel^N
cable^M de transmisión^F

plug
fiche^F
Stecker^M
enchufe^M

CROSS SECTION OF A LIQUID COMPASS
COUPE^F D'UN COMPAS^M MAGNÉTIQUE LIQUIDE
QUERSCHNITT^M DURCH EINEN FLÜSSIGKEITSKOMPASS^M
CORTE^M TRANSVERSAL DE UNA BRÚJULA^F LÍQUIDA

lubber's line
ligne^F de foi^F
Kursstrich^M
línea^F de fe^F

gimbal ring
suspension^F à la Cardan
Kardanring^M
anillo^M balancín

jewel cap
chape^F
Hütchen^N
cubierta^F

float
flotteur^M
Schwimmer^M
flotador^M

expansion diaphragm
diaphragme^M de dilatation^F
Ausdehnungsmembran^F
diafragma^M de expansión

pivot
pivot^M
Pinne^F
pivote^M

magnet
aimant^M
Magnet^M
imán^M

water/alcohol
eau^F/alcool^M
Wasser^N/Alkohol^M
agua^F/alcohol^M

expansion chamber
chambre^F de dilatation^F
Ausdehnungskammer^F
estabilizador^M

485

MARITIME SIGNALS
SIGNALISATION^F MARITIME
SEEZEICHEN^N
SEÑALES^F MARÍTIMAS

LIGHTHOUSE LANTERN
LANTERNE^F DE PHARE^M
LEUCHTTURMLAMPE^F
LINTERNA^F DEL FARO^M

ventilation hood
capuchon^M de ventilation^F
Lüfterkopf^M
capucha^F de ventilación^F

incandescent lamp
lampe^F à incandescence^F
Glühlampe^F
bombilla^F incandescente

dioptric ring
anneau^M dioptrique
dioptrischer Ring^M
anillo^M dióptrico

lamp base
culot^M
Boden^M
base^F de la bombilla^F

housing
boîtier^M
Gehäuse^N
caja^F

LIGHTHOUSE
PHARE^M
LEUCHTTURM^M
FARO^M MARÍTIMO

cupola
coupole^F
Kuppel^F
cúpula^F

lantern
lanterne^F
Laterne^F
linterna^F

lantern pane
vitrage^M
Fenster^N des Scheinwerferraumes^M
vidriera^F

gallery
balcon^M de veille^F
Galerie^F
balcón^M

tower
tour^F
Turm^M
torre^F

CYLINDRICAL BUOY
BOUÉE^F CYLINDRIQUE
STUMPFTONNE^F
BOYA^F CILÍNDRICA

topmark
voyant^M conique
Toppzeichen^N
marca^F de tope^M

light
feu^M
Laterne^F
luz^F

photovoltaic panel
panneau^M photovoltaïque
Photozellenspiegel^M
panel^M fotovoltaico

daymark
marque^F de jour^M
Tagzeichen^N
señal^F diurna

superstructure
superstructure^F
Teil^M über Wasser^N
superestructura^F

flotation section
flotteur^M
Schwimmkörper^M
sección^F de flotación^F

bridle assembly
bride^F de corps-mort^M
Zwickel^M
brida^F de unión^F

mooring chain
chaîne^F de mouillage^M
Ankerkette^F
cadena^F de amarre^M

sinker
corps-mort^M
Tonnenstein^M
plomo^M

light
feu^M
Laterne^F
luz^F

radar reflector
réflecteur^M radar^M
Radarreflektor^M
reflector^M del radar^M

photovoltaic panel
panneau^M photovoltaïque
Photozellenspiegel^M
panel^M fotovoltaico

daymark
marque^F de jour^M
Tagzeichen^N
señal^F diurna

ladder
échelle^F
Leiter^F
escalerilla^F

tubular structure
structure^F tubulaire
Rohrstütze^F
estructura^F tubular

waterline
surface^F de l'eau^F
Wasserlinie^F
línea^F de flotación^F

conical buoy
bouée^F conique
Spitztonne^F
boya^F cónica

pillar buoy
bouée^F charpente^F
Spierentonne^F
boya^F torre^M

MARITIME BUOYAGE SYSTEM
SYSTÈME^M DE BALISAGE^M MARITIME
BETONNUNGSSYSTEM^N
SISTEMA^M DE BOYAS^F MARITIMAS

CARDINAL MARKS
MARQUES^F CARDINALES
KARDINALSEEZEICHEN^N
SEÑALES^F DE LOS PUNTOS^M CARDINALES

topmark
voyant^M conique
Toppzeichen^N
marca^F de tope^M

North
nord^M
Norden^M
norte^M

white light
feu^M blanc
Weißes Feuer^N
luz^F blanca

direction of points
direction^F des pointes^F
Richtungsbezeichnung^F
dirección^F de los puntos^M

Northwest
nord^M-ouest^M
Nordwesten^M
noroeste^M

Northeast
nord^M-est^M
Nordosten^M
noreste^M

West
ouest^M
Westen^M
oeste^M

East
est^M
Osten^M
este^M

Southwest
sud^M-ouest^M
Südwesten^M
suroeste^M

Southeast
sud^M-est^M
Südosten^M
sureste^M

safest water
eaux^F sécuritaires
sicherstes Wasser^N
aguas^F seguras

danger
danger^M
Gefahrenstelle^F
peligro^M

South
sud^M
Süden^M
sur^M

BUOYAGE REGIONS
RÉGIONS^F DE BALISAGE^M
BETONNTE FAHRWASSER^N
REGIONES^F DE BOYAS^F

port hand
bâbord^M
Backbordseite^F
babor^M

starboard hand
tribord^M
Steuerbordseite^F
estribor^M

OPERATIONAL PATTERN OF MARKS BY NIGHT
RYTHME^M DES MARQUES^F DE NUIT^F
LEUCHTFEUERKENNUNG^F
RITMO^M DE LAS SEÑALES^F NOCTURNAS

light
lumière^F
Lichterscheinung^F
luz^F

darkness
obscurité^F
Verdunkelung^F
oscuridad^F

period
période^F
Taktkennung^F
periodo^M

period
période^F
Taktkennung^F
periodo^M

period
période^F
Taktkennung^F
periodo^M

interval
intervalle^M
Unterbrechung^F
intervalo^M

interval
intervalle^M
Unterbrechung^F
intervalo^M

DAYMARKS (REGION B)
MARQUES^F DE JOUR^M (RÉGION^F B)
TAGZEICHEN^N (REGION^F B)
SEÑALES^F DIURNAS (REGIÓN^F B)

starboard hand
tribord^M
Steuerbordseite^F
estribor^M

special mark
marque^F spéciale
Sonderzeichen^N
señal^F especial

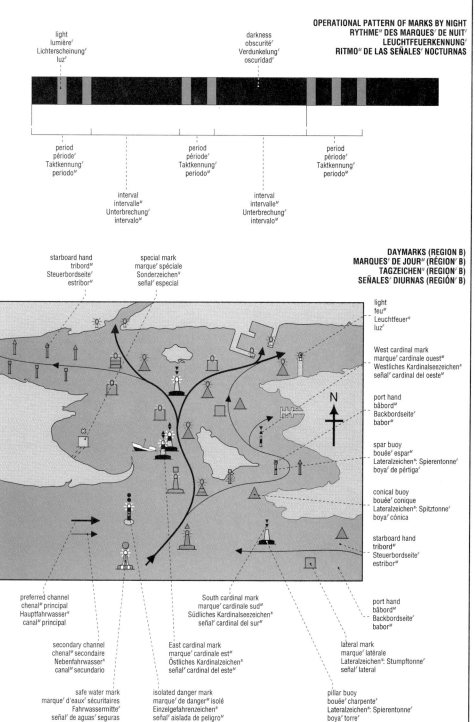

light
feu^M
Leuchtfeuer^N
luz^F

West cardinal mark
marque^F cardinale ouest^M
Westliches Kardinalseezeichen^N
señal^F cardinal del oeste^M

port hand
bâbord^M
Backbordseite^F
babor^M

spar buoy
bouée^F espar^M
Lateralzeichen^N: Spierentonne^F
boya^F de pértiga^F

conical buoy
bouée^F conique
Lateralzeichen^N: Spitztonne^F
boya^F cónica

starboard hand
tribord^M
Steuerbordseite^F
estribor^M

preferred channel
chenal^M principal
Hauptfahrwasser^N
canal^M principal

secondary channel
chenal^M secondaire
Nebenfahrwasser^N
canal^M secundario

South cardinal mark
marque^F cardinale sud^M
Südliches Kardinalseezeichen^N
señal^F cardinal del sur^M

East cardinal mark
marque^F cardinale est^M
Östliches Kardinalzeichen^N
señal^F cardinal del este^M

port hand
bâbord^M
Backbordseite^F
babor^M

lateral mark
marque^F latérale
Lateralzeichen^N: Stumpftonne^F
señal^F lateral

safe water mark
marque^F d'eaux^F sécuritaires
Fahrwassermitte^F
señal^F de aguas^F seguras

isolated danger mark
marque^F de danger^M isolé
Einzelgefahrenzeichen^N
señal^F aislada de peligro^M

pillar buoy
bouée^F charpente^F
Lateralzeichen^N: Spierentonne^F
boya^F torre^F

HARBOUR
PORT^M MARITIME
HAFEN^M
PUERTO^M

gate
porte^F
Tor^N
compuerta^F

transit shed
hangar^M de transit
Transitlagerschuppen^M
depósito^M de mercancía^F en tránsito^M

dry dock
bassin^M de radoub^M
Trockendock^N
dique^M seco

quayside crane
grue^F à flèche^F
Werftkran^M
grúa^F de muelle^M

quay
quai^M
Kai^M
muelle^M

bulk terminal
terminal^M de vrac^M
Massengut-Terminal^M
terminal^M de carga^F

canal lock
écluse^F
Kanalschleuse^F
esclusa^F de canal^M

floating crane
grue^F sur ponton^M
Schwimmkran^M
grúa^F flotante

container-loading bridge
portique^M de chargement^M de conteneurs
Containerbrücke^F
puente^M de carga^F para contenedores^M

silos
silos^M
Silos^M
silos^M

dock
bassin^M
Dock^N
dique^M

quay ramp
rampe^F de quai^M
Kairampe^F
rampa^F del muelle^M

grain terminal
terminal^M à céréales^F
Getreidesilo^M
terminal^M de granos^M

container ship
navire^M porte-conteneurs^M
Containerschiff^N
buque^M portacontenedores

cold store
entrepôt^M frigorifique
Kühlhaus^N
cámara^F frigorífica

ferryboat
transbordeur^M
Hafenfähre^F
transbordador^M

tanker
pétrolier^M
Tanker^M
buque^M cisterna^F

lighthouse
phare^M
Leuchtturm^M
faro^M

passenger terminal
gare^F maritime
Fahrgastanlage^F
terminal^M de pasajeros^M

oil terminal
terminal^M pétrolier
Öllöschbrücke^F
terminal^M de petróleo^M

quayside railway
voie^F ferrée bord^M à quai^M
Hafenbahn^F
ferrocarril^M del muelle^M

road transport
transport^M routier
Straßengüterverkehr^M
transporte^M terrestre

customs house
bureau^M des douanes^F
Hafenzollamt^N
aduana^F

loading bridge
portique^M
Brücke^F
puente^M

office building
bâtiment^M administratif
Bürogebäude^N
oficina^F del puerto^M

container terminal
terminal^M à conteneurs^M
Containerterminal^M
depósito^M de contenedores^M

car park
parking^M
Parkplatz^M
estacionamiento^M

CANAL LOCK
ÉCLUSE^F
KANALSCHLEUSE^F
ESCLUSA^F DE CANAL^M

lower gate
porte^F aval^M
Untertor^N
compuerta^F inferior

bollard
taquet^M d'amarrage^M
Taubesfestigung^F
gancho^M para cuerda^F

side wall
bajoyer^M
Schleusenwand^F
muro^M lateral

approach wall
estacade^F de guidage^M
Vorhafenwand^F
muro^M de abordaje^M

lock emptying system
aqueduc^M de vidange^F
Auslaufschütz^M
sistema^M de esclusas^F de vaciado^M y
desagüe^M

canal bed
radier^M
Kanalsohle^F
lecho^M

lock filling and emptying system
système^M de remplissage^M et de vidange^F
Ein- und Auslaufschütz^M
sistema^M de esclusas^F de vaciado^M y llenado^M

HOVERCRAFT
AÉROGLISSEUR^M
LUFTKISSENFAHRZEUG^N
AERODESLIZADOR^M (HOVERCRAFT^M)

driving propeller
hélice^F de propulsion^F
Luftpropeller^M
hélice^F propulsora

belt drive
courroie^F de transmission^F
Riemenantrieb^M
correa^F de transmisión^F

blade lift fan
ventilateur^M de sustentation^F
Hubgebläse^N
pala^F del ventilador^M de sustentación^F

propeller duct
tuyère^F
Propellerummantelung^F
tubo^M de la helice^F

rudder
dérive^F aérienne
Ruder^N
timón^M

drive shaft
arbre^M de transmission^F
Schraubenwelle^F
eje^M propulsor

diesel propulsion engine
moteur^M diesel de propulsion^F
Dieseltriebwerk^N
motor^M de propulsión^F diésel

luggage racks
soute^F à bagages^M
Gepäckcontainer^M
portaequipajes^M

life raft
canot^M pneumatique de sauvetage^M
Rettungsfloß^N
balsa^F salvavidas

ladder
échelle^f
Leiter^f
escalerilla^f

mitre gate recess
chambre^f de vantail^M
Stemmtornische^f
busco^M

lock filling intake
aqueduc^M de remplissage^M
Einlaufkanal^M
toma^f de llenado^M

flow
courant^M
Strömung^f
flujo^M

lock filling opening
pertuis^M de remplissage^M
Öffnung^f zum Fluten^N der Schleusenkammer^f
abertura^f de llenado^M

upper gate
porte^f amont^M
Obertor^N
compuerta^f de llenado^M

lock filling and emptying opening
pertuis^M de remplissage^M et de vidange^f
ng^f zum Fluten^N und Leeren^N der Schleusenkammer^f
abertura^f de llenado^M y vaciado^M

lower level
tête^f aval^M
niedrigerer Wasserstand^M
nivel^M inferior

lock-chamber
sas^M
Schleusenkammer^f
cámara^f de la esclusa^f

upper level
tête^f amont^M
höherer Wasserstand^M
nivel^M superior

diesel lift engine
moteur^M diesel de sustentation^f
Dieselmotor^M
motor^M de elevación^f diésel

passenger cabin
cabine^f des passagers^M
Passagierkabine^f
compartimiento^M de pasajeros^M

navigation light
feu^M de navigation^f
Positionslicht^N
luz^f de navegación^f

radar
radar^M
Radar^N
radar^M

air intake
prise^f d'air^M
Lufteinlaß^M
boca^f de aspiración^f de aire^M

control deck
cabine^f de pilotage^M
Kommandobrücke^f
cabina^f de mando^M

bow door
porte^f avant
Bugtür^f
puerta^f de proa^f

lift-fan air inlet
entrée^f d'air^M du ventilateur^M
Luftansaugrohr^N für Hubgebläse^N
toma^f de aire^M para el ventilador^M
de sustentación^f

flexible skirt
jupe^f souple
elastische Schürze^f
faldón^M flexible

skirt finger
doigt^M de jupe^f
Schürzenfinger^M
franja^f del faldón^M

FERRY
TRANSBORDEUR^M
FÄHRE^F
TRANSBORDADOR^M

telecommunication antenna
antenne^F de télécommunication^F
Fernmeldeantenne^F
antena^F de telecomunicaciones^F

radar
radar^M
Radar^N
radar^M

radio antenna
antenne^F radio^F
Funkantenne^F
antena^F de radio^M

compass bridge
passerelle^F de navigation^F
Peildeck^N
puente^M de mando^M

heating/air conditioning equipment
conditionnement^M d'air^M
Heizung^F/Klimaanlage^F
equipo^M de climatización^F

bow loading door
porte^F avant
Bugladeklappe^F
puerta^F de proa^F

restaurant
restaurant^M
Restaurant^N
restaurante^M

car deck
compartiment^M des voitures^F
Wagendeck^N
cubierta^F para automóviles^M

passenger cabin
cabine^F des passagers^M
Passagierkabine^F
cabina^F de pasajeros^M

folding ramp
rampe^F d'accès^M
klappbare Laderampe^F
rampa^F plegable

CONTAINER SHIP
CARGO^M PORTE-CONTENEURS^M
CONTAINERSCHIFF^N
CARGUERO^M PORTACONTENEDORES

funnel
cheminée^F
Schornstein^M
chimenea^F

radar
radar^M
Radar^N
radar^M

radio antenna
antenne^F radio^F
Funkantenne^F
antena^F de radio^M

compass bridge
passerelle^F de navigation^F
Peildeck^N
puente^M de mando^M

chart room
salle^F des cartes^F
Kartenraum^M
sala^F de navegación^F

lifeboat
chaloupe^F de sauvetage^M
Rettungsboot^N
bote^M salvavidas

crew quarters
locaux^M du personnel^M
Besatzungsunterkünfte^F
camarotes^M de la tripulación^F

HYDROFOIL BOAT
HYDROPTÈRE^M
TRAGFLÜGELSCHIFF^N
AERODESLIZADOR^M

passenger cabin
cabine^F des passagers^M
Passagierkabine^F
cabina^F de pasajeros^M

radio antenna
antenne^F radio^F
Funkantenne^F
antena^F de radio^M

radar
radar^M
Radar^N
radar^M

compass bridge
passerelle^F de navigation^F
Peildeck^N
puente^M de mando^M

rear foil
aile^F arrière
hinterer Tragflügel^M
ala^F de popa^F

surface-piercing foils
ailes^F en V
teilgetauchte Tragflügel^M
aleta^F de penetración^F superficial

life buoy
bouée^F de sauvetage^M
Rettungsring^M
salvavidas^M

strut
béquille^F
Stütze^F
soporte^M

propeller
hélice^F
Schraube^F
hélice^F

diesel engine
moteur^M diesel
Dieselmotor^M
motor^M diésel

front foil
aile^F avant
vorderer Tragflügel^M
aleta^F de proa^F

propeller shaft
arbre^M de l'hélice^F
Schraubenwelle^F
árbol^M de la hélice^F

gearbox
boîte^F de vitesses^F
Getriebe^N
caja^F de engranajes^M

container
conteneur^M
Container^M
contenedor^M

container hold
cale^F à conteneurs^M
Containerlaschsystem^N
bodega^F de contenedores^M

masthead light
feu^M de tête^F de mât^M
Topplicht^N
luz^F de tope^M

forecastle
plage^F avant
Back^F
castillo^M de proa^F

hawse pipe
écubier^M
Ankerklüse^F
sala^F de molinetes^M del ancla^F

495

CRUISELINER
PAQUEBOT^M
PASSAGIERDAMPFER^M
BUQUE^M TRASATLÁNTICO

hall
salon^M
Saal^M
recibidor^M

funnel
cheminée^F anti-suie
Schornstein^M
chimenea^F

stern
poupe^F
Heck^N
popa^F

lounge
bar^M
Lounge^F
salón^M de pasajeros^M

swimming pool
piscine^F
Swimmingpool^M
piscina^F

quarter-deck
plage^F arrière
Quarterdeck^N
cubierta^F de popa^F

gymnasium
gymnase^M
Sporthalle^F
gimnasio^M

games area
aire^F de jeux^M
Sportplatz^M
zona^F de recreo^M

promenade deck
pont^M-promenade^F
Promenadendeck^N
cubierta^F

lifeboat
chaloupe^F de sauvetage^M
Rettungsboot^N
bote^M salvavidas

propeller
hélice^F
Schraube^F
hélice^F

engine room
salle^F des machines^F
Maschinenraum^M
sala^F de máquinas^F

stabilizer fin
stabilisateur^M de roulis^M
Stabilisierungsflosse^F
aleta^F estabilizadora

rudder
gouvernail^M
Ruder^N
timón^M

cabin
cabine^F
Kabine^F
camarote^M

dining room
salle^F à manger
Speisesaal^M
comedor^M

cinema
cinéma^M
Kino^N
sala^F de cine^M

porthole
hublot^M
Bullauge^N
ojo^M de buey^M

telecommunication antenna
antenne^f de télécommunication^f
Telekommunikationsantenne^f
antena^f de telecomunicaciones^f

radio antenna
antenne^f radio^f
Funkantenne^f
antena^f de radio^M

sundeck
pont^M bain^M de soleil^M
Sonnendeck^N
solárium^M

radar
radar^M
Radar^N
radar^M

open-air terrace
terrasse^f extérieure
Freiluftterrasse^f
terraza^f

compass bridge
passerelle^f de navigation^f
Peildeck^N
puente^M de mando^M

forecastle
plage^f avant
Back^f
castillo^M de proa^f

port hand
bâbord^M
Backbordseite^f
babor^M

bow
proue^f
Bug^M
proa^f

ballroom
salle^f de bal^M
Musiksalon^M
salón^M de baile^M

stem bulb
bulbe^M d'étrave^f
Bugwulst^f
foco^M de proa^f

captain's quarters
appartement^M du commandant^M
Offizierskabine^f
camarote^M del capitán^M

hawse pipe
écubier^M
Ankerklüse^f
sala^f de molinetes^M del ancla^f

bow thruster
propulseur^M d'étrave^f
Bugstrahler^M
propulsor^M de proa^f

starboard hand
tribord^M
Steuerbordseite^f
estribor^M

LONG-RANGE JET AIRLINER
AVION^M LONG-COURRIER^M
LANGSTRECKEN-DÜSENFLUGZEUG^N
AVIÓN^M TURBORREACTOR DE PASAJEROS^M

aileron
aileron^M
Querruder^N
alerón^M

trailing edge
bord^M de fuite^F
Austrittskante^F
borde^M de fuga^F

spoiler
déporteur^M
Störklappe^F
frenos^M

upper deck
pont^M supérieur
Oberdeck^N
cubierta^F superior

trailing edge flap
volet^M de bord^M de fuite^F
Landeklappe^F
aleta^F del borde^M de fuga^F

anticollision light
feu^M anticollision
Warnblinklicht^N
luz^F anticolisión

flight deck
poste^M de pilotage^M
Cockpit^M
cabina^F de mando^M

antenna
antenne^F
Antenne^F
antena^F

nose
nez^M
Bug^M
morro^M

windscreen
pare-brise^M
Windschutzscheibe^F
parabrisas^M

door
porte^F
Tür^F
puerta^F

window
hublot^M
Fenster^N
ventanilla^F

root rib
nervure^F d'emplanture^F
Flügelwurzel^F
costilla^F de encastre^M

wing rib
nervure^F d'aile^F
Versteifungsrippe^F
estructura^F del ala^F

weather radar
radar^M météorologique
Wetterradar^M
radar^M de navegación^F

galley
office^M
Bordküche^F
cocina^F de a bordo^M

spar
longeron^M
Holm^M
larguero^M

first-class cabin
compartiment^M de première classe^F
Passagierraum^M 1. Klasse^F
cabina^F de primera clase^F

nose landing gear
train^M d'atterrissage^M avant
Bugfahrwerk^N
tren^M de aterrizaje^M delantero

TYPES OF TAIL UNIT
TYPES^M D'EMPENNAGES^M
LEITWERKSFORMEN^F
TIPOS^M DE COLAS^F

fuselage-mounted tail unit
empennage^M bas
Rumpfleitwerk^N
guías^F normales

fin-mounted tail unit
empennage^M surélevé
Flossenleitwerk^N
unidad^F cruciforme

triple tail unit
stabilisateur^M à triple plan^M vertical
Dreifachleitwerk^N
triple plano^M vertical

T-tail unit
empennage^M en T
T-Leitwerk^N
guías^F en T

tail fin
dérive^f
Seitenflosse^f
plano^m de deriva^f

tail assembly
empennage^m
Leitwerkⁿ
plano^m vertical

rudder
gouverne^f de direction^f
Seitenruderⁿ
timón^m

fuselage
fuselage^m
Rumpf^m
fuselaje^m

tail
queue^f
Heckⁿ
cola^f

passenger cabin
compartiment^m touriste
Passagierraum^m
cabina^f de clase^f turista

elevator
gouverne^f de profondeur^f
Höhenruderⁿ
timón^m de profundidad^f

tailplane
stabilisateur^m
Höhenflosse^f
plano^m horizontal

cargo hold
compartiment^m à fret^m
Frachtraum^m
bodega^f de equipaje^m

winglet
ailette^f
Wingletⁿ
aleta^f

main landing gear
train^m d'atterrissage^m principal
Hauptfahrwerkⁿ
tren^m de aterrizaje^m principal

wing
aile^f
Tragflügel^m
ala^f

engine mounting pylon
pylône^m du moteur^m
Pylon^m zur Aufhängung^f des
Triebwerksⁿ
pilón^m del turborreactor^m

wing slat
bec^m de bord^m d'attaque^f
Vorflügel^m
aleta^f hipersustentadora

navigation light
feu^m de navigation^f
Positionslichtⁿ
luz^f de navegación^f

turbojet engine
turboréacteur^m
TL-Triebwerkⁿ
turborreactor^m

leading edge
bord^m d'attaque^f
Eintrittskante^f
borde^m de ataque^m

TYPES OF WING
TYPES^m DE VOILURES^f
TRAGFLÜGELFORMEN^f
DIFERENTES FORMAS^f DE ALAS^f

straight wing
voilure^f droite
Rechteckflügel^m
ala^f recta

variable geometry wing
aile^f à géométrie^f variable
Schwenkflügel^m
ala^f variable

swept-back wing
voilure^f en flèche^f
Pfeilflügel^m
ala^f en flecha^f

tapered wing
voilure^f trapézoïdale
Trapezflügel^m
ala^f trapezoidal

delta wing
voilure^f delta^m
Deltaflügel^m
ala^f en delta

LUFTVERKEHR
TRANSPORTE AÉREO

AIR TRANSPORT
TRANSPORT AÉRIEN

landing gear lever
levier^M du train^M d'atterrissage^M
Fahrwerkhebel^M
palanca^F del tren^M de aterrizaje delantero

speaker
haut-parleur^M
Lautsprecher^M
altavoz^M

windscreen
pare-brise^M
Windschutzscheibe^F
parabrisas^M

autopilot controls
commandes^F du pilote^M automatique
Selbststeueranlage^F
controles^M del piloto^M automático

lighting
éclairage^M
Beleuchtung^F
luz^F

standby attitude indicator
horizon^M de secours^M
Reserve-Fluglageanzeige^F
indicador^M de emergencia^F de
inclinación^F

engine and crew alarm display
paramètres^M moteurs^M/alarmes^F
Warnanzeige^F- Besatzung^F und Triebwerke^N
pantalla^F de alarma^F de motor y tripulación^F

overhead switch panel
panneau^M de disjoncteurs^M
Überkopfschaltbrett^N
tablero^M de conmutadores^M

standby airspeed indicator
anémomètre^M de secours^M
Reserve-Fahrtmesser^M
indicador^M de emergencia^F de
velocidad^F

standby altimeter
altimètre^M de secours^M
Reserve-Höhenmesser^M
altímetro^M de emergencia^F

navigation display
informations^F-navigation^F
Navigationsanzeige^F
pantalla^F de navegación^F

primary flight display
informations^F-pilotage^M
Hauptanzeige^F der Flugdaten^N
pantalla^F principal de vuelo^M

control column
manche^M de commande^F
Steuerknüppel^M
columna^F de control^M

control wheel
volant^M de manche^M
Steuerrad^N
timón^M de control^M

speedbrake lever
levier^M des aérofreins^M
Flugbremshebel^M
palanca^F de freno^M

systems display
informations^F-systèmes^M de bord^M
Displayanzeige^F
pantalla^F de los sistemas^M

captain's seat
siège^M du commandant^M
Kapitänssitz^M
asiento^M del capitán^M

throttles
manettes^F de poussée^F
Gashebel^M
válvulas^F de control^M de combustible^M

control console
pupitre^M de commande^F
Steuerpult^N
consola^F de control^M

first officer's seat
siège^M du copilote^M
Kopilotensitz^M
asiento^M del copiloto^M

communication panels
panneaux^M de commandes^F radio^F
Fernmeldeschaltbrett^N
paneles^M de comunicación^F

flap lever
levier^M des volets^M
Klappenhebel^M
palanca^F de los alerones^M de hipersustentación^F

flight management computer
ordinateur^M de gestion^F de vol^M
Flugrechner^M
computador^M de gestión^F de vuelo^M

engine fuel valves
robinets^M de carburant^M
Brennstoffventile^N
válvulas^F de combustible^M del motor^M

air data computer
ordinateur^M des données^F aérodynamiques
Luftdatenrechner^M
computador^M de vuelo^M

TURBOFAN ENGINE
TURBORÉACTEUR^M À DOUBLE FLUX^M
ZWEISTROMTRIEBWERK^N
TURBOREACTOR^M

air intake
entrée^f d'air^M
Lufteintritt^M
entrada^f de aire^M

centrifugal compressor
compresseur^M centrifuge
Turboverdichter^M
compresor^M centrífugo

annular combustion chamber
chambre^f de combustion^f annulaire
Ringbrennkammer^f
cámara^f anular de combustión^f

axial compressor blade
aube^f du compresseur^M axial
Axialverdichterschaufel^f
paletas^f de compresión^f

pipe diffusers
diffuseurs^M tubulaires
Diffusoren^M
tubos^M difusores

bypass duct
canal^M de dérivation^f
Mantelstromführung^f
conducto^M de desviación^f

outer stators
stators^M extérieurs
äußere Leitschaufeln^f
estatores^M externos

turbine-compressor shaft
arbre^M turbine^f-compresseur^M
Turboverdichterwelle^f
árbol^M del turbocompresor^M

cold air
air^M froid
Kaltluft^f
aire^M frío

inner stators
stators^M intérieurs
innere Leitschaufeln^f
estatores^M internos

turbine-compressor shaft

exhaust guide vanes
aubage^M directeur de sortie^f
Abgasleitschaufeln^f
paletas^f del escape^M

nose cone
cône^M d'entrée^f
Spitze^f
cono^M de admisión^f

fuel control
régulateur^M de carburant^M
Brennstoffregelung^f
control^M de combustible^M

power turbines
turbines^f motrices
Arbeitsturbinen^f
turbinas^f de potencia^f

mounting point
point^M d'attache^f
Aufhängung^f
punto^M de montaje^M

compressor turbine
turbine^f du compresseur^M
Verdichterturbine^f
compresor^M de la turbina^f

hot air
air^M chaud
Heißluft^f
aire^M caliente

accessory gear box
relais^M d'accessoires^M
Zusatzgetriebegehäuse^M
caja^f de engranajes^M

ignition box
boîte^f d'allumage^M
Zündanlage^f
caja^f de combustión^f

exhaust duct
tuyère^f d'échappement^M
Austrittsdüse^f
conducto^M de salida^f de aire^M

fan
soufflante^f
Niederdruckverdichtung^f
ventilador^M

compression
compression^f
Verdichtung^f
compresión^f

combustion
combustion^f
Verbrennung^f
combustión^f

exhaust
échappement^M
Abgas^N
escape^M

501

AIRPORT
AÉROPORT[M]
FLUGHAFEN[M]
AEROPUERTO[M]

tower control room
vigie[F]
Kontrollraum[M]
cabina[F] de la torre[F] de control[M]

access road
route[F] d'accès[M]
Zufahrtsstraße[F]
carretera[F] de acceso[M]

high-speed exit taxiway
sortie[F] de piste[F] à grande vitesse[F]
Schnellabrollbahn[F]
salida[F] de la pista[F] de alta velocidad[F]

control tower
tour[F] de contrôle[M]
Kontrollturm[M]
torre[F] de control[M]

taxiway
voie[F] de circulation[F]
Rollbahn[F]
pista[F] de maniobras[F]

by-pass taxiway
bretelle[F]
Überholrollbahn[F]
pista[F] de enlace[M]

apron
aire[F] de trafic[M]
Vorfeld[N]
pista[F] de estacionamiento[M]

apron
aire[F] de manœuvre[F]
Vorfeld[N]
zona[F] de circulación[F]

taxiway
voie[F] de circulation[F]
Rollbahn[F]
pista[F] de maniobras[F]

service road
voie[F] de service[M]
Versorgungsstraße[M]
ruta[F] de servicio[M]

maintenance hangar
hangar^M
Flugzeugwartungshalle^F
hangar^M de mantenimiento^M

passenger terminal
aérogare^F de passagers^M
Passagierterminal^M
terminal^M de pasajeros^M

parking area
aire^F de stationnement^M
Abstellplatz^M
zona^F de estacionamiento^M

telescopic corridor
passerelle^F télescopique
ausziehbare Fluggastbrücke^F
corredor^M telescópico

boarding walkway
quai^M d'embarquement^M
Fluggastbrücke^F
túnel^M de embarque^M

satellite terminal
aérogare^F satellite^M
radiale Einsteigestation^F
terminal^M radial de pasajeros^M

service area
aire^F de service^M
Versorgungsbereich^M
zona^F de servicio^M

taxiway line
marques^F de circulation^F
Rollbahnmarkierung^F
línea^F de pista^F

PASSENGER TERMINAL
AÉROGARE[F]
PASSAGIERTERMINAL[M]
TERMINAL[M] DE PASAJEROS[M]

platform
débarcadère[M]
Bahnsteig[M]
andén[M]

hotel reservation desk
bureau[M] de réservation[F] de chambres[F] d'hôtel[M]
Hotelreservierungsschalter[M]
oficina[F] de reservas[F] de hotel[M]

baggage check-in counter
comptoir[M] d'enregistrement[M]
Check-in-Schalter[M]
recepción[F] de equipaje[M]

automatically-controlled door
porte[F] automatique
automatische Tür[F]
puerta[F] automática

ticket counter
comptoir[M] de vente[F] des billets[M]
Ticketschalter[M]
mostrador[M]

security check
contrôle[M] de sécurité[F]
Sicherheitskontrolle[F]
control[M] de seguridad[F]

lobby
hall[M] public
Eingangshalle[F]
vestíbulo[M]

car park
parc[M] à voitures[F]
Parkplatz[M]
estacionamiento[M]

RESTAURANT

AIR CANADA

baggage claim area
zone[F] de retrait[M] des bagages[M]
Gepäckausgabe[F]
entrega[F] de equipaje[M]

rail shuttle service
navette[F] ferroviaire
Pendelzug[M]
servicio[M] de enlace[M] ferroviario

information counter
comptoir[M] de renseignements[M]
Informationsschalter[M]
puesto[M] de información[F]

conveyor belt
tapis[M] roulant
Förderband[N]
cinta[F] transportadora

RUNWAY
PISTE[F]
START- UND LANDEBAHN[F]
PISTA[F] DE ATERRIZAJE[M] Y DESPEGUE[M]

runway centre line markings
marque[F] d'axe[M] de piste[F]
Pisten-Mittellliniemarkierungen[F]
señal[F] de eje[M] de pista[F]

runway designation marking
marques[F] d'identification[F]
Pistenbezeichnungsmarkierung[F]
señal[F] de identificación[F] de pista[F]

holding area marking
marque[F] de point[M] d'attente[F]
Wartebereichmarkierung[F]
señal[F] de zona[F] de espera[F]

runway side stripe markings
marques[F] latérales de piste[F]
Pistenrandmarkierungen[F]
señales[F] laterales de pista[F]

observation deck
terrasse[f]
Besucherterrasse[f]
mirador[M]

passport control
contrôle[M] des passeports[M]
Paßkontrolle[f]
control[M] de pasaportes[M]

duty-free shop
boutique[f] hors taxe[f]
Duty-free-Shop[M]
tienda[f] libre de impuestos[M]

flight information board
tableau[M] d'affichage[M] des vols[M]
Fluginformationsanzeige[f]
tablero[M] de llegadas[f] y salidas[f]

departure lounge
salle[f] d'embarquement[M]
Abflugwartehalle[f]
sala[f] de espera[f] de embarque[M]

passenger transfer vehicle
transbordeur[M]
Passagiertransferfahrzeug[N]
transbordador[M]

cargo dispatch
expédition[f] du fret[M]
Frachtversand[M]
expedición[f] de carga[f]

customs control
contrôle[M] douanier
Zollkontrolle[f]
aduana[f]

cargo reception
réception[f] du fret[M]
Frachtempfang[M]
recepción[f] de carga[f]

runway touchdown zone marking
marque[f] d'aire[f] de prise[f] de contact[M]
Aufsetzzonenmarkierungen[f]
señal[f] de zona[f] de contacto[M] de pista[f]

exit taxiway
sortie[f] de piste[f]
Abrollbahn[f]
salida[f] de la pista[f]

fixed distance marking
marque[f] de distance[f] constante
Festabstandmarkierung[f]
señal[f] de distancia[f] fija

runway threshold markings
marques[f] de seuil[M] de piste[f]
Schwellenmarkierungen[f]
señales de límite[M] de la pista[f]

505

LUFTVERKEHR
TRANSPORTE AÉREO

AIR TRANSPORT
TRANSPORT AÉRIEN

GROUND AIRPORT EQUIPMENT
ÉQUIPEMENTS^M **AÉROPORTUAIRES**
BODENAUSRÜSTUNG^F
EQUIPO^M **DE TIERRA**^F

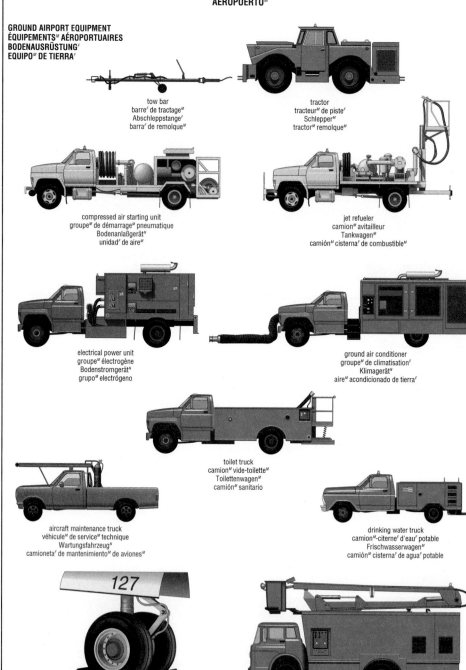

tow bar
barre^F de tractage^M
Abschleppstange^F
barra^F de remolque^M

tractor
tracteur^M de piste^F
Schlepper^M
tractor^M remolque^M

compressed air starting unit
groupe^M de démarrage^M pneumatique
Bodenanlaßgerät^N
unidad^F de aire^M

jet refueler
camion^M avitailleur
Tankwagen^M
camión^M cisterna^F de combustible^M

electrical power unit
groupe^M électrogène
Bodenstromgerät^N
grupo^M electrógeno

ground air conditioner
groupe^M de climatisation^F
Klimagerät^N
aire^M acondicionado de tierra^F

toilet truck
camion^M vide-toilette^M
Toilettenwagen^M
camión^M sanitario

aircraft maintenance truck
véhicule^M de service^M technique
Wartungsfahrzeug^N
camioneta^F de mantenimiento^M de aviones^M

drinking water truck
camion^M-citerne^F d'eau^F potable
Frischwasserwagen^M
camión^M cisterna^F de agua^F potable

wheel chock
cale^F
Bremsklotz^M
calzo^M de la rueda^F

boom truck
nacelle^F élévatrice
Tankwagen^M mit beweglichem Ausleger^M
camioneta^F con canastilla^F telescópica

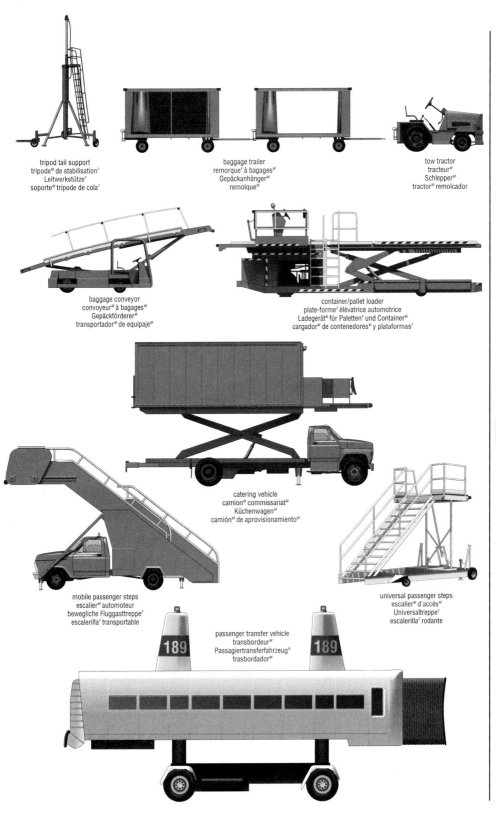

tripod tail support
tripode^M de stabilisation^F
Leitwerkstütze^F
soporte^M trípode de cola^F

baggage trailer
remorque^F à bagages^M
Gepäckanhänger^M
remolque^M

tow tractor
tracteur^M
Schlepper^M
tractor^M remolcador

baggage conveyor
convoyeur^M à bagages^M
Gepäckförderer^M
transportador^M de equipaje^M

container/pallet loader
plate-forme^F élévatrice automotrice
Ladegerät^N für Paletten^F und Container^M
cargador^M de contenedores^M y plataformas^F

catering vehicle
camion^M commissariat^M
Küchenwagen^M
camión^M de aprovisionamiento^M

mobile passenger steps
escalier^M automoteur
bewegliche Fluggasttreppe^F
escalerilla^F transportable

universal passenger steps
escalier^M d'accès^M
Universaltreppe^F
escalerilla^F rodante

passenger transfer vehicle
transbordeur^M
Passagiertransferfahrzeug^N
trasbordador^M

507

HELICOPTER
HÉLICOPTÈRE^M
HUBSCHRAUBER^M
HELICÓPTERO^M

anti-torque tail rotor
rotor^M anticouple
dem Drehmoment^N entgegenwirkender Heckrotor^M
rotor^M de cola^F

tail fin
dérive^F
Seitenflosse^F
aleta^F

tailplane
stabilisateur^M
Höhenflosse^F
estabilizador^M horizontal

drive shaft
arbre^M moteur^M
Steigungseinstellung^F
árbol^M de transmisión^F

tail boom
poutre^F de queue^F
Leitwerksträger^M
estructura^F de cola^F

rotor blade
pale^F de rotor^M
Rotorblatt^N
pala^F del rotor^M

rotor hub
moyeu^M rotor^M
Rotornabe^F
cubo^M del rotor^M

mast
mât^M de rotor^M
Rotormast^M
mástil^M

rotor head
tête^F de rotor^M
Rotorkopf^M
rotor^M

tail skid
béquille^F
Hecksporn^M
patín^M de cola^F

flight deck
poste^M de pilotage^M
Führerraum^M
cabina^F de mando^M

position light
feu^M de position^F
Positionslicht^N
luz^F de navegación^F

exhaust pipe
tuyère^F
Abgasleitung^F
tubo^M de escape^M

luggage compartment
soute^F à bagages^M
Gepäckraum^M
bodega^F de equipaje^M

antenna
antenne^F
Antenne^F
antena^F

fuel tank
réservoir^M à carburant^M
Treibstofftank^M
depósito^M del combustible^M

air intake
entrée^F d'air^M
Lufteinlauf^M
entrada^F de aire^M

control stick
manche^M à balais^M
Steuerknüppel^M
palanca^F de mando^M

boarding step
marchepied^M
Einsteigetreppe^F
estribo^M

landing window
hublot^M d'atterrissage^M
Landefenster^N
ventanilla^F de aterrizaje^M

cabin
cabine^F
Passagierraum^M
cabina^F

landing light
phare^M d'atterrissage^M
Landescheinwerfer^M
luz^F de aterrizaje^M

skid
patin^M
Kufe^F
patín^M de aterrizaje^M

ROCKET
FUSÉE*F*
RAKETE*F*
COHETE*M*

launch escape system
tour*F* de sauvetage*M*
Rettungsturm*M* für die Startphase*F*
torre*F* de escape*M*

command module
module*M* de commande*F*
Kommandokapsel*F*
módulo*M* de mando*M*

service module
module*M* de service*M*
Versorgungskapsel*F*
módulo*M* de servicio*M*

lunar module
module*M* lunaire
Mondlandeinheit*F*
módulo*M* lunar

instrument unit
bloc*M* d'équipement*M*
Instrumenteneinheit*F*
unidad*F* de instrumentos*M*

helium sphere
sphère*F* d'hélium*M*
Heliumsphäre*F*
esfera*F* de helio*M*

J-2 engine
moteur*M* J-2
J-2 Triebwerk*N*
propulsor J-2*M*

liquid hydrogen tank
réservoir*M* d'hydrogène*M* liquide
Flüssigwasserstofftank*M*
tanque*M* de hidrógeno*M* liquido

liquid oxygen tank
réservoir*M* d'oxygène*M* liquide
Flüssigsauerstofftank*M*
tanque*M* de oxígeno*M* liquido

liquid oxygen tank baffle
déflecteur*M* de réservoir*M* d'oxygène*M* liquide
Schlingerwand*F*
deflector*M* del tanque*M* de oxígeno*M* liquido

kerosene tank
réservoir*M* de kérosène*M*
Kerosintank*M*
tanque*M* de keroseno*M*

fuel transfer pipe
conduite*F* de transfert*M* de carburant*M*
Kraftstoffschlauch*M*
tubería*F* de conducción*F* de carburante*M*

stabilizing fin
empennage*M* de stabilisation*F*
Stabilisierungsflosse*F*
estabilizador*M*

nozzle
tuyère*F*
Düse*F*
propulsor*M*

F-1 engine
moteur*M* F-1
F-1 Triebwerk*N*
propulsor F-1*M*

payload
charge*F* utile
Nutzlast*F*
carga*F* útil

third stage
troisième étage*M*
dritte Stufe*F*
tercera etapa*F*

second stage
deuxième étage*M*
zweite Stufe*F*
segunda etapa*F*

first stage
premier étage*M*
erste Stufe*F*
primera etapa*F*

SPACE SHUTTLE AT TAKEOFF
NAVETTE^F SPATIALE AU DÉCOLLAGE^M
RAUMFÄHRE^F BEIM START^M
TRANSBORDADOR^M ESPACIAL EN
POSICIÓN^F DE LANZAMIENTO^M

external fuel tank
réservoir^M externe
Außentank^M
depósito^M externo de combustible^M

booster parachute
parachute^M
Fallschirm^F für die Feststoffrakete^F
paracaídas^F auxiliar

solid-rocket booster
fusée^F à propergol^M solide
Feststoffrakete^F
cohetes^M impulsores

shuttle
navette^F
Raumfähre^F
lanzadera^F

observation window
hublot^M d'observation^F
Sichtfenster^N
ventanilla^F de observación^F

hatch
sas^M
Einstiegsluke^F
escotilla^F

nozzle
tuyère^F
Düse^F
propulsor^M

remote-control arm
bras^M télécommandé
ferngesteuerter Manipulatorarm^M
brazo^M de control^M a larga distancia^F

communication tunnel
tunnel^M de communication^F
Verbindungstunnel^M
túnel^M de comunicación^F

SPACE SHUTTLE IN ORBIT
NAVETTE^F SPATIALE EN ORBITE^F
RAUMFÄHRE^F IN DER UMLAUFBAHN^F
TRANSBORDADOR ESPACIAL EN ÓRBITA

payload bay
soute^F
Ladebucht^F
nave^F de carga^F

flight deck
poste^M de pilotage^M
Cockpit^N
cabina^F de mando^M

surface insulation
revêtement^M thermique
Oberflächenisolierung^F
recubrimiento^M aislante

engines
moteurs^M
Triebwerke^N
motores^M

heat shield
bouclier^M thermique
Hitzeschild^N
cubierta^F térmica

payload bay door
porte^F de la soute^F
Ladeklappen^F
puerta^F a la nave^F de carga^F

radiator panel
panneau^M de refroidissement^M
Radiatoren^M
panel^M radiador

laboratory air lock
sas*M* du laboratoire*M*
Luftschleuse*F*
esclusa*F* científica de aire*M*

scientific instruments
instruments*M* scientifiques
wissenschaftliche Instrumente*N*
instrumentos*M* científicos

rudder
gouvernail*M*
Ruder*N*
timón*M*

manœuvring engine
moteur*M* de manœuvre*F*
Manöver-Triebwerk*N*
propulsor*M* de maniobras*F*

main engines
moteurs*M* principaux
Haupttriebwerk*N*
motores*M* principales

tanks
réservoirs*M*
Behälter*M*
depósitos*M*

body flap
volet*M*
hintere Klappe*F*
aleta*F* de fuselaje*M*

elevon
élevon*M*
Querruder*N*
alerón*M*

spacelab
laboratoire*M* spatial
Raumlaboratorium*N*
laboratorio*M* espacial

instrument pallet
palette*F* porte-instruments*M*
Instrumentenpalette*F*
plataforma*F* de instrumentos*M*

wing
aile*F*
Tragflügel*M*
ala*F*

tile
tuile*F*
Kachel*F*
teja*F*

SPACESUIT
SCAPHANDRE^M SPATIAL
RAUMANZUG^M
TRAJE^M ESPACIAL

35 mm still camera
appareil^M photographique 35 mm
35mm Fotoapparat^M
cámara^F rígida de 35 mm

propellant level gauge
indicateur^M de niveau^M de carburant
Treibstoff-Füllstandanzeige^F
sensor^M de nivel^M de combustible^M

life support system
équipement^M de survie^F
Lebenserhaltungssystem^N
sistema^M de soporte^M vital

solar shield
visière^F antisolaire
Solarschild^N
protector^M solar

helmet ring
collier^M de serrage^M du casque^M
Ringverschluß^M
anillo^M de unión del casco^M

helmet
casque^M
Helm^M
casco^M

computer screen intensity controls
réglage^M de l'écran^M de l'ordinateur^M
Computerbildschirm^M mit Helligkeitsregelung^F
controles^M de intensidad^F de la pantalla^F del
ordenador^M

colour television camera
caméra^F de télévision^F couleurs^F
Farbfernsehkamera^F
cámara^F de televisión^F de color^M

communications volume controls
réglage^M du volume^M des communications^F
Lautstärkerregler^M des
Funkübertragungssystems^N
controles^M de volumen^M de
comunicaciones^F

procedure checklist
aide-mémoire^M des procédures^F
Checkliste^F
lista^F de procedimientos^M

glove
gant^M
Handschuh^M
guante^M

safety suit connection
joint^M de sécurité^F du scaphandre^M
Verbindung^F des Ventilations- und
Kühlsystems^N
conexión^F de seguridad^F del traje^M

safety tether
attache^F de sécurité^F
Sicherheitsriemen^M
correa^F de seguridad^F

tool tether
attache^F pour outils^M
Werkzeughalter^M
correa^F para herramientas^F

reading mirror
miroir^M de lecture^F
Spiegel^M
espejo^M de lectura^F

life support system controls
contrôles^M de l'équipement^M de survie^F
Regelung^F des Lebenserhaltungssystem^N
controles^M del sistema^M de soporte^M vita

body temperature control unit
contrôle^M de la température^F du corps^M
Körpertemperaturregelung^F
unidad^F de control^M de la temperatura^F d
cuerpo^M

oxygen pressure actuator
réglage^M de la pression^F d'oxygène^M
Sauerstoffdruck-Stelleinrichtung^F
accionador^M de presión^F del oxígeno^M

manned manœuvring unit
véhicule^M spatial autonome
bemannte Manövriereinheit^F
unidad^F para maniobras^F en el espacio^M

biomedical monitoring sensor
équipement^M de contrôle^M biomédical
biomedizinischer Sensor^M
sensor^M de control^M biomédico

thruster
propulseur^M
Schubdüse^F
propulsor^M

protection layer
revêtement^M de sécurité^F
Schutzschicht^F
capa^F protectora

liquid cooling and ventilation garment
sous-vêtement^M de contrôle^M thermique
Unteranzug^M zur Kühlung^F und Ventilation^F
líquido^M de enfriamiento^M y ventilación^F del traje^M

insulation layers
sous-vêtement^M d'isolation^F
Isolierschichten^F
capas^F aislantes

OFFICE SUPPLIES

OFFICE AUTOMATION

STATIONERY
ARTICLES^M DE BUREAU^M
SCHREIBWAREN^F
ARTÍCULOS^M DE ESCRITORIO^M

mechanical pencil
porte-mine^M
Druckbleistift^M
portaminas^M

ballpoint pen
stylo^M-bille^F
Kugelschreiber^M
bolígrafo^M

pencil
crayon^M
Bleistift^M
lápiz^M

fountain pen
stylo^M-plume^F
Füllfederhalter^M
estilográfica^F

eraser holder
porte-gomme^M
Radiergummihalter^M
portagomas^M

stick eraser
crayon^M gomme^F
Radierstift^M
lápiz^M borrador^M

marker pen
marqueur^M
Textmarker^M
marcador^M

eraser
gomme^F
Radiergummi^M
goma^F

highlighter pen
surligneur^M
Leuchtstift^M
destacador^M

glue stick
bâtonnet^M de colle^F
Klebestift^M
lápiz^M adhesivo

correction fluid
correcteur^M liquide
Korrekturflüssigkeit^F
liquido^M corrector

clip
pince-notes^M
Papierclip^M
pinza^F

paper clips
trombones^M
Büroklammern^F
presillas^F

stapler
agrafeuse^F
Hefter^M
grapadora^F

paper fasteners
attaches^F parisiennes
Beutelklammern^F
tachuelas^F para papel^M

staples
agrafes^F
Heftklammern^F
grapas^F

letter opener
coupe-papier^M
Brieföffner^M
abrecartas^F

drawing pins
punaises^F
Reißnägel^M
chinchetas^F

pencil sharpener
taille-crayon^M
Bleistiftspitzer^M
sacapuntas^M

correction paper
ruban^M correcteur
Korrekturstreifen^M
papel^M corrector

staple remover
dégrafeuse^F
Entklammerer^M
uñas^F

OFFICE SUPPLIES
FOURNITURES DE BUREAU
BÜROBEDARF
EQUIPO DE OFICINA

rubber stamp
timbre^M caoutchouc^M
Stempel^M
sello^M de goma^F

stamp pad
tampon^M encreur
Stempelkissen^N
cojín para sellos^M

tape dispenser
dévidoir^M de ruban^M adhésif
Klebefilmspender^M
carrete^M de cinta^F adhesiva

date stamp
timbre^M dateur
Datumstempel^M
fechador^M

numbering stamp
numéroteur^M
Numerierstempel^M
foliador^M

stamp rack
porte-timbres^M
Stempelträger^M
portasellos^M

spike file
pique-notes^M
Dornablage^F
pinchador^M

paper punch
perforatrice^F
Locher^M
perforadora^F

label maker
pince^F à étiqueter
Präger^M
rotulador^M

moistener
mouilleur^M
Befeuchter^M
rueda^F humedecedora

rotary file
fichier^M rotatif
Drehkartei^F
fichero^M giratorio

letter scale
pèse-lettres^M
Briefwaage^F
balanza^F para cartas^F

pencil sharpener
taille-crayon^M
Bleistiftspitzer^M
sacapuntas^M

telephone index
répertoire^M téléphonique
Telefonnummernverzeichnis^N
directorio^M telefónico

INDEX CARD DRAWER
TIROIR^M DE FICHIER^M
KARTEISCHUBFACH^N
GAVETA^F DE ARCHIVADOR^M

expanding file
pochette^F de classement^M
Erweiterungskartei^F
archivo^M acordeón

compressor
compresseur^M
Begrenzungseinsatz^M
compresor^M

metal rail
tringle^F métallique
Führungsschiene^F
riel^M metálico

label holder
porte-étiquette^M
Etikettenfenster^N
soporte^M del rótulo^M

book ends
serre-livres^M
Bücherstütze^F
sujetalibros^M

index card cabinet
fichier^M
Karteikasten^M
archivador^M de fichas^F

index cards
fiches^F
Karteikarten^F
fichas^F

filing box
boîte^F-classeur^M
Aktenbox^F
caja^F archivo^M

desk tray
boîte^F à courrier^M
Dokumentenablage^F
bandeja^F de correspondencia^F

517

STATIONERY
ARTICLES^M DE BUREAU^M
SCHREIBWAREN^F
ARTÍCULOS^M DE ESCRITORIO^M

tear-off calendar
calendrier^M-mémorandum^M
Abreißkalender^M
calendario^M de pared^F

appointment book
agenda^M
Terminkalender^M
agenda^F

calendar pad
bloc^M-éphéméride^F
Ringbuchkalender^M
calendario^M de escritorio^M

account book
registre^M de comptabilité^F
Geschäftsbuch^N
agenda^F de caja^F

self-adhesive labels
étiquettes^F autocollantes
Klebeetiketten^N
etiquetas^F adhesivas

memo pad
bloc^M-notes^F
Notizblock^M
libreta^F

tab
onglet^M
Reiter^M
indicador^M

window tab
onglet^M à fenêtre^F
durchsichtiger Reiter^M
indicador^M transparente

archboard
planchette^F à arches^F
Ringablage^F
tabla^F con argollas^F

folder
chemise^F
Aktenmappe^F
carpeta^F de archivo^M

file guides
guides^M de classement^M
Karteiregister^N
guías^F de archivo^M

suspension file
dossier^M suspendu
Hängemappe^F
archivador^M colgante

post binder
reliure^f à vis^f
Hefter^M
carpeta^f de tornillos^M

spring binder
reliure^f à ressort^M
Klemmhefter^M
carpeta^f de costilla^f de resorte^M

clipboard
planchette^f à pince^f
Klemmbrett^N
tabla^f con broche^M de presión^f

ring binder
classeur^M
Ringbuch^N
carpeta^f de argollas^f

document folder
pochette^f d'information^f
Dokumentenmappe^f
carpeta^f con guardas^f

dividers
feuillets^M intercalaires
Registriereinlagen^f
divisores^M

spiral binder
reliure^f spirale^f
Spiralringbuch^N
carpeta^f de espiral^f

clamp binder
reliure^f à pince^f
Aktenordner^M
carpeta^f con mecanismo^M de presión^f

fastener binder
reliure^f à glissière^f
Schnellhefter^M
carpeta^f de broches^M

519

BÜROBEDARF
EQUIPO DE OFICINA

OFFICE SUPPLIES
FOURNITURES DE BUREAU

executive desk
bureau*M* de direction*F*
Chefschreibtisch*M*
escritorio*M* de ejecutivo

swivel-tilter armchair
fauteuil*M* pivotant à bascule*F*
Drehsessel*M*
sillón*M* giratorio

desk pad
sous-main*M*
Schreibunterlage*F*
carpeta*F*

credenza
bahut*M*
Aktenschrank*M*
aparador*M*

partition
cloison*F* amovible
Trennwand*F*
biombo*M*

lateral filing cabinet
classeur*M* à clapets*M*
Hängekartei*F*
archivador*M* lateral

520

COMPUTER TABLE
TABLE^F D'ORDINATEUR^M
COMPUTERTISCH^M
MESA^F DEL ORDENADOR^M

PRINTER TABLE
TABLE^F D'IMPRIMANTE^F
DRUCKERTISCH^M
MESA^F DE LA IMPRESORA^F

paper catcher
panier^M de réception^F
Papierfänger^M
bandeja^F para recoger el papel^M

adjustable shelf
support^M ajustable
verstellbare Tastaturablage^F
plato^M ajustable

paper tray
panier^M d'alimentation^F
Papierablage^F
bandeja^F para el papel^M

modesty panel
panneau^M de modestie^F
Abschlußtafel^F
panel^M

paper feed channel
fente^F d'alimentation^F
Öffnung^F für die Papierzufuhr^F
canal^M de arrastre^M del papel^M

mobile filing unit
classeur^M mobile
fahrbare Aktenablage^F
archivador^M movible

mobile drawer unit
caisson^M
fahrbares Schubladenelement^M
archivador^M movible con cajones^M

typist's chair
chaise^F dactylo^M
Bürodrehstuhl^M
silla^F de secretaria^F

return
retour^M
Winkeltisch^M
aparador^M de escritorio^M

SECRETARIAL DESK
BUREAU^M SECRÉTAIRE^M
ARBEITSPLATZ^M
ESCRITORIO^M DE SECRETARIA^F

521

OFFICE FURNITURE
MOBILIER*M* DE BUREAU*M*
BÜROMÖBEL*N*
MUEBLES*M* DE OFICINA*F*

display cabinet
présentoir*M* à revues*F*
Ausstellungsregal*N*
estante*M* para revistas*F*

coat hook
patère*F*
Kleiderhaken*M*
perchero*M* de pared*F*

stationery cabinet
armoire*F* à papeterie*F*
Schrank*M*
gabinete*M* para papelería*F*

hat stand
porte-manteau*M*
Garderobenständer*M*
perchero*M* de pie

locker
armoire*F*-vestiaire*M*
Kleiderschrank*M*
armario*M*

coat rack
vestiaire*M* de bureau*M*
Garderobe*F*
perchero*M*

CALCULATOR
CALCULATRICE*F*
RECHNER*M*
CALCULADORAS*F*

wallet
étui*M*
Etui*N*
bolsa*F* de cuero*M*

solar cell
alimentation*F* solaire
Solarzelle*F*
célula*F* solar

display
affichage*M*
Anzeige*F*
pantalla*F*

memory recall
rappel*M* de mémoire*F*
Speicheranzeigetaste*F*
retorno*M* a la memoria*F*

memory cancel
effacement*M* de mémoire*F*
Speicherlöschtaste*F*
anulación*F* de la memoria*F*

number key
touche*F* numérique
Zifferntaste*F*
tecla*F* de número*M*

subtract key
soustraction*F*
Subtraktionstaste*F*
tecla*F* de substracción*F*

decimal key
touche*F* de décimale*F*
Kommataste*F*
tecla*F* decimal

POCKET CALCULATOR
CALCULETTE*F*
TASCHENRECHNER*M*
CALCULADORA*F* DE BOLSILLO*M*

subtract from memory
soustraction*F* en mémoire*F*
Speicherlöschtaste*F*
substracción*F* de la memoria*F*

add in memory
addition*F* en mémoire*F*
Speichertaste*F*
adición*F* en la memoria*F*

clear key
effacement*M* total
Löschtaste*F*
tecla*F* para limpiar la pantalla*F*

divide key
division*F*
Divisionstaste*F*
tecla*F* de división*F*

clear-entry key
effacement*M* partiel
Eingabe-Löschtaste*F*
tecla*F* para limpiar la pantalla*F* y
de acceso

square root key
racine*F* carrée
Quadratwurzeltaste*F*
tecla*F* de raíz*F* cuadrada

multiply key
multiplication*F*
Multiplikationstaste*F*
tecla*F* de multiplicación*F*

percent key
pourcentage*M*
Prozenttaste*F*
tecla*F* de porcentaje*M*

add key
addition*F*
Additionstaste*F*
tecla*F* de adición*F*

equals key
touche*F* de résultat*M*
Gleichtaste*F*
tecla*F* de igualdad*F*

change sign key
inverseur*M* de signe*M*
Vorzeichentaste*F*
tecla*F* de cambio*M* de signo*M*

PRINTING CALCULATOR
CALCULATRICE*F* À IMPRIMANTE*F*
TISCHRECHNER*M* MIT DRUCKERTEIL*N*
CALCULADORA*F* CON IMPRESORA*F*

printer
imprimante*F*
Druckerteil*N*
impresora*F*

multiple use key
touche*F* multifonctionnelle
Multifunktionstaste*F*
tecla*F* de utilización*F* múltiple

non-add/subtotal
non addition*F*/total*M* partiel
Zwischensummentaste*F*
subtotal*M*/sin adición*F*

plus/equals key
touche*F* plus*M*-égalité*F*
Addiertaste*F*
tecla*F* de más/igual

number of decimals
nombre*M* de décimales*F*
Kommastellen*F*
número*M* de decimales

paper feed key
commande*F* d'insertion*F* du papier*M*
Papiervorschubtaste*F*
tecla*F* de arrastre*M* del papel*M*

double zero key
touche*F* de double zéro*M*
Doppel-Null-Taste*F*
tecla*F* de doble cero*M*

ELECTRONIC TYPEWRITER
MACHINE^F À ÉCRIRE ÉLECTRONIQUE
ELEKTRISCHE SCHREIBMASCHINE^F
MÁQUINA^F DE ESCRIBIR ELECTRÓNICA

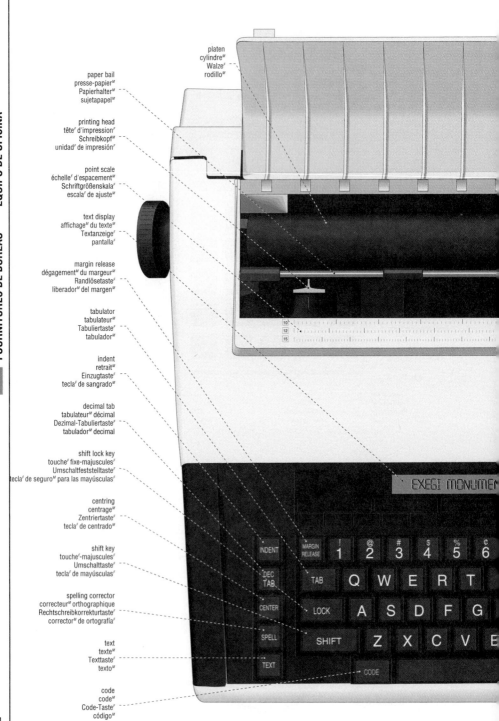

platen
cylindre^M
Walze^F
rodillo^M

paper bail
presse-papier^M
Papierhalter^M
sujetapapel^M

printing head
tête^F d'impression^F
Schreibkopf^M
unidad^F de impresión^F

point scale
échelle^F d'espacement^M
Schriftgrößenskala^F
escala^F de ajuste^M

text display
affichage^M du texte^M
Textanzeige^F
pantalla^F

margin release
dégagement^M du margeur^M
Randlösetaste^F
liberador^M del margen^M

tabulator
tabulateur^M
Tabuliertaste^F
tabulador^M

indent
retrait^M
Einzugtaste^F
tecla^F de sangrado^M

decimal tab
tabulateur^M décimal
Dezimal-Tabuliertaste^F
tabulador^M decimal

shift lock key
touche^F fixe-majuscules^F
Umschaltfeststelltaste^F
tecla^F de seguro^M para las mayúsculas^F

centring
centrage^M
Zentriertaste^F
tecla^F de centrado^M

shift key
touche^F-majuscules^F
Umschalttaste^F
tecla^F de mayúsculas^F

spelling corrector
correcteur^M orthographique
Rechtschreibkorrekturtaste^F
corrector^M de ortografía^F

text
texte^M
Texttaste^F
texto^M

code
code^M
Code-Taste^F
código^M

EXEGI MONUMEN

INDENT

MARGIN RELEASE

DEC TAB

TAB

CENTER

LOCK

SPELL

SHIFT

TEXT

CODE

paper support
support-papier^M
Papierstütze^F
soporte^M del papel^M

paper release lever
levier^M de dégagement^M du papier^M
Papierlösehebel^M
palanca^F de aflojar el papel^M

paper bail release lever
levier^M de dégagement^M du presse-papier^M
Papierfreigabehebel^M
palanca^F para liberar el sujetapapel^M

platen knob
bouton^M d'interligne^M variable
Walzendrehknopf^M
embrague^M de espacios^M

top plate
capot^M
Gehäuseabdeckung^F
lámina^F superior

word correction
correction^F de mots^M
Wortkorrekturtaste^F
corrección^F de palabras^F

character correction
correction^F de caractères^M
Zeichenkorrekturtaste^F
corrección^F de caracteres^M

half indexing
positionnement^M du papier^M
Hoch-/Tiefstelltaste^F
indicador^M de la mitad^F

carriage return
retour^M de chariot^M
Wagenrücklauftaste^F
tecla^F de regreso^M del carro^M

margin control
commande^F de marge^F
Randkontrolltaste^F
control^M del margen^M

tab setting
contrôle^M de tabulation^F
Tabulatoreinstelltaste^F
ajuste^M del tabulador^M

set
validation^F
Tabulatorsetztaste^F
ajuste^M

relocation
repositionnement^M
Fixiertaste^F
otra posición^F

mode
mode^M
Mode-Taste^F
modalidad^F

space bar
barre^F d'espacement^M
Leertaste^F
barra^F espaciadora

CONFIGURATION OF AN OFFICE AUTOMATION SYSTEM
CONFIGURATION^F D'UN SYSTÈME^M BUREAUTIQUE
ZUSAMMENSTELLUNG^F EINES AUTOMATISIERTEN BÜROS^N
CONFIGURACIÓN^F DEL SISTEMA^M DE UNA OFICINA^F AUTOMATIZADA

INPUT DEVICES
PÉRIPHÉRIQUES^M D'ENTRÉE^F
EINGABEGERÄTE^N
UNIDADES^F DE ENTRADA^F DE INFORMACIÓN^F

keyboard
clavier^M
Tastatur^F
teclado^M

mouse
souris^F
Maus^F
ratón^M

joystick
manche^M à balai^M
Joystick^M
palanca^F de mando^M

trackball
boule^F
Rollkugel^F
bola^F de rastreo^M

digitizing pad
tablette^F graphique
Digitalisierungsunterlage^F
almohadilla^F digitalizada

video cassette recorder
magnétoscope^M
Videorekorder^M
videograbadora^F

video camera
caméra^F vídeo
Videokamera^F
cámara^F de vídeo^M

optical scanner
scanneur^M
Scanner^M
explorador^M óptico

CD/ROM player
lecteur^M de disque^M compact
CD-ROM-Laufwerk^N
lector^M de CD-ROM

COMMUNICATION DEVICES
PÉRIPHÉRIQUES^M DE COMMUNICATION^F
ÜBERTRAGUNGSGERÄTE^N
UNIDADES^F DE COMUNICACIÓN^F

modem
modem^M
Modem^N
módem^M

video monitor
écran^M
Bildschirm^M
monitor^M de vídeo^M

personal computer
microordinateur^M
Personalcomputer^M
ordenador^M personal

DATA STORAGE DEVICES
PÉRIPHÉRIQUES^M DE STOCKAGE^M
SPEICHERGERÄTE^N
UNIDADES^F DE ALMACENAMIENTO^F
DE INFORMACIÓN^F

hard disc drive
lecteur^M de disque^M dur
Festplattenlaufwerk^N
unidad^F del disco^M duro

diskette, floppy disc
disquette^F
Diskette^F
diskette^M

floppy disc drive
lecteur^M de disquette^F
Diskettenlaufwerk^N
unidad^F de diskettes^M

cassette
cassette^F
Kassette^F
casete^F

cassette drive
lecteur^M de cassette^F
Kassettenlaufwerk^N
unidad^F de casetes^F

network communication
communication' par réseau^M
Netzwerkkommunikation^F
red' de comunicación'

OUTPUT DEVICES
PÉRIPHÉRIQUES^M DE SORTIE^F
AUSGABEGERÄTE^N
UNIDADES' DE SALIDA' DE INFORMACIÓN'

video monitor
écran^M
Bildschirm^M
monitor^M de vídeo^M

desktop video unit
unité' vidéo
Schreibtisch-Videogerät^N
consola' de la unidad' de vídeo^M

keyboard
clavier^M
Tastatur^F
teclado^M

mouse
souris'
Maus'
ratón^M

laser printer
imprimante' laser^M
Laserdrucker^M
impresora' láser

dot matrix printer
imprimante' matricielle
Nadeldrucker^M
impresora' matriz

film recorder
enregistreur^M de film^M
Filmaufnahmegerät^N
filmadora'

imagesetter
composeuse'
Imagesetter^M
ajuste' de imagen'

cartridge drive
lecteur^M de cartouche'
Magnetbandlaufwerk^N
unidad' de cartuchos^M

cartridge
cartouche'
Magnetband^N
cartucho^M de película'

optical disc drive
lecteur^M de disque^M optique
Bildplattenlaufwerk^N
unidad' de disco^M óptico

optical disc
disque^M optique
Bildplatte'
disco^M óptico

compact disc unit
unité' de disque^M compact
CD-Lesegerät^N
unidad' de disco^M compacto

plotter
traceur^M
Plotter^M
graficador^M

527

BASIC COMPONENTS
SYSTÈME^M DE BASE^F
GRUNDBAUTEILE^N
COMPONENTES^M BÁSICOS

OFFICE AUTOMATION • **BUREAUTIQUE**
BÜROAUTOMATION • **AUTOMATIZACIÓN DE LA OFICINA**

PERSONAL COMPUTER (VIEW FROM ABOVE)
MICRO-ORDINATEUR^M (VUE^F EN PLONGÉE^F)
PERSONALCOMPUTER^M
VISTA^F POR ENCIMA DE UN ORDENADOR^M PERSONAL

expansion connector
connecteur^M d'extension^F
Speichererweiterungsanschluß^M
conector^M de expansión^F

microprocessor
microprocesseur^M
Mikroprozessor^M
microprocesador^M

random access memory (RAM) module
module^M de mémoire^F vive (RAM)
Arbeitsspeicher(RAM)-Modul^N
módulo^M de acceso^M a la memoria^F RAM

battery
pile^F
Batterie^F
batería^F

power supply
bloc^M d'alimentation^F électrique
Netzanschlußgerät^N
fuente^F de alimentación^F

fan
ventilateur^M
Kühlgebläse^N
ventilador^M

sound digitizing processor
processeur^M de sons^M
Klangprozessor^M
procesador^M digital de sonido^M

coprocessor
coprocesseur^M
Ko-Prozessor^M
coprocesador^M

read-only memory (ROM) module
module^M de mémoire^F morte (ROM)
ROM-Modul^N
módulo^M de lectura de memoria^F
ROM unicamente

disc drive port
port^M lecteur^M de disque^M
Anschluß^M für Diskettenlaufwerk^N
conexión^F para unidad^F de disco^M

peripheral device port
port^M périphérique^M
Anschluß^M für Peripheriegeräte^N
conexión^F para unidades^F periféricas

video port
port^M vidéo
Monitoranschluß^M
conexión^F para el vídeo^M

network port
port^M réseau^M
Netzwerkanschluß^M
conexión^F para la red^F

keyboard port
port^M clavier^M
Tastaturanschluß^M
conexión^F para el teclado^M

modem port
port^M modem^M
Modemanschluß^M
conexión^F para el módem^M

printer port
port^M imprimante^F
Druckeranschluß^M
conexión^F para la impresora^F

insulating sheet
surface^F isolante
Isolierabdeckung^F
lámina^F aislante

hard disc bus
bus^M du disque^M dur
Festplattenbus^M
barra^F colectora del disco^M duro

printed circuit
circuit^M imprimé
Platine^F
circuito^M impreso

floppy disc drive
lecteur^M de disquette^F
Diskettenlaufwerk^N
unidad^F del disco^M flexible

hard disc drive
lecteur^M de disque^M dur
Festplattenlaufwerk^N
unidad^F del disco^M duro

data bus
bus^M de données^F
Datenbus^M
barra^F colectora de información^F

VIDEO MONITOR
ÉCRAN*M*
BILDSCHIRMEINHEIT*F*
MONITOR*M* DEL VÍDEO*M*

vertical control
réglage*M* vertical
vertikale Einstellung*F*
control*M* vertical

horizontal control
réglage*M* horizontal
horizontale Einstellung*F*
control*M* horizontal

centring control
réglage*M* de centrage*M*
Zentriereinstellung*F*
control*M* de centrado*M*

contrast control
réglage*M* du contraste*M*
Kontrastregler*M*
control*M* de contraste*M*

power indicator
témoin*M* d'alimentation*F*
Leuchtanzeige*F*
indicador*M* de encendido*M*

power switch
interrupteur*M*
Netzschalter*M*
interruptor*M*

brightness control
réglage*M* de la luminosité*F*
Helligkeitsregler*M*
control*M* de brillo*M*

FLOPPY DISC
DISQUETTE*F* **SOUPLE**
FLOPPY-DISK*F*
DISCO*M* **FLEXIBLE**

jacket
enveloppe*F*
Hülle*F*
cubierta*F*

access window
fenêtre*F* de lecture*F*
Zugriffsöffnung*F*
ventana*F* de acceso*M*

index hole
trou*M*-repère*M*
Indexöffnung*F*
índice*M*

write protect notch
encoche*F* de protection*F*
Schreibschutzöffnung*F*
muesca*F* de protección*F*

disc
disque*M*
Diskette*F*
disco*M*

MINI-FLOPPY DISC
DISQUETTE*F* **RIGIDE**
MINI-DISKETTE*F*
DISCO*M* **FLEXIBLE PEQUEÑO**

access window
fenêtre*F* de lecture*F*
Zugriffsöffnung*F*
ventana*F* de acceso*M*

jacket
enveloppe*F*
Hülle*F*
infraestructura*F*

shutter
volet*M*
Verschluß*M*
obturador*M*

protect tab
taquet*M* de verrouillage*M*
Schreibschutz*M*
lengüeta*F* protectora

disc
disque*M*
Platte*F*
disco*M*

HARD DISC DRIVE
LECTEUR*M* **DE DISQUE***M* **DUR**
FESTPLATTENLAUFWERK*N*
UNIDAD*F* **DEL DISCO***M* **DURO**

actuator arm
guide*M*
Sucharm*M*
brazo*M* actuador

actuator arm motor
moteur*M* de guides*M*
Führungsschienenantrieb*M*
motor*M* del brazo*M* actuador

disc
disque*M*
Platte*F*
disco*M*

disc motor
moteur*M* de disques*M*
Plattenantrieb*M*
motor*M* del disco*M*

read/write head
tête*F* de lecture*F*/écriture*F*
Schreib-/Lesekopf*M*
cabeza*F* de lectura*F* \ escritura*F*

529

BASIC COMPONENTS
SYSTÈME^M DE BASE^F
GRUNDBAUTEILE^N
COMPONENTES^M BÁSICOS

KEYBOARD
CLAVIER^M
TASTATUR^F
TECLADO^M

function key
touche^F programmable
Funktionstasten^F
tecla^F de función^F

return key
touche^F de retour^M
Eingabetaste^F
tecla^F de aceptación^F

start-up key
touche^F de démarrage^M
Reset-Taste^F
tecla^F de corrección^F

tab key
touche^F de tabulateur^M
Tab-Taste^F
tecla^F de tabulación^F

shift lock key
touche^F fixe-majuscules^M
Umschaltfeststelltaste^F
tecla^F seguro^M de mayúsculas^F

delete key
touche^F d'effacement^M
Löschtaste^F
tecla^F de supresión^F

enter key
touche^F d'envoi^M
Eingabetaste^F
tecla^F de entrada^F

extended character range
jeu^M étendu de caractères^M
Taste^F für erweiterten Zeichensatz^M
juego^M extenso de caracteres^M

alphanumeric keyboard
clavier^M alphanumérique
alphanumerisches Tastenfeld^N
teclado^M alfanumérico

numeric keypad
clavier^M numérique
numerisches Tastenfeld^N
teclado^M numérico

control key
touche^F de service^M
Steuerungstaste^F
tecla^F de servicio^M

space bar
barre^F d'espacement^M
Leertaste^F
barra^F espaciadora

cursor movement keys
touches^F de directivité^F
Richtungstasten^F
teclas^F direccionales

shift key
touche^F majuscule^F
Umschalttasten^F
tecla^F de mayúsculas^F

command key
touche^F de commande^F
Befehlstaste^F
tecla^F de mando^M

MOUSE
SOURIS^F
MAUS^F
RATÓN^M

connection cable
câble^M de raccordement^M
Verbindungskabel^N
cable^M de conexión^F

roller
galet^M
Laufrolle^F
rodamiento^M

lock dial
verrou^M
Kugelhalterung^F
retén^M de la esfera^F

button
bouton^M
Taste^F
botón^M

ball
bille^F
Kugel^F
esfera^F

DOT MATRIX PRINTER
IMPRIMANTE^F MATRICIELLE
NADELDRUCKER^M
IMPRESORA^F MATRIZ

OFFICE AUTOMATION
BUREAUTIQUE

BÜROAUTOMATION
AUTOMATIZACIÓN DE LA OFICINA

platen
cylindre^M
Walze^F
rodillo^M

paper bail
presse-papier^M
Papierführungsstange^F
prensapapel^M

paper clamp
presse-ergots^M
Papierklammer^F
abrazadera^F para el papel^M

paper bail roller
galet^M du presse-papier^M
Papierhalterollen^F
guía^F del prensapapel^M

platen knob
molette^F du cylindre^M
Walzendrehknopf^M
perilla^F del rodillo^M

feed pin
ergot^M d'entraînement^M
Papierführungsstachel^M
tractor^M de avance^M

paper advance setting
mode^M d'entraînement^M du papier^M
Papierfreigabehebel^M
ajuste^M de avance^M del papel^M

on/off
select
print quality
line feed
form feed

paper guide
guide-papier^M
Papierführung^F
guía^F del papel^M

ribbon cartridge
cartouche^F de ruban^M
Farbbandkassette^F
cartucho^M para la cinta^F

data bus
bus^M des données^F
Datenbus^M
barra^F colectora de información^F

print head drive
entraînement^M de la tête^F d'impression^F
Druckkopfantrieb^M
unidad^F de la cabeza^F impresora

print head
tête^F d'impression^F
Druckkopf^M
cabeza^F impresora

indicator lights
voyants^M
Leuchtanzeigen^F
luces^F indicadoras

control knobs
boutons^M de commande^F
Einstelltasten^F
botones^M de control^M

PHOTOCOPIER
PHOTOCOPIEURᴹ
FOTOKOPIERERᴹ
FOTOCOPIADORAᶠ

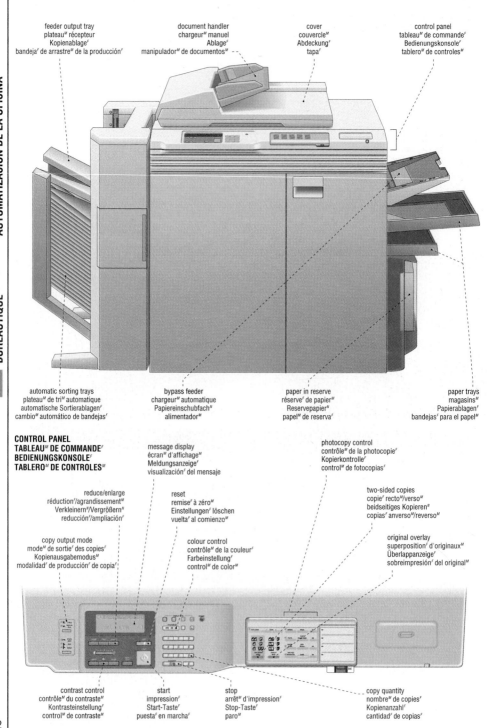

feeder output tray
plateauᴹ récepteurᶠ
Kopienablageᶠ
bandejaᶠ de arrastreᶠ de la producciónᶠ

document handler
chargeurᴹ manuel
Ablageᶠ
manipuladorᴹ de documentosᴹ

cover
couvercleᴹ
Abdeckungᶠ
tapaᶠ

control panel
tableauᴹ de commandeᶠ
Bedienungskonsoleᶠ
tableroᴹ de controlesᴹ

automatic sorting trays
plateauᴹ de triᶠ automatique
automatische Sortierablagenᶠ
cambioᴹ automático de bandejasᶠ

bypass feeder
chargeurᴹ automatique
Papiereinschubfachᴺ
alimentadorᴹ

paper in reserve
réserveᶠ de papierᴹ
Reservepapierᴺ
papelᴹ de reservaᶠ

paper trays
magasinsᴹ
Papierablagenᶠ
bandejasᶠ para el papelᴹ

CONTROL PANEL
TABLEAUᴹ **DE COMMANDE**ᶠ
BEDIENUNGSKONSOLEᶠ
TABLEROᴹ **DE CONTROLES**ᴹ

message display
écranᴹ d'affichageᴹ
Meldungsanzeigeᶠ
visualizaciónᶠ del mensaje

photocopy control
contrôleᶠ de la photocopieᶠ
Kopierkontrolleᶠ
controlᴹ de fotocopiasᶠ

reduce/enlarge
réductionᶠ/agrandissementᴹ
Verkleinernⁿ/Vergrößernⁿ
reducciónᶠ/ampliaciónᶠ

reset
remiseᶠ à zéroᴹ
Einstellungenᶠ löschen
vueltaᶠ al comienzoᴹ

two-sided copies
copieᶠ rectoᴹ/versoᴹ
beidseitiges Kopierenⁿ
copiasᶠ anversoᴹ/reversoᴹ

copy output mode
modeᴹ de sortieᶠ des copiesᶠ
Kopienausgabemodusᴹ
modalidadᶠ de producciónᶠ de copiaᶠ

colour control
contrôleᴹ de la couleurᶠ
Farbeinstellungᶠ
controlᴹ de colorᴹ

original overlay
superpositionᶠ d'originauxᴹ
Überlappanzeigeᶠ
sobreimpresiónᶠ del originalᴹ

contrast control
contrôleᴹ du contrasteᴹ
Kontrasteinstellungᶠ
controlᴹ de contrasteᴹ

start
impressionᶠ
Start-Tasteᶠ
puestaᶠ en marchaᶠ

stop
arrêtᴹ d'impressionᶠ
Stop-Tasteᶠ
paroᴹ

copy quantity
nombreᴹ de copiesᶠ
Kopienanzahlᶠ
cantidadᶠ de copiasᶠ

MUSIK
MÚSICA

MUSIC
MUSIQUE

TRADITIONAL MUSICAL INSTRUMENTS
INSTRUMENTS^M TRADITIONNELS
TRADITIONELLE MUSIKINSTRUMENTE^N
INSTRUMENTOS^M MUSICALES TRADICIONALES

ZITHER
CITHARE^F
ZITHER^F
CÍTARA^F

LYRE
LYRE^F
LYRA^F
LIRA^F

finger board
touche^F
Griffbrett^N
traste^M

soundboard
caisse^F de résonnance^F
Resonanzdecke^F
caja^F sonora

crossbar
traverse^F
Querjoch^N
travesaño^M

arm
montant^M
Jocharm^M
brazo^M

open strings
cordes^F d'accompagnement^M
Freisaiten^F
cuerdas^F de acompañamiento^M

melody strings
cordes^F de mélodie^F
Melodiesaiten^F
cuerdas^F melódicas

soundboard
caisse^F de résonnance^F
Resonanzdecke^F
caja^F sonora

BALALAIKA
BALALAÏKA^F
BALALAIKA^F
BALALAIKA^F

triangular body
caisse^F triangulaire
dreieckiger Korpus^M
caja^F triangular

MANDOLIN
MANDOLINE^F
MANDOLINE^F
MANDOLINA^F

BANJO
BANJO^M
BANJO^N
BANJO^M

circular body
caisse^F circulaire
runder Korpus^M
caja^F circular

pear-shaped body
caisse^F bombée
birnenförmiger Korpus^M
caja^F media pera^F

plectrum
médiator^M
Plektron^N
púa^F

MUSIC
MUSIQUE

MUSIK
MÚSICA

535

TRADITIONAL MUSICAL INSTRUMENTS
INSTRUMENTS^M TRADITIONNELS
TRADITIONELLE MUSIKINSTRUMENTE^N
INSTRUMENTOS^M MUSICALES TRADICIONALES

ACCORDION
ACCORDÉON^M
AKKORDEON^N
ACORDEÓN^M

button
bouton^M
Knopf^M
botón^M

bellows strap
fermeture^F du soufflet^M
Balgenverschluß^M
seguro^M del fuelle^M

treble register
registre^M des aigus^M
Diskantregister^N
registro^M de altos^M

treble keyboard
clavier^M chant^M
Diskanttastatur^F
teclado^M triple

key
touche^F
Taste^F
tecla^F

grille
grille^F
Gitter^M
rejilla^F

bass keyboard
clavier^M accompagnement^M
Baßtastatur^F
teclado^M de los bajos^M

bass register
registre^M des basses^F
Baßregister^N
registros^M de los bajos^M

bellows
soufflet^M
Balg^M
doble fuelle^M

BAGPIPES
CORNEMUSE^F
DUDELSACK^M
GAITA^F

JEW'S HARP
GUIMBARDE^F
MAULTROMMEL^F
BIRIMBAO^M

drone pipe
bourdon^M
Bordunpfeife^F
gran roncón^M

tongue
lame^F
Zunge^F
lengüeta^F de la caña^F

blow pipe
tuyau^M d'insufflation^F
Blaspfeife^F
portaviento^M

frame
cadre^M
Rahmen^M
estructura^F

stock
monture^F
Aufsatzstück^M
cabo^M

harmonica
harmonica^M
Mundharmonika^F
armónica^F

windbag
sac^M
Windsack^M
saco^M de piel^F

panpipe
flûte^F de Pan
Panflöte^F
zampoña^F

chanter
chalumeau^M
Melodiepfeife^F
caramillo^M

STAFF
PORTÉE^F
LINIENSYSTEM^N
PENTAGRAMA^F

ledger line
ligne^F supplémentaire
Hilfslinie^F
línea^F suplementaria

space
interligne^M
Zwischenraum^M
espacio^M

line
ligne^F
Notenlinie^F
línea^F

CLEFS
CLÉS^F
NOTENSCHLÜSSEL^M
CLAVES^F

treble clef
clé^F de sol^M
Violinschlüssel^M
clave^F de sol

bass clef
clé^F de fa^M
Baßschlüssel^M
clave^F de fa

alto clef
clé^F d'ut^M
Altschlüssel^M
clave^F de do

bar line
barre^F de mesure^F
Taktstrich^M
barra^F de compás^M

TIME SIGNATURES
MESURES^F
TAKTARTEN^F
COMPÁS^M

two-two time
mesure^F à deux temps^M
Zweihalbetakt^M
de dos mitades^F

four-four time
mesure^F à quatre temps^M
Vierviertteltakt^M
de cuatro cuartos^M

repeat mark
barre^F de reprise^F
Wiederholungszeichen^N
barra^F de repetición^F

three-four time
mesure^F à trois temps^M
Dreivierteltakt^M
de tres cuartos^M

SCALE
GAMME^F
TONLEITER^F
ESCALA^F

c	d	e	f	g	a	b	c
do^M	ré^M	mi^M	fa^M	sol^M	la^M	si^M	do^M
c	d	e	f	g	a	b	c
do(C)	re(D)	mi(E)	fa^F	sol(G)	la(A)	si(B)	do(C)

INTERVALS
INTERVALLES^M
INTERVALLE^N
INTERVALOS^M

unison
unisson^M
Prime^F
unísono^M

third
tierce^F
Terz^F
tercera^F

fifth
quinte^F
Quinte^F
quinta^F

seventh
septième^F
Septime^F
séptima^F

second
seconde^F
Sekunde^F
segunda^F

fourth
quarte^F
Quarte^F
cuarta^F

sixth
sixte^F
Sexte^F
sexta^F

octave
octave^F
Oktave^F
octava^F

MUSIC
MUSIQUE

MUSIK
MÚSICA

537

MUSIK
MÚSICA

MUSIC
MUSIQUE

CHORD
ACCORD^M
AKKORD^M
ACORDE^M

OTHER SIGNS
AUTRES SIGNES^M
ANDERE ZEICHEN^N
OTROS SIGNOS^M

accent mark
accent^M
Marcato-Zeichen^N
acento^M

arpeggio
arpège^M
Arpeggio^N
arpegio^M

tie
liaison^F
Bindebogen^M
ligadura^F

pause
point^M d'orgue^M
Pause^F
calderón^M

MUSICAL ACCESSORIES
ACCESSOIRES^M
MUSIKZUBEHÖR^N
ACCESORIOS^M MUSICALES

MUSIC STAND
PUPITRE^M À MUSIQUE^F
NOTENSTÄNDER^M
ATRIL^M

tuning fork
diapason^M
Stimmgabel^F
diapasón^M

QUARTZ METRONOME
MÉTRONOME^M À QUARTZ^M
QUARZMETRONOM^N
METRÓNOMO^M DE CUARZO^M

light signal
signal^M lumineux
optisches Signal^N
señal^F luminosa

standard A
la^M universel
Kammerton^M A
pauta^F A

sound signal
signal^M sonore
akkustisches Signal^N
señal^F del sonido^M

music rest
pupitre^M
Notenablage^F
soporte^M plegable

case
boîtier^M
Kasten^M
caja^F

METRONOME
MÉTRONOME^M MÉCANIQUE
METRONOM^N
METRÓNOMO^M

adjusting lever
levier^M de réglage^M
Verstellschraube^F
tornillo^M de ajuste^M

pendulum bar
tige^F de pendule^M
Pendel^N
varilla^F del péndulo^M

rod
tige^F
Stab^M
varilla^F

tempo scale
échelle^F des mouvements^M
Temposkala^F
escala^F de tiempo^M

key spindle
remontoir^M
Schlüssel^M
llave^F

sliding weight
massette^F de réglage^M
Laufgewicht^N
peso^M corredizo

tripod
trépied^M
Dreifuß^M
trípode^M

escapement mechanism
mécanisme^M à échappement^M
Steigradmechanismus^M
mecanismo^M de escape^M

pivot
pivot^M
Pinne^F
pivote^M

fixed weight
masse^F pendulaire
festehendes Gewicht^o
péndulo^M

MUSIK
MÚSICA

MUSIC
MUSIQUE

UPRIGHT PIANO
PIANO^M DROIT
KLAVIER^N
PIANO^M VERTICAL

hammer
marteau^M
Hammer^M
macillo^M

pin block
sommier^M
Stimmstock^M
clavijero^M

muffler felt
feutre^M d'étouffoir^M
Moderatorfilz^M
amortiguador^M de fieltro^M

pressure bar
barre^F de pression^F
Drucksteg^M
ceja^F

key
touche^F
Taste^F
tecla^F

hammer rail
barre^F de repos^M des marteaux^M
Hammerleiste^F
apoyo^M del macillo^M

tuning pin
cheville^F d'accord^M
Stimmnagel^M
clavija^F

case
caisse^F
Gehäuse^N
caja^F

pedal rod
tringle^F de pédale^F
Pedalstange^F
varilla^F del pedal^M

soft pedal
pédale^F douce
Pianopedal^N
pedal^M suave

keybed
plateau^M de clavier^M
Klaviaturboden^M
asiento^M del teclado^M

keyboard
clavier^M
Tastatur^F
teclado^M

sostenuto pedal
pédale^F de sourdine^F
Moderatorpedal^N
pedal^M de amortiguación^F

soundboard
table^F d'harmonie^F
Resonanzboden^M
caja^F harmónica

treble bridge
chevalet^M des aigus^M
Diskantsteg^M
puente^M de los altos^M

sustaining pedal
pédale^F forte
Fortepedal^N
pedal^M de la sordina^F

metal frame
cadre^M métallique
Metallrahmen^M
armazón^M de metal^M

strings
cordes^F
Saitenbezug^M
cuerdas^F

hitch pin
pointe^F d'attache^F
Plattenstift^M
punta^F de sujeción^F

bass bridge
chevalet^M des basses^F
Baßsteg^M
puente^M de los bajos^M

string
corde^F
Saite^F
cuerda^F

damper
étouffoir^M
Dämpfer^M
apagador^M

hammer felt
feutre^M
Hammerfilz^M
macillo^M de fieltro^M

hammer
marteau^M
Hammer^M
macillo^M

damper rail
barre^F d'étouffoir^M
Dämpferpralleiste^F
apoyo^M de la sordina^F

hammer rail
barre^F de repos^M des marteaux^M
Hammerruheleiste^F
apoyo^M del macillo^M

hammer shank
manche^M
Hammerstiel^M
vástago^M del macillo^M

hammer butt
noix^F
Hammernuß^F
cabo^M del macillo^M

catcher
contre-attrape^F
Gegenfänger^M
receptor^M

back check
attrape^F
Fänger^M
descanso^M del macillo^M

bridle tape
lanière^F
Bändchen^N
tirante^M

regulating button
bouton^M d'échappement^M
Auslösepuppe^F
regulador^M

jack spring
ressort^M d'échappement^M
Stoßzungenschraubenfeder^F
resorte^M del martinete^M

damper lever
lame^F d'étouffoir^M
Dämpferarm^M
palanca^F de la sordina^F

hammer jack
levier^M d'échappement^M
Stoßzunge^F
martinete^M

action lever
chevalet^M
Hebeglied^N
mecanismo^M de la palanca^F

capstan button
pilote^M
Pilote^F
cabrestante^M

balance rail
pointe^F
Waagebalken^M
fulcro^M

key
touche^F
Taste^F
tecla^F

MUSIC
MUSIQUE

MUSIK
MÚSICA

ORGAN
ORGUE^M
ORGEL^F
ÓRGANO^M ELECTRONEUMÁTICO

ORGAN CONSOLE
CONSOLE^F D'ORGUE^M
ORGELSPIELTISCH^M
CONSOLA^F

music rest
pupitre^M
Notenablage^F
atril^M

stop knob
bouton^M de registre^M
Registerzug^M
botón^M de registro^M

swell organ manual
clavier^M de récit^M
Manual^N für das Oberwerk^N
teclado^M del órgano^M de expresión^F

coupler-tilt tablet
domino^M d'accouplement^M
Koppel-Kipptaste^F
tableta^F de resonancia^F

choir organ manual
clavier^M de positif^M
Manual^N für das Rückpositiv^N
teclado^M del órgano^M positivo

manuals
claviers^M manuels
Manuale^M
teclados^M manuales

great organ manual
clavier^M de grand orgue^M
Manual^N für das Hauptwerk^N
teclado^M del gran órgano^M

thumb piston
bouton^M de combinaisons^F
Druckknopf^M
botón^M de acoplamiento^M

crescendo pedal
pédale^F crescendo^M
Rollschweller^M
pedal^M crescendo

toe piston
pédale^F de combinaisons^F
Fußtritt^M
acoplamiento^M de pedal^M

pedal key
touche^F de pédalier^M
Pedaltaste^F
tecla^F de pedal^M

swell pedals
pédales^F d'expression^F
Jalousieschweller^M
pedal^M de expresión^F

pedal keyboard
clavier^M à pédales^F
Pedalklaviatur^F
pedalero^M

FLUE PIPE
TUYAU^M À BOUCHE^F
LIPPENPFEIFE^F
CAÑO^M DEL ÓRGANO^M

REED PIPE
TUYAU^M À ANCHE^F
ZUNGENPFEIFE^F
TUBO^M DE LENGÜETA^F

body
corps^M
Körper^M
tapa^F

languid
biseau^M
Kern^M
bisel^M

resonator
pavillon^M
Schallbecher^M
resonador^M

tuning wire
rasette^F
Stimmkrücke^F
afinador^M

upper lip
lèvre^F supérieure
Oberlippe^F
labio^M superior

block
noyau^M
Bleikopf^M
bloque^M

mouth
bouche^F
Aufschnitt^M
boca^F

wedge
coin^M
Keil^M
cuña^F

lower lip
lèvre^F inférieure
Unterlippe^F
labio^M inferior

tongue
languette^F
Zunge^F
lengüeta^F

foot
pied^M
Fuß^M
pie^M

shallot
anche^F
Kehle^F
caña^F

flue
lumière^F
Kernspalte^F
caño^M

boot
pied^M
Stiefel^M
pie^M

foot hole
orifice^M du pied^M
Fußbohrung^F
orificio^M del pie^M

foot hole
orifice^M du pied^M
Fußbohrung^F
orificio^M del pie^M

MECHANISM OF THE ORGAN
MÉCANISME^M DE L'ORGUE^M
ORGELMECHANIK^F
MECANISMO^M DEL ÓRGANO^M

rackboard
faux sommier
Pfeifenrastbrett^N
falso^M secreto^M

upperboard
chape^F
Pfeifenstock^M
tapa^F

rackboard support
pilotin^M
Stützen^F der Pfeifenrastbretter^N
soporte^M del falso^M secreto^M

slider
registre^M coulissant
Registerschleife^F
corredera^F

bearer
faux registre^M
Damm^M
falso^M registro^M

bottomboard
laye^F
Unterbrett^N
caja^F del aire^M

wind supply
alimentation^F en air^M
Windzuleitung^F
soplador^M

wind trunk
porte-vent^M
Windkanal^M
conducto^M del aire^M

pipe
tuyau^M
Pfeife^F
tubo^M

wind chest table
table^F du sommier^M
Fundamenttafel^F
tabla^F harmónica

pallet
soupape^F
Spielventil^N
válvula^F

air sealing gland
boursette^F
Pulpete^F
poma^F

manual
clavier^M manuel
Manual^N
manual^M

key
touche^F
Taste^F
tecla^F

roller board and arms
abrégé^M et pilotes^M
Wellbrett^N und Wellärmchen^N
tablero^M de rodillos^M y brazos^M

tracker
vergette^F
Abstrakte^F
varillas^F

pallet spring
ressort^M de soupape^F
Ventilfeder^F
resorte^M de válvula^F

stop rod
tirant^M de registre^M
Registerleiste^F
varilla^F de registro^M

stop knob
bouton^M de registre^M
Registerzug^M
perilla^F de registro^M

PRODUCTION OF SOUND
PRODUCTION^F DU SON^M
TONERZEUGUNG^F
PRODUCCIÓN^F DEL SONIDO^M

rackboard
faux sommier^M
Pfeifenrastbrett^N
falso^M secreto^{M}

upperboard
chape^F
Pfeifenstock^M
tapa^F superior

wind chest
sommier^M
Windlade^F
caja^F neumática

wind duct
conduit^M
Windkanal^M
conducto^M del aire^M

blower
soufflerie^F
Gebläse^N
fuelle^M

pipework
tuyauterie^F
Pfeifenwerk^N
cañonería^F

wind trunk
porte-vent^M
Windkanal^M
cañón^M de la presión^F

bellow
soufflet^M
Balg^M
bramador^M

reservoir
réservoir^M
Magazinbalg^M
regulador^M de la presión^F

VIOLIN
VIOLON^M
VIOLINE^F
VIOLÍN^M

scroll
volute^F
Schnecke^F
voluta^F

peg
cheville^F
Wirbel^M
clavija^F

peg box
chevillier^M
Wirbelkasten^M
clavijero^M

nut
sillet^F
Sattel^M
cejilla^F

neck
manche^M
Hals^M
mástil^M

finger board
touche^F
Griffbrett^N
diapasón^M

string
corde^F
Saite^F
cuerda^F

soundboard
table^F d'harmonie^F
Resonanzdecke^F
caja^F sonora

purfling
filet^M
Einlage^F
filete^M

waist
échancrure^F
Bügel^M
escotadura^F

bridge
chevalet^M
Steg^M
puente^M

sound hole
ouïe^F
Schalloch^N
abertura^F para el sonido^M

tailpiece
cordier^M
Saitenhalter^M
cordal^M

chin rest
mentonnière^F
Kinnstütze^F
apoyo^M para el mentón^M

end button
bouton^M
Untersattel^M
botón^M

BOW
ARCHET^M
BOGEN^M
ARCO^M

head
tête^F
Kopf^M
cabeza^F

point
pointe^F
Spitze^F
punta^F

stick
baguette^F
Stange^F
vara^F

hair
mèche^F
Haar^N
crin^F

rib
éclisse^F
Zarge^F
reborde^M

handle
poignée^F
Griff^M
mango^M

heel
talon^M
Bogenansatz^M
talón^M

frog
hausse^F
Frosch^M
alza^F

screw
vis^F
Schraube^F
tornillo^M

MUSIK
MÚSICA

MUSIC
MUSIQUE

544

double bass
contrebasse^F
Kontrabaß^M
contrabajo^M

cello
violoncelle^M
Cello^N
violoncelo^M

viola
alto^M
Bratsche^F
viola^F

violin
violon^M
Violine^F
violín^M

HARP
HARPE^F
HARFE^F
ARPA^F

MUSIC
MUSIQUE
MUSIK
MÚSICA

tuning peg
cheville^F
Stimmwirbel^M
clavija^F

neck
console^F
Hals^M
consola^F

crown
chapiteau^M
Krone^F
corona^F

shoulder
crosse^F
Schulter^F
hombrera^F

string
corde^F
Saite^F
cuerda^F

soundboard
table^F d'harmonie^F
Resonanzdecke^F
caja^F sonora

soundbox
caisse^F de résonance^F
Resonanzkörper^M
caja^F de sonido^M

pillar
colonne^F
Baronstange^F
columna^F

pedal
pédale^F
Pedal^N
pedal^M

pedestal
cuvette^F
Sockel^M
pedestal^M

foot
pied^M
Fuß^M
pie^M

545

MUSIC
MUSIQUE
MUSIK
MÚSICA

ACOUSTIC GUITAR
GUITARE^F ACOUSTIQUE
AKUSTISCHE GITARRE^F
GUITARRA^F CLÁSICA

head
tête^F
Kragen^M
cabeza^F

peg
cheville^F
Wirbel^M
clavija^F

nut
sillet^M
Sattel^M
cejilla^F

fret
frette^F
Bund^M
trastes^M

position marker
repère^M de touche^F
Orientierungseinlage^F
marca^F de posisición^F

neck
manche^M
Hals^M
mástil^M

heel
talon^M
Bodenplättchen^N
talón^M

rib
éclisse^F
Zarge^F
reborde^M

rose
rosace^F
Schallrose^F
roseta^F

purfling
filet^M
Einlage^F
filete^M

body
caisse^F
Korpus^M
caja^F

bridge
chevalet^M
Steg^M
puente^M

soundboard
table^F d'harmonie^F
Resonanzdecke^F
caja^F sonora

tuning peg
mécanique^F d'accordage^M
Stimmwirbel^M
clavija^F de afinación^F

head
tête^F
Kragen^M
cabeza^F

nut
sillet^M
Sattel^M
cejilla^F

finger board
touche^F
Griffbrett^N
diapasón^M

position marker
repère^M de touche^F
Orientierungseinlage^F
marca^F de posición^F

fret
frette^F
Bund^M
traste^M

neck
manche^M
Hals^M
mástil^M

pickguard
plaque^F de protection^F
Schlagschutz^M
guardacaptores^M

bass pickup
micro^M de fréquences^F graves
Baß-Tonabnehmer^M
receptor^M de los bajos^M

vibrato arm
levier^M de vibrato^M
Vibratohebel^M
palanca^F de vibración^F

midrange pickup
micro^M de fréquences^F moyennes
Mittellage-Tonabnehmer^M
receptor^M de los intermedios^M

pickup selector
sélecteur^M de micro^M
Tonabnehmer-Wahlschalter^M
selector^M de la recepción^F

treble pickup
micro^M de fréquences^F aiguës
Höhen-Tonabnehmer^M
receptor^M triple

volume control
réglage^M du volume^M
Lautstärkeregler^M
control^M de volumen^M

bridge assembly
ensemble^M du chevalet^M
Saitenaufhängung^F
puente^M de ensamblaje^M

tone control
réglage^M de la tonalité^F
Klangfarbenregler^M
control^M del sonido^M

solid body
caisse^F pleine
massiver Korpus^M
cuerpo^M sólido

output jack
jack^M de sortie^F
Anschlußbuchse^F
conector^M de salida^F

WIND INSTRUMENTS
INSTRUMENTS^M À VENT^M
BLASINSTRUMENTE^N
INSTRUMENTOS^M DE VIENTO^M

SAXOPHONE
SAXOPHONE^M
SAXOPHON^N
SAXOFÓN^M

crook key
clé^F de bocal^M
Griffhebel^M für S-Bogen^M
llave^F del bocal^M

mouthpiece
bec^M
Mundstück^N
boquilla^F

crook
bocal^M
S-Bogen^M
bocal^M

octave mechanism
mécanisme^M d'octave^F
Oktavmechanik^F
mecanismo^M para las octavas^F

reed
anche^F
Blatt^N
caramillo^M

ligature
bague^F de serrage^M
Blattschraube^F
anillo^M de ajuste^M

WOODWIND FAMILY
FAMILLE^F DES BOIS^M
FAMILIE^F DER HOLZBLASINSTRUMENTE^N
FAMILIA^F DE INSTRUMENTOS^M DE MADERA^F

piccolo
piccolo^M
Pikkoloflöte^F
pícolo^M

clarinet
clarinette^F
Klarinette^F
clarinete^M

oboe
hautbois^M
Oboe^F
oboe^M

flute
flûte^F
Querflöte^F
flauta^F

bassoon
basson^M
Fagott^N
fagot^M

saxophone
saxophone^M
Saxophon^N
saxofón^M

cor anglais
cor^M anglais
Englischhorn^N
corno^M inglés

REEDS
ANCHES^F
BLÄTTER^N
CAÑAS^F

single reed
anche^F simple
Rohrblatt^N
caña^F simple

double reed
anche^F double
Doppelblatt^N
doble caña^F

key lever
levier^M de clé^F
Klappenstiel^M
palanca^F

bell
pavillon^M
Trichter^M
pabellón^M

bell brace
attache^F de pavillon^M
Schallbecherstütze^F
sujetador^M del pabellón^M

key
clé^F
Klappe^F
llave^F

key guard
garde^F de clé^F
Klappenschutz^M
dispositivo^M de protección^F

body
corps^M
Korpus^M
cuerpo^M

key finger button
bouton^M de clé^F
Klappendrücker^M
botón^M de la llave^F

thumb rest
support^M de pouce^M
Daumenauflage^F
gancho^M del pulgar^M

breech
culasse^F
Bogen^M
culata^F

breech guard
garde^F de culasse^F
Bogenschutz^M
protector^M de la culata^F

TRUMPET
TROMPETTE*
TROMPETE*
TROMPETA*

finger button
bouton* de piston*
Drücker*
llave*

mouthpipe
branche* d'embouchure*
Mundrohr*
tubo*

mouthpiece receiver
boisseau* d'embouchure*
Mundstückaufnahme*
empate* de la boquilla*

mouthpiece
embouchure*
Mundstück*
boquilla*

thumb hook
crochet* de pouce*
Daumenring*
gancho* del pulgar*

BRASS FAMILY
FAMILLE* DES CUIVRES*****
FAMILIE* DER BLECHBLÄSER*****
FAMILIA* DE LOS METALES*****

first valve slide
coulisse* du premier piston*
erster Ventilzug*
primer pistón* móvil

valve casing
corps* de piston*
Ventilbüchse*
tubo* del pistón*

cornet
cornet* à pistons*
Kornett*
cornetín*

second valve slide
coulisse* du deuxième piston*
zweiter Ventilzug*
segundo pistón* móvil

valve
piston*
Ventil*
pistón*

trumpet
trompette*
Trompete*
trompeta*

bugle
clairon*
Bügelhorn*
clarín*

trombone
trombone*
Posaune*
trombón*

little finger hook
crochet^M de petit doigt^M
Kleinfingerhaken^M
gancho^M del meñique^M

ring
bague^F
Ring^M
anillo^M

bell
pavillon^M
Trichter^M
pabellón^M

tuning slide
coulisse^F d'accord^M
Stimmzug^M
corredera^F de afinamiento^M

third valve slide
coulisse^F du troisième piston^M
dritter Ventilzug^M
tercer pistón^M móvil

water key
soupape^F d'évacuation^F
Wasserklappe^F
llave^F para agua^F

mute
sourdine^F
Dämpfer^M
sordina^F

tuba
tuba^M
Tuba^F
tuba^F

saxhorn
saxhorn^M
Saxhorn^M
bombardino^M

French horn
cor^M d'harmonie^F
Waldhorn^N
corno^M francés

DRUMS
BATTERIE^F
TROMMELN^F
TAMBORES^M

cymbal
cymbale^F suspendue
Becken^N
platillo^M

tom-tom
tam-tam^M
Tomtom^M
tam-tam^M

Charleston cymbal
cymbale^F charleston
Charlestonmaschine^F
platillo^M charleston

superior cymbal
cymbale^F supérieure
oberes Becken^N
platillo^M superior

inferior cymbal
cymbale^F inférieure
unteres Becken^N
platillo^M inferior

drumhead
peau^F de batterie^F
Schlagfell^N
parche^M superior

snare drum
caisse^F claire
kleine Trommel^F
tambor^M

tripod stand
trépied^M
Dreifußständer^M
trípode^M

bass drum
grosse caisse^F
Baßtrommel^F
bombo^M

tension screw
vis^F de tension^F
Stellschraube^F
clavija^F de tensión^F

stand
support^M
Ständer^M
soporte^M

mallet
mailloche^F
Schlegel^M
palillo^M

pedal
pédale^F
Pedal^N
pedal^M

spur
éperon^M
Feststellspitze^F
espolón^M

MUSIK
MÚSICA

MUSIC
MUSIQUE

552

SNARE DRUM
CAISSE^F CLAIRE
KLEINE TROMMEL^F
TAMBOR^M DE TIRANTES^M

lug
attache^F
Böckchen^N
sujetador^M

tension rod
tringle^F de tension^F
Stimmeinrichtung^F
varilla^F de tensión^F

snare
cordes^F de timbre^M
Schnarrsaite^F
cuerdas^F

snare strainer
tendeur^M de timbre^M
Schnarrsaitenspanner^M
tensor^M de las cuerdas^F

snare head
peau^F de timbre^M
Resonanzfell^N
parche^M inferior

sticks
baguettes^F
Stöcke^M
palillos^M

wire brush
balai^M métallique
Jazzbesen^M
escobilla^F metálica

mallets
mailloches^F
Schlegel^M
maza^F

tenor drum
caisse^F roulante
Standtom^N
tamboril^M

KETTLEDRUM
TIMBALE^F
KESSELPAUKE^F
TIMBAL^M

tension screw
tirant^M
Spannschraube^F
barra^F sujetadora

drumhead
peau^F de batterie^F
Schlagfell^N
parche^M superior

metal counterhoop
cercle^M de serrage^M
Metallspannreifen^M
arco^M tensor

tuning gauge
manomètre^M d'accord^M
Stimmanzeiger^M
afinación^F

shell
fût^M
Kessel^M
concha^F

strut
châssis^M
Strebe^F
puntal^M

leg
pied^M
Bein^N
pata^F

tension rod
tringle^F de tension^F
Stimmeinrichtung^F
varilla^F de tensión^F

caster
roulette^F
Rolle^F
ruedecilla^F

crown
couronne^F
Aufhängung^F
corona^F

foot
pied^M
Bodenplatte^F
pata^F

pedal
pédale^F
Pedal^N
pedal^M

MUSIC
MUSIQUE
MUSIK
MÚSICA

553

PERCUSSION INSTRUMENTS
INSTRUMENTS*M* À PERCUSSION*F*
SCHLAGINSTRUMENTE*N*
INSTRUMENTOS*M* DE PERCUSIÓN*F*

TRIANGLE
TRIANGLE*M*
TRIANGEL*M*
TRIÁNGULO*M*

castanets
castagnettes*F*
Kastagnetten*F*
castañuelas*F*

TAMBOURINE
TAMBOUR*M* **DE BASQUE***M*
TAMBURIN*N*
PANDERETA*F*

metal rod
battant*M*
Stahlstab*M*
varilla*F* de acero*M*

jingle
cymbalette*F*
Schelle*F*
cascabel*M*

head
peau*F*
Fell*N*
parche*M*

cymbals
cymbales*F*
Becken*N*
platillos*M*

XYLOPHONE
XYLOPHONE*M*
XYLOPHON*N*
XILÓFONO*M*

tubular bells
carillon*M* tubulaire
Röhrenglocken*F*
campanas*F* tubulares

frame
châssis*M*
Rahmen*M*
armazón*M*

bar
lame*F*
Platte*F*
barra*F*

resonator
tube*M* de résonance*F*
Resonanzröhren*F*
resonador*M*

MUSIK
MÚSICA

MUSIC
MUSIQUE

gong
gong*M*
Gong*M*
gong*M*

ELECTRONIC INSTRUMENTS
INSTRUMENTS^M ÉLECTRONIQUES
ELEKTRONISCHE INSTRUMENTE^N
INSTRUMENTOS^M ELECTRÓNICOS

pitch wheel
modulation^F de la hauteur^F du son^M
Tonhöhenrad^N
rueda^F para ajustar el tono^M

volume control
contrôle^M du volume^M
Lautstärkeregler^M
control^M de volumen^M

SYNTHESIZER
SYNTHÉTISEUR^M
SYNTHESIZER^M
SINTETIZADOR^M

disc drive
lecteur^M de disquette^F
Diskettenlaufwerk^N
unidad^F de discos^M

fast data entry control
modification^F rapide des variables^F
Grobregler^M für Dateneingabe^F
control^M de entrada^F de información^F rápida

sequencer control
contrôle^M du séquenceur^M
Sequenzerregler^M
control^M de secuencias^F

system buttons
fonctions^F système^M
Systemschalter^M
sistema^M de botones^M

fine data entry control
modification^F fine des variables^F
Feinregler^M für Dateneingabe^F
control^M de entrada^F de información^F fina

voice edit buttons
programmation^F des voix^F
Stimmenwahlschalter^M
botones^M para editar la voz^F

modulation wheel
modulation^F du timbre^M du son^M
Modulationsrad^N
rueda^F de modulación^F

program selector
sélecteur^M de programme^M
Programmwahlschalter^M
selector^M de programa^M

keyboard
clavier^M
Tastatur^F
teclado^M

function display
affichage^M des fonctions^F
Funktionsanzeige^F
pantalla^F de funciones^F

power switch
interrupteur^M d'alimentation^F
Netzschalter^M
interruptor^M

music rest
pupitre^M
Notenablage^F
atril^M

rhythm selector
sélecteur^M de rythme^M
Rhythmuswahlschalter^M
selector^M del ritmo^M

ELECTRONIC PIANO
PIANO^M ÉLECTRONIQUE
ELEKTRONISCHES PIANO^N
PIANO^M ELECTRÓNICO

volume control
réglage^M du volume^M
Lautstärkeregler^M
control^M de volumen^M

voice selector
sélecteur^M de voix^F
Stimmenwahlschalter^M
selector^M de la voz^F

tempo control
réglage^M de tempo^M
Temporegler^M
control^M del tiempo^M

headphone jack
prise^F casque^M
Anschlußbuchse^F für Kopfhörer^M
entrada^F para auriculares^M

soft pedal
pédale^F douce
Pianopedal^N
pedal^M de los bajos^M

sustaining pedal
pédale^F forte
Fortepedal^N
pedal^M de la sordina^F

SYMPHONY ORCHESTRA
ORCHESTRE^M SYMPHONIQUE
SINFONIEORCHESTER^N
ORQUESTA^F SINFÓNICA

cornet
cornet^M à pistons^M
Kornett^N
cornetín^M

contrabassoons
contrebassons^M
Kontrafagotte^N
contrafagot^M

tubular bells
carillon^M tubulaire
Röhrenglocken^F
campanas^F tubulares

trumpets
trompettes^F
Trompeten^F
trompetas^F

clarinets
clarinettes^F
Klarinetten^F
clarinetes^M

bass clarinet
clarinette^F basse
Baßklarinette^F
clarinete^M bajo

piano
piano^M
Flügel^M
piano^M

flutes
flûtes^F
Querflöten^F
flautas^F traverseras

harps
harpes^F
Harfen^F
arpas^F

triangle
triangle^M
Triangel^M
triángulo^M

xylophone
xylophone^M
Xylophon^N
xilófono^M

castanets
castagnettes^F
Kastagnetten^F
castañuelas^F

trombones
trombones^M
Posaunen^F
trombones^M

first violins
premiers violons^M
erste Violinen^F
primeros violines^M

second violins
seconds violons^M
zweite Violinen^F
segundos violines^M

violas
altos^M
Bratschen^F
violas^F

conductor's podium
pupitre^M du chef^M d'orchestre^M
Podium^N des Dirigenten^M/der Dirigentin^F
estrado^M del director^M

bassoons
bassons^M
Fagotte^N
fagotes^M

tuba
tuba^M
Tuba^F
tuba^F

cymbals
cymbales^F
Becken^N
platillos^M

snare drum
caisse^F claire
kleine Trommel^F
tarola^F

gong
gong^M
Gong^M
gong^M

timpani
timbales^F
Pauken^F
timbales^M

bass drum
grosse caisse^F
Baßtrommel^F
bombo^M

French horns
cors^M d'harmonie^F
Waldhörner^N
cornos^M franceses

oboes
hautbois^M
Oboen^F
oboes^M

piccolo
piccolo^M
Pikkoflöte^F
pícolo^M

cellos
violoncelles^M
Cellos^N
violoncelos^M

cors anglais
cors^M anglais
Englischhörner^N
cornos^M ingleses

double basses
contrebasses^F
Kontrabasse^M
contrabajos^M

EXAMPLES OF INSTRUMENTAL GROUPS
EXEMPLES^M DE GROUPES^M INSTRUMENTAUX
BEISPIELE^N FÜR INSTRUMENTALGRUPPIERUNGEN^F
EJEMPLOS^M DE CONJUNTOS^M INSTRUMENTALES

duo
duo^M
Duo^N
dúo^M

trio
trio^M
Trio^N
trio^M

quartet
quatuor^M
Quartett^N
cuarteto^M

quintet
quintette^M
Quintett^N
quinteto^M

sextet
sextuor^M
Sextett^N
sexteto^M

jazz band
formation^F de jazz^M
Jazzband^F
banda^F de jazz^M

CREATIVE LEISURE ACTIVITIES
LOISIRS DE CREATION

KREATIVE FREIZEITAKTIVITÄTEN
TRABAJOS MANUALES

SUMMARY

SEWING
COUTURE^F
NÄHEN^N
COSTURA^F

**SEWING MACHINE
MACHINE^F À COUDRE
NÄHMASCHINE^F
MÁQUINA^F DE COSER**

thread guide
guide-fil^M
Fadenleitöse^F
guiahilos^M

spool pin
broche^F porte-bobine^M
Garnrollenstift^M
portacarrete^M

thread take-up lever
releveur^M de fil^M
Fadenhebel^M
tirahilos^M

stitch width selector
réglage^M de largeur^F de point^M
Stichbreitenwähler^M
regulador^M de ancho de puntada^F

arm
bras^M
Arm^M
brazo^M

pressure dial
réglage^M de pression^F
Druckeinsteller^M
regulador^M de presión^F

bobbin winder
bobineur^M
Spuler^M
rebobinador^M

hand wheel
volant^M
Handrad^N
volante^M

needle position selector
positionneur^M
Nadelpositionswähler^M
selector^M de posición^F de aguja^F

stitch length regulator
règle-point^M
Stichlängenwähler^M
regulador^M de largo^M de puntada^F

column
colonne^F
Ständer^M
columna^F

reverse stitch button
bouton^M de point^M arrière
Nährichtungseinsteller^M
botón^M de puntada^F

power/light switch
interrupteur^M moteur^M/éclairage^M
Netz-/Lichtschalter^M
interruptor^M luminoso

stitch selector
sélecteur^M de points^M
Stichwähler^M
selector^M de puntada^F

bedplate
plateau^M
Flachbett^N
placa^F de base^F

tension block
bloc^M-tension^F
Spanneinrichtung^F
regulador^M de tensión^F

head
tête^F
Kopf^M
cabeza^F

needle
aiguille^F
Nadel^F
aguja^F

slide plate
plaque^F-glissière^F
Schiebeplatte^F
placa^F corrediza de la canilla^F

presser foot
pied-de-biche^M
Stoffdrücker^M
prensatelas^M

needle plate
plaque^F à aiguille^F
Stichplatte^F
placa^F de la aguja^F

bobbin
canette^F
Spule^F
canilla^F

**FOOT CONTROL
COMMANDE^F AU PIED^M
TRETPLATTE^F
PEDAL^M ELÉCTRICO**

speed controller
contrôle^M de la vitesse^F
Geschwindigkeitsregelung^F
pedal^M de velocidad^F

connecting socket
prise^F de raccordement^M
Verbindungskabel^N
enchufe^M

561

SEWING
COUTURE^F
NÄHEN^N
COSTURA^F

PRESSER FOOT
PIED^M PRESSEUR
STOFFDRÜCKER^M
PRENSATELAS^M

presser bar
barre^F de pied^M presseur
Stoffdrückerstange^F
barra^F del prensatelas^M

needle bar
barre^F à aiguille^F
Nadelstange^F
barra^F de la aguja^F

needle clamp
pince-aiguille^M
Nadelhalter^M
portaaguja^M

thread guide
guide-fil^M
Fadenleitöse^F
guiahilos^M

needle clamp screw
vis^F de pince-aiguille^M
Nadelhalterschraube^F
tornillo^M de la aguja^F

thread trimmer
coupe-fil^M
Fadenabschneider^M
cortahilos^M

needle
aiguille^F
Nadel^F
aguja^F

feed dog
griffe^F d'entraînement^M
Transporteur^M
dientes^M de la leva^F

presser foot
pied-de-biche^M
Stoffdrücker^M
prensatelas^M

bobbin
canette^F
Spule^F
canilla^F

slide plate
plaque^F-glissière^F
Schiebeplatte^F
placa^F corrediza (cubrecanilla^F)

NEEDLE
AIGUILLE^F
NADEL^F
AGUJA^F

shank
talon^M
Kolben^M
talón^M de aguja^F

groove
rainure^F
Rinne^F
ranura^F

blade
tige^F
Schaft^M
aguja^F

eye
chas^M
Öhr^N
ojo^M

point
pointe^F
Spitze^F
punta^F

TENSION BLOCK
BLOC^M-TENSION^F
SPANNEINRICHTUNG^F
COLUMNA^F DE TENSIÓN^F

thread guide
guide-fil^M
Fadenleitöse^F
guiahilos^M

tension disc
disque^M de tension^F
Spannscheibe^F
disco^M de tensión^F

tension spring
ressort^M compensateur de fil^M
Spannfeder^F
resorte^M de tensión^F

tension dial
indicateur^M de tension^F
Spannungseinsteller^M
regulador^M de tamaño^M de punto^M

BOBBIN CASE
BOÎTE^F À CANETTE^F
SPULENKAPSEL^F
BOBINAS^F

latch
verrou^M
Kapselfinger^M
lengüeta^F

bobbin
canette^F
Spule^F
canilla^F

hook
crochet^M
Greifer^M
portacanilla^M

PIN CUSHION
PELOTE^F
NADELKISSEN^N
ALFILETERO^M

pin
épingle^F
Stecknadel^F
alfiler^M

eye
chas^M
Öhr^N
ojo^M

needle
aiguille^F
Nadel^F
aguja^F

emery pack
coussinet^M d'émeri^M
Schmirgelsäckchen^N
esmeril^M

ACCESSORIES
ACCESSOIRES^M
ZUBEHÖR^N
ACCESORIOS^M

thimble
dé^M
Fingerhut^M
dedal^M

needle threader
enfile-aiguille^M
Einfädler^M
enhebrador^M

magnet
aimant^M
Magnet^M
imán^M

seam gauge
règle^F de couture^F
Saummaß^N
regla^F

TRACING WHEEL
ROULETTE^F
KOPIERRAD^M
MARCADOR^M

wheel
disque^M
Rädchen^N
rueda^F

shank
axe^M
Zubehör^N
vástago^M

handle
manche^M
Griff^M
mango^M

tape measure
mètre^M à ruban^M
Maßband^N
cinta^F métrica

563

CREATIVE LEISURE ACTIVITIES
LOISIRS DE CRÉATION

KREATIVE FREIZEITAKTIVITÄTEN
TRABAJOS MANUALES

ACCESSORIES
ACCESSOIRES^M
ZUBEHÖR^N
ACCESORIOS^M DE COSTURA^F

scissors
ciseaux^M
Schere^F
tijeras^F de modista^F

blade
lame^F
Blatt^N
hoja^F de las tijeras^F

pivot
entablure^F
Schloß^N
eje^M

edge
tranchant^M
Schneide^F
filo^M

shank
branche^F
Halm^M
mango^M

handle
anneau^M
Griff^M
ojo^M

pinking shears
ciseaux^M à denteler
Zickzackschere^F
tijeras^F para rematar

skirt marker
arrondisseur^M
Rockabrunder^M
marcador^M del dobladillo^M

dressmaker's model
mannequin^M
Schneiderbüste^F
maniquí^M

564

LINING FABRICS
TISSUS^M DE SOUTIEN^M
FUTTERSTOFFE^M
FORRO^M Y ENTRETELAS^F

garment fabric
tissu^M du vêtement^M
Kleiderstoff^M
tela^F

interlining
entredoublure^F
Zwischenfutter^N
entretela^F de abrigo^M

lining
doublure^F
Futter^N
forro^M

interfacing
entoilage^M
Einlage^F
entretela^F de armado^M

underlining
triplure^F
Unterfutter^N
entretela^F de refuerzo^M

PATTERN
PATRON^M
SCHNITTMUSTER^N
PATRÓN^M

cutting line
ligne^F de coupe^F
Schnittlinie^F
línea^F de corte^M

seam line
ligne^F de bâti^M
Nahtlinie^F
línea^F de costura^F

marking dot
point^M de repère^M
Markierungspunkt^M
punto^M

seam allowance
rentré^M
Nahtzugabe^F
pestaña^F

alteration line
ligne^F de modification^F
Änderungslinie^F
línea^F para modificaciones^F

dart
pince^F
Abnäher^M
pinzas^F

notch
cran^M
Ausschnitt^M
pico^M muesca^F

fold line
pliure^F
Stoffbruch^M
doblez^M

zip line
ligne^F de piqûre^F de la fermeture^F
Reißverschlußlinie^F
posición^F de la cremallera^F

lengthwise grain
droit fil^M
Längsfaden^M
pinzas^F verticales

hemline
ligne^F d'ourlet^M
Saum^M
línea^F del dobladillo^M

FASTENERS
ATTACHES^F
VERSCHLÜSSE^M
ACCESORIOS^M **PARA CERRAR**

snap fastener
bouton^M**-pression**^F
Druckknopf^M
automático^M

socket
côté^M femelle
Vertiefung^F
hembra^F

shank button
bouton^M à tige^F
Ösenknopf^M
botón^M de fantasía^F

sew-through buttons
boutons^M à trous
gelochte Knöpfe^M
botones^M comunes

stud
côté^M mâle
Erhebung^F
macho^M

hook and eyes
agrafes^F
Haken^M **und Ösen**^F
corchetes^M

buckle
boucle^F
Schnalle^F
hebilla^F

hook
crochet^M
Haken^M
macho^M

round eye
porte^F
runde Öse^F
hembra^F

ring
boucle^F
Ring^M
ojo^M

straight eye
bride^F
gerade Öse^F
enganche^M

tongue
ardillon^M
Dorn^M
pasador^M

safety pin
épingle^F de sûreté^F
Sicherheitsnadel^F
alfiler^M imperdible

ZIP FASTENER
FERMETURE^F **À GLISSIÈRE**^F
REISSVERSCHLUSS^M
CREMALLERA^F

FABRIC STRUCTURE
STRUCTURE^F **DU TISSU**^M
GEWEBESTRUKTUR^F
TEJIDOS^M

teeth
dents^F
Zähne^M
dientes^M

slide
curseur^M
Schieber^M
corredera^F

bias
biais^M
schräg zum Fadenlauf^M
sesgo^M

tab
tirette^F
Griff^M
lengüeta^F

selvage
lisière^F
Webkante^F
orillo^M

tape
ruban^M
Band^N
cinta^F

crosswise grain
trame^F
Querfaden^M
contrahilo^M de la tela^F

lengthwise grain
chaîne^F
Längsfaden^M
hilo^M de la tela^F

stop
butée^F
Endklammer^F
tope^M

KNITTING
TRICOT^M
STRICKEN^N
TEJIDO^M DE PUNTO^M

KNITTING NEEDLES
AIGUILLES^F À TRICOTER
STRICKNADELN^F
AGUJAS^F PARA TEJER

head
tête^F
Kopf^M
cabeza^F

shank
tige^F
Schaft^M
varilla^F

point
pointe^F
Spitze^F
punta^F

crochet hook
crochet^M
Häkelnadel^F
ganchillo^M

hook
bec^M
Haken^M
gancho^M

flat part
méplat^M
flacher Teil^M
parte^F plana

knitting measure
jauge^F à aiguilles^F
Strickmaß^N
regla^F para medir puntos^M

cast-on stitches
mailles^F de montage^M
Maschenanschlag^M
puntos^M de montado^M

circular needle
aiguille^F circulaire
Rundstricknadel^F
aguja^F circular

STITCH PATTERNS
POINTS^M DE TRICOT^M
STRICKMUSTER^N
TIPOS^M DE PUNTO^M

sample
échantillon^M
Maschenprobe^F
muestra^F

stocking stitch
point^M de jersey^M
Glattstrick^M
derecho^M

garter stitch
point^M mousse^F
Krausstrick^M
revés^M

moss stitch
point^M de riz^M
Gerstenkornmuster^N
punto^M de musgo^M

rib stitch
point^M de côtes^F
Perlrippen^F
punto^M de respiguilla^F

basket stitch
point^M de damier^M
Korbstich^M
punto^M de malla^F

cable stitch
point^M de torsades^F
Zopfmuster^N
punto^M de ochos^M

NEEDLE BED AND CARRIAGES
FONTURE^F ET CHARIOTS^M
NADELBETT^N UND SCHLITTEN^M
TRICOTADORAS^F

row counter
compte-rangs^M
Reihenzähler^M
contador^M de pasadas^F

main carriage
chariot^M
Hauptschlitten^M
carro^M principal deslizante

tension dial
cadran^M de tension^F
Spannungseinsteller^M
regulador^M de tensión^F

needle bed groove
rainure^F
Nadelbettrille^F
placa^F de agujas^F

carriage handle
poignée^F de chariot^M
Schiebegriff^M
empuñadura^F del carro^M

accessory box
boîte^F d'accessoires^M
Zubehörfach^N
caja^F de accesorios^M

slide-bar
glissière^F
Führungsschiene^F
barra^F deslizable

arm
chariot^M avant
Strickabstreifer^M
brazo^M

arm nut
bouton^M d'assemblage^M
Strickabstreiferknopf^M
seguro^M del brazo^M

needle bed
fonture^F
Nadelbett^N
lecho^F de agujas^F

lace carriage
chariot^M à dentelle^F
Lochschlitten^M
carro^M de encaje^M

weaving pattern brush
brosse^F de tissage^M
Bürstchen^N für Webeffekt^M
selector^M para regular el tamaño^M de los puntos^M

rail
rail^M
Schiene^F
guía^F

weaving pattern lever
levier^M de tissage^M
Webmustereinstellung^F
palanca^F conmutadora de puntos^M

LATCH NEEDLE
AIGUILLE^F À CLAPET^M
ZUNGENNADEL^F
AGUJA^F CON LENGÜETA^F

latch
clapet^M
Zunge^F
lengüeta^F

butt
talon^M
Nadelfuß^M
talón^M de la aguja^F

shank
tige^F
Schaft^M
vástago^M

hook
crochet^M
Haken^M
gancho^M

row number display
affichage^M du numéro^M de rang^M
Reihenanzeige^F
pantalla^F del contador^M de pasadas^F

stitch pattern memory
mémoire^F des patrons^M
Strickmusterspeicherung^F
memoria^F de tipos^M de puntos^M

latch needle
aiguille^F à clapet^M
Zungennadel^F
aguja^F con lengüeta^F

correction key
touche^F de correction^F
Korrekturtaste^F
tecla^F correctora

variation keys
touches^F de variation^F
Sonderfunktionstasten^F
teclas^F de selección^F

pattern start key
commencement^M du patron^M
Starttaste^F für Strickmuster^N
puesta^F en marcha^F

stitch control buttons
boutons^M de contrôle^M du point^M
Strickarttasten^F
teclas^F conmutadoras de puntos^M

colour display
affichage^M de la couleur^F
Farbanzeige^F
pantalla^F de colores^M

yarn feeder
noix^F
Garnführer^M
cerrojo^M

carriage control dial
commande^F du chariot^M
Schlitteneinstellung^F
mando^M de control^M del carro^M

TENSION BLOCK
BLOC^M-TENSION^F
SPANNEINRICHTUNG^F
SISTEMA^U DE TENSIÓN^F

tension spring
pêcheur^M
Spannfeder^F
resorte^M del tensor^M

tension disc
disque^M de tension^F
Spannscheibe^F
disco^M de tensión^F

yarn tension unit
porte-tension^M
Garnspannungseinheit^F
barra^F tensora

tension dial
bouton^M de tension^F
Spannungseinsteller^M
regulador^M de tensión^F

yarn clip
pince-fil^M
Garnhalter^M
sujetador^M del hilo^M

eyelet
œillet^M
Öse^F
guiahilos^M

yarn rod
support^M de tension^F
Garnstange^F
varilla^F

yarn guide
guide-fil^M
Fadenführung^F
guía^F de tensión^F

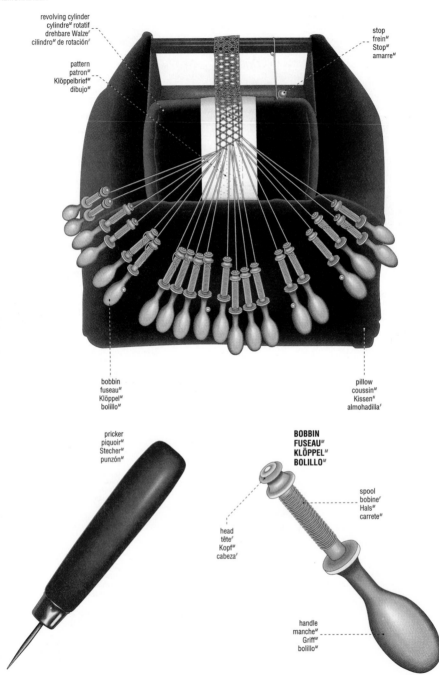

BOBBIN LACE
DENTELLE^F AUX FUSEAUX^M
KLÖPPELSPITZE^F
ENCAJE^M DE BOLILLOS^M

PILLOW
CARREAU^M
KLÖPPELKISSEN^N
ALMOHADILLA^F

revolving cylinder
cylindre^M rotatif
drehbare Walze^F
cilindro^M de rotación^F

pattern
patron^M
Klöppelbrief^M
dibujo^M

stop
frein^M
Stop^M
amarre^M

bobbin
fuseau^M
Klöppel^M
bolillo^M

pillow
coussin^M
Kissen^N
almohadilla^F

pricker
piquoir^M
Stecher^M
punzón^M

BOBBIN
FUSEAU^M
KLÖPPEL^M
BOLILLO^M

spool
bobine^F
Hals^M
carrete^M

head
tête^F
Kopf^M
cabeza^F

handle
manche^M
Griff^M
bolillo^M

EMBROIDERY
BRODERIE^F
STICKEREI^F
BORDADO^M

FRAME
MÉTIER^M À BRODER
RAHMEN^M
BASTIDOR^M

embroidered fabric
tissu^M brodé
bestickter Stoff^M
tela^F bordada

peg
cheville^F
Zapfen^M
espiga^F

tape
tirette^F
Band^N
cinta^F

slat
latte^F
Latte^F
listón^M de madera^F

hoop
tambour^M
runder Stickrahmen^M
lanzadera^F

webbing
coutisse^F
Stoffstreifen^M
tira^F de tela^F

STITCHES
CATÉGORIES^F DE POINTS^M
STICKSTICHE^M
TIPOS^M DE PUNTOS^M

cross stitches
points^M croisés
Kreuzstiche^M
puntos^M de cruz^F

chevron stitch
point^M de chausson^M
Smokstich^M
punto^M de escapulario^M

herringbone stitch
point^M de chevron^M
Hexenstich^M
punto^M de cruz^F

flat stitches
points^M plats
Plattstiche^M
puntos^M de relleno^M

couched stitches
points^M couchés
Überfangstiche^M
bordados^M planos

long and short stitch
point^M passé empiétant
langer und kurzer Spannstich^M
lanzado^M desigual

fishbone stitch
point^M d'arête^F
Zopfstich^M
punto^M de espiga^F

Romanian couching stitch
point^M roumain
rumänischer Überfangstich^M
bordado^M plano

Oriental couching stitch
point^M d'Orient^M
orientalischer Überfangstich^M
relleno^M alternado

knot stitches
points^M noués
Knötchenstiche^M
puntos^M de relleno^M sueltos

loop stitches
points^M bouclés
Schlingstiche^M
puntos^M de malla^F

bullion stitch
point^M de poste^F
Tressenstich^M
pespunte^M

French knot stitch
point^M de nœud^M
französischer Knötchenstich^M
punto^M de nudos^M

chain stitch
point^M de chaînette^F
Kettenstich^M
cadeneta^F

feather stitch
point^M d'épine^F
Krähenfußstich^M
pata^F de gallo^M

WEAVING
TISSAGE^M
WEBEN^N
TELAR^M

LOW WARP LOOM
MÉTIER^M DE BASSE LISSE^F
FLACHWEBSTUHL^M
TELAR^M DE CUATRO MARCOS^M

frame
bâti^M
Rahmen^M
armazón^M

head roller
rouleau^M principal
obere Rolle^F
tambor^M principal

heddles
lisses^F
Litzen^F
lizos^M

harnesses
harnais^M
Geschirr^N
marcos^M

reed
ros^M
Riet^N
peine^M

beater
battant^M
Kammlade^F
batán^M

breast beam
poitrinière^F
Brustbaum^M
travesaño^M frontal

beater sley
semelle^F du battant^F
Ladenbahn^F
travesaño^M intermedio del batán^M

weft
trame^F
Schuß^M
trama^F

cloth roller
ensouple^F de tissu^M
Warenbaum^M
plegador^M del tejido^M

lam
contremarche^F
Seitenschwinge^F
travesaño^M

post
montant^M
Pfosten^M
montante^M

crosspiece
entretoise^F
Querholz^N
travesaño^M

treadle cord
corde^F d'accrochage^M
Schnur^F am Tritt^M
cordón^M del pedal^M

crossbeam
traverse^F
Kantholz^N
travesaño^M frontal interior

treadle
marche^F
Tritt^M
pedal^M

take-up handle
tentoir^M
Spannhandgriff^M
palanca^F de compensación^F

ACCESSORIES
ACCESSOIRESᴹ
ZUBEHÖRᴺ
ACCESORIOSᴹ

upright
support ᴹ du rouleau ᴹ
Säule ᶠ
soporte ᴹ del juego ᴹ de marcos ᴹ

harness
lame ᶠ
Schaft ᴹ
marco ᴹ

beater handtree
chapeau ᴹ du battant ᴹ
Schwenklade ᶠ
travesaño ᴹ superior del batán ᴹ

back beam
porte-fils ᴹ
Streichbaum ᴹ
plegador ᴹ posterior

warp
chaîne ᶠ
Kette ᶠ
urdimbre ᶠ

handle
manivelle ᶠ
Griff ᴹ
manivela ᶠ

warp roller
ensouple ᶠ de chaîne ᶠ
Kettbaum ᴹ
plegador ᴹ de urdimbre ᶠ

ratchet
cliquet ᴹ
Klinke ᶠ
leva ᶠ

ratchet wheel
roue ᶠ dentée
Sperrad ᴺ
engranaje ᴹ

release treadle
pédale ᶠ de frein ᴹ
Trittlöser ᴹ
pedal ᴹ del freno ᴹ

HEDDLES
LISSESᶠ
LITZENᶠ
LIZOSᴹ

eye
œil ᴹ
Fadenauge ᴺ
ojal ᴹ

flat shuttle
réglette ᶠ
Webnadel ᶠ
lanzadera ᶠ plana

reed hooks
passettes ᶠ
Blattstecher ᴹ
ganchos ᴹ peinadores

temple
templet ᴹ
Breithalter ᴹ
templazo ᴹ

SHUTTLE
NAVETTEᶠ
WEBSCHÜTZᴹ
LANZADERAᶠ

rod
tige ᶠ
Dorn ᴹ
varilla ᶠ

bobbin
canette ᶠ
Spule ᶠ
huso ᴹ

eye
œil ᴹ
Fadenauge ᴺ
ojal ᴹ

HIGH WARP LOOM
MÉTIER^M DE HAUTE LISSE^F
HOCHWEBSTUHL^M
TELAR^M DE TAPICERÍA^F

vertical frame
charpente^F verticale
senkrechter Rahmen^M
marco^M vertical

upright
montant^M
Säule^F
montante^M

warp
chaîne^F
Kette^F
urdimbre^F

shed stick
baguette^F d'écartement^M
Trennstab^M
varilla^F de calada^F

heddle rod
barre^F à lisses^F
Litzenstab^M
varilla^F de lizos^M

heddles
lisses^F
Litzen^F
lizos^M

tapestry bobbin
broche^F
Teppichschiffchen^N
lanzadera^F

weft
trame^F
Schuß^M
trama^F

support
support^M
Fuß^M
pata^F

crossbar
traverse^F
Querbalken^M
travesaño^M

leash rod
baguette^F d'encroix^M
Latzenstab^M
varilla^F tensora

comb
peigne^M
Kamm^M
peine^M de tapicería^F

tapestry bobbin
broche^F
Teppichschiffchen^N
lanzadera^F

ACCESSORIES
ACCESSOIRESᴹ
ZUBEHÖRᴺ
ACCESORIOSᴹ

bobbin winder
canetièreᶠ
Handspulgerätᴺ
devanadorᴹ **de bobinas**ᶠ

worm
visᶠ sans finᶠ
Spindelᶠ
tornilloᴹ sinfín

gear
roueᶠ d'engrenageᴹ
Zahnradᴺ
engranajeᴹ

shaft
fuseauᴹ
Dornᴹ
ejeᴹ

swift
dévidoirᴹ
Schirmwindeᶠ
devanaderaᶠ

ball winder
bobinoirᴹ
elektrisches Spulgerätᴺ
devanadorᴹ

driving wheel
roueᶠ d'entraînementᴹ
Spulradᴺ
poleaᶠ de transmisiónᶠ

clamp
serre-jointᴹ
Zwingeᶠ
abrazaderaᶠ

ball
bobineᶠ
Knäuelᴺ
husoᴹ

warping frame
ourdissoirᴹ
Schärbaumᴹ
urdidorᴹ

peg
chevilleᶠ
Zapfenᴹ
espigaᶠ

spool rack
cantreᴹ
Spulengestellᴺ
portabobinasᴹ

575

WEAVING
TISSAGE^M
WEBEN^N
TEJIDOS^M

DIAGRAM OF WEAVING PRINCIPLE
SCHÉMA^M DE PRINCIPE^M DU TISSAGE^M
SCHAUBILD^N FÜR DAS WEBPRINZIP^N
DIAGRAMAS^M DE TEJIDOS^M

weft thread
fil^M de trame^F
Schußfaden^M
hilo^M de trama^F

warp thread
fil^M de chaîne^F
Kettfaden^M
hilo^M de urdimbre^F

BASIC WEAVES
ARMURES^F DE BASE^F
GRUNDBINDUNGEN^F
LIGAMENTOS^M TEXTILES BÁSICOS

plain weave
toile^F
Leinwandbindung^F
tafetán^M

twill weave
sergé^M
Köperbindung^F
sarga^F

satin weave
satin^M
Atlasbindung^F
satén^M

OTHER TECHNIQUES
AUTRES TECHNIQUES^F
ANDERE TECHNIKEN^F
OTROS LIGAMENTOS^M TEXTILES

interlock
croisement^M
Gobelinbindung^F
ligamento^M entrecruzado

slit
fente^F
senkrechte Kelimbindung^F
ligamento^M vertical

hatching
hachure^F
Kelimbindung^F mit wechselnden Wenden^F
ligamento^M de rayas^F

knot
nœud^M
Knoten^M
ligamento^M de nudos^M

FINE BOOKBINDING
RELIURE^F D'ART^M
HANDBUCHBINDEREI^F
ENCUADERNACIÓN^F ARTÍSTICA^F

BOUND BOOK
LIVRE^M RELIÉ
GEBUNDENES BUCH^N
LIBRO^M ENCUADERNADO

headcap
coiffe^F
Häubchen^N
cabecera^F

square
chasse^F
Viereck^N
casilla^F

top edge
tranche^F de tête^F
Kopfsteg^M
canto^M de la cabeza^F

headband
tranchefile^F
Kapitalband^N
cabezada^F

flyleaf
garde^F volante
Vorsatzblatt^N
guarda^F

joint
mors^M
Falz^F
cajo^M

corner
coin^M
Ecke^F
cantonera^F

spine
dos^M
Rücken^M
lomo^M

back board
plat^M verso^M
Hinterdeckel^M
cubierta^F posterior

raised band
nerf^M
erhabenes Band^N
nervio^M

front board
plat^M recto^M
Vorderdeckel^M
cubierta^F frontal

fore edge
tranche^F de gouttière^F
Außensteg^M
canto^M de la cara^F

tail edge
tranche^F de queue^F
Fußsteg^M
canto^M del pie^M

folding stick
plioir^M
Falzbein^N
plegadera^F

signature
cahier^M
Signatur^F
cuadernillo^M

GATHERING
PLAÇURE^F
ZUSAMMENTRAGEN^N
COSIDO^M

endpaper
garde^F
Vorsatzblatt^N
guarda^F

sheet
feuillet^M
Bogen^M
pliego^M

FINE BOOKBINDING
RELIURE^F D'ART^M
HANDBUCHBINDEREI^F
ENCUADERNACIÓN^F ARTÍSTICA

TRIMMING
ÉBARBAGE^M
SCHNEIDEN^N
GUILLOTINA^F

board cutter
cisaille^F
Pappschere^F
cizalla^F

cutting blade
lame^F mobile
Obermesser^N
cuchilla^F móvil

blade lever
levier^M de la lame^F
Obermesserhebel^M
palanca^F de la cuchilla^F

fixed blade
lame^F fixe
festgestelltes Messer^N
cuchilla^F fija

clamp
mordache^F
Preßbalken^M
prensa^F

table
plateau^M
Auflagetisch^M
base^F

gauge
guide^M
Anlegeeinrichtung^F
guía^F para enmarcar

cutting guide
règle^F d'équerrage^M
Schnittführung^F
dispositivo^M para enmarcar

ruler
règle^F
Lineal^N
regla^F

exterior gauge
guide^M extérieur
äußere Formatbegrenzung^F
guía^F externa para enmarcar

SAWING-IN
GRECQUAGE^M
EINSÄGEN^N
ENSAMBLAJE^M **A ESPIGA**^F

tenon saw
scie^F à grecquer
Ansatzsäge^F
sierra^F de ensamblar

SEWING
COUTURE^F
HEFTEN^N
ENCUADERNACIÓN^F **EN RÚSTICA**

groove
grecque^F
Rille^F
muescas^F

sewing frame
cousoir^M
Heftlade^F
bastidor^M de coser

crossbar
traverse^F
Querleiste^F
travesaño^M

cord
ficelle^F
Schnur^F
cuerda^F para el cosido^M

upright
montant^M
Säule^F
montante^M

temple
templet^M
Leiste^F
templador^M

slot
fente^F
Schlitz^M
hendidura^F

bed
table^F
Tisch^M
cama^F

BACKING
ENDOSSURE
BUCHRÜCKENBEARBEITUNG
REDONDEO

BACKING PRESS
ÉTAU À ENDOSSER
BUCHRÜCKENPRESSE
PRENSA DE CAJOS

backing board
ais ferré
Preßbalken
tabla biselada

spine of the book
dos du livre
Buchrücken
lomo del libro

PRESSING
MISE EN PRESSE
PRESSEN
PRENSA

standing press
presse à percussion
Stockpresse
prensa de tornillo

upright
colonne
Säule
montante

central screw
vis centrale
Spindel
husillo

BACKING HAMMER
MARTEAU À ENDOSSER
HAMMER ZUM RUNDKLOPFEN
MARTILLO DE ENCUADERNADOR

claw
panne
Finne
cola

hand-wheel
volant
Schlagrad
volante

handle
manche
Griff
mango

platen
plateau
Preßplatte
prensa

pressing board
ais
Preßbalken
base

face
platine
Hammerbahn
cara

COVERING
COUVRURE
EINBINDEN
CUBIERTA

base
socle
Fußstück
base

bookbinding leather
peau
Einbandleder
piel para encuadernar

foot
patte
Fuß
garra

head
tête
Kopf
cabeza

tail
queue
Schwanz
cola

neck
collet
Hals
lomo

flank
flanc
Seite
costado

butt
croupon
Schild
flor

579

RELIEF PRINTING
IMPRESSION*F* EN RELIEF*M*
HOCHDRUCK*M*
IMPRESIÓN*F* EN RELIEVE*M*

paper
papier*M*
Papier*N*
papel*M*

printed image
image*F* imprimée
Druck*M*
imagen*F* impresa

inked surface
surface*F* encrée
farbige Oberfläche*F*
entintado*M*

raised figure
modèle*M* en relief*M*
hochstehende Form*F*
figura*F* en relieve*M*

INTAGLIO PRINTING
IMPRESSION*F* EN CREUX*M*
TIEFDRUCK*M*
HUECOGRABADO*M*

paper
papier*M*
Papier*N*
papel*M*

printed image
image*F* imprimée
Druck*M*
imagen*F* impresa

inked surface
surface*F* encrée
farbige Oberfläche*F*
entintado*M*

incised figure
modèle*M* en creux*M*
tiefliegende Form*F*
imagen*F* tallada

LITHOGRAPHIC PRINTING
IMPRESSION*F* À PLAT*M*
LITHOGRAPHIE*F*
IMPRESIÓN LITOGRÁFICA

printed image
image*F* imprimée
Druck*M*
imagen*F* impresa

paper
papier*M*
Papier*N*
papel*M*

moist surface
surface*F* mouillée
befeuchtete Oberfläche*F*
superficie*F* humedecida

inked surface
surface*F* encrée
farbige Oberfläche*F*
entintado*M*

plane figure
modèle*M* à plat*M*
Flachform*F*
figura*F* plana

RELIEF PRINTING PROCESS
GRAVURE^F EN RELIEF^M
HOCHDRUCKVERFAHREN^N
IMPRESIÓN^F EN RELIEVE^M

EQUIPMENT
MATÉRIEL^M
AUSSTATTUNG^F
EQUIPO^M

knife
canif^M
Messer^N
cuchillo^M de contornear

U-shaped gouge
gouge^F creuse
Rundeisen^N
gubia^F

mallet
maillet^M
Schlegel^M
maza^F

chisel
ciseau^M
Beitel^M
escoplo^M

burin
burin^M
gerades Hohleisen^N
buril^M

V-shaped gouge
gouge^F en V
Geißfuß^M
cincel^M de rincón^M

dabber
tampon^M
Tampon^M
tampón^M

INKING SLAB
MARBRE^M
FARBSTEIN^M
PLANCHA^F DE ENTINTADO^M

ink
encre^F
Farbe^F
tinta^F

ink
encre^F
Farbe^F
tinta^F

ink roller
rouleau^M d'encrage^M
Farbwalze^F
rodillo^M entintador

spatula
spatule^F
Spachtel^M
espátula^F

woodcut
gravure^F sur bois^M de fil^M
Holzstock^M
bloque^M de madera^F grabado

ETCHING PRESS
PRESSE^F À TAILLE-DOUCE^F
ZYLINDERDRUCKPRESSE^F
PRENSA^F DE AGUAFUERTE^F

pressure screw
vis^F de pression^F
Preßspindel^F
tornillo^M de presión^F

top cylinder
cylindre^M supérieur
Oberwalze^F
cilindro^M superior

press bed
table^F
Drucktisch^M
tímpano^M

blanket
lange^M
Druckbogen^M
fieltro^M

bottom cylinder
cylindre^M inférieur
Antriebswalze^F
cilindro^M inferior

wood engraving
gravure^F sur bois^M debout
Holzschnitt^M
bloque^M de madera^F para grabar

capstan
moulinet^M
Drehkreuz^N
volante^M de aspas^F

INTAGLIO PRINTING PROCESS
GRAVURE*^F* EN CREUX*^M*
TIEFDRUCKVERFAHREN*^N*
IMPRESIÓN*^F* EN HUECOGRABADO*^M*

EQUIPMENT
MATÉRIEL*^M*
AUSSTATTUNG*^F*
EQUIPO*^M*

brush
pinceau*^M*
Pinsel*^M*
bruza*^F*

copperplate
planche*^F* de cuivre*^M*
Kupferplatte*^F*
placa*^F* de cobre*^M*

rocking tool
berceau*^M*
Wiegestahl*^M*
graneador*^M* para el grabado*^M* al humo*^M*

roulette
roulette*^F*
Roulette*^F*
ruleta*^F* estriada

dry point
pointe*^F* sèche
Kaltnadel*^F*
punta*^F* seca

burnisher
brunissoir*^M*
Polierstahl*^M*
bruñidor*^M*

taper
rat*^M* de cave*^F*
dünne Wachskerze*^F*
vela*^F*

hand vice
étau*^M*
Plattenhalter*^M*
pinza*^F*

scraper
ébarboir*^M*
Schaber*^M*
raedor*^M*

smoking-apparatus
enfumoir*^M*
Räucherapparat*^M*
ahumador*^M*

baren
baren*^M*
Baren*^M*
frotador*^M*

tarlatan
tarlatane*^F*
Tarlatan*^M*
tarlatana*^M*

varnish-roller
rouleau*^M* à vernir
Lederwalze*^F*
rodillo*^M* para barnizar

oilstone
pierre*^F* à aiguiser
Ölstein*^M*
piedra*^F* de aceite*^M*

LITHOGRAPHY
LITHOGRAPHIE*F*
LITHOGRAPHIE*F*
LITOGRAFÍA*F*

litho pencil
crayon*M* lithographique
Lithostift*M*
lápiz*M* litográfico

EQUIPMENT
MATÉRIEL*M*
AUSSTATTUNG*F*
EQUIPO*M*

dry-point
pointe*F* sèche
Graviernadel*F*
punta*F* seca

pumice correcting pencil
crayon*M* de pierre*F* ponce
Bimsstein-Korrekturstift*M*
lápiz*M* corrector de piedra*F* pómez

litho crayon
bâton*M* de craie*F*
Lithokreide*F*
jaboncillo*M* litográfico

LEVIGATOR
BOURRIQUET*M*
SCHLEIFSCHEIBE*F*
BARRIQUETE*M*

hole
trou*M*
Loch*N*
agujero*M*

lithographic tusche
encre*F* lithographique
lithographische Tusche*F*
barra*F* diluida al agua*F*

red ochre pencil
sanguine*F*
roter Ockerstift*M*
lápiz*M* corrector de ocre*M* rojo

caliper
compas*M* d'épaisseur*F*
Greifzirkel*M*
calibrador*M*

disc
disque*M*
Scheibe*F*
disco*M*

LITHOGRAPHIC PRESS
PRESSE*F* LITHOGRAPHIQUE
STEINDRUCKPRESSE*F*
PRENSA*F* LITOGRÁFICA

lever
levier*M*
Hebel*M*
palanca*F* de presión*F*

crank handle
poignée*F* de la manivelle*F*
Handkurbel*F*
manivela*F*

pressure screw
vis*F* de pression*F*
Preßspindel*F*
tornillo*M* de presión*F*

scraper bar holder
porte-râteau*M*
Reibergehäuse*N*
brazo*M* del raspador*M*

scraper
râteau*M*
Reiber*M*
raspador*M*

gearbox
mécanisme*M* d'engrenage*M*
Laufrad*N*
caja*F* de engranajes*M*

press bed
table*F*
Drucktisch*M*
platina*F*

frame
bâti*M*
Rahmen*M*
bastidor*M*

lithographic stone
pierre*F* lithographique
Lithographiestein*M*
piedra*F* litográfica

wheel
galet*M*
Rad*N*
rueda*F*

roller
rouleau*M*
Rolle*F*
aplanadora*F*

583

TURNING
TOURNAGE^M
DREHEN^N
TORNO^M

turning wheel
tour^M à pied^M
Drehscheibe^F
torno^M

ball of clay
pâte^F d'argile^F
Hubel^M
arcilla^F de modelar

plaster bat
rondeau^M
Drehteller^M
molde^M

wheel head
girelle^F
Scheibenkopf^M
plato^M

shaft
axe^M
Welle^F
eje^M

seat
siège^M
Sitz^M
asiento^M

flywheel
volant^M
Schwungrad^N
rueda^F de volante^M

footrest
appui-pied^M
Fußstütze^F
estribo^M

SLAB BUILDING
GALETTAGE^M
PLATTEN^F AUSROLLEN
RODILLO^M

COILING
COLOMBIN^M
SPIRALWÜLSTE^F ROLLEN
CORDÓN^M PARA ESPIRALES^F

TOOLS
OUTILS^M
WERKZEUG^N
HERRAMIENTAS^F

ribs
esthèques^F
Drehschiene^F
costillar^M

cutting wire
fil^M à couper la pâte^F
Schneidedraht^M
alambre^M para cortar

banding wheel
tournette^F
Modellierscheibe^F
torneta^F

TOOLS
OUTILS^M
WERKZEUG^N
HERRAMIENTAS^F

wooden modelling tools
ébauchoirs^M
Modellierhölzer^N
espátulas^F de modelar

fettling knife
couteau^M de potier^M
Ausstreichmesser^N
cuchillo^M para desbastar

needle tool
pige^F
Nadelwerkzeug^N
punzón^M

trimming tool
mirette^F
Gipsschlinge^F
raspador^M

stilt
patte^F de coq^M
Ständer^M
soporte^M

pyrometric cone
montre^F
Segerkegel^M
cono^M pirométrico

FIRING
CUISSON^F
BRENNEN^N
COCCIÓN^F

refractory brick
brique^F réfractaire
feuerfester Ziegelstein^M
ladrillo^M refractario

electric kiln
four^M **électrique**
elektrischer Brennofen^M
horno^M **eléctrico**

lid
couvercle^M
Deckel^M
tapa^F

lid brace
cale^F de couvercle^M
Deckelbügel^M
brazo^M extensible

hinge
charnière^F
Scharnier^N
bisagra^F

heating element
élément^M
Heizelement^N
resistencia^F

firing chamber
chambre^F de cuisson^F
Brennraum^M
recámara^F

damper
évent^M
Schieber^M
chimenea^F

temperature control knob
contrôle^M de température^F
Temperatureinsteller^M
control^M de temperatura^F

manual/automatic mode
mode^M manuel/automatique
Manuell-/Automatikeinstellung^F
selector automático/manual

signal lamp
voyant^M lumineux
Kontrolleuchte^F
piloto^M

timer
minuterie^F
Zeituhr^F
reloj^M automático

electrical connections
entrée^F d'électricité^F
Elektroelement^N
enchufe^M

connecting cable
câble^M de raccordement^M
Verbindungskabel^N
cable^M

KREATIVE FREIZEITAKTIVITÄTEN
TRABAJOS MANUALES

CREATIVE LEISURE ACTIVITIES
LOISIRS DE CRÉATION

STEPS
ÉTAPES*F*
SCHRITTE*M*
ETAPAS*F*

drawing
traçage*M*
Zeichnen*N*
diseño*M*

roughing out
dégrossissage*M*
Aussägen*N*
desbaste*M*

carving
sculpture*F*
Schnitzen*N*
talla*F*

finishing
finition*F*
Herausarbeiten*N*
acabado*M*

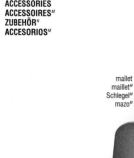

ACCESSORIES
ACCESSOIRES*M*
ZUBEHÖR*N*
ACCESORIOS*M*

carver's bench screw
queue-de-cochon*F*
Schnitzbankschraube*F*
tornillo*M*

mallet
maillet*M*
Schlegel*M*
mazo*M*

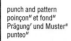

stand
sellette*F*
Bock*M*
taburete*M*

punch and pattern
poinçon*M* et fond*M*
Prägung*F* und Muster*N*
punteo*M*

macaroni
macaroni^M
gebogenes Hohleisen^N
escoplo^M de acanalar

riffler
rifloir^M
Riffelfeile^F
bruñidor^M con rascador^M

burin
burin^M
gerades Hohleisen^N
escoplo^M redondo

U-shaped chisel
fluteroni^M
Kasteneisen^N
escoplo^M de acanalar

knife
couteau^M
Messer^N
cuchillo^M de contornear

firmer chisel
fermoir^M
gerades Balleisen^N
escoplo^M

gouge
gouge^F
Hohlbeitel^M
gubia^F

adze
herminette^F
Dechsel^F
azuela^F para desbastar

rasp
râpe^F
Raspel^F
lima^F

PRINCIPAL TYPES OF CARVING BLADE
PRINCIPALES FORMES^F DE LAMES^F
DIE WICHTIGSTEN SCHNITZEISEN^N
TIPOS^M DE CUCHILLAS^F

blade with two bevelled edges
lame^F à deux biseaux^M
Eisen^N mit zwei schrägen Seiten^F
escoplo^M

spoon blade
lame^F en cuiller^F
Löffeleisen^N
cuchara^F

bent blade
lame^F coudée
gebogenes Eisen^N
curvada

straight blade
lame^F droite
gerades Eisen^N
plana

PAINTING AND DRAWING
PEINTURE*F* ET DESSIN*M*
MALEN*N* UND ZEICHNEN*N*
PINTURA*F* Y DIBUJO*M*

PRINCIPAL TECHNIQUES
PRINCIPALES TECHNIQUES*F*
DIE WICHTIGSTEN TECHNIKEN*F*
TÉCNICAS PRINCIPALES

watercolour and gouache
aquarelle*F* et gouache*F*
Aquarellfarbe*F* und Gouache*F*
acuarela*F* y aguazo*M*

charcoal
fusain*M*
Kohle*F*
carboncillo*M*

oil paint
couleur*F* à l'huile*F*
Ölfarbe*F*
óleo*M*

ink
encre*F*
Tinte*F*
tinta*F* china

tube
tube*M*
Tube*F*
tubo*M*

cakes
pastilles*F*
Kissen*N*
caja*F* de acuarelas*F*

marker pen
marqueur*M*
Marker*M*
marcador*M*

felt tip pen
feutre*M*
Filzstift*M*
rotulador*M*

soft pastel
pastel*M* sec
Pastell*N*
pastel*M*

oil pastel
pastel*M* gras
Ölpastell*N*
pastel*M* de óleo*M*

colouring pencils
crayons*M* de couleur*F*
Buntstifte*M*
lápices*M* de colores*M*

EQUIPMENT
MATÉRIEL^M
AUSSTATTUNG^F
EQUIPO^M

reservoir-nib pen
plume^F
Graphosfeder^F
plumafuente^F

sumie
pinceau^M à sumie^M
Japanpinsel^M
sumie^M

brush
pinceau^M
Pinsel^M
pincel^M

painting knife
couteau^M à peindre
Malspachtel^M
cuchillo^M paleta^F

palette knife
spatule^F
Palettmesser^N
espátula^F

flat brush
brosse^F
Flachpinsel^M
pincel^M plano

fan brush
brosse^F éventail^M
Fächerpinsel^M
brocha^F

SUPPORTS
SUPPORTS^M
BILDTRÄGER^M
LIENZOS^M

paper
papier^M
Papier^N
papel^M

cardboard
carton^M
Malpappe^F
cartón^M

canvas
toile^F
Leinwand^F
lienzo^M

panel
panneau^M
Platte^F
tabla^F

PAINTING AND DRAWING
PEINTURE^F ET DESSIN^M
MALEN^N UND ZEICHNEN^N
PINTURA^F Y DIBUJO^M

AIRBRUSH
AÉROGRAPHE^M
SPRITZPISTOLE^F
PISTOLA^F **DE PINTAR**

trigger
gâchette^F
Hebel^M
palanca^F principal

cap
couvercle^M
Deckel^M
tapa^F

paint cup
godet^M à couleur^F
Farbbehälter^M
cazoleta^F

air hose
flexible^M d'air^M
Luftschlauch^M
conducto^M de aire^M comprimido

crown
couronne^F
Düsenkappe^F
corona^F

CROSS SECTION OF AN AIRBRUSH
COUPE^F **D'UN AÉROGRAPHE**^M
QUERSCHNITT^M **DURCH EINE SPRITZPISTOLE**^F
CORTE^M **TRANSVERSAL DE UNA PISTOLA**^F **DE PINTAR**

needle assembly
bloc^M aiguille^F
Nadelklemmschraube^F
enganche^M de conducto^M

trigger
gâchette^F
Hebel^M
palanca^F principal

paint cup
godet^M à couleur^F
Farbbehälter^M
cazoleta^F

pivot
pivot^M
Pinne^F
pivote^M

needle
aiguille^F
Nadel^F
conducto^M

nozzle
buse^F
Düse^F
pulverizador^M

air flow
jet^M d'air^M
Luftstrom^M
aire^M comprimido

air valve
soupape^F d'arrivée^F d'air^M
Luftventil^N
válvula^F de aire^M

paint spray
jet^M de couleur^F
Farbspray^M
color^M vaporizado

DRAWING BOARD
TABLE^F À DESSIN^M
REISSBRETT^N
TABLERO^M DE DIBUJO^M

ruler
règle^F
Lineal^N
regla^F de escuadra^F

storage tray
plateau^M de rangement^M
Ablagebrett^N
tablero^M de accesorios^M

drafting machine
appareil^M à dessiner
Zeichenmaschine^F
máquina^F de dibujar con guía^F

adjustment pedal
pédale^F d'ajustement^M
Pedal^N zur Verstellung^F
pedal^M de ajuste^M

easel
chevalet^M
Staffelei^F
caballete^M

maulstick
appui-main^M
Malstock^M
tiento^M

591

KREATIVE FREIZEITAKTIVITÄTEN
TRABAJOS MANUALES

CREATIVE LEISURE ACTIVITIES
LOISIRS DE CRÉATION

ACCESSORIES
ACCESSOIRES^M
ZUBEHÖR^N
ACCESORIOS^M

colour chart
nuancier^M
Farbtafel^F
gama^F de colores^M

palette with hollows
palette^F à alvéoles^F
Palette^F mit Vertiefungen^F
paleta^F con huecos^M para pintura^F

dipper
godet^M
Stecker^M
tarrito^M para pincel^M

palette with dipper
palette^F avec godet^M
Palette^F mit Stecker^M
paleta^F con tarrito^M

articulated mannequin
mannequin^M articulé
Gliederpuppe^F
maniquí^M

USEFUL LIQUIDS
LIQUIDES^M D'APPOINT^M
HILFSMITTEL^N
LÍQUIDOS^M ACCESORIOS

varnish
vernis^M
Firnis^M
barniz^M

linseed oil
huile^F de lin^M
Leinöl^N
aceite^M de linaza^F

turpentine
térébenthine^F
Terpentin^N
aguarrás^M

fixative
fixatif^M
Fixativ^N
fijador^M

SPORTARTEN
DEPORTES

SPORTS
SPORTS

594

BASEBALL
BASEBALL^M
BASEBALL^M
BÉISBOL^M

CATCHER
RECEVEUR^M
FÄNGER^M
RECEPTOR^M

BATTER
FRAPPEUR^M
SCHLAGMANN^M
BATEADOR^M

batter's helmet
casque^M de frappeur^M
Schlagmannshelm^M
casco^M del bateador^M

frame
grille^F
Visiergestell^N
armazón^M de la máscara^F

team shirt
chandail^M d'équipe^F
Mannschaftstrikot^N
camiseta^F

bat
bâton^M
Schläger^F
bate^M

mask
masque^M
Maske^F
máscara^F

batting glove
gant^M de frappeur^M
Schlaghandschuh^M
guante^M de bateo^M

throat protector
protège-gorge^M
Halsschutz^M
protector^M de la garganta^F

undershirt
chandail^M de dessous^M
Unterhemd^N
camiseta^F interior

catcher's glove
gant^M de receveur^M
Fanghandschuh^M
guante^M del receptor^M

stirrup sock
chaussette^F-étrier^M
Stutzen^M
calcetín^M con tirante^M

shin guard
protège-tibia^M
Schienbeinschützer^M
espinillera^F

chest protector
protecteur^M de poitrine^F
Brustschutz^M
peto^M

trousers
pantalon^M
Hose^F
pantalón^M

toe guard
protège-orteils^M
Zehenschützer^M
protector^M del pie^M

knee pad
genouillère^F
Knieschützer^M
rodillera^F

spiked shoe
chaussure^F à crampons^M
Stollenschuh^M
zapatilla^F con tacos^M

BAT
BÂTON^M
SCHLÄGER^M
BATE^M

knob
pommeau^M
Knauf^M
puño^M

handle
manche^M
Griff^M
empuñadura^F

MANNSCHAFTSSPORTARTEN
DEPORTES DE EQUIPO

TEAM GAMES
SPORTS D'ÉQUIPE

crest
écusson^M
Wappen^N
emblema^M

hitting area
surface^F de frappe^F
Schlagbereich^M
cuadro^M de bateo^M

BASEBALL
BALLE^F **DE BASEBALL**^M
BASEBALL^M
BÉISBOL^M

71 – 74 mm

CROSS SECTION OF A BASEBALL
COUPE^F **DE LA BALLE**^F
BASEBALL^M **IM QUERSCHNITT**
CORTE^M **TRANSVERSAL DE LA PELOTA**^F

yarn ball
balle^F de fil^M
Garnball^M
bola^F de hilo^M

cork ball
balle^F de liège^M
Korkball^M
bola^F de corcho^M

cover
enveloppe^F
Außenschicht^F
forro^M

stitches
couture^F
Nähte^F
costura^F

FIELDER'S GLOVE
GANT^M
HANDSCHUH^M
GUANTE^M **DE RECOGIDA**^F

web
panier^M
Netz^N
canasta^F

finger
doigt^M
Finger^M
dedo^M

strap
patte^F
Riemen^M
trabilla^F

thumb
pouce^M
Daumen^M
pulgar^M

palm
paume^F
Handfläche^F
palma^F

heel
talon^M
Handwurzel^F
talón^M

lace
lacet^M
Schnürband^N
cordón^M

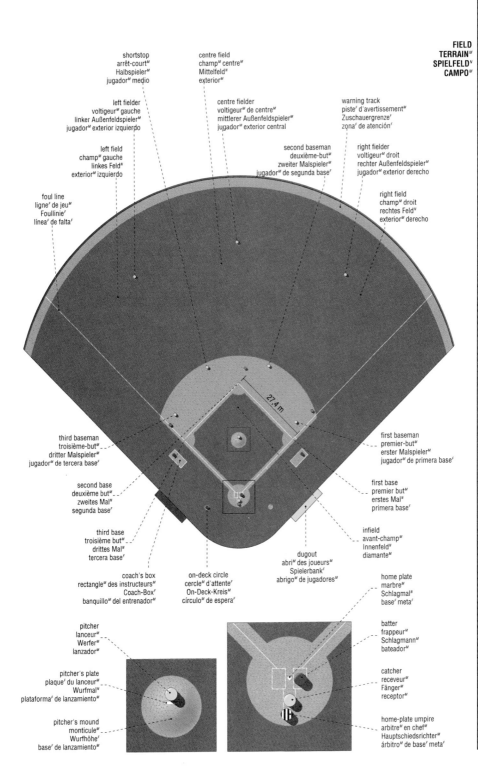

shortstop
arrêt-court^M
Halbspieler^M
jugador^M medio

centre field
champ^M centre^M
Mittelfeld^N
exterior^M

left fielder
voltigeur^M gauche
linker Außenfeldspieler^M
jugador^M exterior izquierdo

centre fielder
voltigeur^M de centre^M
mittlerer Außenfeldspieler^M
jugador^M exterior central

warning track
piste^F d'avertissement^M
Zuschauergrenze^F
zona^F de atención^F

left field
champ^M gauche
linkes Feld^N
exterior^M izquierdo

second baseman
deuxième-but^M
zweiter Malspieler^M
jugador^M de segunda base^F

right fielder
voltigeur^M droit
rechter Außenfeldspieler^M
jugador^M exterior derecho

foul line
ligne^F de jeu^M
Foullinie^F
línea^F de falta^F

right field
champ^M droit
rechtes Feld^N
exterior^M derecho

27.4 m

third baseman
troisième-but^M
dritter Malspieler^M
jugador^M de tercera base^F

first baseman
premier-but^M
erster Malspieler^M
jugador^M de primera base^F

second base
deuxième but^M
zweites Mal^N
segunda base^F

first base
premier but^M
erstes Mal^N
primera base^F

third base
troisième but^M
drittes Mal^N
tercera base^F

infield
avant-champ^M
Innenfeld^N
diamante^M

coach's box
rectangle^M des instructeurs^M
Coach-Box^F
banquillo^M del entrenador^M

on-deck circle
cercle^M d'attente^F
On-Deck-Kreis^M
círculo^M de espera^F

dugout
abri^M des joueurs^M
Spielerbank^F
abrigo^M de jugadores^M

home plate
marbre^M
Schlagmal^N
base^F meta^F

pitcher
lanceur^M
Werfer^M
lanzador^M

batter
frappeur^M
Schlagmann^M
bateador^M

pitcher's plate
plaque^F du lanceur^M
Wurfmal^N
plataforma^F de lanzamiento^M

catcher
receveur^M
Fänger^M
receptor^M

pitcher's mound
monticule^M
Wurfhöhe^F
base^F de lanzamiento^M

home-plate umpire
arbitre^M en chef^M
Hauptschiedsrichter^M
árbitro^M de base^F meta^F

CRICKET
CRICKET^M
CRICKET^N
CRICKET^M

CRICKET PLAYER
JOUEUR^M DE CRICKET^M
CRICKETSPIELER^M
JUGADOR^M DE CRICKET^M

BAT
BATTE^F
SCHLAGHOLZ^N
PALA^F

glove
gant^M
Handschuh^M
guante^M

bat
batte^F
Schlagholz^N
pala^F

handle
manche^M
Griff^M
mango^M

ball
balle^F
Ball^M
pelota^F

stump
piquet^M
Stab^M
rastrillo^M con los travesaños^M

willow
plat^M
Weidenholz^N
pala^F

pad
jambière^F
Polster^N
protector^M

cricket shoe
chaussure^F
Cricketschuh^M
zapatilla^F

CRICKET BALL
BALLE^F DE CRICKET^M
CRICKETBALL^M
PELOTA^F DE CRICKET^M

studs
crampons^M
Stollen^M
tacos^M

seam
couture^F
Saum^M
costura^F

leather skin
enveloppe^F
Lederhaut^F
forro^M de cuero^M

70 – 73 mm

groove
rainure^F
Rille^F
ranura^F guía^F

TEAM GAMES
SPORTS D'ÉQUIPE

MANNSCHAFTSSPORTARTEN
DEPORTES DE EQUIPO

WICKET
GUICHET^M
MAL^N
RASTRILLO^M **CON LOS TRAVESAÑOS**^M

bail
barrette^F
Querholz^N
travesaño^M

stump
piquet^M
Stab^M
rastrillo^M

FIELD
TERRAIN^M
FELD^N
CAMPO^M

wicketkeeper
garde-guichet^M
Torwächter^M
portero^M del equipo^M receptor

umpire
arbitre^M
Schiedsrichter^M
árbitro^M

fielders
équipe^F au champ^M
Spieler^M der Feldseite^F
equipo^M receptor

batsman
batteur^M
Schlagmann^M
bateador^M

pitch
livrée^F
Spielfeld^N
terreno^M de juego^M

bowler
lanceur^M
Werfer^M
lanzador^M

batsman
batteur^M
Schlagmann^M
bateador^M

umpire
arbitre^M
Schiedsrichter^M
árbitro^M

PITCH
LIVRÉE^F
SPIELFELD^N
TERRENO^M **DE JUEGO**^M

wicketkeeper
garde-guichet^M
Torwächter^M
portero^M del equipo^M receptor

wicket
guichet^M
Mal^N
rastrillo^M con los travesaños^M

run
course^F
Lauf^M
carrera^F

batsman
batteur^M
Schlagmann^M
bateador^M

return crease
limite^F de retour^M
Rückwurflinie^F
línea^F de devolución^F

batsman
batteur^M
Schlagmann^M
bateador^M

20,12 m

popping crease
limite^F du batteur^M
Schlagmallinie^F
línea^F de carrera^F

bowling crease
ligne^F de retrait^M
Wurflinie^F
línea^F del rastrillo^M

bowler
lanceur^M
Werfer^M
lanzador^M

ASSOCIATION FOOTBALL
FOOTBALL*M*
FUSSBALL*M*
FÚTBOL*M*

FOOTBALLER
FOOTBALLEUR*M*
FUSSBALLSPIELER*M*
FUTBOLISTA*M/F*

FOOTBALL
BALLON*M* **DE FOOTBALL***M*
FUSSBALL*M*
BALÓN*M*

218 mm

team shirt
chandail*M* d'équipe*F*
Trikot*N*
camiseta*F* de equipo*M*

shorts
short*M*
Hose*F*
pantalones*M*

shin guard
protège-tibia*M*
Schienbeinschützer*M*
espinillera*F*

football boot
chaussure*F* de football*M*
Fußballschuh*M*
bota*F*

screw-in studs
crampons*M* interchangeables
Schraubstollen*M*
tacos*M* de rosca*F*

600

penalty spot
point^M de penalty^M
Elfmeterpunkt^M
punto^M de pénalty^M

goal
but^M
Tor^N
portería^F

penalty area
surface^F de réparation^F
Strafraum^M
área^F de penalty^M

goal area
surface^F de but^M
Torraum^M
área^F pequeña

45 – 90 m

penalty area marking
ligne^F de surface^F de réparation^F
Strafraumlinie^F
línea^F de área^F de penalty^M

corner flag
drapeau^M de coin^M
Eckballfahne^F
banderín^M de córner^M

penalty arc
arc^M de cercle^M
Strafraumbogen^M
semicírculo^M del área^F

corner arc
surface^F de coin^M
Eckbogen^M
córner^M

centre circle
cercle^M central
Mittelkreis^M
círculo^M central

referee
arbitre^M
Schiedsrichter^M
árbitro^M

halfway line
ligne^F médiane
Mittellinie^F
línea^F central

centre flag
drapeau^M de centre^M
Mittelfahne^F
banderín^M de córner^M

90 – 120 m

left wing
ailier^M gauche
Linksaußen^M
extremo^M izquierdo

right wing
ailier^M droit
Rechtsaußen^M
extremo^M derecho

touch line
ligne^F de touche^F
Seitenauslinie^F
banda^F

centre spot
centre^M
Anstoßpunkt^M
centro^M del campo^M

centre back
demi^M gauche
Vorstopper^M
medio^M izquierdo

linesman
juge^M de touche^F
Linienrichter^M
juez^M de línea^F

fullback
arrière^M gauche
Verteidiger^M
defensa^M izquierdo

centre-back
demi^M droit
Vorstopper^M
medio^M derecho

midfield
intérieur^M gauche
Mittelfeldspieler^M
interior^M izquierdo

fullback
arrière^M droit
Verteidiger^M
defensa^M derecho

centre forward
avant^M centre
Mittelstürmer^M
delantero^M centro

midfield
intérieur^M droit
Mittelfeldspieler^M
interior^M derecho

central defender
arrière^M central
Libero^M
defensa^M central

goalkeeper
gardien^M de but^M
Torwart^M
portero^M

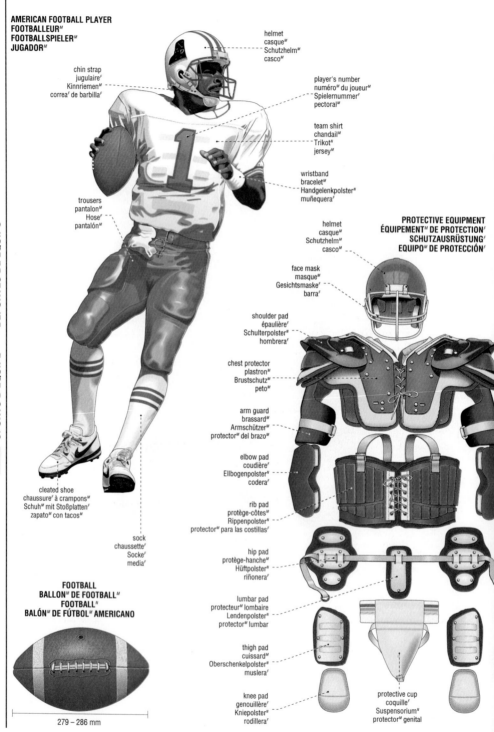

AMERICAN FOOTBALL
FOOTBALL^M AMÉRICAIN
FOOTBALL^N
FÚTBOL^M AMERICANO

AMERICAN FOOTBALL PLAYER
FOOTBALLEUR^M
FOOTBALLSPIELER^M
JUGADOR^M

helmet
casque^M
Schutzhelm^M
casco^M

chin strap
jugulaire^F
Kinnriemen^M
correa^F de barbilla^F

player's number
numéro^M du joueur^M
Spielernummer^F
pectoral^M

team shirt
chandail^M
Trikot^N
jersey^M

wristband
bracelet^M
Handgelenkpolster^N
muñequera^F

trousers
pantalon^M
Hose^F
pantalón^M

PROTECTIVE EQUIPMENT
ÉQUIPEMENT^M DE PROTECTION^F
SCHUTZAUSRÜSTUNG^F
EQUIPO^M DE PROTECCIÓN^F

helmet
casque^M
Schutzhelm^M
casco^M

face mask
masque^M
Gesichtsmaske^F
barra^F

shoulder pad
épaulière^F
Schulterpolster^N
hombrera^F

chest protector
plastron^M
Brustschutz^M
peto^M

arm guard
brassard^M
Armschützer^M
protector^M del brazo^M

elbow pad
coudière^F
Ellbogenpolster^N
codera^F

rib pad
protège-côtes^M
Rippenpolster^N
protector^M para las costillas^F

cleated shoe
chaussure^F à crampons^M
Schuh^M mit Stoßplatten^F
zapato^M con tacos^M

hip pad
protège-hanche^M
Hüftpolster^N
riñonera^F

sock
chaussette^F
Socke^F
media^F

lumbar pad
protecteur^M lombaire
Lendenpolster^N
protector^M lumbar

FOOTBALL
BALLON^M DE FOOTBALL^M
FOOTBALL^N
BALÓN^M DE FÚTBOL^M AMERICANO

thigh pad
cuissard^M
Oberschenkelpolster^N
muslera^F

knee pad
genouillère^F
Kniepolster^N
rodillera^F

protective cup
coquille^F
Suspensorium^N
protector^M genital

279 – 286 mm

offence
attaque^F
angreifende Mannschaft^F
ataque^M

defence
défense^F
verteidigende Mannschaft^F
defensa^F

line judge
second juge^M de ligne^F
Linienrichter^M
juez^M de línea^F

tight end
ailier^M rapproché
Tight-End^M
ala^M cerrado

neutral zone
zone^F neutre
neutrale Zone^F
zona^F neutral

left tackle
bloqueur^M gauche
linker Angriffsspieler^M
tacle^M izquierdo

right cornerback
demi^M de coin^M droit
rechter Cornerback^M
esquinero^M derecho

referee
arbitre^M en chef^M
erster Schiedsrichter^M
árbitro^M

outside linebacker
secondeur^M extérieur droit
äußerer Linebacker^M
apoyador^M exterior

left guard
garde^M gauche
linker Guard^M
guardia^M izquierdo

right defensive end
ailier^M défensif droit
rechter Defensive-End^M
ala^M defensivo derecho

left halfback
demi^M gauche
linker Halfback^M
corredor^M izquierdo

right safety
demi^M de sûreté^F droit
rechter Safety^M
profundo^M derecho

quarterback
quart-arrière^M
Quarterback^M
quarterback^M

umpire
arbitre^M
zweiter Schiedsrichter^M
juez^M

fullback
arrière^M
Fullback^M
corredor^M de poder^M

left safety
demi^M de sûreté^F gauche
linker Safety^M
profundo^M izquierdo

right halfback
demi^M droit
rechter Halfback^M
corredor^M derecho

back judge
juge^M de champ^M arrière
Rückfeldschiedsrichter^M
árbitro^M de la defensa^F

centre
centre^M
Centre^M
central^M

middle linebacker
secondeur^M au centre^M
mittlerer Linebacker^M
apoyador^M

right guard
garde^M droit
rechter Guard^M
guardia^M derecho

right defensive tackle
plaqueur^M droit
rechter Defensive-Tackle^M
tacle^M defensivo derecho

right tackle
bloqueur^M droit
rechter Angriffsspieler^M
tacle^M derecho

inside linebacker
secondeur^M extérieur gauche
Inside-Linebacker^M
apoyador^M interior

split end
ailier^M éloigné
Split-End^M
receptor^M abierto

head linesman
premier juge^M de ligne^F
Hauptlinienrichter^M
juez^M de línea^F

left defensive end
ailier^M défensif gauche
linker Defensive-End^M
ala^M defensivo izquierdo

left defensive tackle
plaqueur^M gauche
linker Defensive-Tackle^M
tacle^M defensivo izquierdo

line of scrimmage
ligne^F de mêlée^F
Scrimmagelinie^F
línea^F de melé^M

left cornerback
demi^M de coin^M gauche
linker Cornerback^M
esquinero^M izquierdo

AMERICAN/CANADIAN FOOTBALL
FOOTBALL^M
FOOTBALL^N
FÚTBOL^M AMERICANO

PLAYING FIELD FOR AMERICAN FOOTBALL
TERRAIN^M DE FOOTBALL^M AMÉRICAIN
SPIELFELD^N FÜR AMERIKANISCHES FOOTBALL^N
CAMPO^M DE JUEGO^M DE FÚTBOL^M AMERICANO

players' bench
banc^M des joueurs^M
Spielerbank^F
banquillo^M de jugadores^M

sideline
ligne^F de touche^F
Seitenlinie^F
banda^F

goalpost
poteau^M de but^M
Torpfosten^M
poste^M

goal line
ligne^F de but^M
Torlinie^F
línea^F de gol^M

centre line
ligne^F de centre^M
Mittellinie^F
línea^F media

goal
but^M
Tor^N
gol^M

MANNSCHAFTSSPORTARTEN
DEPORTES DE EQUIPO

TEAM GAMES
SPORTS D'ÉQUIPE

49 m

9,1 m

91,4 m

end line
ligne^F de fond^M
Endlinie^F
línea^F de fondo^M

inbound line
trait^M de mise^F au jeu^M
Inbound-Linie^F
línea^F límite^M de inicio^M de jugada^F

yard line
ligne^F des verges^F
Yardlinie^F
yardas^F

end zone
zone^F de but^M
Endzone^F
zona^F de anotación^F

PLAYING FIELD FOR CANADIAN FOOTBALL
TERRAIN^M DE FOOTBALL^M CANADIEN
SPIELFELD^N FÜR KANADISCHES FOOTBALL^N
CAMPO^M DE JUEGO^M DE FÚTBOL^M CANADIENSE

60 m

18,2 m

100 m

SCRIMMAGE IN CANADIAN FOOTBALL
MÊLÉE^F AU FOOTBALL^M CANADIEN
SCRIMMAGE^N IM KANADISCHEN FOOTBALL^M
MELÉ^M EN EL FÚTBOL^M CANADIENSE

offence
attaque^F
angreifende Mannschaft^F
ataque^M

line of scrimmage
ligne^F de mêlée^F
Scrimmagelinie^F
línea^F de disputa^F

line judge
juge^M de mêlée^F
erster Linienrichter^M
juez^M de línea^F

defence
défense^F
verteidigende Mannschaft^F
defensa^F

neutral zone
zone^F neutre
neutrale Zone^F
zona^F neutral

right outside linebacker
secondeur^M extérieur droit
Rechtsaußen-Linebacker^M
apoyador^M externo derecho

tight end
ailier^M rapproché
Tight-End^M
ala^M cerrado

back judge
juge^M de champ^M arrière
Rückfeldrichter^M
juez^M de campo^M

left tackle
bloqueur^M gauche
linker Tackle^M
tacle^M izquierdo

right cornerback
demi^M de coin^M droit
rechter Cornerback^M
esquinero^M derecho

referee
arbitre^M en chef^M
erster Schiedsrichter^M
árbitro^M

right defensive end
ailier^M défensif droit
rechter Defensive-End^M
ala^M defensivo derecho

left guard
garde^M gauche
linker Guard^M
guardia^M izquierdo

right defensive tackle
plaqueur^M droit
rechter Defensive-Tackle^M
tacle^M defensivo derecho

slotback
demi-inséré^M
Slotback^M
flanqueador^M izquierdo

umpire
arbitre^M
zweiter Schiedsrichter^M
juez^M

fullback
arrière^M
Fullback^M
corredor^M de poder^M

right safety back
demi^M de sûreté^F droit
rechter Safetyback^M
profundo^M derecho

halfback
demi^M
Halfback^M
corredor^M ligero

monster
demi^M en maraude^F
Monster^M
profundo^M libre

flanker
flanqueur^M
Flanker^M
flanqueador^M derecho

left safety back
demi^M de sûreté^F gauche
linker Safetyback^M
profundo^M izquierdo

quarterback
quart-arrière^M
Quarterback^M
quarterback^M

middle linebacker
secondeur^M au centre^M
mittlerer Linebacker^M
apoyador^M central

centre
centre^M
Centre^M
centro^M

field judge
juge^M de passes^F et de bottés^M
Feldrichter^M
árbitro^M

right guard
garde^M droit
rechter Guard^M
guardia^M derecho

left defensive tackle
plaqueur^M gauche
linker Defensive-Tackle^M
tacle^M defensivo izquierdo

right tackle
bloqueur^M droit
rechter Tackle^M
tacle^M derecho

split end
ailier^M éloigné
Split-End^M
receptor^M abierto

left outside linebacker
secondeur^M extérieur gauche
Linksaußen-Linebacker^M
apoyador^M externo izquierdo

left cornerback
demi^M de coin^M gauche
linker Cornerback^M
esquinero^M izquierdo

linesman
juge^M de ligne^F
zweiter Linienrichter^M
juez^M de línea^F

left defensive end
ailier^M défensif gauche
linker Defensive-End^M
ala^M defensivo izquierdo

side judge
juge^M de touche^F
Seitenlinienrichter^M
juez^M de línea^F

FIELD
TERRAIN^M
SPIELFELD^N
CAMPO^M DE JUEGO^M

MANNSCHAFTSSPORTARTEN
DEPORTES DE EQUIPO

TEAM GAMES
SPORTS D'ÉQUIPE

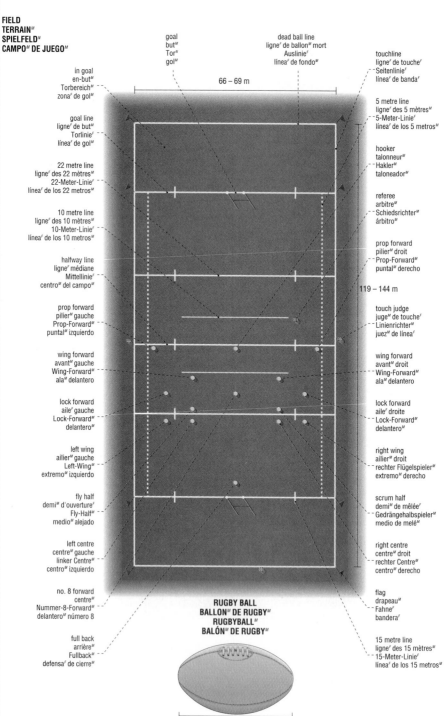

goal
but^M
Tor^N
gol^M

dead ball line
ligne^F de ballon^M mort
Auslinie^F
línea^F de fondo^M

touchline
ligne^F de touche^F
Seitenlinie^F
línea^F de banda^F

in goal
en-but^M
Torbereich^M
zona^F de gol^M

66 – 69 m

5 metre line
ligne^F des 5 mètres^M
5-Meter-Linie^F
línea^F de los 5 metros^M

goal line
ligne^F de but^M
Torlinie^F
línea^F de gol^M

hooker
talonneur^M
Hakler^M
taloneador^M

22 metre line
ligne^F des 22 mètres^M
22-Meter-Linie^F
línea^F de los 22 metros^M

referee
arbitre^M
Schiedsrichter^M
árbitro^M

10 metre line
ligne^F des 10 mètres^M
10-Meter-Linie^F
línea^F de los 10 metros^M

prop forward
pilier^M droit
Prop-Forward^M
puntal^M derecho

halfway line
ligne^F médiane
Mittellinie^F
centro^M del campo^M

119 – 144 m

prop forward
pilier^M gauche
Prop-Forward^M
puntal^M izquierdo

touch judge
juge^M de touche^F
Linienrichter^M
juez^M de línea^F

wing forward
avant^M gauche
Wing-Forward^M
ala^M delantero

wing forward
avant^M droit
Wing-Forward^M
ala^M delantero

lock forward
aile^F gauche
Lock-Forward^M
delantero^M

lock forward
aile^F droite
Lock-Forward^M
delantero^M

left wing
ailier^M gauche
Left-Wing^M
extremo^M izquierdo

right wing
ailier^M droit
rechter Flügelspieler^M
extremo^M derecho

fly half
demi^M d'ouverture^F
Fly-Half^M
medio^M alejado

scrum half
demi^M de mêlée^F
Gedrängehalbspieler^M
medio de melé^M

left centre
centre^M gauche
linker Centre^M
centro^M izquierdo

right centre
centre^M droit
rechter Centre^M
centro^M derecho

no. 8 forward
centre^M
Nummer-8-Forward^M
delantero^M número 8

flag
drapeau^M
Fahne^F
bandera^F

RUGBY BALL
BALLON^M DE RUGBY^M
RUGBYBALL^M
BALÓN^M DE RUGBY^M

full back
arrière^M
Fullback^M
defensa^F de cierre^M

15 metre line
ligne^F des 15 mètres^M
15-Meter-Linie^F
línea^F de los 15 metros^M

28 cm

FIELD HOCKEY
HOCKEY^M SUR GAZON^M
HOCKEY^N
HOCKEY^M SOBRE HIERBA^F

PLAYING FIELD
TERRAIN^M
SPIELFELD^N
CAMPO^M DE JUEGO^M

54,9 m

goal line
ligne^F de but^M
Torlinie^F
línea^F de meta^F

corner flag
drapeau^M de coin^M
Eckfahne^F
banderín^M de esquina^F

22,9 metre line
ligne^F des 22,9 mètres^M
22,9-Meter-Linie^F
línea^F de los 22,9 metros^M

goal
but^M
Tor^N
portería^F

centre line
ligne^F de centre^M
Mittellinie^F
línea^F media

striking circle
cercle^M d'envoi^M
Schußkreis^M
área^F de pénalty^M

left inner
avant^M gauche
linker Innenfeldspieler^M
interior^M izquierdo

sideline
ligne^F de touche^F
Seitenlinie^F
banda^F

91,4 m

left wing
ailier^M gauche
linker Flügelspieler^M
centro^M del campo^M

right wing
ailier^M droit
rechter Flügelspieler^M
extremo^M derecho

left half
demi^M gauche
linker Mittelfeldspieler^M
defensa^M central izquierdo

right inner
avant^M droit
halbrechter Läufer^M
interior^M derecho

centre half
demi^M centre
Mittelfeldspieler^M
medio^M central

centre forward
avant^M centre
Mittelstürmer^M
centro^M delantero

left back
arrière^M gauche
linker Verteidiger^M
defensa^M lateral izquierdo

right half
demi^M droit
rechter Mittelfeldspieler^M
medio punta^F

goalkeeper
gardien^M de but^M
Torwart^M
portero^M

right back
arrière^M droit
rechter Verteidiger^M
defensa^M lateral derecho

handle
manche^M
Griff^M
mango^M

STICK
CROSSE^F
SCHLÄGER^M
STICK^M

tape
ruban^M adhésif
Klebeband^N
cinta^F

HOCKEY BALL
BALLE^F DE HOCKEY^M
HOCKEYBALL^M
PELOTA^F DE HOCKEY^M

blade
tête^F
Schlägerblatt^N
pala^F

66 – 74 mm

607

ICE HOCKEY
HOCKEY*M* SUR GLACE*F*
EISHOCKEY*N*
HOCKEY*M* SOBRE HIELO

RINK
PATINOIRE*F*
EISFLÄCHE*F*
PISTA*F*

26 – 30 m

goal line
ligne*F* de but*M*
Torlinie*F*
línea*F* de gol*M*

face-off spot
point*M* de mise*F* au jeu*M*
Anspielpunkt*M*
punto*M* de saque*M*

face-off circle
cercle*M* de mise*F* au jeu*M*
Anspielpunkt*M*
círculo*M* de reanudación*F* del juego*M*

neutral zone
zone*F* neutre
neutrale Zone*F*
zona*F* neutral

left wing
ailier*M* gauche
linker Stürmer*M*
extremo*M* izquierdo

penalty bench
banc*M* des pénalités*M*
Strafbank*F*
banquillo*M* de castigo

officials' bench
banc*M* des officiels*M*
Offiziellenbank*F*
mesa*F* arbitral

centre
centre*M*
Sturmspitze*F*
centro*M*

centre face-off circle
cercle*M* central
mittlerer Anspielpunkt*M*
círculo*M* de saque*M* inicial

left defence
défenseur*M* gauche
linker Verteidiger*M*
defensa*M* izquierdo

defending zone
zone*F* de défense*F*
Verteidigungszone*F*
zona*F* de defensa*F*

boards
bande*F*
Bande*F*
valla*F* de madera*F*

goal
but*M*
Tor*N*
portería*F*

goal crease
zone*F* de but*M*
Torraum*M*
zona*F* de la portería*F*

attacking zone
zone*F* d'attaque*F*
Angriffszone*F*
zona*F* de ataque*M*

blue line
ligne*F* bleue
blaue Linie*F*
línea*F* azul

referee
arbitre*M*
Schiedsrichter*M*
árbitro*M*

players' bench
banc*M* des joueurs*M*
Spielerbank*F*
banquillo*M* de los jugadores*M*

61 m

centre line
ligne*F* centrale
Mittellinie*F*
línea*F* media

right wing
ailier*M* droit
rechter Stürmer*M*
extremo*M* derecho

linesman
juge*M* de ligne*F*
Linienrichter*M*
juez*M* de línea*F*

right defence
défenseur*M* droit
rechter Verteidiger*M*
defensa*M* derecho

goalkeeper
gardien*M* de but*M*
Torwart*M*
portero*M*

rink corner
coin*M* de patinoire*F*
Ecke*F*
esquina*F*

PUCK
RONDELLE*F*
PUCK*M*
DISCO*M*

25 mm

76 mm

goal judge
juge*M* de but*M*
Torrichter*M*
juez*M* de gol*M*

608

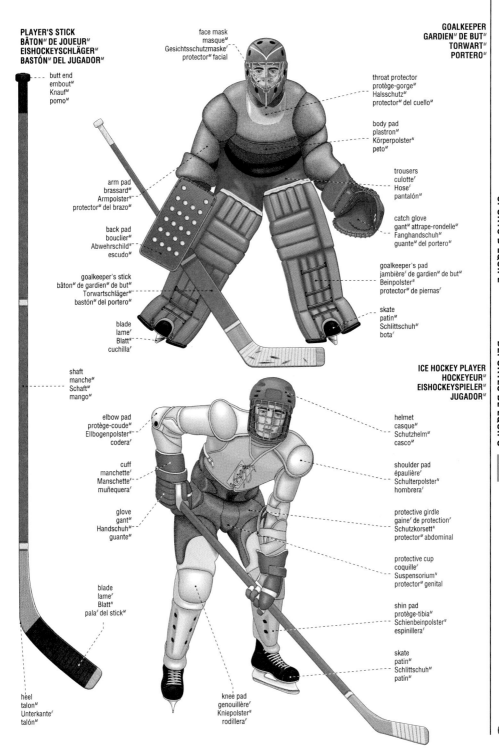

PLAYER'S STICK
BÂTON^M DE JOUEUR^M
EISHOCKEYSCHLÄGER^M
BASTÓN^M DEL JUGADOR^M

butt end
embout^M
Knauf^M
pomo^M

face mask
masque^M
Gesichtsschutzmaske^F
protector^M facial

throat protector
protège-gorge^M
Halsschutz^M
protector^M del cuello^M

body pad
plastron^M
Körperpolster^N
peto^M

arm pad
brassard^M
Armpolster^N
protector^M del brazo^M

trousers
culotte^F
Hose^F
pantalón^M

back pad
bouclier^M
Abwehrschild^N
escudo^M

catch glove
gant^M attrape-rondelle^M
Fanghandschuh^M
guante^M del portero^M

goalkeeper's stick
bâton^M de gardien^M de but^M
Torwartschläger^M
bastón^M del portero^M

goalkeeper's pad
jambière^F de gardien^M de but^M
Beinpolster^N
protector^M de piernas^F

blade
lame^F
Blatt^N
cuchilla^F

skate
patin^M
Schlittschuh^M
bota^F

shaft
manche^M
Schaft^M
mango^M

ICE HOCKEY PLAYER
HOCKEYEUR^M
EISHOCKEYSPIELER^M
JUGADOR^M

elbow pad
protège-coude^M
Ellbogenpolster^N
codera^F

helmet
casque^M
Schutzhelm^M
casco^M

cuff
manchette^F
Manschette^F
muñequera^F

shoulder pad
épaulière^F
Schulterpolster^N
hombrera^F

glove
gant^M
Handschuh^M
guante^M

protective girdle
gaine^F de protection^F
Schutzkorsett^N
protector^M abdominal

protective cup
coquille^F
Suspensorium^N
protector^M genital

blade
lame^F
Blatt^N
pala^F del stick^M

shin pad
protège-tibia^M
Schienbeinpolster^N
espinillera^F

skate
patin^M
Schlittschuh^M
patín^M

heel
talon^M
Unterkante^F
talón^M

knee pad
genouillère^F
Kniepolster^N
rodillera^F

COURT
TERRAIN^M
SPIELFELD^N
CANCHA^F

basket
panier^M
Korb^M
canasta^F

restricted area
zone^F réservée
begrenzte Zone^F
zona^F de tres segundos^M

end line
ligne^F de fond^M
Endlinie^F
línea^F de fondo^M

restricting circle
cercle^M restrictif
Begrenzungskreis^M
círculo^M central

15 m

free throw lane
couloir^M de lancer^M franc
Freiwurfbahn^F
zona^F

players' bench
banc^M des joueurs^M
Spielerbank^F
banquillo^M de los jugadores^M

semi-circle
demi-cercle^M
Halbkreis^M
semicírculo^M de la zona^F de tiro^F libre

left forward
avant^M gauche
linker Angriffsspieler^M
alero^M izquierdo

referee
arbitre^M
Schiedsrichter^M
árbitro^M

timekeeper
chronométreur^M
Zeitnehmer^M
cronometrador^M

right forward
avant^M droit
rechter Angriffsspieler^M
alero^M derecho

clock operator
chronométreur^M des trente
secondes^F
Uhrenmeister^M
operador^M del reloj^M de 30
segundos^M

28 m

centre line
ligne^F médiane
Mittellinie^F
línea^F media

scorer
marqueur^M
Anschreiber^M
anotador^M

right guard
arrière^M droit
rechte Deckung^F
escolta^M derecho

left guard
arrière^M gauche
linke Deckung^F
escolta^M izquierdo

referee
aide^M-arbitre^M
Schiedsrichter^M
árbitro^M

centre circle
cercle^M central
Mittelkreis^M
círculo^M central

centre
centre^M
mittlerer Angriffsspieler^M
pívot^M

free throw line
ligne^F de lancer^M franc
Freiwurflinie^F
línea^F de tiro^F libre

sideline
ligne^F de touche^F
Seitenlinie^F
banda^F

second space
deuxième espace^M
zweiter Raum^M
segundo espacio^M

first space
premier espace^M
erster Raum^M
primer espacio^M

three-point line
ligne^F des trois points^M
Drei-Punkte-Linie^F
línea^F de tres puntos^M

BASKET
PANIER^M
KORB^M
CANASTA^F

BASKETBALL
BALLON^M **DE BASKET**^M
BASKETBALL^M
BALÓN^M **DE BALONCESTO**^M

rim
anneau^M
Korbring^M
aro^M

backboard
panneau^M
Korbbrett^N
tablero^M

net
filet^M
Netz^N
red^F

244 mm

NETBALL
NETBALL[M]
NETZBALLSPIEL[N]
BALONCESTO[M] DE MUJERES[F]

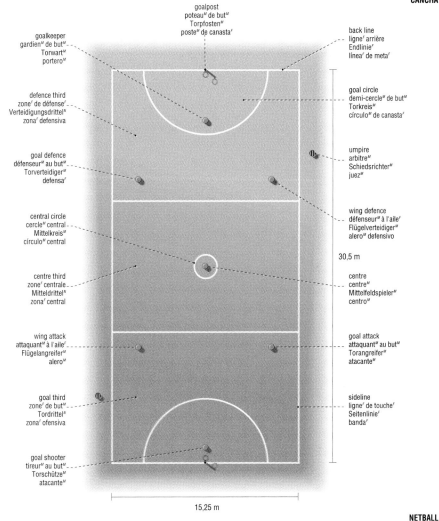

goalpost
poteau[M] de but[M]
Torpfosten[M]
poste[M] de canasta[F]

goalkeeper
gardien[M] de but[M]
Torwart[M]
portero[M]

back line
ligne[F] arrière
Endlinie[F]
línea[F] de meta[F]

defence third
zone[F] de défense[F]
Verteidigungsdrittel[N]
zona[F] defensiva

goal circle
demi-cercle[M] de but[M]
Torkreis[M]
círculo[F] de canasta[F]

goal defence
défenseur[M] au but[M]
Torverteidiger[M]
defensa[F]

umpire
arbitre[M]
Schiedsrichter[M]
juez[M]

central circle
cercle[M] central
Mittelkreis[M]
círculo[M] central

wing defence
défenseur[M] à l'aile[F]
Flügelverteidiger[M]
alero[M] defensivo

30,5 m

centre third
zone[F] centrale
Mitteldrittel[N]
zona[F] central

centre
centre[M]
Mittelfeldspieler[M]
centro[M]

wing attack
attaquant[M] à l'aile[F]
Flügelangreifer[M]
alero[M]

goal attack
attaquant[M] au but[M]
Torangreifer[M]
atacante[M]

goal third
zone[F] de but[M]
Tordrittel[N]
zona[F] ofensiva

sideline
ligne[F] de touche[F]
Seitenlinie[F]
banda[F]

goal shooter
tireur[M] au but[M]
Torschütze[M]
atacante[M]

15,25 m

NETBALL
BALLON[M] DE NETBALL[M]
NETZBALLSPIEL[N]
BALÓN[M]

218 – 226 mm

COURT
TERRAIN^M
SPIELFELD^N
CANCHA^F

goalkeeper
gardien^M de but^M
Torhüter^M
portero^M

20 m

penalty line
ligne^F des sept mètres^M
Penalty-Linie^F
línea^F de pénalty^M

guide mark
repère^M
Torhütermarkierung^F
límite^M de salida^F del portero^M

centre back
demi-centre^M
zurückgezogener Mittelfeldspieler^M
central^M

right back
arrière^M droit
zurückgezogener rechter Feldspieler^M
interior^M derecho

left back
arrière^M gauche
zurückgezogener linker Feldspieler^M
interior^M izquierdo

goal line referee
arbitre^M de ligne^F de but^M
Linienrichter^M
árbitro^M auxiliar

substitute corridor
couloir^M des remplacements^M
Wechselraum^M
zona^F de cambio^M

right winger
ailier^M droit
rechter Angriffsfeldspieler^M
extremo^M derecho

secretary
secrétaire^M
Schriftführer^M
secretario^M

40 m

centre line
ligne^F médiane
Mittellinie^F
línea^F central

timekeeper
chronométreur^M
Zeitnehmer^M
cronometrador^M

court referee
arbitre^M de champ^M
Feldschiedsrichter^M
árbitro^M principal

players' bench
banc^M des joueurs^M
Spielerbank^F
banquillo^M de jugadores^M

free throw line
ligne^F de jet^M franc
Freiwurflinie^F
línea^F de tiro^M libre

left winger
ailier^M gauche
linker Angriffsfeldspieler^M
extremo^M izquierdo

goal area line
ligne^F de surface^F de but^M
Torraumlinie^F
línea^F del área^F de gol^M

centre forward
avant-centre^M
Mittelfeldangriffsspieler^M
pivote^M

goal line
ligne^F de but^M
Torlinie^F
línea^F de gol^M

sideline
ligne^F de touche^F
Seitenlinie^F
banda^F

goal area
surface^F de but^M
Torraum^M
área^F de gol^M

goal
but^M
Tor^N
portería^F

net
filet^M
Netz^N
red^F

TEAM GAMES
SPORTS D'ÉQUIPE
MANNSCHAFTSSPORTARTEN
DEPORTES DE EQUIPO

HANDBALL
BALLON^M **DE HANDBALL**^M
HANDBALL^M
BALÓN^M **DE BALONMANO**^M

♀ 173 – 178 mm

♂ 183 – 188 mm

612

VOLLEYBALL
VOLLEYBALL[M]
VOLLEYBALLSPIEL[N]
BALÓN[M] VOLEA

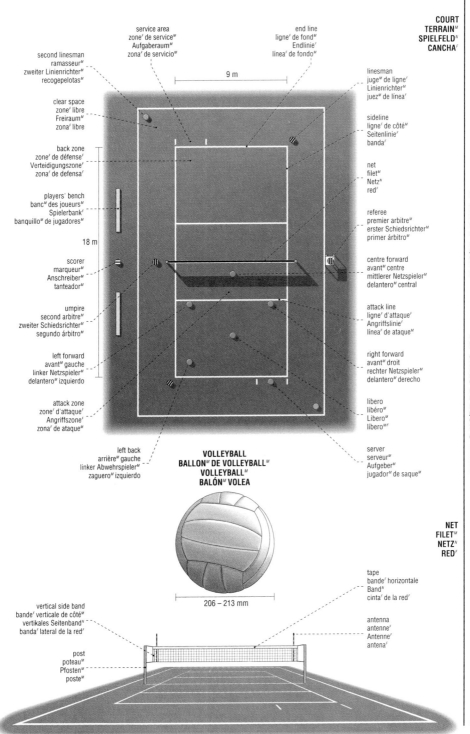

COURT
TERRAIN[M]
SPIELFELD[N]
CANCHA[F]

TEAM GAMES
SPORTS D'ÉQUIPE

MANNSCHAFTSSPORTARTEN
DEPORTES DE EQUIPO

service area
zone[F] de service[M]
Aufgaberaum[M]
zona[F] de servicio[M]

end line
ligne[F] de fond[M]
Endlinie[F]
línea[F] de fondo[M]

second linesman
ramasseur[M]
zweiter Linienrichter[M]
recogepelotas[M]

9 m

linesman
juge[M] de ligne[F]
Linienrichter[M]
juez[M] de línea[F]

clear space
zone[F] libre
Freiraum[M]
zona[F] libre

sideline
ligne[F] de côté[M]
Seitenlinie[F]
banda[F]

back zone
zone[F] de défense[F]
Verteidigungszone[F]
zona[F] de defensa[F]

net
filet[M]
Netz[N]
red[F]

players' bench
banc[M] des joueurs[M]
Spielerbank[F]
banquillo[M] de jugadores[M]

referee
premier arbitre[M]
erster Schiedsrichter[M]
primer árbitro[M]

18 m

scorer
marqueur[M]
Anschreiber[M]
tanteador[M]

centre forward
avant[M] centre
mittlerer Netzspieler[M]
delantero[M] central

umpire
second arbitre[M]
zweiter Schiedsrichter[M]
segundo árbitro[M]

attack line
ligne[F] d'attaque[F]
Angriffslinie[F]
línea[F] de ataque[M]

left forward
avant[M] gauche
linker Netzspieler[M]
delantero[M] izquierdo

right forward
avant[M] droit
rechter Netzspieler[M]
delantero[M] derecho

attack zone
zone[F] d'attaque[F]
Angriffszone[F]
zona[F] de ataque[M]

libero
libéro[M]
Libero[M]
líbero[M,F]

left back
arrière[M] gauche
linker Abwehrspieler[M]
zaguero[M] izquierdo

server
serveur[M]
Aufgeber[M]
jugador[M] de saque[M]

VOLLEYBALL
BALLON[M] DE VOLLEYBALL[M]
VOLLEYBALL[M]
BALÓN[M] VOLEA

206 – 213 mm

tape
bande[F] horizontale
Band[N]
cinta[F] de la red[F]

vertical side band
bande[F] verticale de côté[M]
vertikales Seitenband[N]
banda[F] lateral de la red[F]

antenna
antenne[F]
Antenne[F]
antena[F]

post
poteau[M]
Pfosten[M]
poste[M]

TENNIS
TENNIS^M
TENNIS^N
TENIS^M

COURT
TERRAIN^M
TENNISPLATZ^M
CANCHA^F

8,23 m

linesman
juge^F de ligne^F
Linienrichter^M
juez^M de línea^F

receiver
receveur^M
Rückschläger^M
restador^M

backcourt
arrière court^M
Rückfeld^N
cancha^F de fondo^M

centre service line
ligne^F médiane de service^M
mittlere Aufschlaglinie^F
línea^F central de servicio^M

forecourt
avant court^M
Vorderfeld^N
cuadro^M de saque^M

23,8 m

umpire
arbitre^M
Schiedsrichter^M
juez^M de silla^F

left service court
court^M de service^M gauche
linkes Aufschlagfeld^N
zona^F de saque^M izquierda

alley
couloir^M
Gasse^F
banda^F para dobles^M

server
serveur^M
Aufschläger^M
jugador^M con el servicio^M

ball boy
ramasseur^M
Balljunge^M
recogepelotas^M

centre mark
marque^F centrale
Mittelzeichen^N
marca^F central

baseline
ligne^F de fond^M
Grundlinie^F
línea^F de fondo^M

service line
ligne^F de service^M
Aufschlaglinie^F
línea^F de servicio^M

service judge
juge^M de service^M
Aufschlagrichter^M
juez^M de servicio^M

singles sideline
ligne^F de simple^M
Seitenlinie^F für das Einzelspiel
línea lateral^F de individuales^M

net judge
juge^M de filet^M
Netzrichter^M
juez^M de red^F

net
filet^M
Netz^N
red^F

right service court
court^M de service^M droit
rechtes Aufschlagfeld^N
zona^F de saque^M derecha

foot fault judge
juge^M de faute^F de pieds^M
Grundlinienrichter^M
juez^M de faltas^F de pie^M

doubles sideline
ligne^F de double^M
Seitenlinie^F für das Doppelspiel
línea^F de dobles^M

11 m

NET
FILET^M
NETZ^N
RED^F

centre strap
sangle^F
Mittelstreifen^M
cinta^F central

singles pole
poteau^M de simple^M
Pfosten^M für das Einzelspiel
poste^M de individuales^M

net band
bande^F de filet^M
Netzband^N
cinta^F de la red^F

doubles pole
poteau^M de double^M
Pfosten^M für das Doppelspiel
poste^M de dobles^M

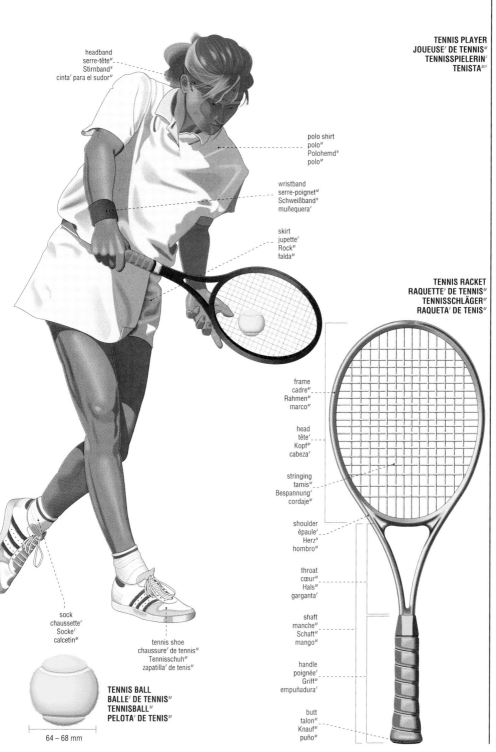

headband
serre-tête^M
Stirnband^N
cinta^F para el sudor^M

polo shirt
polo^M
Polohemd^N
polo^M

wristband
serre-poignet^M
Schweißband^N
muñequera^F

skirt
jupette^F
Rock^M
falda^M

TENNIS RACKET
RAQUETTE^F DE TENNIS^M
TENNISSCHLÄGER^M
RAQUETA^F DE TENIS^M

frame
cadre^M
Rahmen^M
marco^M

head
tête^F
Kopf^M
cabeza^F

stringing
tamis^M
Bespannung^F
cordaje^M

shoulder
épaule^F
Herz^N
hombro^M

throat
cœur^M
Hals^M
garganta^F

shaft
manche^M
Schaft^M
mango^M

handle
poignée^F
Griff^M
empuñadura^F

butt
talon^M
Knauf^M
puño^M

sock
chaussette^F
Socke^F
calcetín^M

tennis shoe
chaussure^F de tennis^M
Tennisschuh^M
zapatilla^F de tenis^M

TENNIS BALL
BALLE^F DE TENNIS^M
TENNISBALL^M
PELOTA^F DE TENIS^M

64 – 68 mm

615

SQUASH
SQUASHᴹ
SQUASHᴺ
SQUASHᴹ

SQUASH BALL
BALLEᶠ **DE SQUASH**ᴹ
SQUASHBALLᴹ
PELOTAᶠ **DE SQUASH**ᴹ

45 mm

SQUASH RACKET
RAQUETTEᶠ **DE SQUASH**ᴹ
SQUASHSCHLÄGERᴹ
RAQUETAᶠ **DE SQUASH**ᴹ

INTERNATIONAL SINGLES COURT
TERRAINᴹ **INTERNATIONAL DE SIMPLES**ᴹ
INTERNATIONALES EINZELSPIELFELDᴺ
CANCHAᶠ **INTERNACIONAL DE INDIVIDUALES**ᴹ

outer boundary line
limite ʳ hors-terrain
äußere Begrezungslinie ʳ
línea ʳ superior

ceiling
plafond ᴹ
Decke ʳ
techo ᴹ

side wall line
ligne ʳ latérale
Seitenwandlinie ʳ
línea ʳ lateral

front wall
mur ᴹ avant
Vorderwand ʳ
pared ʳ frontal

side wall
mur ᴹ latéral
Seitenwand ʳ
pared ʳ lateral

6,4 m

9,75 m

receiver
receveur ᴹ
Rückschläger ᴹ
restador ᴹ

right service court
zone ʳ de service ᴹ droite
rechtes Aufschlagfeld ᴺ
área ʳ derecha de recepción ʳ de servicio ᴹ

4,57 m

service line
ligne ʳ de service ᴹ
Aufschlaglinie ʳ
línea ʳ de servicio ᴹ

telltale
plaque ʳ de tôle ʳ
Dämpfer ᴹ
resonador ᴹ

floor
plancher ᴹ
Boden ᴹ
piso ᴹ

short line
ligne ʳ des courtes ʳ
Shortline ʳ
línea ʳ de servicio ᴹ

half court line
ligne ʳ de demi-court ᴹ
Mittellinie ʳ
línea ʳ divisoria central

service box
boîte ʳ de service ᴹ
Angaberaum ᴹ
cajón ᴹ de servicio ᴹ

left service court
zone ʳ de service ᴹ gauche
linkes Aufschlagfeld ᴺ
área ʳ izquierda de recepción ʳ de servicio ᴹ

server
serveur ᴹ
Aufschläger ᴹ
jugador ᴹ de saque ᴹ

back wall
mur ᴹ arrière
Hinterwand ʳ
muro ʳ de rebote ᴹ

616

RACQUETBALL
RACQUETBALL^M
RACQUETBALLSPIEL^N
RAQUETBOL^M

RACQUETBALL RACKET
RAQUETTE^F DE RACQUETBALL^M
RACQUETBALLSCHLÄGER^M
RAQUETA^F DE RAQUETBOL^M

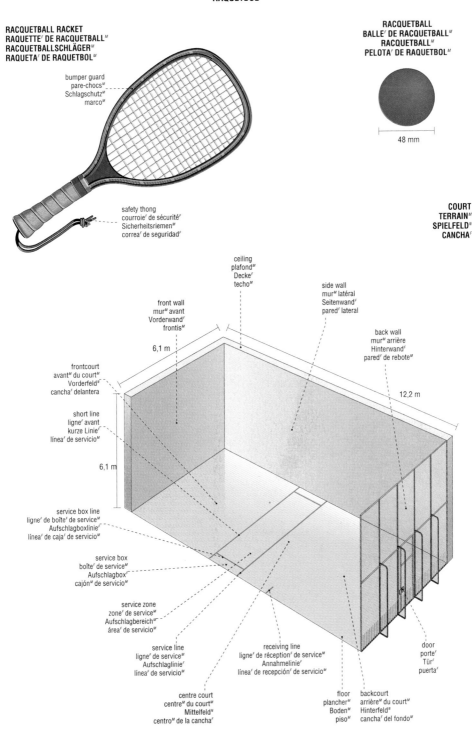

bumper guard
pare-chocs^M
Schlagschutz^M
marco^M

safety thong
courroie^F de sécurité^F
Sicherheitsriemen^M
correa^F de seguridad^F

RACQUETBALL
BALLE^F DE RACQUETBALL^M
RACQUETBALL^M
PELOTA^F DE RAQUETBOL^M

48 mm

COURT
TERRAIN^M
SPIELFELD^N
CANCHA^F

ceiling
plafond^M
Decke^F
techo^M

side wall
mur^M latéral
Seitenwand^F
pared^F lateral

front wall
mur^M avant
Vorderwand^F
frontis^M

back wall
mur^M arrière
Hinterwand^F
pared^F de rebote^M

6,1 m

frontcourt
avant^M du court^M
Vorderfeld^N
cancha^F delantera

12,2 m

short line
ligne^F avant
kurze Linie^F
línea^F de servicio^M

6,1 m

service box line
ligne^F de boîte^F de service^M
Aufschlagboxlinie^F
línea^F de caja^F de servicio^M

service box
boîte^F de service^M
Aufschlagbox^F
cajón^M de servicio^M

service zone
zone^F de service^M
Aufschlagbereich^M
área^F de servicio^M

service line
ligne^F de service^M
Aufschlaglinie^F
línea^F de servicio^M

receiving line
ligne^F de réception^F de service^M
Annahmelinie^F
línea^F de recepción^F de servicio^M

door
porte^F
Tür^F
puerta^F

centre court
centre^M du court^M
Mittelfeld^N
centro^M de la cancha^F

floor
plancher^M
Boden^M
piso^M

backcourt
arrière^M du court^M
Hinterfeld^N
cancha^F del fondo^M

BADMINTON
BADMINTON^M
BADMINTON^N
BÁDMINTON^M

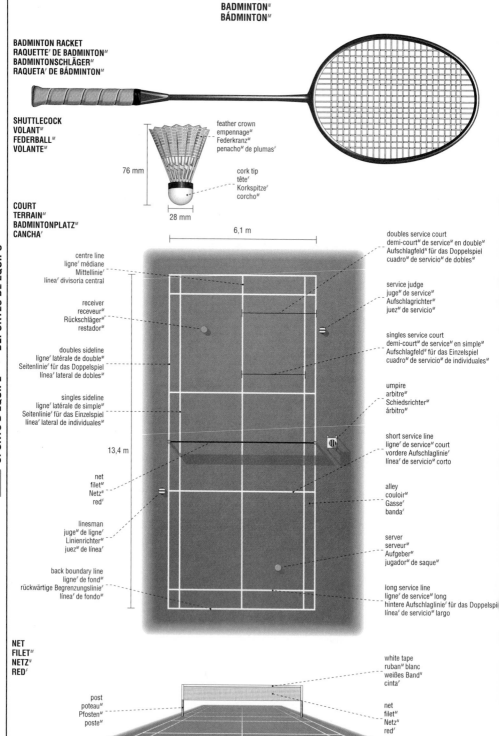

BADMINTON RACKET
RAQUETTE^F DE BADMINTON^M
BADMINTONSCHLÄGER^M
RAQUETA^F DE BÁDMINTON^M

SHUTTLECOCK
VOLANT^M
FEDERBALL^M
VOLANTE^M

feather crown
empennage^M
Federkranz^M
penacho^M de plumas^F

76 mm

cork tip
tête^F
Korkspitze^F
corcho^M

28 mm

COURT
TERRAIN^M
BADMINTONPLATZ^M
CANCHA^F

6,1 m

doubles service court
demi-court^M de service^M en double^M
Aufschlagfeld^N für das Doppelspiel
cuadro^M de servicio^M de dobles^M

centre line
ligne^F médiane
Mittellinie^F
línea^F divisoria central

service judge
juge^M de service^M
Aufschlagrichter^M
juez^M de servicio^M

receiver
receveur^M
Rückschläger^M
restador^M

singles service court
demi-court^M de service^M en simple^M
Aufschlagfeld^N für das Einzelspiel
cuadro^M de servicio^M de individuales^M

doubles sideline
ligne^F latérale de double^M
Seitenlinie^F für das Doppelspiel
línea^F lateral de dobles^M

umpire
arbitre^M
Schiedsrichter^M
árbitro^M

singles sideline
ligne^F latérale de simple^M
Seitenlinie^F für das Einzelspiel
línea^F lateral de individuales^M

short service line
ligne^F de service^M court
vordere Aufschlaglinie^F
línea^F de servicio^M corto

13,4 m

net
filet^M
Netz^N
red^F

alley
couloir^M
Gasse^F
banda^F

linesman
juge^M de ligne^F
Linienrichter^M
juez^M de línea^F

server
serveur^M
Aufgeber^M
jugador^M de saque^M

back boundary line
ligne^F de fond^M
rückwärtige Begrenzungslinie^F
línea^F de fondo^M

long service line
ligne^F de service^M long
hintere Aufschlaglinie^F für das Doppelspiel
línea^F de servicio^M largo

NET
FILET^M
NETZ^N
RED^F

white tape
ruban^M blanc
weißes Band^N
cinta^F

post
poteau^M
Pfosten^M
poste^M

net
filet^M
Netz^N
red^F

618

TABLE TENNIS
TENNIS*M* DE TABLE*F*
TISCHTENNIS*N*
PING PONG*M*

TABLE
TABLE*F*
TISCHTENNISPLATTE*F*
MESA*F*

mesh
maille*F*
Maschen*F*
malla*F*

side line
ligne*F* latérale
Seitenlinie*F*
línea*F* de banda*F*

net
filet*M*
Netz*N*
red*F*

playing surface
surface*F* de jeu*M*
Spielfläche*F*
superficie*F* de juego*M*

upper edge
arête*F* supérieure
Oberkante*F*
moldura*F* superior

white tape
bordure*F* blanche
weißes Band*N*
cinta*F*

centre line
ligne*F* centrale
Mittellinie*F*
línea*F* divisoria central

end line
ligne*F* de fond*M*
Endlinie*F*
línea*F* de fondo

net support
support*M*
Netzhalter*M*
soporte*M* de la red*F*

153 mm

2,74 m

1,52 m

leg
pied*M*
Bein*N*
pata*F* de la mesa*F*

38 mm

table tennis ball
balle*F* de tennis*M* de table*F*
Tischtennisball*M*
pelota*F* de ping pong*M*

TYPES OF GRIP
TYPES*M* DE PRISES*F*
GRIFFTECHNIKEN*F*
FORMAS*F* DE ASIR LA PALETA*F*

penholder grip
prise*F* porte-plume*M*
Penholdergriff*M*
oriental

TABLE TENNIS BAT
RAQUETTE*F* DE TENNIS*M* DE TABLE*F*
TISCHTENNISSCHLÄGER*M*
PALETA*F* DE PING PONG*M*

face
face*F*
Oberfläche*F*
cara*F*

covering
revêtement*M*
Beschichtung*F*
revestimiento*M*

handle
manche*M*
Griff*M*
mango*M*

blade
palette*F*
Blatt*N*
paleta*F*

shake-hands grip
prise*F* classique
Shake-Hands-Griff*M*
occidental

CURLING STONE
PIERRE^F DE CURLING^M
CURLINGSTEIN^M
PIEDRA^F DE CURLING^M

RINK
TERRAIN^M
EISBAHN^F
PISTA^F

handle
poignée^F
Griff^M
mango^M

114 mm

292 mm

rink
équipe^F
Abspielraum^M
pista^F

number two
deuxième joueur^M
Zweiter^M
segundo jugador^M

number three
troisième joueur^M
Dritter^M
tercer jugador^M

lead
meneur^M
Lead^M
líder^M

skip
capitaine^M
Skip^M
capitán^M

sweeping score line
ligne^F de balayage^M
Sweeping-Line^F
línea^F de barrido^M

back score line
ligne^F arrière
Back-Line^F
línea^F de fondo^M

hog score line
ligne^F de jeu^M
Hog-Line^F
línea^F de juego^M

CURLING BROOMS
BALAIS^M DE CURLING^M
CURLINGBESEN^M
ESCOBAS^F DE CURLING^M

44,5 – 50,3 m

centre line
ligne^F de centre^M
Mittellinie^F
línea^F central

area of ice
surface^F de glace^F
Eisfeld^N
pista^F de hielo^M

lateral line
ligne^F latérale
Seitenlinie^F
línea^F de banda^F

outer circle
cercle^M extérieur
Außenkreis^M
círculo^M exterior

tee
centre^M
Tee^N
marca^F central

inner circle
cercle^M intérieur
Innenkreis^M
círculo^M central

house
maison^F
Haus^N
casa^F

curler
curleur^M
Curlingstein^M
primer jugador^M

foot score line
ligne^F de départ^M
Foot-Line^F
línea^F de salida^F

hack
appui-pieds^M
Hack^M
percha^F

4,3 m

SWIMMING
NATATION[F]
SCHWIMMEN[N]
NATACIÓN[F]

COMPETITIVE COURSE
BASSIN[N] DE COMPÉTITION[F]
WETTKAMPFBECKEN[N]
PISCINA[F] OLÍMPICA

23 m

50 m

chief timekeeper
chronométreur[M] principal
Hauptzeitnehmer[M]
jefe[M] de cronometradores[M]

placing judge
juge[M] de classement[M]
Plazierungsrichter[M]
juez[M] de llegada[F]

lane number
numéro[M] de couloir[M]
Bahnnummer[F]
número[M] de calle[F]

recorder
enregistreur[M]
Protokollant[M]
anotador[M]

starting block
plot[M] de départ[M]
Startblock[M]
podio[M] de salida[F]

referee
arbitre[M]
Schiedsrichter[M]
árbitro[M]

stroke judge
juge[M] de nages[F]
Zugrichter[M]
juez[M] de brazado[M]

swimming pool
bassin[M]
Schwimmbecken[N]
piscina[F]

lane
couloir[M]
Bahn[F]
calle[F]

turning judge
juge[M] de virages[M]
Wenderichter[M]
juez[M] de viraje[M]

lane timekeeper
chronométreur[M] de couloir[M]
Bahnzeitnehmer[M]
cronometrador[M] de calle[F]

starter
juge[M] de départ[M]
Starter[M]
juez[M] de salida[F]

end wall
mur[M] d'extrémité[F]
Abschlußwand[F]
pared[F] de fondo[M]

side wall
mur[M] latéral
Seitenwand[F]
pared[F] lateral

bottom line
ligne[F] de fond[M]
Bodenlinie[F]
línea[F] del fondo[M] de la piscina[F]

lane rope
corde[F] de couloir[M]
Bahnseil[N]
corderas[F]

backstroke turn indicator
repère[M] de virage[M] de dos[M]
Wechselanzeige[F] für die Rückenlage
indicador[M] para viraje[M] en nado[M]

turning wall
mur[M] de virage[M]
Wendewand[F]
pared[F] de viraje[M]

STARTING BLOCK
PLOT[M] DE DÉPART[M]
STARTBLOCK[M]
PODIO[M] DE SALIDA[F]

platform
plate-forme[F]
Plattform[F]
podio[M] de salida[F]

column
colonne[F]
Säule[F]
pilar[M]

starting bar (backstroke)
barre[F] de départ[M] (dos[M])
Startstange[F] für die Rückenlage
barra[F] de salida[F] de espalda[F]

start wall
mur[M] de départ[M]
Startwand[F]
línea[F] de salida[F]

WATER SPORTS
SPORTS NAUTIQUES
WASSERSPORT
DEPORTES ACUÁTICOS

621

WASSERSPORT
DEPORTES ACUÁTICOS

WATER SPORTS
SPORTS NAUTIQUES

TYPES OF STROKE
TYPES[M] DE NAGES[F]
VERSCHIEDENE SCHWIMMSTILE[M]
ESTILOS[M] DE NATACIÓN[F]

starting dive
plongeon[M] de départ[M]
Startsprung[M]
salto[M] de salida[F]

CRAWL STROKE
CRAWL[M]
KRAULEN[N]
ESTILO[M] DE CROL[M]

crawl kick
coup[M] de pied[M] de crawl[M]
Beinarbeit[F] beim Kraulen[N]
patada[F] de crol[M]

breathing in
inspiration[F]
Einatmen[N]
inhalación[F]

breathing out
expiration[F]
Ausatmen[N]
exhalación[F]

flip turn
virage[M]-culbute[F]
Wende[F]
vuelta[F] de campana[F]

turning wall
mur[M] de virage[M]
Bahnende[N]
pared[F] de viraje[M]

BREASTSTROKE
BRASSE[F]
BRUSTSCHWIMMEN[N]
ESTILO[M] DE PECHO[M]

breaststroke kick
coup[M] de pied[M] de brasse[F]
Beinarbeit[F] beim Brustschwimmen[N]
patada[F] de rana[F]

breaststroke turn
virage[M] de brasse[F]
Wende[F] beim Brustschwimmen[N]
viraje[M] (toque[M]) con dos manos[F]

BUTTERFLY STROKE
PAPILLON^M
BUTTERFLYSCHWIMMSTIL^M
ESTILO^M **DE MARIPOSA**^F

butterfly kick
coup^M de pied^M de papillon^M
Beinarbeit^F beim Butterflyschwimmstil^M
patada^F de mariposa^F

butterfly turn
virage^M de papillon^M
Butterflywende^F
viraje^M de mariposa^F

BACKSTROKE START
DÉPART^M **DE DOS**^M
START^M **BEIM RÜCKENSCHWIMMEN**^N
POSICIÓN^F **DE SALIDA**^F **DE ESPALDA**^F

BACKSTROKE
NAGE^F **SUR LE DOS**^M
RÜCKENSCHWIMMEN^N
ESTILO^M **DE ESPALDA**^F

flip turn
virage^M-culbute^F
Wende^F
vuelta^F de campana^F

623

DIVING
PLONGEON^M
KUNSTSPRINGEN^N
SALTO^M

DIVING APPARATUS
PLONGEOIR^M
SPRINGEINRICHTUNGEN^F
TORRE^F **DE SALTOS**^{M}

diving tower
tour^F du plongeoir^M
Sprungturm^M
torre^F de saltos^M

10 m platform
plate-forme^F de 10 m
10-Meter-Turm^M
palanca^F de 10 m

7,5 m platform
plate-forme^F de 7,5 m
7,5-Meter-Turm^M
palanca^F de 7,5 m

5 m platform
plate-forme^F de 5 m
5-Meter-Turm^M
palanca^F de 5 m

3 m springboard
tremplin^M de 3 m
3-Meter-Brett^N
palanca^F de 3 m

3 m platform
plate-forme^F de 3 m
3-Meter-Turm^M
palanca^F de 3 m

fulcrum
pivot^M
Stützpunkt^M
punto^M de apoyo^M variable

1 m springboard
tremplin^M de 1 m
1-Meter-Brett^N
palanca^F de 1 m

surface of the water
surface^F de l'eau^F
Wasseroberfläche^F
superficie^F del agua^F

STARTING POSITIONS
POSITIONS^F **DE DÉPART**^{M}
STARTPOSITIONEN^F
POSICIONES^F **DE SALTO**^{M}

forward
avant
vorwärts
salto^M al frente^M

backward
arrière
rückwärts
salto^M atrás

armstand
en équilibre^M
Handstand^M
equilibrio^M

FLIGHTS
VOLS^M
SPRUNGFIGUREN^F
SALTOS^M

pike position
position^F carpée
Hechtsprungstellung^F
posición^F B - hacer la carpa^F

straight position
position^F droite
Bohrerstellung^F
posición^F A - derecho

tuck position
position^F groupée
Saltostellung^F
posición^F C - cuerpo^M encogido

ENTRIES
ENTRÉES^F **DANS L'EAU**^{F}
EINTAUCHSTELLUNGEN^F
ENTRADAS^F **AL AGUA**^{F}

head-first entry
entrée^F tête^F première
Kopf^M voraus
entrada^F de cabeza^F

feet-first entry
entrée^F pieds^M premiers
Füße^M voraus
entrada^F de pie^M

FORWARD DIVE
PLONGEON^M EN AVANT
KOPFSPRUNG^M VORWÄRTS
SALTO^M AL FRENTE^M EN POSICIÓN^F A

BACKWARD DIVE
PLONGEON^M EN ARRIÈRE
KOPFSPRUNG^M RÜCKWÄRTS
SALTO^M ATRÁS EN POSICIÓN^F A

ARMSTAND DIVE
PLONGEON^M EN ÉQUILIBRE^M
HANDSTANDSPRUNG^M
SALTO^M EN EQUILIBRIO^M

leg position
position^F des jambes^F
Beinhaltung^F
posición^F de las piernas^F

arm position
position^F des bras^M
Armhaltung^F
posición^F de los brazos^M

starting position
position^F de départ^M
Ausgangsposition^F
posición^F de salida^F

entry
entrée^F
Eintauchmoment^M
entrada^F

TWIST DIVE
TIRE-BOUCHON^M
SCHRAUBE^F
SALTO^M TIRABUZÓN^M EN POSICIÓN^F A

REVERSE DIVE
PLONGEON^M RENVERSÉ
SALTO^M
SALTO^M INVERSO EN POSICIÓN^F B

INWARD DIVE
PLONGEON^M RETOURNÉ
KLAPPMESSERSPRUNG^M
SALTO^M INTERIOR EN POSICIÓN^F B

height of the dive
hauteur^F du plongeon^M
Scheitelpunkt^M
altura^F de salto^M

flight
vol^M
Flug^M
vuelo^M

entry
entrée^F
Eintauchmoment^M
entrada^F

WATER SPORTS
SPORTS NAUTIQUES
WASSERSPORT
DEPORTES ACUÁTICOS

625

WATER POLO
WATER-POLO^M
WASSERBALLSPIEL^N
WATERPOLO^M

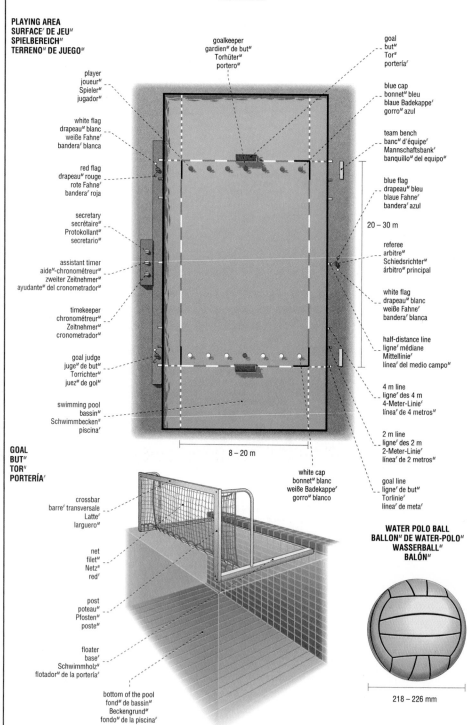

PLAYING AREA
SURFACE^F DE JEU^M
SPIELBEREICH^M
TERRENO^M DE JUEGO^M

goalkeeper
gardien^M de but^M
Torhüter^M
portero^M

goal
but^M
Tor^N
portería^F

player
joueur^M
Spieler^M
jugador^M

blue cap
bonnet^M bleu
blaue Badekappe^F
gorro^M azul

white flag
drapeau^M blanc
weiße Fahne^F
bandera^F blanca

team bench
banc^M d'équipe^F
Mannschaftsbank^F
banquillo^M del equipo^M

red flag
drapeau^M rouge
rote Fahne^F
bandera^F roja

blue flag
drapeau^M bleu
blaue Fahne^F
bandera^F azul

secretary
secrétaire^M
Protokollant^M
secretario^M

20 – 30 m

assistant timer
aide^M-chronométreur^M
zweiter Zeitnehmer^M
ayudante^M del cronometrador^M

referee
arbitre^M
Schiedsrichter^M
árbitro^M principal

timekeeper
chronométreur^M
Zeitnehmer^M
cronometrador^M

white flag
drapeau^M blanc
weiße Fahne^F
bandera^F blanca

goal judge
juge^M de but^M
Torrichter^M
juez^M de gol^M

half-distance line
ligne^F médiane
Mittellinie^F
línea^F del medio campo^M

swimming pool
bassin^M
Schwimmbecken^N
piscina^F

4 m line
ligne^F des 4 m
4-Meter-Linie^F
línea^F de 4 metros^M

8 – 20 m

2 m line
ligne^F des 2 m
2-Meter-Linie^F
línea^F de 2 metros^M

GOAL
BUT^M
TOR^N
PORTERÍA^F

white cap
bonnet^M blanc
weiße Badekappe^F
gorro^M blanco

goal line
ligne^F de but^M
Torlinie^F
línea^F de meta^F

crossbar
barre^F transversale
Latte^F
larguero^M

WATER POLO BALL
BALLON^M DE WATER-POLO^M
WASSERBALL^M
BALÓN^M

net
filet^M
Netz^N
red^F

post
poteau^M
Pfosten^M
poste^M

floater
base^F
Schwimmholz^N
flotador^M de la portería^F

bottom of the pool
fond^M de bassin^M
Beckengrund^M
fondo^M de la piscina^F

218 – 226 mm

SCUBA DIVING
PLONGÉE^F SOUS-MARINE
TAUCHEN^N
BUCEO^M

SCUBA DIVER
PLONGEUR^M
TAUCHER^M
BUCEADOR^M

mask
masque^M
Maske^F
gafas^F

hood
cagoule^F
Mütze^F
caperuza^F

snorkel
tuba^M
Schnorchel^M
tubo^M

harness
harnais^M
Gurtwerk^N
correas^F de los aparatos^M de buceo^M

regulator second stage
détendeur^M second étage^M
Druckregulierung^F
regulador^M de la 2ª etapa^F de descompresión^F

inflator
gonfleur^M
Aufblasteil^N
bomba^F de aire^M comprimido

regulator first stage
détendeur^M premier étage^M
Druckminderer^M
regulador^M de la 1ª etapa^F de descompresión^F

inflator valve
soupape^F de gonflage^M
Aufblasventil^N
válvula^F de aire^M comprimido

air hose
tuyau^M d'air^M
Luftschlauch^M
tubo^M de aire^M

mouthpiece
embout^M
Mundstück^N
boquilla^F

weight belt
ceinture^F lestée
Bleigürtel^M
cinturón^M lastrado

purge valve
soupape^F de purge^F
Überdruckventil^N
descompresor^M

buoyancy compensator
gilet^M de stabilisation^F
Auftriebsausgleich^M
compensador^M de flotación^F

information console
console^F d'instruments^M
Anzeigeeinheit^F
instrumentos^M de inmersión^F

compressed-air cylinder
bouteille^F d'air^M comprimé
Druckluftflasche^F
tanque^M de aire^M comprimido

thermometer
thermomètre^M
Thermometer^N
termómetro^M

emergency regulator
détendeur^M de secours^M
Notregulierung^F
regulador^M de emergencia^F

pressure gauge
manomètre^M
Druckanzeiger^M
manómetro^M

diving glove
gant^M de plongée^F
Taucherhandschuh^M
guante^M de buceo^M

depth gauge
profondimètre^M
Tiefenmesser^M
batímetro^M (medidor^M) de profundidad^F

wet suit
vêtement^M isothermique
Tauchanzug^M
traje^M isotérmico

fin
palme^F
Flosse^F
aleta^F

boot
bottillon^M
Schuh^M
bota^F

blade
voilure^F
Blatt^N
palma^F

foot pocket
chausson^M
Einstieg^M
bota^F de la aleta^F

rail
nervure^F
Rand^M
borde^M

harpoon gun
fusil^M à air^M comprimé
Harpune^F
arpón^M submarino

SAILING
VOILE^F
SEGELSPORT^M
VELA^F

SAILING BOAT
DÉRIVEUR^M
SEGELBOOT^N
VELERO^M

wind indicator
girouette^F
Verklicker^M
veleta^F (grímpola)

mast
mât^M
Mast^M
mástil^M

batten pocket
gousset^M de latte^F
Segeltasche^F
funda^F del sable^M

forestay
étai^M avant
Vorstag^M
estay^M de proa^F

batten
latte^F
Segellatte^F
sable^M

jib
foc^M
Klüver^M
foque^M

mainsail
grand-voile^F
Hauptsegel^N
vela^F mayor

shroud
hauban^M
Want^F
obenque^M

sail panel
laize^F
Segelkleid^N
panel^M de la vela^F

crosstree
barre^F de flèche^F
Saling^F
cruceta^F

telltale
pennon^M
Windanzeiger^M
axiómetro^M

boom vang
halebas^M
Halstalje^F
botavara^F

boom
bôme^F
Baum^M
botalón^M

jibsheet
écoute^F de foc^M
Vorsegelschot^N
escota^F foque^M

tiller
barre^F
Pinne^F
caña^F del timón^M

cleat
taquet^M
Klampe^F
escotera^F

mainsheet
écoute^F de grand-voile^F
Großschot^N
escota^F mayor

bow
étrave^F
Bug^M
proa^F

rudder
gouvernail^M
Ruderblatt^N
pala^F del timón^M

hull
coque^F
Rumpf^M
casco^M

cockpit
cockpit^M
Cockpit^N
bañera^F

centreboard
dérive^F
Schwert^N
orza^F de quilla^F

traveller
barre^F d'écoute^F
Traveller^M
escotero^M

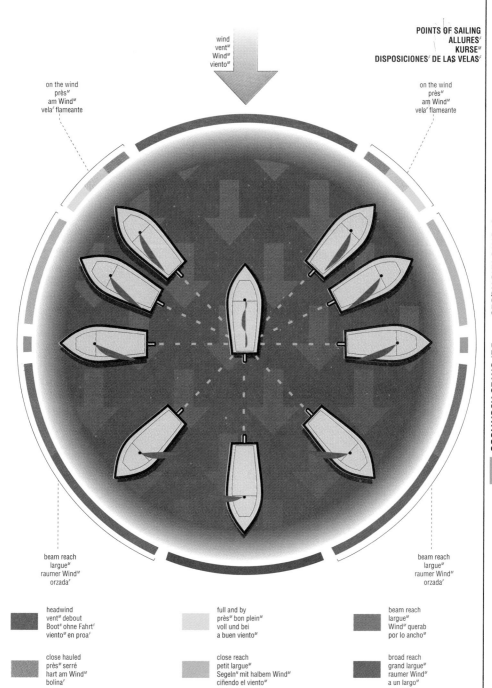

POINTS OF SAILING
ALLURES^F
KURSE^M
DISPOSICIONES^F DE LAS VELAS^F

wind
vent^M
Wind^M
viento^M

on the wind
près^M
am Wind^M
vela^F flameante

on the wind
près^M
am Wind^M
vela^F flameante

beam reach
largue^M
raumer Wind^M
orzada^F

beam reach
largue^M
raumer Wind^M
orzada^F

headwind
vent^M debout
Boot^N ohne Fahrt^F
viento^M en proa^F

full and by
près^M bon plein^M
voll und bei
a buen viento^M

beam reach
largue^M
Wind^M querab
por lo ancho^M

close hauled
près^M serré
hart am Wind^M
bolina^F

close reach
petit largue^M
Segeln^N mit halbem Wind^M
ciñendo el viento^M

broad reach
grand largue^M
raumer Wind^M
a un largo^M

on the wind
près^M
am Wind^M
viento^M contrario

wind abeam
vent^M de travers^M
halber Wind^M
viento^M de través

down wind
vent^M arrière
mit dem Wind^M
viento^M en popa^F

629

SAILING
VOILE^F
SEGELSPORT^M
VELA^F

UPPERWORKS
ACCASTILLAGE^M
BESCHLÄGE^M
OBRA^F **MUERTA**

hank
mousqueton^M
Gelenkschäkel^M
mosquetón^M

snap shackle
mousqueton^M à ressort^M
Karabinerhaken^M
grillete^M de resorte^M

shackle
manille^F
Schraubschäkel^M
grillete^M

fairlead
chaumard^M
Lippe^F
guía^F

cleat
taquet^M
Klampe^F
abrazadera^F

clam cleat
taquet^M coinceur
Curryklemme^F
escotera^F

winch
winch^M
Winsch^F
manubrio^M

turnbuckle
ridoir^M
Wantenspanner^M
tensor^M

sheet lead
filoir^M d'écoute^F
Leitöse^F
guía^F de escotas^F

TRAVELLER
BARRE^F **D'ÉCOUTE**^F
TRAVELLER^M
BARRA^F **DE ESCOTAS**^F

sliding rail
rail^M de glissement^M
Schlitten^M
riel^M corredizo

car
chariot^M
Wagen^M
carro^M

clam cleat
taquet^M coinceur
Curryklemme^F
abrazadera^F

end stop
butée^F
Anschlag^M
amarre^M

SAILBOARD
PLANCHE^F À VOILE^M
SURFBRETT^N
PLANCHA^F DE WINDSURF^M

sail
voile^F
Segel^N
vela^F

masthead
tête^F de mât^M
Mastspitze^F
cabeza^F de mástil^M

mast sleeve
fourreau^M
Masttasche^F
funda^F de mástil^M

luff
guindant^M
Vorliek^N
caída de proa^F

batten
latte^F
Segellatte^F
sable^M

batten pocket
gousset^M de latte^F
Segeltasche^F
funda^F del sable^M

leech
chute^F
Latte^F
caída^F de popa^F

window
fenêtre^F
Fenster^N
ventana^F

clew
point^M d'écoute^F
Horn^N
puño^M de escota^F

wishbone boom
wishbone^M
Gabelbaum^M
botavara^F

mast
mât^M
Mast^M
mástil^M

uphaul
tire-veille^M
Strang^M
tirante^M de la botavara^F

tack
point^M d'amure^F
Hals^M
puño^M de amura^F

foot
bordure^F
Fuß^M
pujamen^M

mast foot
pied^M de mât^M
Mastlager^N
cojinete^M móvil

daggerboard well
puits^M de dérive^F
Hauptschwerteinzug^M
caja^F orza^F de quilla^F

board
flotteur^M
Brett^N
tabla^F de surf^M

foot strap
arceau^M
Fußschlaufe^F
correa^F

stern
poupe^F
Heck^N
popa^F

skeg
aileron^M
Hilfsschwert^N
orza^F de popa^F

daggerboard
dérive^F
Hauptschwert^N
orza^F de quilla^F

bow
proue^F
Bug^M
proa^F

ROWING AND SCULLING
AVIRON^M
RUDERN^N UND SKULLEN^N
REMO^M

SCULLING (TWO OARS)
AVIRONS^M À COUPLE^M
SKULLEN^N (ZWEI SKULLS^N)
SKIF^M

shaft
manche^M
Schaft^M
cuello^M del remo^M

grip
poignée^F
Griff^M
guión^M

rowlock
dame^F de nage^F
Dolle^F
chumalera^F giratoria

stop
bourrelet^M
Anschlag^M
tope^M

outrigger
portant^M
Ausleger^M
arbotante^M

leather sheath
manchon^M
Belederung^F
luchadero^M

ROWING (ONE OAR)
AVIRON^M EN POINTE^F
RUDERN^N (EIN RIEMEN^M)
REMO^M

TYPES OF OAR
TYPES^M D'AVIRONS^M
RIEMENARTEN^F
TIPOS DE REMOS^M

needle
aviron^M de pointe^F
Nadelriemen^M
cuello^M del remo^M

blade
pelle^F
Blatt^N
pala^F

SCULLING BOATS
BATEAUX^M DE COUPLE^M
SKULLBOOTE^N
SKIF^M

single scull
skiff^M
Einer^M
skif^M unipersonal

double scull
double-scull^M
Zweier^M
skif^M doble

spade
aviron^M de couple^M
Spatenriemen^M
timón^M

blade
pelle^F
Blatt^N
pala^F

ROWING BOATS
BATEAUX^M DE POINTE^F
RUDERBOOTE^N
OUTRIGGERS^M

coxless pair
deux sans barreur^M
Zweier^M ohne Steuermann^M
el dos

coxed pair
deux avec barreur^M
Zweier^M mit Steuermann^M
el dos con timonel^M

coxless four
quatre sans barreur^M
Vierer^M ohne Steuermann^M
el cuatro

coxed four
quatre avec barreur^M
Vierer^M mit Steuermann^M
el cuatro con timonel^M

eight
huit
Achter^M
bote^M de a ocho (con timonel^M)

WATER SKIING
SKI^M NAUTIQUE
WASSERSKI^N
ESQUÍ^M ACUÁTICO

twin skis
ski^M de tourisme^M
Monoski^M
esquí^M normal

tip
spatule^F
Spitze^F
punta^F

toe piece
sabot^M
Vorfußgummi^N
bota^F del pie^M delantero

binding
fixation^F
Bindung^F
fijación^F

heel piece
talonnière^F
Stegschlaufe^F für zweiten Fuß^M
goma^F de sujeción^F del talón^M

fin
dérive^F
Kiel^M
aleta^F estabilizador^M

slalom ski
ski^M de slalom^M
Slalomski^M
esquí^M de eslálom^M

figure ski
ski^M de figure^F
Figurenski^M
esquí^M de figuras^F

bottom
semelle^F
Unterseite^F
suela^F

TYPES OF SKI
TYPES^M DE SKIS^M
ARTEN VON WASSERSKI^M
TIPOS^M DE ESQUÍS^M

jump ski
ski^M de saut^M
Sprungski^M
esquí^M de salto^M

front binding
fixation^F avant
Vorderbindung^F
sujeción^F delantera

back binding
fixation^F arrière
Hinterbindung^F
sujeción^F trasera

tail
queue^F
Endstück^N
talón^M

TYPES OF HANDLE
TYPES^M DE TRAPÈZES^M
HANTELARTEN^F
EMPUÑADURAS^F PARA ESQUÍ^M

figure skiing handle
trapèze^M de figure^F
Figurenhantel^F
empuñaduras^F para esquí^M de figuras^F

double handles
palonnier^M de slalom^M
Paarlaufhantel^F
cuerdas^F para eslálom^M

handle
trapèze^M
Hantel^F
empuñadura^F

tow line
remorque^F
Schleppseil^N
cable^M de arrastre^M

toe strap
lanière^F
Vorfußriemen^M
correa^F para el pie^M

tow bar
barre^F
Hantelgriff^M
barra^F

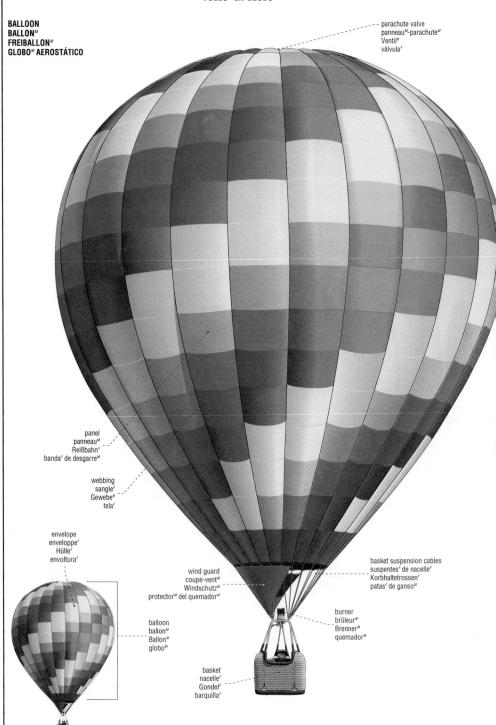

BALLOON
BALLON[M]
FREIBALLON[M]
GLOBO[M] **AEROSTÁTICO**

parachute valve
panneau[M]-parachute[M]
Ventil[N]
válvula[F]

panel
panneau[M]
Reißbahn[F]
banda[F] de desgarre[M]

webbing
sangle[F]
Gewebe[N]
tela[F]

envelope
enveloppe[F]
Hülle[F]
envoltura[F]

balloon
ballon[M]
Ballon[M]
globo[M]

wind guard
coupe-vent[M]
Windschutz[M]
protector[M] del quemador[M]

basket suspension cables
suspentes[F] de nacelle[F]
Korbhaltetrossen[F]
patas[F] de ganso[M]

burner
brûleur[M]
Brenner[M]
quemador[M]

basket
nacelle[F]
Gondel[F]
barquilla[F]

burner
brûleur^M
Brenner^M
quemador^M

fuel lines
flexibles^M d'alimentation^F
Treibstoffzufuhrleitungen^F
cañerías^F

basket support
cadre^M de charge^F
Korbtragerohr^N
armazón^M

variometer
variomètre^M
Variometer^N
variómetro^M

altimeter
altimètre^M
Höhenmesser^M
altímetro^M

wicker basket
nacelle^F d'osier^M
Weidenkorb^M
barquilla^F de mimbre^M

hardwood base
base^F en bois^M
Holzboden^M
suelo^M de madera^F

**BASKET
NACELLE^F
GONDEL^F
BARQUILLA^F**

heating coil
serpentin^M
Heizspirale^F
calentador^M

blast valve
soupape^F d'admission^F
Heizventil^N
válvula^F del quemador^M

flight instruments
instruments^M de vol^M
Bordinstrumente^N
instrumentos^M

thermometer
thermomètre^M
Thermometer^N
termómetro^M

padding
rembourrage^M
Polsterung^F
revestimiento^M

basket handle
poignée^F de nacelle^F
Gondelhaltegriff^M
asa^F de la barquilla^F

**SKY DIVING
CHUTE^F LIBRE
FALLSCHIRMSPRINGEN^N
PARACAIDISMO^M**

**SKY DIVER
SAUTEUR^M
FALLSCHIRMSPRINGER^M
PARACAIDISTA^{M/F}**

helmet
casque^M de saut^M
Schutzhelm^M
casco^M

main parachute
parachute^M dorsal
Hauptfallschirm^M
paracaídas^F principal

jumping boot
botte^F de saut^M
Springerstiefel^M
bota^F

harness
harnais^M
Gurtwerk^N
arnés^M

glove
gant^M
Handschuh^M
guante^M

goggles
lunettes^F de vol^M
Schutzbrille^F
gafas^F

altimeter
altimètre^M
Höhenmesser^M
altímetro^M

reserve parachute
parachute^M de secours^M
Reservefallschirm^M
paracaídas^F ventral

one-piece coverall
combinaison^F de vol^M
einteiliger Overall^M
traje^M de vuelo

PARAGLIDING
PARAPENTE^M
GLEITSCHIRMFLIEGEN^N
PLANEADOR^M

CANOPY
AILE^F
GLEITSCHIRM^M
CASQUETE^M

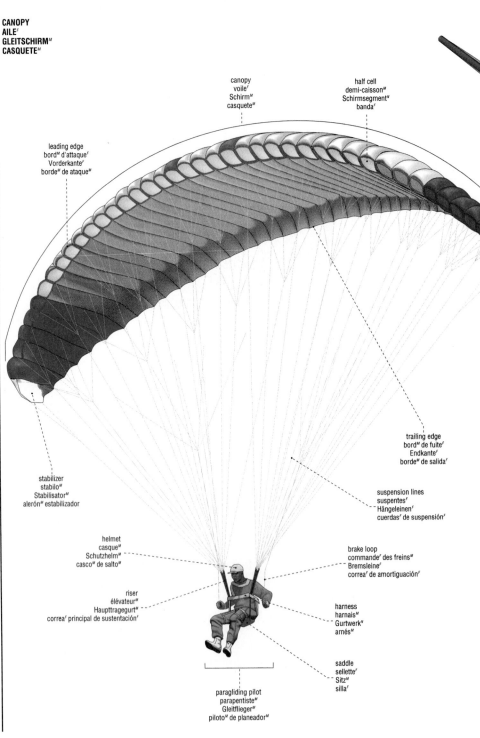

canopy
voile^F
Schirm^M
casquete^M

half cell
demi-caisson^M
Schirmsegment^N
banda^F

leading edge
bord^M d'attaque^F
Vorderkante^F
borde^M de ataque^M

trailing edge
bord^M de fuite^F
Endkante^F
borde^M de salida^F

suspension lines
suspentes^F
Hängeleinen^F
cuerdas^F de suspensión^F

stabilizer
stabilo^M
Stabilisator^M
alerón^M estabilizador

helmet
casque^M
Schutzhelm^M
casco^M de salto^M

brake loop
commande^F des freins^M
Bremsleine^F
correa^F de amortiguación^F

riser
élévateur^M
Haupttragegurt^M
correa^F principal de sustentación^F

harness
harnais^M
Gurtwerk^N
arnés^M

saddle
sellette^F
Sitz^M
silla^F

paragliding pilot
parapentiste^M
Gleitflieger^M
piloto^M de planeador^M

636

HANG GLIDER
AILE^F LIBRE
FLUGDRACHEN^M
AERODESLIZADOR^M

crossbar
tube^M transversal
Querstange^F
barra^F transversal

sail
voilure^F
Tragsegel^N
ala^F delta

leading edge tube
tube^M de bord^M d'attaque^F
Vorderstangentasche^F
tubo^M del borde^M de ataque^M

batten
latte^F
Längslatte^F
sable^M

keel
quille^F
Kielstange^F
quilla^F

king post
mât^M
Spannmast^M
mástil^M

nose
nez^M
Nase^F
proa^F

rigging wire
hauban^M
Rigg-Stahlseil^N
tirante^M de fijación^F

wing
aile^F
Flügel^M
ala^F

airframe
trapèze^M
Steuerbügel^M
trapecio^M

control bar
barre^F de commande^F
Lenkstange^F
barra^F de dirección^F

hang point
point^M d'ancrage^M
Aufhängepunkt^M
arzón^M de amarre^M

flight bag
fourreau^M
Schlafsack^M mit Rettungssystem^N
saco^M de pilotaje^M

trailing edge
bord^M de fuite^F
Endkante^F
caída^F de popa^F

harness
harnais^M
Gurtwerk^N
arnés^M

pilot
pilote^M
Pilot^M
piloto^M

wingtip
bout^M d'aile^F
Flügelspitze^F
punta^F del ala^F

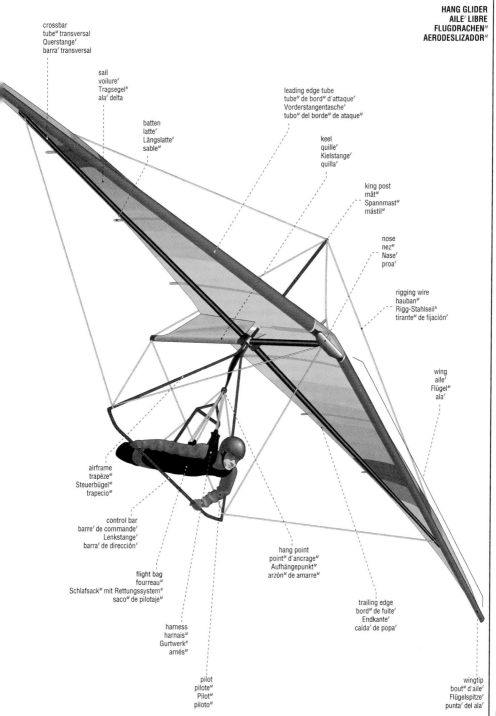

AERIAL SPORTS
SPORTS AÉRIENS

LUFTSPORT
DEPORTES AÉREOS

637

GLIDER
PLANEUR^M
SEGELFLUGZEUG^N
PLANEADOR^M

air brake
aérofrein^M
Bremsklappe^L
trampilla^F de freno^M aerodinámico

aileron
aileron^M
Querruder^{NL}
alerón^M

cockpit canopy
verrière^F
Kanzel^F
cubierta^F de la cabina^F

nose
nez^M
Nase^F
morro^M

leading edge
bord^M d'attaque^F
Vorderkante^L
borde^M de ataque^M

trailing edge
bord^M de fuite^F
Hinterkante^F
borde^M de salida^F

wingtip
saumon^M d'aile^F
Flügelspitze^F
borde^M marginal

wing
ailes^F
Flügel^M
ala^F

tail
queue^F
Leitwerk^N
grupo^M de cola^F

rudder
gouvernail^M de direction^F
Seitenruder^N
timón^M de dirección^F

fin
dérive^F
Seitenflosse^F
estabilizador^M de dirección^F

fuselage
fuselage^M
Rumpf^M
fuselaje^M

elevator
gouvernail^M de profondeur^F
Höhenruder^N
timón^M de profundidad^F

tailplane
stabilisateur^M
Höhenflosse^F
estabilizador^M horizontal

COCKPIT
CABINE^F DE PILOTAGE^M
COCKPIT^N
CABINA^F DEL PILOTO^M

altimeter
altimètre^M
Höhenmesser^M
altímetro^M

airspeed indicator
anémomètre^M
Geschwindigkeitsanzeige^F
anemómetro^M

compass
compas^M
Kompass^M
brújula^F

turn and bank indicator
indicateur^M de virage^M et d'inclinaison^F latérale
Wendezeiger^M
indicador^M de viraje^M

electric variometer
variomètre^M électrique
Elektrovariometer^N
variómetro^M eléctrico

cockpit ventilation
ventilation^F de la cabine^F
Frischluftzufuhr^F
ventilador^M de cabina^F

mechanical variometer
variomètre^M mécanique
mechanisches Variometer^N
variómetro^M mecánico

oxygen indicator
contrôle^M d'alimentation^F en oxygène^M
Sauerstoffzufuhranzeige^F
control^M de alimentador^M de oxígeno^M

tow release knob
commande^F de largage^M de câble^M
Ausklinkhebel^M
liberador^M del cable^M de remolque^M

oxygen supply regulator
commande^F d'alimentation^F en oxygène^M
Sauerstoffzufuhrregler^M
palanca^F de alimentador^M de oxígeno^M

rudder pedal
pédale^F de palonnier^M
Seitenruderpedal^N
pedal^M del timón^M de mando^M

microphone
microphone^M
Mikrofon^N
micrófono^M

air brake handle
commande^F d'aérofrein^M
Bremsklappenhebel^M
mando^M del freno^M aerodinámico

canopy release knob
commande^F de largage^M de la verrière^F
Kanzellösehebel^M
eyector^M del protector^M de cabina^F

turn and bank knob
commande^F de virage^M et d'inclinaison^F latérale
Wendehebel^M
palanca^F de viraje^M

control stick
manche^M à balai^M
Steuerknüppel^M
palanca^F de mando^M

radio
radio^F
Fungerät^N
radio^M

seat
siège^M
Sitz^M
asiento^M

639

ALPINE SKIING
SKI^M ALPIN
ALPINES SKILAUFEN^N
ESQUÍ^M ALPINO

ALPINE SKIER
SKIEUR^M ALPIN
ALPINER SKILÄUFER^M
ESQUIADOR^M ALPINO

ski hat
bonnet^M
Skimütze^F
gorro^M de esquí^M

ski goggles
lunettes^F de ski^M
Skibrille^F
gafas^F de esquí^M

ski suit
combinaison^F de ski^M
Skianzug^M
traje^M de esqui

ski glove
gant^M de ski^M
Skihandschuhe^M
guante^M de esquí^M

handle
poignée^F
Griff^M
puño^M

wrist strap
dragonne^F
Handschlaufe^F
correa^F para la mano^F

ski pole
bâton^M de ski^M
Skistock^M
bastón^M de esquí^M

bottom face
semelle^F
Laufsohle^F
superficie^F de deslizamiento^M

ski stop
frein^M
Skibremse^F
freno^M del esquí^M

shovel
spatule^F
Schaufel^F
pala^F

edge
carre^F
Stahlkante^F
canto^M

heel piece
talonnière^F
Fersenstütze^F
pieza^F automática del talón^M

ski boot
chaussure^F de ski^M
Skistiefel^M
bota^F

tip
pointe^F
Spitze^F
punta^F

toe piece
butée^F
Kopfautomatik^F
pieza^F de sujeción^F de la punta^F del pie^M

SAFETY BINDING
FIXATION^F DE SÉCURITÉ^F
SICHERHEITSBINDUNG^F
FIJACIÓN^F DE SEGURIDAD^F DEL ESQUÍ^M

manual release
pédale^F de déchaussage^M
Handlöser^M
desenganchador^M manual

release setting screw
vis^F de réglage^M de libération^F
Löseeinstellschraube^F
ajustador^M de desenganche^M
automático

anti-friction pad
plaque^F antifriction^M
Gleitschutz^M
placa^F antifricción

brake pedal
plaque^F de frein^M
Fersenautomatik^F
placa^F de freno^M

setting indicator
indicateur^M de réglage^M
Einstellanzeige^F
indicador^M de ajuste^M

height adjustment screw
vis^F de réglage^M de hauteur^F
Höhenverstellschraube^F
ajustador^M de altura^F

base plate
embase^F
Grundplatte^F
placa^F base^F

ski stop
frein^M
Skibremse^F
freno^M

heel-piece
talonnière^F
Absatzteil^N
pieza^F automática del talón^M

SKI BOOT
CHAUSSURE^F DE SKI^M
SKISTIEFEL^M
BOTAS^F PARA ESQUIAR

toe-piece
butée^F
Kopfautomatik^F
puntera^F

inner boot
chausson^M intérieur
Innenstiefel^M
bota^F interior

setting indicator
indicateur^M de réglage^M
Einstellanzeige^F
indicador^M de ajuste^M

upper cuff
collier^M
obere Manschette^F
guarnición^F

basket
rondelle^F
Stockteller^M
arandela^F

upper
tige^F
Rücklagenstütze^F
alto^M de caña^F

tongue
languette^F
Zunge^F
lengüeta^F

buckle
boucle^F
Verschluß^M
hebilla^F

upper strap
courroie^F de tige^F
oberes Verschlußband^N
correa^F de ajuste^M

upper shell
coque^F supérieure
obere Schale^F
caña^F

tail
talon^M
Ende^N
cola^F

wire
câble^M
Spanndraht^M
trabilla^F

groove
rainure^F
Führungsrille^F
ranura^F guía^F

ski
ski^M
Ski^M
esquí^M

hinge
charnière^F
Gelenk^N
pivote^M

adjustable catch
cran^M de réglage^M
Einstellkerbe^F
ajustador^M de la bota^F

lower shell
coque^F inférieure
untere Schale^F
contrafuerte^M

sole
semelle^F
Sohle^F
suela^F rígida

641

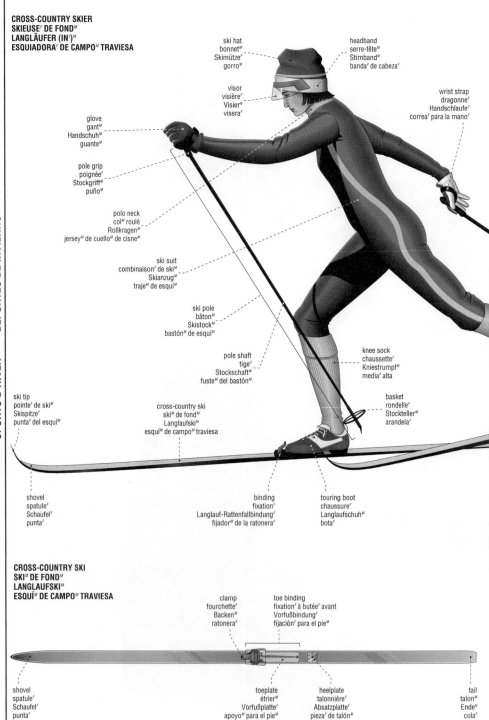

CROSS-COUNTRY SKIING
SKI^M DE FOND^M
SKILANGLAUF^M
ESQUÍ^M DE FONDO^M

WINTERSPORT
DEPORTES DE INVIERNO

WINTER SPORTS
SPORTS D'HIVER

CROSS-COUNTRY SKIER
SKIEUSE^F DE FOND^M
LANGLÄUFER (IN^F)^M
ESQUIADORA^F DE CAMPO^M TRAVIESA

ski hat
bonnet^M
Skimütze^F
gorro^M

headband
serre-tête^M
Stirnband^N
banda^F de cabeza^F

visor
visière^F
Visier^N
visera^F

wrist strap
dragonne^F
Handschlaufe^F
correa^F para la mano^F

glove
gant^M
Handschuh^M
guante^M

pole grip
poignée^F
Stockgriff^M
puño^M

polo neck
col^M roulé
Rollkragen^M
jersey^M de cuello^M de cisne^M

ski suit
combinaison^F de ski^M
Skianzug^M
traje^M de esquí^M

ski pole
bâton^M
Skistock^M
bastón^M de esquí^M

knee sock
chaussette^F
Kniestrumpf^M
media^F alta

pole shaft
tige^F
Stockschaft^M
fuste^M del bastón^M

ski tip
pointe^F de ski^M
Skispitze^F
punta^F del esquí^M

cross-country ski
ski^M de fond^M
Langlaufski^M
esquí^M de campo^M traviesa

basket
rondelle^F
Stockteller^M
arandela^F

shovel
spatule^F
Schaufel^F
punta^F

binding
fixation^F
Langlauf-Rattenfallbindung^F
fijador^M de la ratonera^F

touring boot
chaussure^F
Langlaufschuh^M
bota^F

CROSS-COUNTRY SKI
SKI^M DE FOND^M
LANGLAUFSKI^M
ESQUÍ^M DE CAMPO^M TRAVIESA

clamp
fourchette^F
Backen^M
ratonera^F

toe binding
fixation^F à butée^F avant
Vorfußbindung^F
fijación^F para el pie^M

shovel
spatule^F
Schaufel^F
punta^F

toeplate
étrier^M
Vorfußplatte^F
apoyo^M para el pie^M

heelplate
talonnière^F
Absatzplatte^F
pieza^F de talón^M

tail
talon^M
Ende^N
cola^F

LUGE
LUGE^F
RENNRODEL^M
LUGE^M

face mask
masque^M protecteur
Gesichtsmaske^F
protector^M facial

one-piece suit
combinaison^F
einteiliger Anzug^M
traje^M de una sola pieza^F

sled
traîneau^M
Rodel^M
trineo^M

crash helmet
casque^M protecteur
Sturzhelm^M
casco^M protector

runner
patin^M
Kufe^F
patín^M

glove
gant^M
Handschuh^M
guante^M

blade
arête^F
Schiene^F
canto^M

heelplate
talonnière^F
Fersenplatte^F
pieza^F de talón^M

pole tip
pointe^F de bâton^M
Stockspitze^F
punta^F del bastón^M

tail
talon^M
Ende^N
cola^F

BOBSLEIGH
BOBSLEIGH^M
BOBSCHLITTEN^M
BOBSLEIGH^M

handle
poignée^F
Griff^M
asa^F

driver
capitaine^M
Steuermann^M
capitán^M

shell
coque^F
Gehäuse^N
bob^M

front runner
patin^M avant
vordere Kufe^F
patín^M delantero

brakeman
freineur^M
Bremser^M
guardafrenos^M

rear runner
patin^M arrière
hintere Kufe^F
patín^M trasero

SKATING
PATINAGE^M
EISLAUFEN^N
PATINAJE^M

FIGURE SKATE
PATÍN^M **DE FIGURE**^F
EISKUNSTLAUFSTIEFEL^M
PATÍN^M **PARA FIGURAS**^F

tongue
languette^F
Zunge^F
lengüeta^F

lining
doublure^F
Futter^N
forro^M

hook
crochet^M
Schnürhaken^M
corchete^M

backstay
tige^F
Rückenverstärkung^F
contrafuerte^M

lace
lacet^M
Schnürsenkel^M
cordón^M

boot
chaussure^F
Stiefel^M
bota^F

eyelet
œillet^M
Schnüröse^F
ojal^M

heel
talon^M
Absatz^M
tacón^M

sole
semelle^F
Sohle^F
suela^F

stanchion
montant^M
Träger^M
montante^M

toe pick
dent^F
Abstoßsäge^F
dientes^M

edge
carre^F
Schneide^F
canto^M

blade
lame^F
Kufe^F
hoja^F de cuchilla^F

HOCKEY SKATE
PATÍN^M **DE HOCKEY**^M
EISHOCKEYSCHLITTSCHUH^M
PATÍN^M **DE HOCKEY**^M

speed skate
patin^M de course^F
Schnellaufschlittschuh^M
patín^M de velocidad^F

tendon guard
protège-tendon^M
Sehnenschützer^M
protector^M del tendón^M

boot
chaussure^F
Stiefel^M
bota^F de salto^M

toecap
renfort^M de pointe^F
Kappe^F
puntera^F reforzada

skate guard
protège-lame^M
Schlittschuhschoner^M
funda^F protectora de la cuchilla^F

point
pointe^F
Spitze^F
puntera^F

blade
lame^F
Kufe^F
hoja^F de cuchilla^F

SNOWSHOE
RAQUETTE^F
SCHNEESCHUH^M
RAQUETA^F

MICHIGAN SNOWSHOE
RAQUETTE^F ALGONQUINE
MICHIGAN-SCHNEESCHUH^M
TIPO^M MICHIGAN

body
pied^M
Korpus^M
cuerpo^M

harness
harnais^M
Befestigungsriemen^M
correa^F

toe hole
porte^F
Zehenloch^N
puntera^F

tip
tête^F
Spitze^F
cabeza^F

lacing
lacis^M
Bespannung^F
cordaje^M

frame
cadre^M
Rahmen^M
marco^M

tail
queue^F
Hinterteil^N
cola^F

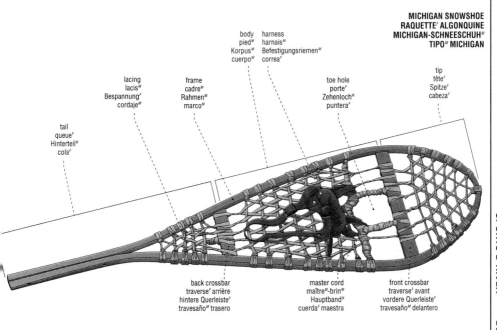

back crossbar
traverse^F arrière
hintere Querleiste^F
travesaño^M trasero

master cord
maître^M-brin^M
Hauptband^N
cuerda^F maestra

front crossbar
traverse^F avant
vordere Querleiste^F
travesaño^M delantero

ROLLER SKATE
PATIN^M À ROULETTES^F
ROLLSCHUH^M
PATÍN^M DE RUEDAS^F

inner boot
chausson^M intérieur
Innenstiefel^M
bota^F interior

adjustable buckle
boucle^F de réglage^M
Einstellspanner^M
hebilla^F de ajuste^M

upper shell
coque^F supérieure
Oberschale^F
caña^F

boot
chaussure^F
Stiefel^M
bota^F

heel stop
frein^M de talon^M
Absatzstopper^M
freno^M trasero

wheel
roulette^F
Rolle^F
rueda^F

truck
bloc^M-essieu^M
Wagen^M
bogie^M

axle
essieu^M
Achse^F
eje^M

SHOW-JUMPING
ÉQUITATION[F]
REITEN[N]
EQUITACIÓN[F]: CONCURSO[M] DE SALTOS[M]

SHOW-JUMPING COURSE
PARCOURS[M] D'OBSTACLES[M]
WETTKAMPFPARCOURS[M]
PISTA[F] PARA PRUEBA[F] DE OBSTÁCULOS[M]

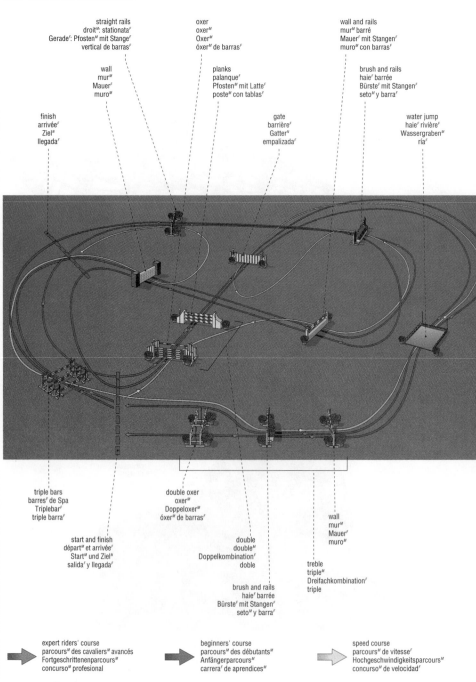

straight rails
droit[M]: stationata[F]
Gerade[F]: Pfosten[M] mit Stange[F]
vertical de barras[F]

oxer
oxer[M]
Oxer[M]
óxer[M] de barras[F]

wall and rails
mur[M] barré
Mauer[F] mit Stangen[F]
muro[M] con barras[F]

wall
mur[M]
Mauer[F]
muro[M]

planks
palanque[F]
Pfosten[M] mit Latte[F]
poste[M] con tablas[F]

brush and rails
haie[F] barrée
Bürste[F] mit Stangen[F]
seto[M] y barra[F]

finish
arrivée[F]
Ziel[N]
llegada[F]

gate
barrière[F]
Gatter[N]
empalizada[F]

water jump
haie[F] rivière[F]
Wassergraben[M]
ría[F]

REITSPORT
DEPORTES ECUESTRES

EQUESTRIAN SPORTS
SPORTS ÉQUESTRES

triple bars
barres[F] de Spa
Triplebar[F]
triple barra[F]

double oxer
oxer[M]
Doppeloxer[M]
óxer[M] de barras[F]

wall
mur[M]
Mauer[F]
muro[M]

start and finish
départ[M] et arrivée[F]
Start[M] und Ziel[N]
salida[F] y llegada[F]

double
double[F]
Doppelkombination[F]
doble

treble
triple[M]
Dreifachkombination[F]
triple

brush and rails
haie[F] barrée
Bürste[F] mit Stangen[F]
seto[M] y barra[F]

expert riders' course
parcours[M] des cavaliers[M] avancés
Fortgeschrittenenparcours[M]
concurso[M] profesional

beginners' course
parcours[M] des débutants[M]
Anfängerparcours[M]
carrera[F] de aprendices[M]

speed course
parcours[M] de vitesse[F]
Hochgeschwindigkeitsparcours[M]
concurso[M] de velocidad[F]

646

planks
palanque^F
Pfosten^M mit Latte^F
vertical de desviadores^M

rails
stationata^F
Pfosten^M mit Stange^F
vertical^M de barras^F

gate
barrière^F
Gatter^N
empalizada^F

brush and rails
haie^F barrée
Bürste^F mit Stangen^F
valla^F sobre seto^M

double oxer
oxer^M
Doppeloxer^M
óxer^M de barras^F

wall
mur^M
Mauer^F
muro^M

triple bars
barres^F de Spa
Triplebar^F
triple de barras^F

wall and rails
mur^M barré
Mauer^F mit Stangen^F
valla^F sobre muro^M

water jump
haie^F rivière^F
Wassergraben^M
ría^F

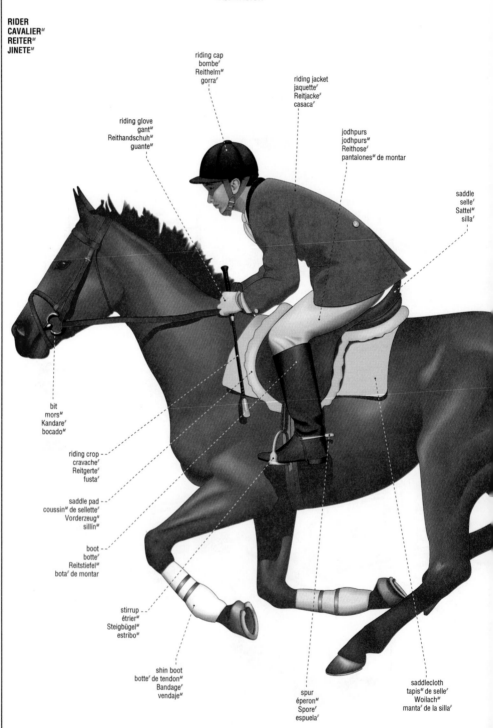

RIDER
CAVALIER^M
REITER^M
JINETE^M

riding cap
bombe^F
Reithelm^N
gorra^F

riding jacket
jaquette^F
Reitjacke^F
casaca^F

riding glove
gant^M
Reithandschuh^M
guante^M

jodhpurs
jodhpurs^M
Reithose^F
pantalones^M de montar

saddle
selle^F
Sattel^M
silla^F

bit
mors^M
Kandare^F
bocado^M

riding crop
cravache^F
Reitgerte^F
fusta^F

saddle pad
coussin^M de sellette^F
Vorderzeug^N
sillín^M

boot
botte^F
Reitstiefel^M
bota^F de montar

stirrup
étrier^M
Steigbügel^M
estribo^M

shin boot
botte^F de tendon^M
Bandage^F
vendaje^M

spur
éperon^M
Spore^F
espuela^F

saddlecloth
tapis^M de selle^F
Woilach^M
manta^F de la silla^F

SADDLE
SELLE*F*
SATTEL*M*
SILLA*F* DE MONTAR

pommel
pommeau*M*
Vorderzwiesel*M*
borrén*M*

tree
arcade*F*
Baum*M*
arzón*M*

seat
siège*M*
Sitz*M*
sillín*M*

skirt
petit quartier*M*
Schnallenabdeckung*F*
faldoncillo*M*

panel
faux quartier*M*
Schweißblatt*N*
rodillera*F*

girth strap
contre-sanglon*M*
Gurtstrippe*F*
latiguillo*M*

girth
sangle*F*
Sattelgurt*M*
cincha*F*

cantle
trousequin*M*
Hinterzwiesel*F*
borrén*M* trasero

panel
matelassure*F*
Sattelpolster*N*
forro*M*

flap
quartier*M*
Pausche*F*
hoja*F* del faldón*M* lateral

stirrup leather
étrivière*F*
Bügelriemen*M*
correa*F*

eye
œil*M*
Auge*N*
ojo*M*

arch
branche*F*
Bügel*M*
aro*M*

girth buckle
sanglon*M*
Gurtschnalle*F*
correa*F* de la cincha*F*

tread
plancher*M*
Trittfläche*F*
hondón*M*

BRIDLE
BRIDE*F*
ZAUMZEUG*N*
BRIDA*F*

crownpiece
têtière*F*
Genickstück*N*
cabezada*F*

throat lash
sous-gorge*M*
Kehlriemen*M*
ahogadero*M*

browband
frontal*M*
Stirnriemen*M*
frontalera*F*

cheek strap
montant*M* de bride*F*
Backenriemen*M*
trabilla*F*

snaffle strap
montant*M* de filet*M*
Gebißriemen*M*
quijera*F*

noseband
muserolle*F*
Nasenriemen*M*
muserola*F*

curb bit
mors*M* de bride*F*
Kandare*F*
cambocadura*F*

curb chain
gourmette*F*
Kandarenkette*F*
freno*M*

snaffle rein
rêne*F* de filet*M*
Trensenzügel*M*
rienda*F* del freno*M*

curb rein
rêne*F* de bride*F*
Kandarenzügel*M*
rienda*F* del bocado*M*

snaffle bit
mors*M* de filet*M*
Trense*F*
barbada*F*

SNAFFLE BIT
MORS^M DE FILET^M
TRENSE^F
BOCADO^M ACODADO

jointed mouth
canon^M brisé
Wassertrense^F
bocado^M articulado

rein ring
anneau^M de rêne^F
Zügelring^M
anillo^M de las riendas^F

egg butt snaffle bit
filet^M à olives^F
Olivenkopftrense^F
bocado^M ovoide acodado

rubber snaffle bit
filet^M en caoutchouc^M
Gummigebiß^N
bocado^M acodado elástico

full cheek snaffle bit with keys
filet^M à jouets^M
Spielertrense^F
freno^M de quijada^F acodado

full cheek snaffle bit
filet^M à aiguilles^F
Knebeltrense^F
bocado^M de quijada^F acodado

keys
jouets^M
Knebel^M
caireles^M

CURB BIT
MORS^M DE BRIDE^F
KANDARE^F
BOCADO^M CON LA BARBADA^F

port
liberté^F de langue^F
Brücke^F
puente^M

cheek ring
anneau^M de montant^M
Anzugring^M
anillo^M de quijada^F

upper cheek
branche^F supérieure
oberer Anzug^M
quijada^F superior

curb hook
crochet^M de gourmette^F
Kinnkettenhaken^M
gancho^M de la barbada^F

curb chain
gourmette^F
Kinnkette^F
cadenilla^F de la barbada^F

lip strap ring
anneau^M de branche^F
Zügelring^M
anillo^M de carrillera^F

mouth
canon^M
Gebiß^N
boca^F

lower cheek
branche^F inférieure
unterer Anzug^M
quijada^F inferior

rein ring
anneau^M de rêne^F
Zügelring^M
anillo^M de las riendas^F

Pelham bit
mors^M à canon^M brisé
Pelham-Kandare^F
bocado^M articulado

Liverpool bit
mors^M anglais
Ellenbogenkandare^F
bocado^M de codo^M militar

sliding cheek bit
mors^M à pompe^F
einfache Kandare^F
bocado^M corredizo

HORSE RACING
COURSE^F DE CHEVAUX^M
GALOPPRENNEN^N
CARRERA^F DE CABALLOS^M

riding cap
casque^M
Reitkappe^F
gorra^F

jockey
jockey^M
Jockey^M
jockey^M

sheepskin noseband
mouton^M
Nasenschoner^M
musarola^F

saddle
selle^F
Sattel^M
silla^F

rein
rêne^F
Zügel^M
rienda^F

saddlecloth
tapis^M de selle^F
Satteltuch^N
sudadero^M

whip
cravache^F
Reitgerte^F
fusta^F

girth
sangle^F
Bauchgurt^M
cincha^F

STAND AND TRACK
ESTRADE^F ET PISTE^F
GALOPPRENNBAHN^F MIT TRIBÜNE^F
TRIBUNAS^F Y PISTA^F

far turn
grand tournant^M
Kurve^F
curva^F lejana

distance post
repère^M de distance^F
Längenpfosten^M
poste^M indicador

back straight
montée^F arrière
hintere Gerade^F
recta^F de fondo^M

stable
écurie^F
Stall^M
caballerizas^F

clubhouse
club-house^M
Klubhaus^N
jockey club^M

clubhouse turn
tournant^M de club-house^M
Klubhauskurve^F
curva^F del club^M

tote board
tableau^M indicateur^M
Totalisator^M
tablero^M indicador

judge's stand
tribune^F des juges^M
Kampfrichtertribüne^F
tribuna^F de los jueces^M

finishing line
fil^M d'arrivée^F
Ziellinie^F
linea^F de llegada^F

paddock
paddock^M
Sattelplatz^M
cercado^M para entrenar los caballos^M

grandstand
tribune^F populaire
Haupttribüne^F
tribuna^F para el público^M

home straight
dernier droit^M
Zielgerade^F
última^F recta^F

starting furlong
chute^F de départ^M
Achtelmeileneinlauf^M
salida^F de la pista^F

STANDARDBRED PACER
AMBLEUR^M SOUS HARNAIS^M
SULKY^M
ARNESES^M PARA TROTONES^M

sulky
sulky^M
Sulky^M
sulky^M

driver
conducteur^M
Fahrer^M
conductor^M

handhold
courroie^F de rêne^F
Halteriemen^M
asidera^F de la rienda^F

shaft
brancard^M
Schaft^M
limonera^F

hobble hanger
support^M d'entrave^F
Fußfesselriemen^M
sostén^M de la traba^F

hobble
entrave^F
Fußfessel^F
traba^F

seat
siège^M
Sitz^M
asiento^M

spoked wheel
roue^F à rayons^M
Speichenrad^N
rueda^F de radios^M

shin boot
botte^F de tendon^M
Gummischutz^M
polaina^F

bridle
bride^F
Zaumzeug^N
brida^F

head number
numéro^M de tête^F
Startnummer^F
número^M de salida^F

overcheck
rétenteur^M
Overcheck^M
tirante^M de la cabeza^F

blinker
œillère^F
Scheuklappe^F
anteojera^F

back strap
dossière^F
Rückenlasche^F
lomera^F

head pole
perche^F de tête^F
Kopfstab^M
varal^M de la cabeza^F

back pad
sellette^F
Rückenpolster^N
sillín^M

breast collar
collier^M
Brustriemen^M
petral^M

knee boot suspender
bretelle^F pour botte^F de genou^M
Kniemanschettenhalter^M
tirante^M de la rodillera^F

knee boot
botte^F de genou^M
Kniemanschette^F
rodillera^F

shaft holder
sangle^F de brancard^M
Schaftführung^F
cincha^F de la limonera^F

surcingle
sangle^F sous-ventrière
Bauchgurt^M
sobrecincha^F

coronet boot
botte^F de couronne^F
Springglocke^F
bota^F de la corona^F del casco^M

TRACK AND FIELD ATHLETICS
ATHLÉTISME^M
LEICHTATHLETIK^F
ATLETISMO^M DE CAMPO^M Y PISTA^F

ARENA
STADE^M
STADION^N
ESTADIO^M

EINZELSPORTARTEN
ATLETISMO

ATHLETICS
SPORTS ATHLÉTIQUES

finish line
ligne^F d'arrivée^F
Ziellinie^F
llegada^F

finishing post
poteau^M d'arrivée^F
Zielpfosten^M
poste^M de llegada^F

running
course^F
Laufbahn^F
pista^F de carreras^F

high jump
saut^M en hauteur^F
Hochsprung^M
salto^M de altura^F

javelin
lancer^M du javelot^M
Speerwurf^M
lanzamiento^M de jabalina^F

run-up
piste^F d'élan^M
Anlaufstrecke^F
pista^F de lanzamiento^M

throwing circle
cercle^M
Wurfkreis^M
círculo^M de lanzamiento^M

safety cage
cage^F
Schutzkäfig^M
jaula^F de protección^F

discus and hammer
lancer^M disque^M et marteau^M
Diskus- und Hammerwerfen^N
disco^M y martillo^M (lanzamiento^M)

triple jump take-off board
planche^F d'appel^M triple saut^M
Absprungholz^N beim Dreisprung^M
tabla^F de triple salto^M

triple jump take-off line
ligne^F d'appel^M triple saut^M
Absprunglinie^F beim Dreisprung^M
línea^F de triple salto^M

indicator board
planche^F témoin^M
Anzeigefläche^F
tablero^M de información^F

pole vault
saut^M à la perche^F
Stabhochsprung^M
salto^M de pértiga^F

throwing circle
cercle^M
Wurfkreis^M
círculo^M de lanzamiento^M

starting line
ligne^F de départ^M
Startlinie^F
línea^F de salida^F

shot put
lancer^M du poids^M
Kugelstoßen^N
lanzamiento^M de peso^M

landing area
zone^F de chute^F
Landebereich^M
área^F de caída^F

steeplechase
steeple^M
Hürdenlauf^M
curva^F para carrera^F steeplechase^M

lane
couloir^M
Bahn^F
calle^F

run-up
piste^F d'élan^M
Anlaufstrecke^F
pista^F de impulso^M

long jump take-off board
planche^F d'appel^M saut^M en longueur^F
Absprungholz^N für Weitsprung^M
tabla^F de impulso^M de salto^M de longitud^F

landing area
zone^F de chute^F
Landebereich^M
área^F de caída^F

TRACK AND FIELD ATHLETICS
ATHLÉTISME^M
LEICHTATHLETIK^F
ATLETISMO^M DE CAMPO^M Y PISTA^F

STARTING BLOCK
BLOC^M DE DÉPART^M
STARTBLOCK^M
TACO^M DE SALIDA^F

shirt
maillot^M
Hemd^N
camiseta^F

number
dossard^M
Startnummer^F
número^M dorsal

shorts
short^M
Sporthose^F
pantalón^M

running shoe
chaussure^F de piste^F
Laufschuh^M
zapatilla^F

anchor
fixation^F
Anker^M
tornillo^M de anclaje^M

start line
ligne^F de départ^M
Startlinie^F
línea^F de salida^F

rack
crémaillère^F
Schiene^F
bloque^M de salida^F

base
embase^F
Basis^F
pedestal^M

lane line
ligne^F de couloir^M
Bahnmarkierung^F
calle^F

notch
cran^M
Raste^F
ranura^F

pedal
sabot^M
Fußstütze^F
soporte^M del pie^M

spike
pointe^F
Stollen^M
tacos^M

block
bloc^M
Block^M
bloque^M

hurdle
haie^F
Hürde^F
valla^F

steeplechase hurdle
haie^F de steeple^M
Hindernislaufhürde^F
valla^F de la carrera^F de obstáculos^M

656

pole
perche^F
Stab^M
pértiga^F

HIGH JUMP
SAUT^M EN HAUTEUR^F
HOCHSPRUNG^M
SALTO^M DE ALTURA^F

crossbar
barre^F
Sprunglatte^F
listón^M

landing area
zone^F de chute^F
Sprungkissen^N
colchón^M

upright
montant^M
Sprungständer^M
poste^M de salto^M

POLE VAULT
SAUT^M À LA PERCHE^F
STABHOCHSPRUNG^M
SALTO^M DE PÉRTIGA^F

upright
montant^M
Sprungständer^M
poste^M de salto^M

crossbar
barre^F
Sprunglatte^F
listón^M

landing area
zone^F de chute^F
Sprungkissen^N
colchoneta^F

box
butoir^M de saut^M
Einstichkasten^M
cajón^M de batir

run-up
piste^F d'élan^M
Anlaufstrecke^F
pista^F de impulso^M

EINZELSPORTARTEN
ATLETISMO

ATHLETICS
SPORTS ATHLÉTIQUES

THROWING APPARATUS
LANCERS^M
WURFGERÄTE^N
LANZAMIENTOS^M

javelins
javelots^M
Speere^M
jabalina^F

♂

hammer
marteau^M
Hammer^M
martillo^M

wire
câble^M
Verbindungsdraht^M
cable^M

tip
pointe^F
Speerspitze^F
punta^F

♀

metal head
tête^F de métal^M
Metallkopf^M
cabeza^F de metal^M

handle
poignée^F
Hammergriff^M
mango^M

shaft
corps^M
Schaft^M
fuste^M

swivel
pivot^M
Ösenverbindung^F
pivote^M

head
tête^F
Hammerkopf^M
cabeza^F del martillo^M

102 – 120 mm

shot
poids^M
Kugeln^F
peso^M

♂

cord grip
corde^F de prise^F
Kordgriff^M
empuñadura^F

♀

110 – 130 mm

95 – 110 mm

2,2 – 2,3 m

2,6 – 2,7 m

discus
disques^M
Diskus^M
disco^M

weight
poids^M
Gewicht^N
peso^M

♂

rim
jante^F
Rand^M
canto^M

♀

body
corps^M
Korpus^M
cuerpo^M

219 – 221 mm

180 – 182 mm

GYMNASTICS
GYMNASTIQUE*F*
GERÄTETURNEN*N*
GIMNASIA*F*

ASYMMETRICAL BARS
BARRES*F* ASYMÉTRIQUES
STUFENBARREN*M*
BARRAS*F* ASIMÉTRICAS

vaulting horse
cheval*M*-sautoir*M*
Sprungpferd*N*
potro*M*

top bar
barre*F* supérieure
oberer Holm*M*
barra*F* alta

lower bar
barre*F* inférieure
unterer Holm*M*
barra*F* baja

adjusting tube
tube*M* d'ajustement*M*
Rohrführung*F* mit Verstellmöglichkeit*F*
tubo*M* de ajuste*M*

springboard
tremplin*M*
Sprungbrett*N*
plancha*F* de muelles*M*

BALANCE BEAM
POUTRE*F* D'ÉQUILIBRE*M*
SCHWEBEBALKEN*M*
BARRA*F* DE EQUILIBRIO*M*

beam
poutre*F*
Balken*M*
barra*F*

upright
montant*M*
Ständer*M*
montante*M*

height adjustment
réglage*M* de la hauteur*F*
Höhenverstellung*F*
regulador*M* de altura*F*

safety pad
coussin*M* de protection*F*
Schutzpolster*N*
protector*M*

bed
toile*F* de saut*M*
Sprungtuch*N*
cama*F*

TRAMPOLINE
TRAMPOLINE*F*
TRAMPOLIN*N*
CAMA*F* ELÁSTICA

leg
pied*M*
Bein*N*
pata*F*

spring
ressort*M*
Feder*F*
muelle*M*

frame
cadre*M*
Rahmen*M*
marco*M*

RINGS
ANNEAUX[M]
RINGE[M]
ANILLAS[M]

frame
portique[M]
Rahmen[M]
bastidor[M]

cable
câble[M]
Tau[N]
cable[M]

strap
sangle[F]
Riemen[M]
correa[F]

guy wire
câble[M] de haubanage[M]
Verspannung[F]
tensor[M]

ring
anneau[M]
Ring[M]
anilla[F]

ATHLETICS
SPORTS ATHLÉTIQUES

EINZELSPORTARTEN
ATLETISMO

HORIZONTAL BAR
BARRE[F] **FIXE**
RECK[N]
BARRA[F] **FIJA**

steel bar
barre[F] d'acier[M]
Reckstange[F]
barra[F] de acero[M]

upright
montant[M]
Recksäule[F]
soporte[M]

guy wire
câble[M] de haubanage[M]
Verspannung[F]
tensor[M]

POMMEL HORSE
CHEVAL^M D'ARÇONS^M
PAUSCHENPFERD^N
CABALLO^M DE ARZÓN^M

neck
cou^M
Hals^M
cabeza^F

saddle
selle^F
Sattel^M
silla^F

croup
croupe^F
Kruppe^F
grupa^F

pommel
arçon^M
Pausche^F
arzón^M

height adjustment
réglage^M de la hauteur^F
Höhenverstellung^F
regulador^M de altura^F

chain
chaîne^F
Kette^F
cadena^F

upright
montant^M
Stütze^F
soporte^M

anti-slip shoe
patin^M antidérapant
rutschfester Sockel^M
zapata^F antideslizante

horse
cheval^M
Pferd^M
caballo^M

base
piètement^M
Sockel^M
base^F

anchorage
système^M d'ancrage^M
Befestigungssystem^N
placa^F de amarre^M

tensioner
tendeur^M
Spanner^M
tensor^M

PARALLEL BARS
BARRES^F PARALLÈLES
PARALLELBARREN^M
BARRAS^F PARALELAS

wooden bar
barre^F de bois^M
hölzerner Barrenholm^M
barra^F de madera^F

adjustable support
tube^M d'ajustement^M
Rohrführung^F mit Verstellmöglichkeit^F
tubo^M de ajuste^M

base
base^F
Sockel^M
base^F

WEIGHTLIFTING
HALTÉROPHILIE*F*
GEWICHTHEBEN*N*
HALTEROFILIA*F*

WEIGHTLIFTER
HALTÉROPHILE*M*
GEWICHTHEBER*M*
LEVANTADOR*M* **DE PESAS***F*

bar
manchon*M*
Hantelstange*F*
barra*F*

gauze bandage
bandage*M* de gaze*F*
Bandage*F*
muñequera*F*

singlet
maillot*M* de corps*M*
ärmelloses Sporthemd*N*
camiseta*F* sin mangas*F*

weightlifting belt
ceinture*F* d'haltérophilie*F*
Gewichthebergürtel*M*
cinturón*M*

shorts
culotte*F*
Hose*F*
pantalón*M*

weightlifting shoe
chaussure*F* d'haltérophilie*F*
Gewichtheberschuh*M*
zapatilla*F*

strap
lanière*F*
Riemen*M*
correa*F*

TWO-HAND SNATCH
ARRACHÉ*M* **À DEUX BRAS***M*
ZWEIARMIGES REISSEN*N*
MODALIDAD*F* **ARRANQUE***M*

TWO-HAND CLEAN AND JERK
ÉPAULÉ*M*-**JETÉ***M* **À DEUX BRAS***M*
ZWEIARMIGES STOSSEN*N* **MIT AUSFALLSCHRITT***M*
MODALIDAD*F* **CON IMPULSO***M* **EN DOS TIEMPOS***M*

FITNESS EQUIPMENT
APPAREILS^M DE CONDITIONNEMENT^M PHYSIQUE
FITNESSGERÄTE^N
APARATOS^M DE EJERCICIOS^M

WEIGHT TRAINER
BANC^M DE MUSCULATION^F
MULTITRAINER^M
UNIDAD^F DE PESAS^F

wire
câble^M
Draht^M
cable^M

pectoral deck
presse^F à pectoraux^M
Butterfly^M
pectoral^M

lateral bar
barre^F à dorsaux^M
Latissimuszug^M
barra^F lateral

bench
planche^F
Bank^F
banco^M

press bar
barre^F à pectoraux^M
Drückstange^F
presión^F

leg curl bar
balancier^M de traction^F
Beincurler^M
barra^F de flexión^F de piernas^F

leg extension bar
balancier^M d'extension^F
Beinstreckerzug^M
barra^F de extensión^F de piernas^F

triceps bar
barre^F à triceps^M
Trizepszug^M
barra^F de triceps^M

weights
poids^M
Gewichte^N
pesas^F

BARBELL
HALTÈRE^M LONG
HANTEL^F
HALTERA^F

bar
barre^F
Stange^F
barra^F

disc
disque^M
Scheibe^F
disco^M

collar
collier^M de serrage^M
Manschette^F
collarín^M

sleeve
manchon^M
Hantelstange^F
manguito^M

FITNESS EQUIPMENT
APPAREILS^M DE CONDITIONNEMENT^M PHYSIQUE
FITNESSGERÄTE^N
APARATOS^M DE EJERCICIOS^M

EXERCISE CYCLE
VÉLO^M D'EXERCICE^M
HEIMTRAINER^M
BICICLETA^F ESTÁTICA

resistance adjustment
réglage^M de la résistance^F
Widerstandseinstellung^F
ajuste^M de resistencia^F

handlebar
guidon^M
Lenkstange^F
manillar^M

timer
minuteur^M
Timer^M
reloj^M

speedometer
indicateur^M de vitesse^F
Tachometer^M
velocímetro^M

seat
selle^F
Sitz^M
asiento^M

height adjustment
réglage^M de la hauteur^F
Höhenverstellung^F
ajuste^M de altura^F

stepper
simulateur^M d'escalier^M
Climber^M
escalera^F

footstrap
sangle^F
Fußriemen^M
trabilla^F para el pie^M

pedal
pédale^F
Pedal^N
pedal^M

brake
frein^M
Bremse^F
freno^M

flywheel
volant^M d'inertie^F
Schwungrad^N
rueda^F

ROWING MACHINE
RAMEUR^M
RUDERGERÄT^N
REMO^M

push-up stand
poignée^F d'appui^M
Pushup-Griff^M
anillas^F para flexiones^F

oar
rame^F
Ruder^N
remo^M

hydraulic resistance
résistance^F hydraulique
hydraulischer Widerstand^M
resorte^M hidráulico

foot plate
cale-pied^M
Fußstütze^F
soporte^M del pie^M

sliding seat
siège^M coulissant
freilaufender Sitz^M
asiento^M de corredera^F

DUMBBELL
HALTÈRE^M COURT
HANTEL^F
PESAS^F

handgrips
poignée^F à ressort^M
Handmuskeltrainer^M
empuñaderas^F

weight
poids^M
Gewicht^N
pesas^F

bar
barre^F
Griff^M
barra^F

ankle/wrist weight
bracelet^M lesté
Fuß-/Handgelenksgewicht^N
pesas^F para muñecas^F y tobillos^M

skipping-rope
corde^F à sauter
Springseil^N
cuerda^F

TWIST BAR
RESSORT^M ATHLÉTIQUE
FEDERSTANGE^F
BARRA^F DE TORSIÓN^F

grip
poignée^F
Griff^M
empuñadura^F

tension spring
ressort^M de tension^F
Spannfeder^F
resorte^M de tensión^F

chest expander
extenseur^M
Expander^M
tensores^M pectorales

PARTS OF THE WEAPON
PARTIES*F* DE L'ARME*F*
TEILE DER WAFFE*F*
PARTES*F* DEL ARMA*F*

blade
lame*F*
Klinge*F*
cuerpo*M*

button
bouton*M*
Spitzenkopf*M*
botón*M*

guard
coquille*F*
Glocke*F*
guarnición*F*

foible
faible*M*
Klingenschwäche*F*
zona*F* débil de la hoja*F*

mounting
monture*F*
Handteil*N*
empuñadura*F*

medium
moyen*M*
Klingenmitte*F*
zona*F* media

forte
fort*M*
Klingenstärke*F*
zona*F* fuerte de la hoja*F*

FENCING WEAPONS
ARMES*F*
FECHTWAFFEN*N*
ARMAS*F*

martingale
martingale*F*
Handschlaufe*F*
fiador*M*

épée
épée*F*
Degen*M*
espada*F*

handle
poignée*F*
Griff*M*
puño*M*

foil
fleuret*M*
Florett*N*
florete*M*

pommel
pommeau*M*
Knauf*M*
pomo*M*

sabre
sabre*M*
Säbel*M*
sable*M*

PISTE
PISTE*F*
FECHTBAHN*F*
PISTA*F* DE ESGRIMA*F*

sabre and épée warning line
ligne*F* d'avertissement*M*- épée*F* et sabre*M*
Warnlinie*F* beim Säbel- und Degenfechten*N*
línea*F* de puesta*F* en guardia*F* de sable*M* y espada*F*

centre line
ligne*F* médiane
Mittellinie*F*
línea*F* del centro*M*

on guard line
ligne*F* de mise*F* en garde*F*
Startlinie*F*
línea*F* de puesta*F* en guardia*F*

rear limit line
ligne*F* de limite*F* arrière
hintere Begrenzungslinie*F*
línea*F* límite*M* de salida*F*

electric foil
fleuret*M* électrique
Elektroflorett*N*
florete*M* eléctrico

electrical scoring apparatus
compte-touches*M* électrique
Elektrometer*N*
equipo*M* marcador electrónico

body wire
fil*M* de corps*M*
Kabel*N*
cable*M* del esgrimidor*M*

foil warning line
ligne*F* d'avertissement*M*- fleuret*M*
Warnlinie*F* beim Florettfechten*N*
línea*F* de puesta*F* en guardia*F* de florete*M*

scoring light
lampe*F*-témoin*M*
Trefferanzeige*F*
lámpara indicadora de tocado*M*

timekeeper
chronométreur*M*
Zeitnehmer*M*
cronometrador*M*

reel
enrouleur*M*
Kabelrolle*F*
carrete*M* del cable*M*

judge
juge*M*
Kampfrichter*M*
juez*M*

scorer
marqueur*M*
Anschreiber*M*
marcador*M*

president
président*M*
Obmann*M*
presidente*M*

TARGET AREAS
CIBLES^F
TREFFLÄCHEN^F
ÁREAS^F **VÁLIDAS DE TOCADO**^M

épéeist
épéiste^M
Degenfechter^M
tirador^M de espada^F

foilist
fleurettiste^M
Florettfechter^M
tirador^M de florete^M

sabreur
sabreur^M
Säbelfechter^M
tirador^M de sable^M

FENCER
ESCRIMEUR^M
FECHTER^M
FLORETISTA^M

mask
masque^M
Fechtmaske^F
careta^F de esgrima^F

bib
bavette^F
Latz^M
gola^F

metallic plastron
plastron^M métallique
Elektroweste^F
peto^M metálico

jacket
veste^F
Fechtjacke^F
chaqueta^F blanca de esgrima^F

breeches
culotte^F
Fechthose^F
calzón^M

sleeve
crispin^M
Ärmelaufschlag^M
manga^F

glove
gant^M
Fechthandschuh^M
guante^F de esgrima^F

stocking
chaussette^F
Kniestrumpf^M
media^F

fencing shoe
chaussure^F d'escrime^F
Fechtschuh^M
zapatillas^F de esgrima^F

POSITIONS
POSITIONS^F
EINLADUNGEN^F
POSICIONES^F

tierce
tierce^F
Blöße^F bei der Terz-Einladung^F
tercera^F

sixte
sixte^F
Blöße^F bei der Sixt-Einladung^F
sexta^F

quinte
quinte^F
Blöße^F bei der Quint-Einladung^F
quinta^F

quarte
quarte^F
Blöße^F bei der Quart-Einladung^F
cuarta^F

prime
prime^F
Blöße^F bei der Prim-Einladung^F
primera^F

seconde
seconde^F
Blöße^F bei der Second-Einladung^F
segunda^F

septime
septime^F
Blöße^F bei der Septim-Einladung^F
séptima^F

octave
octave^F
Blöße^F bei der Oktav-Einladung^F
octava^F

KAMPFSPORTARTEN
DEPORTES DE COMBATE

COMBAT SPORTS
SPORTS DE COMBAT

JUDO SUIT
COSTUME^M DE JUDO^M
JUDOANZUG^M
JUDOKA^M

jacket
veste^F
Jacke^F
kimono^M

belt
ceinture^F
Gurt^M
obi (cinta^F)

trousers
pantalon^M
Hose^F
pantalón^M

EXAMPLES OF HOLDS
EXEMPLES^M DE PRISES^F
GRIFF- UND WURFBEISPIELE^N
EJEMPLOS^M DE LLAVES^F

arm lock
clé^F de bras^M
Armhebel^M
presa^F de brazo^M

major outer reaping throw
grand fauchage^M extérieur
Große Außensichel^F
osoto-gari (gran siega^F) exterior

major inner reaping throw
grand fauchage^M intérieur
Große Innensichel^F
o-uchi-gari (gran siega^F) interior

stomach throw
projection^F en cercle^M
Kopfwurf^M
proyección^F en círculo^M

holding
immobilisation^F
Haltegriffe^M
presa^F

one-arm shoulder throw
projection^F d'épaule^F par un côté^M
einarmiger Schulterwurf^M
ippon-seoi-nage (proyección^F) por
encima del hombro^M con una mano^F

naked strangle
étranglement^M
Halsumklammerung^F
estrangulación^F

sweeping hip throw
hanche^F ailée
Hüftwurf^M
proyección^F primera de cadera^F

MAT
TAPIS^M
MATTE^F
TATAMI^M

danger area
zone^F de danger^M
Gefahrenbereich^M
área^F de peligro^M

contestant
combattant^M
Judokämpfer^M
uke (defensor^M)

referee
arbitre^M
Schiedsrichter^M
judoka^M neutral

contest area
surface^F de combat^M
Kampfbereich^M
área^F de combate^M

safety area
surface^F de sécurité^F
Sicherheitsbereich^M
área^F de seguridad^F

red flag
drapeau^M rouge
rote Fahne^F
bandera roja^F

timekeeper
chronométreur^M
Zeitnehmer^M
cronometrador^M

holding timekeeper
chronométreur^M des immobilisations^F
Griffzeitnehmer^M
cronometrador^M de presas^F

scorer
marqueur^M
Punktezähler^M
anotador^M

judge
juge^M
Kampfrichter^M
juez^M

RING
RING^M
RING^M
RING^M **DE BOXEO**^M

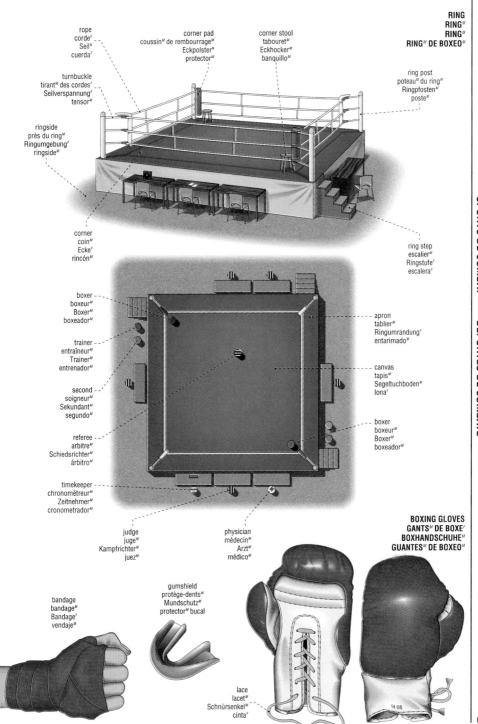

rope
corde^F
Seil^N
cuerda^F

corner pad
coussin^M de rembourrage^M
Eckpolster^N
protector^M

corner stool
tabouret^M
Eckhocker^M
banquillo^M

ring post
poteau^M du ring^M
Ringpfosten^M
poste^M

turnbuckle
tirant^M des cordes^F
Seilverspannung^F
tensor^M

ringside
près du ring^M
Ringumgebung^F
ringside^M

corner
coin^M
Ecke^F
rincón^M

ring step
escalier^M
Ringstufe^F
escalera^F

boxer
boxeur^M
Boxer^M
boxeador^M

apron
tablier^M
Ringumrandung^F
entarimado^M

trainer
entraîneur^M
Trainer^M
entrenador^M

canvas
tapis^M
Segeltuchboden^M
lona^F

second
soigneur^M
Sekundant^M
segundo^M

referee
arbitre^M
Schiedsrichter^M
árbitro^M

boxer
boxeur^M
Boxer^M
boxeador^M

timekeeper
chronométreur^M
Zeitnehmer^M
cronometrador^M

judge
juge^M
Kampfrichter^M
juez^M

physician
médecin^M
Arzt^M
médico^M

BOXING GLOVES
GANTS^M **DE BOXE**^F
BOXHANDSCHUHE^M
GUANTES^M **DE BOXEO**^M

gumshield
protège-dents^M
Mundschutz^M
protector^M bucal

bandage
bandage^M
Bandage^F
vendaje^M

lace
lacet^M
Schnürsenkel^M
cinta^F

14 OZ

COMBAT SPORTS
SPORTS DE COMBAT

KAMPFSPORTARTEN
DEPORTES DE COMBATE

669

FLY ROD
CANNE^F À MOUCHE^F
FLIEGENRUTE^F
CAÑA^F PARA MOSCA^F

male ferrule
virole^F mâle
Innensteckhülse^F
ensamble^M macho^M

keeper ring
accroche-mouche^M
Hakenhalteöse^F
anilla^F de sujeción^F

butt section
talon^M
Rückgrat^N
talón^M

tip-ring
tête^F de scion^M
Abschlußring^M
guía^F de la punta^F

hand grip
poignée^F
Griff^M
empuñadura^F

guide ring
anneau^M
Führungsring^M
anilla^F guía^F

reel seat
porte-moulinet^M
Rollenhalterung^F
portacarrete^M

tip section
scion^M
Spitze^F
rabiza^F

FLY REEL
MOULINET^M À MOUCHE^F
FLIEGENROLLE^F
CARRETE^M GIRATORIO

screw locking nut
écrou^M de blocage^M
Haltemutter^F
tuerca^F de sujeción^F

foot
pied^M
Rollenfuß^M
pie^M

female ferrule
virole^F femelle
Außensteckhülse^F
ensamble^M hembra^F

catch
cran^M
Knarre^F
matraca^F

butt cap
embout^M
Abschlußkappe^F
contera^F

handle
poignée^F
Drehknopf^M
manivela^F

fly line
soie^F
Fliegenschnur^F
sedal^M

spool
tambour^M
Spule^F
bobina^F

drag
frein^M
Bremse^F
freno^M

ARTIFICIAL FLY
MOUCHE^F ARTIFICIELLE
KUNSTFLIEGE^F
MOSCA^F ARTIFICIAL

veil
voile^M
Schleier^M
velo^M

wing
aile^F
Flügel^M
ala^F

topping
coiffe^F
Oberpartie^F
copete^M

cheek
joue^F
Wange^F
carrillo^M

tail
cerques^M
Schwanz^M
cola^F

shoulder
épaule^F
Schulter^F
hombro^M

tip
bout^M
Hinterpartie^F
cabo^M

head
tête^F
Kopf^M
cabeza^F

butt
talon^M
Stummel^M
talón^M

hackle
hackle^M
Nackenfeder^F
pelillo^M

fishhook
hameçon^M
Angelhaken^M
anzuelo^M

body
corps^M
Körper^M
cuerpo^M

ribbing
côte^F
Wicklung^F
costilla^F

joint
articulation^F
Spiralbindung^F
articulación^F

FREIZEITSPORT
DEPORTES RECREATIVOS

LEISURE SPORT
SPORTS DE LOISIR

SPINNING ROD
CANNE*ᶠ* **À LANCER***ᴹ*
SPINNRUTE*ᶠ*
CAÑA*ᶠ* **PARA LANZAR**

butt guide
anneau*ᴹ* de départ*ᴹ*
erster Führungsring*ᴹ*
anilla*ᶠ* para lanzamiento*ᴹ* largo

reel seat
porte-moulinet*ᴹ*
Rollenhalterung*ᶠ*
portacarrete*ᴹ*

butt grip
poignée*ᶠ* arrière
Rutengriff*ᴹ*
mango*ᴹ* posterior

tip-ring
anneau*ᴹ* de tête*ᶠ*
Abschlußring*ᴹ*
guía*ᶠ* de la punta*ᶠ*

screw locking nut
écrou*ᴹ* de blocage*ᴹ*
Haltemutter*ᶠ*
fijador*ᴹ* de carrete*ᴹ*

OPEN-FACE SPINNING REEL
MOULINET*ᴹ* **À TAMBOUR***ᴹ* **FIXE**
OFFENE SPINNROLLE*ᶠ*
CARRETE*ᴹ* **DE BOBINA***ᶠ* **FIJA**

foot
talon*ᴹ*
Rollenhaltepartie*ᶠ*
talón*ᴹ*

leg
pied*ᴹ*
Rollenfuß*ᴹ*
pata*ᶠ*

bail arm opening mechanism
mécanisme*ᴹ* d'ouverture*ᶠ* de l'anse*ᶠ*
Bügelspannmechanismus*ᴹ*
freno*ᴹ*

line guide
guide-ligne*ᴹ*
Schnurlaufröllchen*ᴺ*
asa*ᶠ*

FISHHOOK
HAMEÇON*ᴹ*
ANGELHAKEN*ᴹ*
ANZUELO*ᴹ*

bail arm
anse*ᶠ*
Schnurfangbügel*ᴹ*
devanador*ᴹ*

spool
tambour*ᴹ*
Spule*ᶠ*
bobina*ᶠ*

eye
œillet*ᴹ*
Öse*ᶠ*
ojete*ᴹ*

shank
hampe*ᶠ*
Schenkel*ᴹ*
caña*ᶠ*

crank
manivelle*ᶠ*
Kurbel*ᶠ*
manivela*ᶠ*

gear housing
carter*ᴹ*
Übersetzungsgehäuse*ᴺ*
caja*ᶠ*

gap
ouverture*ᶠ*
Hakeninnenweite*ᶠ*
abertura*ᶠ*

tension adjustment
réglage*ᴹ* de la tension*ᶠ*
einstellbare Bremse*ᶠ*
tensor*ᴹ*

throat
gorge*ᶠ*
Hakenbogentiefe*ᶠ*
garganta*ᶠ*

handle
poignée*ᶠ*
Drehknopf*ᴹ*
mango*ᴹ*

point
pointe*ᶠ*
Hakenspitze*ᶠ*
punta*ᶠ*

barb
ardillon*ᴹ*
Widerhaken*ᴹ*
barbilla*ᶠ*

bend
courbure*ᶠ*
Hakenbogen*ᴹ*
curva*ᶠ*

FISHING
PÊCHE^F
SPORTFISCHEREI^F
PESCA^F

SPINNER
CUILLER^F
BLINKER^M
CUCHARA^F

swivel
émerillon^M
Wirbel^M
destorcedor^M

treble fishhook
hameçon^M triple
Drillingshaken^M
anzuelo^M

split link
anneau^M brisé
Sprengring^M
anillo^M de articulación^F

blade
palette^F
Löffel^M
cuchara^F

TERMINAL TACKLES
BAS^M **DE LIGNE**^F
FANGZUBEHÖR^N
APAREJO^M

float
flotteur^M
Schwimmer^M
flotador^M

swivel
émerillon^M
Wirbel^M
destorcedor^M

leader
avançon^M
Vorfach^N
hijuela^F

sinker
plomb^M
Sinkblei^N
plomo^M

snap
mousqueton^M
Karabiner^M
mosquetón^M

snelled fishhook
hameçon^M monté
Angelhaken^M mit Vorfach^N
anzuelo^M

FISHING WEAR
VÊTEMENTS^M
ANGELBEKLEIDUNG^F
VESTIDO^M **DE PESCADOR**^M

fishing jacket
veste^F de pêche^F
Anglerweste^F
chaleco^M de pescador^M

waders
cuissardes^F
Watstiefel^M
botas^F altas

disgorger
dégorgeoir^M
Hakenlöser^M
sacaanzuelos^M

ACCESSORIES
ACCESSOIRES^M
ZUBEHÖR^N
ACCESORIOS^M

tackle box
boîte^F à leurres^M
Spinnerschachtel^F
caja^F de pesca^F

creel
panier^M
Fischkorb^M
cesta^F de pescador^M

landing net
épuisette^F
Unterfangkescher^M
red^F de mano^F

BILLIARDS
BILLARD[M]
BILLIARD[N]
BILLAR[M]

CAROM BILLIARDS
BILLARD[M] FRANÇAIS
KARAMBOLAGEBILLARD[N]
CARAMBOLA[F]

cue ball
bille[F] de choc[M]
Spielball[M]
bola[F] blanca

red ball
bille[F] rouge
roter Stoßball[M]
bola[F] roja

white spot ball
bille[F] de visée[F] blanche
weißer Punktball[M]
bola[F] pinta

2,27 – 3 m

1,13 – 1,5 m

POOL
BILLARD[M] POOL
POOL[N]
POOL[M]

object balls
billes[F] numérotées
Zielbälle[M]
bolas[F] numeradas

pocket
poche[F]
Tasche[F]
bolsillo[M]

cue ball
bille[F] de choc[M]
Spielball[M]
bola[F] blanca

2,1 – 3 m

1,06 – 1,5 m

ENGLISH BILLIARDS
BILLARD[M] ANGLAIS
LOCHBILLARD[N]
BILLAR[M] INGLÉS

white cue ball
bille[F] blanche
weißer Spielball[M]
bola[F] blanca

white spot ball
bille[F] blanche mouchetée
weißer Punktball[M]
bola[F] pinta

red ball
bille[F] rouge
roter Ball[M]
bola[F] roja

3,7 m

1,86 m

SNOOKER
SNOOKER[M]
SNOOKER[N]
SNOOKER[M]

brown ball
bille[F] brune
brauner Ball[M]
bola[F] café

green ball
bille[F] verte
grüner Ball[M]
bola[F] verde

cue ball
bille[F] de choc[M]
Spielball[M]
bola[F] blanca

yellow ball
bille[F] jaune
gelber Ball[M]
bola[F] amarilla

blue ball
bille[F] bleue
blauer Ball[M]
bola[F] azul

pink ball
bille[F] rose
rosa Ball[M]
bola[F] rosa

red balls
billes[F] rouges
rote Bälle[M]
bolas[F] rojas

black ball
bille[F] noire
schwarzer Ball[M]
bola[F] negra

3,7 m

1,86 m

ENGLISH BILLIARDS AND SNOOKER
BILLARD^M ANGLAIS ET SNOOKER^M
LOCHBILLARD^N UND SNOOKER^N
BILLAR^M INGLÉS Y SNOOKER^M

TABLE
TABLE^F
BILLARDTISCH^M
MESA^F

baulk line spot
mouche^F de ligne^F de cadre^M
Anstoßpunkt^M
mosca^F de la línea^F de cuadro^M

centre spot
mouche^F centrale
Mittelpunkt^M
mosca^F central

baulk
cadre^M
Anstoßraum^M
cuadro^M

«D»
«D»^M
«D»^N
semicírculo^M

bottom pocket
poche^F inférieure
untere Tasche^F
bolsillo^M

bottom cushion
coussin^M de tête^F
Endbande^F
banda^F de goma^F

baulk line
ligne^F de cadre^M
Anstoßlinie^F
línea^F de cuadro^M

hook
crochet^M
Haken^M
vástago^M

centre pocket
poche^F centrale
Mitteltasche^F
bolsillo^M

BRIDGE
RÂTEAU^M
STEG^M
BURRA^F

shaft
manche^M
Stiel^M
mango^M

rack
triangle^M
Dreieck^N
triángulo^M

notch
dent^F
Kerbe^F
muesca^F

end-piece
tête^F
Endstück^N
cabeza^F

674

baize
tapis^M
Bespannung^F
tapete^M

pyramid spot
mouche^F supérieure
Aufstellpunkt^M
mosca^F superior

billiard spot
mouche^F
Aufstellpunkt^M
mosca^F

top cushion
coussin^M arrière
Stirnbande^F
banda^F de la cabecera^F

top pocket
poche^F supérieure
obere Tasche^F
bolsillo^M

rail
bande^F
Rahmen^M
baranda^F

chalk
craie^F
Kreide^F
tiza^F

BILLIARD CUE
QUEUE^F DE BILLARD^M
BILLARDQUEUE^M
TACO^M DE BILLAR^M

tip
procédé^M
Kuppe^F
suela^F

ferrule
virole^F
Kuppenring^M
casquillo^M

shaft
flèche^F
Schaft^M
mango^M

joint
tourillon^M
Gewinde^N
articulación^F

butt
talon^M
Griffteil^N
maza^F

GOLF
GOLF^M
GOLFSPIEL^N
ACCESORIOS^M DE GOLF^M

COURSE
PARCOURS^M
GOLFPLATZ^M
CAMPO^M **DE GOLF**^M

path
chemin^M
Feldweg^M
vereda^F

green
vert^M
Puttergrün^N
césped^M

hole
trou^M
Loch^N
zona^F del hoyo^M

clubhouse
chalet^M
Klubhaus^N
casa^F club^M

practice green
vert^M d'entraînement^M
Übungsgrün^N
green^M de entrenamiento^M

fairway
allée^F
Fairway^N
pista^F

rough
rough^M
Rauh^N
maleza^F

water hazard
obstacle^M d'eau^F
Wasserhindernis^N
trampa^F de agua^F

stream
ruisseau^M
Bach^M
ría^F

bunker
fosse^F de sable^M
Bunker^M
trampa^F de arena^F

trees
arbres^M
Bäume^M
árboles^M

teeing ground
départ^M
Abschlagplatz^M
punto^M de salida^F

CROSS SECTION OF A GOLF BALL
COUPE^F D'UNE BALLE^F DE GOLF^M
GOLFBALL^M IM QUERSCHNITT
CORTE^M TRANSVERSAL DE UNA PELOTA^F DE GOLF^M

4,1 – 4,2 cm

cover
enveloppe^F
Hülle^F
revestimiento^M

rubber thread
ruban^M de caoutchouc^M
Gummieinsatz^M
núcleo^M

core
noyau^M
Kern^M
caucho^M central

GOLF BALL
BALLE^F DE GOLF^M
GOLFBALL^M
PELOTA^F DE GOLF^M

cover
enveloppe^F
Hülle^F
revestimiento^M

dimple
alvéole^M
Delle^F
hoyuelo^M

tee
té^M
Tee^N
tee^M

grip
poignée^F
Griff^M
empuñadura^F

TYPES OF GOLF CLUB
TYPES^M DE BÂTONS^M DE GOLF^M
ARTEN VON GOLFSCHLÄGER^M
BASTONES^M

shaft
manche^M
Schaft^M
mango^M

head
tête^F
Kopf^M
cabeza^F

putter
fer^M droit
Putter^M
putter^M

iron
fer^M
Eisenschläger^M
iron^M

wood
bois^M
Holzschläger^M
madera^F

face
face^F
Schlagfläche^F
cara^F

WOOD
BOIS^M
HOLZ^N
PALO^M

IRON
FER^M
EISEN^N
HIERRO^M

whipping
bandage^M
Whipping^N
refuerzo^M embobinado

ferrule
bague^F
Verbindungshülse^F
contera^F

neck
col^M
Hals^M
cuello^M

toe
pointe^F
Spitze^F
punta^F

toe
pointe^F
Spitze^F
toe^M

neck
col^M
Hals^M
pescuezo^M

groove
rainure^F
Rille^F
superficie^F acanalada

heel
talon^M
Lage^F
talón^M

groove
rainure^F
Rille^F
surco^M

heel
talon^M
Lage^F
talón^M

sole
semelle^F
Sohle^F
zapata^F

sole
semelle^F
Sohle^F
zapata^F

FREIZEITSPORT
DEPORTES RECREATIVOS

LEISURE SPORTS
SPORTS DE LOISIR

GOLF CLUBS
BÂTONS^M DE GOLF^M
GOLFSCHLÄGER^M
HIERROS^M Y PALOS^M

no. 1 wood
bois^M n° 1
Holz^N 1
driver^M, palo^M núm. 1

no. 3 wood
bois^M n° 3
Holz^N 3
madera^F núm.3

no. 5 wood
bois^M n° 5
Holz^N 5
madera^F núm.5

no. 3 iron
fer^M n° 3
Eisen^N 3
iron^M núm.3

no. 4 iron
fer^M n° 4
Eisen^N 4
iron^M núm.4

no. 5 iron
fer^M n° 5
Eisen^N 5
iron^M núm.5

no. 6 iron
fer^M n° 6
Eisen^N 6
iron^M núm.6

no. 7 iron
fer^M n° 7
Eisen^N 7
iron^M núm.7

no. 8 iron
fer^M n° 8
Eisen^N 8
iron^M núm.8

no. 9 iron
fer^M n° 9
Eisen^N 9
niblick^M, hierro^M núm. 9

pitching wedge
cocheur^M d'allée^F
Pitching-Wedge^N
wedge^M para rough^M

sand wedge
cocheur^M de sable^M
Sand-Wedge^N
wedge^M para arena^F

putter
fer^M droit
Putter^M
putter^M

golf glove
gant^M de golf^M
Golfhandschuh^M
guante^M de golf^M

head cover
capuchon^M
Schlägerabdeckung^F
capuchón^M de bastones^M

golf shoe
chaussure^F de golf^M
Golfschuh^M
zapato^M de golf^M

golf trolley
chariot^M
Golfwagen^M
carrito^M de golf^M

GOLF BAG
SAC^M DE GOLF^M
GOLFTASCHE^F
BOLSA^F DE GOLF^M

umbrella ring
porte-parapluie^M
Regenschirmhalter^M
portaparaguas^M

handle
poignée^F
Griff^M
empuñadura^F

shoulder strap
sangle^F
Schultergurt^M
correa^F

pocket
poche^F
Seitentasche^F
bolsillo^M

bag well
porte-sac^M
Taschenträger^M
portabolsa^F

ELECTRIC GOLF CART
VOITURETTE^F DE GOLF^M ÉLECTRIQUE
ELEKTRISCHER GOLFWAGEN^M
CARRO^M DE GOLF^M ELÉCTRICO

MOUNTAINEER
ALPINISTE^M
BERGSTEIGER^M
ALPINISTA^M

helmet
casque^M
Steinschlaghelm^M
casco^M

helmet lamp
lampe^F frontale
Helmlampe^F
lámpara^F del casco^M

hood
cagoule^F
Kapuze^F
buzo^M

rucksack
sac^M à dos^M
Rucksack^M
mochila^F

rope
corde^F
Seil^N
soga^F

parka
anorak^M
Anorak^M
parka^M

karabiner
mousqueton^M
Karabinerhaken^M
mosquetón^M

climbing harness
baudrier^M
Klettergürtel^M
cinturón^M de alpinista^M

piton-carrier
porte-pitons^M
Hakenhalter^M
portapitones^M

chock
coinceur^M
Klemmschlaufe^F
obturador^M

mountaineering shovel
pelle^F de montagne^F
Bergsteigerspaten^M
pala^F

mitten
moufle^F
Handschuh^M
manopla^F

hammer axe
marteau^M-piolet^M
Kombihammer^M
martillo^M mixto

ice axe
piolet^M
Eispickel^M
piolet^M

ice piton
piton^M à glace^F
Eishaken^M
pitón^M de rosca^F

ice screw
vis^F à glace^F
Eisschraube^F
pitón^M de rosca^F

trousers
pantalon^M
Kletterhose^F
pantalón^M

crampon strap
lanière^F
Steigeisenriemen^M
correa^F de crampones^M

legging
jambière^F
Schneegamaschen^F
polaina^F

front point
pointe^F antérieure
Frontalzacken^M
punta^F delantera

spike
pointe^F
Spike^M
clavo^M

mountaineering boot
chaussure^F d'alpinisme^M
Bergsteigerstiefel^M
bota^F alpina

HAMMER AXE
MARTEAU^M-PIOLET^M
KOMBIHAMMER^M
MARTILLO^M PARA HIELO^M

hammer head
tête^F de marteau^M
Hammerkopf^M
cabeza^F del martillo^M

KARABINER
MOUSQUETON^M
KARABINER^M
MOSQUETÓN^M

latch
bec^M
Haken^M
traba^F

gate
doigt^M
Schraubfeder^F
dedo^M

screwsleeve
bague^F filetée
Manschette^F
cierre^M de rosca^F

TUBULAR ICE SCREW
VIS^F À GLACE^F
HOHLE EISSCHRAUBE^F
PITÓN^M PARA HIELO^M

pick
pointe^F
Haue^F
pico^M

ring
anneau^M
Ring^M
anillo^M

ICE AXE
PIOLET^M
EISPICKEL^M
PIOLET^M

head
tête^F
Kopf^M
cabeza^F

descender
descendeur^M
Abseilhaken^M
pitón^M para el descenso^M

adze
panne^F
Schaufel^F
pala^F

pick
pointe^F
Haue^F
pico^M

CHOCK
COINCEUR^M
KLEMMSCHLAUFE^F
CUÑA^F

wrist sling
dragonne^F
Handschlaufe^F
correa^F de muñeca^F

wire sling
câble^M d'acier^M
Drahtschlinge^F
cable^M de acero^M

shaft
manche^M
Stiel^M
mango^M

PITON
PITON^M
KLETTERHAKEN^M
PITÓN^M

blade
lame^F
Spitze^F
pata^F

eye
œil^M
Auge^N
ojo^M

spike
pique^F
Dorn^M
regatón^M

BOWLS AND PETANQUE
BOULES^F ANGLAISES ET PÉTANQUE^F
BOULE^N UND PETANQUE^N
BOLOS^M Y PETANCA^F

GREEN
PELOUSE^F
GRÜN^N
BOLERA^F EN EL CÉSPED^M

dead bowl area
zone^F de boule^F morte
Ausbereich^M
calle^F

corner pin
piquet^M de coin^M
Eckholz^N
esquina^F de calle^F

mat
tapis^M
Matte^F
esterilla^F de lanzamiento^M

corner pin
piquet^M de coin^M
Eckholz^N
esquina^F de calle^F

jack
cochonnet^M
Zielkugel^F
boliche^M

rink
surface^F de jeu^M
Abwurfstelle^F
pista^F

centre line
ligne^F de centre^M
Mittellinie^F
línea^F central

ditch
rigole^F
Graben^M
cuneta^F

DELIVERY
LANCEMENT^M DE LA BOULE^F
ABWURF^M
LANZAMIENTO^M

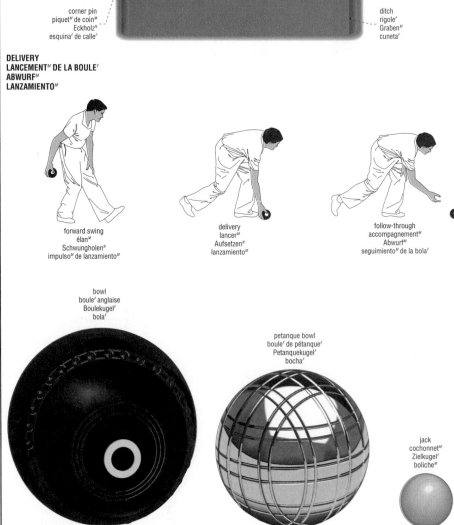

forward swing
élan^M
Schwungholen^N
impulso^M de lanzamiento^M

delivery
lancer^M
Aufsetzen^N
lanzamiento^M

follow-through
accompagnement^M
Abwurf^M
seguimiento^M de la bola^F

bowl
boule^F anglaise
Boulekugel^F
bola^F

petanque bowl
boule^F de pétanque^F
Petanquekugel^F
bocha^F

jack
cochonnet^M
Zielkugel^F
boliche^M

BOWLING
JEU^M DE QUILLES^F
BOWLING^N
JUEGO^M DE BOLOS^M

BOWLING BALL
BOULE^F DE QUILLES^F
BOWLINGKUGEL^F
BOLA^F

TYPES OF PINS
TYPES^M DE QUILLES^F
VERSCHIEDENE PINS^M
TIPOS^M DE BOLOS^M

duckpin
Dauphine^F américaine
Duckpin^M
bolo^M chico

duckpin
Dauphine^F canadienne
Duckpin^M
bolo^M chico

tenpin
grosse quille^F
Zehnerpin^M
bolo^M

candlepin
quille^F chandelle^F
Candlepin^M
bolo^M cilíndrico

fivepin
petite quille^F
Fünferpin^M
bolo^M pequeño

SET-UP
QUILLIER^M
AUFSTELLUNG^F
DISPOSICIÓN^F DE LOS BOLOS^M

pin
quille^F
Pin^M
bolo^M

pocket
poche^F
Gasse^F
separación^F entre bolos^M

headpin
quille^F-reine^F
Vordereckpin^M
bolo^M delantero

LANE
PISTE^F
BAHN^F
PISTA^F

score-console
tableau^M marqueur^M
Punktekonsole^F
marcador^M

ball return
monte-boules^M
Kugelrücklaufkasten^M
devolvedor^M

keyboard
clavier^M
Kontrollkonsole^F
teclado^M

ball stand
boulier^M
Kugelträger^M
stand^M de bolos^M

set-up
quillier^M
Aufstellmaschine^F
disposición^F de los bolos^M

pit
fosse^F de réception^F
Grube^F
foso^M de recepción^F

marker
point^M de repère^M
Ziellinie^F
línea^F de tiro^M

gutter
dalot^M
Rinne^F
canal^M

foul line
ligne^F de jeu^M
Foullinie^F
línea^F de lanzamiento^M

approach
piste^F d'élan^M
Anlaufstrecke^F
antepista^F

ball
boule^F
Kugel^F
bola^F

ARCHERY
TIR^M À L'ARC^M
BOGENSCHIESSEN^N
TIRO^M AL ARCO^M

ARROW
FLÈCHE^F
PFEIL^M
FLECHA^F

shaft
fût^M
Schaft^M
flecha^F

nock
encoche^F
Nocke^F
muesca^F

point
pointe^F
Pfeilspitze^F
punta^F

fletching
empennage^M
Steuerfedern^F
pluma^F de dirección^F

COMPOUND BOW
ARC^M À POULIES^F
COMPOUND-BOGEN^M
ARCO^M DE COMPETICIÓN^F

ARCHER
ARCHER^M
BOGENSCHÜTZE^M
ARQUERO^M

chest protector
plastron^M
Brustschutz^M
protector^M pectoral

armguard
bracelet^M
Armschutz^M
protector^M de brazo^M

tensioning wire
câble^M
Spannkabel^M
cable^M

nocking point
point^M d'encochage^M
Nockenpunkt^M
punto^M de inserción^F

mounting bracket
écrou^M de montage^M
Aufsetzbacke^F
alza^F

sight
mire^F
Visier^N
mira^F

arrow rest
appui-flèche^M
Pfeilstütze^F
soporte^M de flecha^F

accessory pouch
sac^M pour accessoires^M
Zubehörtasche^F
accesorios^M

quiver
carquois^M
Köcher^M
carcaj^M

grip
poignée^F
Griff^M
empuñadura^F

TARGET
CIBLE^F
ZIELSCHEIBE^F
BLANCO^M

stabilizer
stabilisateur^M
Stabilisator^M
estabilizador^M

cable guard
espaceur^M de câbles^M
Spannkabelhalter^M
cable^M de dirección^F

bowstring
corde^F
Bogensehne^F
cuerda^F

bull's-eye
centre^M
Mouche^F
centro^M del blanco^M

limb
branche^F
Bogenarm^M
brazo^M elástico

wheel
poulie^F
Rolle^F
polea^F

TWO-PERSON TENT
TENTE^F DEUX PLACES^F
ZWEIPERSONENZELT^N
TIENDA^F PARA DOS

flysheet
double toit^M
Überdach^N
doble techo^M

door
porte^F
Eingang^M
puerta^F

canopy
auvent^M
Vordach^N
toldo^M delantero

tension adjuster
tendeur^M
Spanner^M
fiador^M

zip
fermeture^F à glissière^F
Reißverschluß^M
cierre^M

inner tent
tente^F intérieure
Innenzelt^N
tienda^F interior

elastic loop
Sandow®^M
Gummispannring^M
fiador^M elástico

guy line
hauban^M
Zeltspannleine^F
viento^M

peg
piquet^M
Hering^M
estaquilla^F

FAMILY TENT
TENTE^F FAMILIALE
FAMILIENZELT^N
TIENDA^F DE CAMPAÑA^F TAMAÑO^M FAMILIAR

living room
séjour^M
Wohnraum^M
cuarto^M de estar

bedroom
chambre^F
Schlafraum^M
dormitorio^M

window awning
auvent^M de fenêtre^F
Fensterüberdachung^F
toldo^M de ventana^F

screen window
fenêtre^F moustiquaire^F
Fliegenfenster^N
ventana^F-mosquitero^M

elastic loop
Sandow®^M
Gummispannring^M
fiador^M elástico

sewn-in groundsheet
tapis^M de sol^M cousu
eingenähter Boden^M
piso^M cosido

wall
mur^M
Zeltwand^F
muro^M

guy line
hauban^M
Zeltspannleine^F
viento^M

canvas divider
cloison^F
Raumteiler^M
lona^F de separación^F

frame
armature^F
Gestänge^N
armadura^F

peg loop
boucle^F de piquet^M
Heringsschlaufe^F
presilla^F de estaquilla^F

RIDGE TENT
TENTE^{F} **CANADIENNE**
HAUSZELT^{N}
TIENDA^{F} **DE CAMPAÑA**^{F} **CLÁSICA**

flysheet
double toit^{M}
Überdach^{N}
doble toldo^{M}

inner tent
tente^{F} intérieure
Innenzelt^{N}
tienda^{F} interior

roof pole
mât^{M} de toit^{M}
Zeltstange^{F}
palo^{M} de la tienda^{F}

door
porte^{F}
Eingang^{M}
puerta^{F}

elastic strainer
Sandow®^{M}
Gummispannring^{M}
fiador^{M} elástico

sewn-in groundsheet
tapis^{M} de sol^{M} cousu
eingenähter Boden^{M}
piso^{M} cosido

peg loop
boucle^{F} de piquet^{M}
Heringsschlaufe^{F}
presilla^{F} de estaquilla^{F}

peg
piquet^{M}
Hering^{M}
estaquilla^{F}

PRINCIPAL TYPES OF TENT
PRINCIPAUX TYPES^{M} **DE TENTES**^{F}
DIE WICHTIGSTEN ZELTARTEN^{F}
TIPOS^{M} **DE TIENDAS**^{F}

wagon tent
tente^{F} grange^{F}
Mannschaftszelt^{N}
tienda^{F} tipo^{M} vagón^{M}

wall tent
tente^{F} rectangulaire
Steilwandzelt^{N}
tienda^{F} rectangular

dome tent
tente^{F} dôme^{M}
Kuppelzelt^{N}
tienda^{F} tipo^{M} domo^{M}

one-person tent
tente^{F} individuelle
Einpersonenzelt^{N}
tienda^{F} unipersonal

igloo tent
tente^{F} igloo^{M}
aufklappbares Igluzelt^{N}
tienda^{F} tipo^{M} iglú^{M}

BED AND MATTRESS
LIT^M **ET MATELAS**^M
BETT^N **MIT MATRATZE**^F
CAMAS^F **Y COLCHONETAS**^F

foam pad
matelas^M mousse^F
Schaumgummimatratze^F
colchón^M de espuma^F

self-inflating mattress
matelas^M autogonflant
Luftmatratze^F
colchón^M aislante

air mattress
matelas^M pneumatique
Luftmatratze^F
colchón^M de aire^M

inflator
gonfleur^M
Blasebalg^M
inflador^M

inflator-deflator
gonfleur^M-dégonfleur^M
Kombipumpe^F
muelle^F para inflar y desinflar

camp bed
lit^M de camp^M pliant
Faltfeldbett^N
catre^M desmontable

SLEEPING BAGS
SACS^M **DE COUCHAGE**^M
SCHLAFSÄCKE^M
SACOS^M **DE DORMIR**

mummy
à cagoule^F
Mumienschlafsack^M
de momia^F

semi-mummy
semi-rectangulaire
Halbmumienschlafsack^M
saco^M semirrectangular

rectangular
rectangulaire
Rechteckschlafsack^M
saco^M rectangular

CAMPING EQUIPMENT
MATÉRIEL*^M* DE CAMPING*^M*
CAMPINGAUSRÜSTUNG*^F*
EQUIPO*^M* PARA ACAMPAR

SWISS ARMY KNIFE
COUTEAU*^M* SUISSE
SCHWEIZER OFFIZIERSMESSER*^N*
NAVAJA*^F* TIPO*^M* SUIZO

scissors
ciseaux*^M*
Schere*^F*
tijeras*^F*

ruler
règle*^F* graduée
Lineal*^N*
regla*^F*

fish scaler
écailleur*^M*
Fischschupper*^M*
descamador*^M*

magnifier
loupe*^F*
Lupe*^F*
lupa*^F*

file
lime*^F*
Feile*^F*
lima*^F*

small blade
petite lame*^F*
kleine Klinge*^F*
hoja*^F* corta

cross-tip screwdriver
tournevis*^M* cruciforme
Kreuzschlitzschraubenzieher*^M*
destornillador*^M* de cruceta*^F*

screwdriver
tournevis*^M*
Schraubenzieher*^M*
destornillador*^M*

large blade
grande lame*^F*
große Klinge*^F*
hoja*^F* larga

nail groove
onglet*^M*
Nagelzieher*^M*
lima*^F*

screwdriver
tournevis*^M*
Schraubenzieher*^M*
destornillador*^M*

bottle opener
décapsuleur*^M*
Flaschenöffner*^M*
abrebotellas*^M*

awl
poinçon*^M*
Ahle*^F*
punzón*^M*

corkscrew
tire-bouchon*^M*
Korkenzieher*^M*
sacacorchos*^M*

tin opener
ouvre-boîtes*^M*
Dosenöffner*^M*
abrelatas*^M*

COOKING SET
POPOTE*^F*
KOCHGESCHIRR*^N*
UTENSILIOS*^M* DE COCINA*^F*

cup
tasse*^F*
Tasse*^F*
taza*^F*

coffee pot
cafetière*^F*
Kaffeekanne*^F*
cafetera*^F*

saucepan
faitout*^M*
Kochtopf*^M*
olla*^F*

handle
queue*^F*
Griff*^M*
mango*^M*

frying pan
poêle*^F*
Bratpfanne*^F*
sartén*^F*

plate
assiette*^F* plate
Teller*^M*
plato*^M*

CUTLERY SET
USTENSILES*^M* DE CAMPEUR*^M*
ESSBESTECK*^N*
CUBERTERÍA*^F*

spoon
cuiller*^F*
Löffel*^M*
cuchara*^F*

belt loop
ganse*^F*
Gürtelschlaufe*^F*
presilla*^F*

fork
fourchette*^F*
Gabel*^F*
tenedor*^M*

knife
couteau*^M*
Messer*^N*
cuchillo*^M*

pouch
étui*^M*
Hülle*^F*
funda*^F*

lantern
lanterne[f]
Lampe[f]
linterna[f]

globe
globe[m]
Glas[n]
globo[m]

burner frame
bâti[m] du brûleur[m]
Brennsockel[m]
armazón[m] del quemador[m]

pressure regulator
régulateur[m] de pression[f]
Gasstromregulierung[f]
regulador[m] de presión[f]

leakproof cap
bouchon[m] antifuite
Dichtverschluß[m]
tapón[m] hermético

gas container
réservoir[m]
Gasbehälter[m]
tanque[m]

pump
pompe[f]
Pumpe[f]
bomba[f]

PROPANE OR BUTANE APPLIANCES
ACCESSOIRES[M] AU PROPANE[M] OU AU BUTANE[M]
PROPAN-/BUTANGASBETRIEBENE GERÄTE[N]
EQUIPO[M] DE GAS[M]

heater
chaufferette[f]
Heizstrahler[M]
calentador[M]

single-burner camp stove
réchaud[M] à un feu[M]
einflammiger Gasbrenner[M]
camping[M] gas[M]

two-burner camp stove
réchaud[M] à deux feux[M]
zweiflammiger Gasbrenner[M]
cocina[f]

burner
brûleur[M]
Brenner[M]
quemador[M]

control valve
robinet[M] relais[M]
Reglerventil[N]
válvula[f] de control[M]

wire frame
grille[f] stabilisatrice
Metallaufsatz[M]
parrilla[f] estabilizadora

gas container
réservoir[M]
Gasbehälter[M]
bombona[f] de gas[M]

CAMPING EQUIPMENT
MATÉRIEL*M* DE CAMPING*M*
CAMPINGAUSRÜSTUNG*F*
EQUIPO*M* PARA ACAMPAR

vacuum flask
bouteille*f* isolante
Thermosflasche*f*
termos*M*

water carrier
cruche*f*
Wasserkanister*M*
termos*M* con llave*f* de servicio*M*

canteen
gourde*f*
Feldflasche*f*
cantimplora*f*

hurricane lamp
lampe*f*-tempête*f*
Sturmlampe*f*
lámpara*f* de petróleo*M*

cooler
glacière*f*
Kühlbox*f*
nevera*f*

folding grill
gril*M* pliant
Faltgrill*M*
parrilla*f* plegable

TOOLS
OUTILS*M*
WERKZEUG*N*
HERRAMIENTAS*F*

hatchet
hachette*f*
Beil*N*
hacha*f*

leather sheath
étui*M* de cuir*M*
Lederschutz*M*
funda*f* de cuero*M*

sheath
gaine*f*
Scheide*f*
funda*f*

folding shovel
pelle*f*-pioche*f* pliante
Klappspaten*M*
pala*f* plegable

knife
couteau*M*
Messer*N*
cuchillo*M*

bow saw
scie*f* de camping*M*
Bogensäge*f*
sierra*f* de campo*M*

KNOTS
NŒUDS*M*
KNOTEN*M*
NUDOS*M*

reef knot
nœud*M* plat
Kreuzknoten*M*
nudo*M* de rizo*M*

overhand knot
nœud*M* simple
Hausfrauenknoten*M*
nudo*M* llano

granny knot
nœud*M* de vache*F*
Altweiberknoten*M*
nudo*M* de tejedor*M*

running bowline
nœud*M* coulant
laufender Pahlstek*M*
balso*M*

sheet bend
nœud*M* d'écoute*F* simple
einfacher Schotstek*M*
vuelta*F* de escota*F*

double sheet bend
nœud*M* d'écoute*F* double
doppelter Schotstek*M*
vuelta*F* de escota*F* doble

sheepshank
nœud*M* de jambe*F* de chien*M*
Verkürzungsstek*M*
margarita*F*

cow hitch
demi-clé*F* renversée
Kuhstek*M*
vuelta*F* de cabo*M*

heaving line knot
noeud*M* de Franciscain*M*
Wurflinienknoten*M*
nudo*M* de guía*M*

fisherman's knot
nœud*M* de pêcheur*M*
Fischerknoten*M*
nudo*M* de pescador*M*

clove hitch
nœud*M* de cabestan*M*
Slipstek*M*
nudo*M* de dos cotes*M*

figure-eight knot
nœud*M* d'arrêt*M*
Achtknoten*M*
lasca*F* doble

common whipping
surliure*F*
einfacher Takling*M*
sobrenudo*M*

bowline
nœud*M* de chaise*F* simple
Pahlstek*M*
as*M* de guía*F*

bowline on a bight
nœud*M* de chaise*F* double
doppelter Pahlstek*M*
as*M* de guía*F* de eslinga*F* doble

KNOTS
NŒUDS[M]
KNOTEN[M]
NUDOS[M] NÁUTICOS

SHORT SPLICE
ÉPISSURE[F] COURTE
SPLEISS[M]
EMPALMADURA[F]

forming
début[M]
Flechten[N]
conformación[F]

completion
fin[F]
fertige Verbindung[F]
acabado[M]

CABLE
CÂBLE[M]
TAUWERK[N]
CABLE[M]

TWISTED ROPE
CORDAGE[M] COMMIS
GEDREHTES SEIL[N]
CABLE[M] TORCIDO

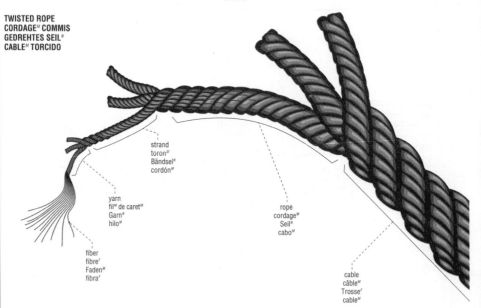

strand
toron[M]
Bändsel[N]
cordón[M]

yarn
fil[M] de caret[M]
Garn[N]
hilo[M]

rope
cordage[M]
Seil[N]
cabo[M]

fiber
fibre[F]
Faden[M]
fibra[F]

cable
câble[M]
Trosse[F]
cable[M]

BRAIDED ROPE
CORDAGE[M] TRESSÉ
GEFLOCHTENES SEIL[N]
CABLE[M] TRENZADO

core
âme[F]
Kern[M]
núcleo[M]

sheath
gaine[F]
Mantel[M]
forro[M]

SUMMARY

SPIELE
JUEGOS DE INTERIOR

INDOOR GAMES
JEUX DE SOCIÉTÉ

CARD GAMES
CARTES^F
KARTENSPIELE^N
BARAJA^F

SYMBOLS
SYMBOLES^M
FARBEN^F
SÍMBOLOS^M

heart
cœur^M
Herz^N
corazón^M

diamond
carreau^M
Karo^N
diamante^M

club
trèfle^M
Kreuz^N
trébol^M

spade
pique^M
Pik^N
espada^F

Joker
Joker^M
Joker^M
comodín^M

Ace
As^M
Ass^N
as^M

King
Roi^M
König^M
rey^M

Queen
Dame^F
Dame^F
reina^F

Jack
Valet^M
Bube^M
jota^F

STANDARD POKER HANDS
COMBINAISONS^F AU POKER^M
NORMALE POKERBLÄTTER^N
MANOS^F DE PÓQUER^M

royal flush
quinte^F royale
Royal Flush^M
escalera^F real

straight flush
quinte^F
Straight Flush^M
escalera^F de color^M

four-of-a-kind
carré^M
Vierling^M
póquer^M

full house
main^F pleine
Full House^N
full

flush
couleur^F
Flush^M
color^M

straight
séquence^F
Straße^F
escalera^F

three-of-a-kind
brelan^M
Drilling^M
trío^M

two pairs
double paire^F
zwei Pärchen^N
dos pares^M

one pair
paire^F
ein Pärchen^N
un par^M

high card
carte^F isolée
höchste Karte^F
cartas^F altas

DOMINOES
DOMINOS^M
DOMINO^N
DOMINÓ^M

doublet
double^M
Doublette^F
dos^M doble

blank
blanc^M
Blank^N
blanca^F

pip
point^M
Auge^N
punto^M

double-six
double-six^M
Sechserpasch^M
seis^M doble

double-blank
double-blanc^M
Doppelblank^N
blanca^F doble

CHESS
ÉCHECS^M
SCHACH^N
AJEDREZ^M

INDOOR GAMES
JEUX DE SOCIÉTÉ

SPIELE
JUEGOS DE INTERIOR

CHESSBOARD
ÉCHIQUIER^M
SCHACHBRETT^N
TABLERO^M **DE AJEDREZ**^M

Queen's side
aile^F Dame^F
Damenflanke^F
lado^M de la dama^F

King's side
aile^F Roi^M
Königsflanke^F
lado^M del rey^M

Black
Noirs^M
Schwarz^N
negras^F

white square
case^F blanche
weißes Feld^N
escaque^M blanco

black square
case^F noire
schwarzes Feld^N
escaque^M negro

White
Blancs^M
Weiß^N
blancas^F

chess notation
notation^F algébrique
Notation^F
notación^F del ajedrez^M

TYPES OF MOVE
TYPES^M **DE DÉPLACEMENTS**^M
GANGARTEN^F
TIPOS^M **DE MOVIMIENTOS**^M

diagonal move
déplacement^M diagonal
diagonaler Zug^M
movimiento^M diagonal

square move
déplacement^M en équerre^F
Rösselsprung^M
movimiento^M en ángulo^M

vertical move
déplacement^M vertical
vertikaler Zug^M
movimiento^M vertical

horizontal move
déplacement^M horizontal
horizontaler Zug^M
movimiento^M horizontal

MEN
PIÈCES^F
FIGUREN^F
PIEZAS^F

Pawn
Pion^M
Bauer^M
peón^M

Castle
Tour^F
Turm^M
torre^F

King
Roi^M
König^M
rey^M

Queen
Dame^F
Dame^F
reina^F

Bishop
Fou^M
Läufer^M
alfil^M

Knight
Cavalier^M
Pferd^N
caballo^M

BACKGAMMON
JACQUET^M
BACKGAMMON^N
BACKGAMMON^M

doubling die
dé^M doubleur^M
Dopplerwürfel^M
dado^M doble

outer table
jan^M extérieur
Außenbrett^N
base^F exterior

inner table
jan^M intérieur
Innenbrett^N
base^F interior

dice cup
cornet^M à dés^M
Würfelbecher^M
cubilete^M

Red
Rouges^M
Rot^N
roja^F

die
dé^M
Würfel^M
dado^M

point
flèche^F
Feld^N
punta^F

White
Blancs^M
Weiß^N
blanca^F

bar
cloison^F
Bar^F
barra^F

men
dames^F
Steine^M
dama^F

runner
postillon^M
Läufer^M
jugador^M

GO
GO^M
GO^N
GO(SUN-TSE)

BOARD
TERRAIN^M
SPIELBRETT^N
TABLERO^M

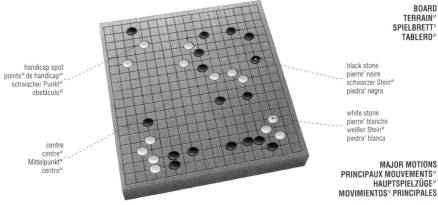

handicap spot
points^M de handicap^M
schwacher Punkt^M
obstáculo^M

black stone
pierre^F noire
schwarzer Stein^M
piedra^F negra

white stone
pierre^F blanche
weißer Stein^M
piedra^F blanca

centre
centre^M
Mittelpunkt^M
centro^M

MAJOR MOTIONS
PRINCIPAUX MOUVEMENTS^M
HAUPTSPIELZÜGE^M
MOVIMIENTOS^M PRINCIPALES

capture
capture^F
Fangen^N
captura^F

contact
contact^M
Berührung^F
contacto^M

connection
connexion^F
Verbindung^F
conexión^F

697

GAME OF DARTS
JEU^M DE FLÉCHETTES^F
DARTSPIEL^N
JUEGO^M DE DARDOS^M

DARTBOARD
CIBLE^F
DARTSCHEIBE^F
DIANA^F

segment score number
valeur^F des segments^M
Segmentpunktzahl^F
segmento^M de marcas^F

double ring
score^M doublé
Double^M
círculo^M doble

bull's-eye
50 points^M
Bull's eye^N
blanco^M

treble ring
score^M triplé
Treble^M
círculo^M triple

25 ring
25 points^M
äußerer Bull^M
círculo^M 25

DART
FLÉCHETTE^F
WURFPFEIL^M
DARDO^M

point
pointe^F
Spitze^F
punta^F

barrel
corps^M
Rumpf^M
cañón^M

shaft
fût^M
Schaft^M
asta^F

flight
empennage^M
Steuerfeder^F
volador^M

PLAYING AREA
AIRE^F **DE JEU**^M
SPIELBEREICH^M
ÁREA^F **DE JUEGO**^M

protective surround
fond^M de protection^F
Schutzumrandung^F
protector^M

scoreboard
tableau^M des scores^M
Punktetabelle^F
tablero^M de notación^F

1,74 m

oche
ligne^F de jeu^M
Hockey^M
demarcación^F

2,37 m

698

VIDEO ENTERTAINMENT SYSTEM
SYSTÈME*ᴹ* DE JEUX*ᴹ* VIDÉO
VIDEOSPIELSYSTEM*ᴺ*
SISTEMA*ᴹ* DE JUEGOS*ᴹ* DE VÍDEO*ᴹ*

visual display
écran*ᴹ*
Monitor*ᴹ*
pantalla*ᶠ*

control pad
bloc*ᴹ* de commande*ᶠ*
Steuereinheit*ᶠ*
mecanismo*ᴹ* de control

function button
bouton*ᴹ* de fonction*ᶠ*
Funktionstaste*ᶠ*
botón*ᴹ* de funcionamiento*ᴹ*

control deck
console*ᶠ* de traitement*ᴹ*
Kontrollgerät*ᴺ*
cubierta*ᶠ* de control*ᴹ*

game cartridge
cartouche*ᶠ* de jeu*ᴹ*
Spielcassette*ᶠ*
casete*ᴹ* de juego*ᴹ*

INDOOR GAMES
JEUX DE SOCIÉTÉ

SPIELE

JUEGOS DE INTERIOR

DICE
DÉS*ᴹ*
WÜRFEL*ᴹ*
DADOS*ᴹ*

poker die
dé*ᴹ* à poker*ᴹ*
Pokerwürfel*ᴹ*
dado*ᴹ* de póquer*ᴹ*

ordinary die
dé*ᴹ* régulier
gewöhnlicher Würfel*ᴹ*
dado*ᴹ* común

ROULETTE TABLE
TABLE^F DE ROULETTE
ROULETTESPIELTISCH^M
MESA^F DE LA RULETA^F

AMERICAN ROULETTE WHEEL
ROULETTE^F AMÉRICAINE
AMERIKANISCHES ROULETTE^N
RULETA^F AMERICANA

double zero
double zéro^M
Double-zero^N
doble^M cero

AMERICAN BETTING LAYOUT
TABLEAU^M AMÉRICAIN DES MISES^F
AMERIKANISCHER ROULETTESPIELPLAN^M
DISTRIBUCIÓN^F DE APUESTA^F AMERICANA

main section
bande^F centrale
Hauptabschnitt^M
banda^F central

low (1 to 18)
manque^M (1 à 18)
Manque^N (1 bis 18)
falta^F (1 a 18)

single zero
zéro^M
Zero^N
cero^M

dozen (1 to 12)
douzaine^F (1 à 12)
Douze premier^N (1 bis 12)
docena^F (1 a 12)

double zero
double zéro^M
Double zero^N
doble cero^M

even
pair^M
Pair^N
par^M

square bet
carré^M
Carré^N
apuesta^F en cuadro^M

red
rouge^M
Rouge^N
roja^F

split bet
à cheval^M sur deux numéros^M
Cheval^N
partido^M

dozen (13 to 24)
douzaine^F (13 à 24)
Douze milieu^N (13 bis 24)
docena^F (13 a 24)

line
sixain^M
Transversale simple^F
línea^F

black
noir^M
Noir^N
negra^F

five-number bet
quinte^F
fünf Nummern^F
apuesta^F de cinco números^M

en prison
en prison^F
en prison
en prisión^F

straight bet
numéro^M plein
Plein^N
seco^M

odd
impair^M
Impair^N
impar^M

street bet
transversale^F pleine
Transversale pleine^F
apuesta^F libre

high (19 to 36)
passe^F (19 à 36)
Passe^N (19 bis 36)
pasa^F (19 a 36)

two columns split bet
à cheval^M sur deux colonnes^F
zwei Kolonnen Cheval^N
apuesta^F sobre dos columnas^F

dozen (25 to 36)
douzaine^F (25 à 36)
Douze dernier^N (25 bis 36)
docena^F (25 a 36)

column
colonne^F
Kolonne^F
columna^F

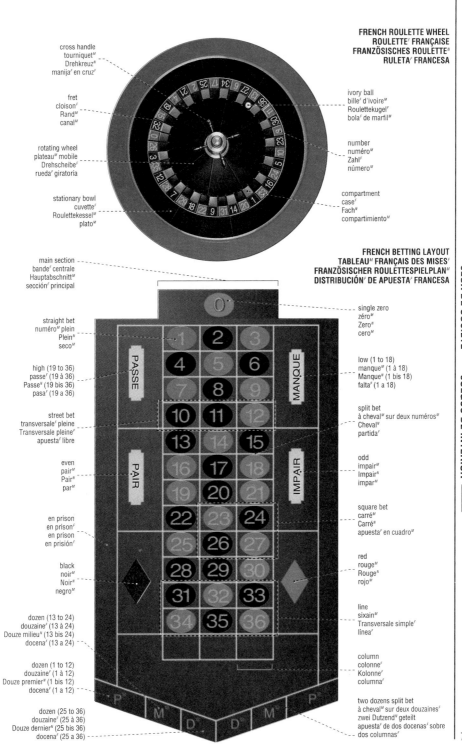

FRENCH ROULETTE WHEEL
ROULETTE^F FRANÇAISE
FRANZÖSISCHES ROULETTE^N
RULETA^F FRANCESA

cross handle
tourniquet^M
Drehkreuz^N
manija^F en cruz^F

fret
cloison^F
Rand^M
canal^M

rotating wheel
plateau^M mobile
Drehscheibe^F
rueda^F giratoria

stationary bowl
cuvette^F
Roulettekessel^M
plato^M

ivory ball
bille^F d'ivoire^M
Roulettekugel^F
bola^F de marfil^M

number
numéro^M
Zahl^F
número^M

compartment
case^F
Fach^N
compartimiento^M

FRENCH BETTING LAYOUT
TABLEAU^M FRANÇAIS DES MISES^F
FRANZÖSISCHER ROULETTESPIELPLAN^M
DISTRIBUCIÓN^F DE APUESTA^F FRANCESA

**INDOOR GAMES
JEUX DE SOCIÉTÉ**

**SPIELE
JUEGOS DE INTERIOR**

main section
bande^F centrale
Hauptabschnitt^M
sección^F principal

straight bet
numéro^M plein
Plein^N
seco^M

high (19 to 36)
passe^F (19 à 36)
Passe^N (19 bis 36)
pasa^F (19 a 36)

street bet
transversale^F pleine
Transversale pleine^F
apuesta^F libre

even
pair^M
Pair^N
par^M

en prison
en prison^F
en prison
en prisión^F

black
noir^M
Noir^N
negro^M

dozen (13 to 24)
douzaine^F (13 à 24)
Douze milieu^N (13 bis 24)
docena^F (13 a 24)

dozen (1 to 12)
douzaine^F (1 à 12)
Douze premier^N (1 bis 12)
docena^F (1 a 12)

dozen (25 to 36)
douzaine^F (25 à 36)
Douze dernier^N (25 bis 36)
docena^F (25 a 36)

single zero
zéro^M
Zero^N
cero^M

low (1 to 18)
manque^M (1 à 18)
Manque^N (1 bis 18)
falta^F (1 a 18)

split bet
à cheval^M sur deux numéros^M
Cheval^N
partida^F

odd
impair^M
Impair^N
impar^M

square bet
carré^M
Carré^N
apuesta^F en cuadro^M

red
rouge^M
Rouge^N
rojo^M

line
sixain^M
Transversale simple^F
línea^F

column
colonne^F
Kolonne^F
columna^F

two dozens split bet
à cheval^M sur deux douzaines^F
zwei Dutzend^N geteilt
apuesta^F de dos docenas^F sobre
dos columnas^F

701

FRUIT MACHINE
MACHINE^F À SOUS^M
EINARMIGER BANDIT^M
TRAGAPERRAS^M

casing
boîtier^M
Gehäuse^N
caja^F

coin slot
fente^F à monnaie^F
Münzeinwurf^M
ranura^F para monedas^F

symbol
symbole^M
Symbol^N
símbolo^M

lever
bras^M
Hebel^M
palanca^F

coin reject slot
réceptacle^M pour les pièces^F refusées
Münzrückgabe^F
devolución^F de monedas^F rechazadas

winning line
combinaison^F gagnante
Gewinnkombination^F
combinación^F ganadora

payout tray
plateau^M réceptacle^M de paiement^M
Auszahlungsschale^F
bandeja^F de pago^M

CROSS SECTION
COUPE^F
QUERSCHNITT
CORTE^M TRANSVERSAL

reel plate
plaque^F de rouleau^M
Drehkranz^M
engranaje^M

payout trigger
déclencheur^M de paiement^M
Auszahlungshebel^M
disparador^M de pago^M

reel
rouleau^M
Glücksrad^N
tambor^M

spring linkage
levier^M à ressort^M
Federverbindung^F
resorte^M del sistema^M articulado

coin chute
conduite^F des pièces^F
Münzleitung^F
conducto^M de monedas^F

jackpot feed
alimentation^F jackpot^M
Jackpot-Leitung^F
selector^M del premio^M

strongbox
caisse^F blindée
Gehäuseverstärkung^F
caja^F fuerte

jackpot box
boîte^F jackpot^M
Jackpot-Kasten^M
casilla^F del dinero^M

electrical payout linkage
commande^F électrique de paiement^M
elektrisches Auszahlungselement^N
control^M eléctrico de pago^M

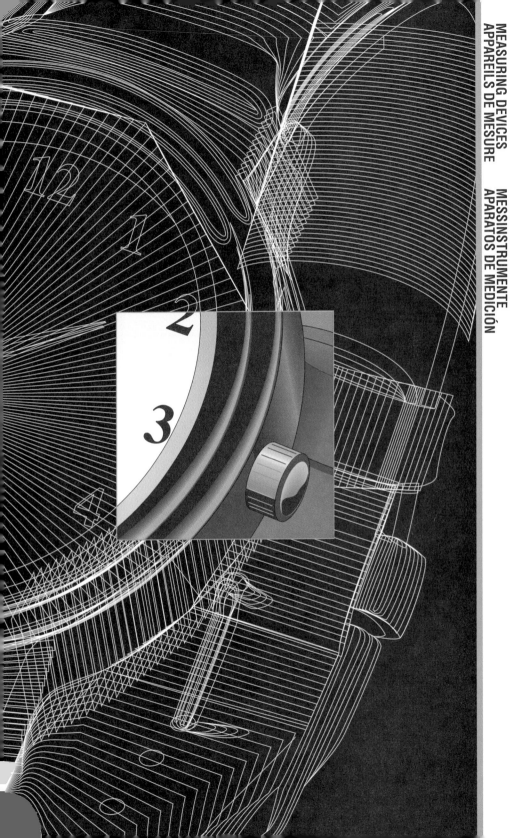

MESSINSTRUMENTE
APARATOS DE MEDICIÓN

MEASURING DEVICES
APPAREILS DE MESURE

MEASURE OF TEMPERATURE
MESURE^F DE LA TEMPÉRATURE^F
TEMPERATURMESSUNG^F
MEDICIÓN^F DE LA TEMPERATURA^F

THERMOMETER
THERMOMÈTRE^M
THERMOMETER^N
TERMÓMETRO^M

Fahrenheit scale
échelle^F Fahrenheit
Fahrenheitskala^F
escala^F Fahrenheit

Celsius scale
échelle^F Celsius
Celsiusskala^F
escala^F Celsius

degrees Fahrenheit
°F
Grad^M Fahrenheit
grados^M F

degrees Celsius
°C
Grad^M Celsius
grados^M C

alcohol column
colonne^F d'alcool^M
Alkoholsäule^F
columna^F de alcohol^M

alcohol bulb
réservoir^M d'alcool^M
Alkoholkolben^M
cubeta^F de alcohol^M

CLINICAL THERMOMETER
THERMOMÈTRE^M MÉDICAL
FIEBERTHERMOMETER^N
TERMÓMETRO^M CLÍNICO

expansion chamber
chambre^F d'expansion^F
Ausdehnungskammer^F
cámara^F de expansión^F

capillary tube
tube^M capillaire
Kapillarröhrchen^N
tubo^M capilar

stem
tige^F
Röhre^F
tubo^M de cristal^M

scale
graduation^F
Skala^F
escala^F de temperaturas^F

column of mercury
colonne^F de mercure^M
Quecksilbersäule^F
columna^F de mercurio^M

constriction
étranglement^M
Verengung^F
estrechamiento^M

mercury bulb
réservoir^M de mercure^M
Quecksilberkolben^M
cubeta^F de mercurio^M

BIMETALLIC THERMOMETER
THERMOMÈTRE^M BIMÉTALLIQUE
BIMETALL-THERMOMETER^N
TERMÓMETRO^M BIMETÁLICO

pointer
aiguille^F
Zeiger^M
aguja^F

case
boîtier^M
Gehäuse^N
caja^F

dial
cadran^M
Anzeigeskala^F
cuadrante^M

shaft
arbre^M
Welle^F
barra^F

bimetallic helix
élément^M bimétallique hélicoïdal
Bimetallfeder^F
hélice^F bimetálica

ROOM THERMOSTAT
THERMOSTAT^M D'AMBIANCE^F
RAUMTHERMOSTAT^M
TERMOSTATO^M AMBIENTAL

cover
couvercle^M
Abdeckung^F
tapa^F

desired temperature
température^F désirée
gewünschte Temperatur^F
marcador^M de temperatura^F

temperature set point knob
réglage^M de la température^F
Temperaturregler^M
botón^M para fijar la temperatura^F

actual temperature
température^F ambiante
tatsächliche Temperatur^F
temperatura^F real

pointer
aiguille^F
Zeiger^M
aguja^F

MESSINSTRUMENTE / APARATOS DE MEDICIÓN

MEASURING DEVICES / APPAREILS DE MESURE

STOPWATCH
CHRONOMÈTRE^M
STOPPUHR^F
CRONÓMETRO^M

ring
anneau^M
Ring^M
anilla^F

reset button
poussoir^M de remise^F à zéro^M
Rückstellknopf^M
botón^M de inicio^M del contador^M

start button
poussoir^M de mise^F en marche^F
Startknopf^M
botón^M de inicio^M de marcha^F

second hand
trotteuse^F
Sekundenzeiger^M
segundero^M

stop button
poussoir^M d'arrêt^M
Stoppknopf^M
botón^M de parada^F

1/10th second hand
aiguille^F des dixièmes^M de seconde^F
Zehntelsekundenzeiger^M
aguja^F de décimas^F de segundo^M

minute hand
aiguille^F des minutes^F
Minutenzeiger^M
minutero^M

case
boîtier^M
Gehäuse^N
estuche^M

MECHANICAL WATCH
MONTRE^F MÉCANIQUE
MECHANISCHE UHR^F
RELOJ^M MECÁNICO

strap
bracelet^M
Uhrband^N
correa^F

jewel
rubis^M
Stein^M
rubí^M

ANALOGUE WATCH
MONTRE^F À AFFICHAGE^M ANALOGIQUE
ANALOGUHR^F
RELOJ^M DE PULSERA^F

escape wheel
roue^F d'échappement^M
Hemmrad^N
rueda^F de escape^M

fourth wheel
roue^F de champ^M
Ankerrad^N
rueda^F de los segundos^M

hairspring
spiral^M
Spiralfeder^F
espiral^M

third wheel
roue^F petite moyenne
Antriebswerk^N
rueda^F media

centre wheel
roue^F de centre^M
Spannrad^N
rueda^F central

crown
couronne^F
Krone^F
corona^F

barrel
rochet^M
Federhaus^N
rueda^F de trinquete^M

winder
remontoir^M
Aufzugsrad^N
cuerda^F

dial
cadran^M
Ziffernblatt^N
cuadrante^M

click
cliquet^M
Sperrstift^M
trinquete^M

DIGITAL WATCH
MONTRE^F À AFFICHAGE^M NUMÉRIQUE
DIGITALUHR^F
RELOJ^M DIGITAL

SUNDIAL
CADRAN^M SOLAIRE
SONNENUHR^F
RELOJ^M DE SOL^M

gnomon
style^M
Gnomon^M
estilo^M

dial
cadran^M
Ziffernblatt^N
cuadrante^M

shadow
ombre^F
Schatten^M
sombra^F

liquid-crystal display
cristaux^M liquides
LCD-Anzeige^F
registro^M de cristal^M líquido

GRANDFATHER CLOCK
HORLOGE^F DE PARQUET^M
STANDUHR^F
RELOJ^M DE PÉNDULO^M

pediment
corniche^F
Giebeldreieck^N
frontón^M

body
caisse^F
Gehäuse^N
caja^F

hour hand
aiguille^F des heures^F
Sekundenzeiger^M
manecilla^F de las horas^F

dial
cadran^M
Ziffernblatt^N
esfera^F

plinth
socle^M
Plinthe^F
zócalo^M

moon dial
cadran^M des phases^F de la Lune^F
Mondphasenzeiger^M
esfera^F lunar

minute hand
aiguille^F des minutes^F
Minutenzeiger^M
minutero^M

weight
poids^M
Gewicht^N
pesa^F

pendulum
pendule^M
Pendel^N
péndulo^M

chain
chaîne^F
Kette^F
cadena^F

WEIGHT-DRIVEN CLOCK MECHANISM
MÉCANISME^M DE L'HORLOGE^F À POIDS^M
ZUGGETRIEBENES UHRWERK^N
MECANISMO^M DEL RELOJ^M DE PESAS^F

suspension spring
lame^F de suspension^F
Aufhängefeder^F
resorte^M de suspensión^F

pinion
pignon^M
Ritzel^N
piñón^M

fork
fourchette^F
Gabel^F
diapasón^M

centre wheel
roue^F de centre^M
Spannrad^N
rueda^F central

pendulum rod
tige^F
Pendelstab^M
varilla^F del péndulo^M

click
cliquet^M
Sperrstift^M
trinquete^M

pendulum
lentille^F
Pendel^N
péndulo^M

main wheel
roue^F motrice
Hauptrad^M
rueda^F motriz

pallet
ancre^F
Hemmungslappen^M
áncora^F

ratchet wheel
rochet^M
Sperrad^N
rueda^F de trinquete^M

weight
poids^M
Gewicht^N
pesa^F

escape wheel
roue^F d'échappement^M
Hemmrad^N
rueda^F de escape^M

spindle
arbre^M
Spindel^F
eje^M

third wheel
roue^F petite moyenne
Antriebswerk^N
rueda^F de corona^F

minute hand
aiguille^F des minutes^F
Minutenzeiger^M
minutero^M

hour hand
aiguille^F des heures^F
Stundenzeiger^M
manecilla^F de las horas^F

winding mechanism
remontoir^M
Aufzugsmechanismus^M
mecanismo^M de cuerda^F

drum
tambour^M
Trommel^F
cilindro^M

MEASUREMENT OF WEIGHT
MESURE^F DE LA MASSE^F
WIEGEN^N
MEDICIÓN^F DEL PESO^M

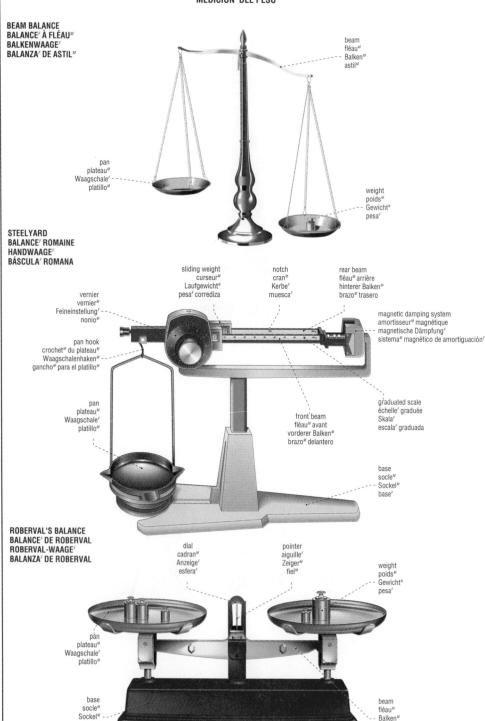

BEAM BALANCE
BALANCE^F À FLÉAU^M
BALKENWAAGE^F
BALANZA^F DE ASTIL^M

beam
fléau^M
Balken^M
astil^M

pan
plateau^M
Waagschale^F
platillo^M

weight
poids^M
Gewicht^N
pesa^F

STEELYARD
BALANCE^F ROMAINE
HANDWAAGE^F
BÁSCULA^F ROMANA

sliding weight
curseur^M
Laufgewicht^N
pesa^F corrediza

notch
cran^M
Kerbe^F
muesca^F

rear beam
fléau^M arrière
hinterer Balken^M
brazo^M trasero

vernier
vernier^M
Feineinstellung^F
nonio^M

magnetic damping system
amortisseur^M magnétique
magnetische Dämpfung^F
sistema^M magnético de amortiguación^F

pan hook
crochet^M du plateau^M
Waagschalenhaken^M
gancho^M para el platillo^M

graduated scale
échelle^F graduée
Skala^F
escala^F graduada

pan
plateau^M
Waagschale^F
platillo^M

front beam
fléau^M avant
vorderer Balken^M
brazo^M delantero

base
socle^M
Sockel^M
base^F

ROBERVAL'S BALANCE
BALANCE^F DE ROBERVAL
ROBERVAL-WAAGE^F
BALANZA^F DE ROBERVAL

dial
cadran^M
Anzeige^F
esfera^F

pointer
aiguille^F
Zeiger^M
fiel^M

weight
poids^M
Gewicht^N
pesa^F

pan
plateau^M
Waagschale^F
platillo^M

base
socle^M
Sockel^M
base^F

beam
fléau^M
Balken^M
astil^M

SPRING BALANCE
PESON^M
FEDERWAAGE^F
DINAMÓMETRO^M

ring
anneau^M
Halterung^F
anilla^F

pointer
index^M
Zeiger^M
fiel^M

graduated scale
échelle^F graduée
Anzeigeskala^F
escala^F graduada

hook
crochet^M
Haken^M
gancho^M

ELECTRONIC SCALES
BALANCE^F **ÉLECTRONIQUE**
ELEKTRONISCHE WAAGE^F
BÁSCULA^F **ELECTRÓNICA**

weight
poids^M
Gewicht^N
peso^M

unit price
prix^M à l'unité^F
Preis^M pro Einheit^F
precio^M unitario

POIDS/WEIGHT

PRIX/PRICE/kg

TOTAL

display
afficheur^M
Anzeige^F
indicador^M luminoso

total
prix^M à payer
Summe^F
precio^M total

platform
plateau^M
Wiegefläche^F
platillo^M

function keys
touches^F de fonctions
Funktionstasten^F
teclado^M de funciones^F

numeric keyboard
clavier^M numérique
numerisches Tastenfeld^N
teclado^M numérico

product code
code^M des produits^M
Warencode^M
código^M del producto^M

printout
étiquette^F
Wiegeetikett^N
recibo^M

ANALYTICAL BALANCE
BALANCE^F **DE PRÉCISION**^F
PRÄZISIONSWAAGE^F
BALANZA^F **DE PRECISIÓN**^F

BATHROOM SCALES
PÈSE-PERSONNE^M
PERSONENWAAGE^F
BÁSCULA^F **DE BAÑO**^M

digital display
affichage^M numérique
Digitalanzeige^F
indicador^M digital

glass case
cage^F vitrée
Glasgehäuse^N
urna^F

access door
porte^F
Schiebeöffnung^F
puerta^F

pan
plateau^M
Waagschale^F
platillo^M

weighing platform
plate-forme^F
Wiegefläche^F
plataforma^F

levelling screw
vis^F calante
Ausrichtschraube^F
tornillo^M nivelador

4.4956 g

MEASUREMENT OF PRESSURE
MESURE*F* DE LA PRESSION*F*
DRUCKMESSUNG*F*
MEDICIÓN*F* DE LA PRESIÓN*F*

BAROMETER/THERMOMETER
BAROMÈTRE*M*/THERMOMÈTRE*M*
BAROMETER*N*/THERMOMETER*N*
BARÓMETRO*M*/TERMÓMETRO*M*

indicator
repère*M*
Indikator*M*
indicador*M*

barometer scales
échelles*F* barométriques
Barometerskalen*F*
escalas*F* barométricas

graduated scale
cadran*M* gradué
Anzeigeskala*F*
esfera*F* graduada

needle
aiguille*F*
Zeiger*M*
aguja*F*

vacuum chamber
caisse*F* cylindrique
Vakuumkammer*F*
vacío*M* barométrico

temperature scales
échelles*F* de la température*F*
Temperaturskalen*F*
escalas*F* de temperatura*F*

case
boîtier*M*
Gehäuse*N*
caja*F*

SPHYGMOMANOMETER
TENSIOMÈTRE*M*
BLUTDRUCKMESSGERÄT*N*
TENSIÓMETRO*M*

digital display
affichage*M* numérique
Digitalanzeige*F*
indicador*M* digital

pressure gauge
manomètre*M*
Druckmeßgerät*N*
manómetro*M*

tube
tube*M*
Schlauch*M*
tubo*M*

air-pressure pump
poire*F* de gonflage*M*
Handblasebalg*M*
pera*F* de goma*F* para inyectar aire*M*

pneumatic armlet
brassard*M* pneumatique
aufblasbare Manschette*F*
brazalete*M* neumático

pressure control valve
soupape*F* d'évacuation*F*
Ablaßschraube*F*
tornillo*M* de ajuste*M*

MESSINSTRUMENTE
APARATOS DE MEDICIÓN

MEASURING DEVICES
APPAREILS DE MESURE

MEASUREMENT OF LENGTH
MESURE^F DE LA LONGUEUR^F
LÄNGENMESSUNG^F
MEDICIÓN^F DE LA LONGITUD^F

TAPE MEASURE
MÈTRE^M À RUBAN^M
MESSBAND^N
CINTA^F MÉTRICA

tape lock
bouton^M de blocage^M
Bandsperre^F
botón^M de bloqueo^M

scale
graduation^F
Skala^F
escala^F

hook
crochet^M
Haken^M
gancho^M

case
boîtier^M
Gehäuse^N
estuche^M

tape
ruban^M
Maßband^N
cinta^F

MEASUREMENT OF DISTANCE
MESURE^F DE LA DISTANCE^F
ENTFERNUNGSMESSUNG^F
MEDICIÓN^F DE LA DISTANCIA^F

PEDOMETER
PODOMÈTRE^M
PEDOMETER^N
ODÓMETRO^M

reset button
bouton^M de remise^F à zéro^M
Rückstellknopf^M
botón^M de inicio^M del contador^M

distance travelled
distance^F parcourue
zurückgelegte Strecke^F
distancia^F recorrida

step setting
réglage^M du pas^M
Schrittlängeneinstellung^F
contador^M

clip
agrafe^F
Befestigungsclip^M
pinza^F

case
boîtier^M
Gehäuse^N
caja^F

MEASUREMENT OF THICKNESS
MESURE^F DE L'ÉPAISSEUR^F
DICKEMESSUNG^F
MEDICIÓN^F DEL ESPESOR^M

MICROMETER CALIPER
MICROMÈTRE^M PALMER^M
MIKROMETERSCHRAUBE^F
MICRÓMETRO^M

spindle
touche^F mobile
Meßspindel^F
tope^M móvil

anvil
touche^F fixe
Anschlag^M
tope^M fijo

finely threaded screw
vis^F micrométrique
Filigrangewinde^N
rosca^F

thimble
tambour^M
Meßtrommel^F
tambor^M

lock nut
bague^F de blocage^M
Feststellschraube^F
tuerca^F de bloqueo^M

ratchet knob
bouton^M à friction^F
Sperrdrehknopf^M
husillo^M

frame
corps^M
Meßbügel^M
cuerpo^M

WATT-HOUR METER
WATTHEUREMÈTRE[M]
STROMZÄHLER[M]
VATÍMETRO[M]

EXTERIOR VIEW
VUE[F] EXTÉRIEURE
AUSSENANSICHT[F]
VISTA[F] EXTERIOR

cover
couvercle[M]
Abdeckung[F]
tapa[F]

full-load adjustment screw
vis[F] de réglage[M] de grand débit[M]
Vollbelastungseinstellschraube[F]
tornillo[M] de regulación[F] para carga[F] completa

register
minuterie[F]
Registriereinheit[F]
registro[M]

dial
cadran[M]
Ziffernblatt[N]
cuadrante[M]

name plate
plaque[F] signalétique
Kennplakette[F]
placa[F] indicadora

disc
disque[M]
Drehscheibe[F]
disco[M]

light-load adjustment screw
vis[F] de réglage[M] de petit débit[M]
Leichtbelastungseinstellschraube[F]
tornillo[M] de regulación[F] para carga[F] ligera

consumer number
numéro[M] de l'abonné[M]
Stromverbrauchernummer[F]
número[M] del consumidor[M]

MECHANISM
MÉCANISME[M]
MECHANISMUS[M]
MECANISMO[M]

magnetic suspension
palier[M] magnétique
Magnetaufhängung[F]
suspension[F] magnética

register
minuterie[F]
Registriereinheit[F]
registro[M]

spindle
arbre[M]
Spindel[F]
árbol[M]

retarding magnet
aimant[M]-frein[M]
Retardiermagnet[M]
imán[M] frenador

potential coil
bobine[F] de tension[F]
Potentialspule[F]
bobina[F] de tensión[F]

cover
couvercle[M]
Abdeckung[F]
tapa[F]

disc
disque[M]
Drehscheibe[F]
disco[M]

current coil
bobine[F] de courant[M]
Stromspule[F]
bobina[F] de corriente[F]

base
socle[M]
Grundplatte[F]
base[F]

MEASURE OF ANGLES
MESURE*F* DES ANGLES*M*
WINKELMESSUNG*F*
MEDICIÓN*F* DE ÁNGULOS*M*

THEODOLITE
THÉODOLITE*M*
THEODOLIT*M*
TEODOLITO*M*

alidade
alidade*F*
Alhidade*F*
alidada*F* móvil

adjustment for vertical-circle image
ajustement*M* de l'image*F* du cercle*M* vertical
Höhenfeintrieb*M*
botón*M* para ajustar la imágen*F* verticalmente

micrometer screw
bouton*M* de réglage*M* du micromètre*M* optique
Mikrometerknopf*M*
tornillo*M* micrométrico

adjustment for horizontal-circle image
ajustement*M* de l'image*F* du cercle*M* horizontal
Seitenfeintrieb*M*
botón*M* para ajustar la imágen*F* horizontalmente

horizontal clamp
blocage*M* du pivotement*M*
Seitenklemme*F*
tornillo*M* de fijación*F* horizontal

levelling head level
nivelle*F* d'embase*F*
Ausrichtkopfebene*F*
nivelador*M* principal

levelling head
embase*F*
Ausrichtknopf*M*
nivelación*F* principal

optical sight
viseur*M*
Mikroskopokular*N*
visor*M*

telescope
lunette*F*
Fernrohr*N*
telescopio*M*

illumination mirror
miroir*M* d'éclairage*M*
Beleuchtungsspiegel*M*
espejo*M* iluminador

alidade level
nivelle*F* d'alidade*F*
Alhidadenebene*F*
nivelador*M* de la alidada*F*

levelling screw
vis*F* calante
Ausrichtschraube*F*
tornillo*M* nivelador

base plate
plaque*F* de fixation*F*
Sockelplatte*F*
placa*F* de fijación*F*

levelling head locking knob
bouton*M* de verrouillage*M* de l'embase*F*
Ausrichtkopfblockierung*F*
botón*M* de fijación*F* del nivel*M* principal

bevel square
fausse-équerre*F*
Schrägmaß*N*
falsa escuadra*F*

protractor
rapporteur*M* d'angle*M*
Winkelmesser*M*
transportador*M*

MEASUREMENT OF SEISMIC WAVES
MESUREᶠ DES ONDESᶠ SISMIQUES
MESSUNGᶠ SEISMISCHER WELLENᶠ
MEDICIÓNᶠ DE ONDASᶠ SÍSMICAS

DETECTION OF SEISMIC WAVES
DÉTECTIONᶠ DES ONDESᶠ SISMIQUES
REGISTRIERUNGᶠ SEISMISCHER WELLENᶠ
DETECCIÓNᶠ DE ONDASᶠ SÍSMICAS

horizontal seismograph
sismographeᴹ horizontal
Horizontalseismographᴹ
sismógrafoᴹ horizontal

concrete base
baseᶠ de bétonᴹ
Betonsockelᴹ
baseᶠ de cementoᴹ

pillar
pilierᴹ
Pendelaufhängungᶠ
pilarᴹ

transmission of the electric current
transmissionᶠ du courantᴹ induit
Stromweiterleitungᶠ
transmisiónᶠ de la corrienteᶠ eléctrica

mass
masseᶠ
Masseᶠ
masaᶠ inerte

wire
filᴹ
Drahtᴹ
alambreᴹ

bedrock
rocᴹ
Grundgesteinᴺ
rocaᶠ firme

stand
socleᴹ
Standsockelᴹ
plataformaᶠ

coil
bobineᶠ
Federᶠ
bobinaᶠ

magnet
aimantᴹ
Magnetᴹ
imánᴹ

AMPLIFICATION OF SEISMIC WAVES
AMPLIFICATIONᶠ DES ONDESᶠ SISMIQUES
VERSTÄRKUNGᶠ SEISMISCHER WELLENᶠ
AMPLIFICACIÓNᶠ DE ONDASᶠ SÍSMICAS

amplifier
amplificateurᴹ
Verstärkerᴹ
amplificadorᴹ

clock
horlogeᶠ
Uhrᶠ
relojᴹ

TRANSCRIPTION OF SEISMIC WAVES
TRANSCRIPTIONᶠ DES ONDESᶠ SISMIQUES
AUFZEICHNUNGᶠ SEISMISCHER WELLENᶠ
TRANSCRIPCIÓNᶠ DE ONDASᶠ SÍSMICAS

visualization of seismic waves
visualisationᶠ des ondesᶠ sismiques
Sichtbarmachungᶠ seismischer Wellenᶠ
visualizaciónᶠ de las ondasᶠ sísmicas

seismogram
sismogrammeᴹ
Seismogrammᴺ
sismogramaᴹ

rotating drum
cylindreᴹ enregistreur
Drehwalzeᶠ
tamborᴹ rotativo

pen
plumeᶠ
Schreibspitzeᶠ
punta grabadoraᶠ

drum
tambourᴹ
Walzeᶠ
tamborᴹ

sheet of paper
feuilleᶠ de papierᴹ
Registrierpapierᴺ
papelᴹ

SUMMARY

OPTISCHE INSTRUMENTE
INSTRUMENTOS ÓPTICOS

OPTICAL INSTRUMENTS
APPAREILS DE VISION

ELECTRON MICROSCOPE
MICROSCOPE^M ÉLECTRONIQUE
ELEKTRONENMIKROSKOP^N
MICROSCOPIO^M DE ELECTRONES

CROSS SECTION OF AN ELECTRON MICROSCOPE
COUPE^F D'UN MICROSCOPE^M ÉLECTRONIQUE
QUERSCHNITT^M DURCH EIN ELEKTRONENMIKROSKOP^N
CORTE^M TRANSVERSAL DE UN MICROSCOPIO^M DE ELECTRONES^M

electron gun
canon^M à électrons^M
Elektronenkanone^F
cañón^M de electrones^M

vacuum manifold
canalisation^F de pompage^M
Vakuumrohr^N
canalización^F de vacío^M

condenser
condenseur^M
Kondensor^M
condensador^M

aperture changer
commande^F de sélection^F de l'ouverture^F
Aperturblende^F
abertura^F para el cambio^M de gases^M

aperture diaphragm
diaphragme^M d'ouverture^F
Blendeneinsteller^M
abertura^F del diafragma^M

stage
porte-spécimen^M
Objekttisch^M
platina^F

electron beam
faisceau^M d'électrons^M
Elektronenstrahl^M
haz^M de electrones^M

electron beam positioning
alignement^M du faisceau^M dans l'axe^M
Elektronenstrahljustierung^F
posición^F del haz^M de electrones^M

beam diameter reduction
concentration^F du faisceau^M
Verminderung^F des Strahlendiameters^M
reducción^F del diámetro^M del haz^M

focusing lenses
lentilles^F de mise^F au point^M
elektronoptische Linsen^F
lentes^F de enfoque^M

visual transmission
transmission^F de l'image^F
Einblicklupe^F
transmisión^F visual

vacuum chamber
chambre^F à vide^M
Vakuumkammer^F
cámara^F de vacío^M

ELECTRON MICROSCOPE ELEMENTS
COMPOSANTES^F D'UN MICROSCOPE^M ÉLECTRONIQUE
TEILE^N DES ELEKTRONENMIKROSKOPS^N
ELEMENTOS^M DEL MICROSCOPIO^M DE ELECTRONES^M

liquid nitrogen tank
réservoir^M d'azote^M liquide
Behälter^M mit flüssigem Stickstoff^M
tanque^M del nitrógeno^M

spectrometer
spectromètre^M
Spektrometer^M
espectrómetro^M

specimen chamber
chambre^F d'observation^F
Probenkammer^F
cámara^F para la muestra^F

vacuum system console
bâti^M de la pompe^F à vide^M
Vakuumpumpe^F
consola^F para el sistema^M de vacío^M

specimen positioning control
commande^F de positionnement^M du specimen^M
Bedienungselement^N für Objektbewegung^F
control^M de posición^F de la muestra^F

control panel
tableau^M de commandes^F
Bedienpult^N
tablero^M de control^M

photographic chamber
chambre^F photographique
Aufnahmekammer^F
cámara^F de fotografía^F

electron gun
canon^M à électrons^M
Elektronenkanone^F
cañón^M de electrones^M

monitor screen
écran^M de contrôle^M
Kontrollbildschirm^M
pantalla^F de control^M

data record system
saisie^F des données^F
Datenspeicherung^F
sistema^M de registro^M de la información^F

717

BINOCULAR MICROSCOPE
MICROSCOPE^M BINOCULAIRE
BINOKULARMIKROSKOP^N
MICROSCOPIO^M BINOCULAR

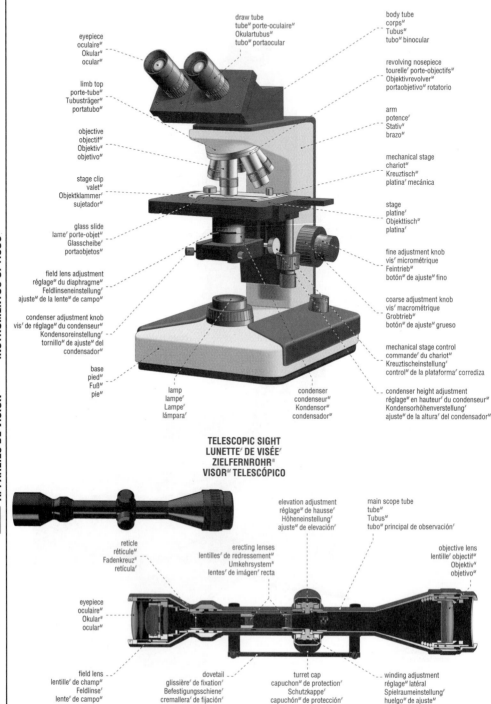

eyepiece
oculaire^M
Okular^N
ocular^M

limb top
porte-tube^M
Tubusträger^M
portatubo^M

objective
objectif^M
Objektiv^N
objetivo^M

stage clip
valet^M
Objektklammer^F
sujetador^M

glass slide
lame^F porte-objet^M
Glasscheibe^F
portaobjetos^M

field lens adjustment
réglage^M du diaphragme^M
Feldlinseneinstellung^F
ajuste^M de la lente^F de campo^M

condenser adjustment knob
vis^F de réglage^M du condenseur^M
Kondensoreinstellung^F
tornillo^M de ajuste^M del
condensador^M

base
pied^M
Fuß^M
pie^M

draw tube
tube^M porte-oculaire^M
Okulartubus^M
tubo^M portaocular

lamp
lampe^F
Lampe^F
lámpara^F

condenser
condenseur^M
Kondensor^M
condensador^M

body tube
corps^M
Tubus^M
tubo^M binocular

revolving nosepiece
tourelle^F porte-objectifs^M
Objektivrevolver^M
portaobjetivo^M rotatorio

arm
potence^F
Stativ^N
brazo^M

mechanical stage
chariot^M
Kreuztisch^M
platina^F mecánica

stage
platine^F
Objekttisch^M
platina^F

fine adjustment knob
vis^F micrométrique
Feintrieb^M
botón^M de ajuste^M fino

coarse adjustment knob
vis^F macrométrique
Grobtrieb^M
botón^M de ajuste^M grueso

mechanical stage control
commande^F du chariot^M
Kreuztischeinstellung^F
control^M de la plataforma^F corrediza

condenser height adjustment
réglage^M en hauteur^F du condenseur^M
Kondensorhöhenverstellung^F
ajuste^M de la altura^F del condensador^M

TELESCOPIC SIGHT
LUNETTE^F DE VISÉE^F
ZIELFERNROHR^N
VISOR^M TELESCÓPICO

reticle
réticule^M
Fadenkreuz^N
retícula^F

eyepiece
oculaire^M
Okular^N
ocular^M

field lens
lentille^F de champ^M
Feldlinse^F
lente^F de campo^M

elevation adjustment
réglage^M de hausse^F
Höheneinstellung^F
ajuste^M de elevación^F

erecting lenses
lentilles^F de redressement^M
Umkehrsystem^N
lentes^F de imágen^F recta

dovetail
glissière^F de fixation^F
Befestigungsschiene^F
cremallera^F de fijación^F

main scope tube
tube^M
Tubus^M
tubo^M principal de observación^F

objective lens
lentille^F objectif^M
Objektiv^N
objetivo^M

turret cap
capuchon^M de protection^F
Schutzkappe^F
capuchón^M de protección^F

winding adjustment
réglage^M latéral
Spielraumeinstellung^F
huelgo^M de ajuste^M

PRISM BINOCULARS
JUMELLES*F* À PRISMES*M*
PRISMENFERNGLAS*N*
PRISMÁTICOS*M* BINOCULARES

eyepiece
oculaire*M*
Okular*N*
ocular*M*

lens system
système*M* de lentilles*F*
Linsensystem*N*
sistema*M* de lentes*F*

Porro prism
prisme*M* de Porro
Porro-Prismensystem*N*
prisma*M* de Porro

hinge
charnière*F*
Scharnier*N*
bisagra*F*

objective lens
lentille*F* objectif*M*
Objektiv*N*
objetivo*M*

focusing ring
bague*F* de correction*F* dioptrique
Scharfstellring*M*
anillo*M* de enfoque*M*

central focusing wheel
molette*F* de mise*F* au point*M*
zentrales Scharfstellrad*N*
rueda*F* central de enfoque*M*

bridge
pont*M*
Brücke*F*
puente*M*

body
tube*M*
Tubus*M*
tubo*M*

MAGNETIC COMPASS
BOUSSOLE*F* MAGNÉTIQUE
MAGNETKOMPASS*M*
BRÚJULA*F* MAGNÉTICA

sighting mirror
miroir*M*
Spiegel*M*
espejo*M*

cover
couvercle*M*
Deckel*M*
tapa*F*

edge
pointeur*M*
Kante*F*
puntero*M*

compass meridian line
ligne*F* méridienne
Meridianlinie*F*
línea*F* meridiana

compass card
cadran*M*
Kompaßrose*F*
rosa*F* de los vientos*M*

graduated dial
graduation*F*
Gradeinteilung*F*
esfera*F* graduada

sight
mire*F*
Visier*N*
punto*M* de mira*F*

sighting line
ligne*F* de visée*F*
Sichtlinie*F*
línea*F* de visión*F*

magnetic needle
aiguille*F* aimantée
Magnetnadel*F*
aguja*F* imantada

pivot
pivot*M*
Pinne*F*
pivote*M*

scale
échelle*F*
Skala*F*
escala*F*

base line
repère*M* de ligne*F* de marche*F*
Markierungslinie*F*
línea*F* de referencia*F*

base plate
base*F*
Bodenplatte*F*
soporte*M*

REFLECTING TELESCOPE
TÉLESCOPE*M*
SPIEGELTELESKOP*N*
TELESCOPIO*M* REFLECTOR

support
support*M* de fixation*F*
Stütze*F*
soporte*M*

finderscope
chercheur*M*
Sucher*M*
anteojo*M* buscador

eyepiece
oculaire*M*
Okular*N*
ocular*M*

cradle
bride*F* de fixation*F*
Wiege*F*
abrazadera*F*

main tube
tube*M*
Tubus*M*
tubo*M* principal

focusing knob
bouton*M* de mise*F* au point*M*
Scharfeinstellung*F*
botón*M* de enfoque*M*

declination setting scale
cercle*M* de déclinaison*F*
Einstellung*F* der Deklinationsachse*F*
disco*M* de ajuste*M* de declinación*F*

right ascension setting scale
cercle*M* d'ascension*F* droite
Einstellung der Rektaszensionsachse*F*
disco*M* de ajuste*M* de ascención*F* recta

azimuth clamp
vis*F* de blocage*M* (azimut*M*)
Azimutfeststeller*M*
bloqueo*M* del ajuste*M* del acimut*M*

azimuth fine adjustment
réglage*M* micrométrique (azimut*M*)
Azimutfeineinstellung*F*
ajuste*M* fino del acimut*M*

altitude clamp
vis*F* de blocage*M* (latitude*F*)
Höhenfeststeller*M*
bloqueo*M* del ajuste*M* de la altura*F*

altitude fine adjustment
réglage*M* micrométrique (latitude*F*)
Höhenfeineinstellung*F*
ajuste*M* fino de la altura*F*

CROSS SECTION OF A REFLECTING TELESCOPE
COUPE*F* D'UN TÉLESCOPE*M*
QUERSCHNITT*M* DURCH EIN SPIEGELTELESKOP*N*
CORTE*M* TRANSVERSAL DE UN TELECOPIO*M* REFLECTOR

eyepiece
oculaire*M*
Okular*N*
ocular*M*

main tube
tube*M*
Tubus*M*
tubo*M* principal

light
lumière*F*
Licht*N*
luz*F*

flat mirror
miroir*M* plan*M*
Umlenkspiegel*M*
espejo*M* plano

main mirror
miroir*M* primaire parabolique
Hauptspiegel*M*
espejo*M* principal

REFRACTING TELESCOPE
LUNETTE^F ASTRONOMIQUE
LINSENFERNROHR^N
TELESCOPIO^M REFRACTOR

cradle
bride^F de fixation^F
Wiege^F
abrazadera^F

lens hood
pare-soleil^M
Sonnenblende^F
protección^F contra el vaho^M

objective lens
lentille^F objectif^M
Objektiv^N
objetivo^M

finderscope
chercheur^M
Sucher^M
anteojo^M buscador

main tube
tube^M
Tubus^M
tubo^M principal

eyepiece
oculaire^M
Okular^N
ocular^M

eyepiece holder
tube^M porte-oculaire^M
Okularträger^M
portaocular^M

declination setting scale
cercle^M de déclinaison^F
Einstellung^F der Deklinationsachse^F
disco^M de ajuste^M de declinación^F

star diagonal
oculaire^M coudé
Coudé-Okular^N
ocular^M acodado

azimuth clamp
vis^F de blocage^M (azimut^M)
Azimutfesteller^M
bloqueo^M del ajuste^M del acimut^M

focusing knob
bouton^M de mise^F au point^M
Scharfeinstellung^F
botón^M de enfoque^M

altitude clamp
vis^F de blocage^M (latitude^F)
Höhenfeststeller^M
bloqueo^M del ajuste^M de la altura^F

azimuth fine adjustment
réglage^M micrométrique (azimut^M)
Azimutfeineinstellung^F
ajuste^M fino del acimut^M

right ascension setting scale
cercle^M d'ascension^F droite
Einstellung^F der Rektaszensionsachse^F
disco^M de ajuste^M de ascención^F recta

altitude fine adjustment
réglage^M micrométrique (latitude^F)
Höhenfeineinstellung^F
ajuste^M fino de la altura^F

counterweight
contrepoids^M
Massestück^N
contrapeso^M

fork
fourche^F
Gabel^F
horquilla^F

tripod
trépied^M
Stativ^N
trípode^M

tripod accessories shelf
plateau^M pour accessoires^M
Stativablage^F
repisa^F para accesorios^M

CROSS SECTION OF A REFRACTING TELESCOPE
COUPE^F D'UNE LUNETTE^F ASTRONOMIQUE
QUERSCHNITT^M DURCH EIN LINSENFERNROHR^N
CORTE^M TRANSVERSAL DE UN TELESCOPIO^M REFRACTOR

eyepiece
oculaire^M
Okular^N
ocular^M

light
lumière^F
Licht^N
luz^F

main tube
tube^M
Tubus^M
tubo^M principal

objective lens
lentille^F objectif^M
Objektiv^N
objetivo^M

721

LENSES
LENTILLES^F
LINSEN^F
LENTES^F

CONVERGING LENSES
LENTILLES^F CONVERGENTES
SAMMELLINSEN^F
LENTES^F CONVERGENTES

convex lens
lentille^F convexe
konvexe Linse^F
lentes^F convexas

biconvex lens
lentille^F biconvexe
bikonvexe Linse^F
lentes^F biconvexas

positive meniscus
ménisque^M convergent
konkavkonvexe Linse^F
menisco^M convergente

plano-convex lens
lentille^F plan^M-convexe
plankonvexe Linse^F
lente^F convexo-plana

DIVERGING LENSES
LENTILLES^F DIVERGENTES
ZERSTREUUNGSLINSEN^F
LENTES^F DIVERGENTES

concave lens
lentille^F concave
konkave Linse^F
lentes^F cóncavas

biconcave lens
lentille^F biconcave
bikonkave Linse^F
lentes^F bicóncavas

negative meniscus
ménisque^M divergent
konvexkonkave Linse^F
menisco^M divergente

plano-concave lens
lentille^F plan^M-concave
plankonkave Linse^F
lentes^F cóncavo-planas

RADAR
RADAR^M
RADAR^N
RADAR^M

OPTISCHE INSTRUMENTE
INSTRUMENTOS ÓPTICOS

OPTICAL INSTRUMENTS
APPAREILS DE VISION

transmitted pulse
impulsion^F
Sendeimpuls^M
impulso^M electromagnético

aircraft
avion^M
Flugzeug^N
aeroplano^M

echo
écho^M
Echo^N
eco^M

adjustable antenna
antenne^F orientable
rotierende Antenne^F
antena^F regulable

transmitting station
station^F d'émission^F
Übertragungsstation^F
estación^F de transmisión^F

receiving station
station^F de réception^F
Empfängerstation^F
estación^F receptora

information processing
traitement^M de l'information^F
Datenverarbeitung^F
procesamiento^M de la información^F

SUMMARY

HEALTH AND SAFETY
SANTÉ ET SÉCURITÉ

GESUNDHEIT UND UNFALLSCHUTZ
SALUD Y SEGURIDAD

FIRST AID KIT
TROUSSE^F DE SECOURS^M
ERSTE-HILFE-KASTEN^M
BOTIQUÍN^M DE PRIMEROS AUXILIOS^M

splints
attelles^F
Schienen^F
tablillas^F

aspirin
aspirine^F
Aspirin^N
aspirina^F

peroxide
peroxyde^M
Peroxyd^N
peróxido^M

adhesive tape
ruban^M de tissu^M adhésif
Heftpflaster^N
cinta^F adhesiva

pure alcohol
alcool^M à 90°
antiseptische Flüssigkeit^F
alcohol^M para friccionar

triangular bandage
bandage^M triangulaire
Dreiecktuch^N
venda^F triangular

sterile dressing
compresse^F stérilisée
sterile Wundauflage^F
cojinete^M estéril de gasa^F

cotton applicators
coton^M-tige^F
Wattestäbchen^N
aplicadores^M de algodón^M

plaster dressing
pansement^M adhésif
Gipsbinden^F
curitas^F

gauze roller bandage
bande^F de gaze^F
Mullverband^M
venda^F de gasa^F

first aid manual
manuel^M de premiers soins^M
Erste-Hilfe-Anleitung^F
manual^M de primeros auxilios^M

antiseptic
antiseptique^M
Antiseptikum^N
antiséptico^M

scissors
ciseaux^M
Schere^F
tijeras^F

elastic support bandage
bande^F de tissu^M élastique
elastische Binde^F
venda^F elástica

tweezers
pince^F à échardes^F
Pinzette^F
pinzas^F

cotton wool ball
coton^M hydrophile
Wattetupfer^M
algodón^M absorbente

ampoule
ampoule^F
Ampulle^F
ampolleta^F

capsule
capsule^F
Kapsel^F
cápsula^F

tablet
comprimé^M
Tablette^F
tableta^F

gelatin capsule
gélule^F
Gelatinekapsel^F
cápsula^F de gelatina^F

STETHOSCOPE
STÉTHOSCOPE*M*
STETHOSKOP*N*
ESTETOSCOPIO*M*

Y-tube
tube*M* en Y*M*
Y-Schlauch*M*
tubo*M* en Y

sound receiver
récepteur*M* de son*M*
Höraufsatz*M*
receptor*M* del sonido*M*

branch clip
lame*F*-ressort*M*
Verbindungsclip*M*
muelle*M*

tip protector
protecteur*M* d'embout*M*
Schutzkappe*F*
protector*M*

hollow barrel
corps*M* de pompe*F*
Spritzenkörper*M*
cilindro*M*

flexible tube
tube*M* flexible
Gummischlauch*M*
tubo*M* flexible

branch
branche*F*
Rohrstück*N*
rama*F*

earpiece
embout*M* auriculaire
Ohrstöpsel*M*
auricular*M*

finger flange
anneau*M* de retenue*F*
Fingerrand*M*
pestaña*F* de arrojo*M*

syringe for irrigation
seringue*F* pour lavage*M* de cavités*F*
Klistierspritze*F*
jeringa*F* de irrigación*F*

SYRINGE
SERINGUE*F*
SPRITZE*F*
JERINGA*F*

needle
aiguille*F*
Kanüle*F*
aguja*F*

bevel
biseau*M*
Schräge*F*
bisel*M*

needle hub
pavillon*M*
Kanülenansatz*M*
portaagujas*M*

Luer-Lock tip
embout*M* Luer Lock
Luer-Lock-Spitze*F*
jeringa*F* de Luer-Lock

rubber bulb
bouchon*M*
Gummipfropfen*M*
pera*F* de goma*F*

scale
graduation*F*
Skala*F*
escala*F*

plunger
piston*M*
Spritzenkolben*M*
émbolo*M*

thumb rest
poussoir*M*
Daumenteil*M*
apoyo*M* del pulgar*M*

HOSPITAL TROLLEY
CIVIÈRE*F*
FAHRTRAGE*F*
CAMILLA*F*

reclining back
dossier*M* inclinable
verstellbares Rückenteil*N*
respaldo*M* reclinatorio

frame
cadre*M*
Gestell*N*
chasis*M*

mattress
matelas*M*
Polsterauflage*F*
colchón*M*

telescopic leg
pied*M* télescopique
Teleskoptragebein*N*
pata*F* telescópica

stretcher
brancard*M*
Krankentrage*F*
camilla*F*

pulling ring
anneau*M* de traction*F*
Ziehbügel*M*
argolla*F* para tirar

hook
crochet*M*
Haken*M*
gancho*M* de tracción*F*

WHEELCHAIR
FAUTEUIL^M ROULANT
ROLLSTUHL^M
SILLA^F DE RUEDAS^F

back
dossier^M
Rückenlehne^F
respaldo^M

handle
poignée^F de conduite^F
Schiebegriff^M
puño^M

seat
siège^M
Sitz^M
asiento^M

armrest
accoudoir^M
Armstütze^F
descansabrazos^M

clothing guard
panneau^M de protection^F latéral
Kleiderschutz^M
panel^M protector

arm
bras^M
Arm^M
brazo^M

brake
poignée^F de frein^M
Bremse^F
freno^M

spacer
barre^F d'espacement^M
Abstandstück^N
separador^M

hub
moyeu^M
Nabe^F
cubo^M

push rim
main^F courante
Schieberad^N
aro^M de impulso^M

large wheel
roue^F
Großrad^N
rueda^F

cross brace
croisillon^M
Querstrebe^F
travesaño^M

front wheel
roue^F pivotante
Vorderrad^N
rueda^F de la dirección^F

stabilizer
dispositif^M anti-bascule
Kipphebel^M
palanca^F estabilizadora

footrest
repose-pied^M
Fußablage^F
descanso^M del pie^M

heel loop
butée^F talonnière^F
Fersenstütze^F
talón^M

hanger bracket
potence^F
Haltebügel^M
soporte^M colgante

WALKING AIDS
AIDES^F À LA MARCHE^F
GEHHILFEN^F
AUXILIARES^M ORTOPÉDICOS PARA CAMINAR

FOREARM CRUTCH
BÉQUILLE^F D'AVANT-BRAS^M
GEHKRÜCKE^F
MULETA^F DE ANTEBRAZO^M

UNDERARM CRUTCH
BÉQUILLE^F COMMUNE
ACHSELKRÜCKE^F
MULETA^F DE SOBACO^M

forearm support
embrasse^F
Unterarmstütze^F
soporte^M para el antebrazo^M

underarm rest
crosse^F
Achselstütze^F
soporte^M para el sobaco^M

handgrip
poignée^F
Griff^M
asidero^M

crosspiece
traverse^F
Querstück^N
travesaño^M

upright
montant^M
Holm^M
montante^M

adjuster
réglage^M
Längenverstellung^F
tubo ajustable^M

rubber ferrule
embout^M de caoutchouc^M
Gummikappe^F
contera^F de caucho^M

English stick
canne^F en T^M
englischer Stock^M
bastón^M inglés

STICKS
CANNES^F
STÖCKE^M
BASTONES^M

walking frame
cadre^M de marche^F
Gehgestell^N
andador^M

quadruped stick
canne^F avec quadripode^M
vierfüßiger Stock^M
bastón^M cuadrangular

ortho-stick
canne^F avec poignée^F orthopédique
orthopädischer Stock^M
bastón^M ortopédico

walking stick
canne^F en C^M
Gehstock^M
bastón^M para caminar

GESUNDHEIT UND UNFALLSCHUTZ
SALUD Y SEGURIDAD

HEALTH AND SAFETY
SANTÉ ET SÉCURITÉ

EAR PROTECTION
PROTECTION*F* DE L'OUÏE*F*
GEHÖRSCHUTZ*M*
PROTECCIÓN*F* PARA LOS OÍDOS*M*

SAFETY EARMUFF
SERRE-TÊTE*M* ANTIBRUIT
SICHERHEITSOHRENSCHÜTZER*M*
OREJERA*F* DE SEGURIDAD*F*

headband
serre-tête*M*
Kopfband*N*
diadema*F*

ear plugs
protège-tympan*M*
Ohrschützer*M*
protector*M* de oídos*M*

foam cushion
coussinet*M* en mousse*F*
Schaumgummipolsterung*F*
resguardo*M* de espuma*F*

EYE PROTECTION
PROTECTION*F* DES YEUX*M*
AUGENSCHUTZ*M*
PROTECCIÓN*F* PARA LOS OJOS*M*

safety glasses
lunettes*F* de sécurité*F*
Schutzbrille*F*
anteojos*M* de seguridad*F*

safety goggles
lunettes*F* de protection*F*
Schutzmaske*F*
anteojos*M* protectores

HEAD PROTECTION
PROTECTION*F* DE LA TÊTE*F*
KOPFSCHUTZ*M*
PROTECCIÓN*F* PARA LA CABEZA*F*

HARD HAT
CASQUE*M* DE SÉCURITÉ*F*
SCHUTZHELM*M*
CASCO*M* DE SEGURIDAD*F*

suspension band
sangle*F* d'amortissement*M*
Trageband*N*
banda*F* de suspensión*F*

headband
tour*M* de tête*F*
Kopfband*N*
cinta*F*

rib
nervure*F*
Verstärkungsschwelle*F*
refuerzo*M*

neck strap
sangle*F* de nuque*F*
Genicklasche*F*
correa*F* para el cuello*M*

peak
visière*F*
Schild*N*
visera*F*

RESPIRATORY SYSTEM PROTECTION
PROTECTION^F DES VOIES^F RESPIRATOIRES
ATEMSCHUTZ^M
PROTECCIÓN^F PARA EL SISTEMA^M RESPIRATORIO^M

RESPIRATOR
MASQUE^M **RESPIRATOIRE**
GASMASKE^F
MÁSCARA^F **DE GAS**^M

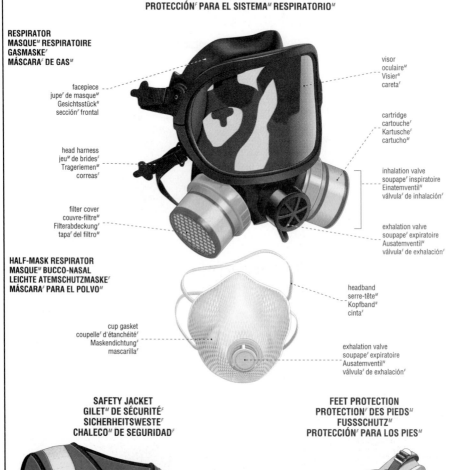

facepiece
jupe^F de masque^M
Gesichtsstück^N
sección^F frontal

head harness
jeu^M de brides^F
Trageriemen^M
correas^F

filter cover
couvre-filtre^M
Filterabdeckung^F
tapa^F del filtro^M

visor
oculaire^M
Visier^N
careta^F

cartridge
cartouche^F
Kartusche^F
cartucho^M

inhalation valve
soupape^F inspiratoire
Einatemventil^N
válvula^F de inhalación^F

exhalation valve
soupape^F expiratoire
Ausatemventil^N
válvula^F de exhalación^F

HALF-MASK RESPIRATOR
MASQUE^M **BUCCO-NASAL**
LEICHTE ATEMSCHUTZMASKE^F
MÁSCARA^F **PARA EL POLVO**^M

cup gasket
coupelle^F d'étanchéité^F
Maskendichtung^F
mascarilla^F

headband
serre-tête^M
Kopfband^N
cinta^F

exhalation valve
soupape^F expiratoire
Ausatemventil^N
válvula^F de exhalación^F

SAFETY JACKET
GILET^M **DE SÉCURITÉ**^F
SICHERHEITSWESTE^F
CHALECO^M **DE SEGURIDAD**^F

FEET PROTECTION
PROTECTION^F **DES PIEDS**^M
FUSSSCHUTZ^M
PROTECCIÓN^F **PARA LOS PIES**^M

toe guard
protège-orteils^M
Zehenschützer^M
puntera^F protectora

SAFETY BOOT
BRODEQUIN^M **DE SÉCURITÉ**^F
SICHERHEITSSCHUH^M
BOTA^F **DE SEGURIDAD**^F

reinforced toe
embout^M de protection^F
Stahlkappe^F
tope^M

reflective stripe
bande^F réfléchissante
Leuchtstreifen^M
banda^F reflectora

GESUNDHEIT UND UNFALLSCHUTZ
SALUD Y SEGURIDAD

HEALTH AND SAFETY
SANTÉ ET SÉCURITÉ

SUMMARY

ENERGIE
ENERGÍA

ENERGY
ÉNERGIES

COAL MINE
MINE^F DE CHARBON^M
KOHLEBERGWERK^N
MINAS^F DE CARBÓN^M

OPEN-PIT MINE
CARRIÈRE^F EN ENTONNOIR^M
OFFENE GRUBE^F
MINA^F A CIELO^M ABIERTO

face
front^M de taille^F
Streb^M
frente^M de corte^M

bench
gradin^M
Bank^F
antepecho^M

ground surface
terrain^M naturel
Erdoberfläche^F
superficie^F del terreno^M

overburden
morts-terrains^M
Obergestein^N
relleno^M exterior

bench height
hauteur^F du gradin^M
Bankhöhe^F
altura^F del antepecho^M

ramp
rampe^F
Rampe^F
talud^M

haulage road
voie^F de transport^M
Straße^F für den Abtransport^M
camino^M de arrastrre^M

crater
cratère^M
Krater^M
cráter^M

ore
minerai^M
Erz^N
mineral^M

OPENCAST STRIP MINE
CARRIÈRE^F EXPLOITÉE EN CHASSANT
ÜBERTAGEABBAU^M
EXCAVACIÓN^F A CIELO^M ABIERTO

dump
terril^M
Bergehalde^F
basurero^M

conveyor
convoyeur^M
Förderband^N
banda^F transportadora

mechanical shovel
pelle^F mécanique
Standbagger^M
pala^F mecánica

bucket wheel excavator
excavatrice^F à roue^F
Schaufelradbagger^M
excavadora^F de rueda^F de
cangilones^M

belt loader
sauterelle^F
Ladeband^N
banda^F de carga^F

overburden
morts-terrains^M
Obergestein^N
relleno exterior^M

roof
toit^M de la couche^F
Dach^N
terreno^M de recubrimiento

trench
tranchée^F
Graben^M
zanja^F

bulldozer
bouteur^M
Bulldozer^M
tractor^M nivelador

face
front^M
Streb^M
frente^M de corte^M

ENERGY
ÉNERGIES

ENERGIE
ENERGÍA

733

COAL MINE
MINE^F DE CHARBON^M
KOHLEBERGWERK^N
MINA^F DE CARBÓN^M SUBTERRÁNEA

JACKLEG DRILL
MARTEAU^M PERFORATEUR À POUSSOIR^M PNEUMATIQUE
BOHRHAMMER^M
TALADRO^M DE POSTE^M EXTENSIBLE

hammer drill
marteau^M perforateur
Schlagbohrer^M
taladro^M de percusión^F

water hose
flexible^M d'eau^F
Wasserschlauch^M
manguera^F para agua^F

bit
taillant^M
Bohrkopf^M
broca^F

drill rod
fleuret^M
Bohrstange^F
barrena^F

air leg
poussoir^M pneumatique
Druckluft-Bohrknecht^M
cilindro^M neumático

air hose
flexible^M d'air^M
Luftschlauch^M
manguera^F de aire^M

water separator
séparateur^M d'eau^F
Wasserabscheider^M
separador de agua^F

oiler
graisseur^M
Ölbehälter^M
aceitera^F

PITHEAD
CARREAU^M DE MINE^F
ÜBERTAGEANLAGEN^F
PLANTA^F EXTERIOR

maintenance shop
atelier^M d'entretien^M
Maschinenhaus^N
taller^M de mantenimiento^M

slagheap
terril^M
Bergehalde^F
basurero^M

main fan
ventilateur^M principal
Hauptlüfter^M
ventilador^M principal

loading bunker
silo^M de chargement^M
Schachtgebäude^N
carbonera^F de carga^F

ENERGIE
ENERGÍA

ENERGY
ÉNERGIES

734

control lever
levier^M de commande^F
Steuerhebel^M
palanca^F de control^M

throttle valve
soupape^F
Druckventil^N
válvula^F de aceleración^F

PNEUMATIC DRILL
MARTEAU^M PNEUMATIQUE
PRESSLUFTBOHRER^M
MARTILLO^M NEUMÁTICO

flexible hose connection
raccordement^M du flexible^M
Anschluß^M für Gummischlauch^M
manguera^F de conexión^F

handle
poignée^F
Griff^M
mango^M

flexible hose
tuyau^M flexible
Gummischlauch^M
manguera^F flexible

lubricator
injecteur^M de lubrifiant^M
Schmierknopf^M
lubrificador^M

chuck
porte-outil^M
Spannfutter^N
mandril^M

silencer
silencieux^M
Geräuschdämpfer^M
silenciador^M

retainer
système^M de fixation^F
Halterung^F
retén^M

shaft head
tête^F de puits^M
Fördergerüst^N
pozo^M principal

exhaust port
orifice^M d'échappement^M
Luftaustritt^M
abertura^F de escape^M

miners' changing-room
vestiaire^M des mineurs^M
Umkleideraum^M
guardarropa^M de los mineros^M

treatment plant
usine^F de traitement^M
Aufbereitungsanlage^F
planta^F de tratamiento^M

conveyor
convoyeur^M
Förderband^N
banda^F transportadora

tool
outil^M
Einsatz^M
barrena^F

winding tower
tour^F d'extraction^F
Förderturm^M
torre^F de extracción^F

winder house
salle^F du treuil^M
Fördergebäude^N
sala^F del montacargas^M

rail track
voie^F ferrée
Bahngleise^N
vía^F férrea

water transport
transport^M maritime
Abtransport^M per Schiff^N
transporte^M marítimo

COAL MINE
MINE^F DE CHARBON^M
KOHLEBERGWERK^N
MINA^F DE CARBÓN^M

UNDERGROUND MINE
MINE^F SOUTERRAINE
GRUBE^F
MINA^F SUBTERRÁNEA

headframe
chevalement^M
Schachtfördergerüst^N
castillete^M de extracción^F

lift
ascenseur^M
Aufzug^M
montacargas^M

vertical shaft
puits^M vertical
Richtschacht^M
tiro^M vertical

pithead
tour^F d'extraction^F
Übertageanlage^F
boca^F de pozo^M

winding shaft
puits^M d'extraction^F
Förderschacht^M
pozo^M de extracción^F

pillar
pilier^M
Abbaupfeiler^M
pilar^M

room
chambre^F
Kammer^F
cámara^F

level
niveau^M
Sohle^F
nivel^M

top road
voie^F de tête^F
Kopfstrecke^F
galería^F superior

deck
étage^M
Förderkorbstockwerk^N
plataforma^F de jaula^F

skip
skip^M
Förderkübel^M
jaula^F de extracción^F

ore pass
cheminée^F à minerai^M
Erzgang^M
chimenea^F de evacuación^F

panel
panneau^M
Streb^M
pared^F

landing
recette^F
Landung^F
plataforma^F de carga^F

sump
puisard^M
Schachtsumpf^M
sumidero^M

bottom road
voie^F de fond^M
Sohlenstrecke^F
galería^M inferior

manway
galerie^F de circulation^F
Einstiegschacht^M
galería^F de acceso^M

chute
cheminée^F
Rutsche^F
resbaladero^M

winze
descenderie^F
Blindschacht^M
pozo^M ciego^M

drift
galerie^F en direction^F
Seitenstollen^M
galería^F de arrastre^M

cross cut
travers-banc^M
Querschlag^M
galería^F transversal

face
front^M de taille^F
Kopfseite^F
frente^M de corte^M

OIL
PÉTROLE^M
ERDÖL^N
PETRÓLEO^M

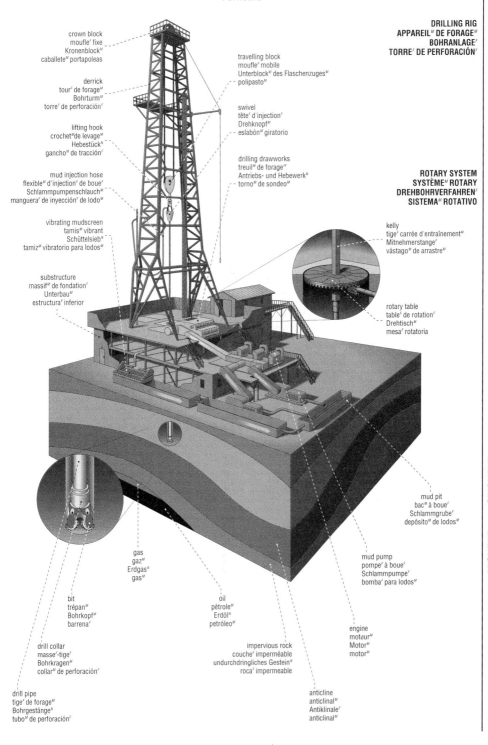

crown block
moufle^F fixe
Kronenblock^M
caballete^M portapoleas

derrick
tour^F de forage^M
Bohrturm^M
torre^F de perforación^F

lifting hook
crochet^Mde levage^M
Hebestück^N
gancho^M de tracción^F

mud injection hose
flexible^M d'injection^F de boue^F
Schlammpumpenschlauch^M
manguera^F de inyección^F de lodo^M

vibrating mudscreen
tamis^M vibrant
Schüttelsieb^N
tamiz^M vibratorio para lodos^M

substructure
massif^M de fondation^F
Unterbau^M
estructura^F inferior

DRILLING RIG
APPAREIL^M DE FORAGE^M
BOHRANLAGE^F
TORRE^F DE PERFORACIÓN^F

travelling block
moufle^F mobile
Unterblock^M des Flaschenzuges^M
polipasto^M

swivel
tête^F d'injection^F
Drehknopf^M
eslabón^M giratorio

drilling drawworks
treuil^M de forage^M
Antriebs- und Hebewerk^N
torno^M de sondeo^M

ROTARY SYSTEM
SYSTÈME^M ROTARY
DREHBOHRVERFAHREN^F
SISTEMA^M ROTATIVO

kelly
tige^F carrée d'entraînement^M
Mitnehmerstange^F
vástago^M de arrastre^M

rotary table
table^F de rotation^F
Drehtisch^M
mesa^F rotatoria

mud pit
bac^M à boue^F
Schlammgrube^F
depósito^M de lodos^M

mud pump
pompe^F à boue^F
Schlammpumpe^F
bomba^F para lodos^M

gas
gaz^M
Erdgas^N
gas^M

bit
trépan^M
Bohrkopf^M
barrena^F

oil
pétrole^M
Erdöl^N
petróleo^M

engine
moteur^M
Motor^M
motor^M

drill collar
masse^F-tige^F
Bohrkragen^M
collar^M de perforación^F

impervious rock
couche^F imperméable
undurchdringliches Gestein^N
roca^F impermeable

drill pipe
tige^F de forage^M
Bohrgestänge^N
tubo^M de perforación^F

anticline
anticlinal^M
Antiklinale^F
anticlinal^M

PRODUCTION PLATFORM
PLATE-FORME*F* DE PRODUCTION*F*
BOHRINSEL*F*
PLATAFORMA*F* DE PRODUCCIÓN*F*

crane
grue*F*
Kran*M*
grúa*F*

derrick
tour*F* de forage*M*
Bohrturm*M*
torre*F* de perforación*F*

gas lift module
module*M* d'injection*F* de gaz*M*
Druckgasförderanlage*F*
módulo*M* para liberar el gas*M*

flare
torche*F*
Abfackelung*F*
quemador*M*

oil processing area
section*F* raffinerie*F*
Ölverarbeitungsbereich*M*
área*F* de procesamiento*M* del petróleo

helipad
hélisurface*F*
Hubschrauberlandeplatz*M*
helipuerto*M*

oil/gas separator
séparateur*M* de gaz*M*
Gasabscheider*M*
separador*M* de petróleo*M* y gas*M*

radio mast
antenne*F* radio*F*
Funkmast*M*
antena*F* de radio*M*

lifeboat
canot*M* de sauvetage*M*
Rettungsboot*N*
bote*M* salvavidas

anchor wires
chaînes*F* d'ancrage*M*
Ankerketten*F*
cables*M* de anclaje*M*

pontoon
ponton*M*
Ponton*M*
pontón*M*

hull column
colonne*F* de stabilisation*F*
Tragsäule*F*
columna*F* de soporte*M*

tubular member
section*F* tubulaire
Rohrquerstrebe*F*
estructura*F* tubular

production/export riser system
tubage*M* de production*F*/expédition*F*
Förder-/Exportsteigsystem*M*
sistema*M* de tubería montante para sacar la producción*F*

manifold
manifold*M*
Rohrverteilerstück*N*
múltiple

export pipeline
oléoduc*M* d'évacuation*F*
Exportpipeline*F*
oleoducto*M* de salida*F*

surface pipe
tube*M* conducteur
Standrohr*N*
tubería*F* del caudal*M* del pozo*M*

template
plaque*F* de base*F*
Träger*M*
guía*F*

Christmas tree
arbre*M* de Noël*M*
Erdöleruptionskranz*M*
árbol*M* de conexiones*F*

pier
jetée*F*
Pier*F*
muelle*M* saliente

emergency support vessel
barge*F* de service*M* d'urgence*F*
Hilfs- und Rettungsschiff*N*
embarcación*F* de emergencia*F*

jack-up platform
plate-forme*F* auto-élévatrice
Hubplattform*F*
plataforma*F* montada en gatos*M* mecánicos

fixed platform
plate-forme*F* fixe
Festplattform*F*
plataforma*F* fija

semi-submersible platform
plate-forme*F* semi-submersible
Halbtaucher*M*
plataforma*F* semisumergida

drill ship
navire*M* de forage*M*
Bohrschiff*N*
barco*M* perforador

OIL
PÉTROLE^M
ERDÖL^N
PETRÓLEO^M

CHRISTMAS TREE
ARBRE^M DE NOËL^M
ERDÖLERUPTIONSKRANZ^M
ÁRBOL^M DE CONEXIONES^F

pressure gauge
manomètre^M
Druckmesser^M
manómetro^M

master gate valve
vanne^F maîtresse
Hauptschieber^M
válvula^F maestra

flow bean
duse^F
Eruptionsdüse^F
reductor^M de flujo^M

pipeline
oléoduc^M
Pipeline^F
oleoducto^M

tubing head
tête^F de puits^M
Steigrohrkopf^M
cabeza^F de la tubería^F

tubing valve
vanne^F de production^F
Steigrohrventil^N
válvula^F de la tubería^F

tubing
colonne^F de production^F
Steigrohr^N
tubería^F

casing first string
tubage^M de surface^F
Rohrfahrteingang^M
recubrimiento^M de la primera tubería^F

CRUDE-OIL PIPELINE
RÉSEAU^M D'OLÉODUCS^M
ROHÖLPIPELINE^F
OLEODUCTO^M PARA PETRÓLEO^M CRUDO

offshore well
puits^M sous-marin
Bohranlage^F vor der Meeresküste^F
pozo^M marino

production platform
plate-forme^F de production^F
Förderplattform^F
plataforma^F de producción^F

derrick
tour^F de forage^M
Bohrturm^M
torre^F de perforación^F

submarine pipeline
oléoduc^M sous-marin
Unterwasserpipeline^F
oleoducto^M submarino

Christmas tree
arbre^M de Noël^M
Erdöleruptionskranz^M
árbol^M de conexiones^F

pumping station
station^F de pompage^M
Pumpstation^F
planta^F de bombeo^M

buffer tank
réservoir^M tampon^M
Puffertank^M
tanque^M de regulación^F de presión^F

tank farm
parc^M de stockage^M
Tankanlage^F
patio^M de tanques^M

central pumping station
station^F de pompage^M principale
zentrale Pumpstation^F
estación^F central de bombeo^M

aboveground pipeline
oléoduc^M surélevé
überirdische Pipeline^F
oleoducto^M de superficie^F

pipeline
oléoduc^M
Pipeline^F
oleoducto^M

terminal
parc^M de stockage^M terminal
Erdölterminal^N
terminal^M

intermediate booster station
station^F de pompage^M intermédiaire
Druckverstärkerpumpanlage^F
planta^F intermedia de refuerzo^M

refinery
raffinerie^F
Raffinerie^F
refinería^F

breather valve
soupape' à pression' et dépression'
Entlüftungsventil"
respiradero"

spray nozzle
gicleur"
Zerstäuber"
boquilla' rociadora

tank gauge float
flotteur"
Füllanzeigeschwimmer"
flotador" del medidor"

lagging
revêtement"
Isoliermaterial"
empaque"

manometer
manomètre"
Manometer"
manómetro"

splash plate
tôle' pare-gouttes"
Spritzblech"
colector"

manhole
trou" d'homme"
Mannloch"
boca' de acceso"

manhole
trou" d'homme"
Mannloch"
boca' de acceso"

automatic tank gauge
jauge' magnétique à lecture' directe
automatische Füllanzeige'
medidor" automático

spiral staircase
escalier" en spirale'
Wendeltreppe'
escalera' de caracol"

secondary inlet
conduite' d'admission' secondaire
Nebeneinfüllstutzen"
toma' secundaria

drain valve
robinet" de vidange'
Ablaßventil"
válvula' de vaciado"

bund wall
merlon" de protection'
Tankwall"
tabique" cortafuego

main inlet
conduite' d'admission' principale
Haupteinfüllstutzen"
toma' principal de llenado"

concrete drain
canal' d'écoulement"
Betonauslauf"
canal"

ground
conduite' à la terre'
Erdung'
conexión' eléctrica a tierra'

stairs
escalier"
Treppenaufgang"
escalera'

manhole
trou" d'homme"
Mannloch"
boca' de acceso"

floating roof
toit" flottant
Schwimmdach"
tapa' flotante

sealing ring
joint" d'étanchéité'
Dichtring"
anillo" sellador

top deck
pont" supérieur
Oberdeck"
cubierta' superior

shell
robe'
Mantelblech"
casco"

ladder
échelle'
Leiter'
escalerilla'

drain valve
robinet" de vidange'
Ablaßventil"
válvula' de vaciado"

thermometer
thermomètre"
Thermometer"
termómetro"

bottom deck
pont" inférieur
Unterdeck"
cubierta' inferior

filling inlet
remplissage"
Einfüllstutzen"
válvula' de llenado"

OIL
PÉTROLE[M]
ERDÖL[N]
PETRÓLEO[M]

ROAD TANKER
SEMI-REMORQUE[F] CITERNE[F]
TANKLASTZUG[M]
CAMIÓN[M] CISTERNA[F]

manhole
trou[M] d'homme[M]
Mannloch[N]
boca[F] de acceso[M]

semitrailer
semi-remorque[F]
Tankaufsatz[M]
semirremolque[M]

tank
citerne[F]
Tank[M]
tanque[M]

tractor
tracteur[M]
Zugmaschine[F]
tractor[M]

tank wall
cloison[F] de citerne[F]
Tankwand[F]
pared[F] del tanque[M]

discharge system
système[M] de dépotage[M]
Auslaßrohr[N]
tubo[M] de descarga[F]

baffle
brise-lame[M]
Prallblech[N]
deflector[M]

TANKER
PÉTROLIER[M]
TANKER[M]
BARCO[M] PETROLERO

radio antenna
antenne[F] radio[F]
Funkantenne[F]
antena[F] de radio[F]

separator
séparateur[M]
Ausscheider[M]
separador[M]

gangway
coupée[F]
Gangway[F]
pasarela[F]

radar mast
mât[M] radar[M]
Radarmast[M]
poste[M] del radar[M]

davit
bossoir[M]
Ladebaum[M]
pescante[M]

stern post
étambot[M]
Wellenhose[F]
codaste[M]

propeller
hélice[F]
Schiffsschraube[F]
hélice[F]

pump room
chambre[F] des pompes[F]
Pumpenraum[M]
sala[F] de bombeo[M]

lengthways bulkhead
cloison[F] longitudinale
Längsschott[N]
tabique[M] de contención[M] longitudinal

rudder
gouvernail[M]
Ruder[N]
timón[M]

engine room
salle[F] de contrôle[M] des machines[F]
Maschinenraum[M]
sala[F] de máquinas[F]

transverse bulkhead
cloison[F] transversale
Querschott[N]
pared[F] transversal de contención[F]

tank
citerne*F*
Tank*M*
tanque*M*

top central manhole
dôme*M*
Hauptmannloch*N*
boca*F* de acceso*M*

contents identification board
porte-étiquette*M* de contenu*M*
Ladekennziffer-Plakette*F*
rótulo*M* de identificación*F*

route board
porte-étiquette*M* d'acheminement*M*
Streckenplakette*F*
rótulo*M* de destino*M*

bitt
bitte*F*
Poller*M*
bita*F*

derrick
mât*M* de charge*F*
Ladebaum*M*
grúa*F*

air relief valve
dégagement*M* d'air*M* des citernes*F*
Entlüftungsventil*N*
válvula*F* de liberación*F* de aire*M*

derrick mast
mâtereau*M*
Lademast*M*
poste*M* de la grúa*F*

foam gun
canon*M* à mousse*F*
Schaumanzeiger*M*
tubo*M* expulsor de espuma*F*

tank hatch
panneau*M* de citerne*F*
Tankluke*F*
compuerta*F* del tanque*M*

foremast
mât*M* avant
Vordermast*M*
palo*M* de trinquete*M*

ship's side
muraille*F*
Geradseite*F*
pared*F* lateral

main deck
pont*M* principal
Hauptdeck*N*
cubierta*F* principal

crossover cargo deck line
traverse*F* de chargement*M*
Umladeabschnitt*M*
zona*F* de traspaso*M* de carga*F*

web frame
porque*F*
Rahmenspant*M*
cuaderna*F*

mooring winch
treuil*M* d'amarrage*M*
Festmachwinsch*N*
amarra*F*

tank
citerne*F*
Tank*M*
tanque*M*

centre Keelson
carlingue*F* centrale
Mittelkielschwein*N*
contraquilla*F*

bulb
bulbe*M* d'étrave*F*
Wulst*M*
bulbo*M*

OIL
PÉTROLE*M*
ERDÖL*N*
PETRÓLEO*M*

REFINERY PRODUCTS
PRODUITS*M* DE LA RAFFINERIE*F*
RAFFINERIEERZEUGNISSE*N*
PRODUCTOS*M* DEL REFINADO*M*

petrochemical industry
usine*F* pétrochimique
petrochemische Industrie*F*
industría*F* petroquímica

gas
gaz*M*
Gas*N*
gas*M*

cooling
refroidissement*M*
Kühlung*F*
refrigerante*M*

catalytic reforming plant
réformeur*M* catalytique
katalytische Reformieranlage*F*
planta*F* de reforma*F* catalítica

petroleum
essence*F*
Erdöl*N*
gasolina*F*

fractionating tower
tour*F* de fractionnement*M*
Fraktionierturm*M*
torre*F* fraccionadora

kerosene
kérosène*M*
Kerosin*N*
queroseno*M*

heavy petroleum
essence*F* lourde
Schweröl*M*
gasolina*F* pesada

fuel oil
gazole*M*
Gasöl*N*
petróleo*M* diáfano

fractionating tower
tour*F* de fractionnement*M*
Fraktionierturm*M*
torre*F* fraccionadora

tubular heater
four*M* tubulaire
Röhrenkessel*M*
calentador*M* tubular

solvent extraction unit
unité*F* d'extraction*F* par solvant*M*
Solvent-Extraktionsanlage*F*
unidad*F* de extracción*F* de solventes*M*

ENERGIE
ENERGÍA

long residue
fond*M* de tour*M*
Toprückstand*M*
residuos*M* primarios

ENERGY
ÉNERGIES

vacuum distillation
distillation*F* sous vide*M*
Vakuumdestillation*F*
unidad*F* de destilación*F* al vacío*M*

storage tank
réservoir*M* de brut*M*
Lagertank*M*
tanque*M* de almacenamiento*M*

crude oil
pétrole*M* brut
Rohöl*N*
petróleo*M* crudo

asphalt still
usine*F* à asphalte*M*
Asphalt-Destillationsanlage*F*
destilador*M* para asfalto*M*

chemical treatment
traitement^M chimique
chemische Behandlung^F
tratamiento^M químico

petrochemicals
produits^M pétrochimiques
Petrochemikalien^F
productos^M petroquímicos

jet fuel
carburéacteur^M
Düsenflugzeugbenzin^N
combustible^M para aviones^M

petrol
essence^F
Benzin^N
gasolina^F

paraffin
kérosène^M
Petroleum^N
queroseno^M

methylated spirits
mazout^M léger
Brennspiritus^M
petróleo^M

diesel oil
carburant^M diesel^M
Dieselkraftstoff^M
diésel^M

heating oil
mazout^M domestique
Heizöl^N
petróleo^M para calefacción^F

bunker oil
mazout^M lourd
Bunkeröl^N
petróleo^M para calderas^F

marine diesel
diesel^M-navire^M
Marine-Dieselkraftstoff^M
diésel^M para barcos

greases
graisses^F
Fette^N
grasas^F

lubricating oils
huiles^F lubrifiantes
Schmieröle^N
aceites^M lubricantes

paraffins
paraffines^F
Paraffine^N
parafinas^F

asphalt
asphalte^M
Asphalt^M
asfalto^M

lubricants plant
usine^F des lubrifiants^M
Schmiermittelraffinerie^F
planta^F de lubricantes^M

HYDROELECTRIC COMPLEX
COMPLEXE^M **HYDROÉLECTRIQUE**
WASSERKRAFTWERK^N
COMPLEJO^M **HIDROELÉCTRICO**

spillway gate
vanne^F
Überlauftor^N
compuerta^F del aliviadero

penstock
conduite^F forcée
Falleitung^F
tubería^F de carga^F

crest of spillway
seuil^M de déversoir^M
Überlaufkrone^F
cresta^F del aliviadero^M

top of dam
crête^F
Dammkrone^F
cresta^F de la presa^F

headbay
bief^M d'amont^M
Oberwasser^N
embalse^M

spillway
déversoir^M
Überlaufwehr^N
aliviadero^M

reservoir
réservoir^M
Stausee^M
embalse^M

gantry crane
portique^M
Bockkran^M
grúa^F de caballete^M

log chute
passe^F à billes^F
Trift^F
rebosadero^M

control room
salle^F de commande^F
Steuerzentrale^F
sala^F de control^M

diversion channel
canal^M de dérivation^F
Ablenkkanal^M
canal^M de derivación^F

dam
barrage^M
Damm^M
presa^F

afterbay
bief^M d'aval^M
Unterwasser^N
cámara^F de salida^F

spillway chute
coursier^M d'évacuateur^M
Überfallrinne^F
canal^M del aliviadero^M

bushing
traversée^F de transformateur^M
Stromführung^F
boquilla^F reducidora

training wall
mur^M bajoyer^M
Leitwerk^N
muro^M de encauzamiento^M

powerhouse
centrale^F
Kraftwerk^N
central^F hidroeléctrica

machine hall
salle^F des machines^F
Maschinenhalle^F
sala^F de máquinas^F

gate
vanne'
Schieber^M
compuerta'

circuit breaker
disjoncteur^M
Abschalter^M
interruptor^M automático

gantry crane
portique^M
Bockkran^M
grúa' de caballete^M

bushing
traversée' de transformateur^M
Stromführung'
boquilla' reducidora

transformer
transformateur^M
Transformator^M
transformador^M

lightning conductor
parafoudre^M
Blitzableiter^M
pararrayos^M

travelling crane
pont^M roulant
Laufkran^M
grúa' de puente^M

machine hall
salle' des machines'
Maschinenhalle'
sala' de máquinas'

access gallery
galerie' de visite'
Zugang^M
galería' de acceso^M

gantry crane
portique^M
Bockkran^M
grúa' de caballete^M

scroll case
bâche' spirale
Umlaufgehäuse^N
caja' de caracol^M

gate
vanne'
Rechen^M
compuerta'

afterbay
bief^M d'aval^M
Unterwasser^N
cámara' de salida'

tailrace
canal^M de fuite'
Auslaufrohr^N
canal^M de descarga'

generator unit
groupe^M turbo-alternateur^M
Generatoreinheit'
turbinas'

water intake
prise' d'eau'
Wassereinlaß^M
entrada' de agua'

draught tube
aspirateur^M
Saugrohr^N
tubo^M de aspiración'

screen
grille'
Rechen^M
enrejado^M

busbar
barre' blindée
Sammelschiene'
barra' colectora

reservoir
réservoir^M
Stausee^M
embalse^M de la presa'

penstock
conduite' forcée
Falleitung'
tubería' de carga'

EMBANKMENT DAM
BARRAGE[M] EN REMBLAI[M]
UFERDAMM[M]
DIQUE[M] DE TERRAPLÉN[M]

CROSS SECTION OF AN EMBANKMENT DAM
COUPE[F] D'UN BARRAGE[M] EN REMBLAI[M]
UFERDAMM[M] IM QUERSCHNITT[M]
CORTE[M] TRANSVERSAL DE UN DIQUE[M] DE TERRAPLÉN[M]

top of dam
crête[F]
Dammkrone[F]
tope[M] del dique[M]

clay core
noyau[M] d'argile[F]
Lehmkern[M]
núcleo[M] de greda[F]

pitching
perré[M]
Neigung[F]
revestimiento[M]

wave wall
mur[M] de batillage[M]
Wellenmauer[F]
parapeto[M] contra olas[F]

sand
sable[M]
Sand[M]
arena[F]

reservoir
réservoir[M]
Stausee[M]
embalse[M]

berm
risberme[F]
Berme[F]
berma[F]

drainage layer
couche[F] drainante
Drainage-Schicht[F]
capa[F] de desagüe[M]

downstream toe
pied[M] aval
Trockenseite[F]
pie[M] del talud[M]

upstream toe
pied[M] amont
Dammbrust[F]
pie[M] del talud[M]

upstream shoulder
recharge[F] amont
Oberstützmauer[F]
talud[M] de aguas[F] contenidas

downstream shoulder
recharge[F] aval
Unterstützmauer[F]
talud[M] de aguas[F] abajo

drainage blanket
tapis[M] drainant
Drainage-Decke[F]
plantilla[F] de desagüe[M]

upstream blanket
tapis[M] amont
Oberwasserdecke[F]
plantilla[F] de arcilla[F]

cut-off trench
parafouille[M]
Dichtungsschleier[M]
cortina[F] de inyecciones[F]

dam foundation
terrain[M] de fondation[F]
Dammsockel[M]
cimientos[M] del dique[M]

ENERGIE
ENERGÍA

ENERGY
ÉNERGIES

CROSS SECTION OF A GRAVITY DAM
COUPE*ᶠ* **D'UN BARRAGE***ᴹ***-POIDS***ᴹ*
GEWICHTSSTAUDAMM*ᴹ* **IM QUERSCHNITT***ᴹ*
CORTE*ᴹ* **TRANSVERSAL DE UNA PRESA***ᶠ*

upstream face
parement*ᴹ* amont
Oberwassermauer*ᶠ*
paramento*ᴹ* de aguas*ᶠ* contenidas

top of dam
couronnement*ᴹ*
Dammkrone*ᶠ*
tope*ᴹ* del dique*ᴹ*

downstream face
parement*ᴹ* aval
Unterwassermauer*ᶠ*
paramento*ᴹ* de aguas*ᶠ* corrientes

afterbay
bief*ᴹ* aval
Unterwasser*ᴺ*
cámara*ᶠ* de salida*ᶠ*

reservoir
réservoir*ᴹ*
Stausee*ᴹ*
embalse*ᴹ*

cut-off trench
parafouille*ᴹ*
Dichtungsschleier*ᴹ*
cortina*ᶠ* de inyecciones*ᶠ*

ENERGY
ÉNERGIES

ENERGIE
ENERGÍA

749

ARCH DAM
BARRAGE*M***-VOÛTE***F*
BOGENSTAUDAMM*M*
PRESA*F* **DE ARCO***M*

CROSS SECTION OF AN ARCH DAM
COUPE*F* **D'UN BARRAGE***M***-VOÛTE***F*
BOGENSTAUDAMM*M* **IM QUERSCHNITT***M*
CORTE*M* **TRANSVERSAL DE UNA PRESA***F* **DE ARCO***M*

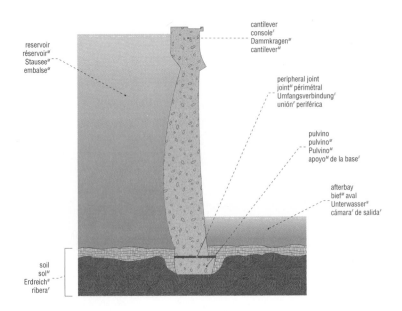

reservoir
réservoir*M*
Stausee*M*
embalse*M*

cantilever
console*F*
Dammkragen*M*
cantilever*M*

peripheral joint
joint*M* périmétral
Umfangsverbindung*F*
unión*F* periférica

pulvino
pulvino*M*
Pulvino*M*
apoyo*M* de la base*F*

afterbay
bief*M* aval
Unterwasser*N*
cámara*F* de salida*F*

soil
sol*M*
Erdreich*N*
ribera*F*

CROSS SECTION OF A BUTTRESS DAM
COUPE^F **D'UN BARRAGE**^{M} **À CONTREFORTS**^{M}
STÜTZPFEILERSTAUDAMM^M **IM QUERSCHNITT**^{M}
CORTE^M **TRANSVERSAL DE UN DIQUE**^{M} **DE MACHONES**^{M}

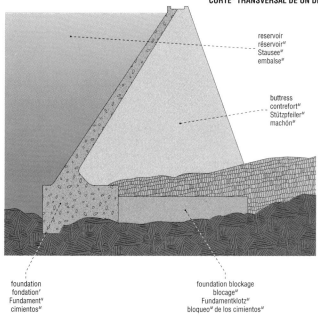

reservoir
réservoir^M
Stausee^M
embalse^M

buttress
contrefort^M
Stützpfeiler^M
machón^M

foundation
fondation^F
Fundament^N
cimientos^M

foundation blockage
blocage^M
Fundamentklotz^M
bloqueo^M de los cimientos^M

TIDAL POWER PLANT
USINE*F* MARÉMOTRICE
GEZEITENKRAFTWERK*N*
CENTRAL*F* MAREMOTRIZ

operating dam
barrage*M* mobile
Stromerzeugungsabschnitt*M*
dique*M* de operación*F*

bank
rive*F*
Ufer*N*
orilla*F*

sea
mer*F*
Meer*N*
mar*M* abierto

power station
usine*F*
Kraftwerk*N*
planta*F* maremotriz

lock
écluse*F*
Schleuse*F*
esclusa*F*

administrative building
bâtiment*M* administratif
Verwaltungsgebäude*N*
edificio*M* de la administración*F*

substation
poste*M*
Umspannwerk*N*
subestación*F*

basin
bassin*M*
Becken*N*
embalse*M*

inactive dyke
digue*F* morte
unbewegter Deich*M*
dique*M* inerte

gate
vanne*F*
Rechen*M*
compuerta*F*

CROSS SECTION OF A POWER PLANT
COUPE*F* DE L'USINE*F*
KRAFTWERK*N* IM QUERSCHNITT*M*
CORTE*M* TRANSVERSAL DE UNA PLANTA*F* MAREMOTRIZ

top of dam
couronnement*M* du barrage*M*
Deichkrone*F*
tope*M* del dique*M*

operating floor
étage*M* d'exploitation*F*
Betriebsebene*F*
piso*M* de operaciones*F*

sea side
côté*M* mer*F*
Meeresseite*F*
lado*M* del mar*M*

access shaft
puits*M* d'accès*M*
Zugangschacht*M*
pozo*M* de acceso*M*

bulb unit
groupe*M* bulbe*M*
Rohrturbine*F*
bulbo*M*

runner blade
pale*F*
Laufblatt*N*
paleta*F* del rotor*M*

turbine runner
roue*F* de turbine*F*
Turbinenläufer*M*
rotor*M* de la turbina*F*

penstock
conduite*F* forcée
Falleitung*F*
canal*M* de carga*F*

basin side
côté*M* bassin*M*
Beckenseite*F*
lado*M* hacia el embalse*M*

GENERATOR UNIT
GROUPE^M TURBO-ALTERNATEUR^M
STROMGENERATOR^M
UNIDAD^F GENERADORA

thrust bearing
palier^M de butée^F
Drucklager^N
rodamiento^M

collector
collecteur^M
Kollektor^M
colector^M

rotor
rotor^M
Rotor^M
cilindro^M interno

stator
stator^M
Stator^M
cilindro^M externo

gate operating ring
cercle^M de vannage^M
Einlaufsteuerring^M
anillo^M regulador

shaft
arbre^M
Welle^F
árbol^M

ring gate
vanne^F fourreau^M
Ringzugang^M
compuerta^F de toma^F

turbine headcover
couvercle^M de la turbine^F
Turbinenummantelung^F
cubierta^F superior de la turbina^F

stay vane blade
aube^F avant-directrice
Schaufelblatt^N
paletas^F de la turbina^F

spiral case
bâche^F spirale
Spiralgehäuse^N
caja^F espiral

wicket gate
aube^F directrice
Einlaßtor^N
álabe^M

stay ring
avant-distributeur^M
Stützring^M
anillo^M distribuidor

runner blade
aube^F de roue^F
Laufblatt^N
paleta^F de la turbina^F

runner
roue^F
Läufer^M
cojinete^M de rodamiento^M

draught tube
aspirateur^M
Saugrohr^N
tubo^M de aspiración^F

bottom ring
flasque^F inférieur
Grundring^M
anillo^M inferior

draught tube liner
blindage^M d'aspirateur^M
Ausströmmantel^M
calza^F de descarga^F

generator
alternateur^M
Generator^M
generador^M

turbine
turbine^F
Turbine^F
turbina^F

FRANCIS RUNNER
ROUE^F **FRANCIS**
FRANCISTURBINE^F
TURBINA^F **FRANCIS**

ring
flasque^F
Ring^M
anillo^M

blade
aube^F
Blatt^N
paleta^F

KAPLAN RUNNER
ROUE^F **KAPLAN**
KAPLANTURBINE^F
TURBINA^F **KAPLAN**

runner blade
pale^F
Laufblatt^N
paleta^F del rotor^M

hub
moyeu^M
Nabe^F
cubo^M

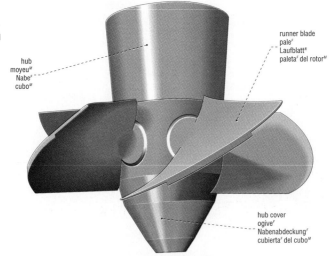

hub cover
ogive^F
Nabenabdeckung^F
cubierta^F del cubo^M

PELTON RUNNER
ROUE^F **PELTON**
PELTONTURBINE^F
TURBINA^F **PELTON**

bucket ring
couronne^F d'aubage^M
Zellenring^M
rueda^F de cangilones^M

bucket
auget^M
Zelle^F
cangilón^M

coupling bolt
boulon^M d'accouplement^M
Kupplungsbolzen^M
perno^M de acoplamiento^M

distribution to consumers
transport" vers les usagers"
Stromabgabe' an Verbraucher"
distribución' al consumidor"

voltage decrease
abaissement" de la tension'
Spannungsreduzierung'
reductor" de voltaje"

power fed into the distribution network
intégration' de l'électricité' au réseau" de transport"
Einspeisung' in das Stromnetz"
paso" de la energía' hacia la red' de transmisión'

power supply at generator voltage
transport" de l'énergie' à la tension' de l'alternateur"
Generatorspannungsübertragung'
transmisión' de energía' al generador" de voltaje"

high-tension electricity transmission
transport" de l'électricité' à haute tension'
Hochspannungsleitung'
transmisión' de electricidad' de alto voltaje"

voltage increase
élévation' de la tension'
Spannungserhöhung'
amplificador" de voltaje"

supply of water
provision' d'eau'
Wasservorrat"
suministro" de agua'

head of water
hauteur' de chute'
Wasserstand'
volumen" de agua'

production of electricity by the generator
production' d'électricité' par l'alternateur"
Stromerzeugung' durch den Generator"
producción' de electricidad' por generador"

water under pressure
eau' sous pression'
Druckwasser"
agua' a presión'

turbined water draining
évacuation' de l'eau' turbinée
Turbinenwasserabfluß"
desagüe" de la turbina'

transformation of mechanical work into electricity
conversion' du travail" mécanique en électricité'
Umwandlung' von Bewegungsenergie' in Elektrizität'
transformación' del trabajo" mecánico en electricidad'

rotation of the turbine
mouvement" rotatif de la turbine'
Turbinendrehung'
rotación' de la turbina'

transmission of the rotary motion to the rotor
transmission' du mouvement" au rotor"
Übertragung' der Drehbewegung' auf den Rotor"
transmisión' del movimiento" hacia el rotor"

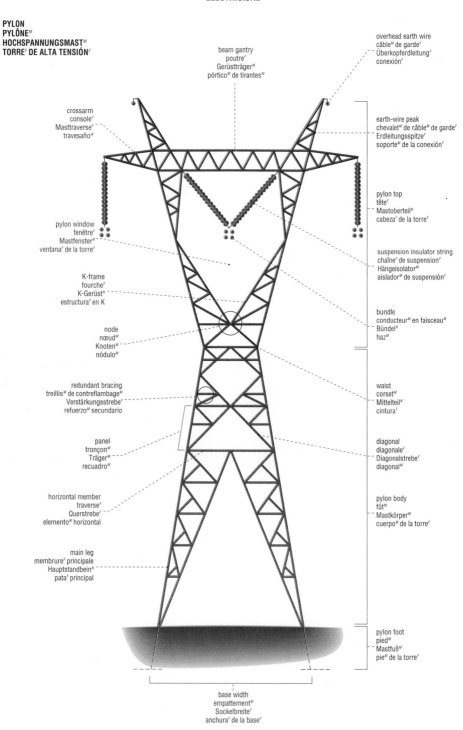

PYLON
PYLÔNE*M*
HOCHSPANNUNGSMAST*M*
TORRE*F* DE ALTA TENSIÓN*F*

beam gantry
poutre*F*
Gerüstträger*M*
pórtico*M* de tirantes*M*

overhead earth wire
câble*M* de garde*F*
Überkopferdleitung*F*
conexión*F*

crossarm
console*F*
Masttraverse*F*
travesaño*M*

earth-wire peak
chevalet*M* de câble*M* de garde*F*
Erdleitungsspitze*F*
soporte*M* de la conexión*F*

pylon top
tête*F*
Mastoberteil*N*
cabeza*F* de la torre*F*

pylon window
fenêtre*F*
Mastfenster*N*
ventana*F* de la torre*F*

suspension insulator string
chaîne*F* de suspension*F*
Hängeisolator*M*
aislador*M* de suspensión*F*

K-frame
fourche*F*
K-Gerüst*N*
estructura*F* en K

bundle
conducteur*M* en faisceau*M*
Bündel*N*
haz*M*

node
nœud*M*
Knoten*M*
nódulo*M*

redundant bracing
treillis*M* de contreflambage*M*
Verstärkungsstrebe*F*
refuerzo*M* secundario

waist
corset*M*
Mittelteil*N*
cintura*F*

panel
tronçon*M*
Träger*M*
recuadro*M*

diagonal
diagonale*F*
Diagonalstrebe*F*
diagonal*M*

horizontal member
traverse*F*
Querstrebe*F*
elemento*M* horizontal

pylon body
fût*M*
Mastkörper*M*
cuerpo*M* de la torre*F*

main leg
membrure*F* principale
Hauptstandbein*N*
pata*F* principal

pylon foot
pied*M*
Mastfuß*M*
pie*M* de la torre*F*

base width
empattement*M*
Sockelbreite*F*
anchura*F* de la base*F*

ELECTRICITY DISTRIBUTION
TRANSPORT^M DE L'ÉLECTRICITÉ^F
STROMTRANSPORT^M
TRANSMISIÓN^F DE ELECTRICIDAD^F

medium tension distribution line
ligne^F de distribution^F à moyenne tension^F
Mittelspannungsleitung^F
cables^M de tensión^F mediana

high tension connector
connecteur^M à serrage^M mécanique
Anschluß^M für Hochspannungsleitung^F
conector^M de línea^F cargada

insulator
isolateur^M
Isolator^M
aislador^M

crossarm
traverse^F
Traverse^F
travesaño^M

brace
contrefiche^F
Stütze^F
puntal^M

lightning conductor
parafoudre^M
Blitzableiter^M
pararrayos^M

fuse
fusible^M
Sicherung^F
fusible^M

fuse holder
porte-fusible^M
Sicherungsträger^M
portafusible^M

fuse cutout
coupe-circuit^M
Sicherungsabschnitt^M
placa^F para fusibles^M

bushing
traversée^F
Durchführung^F
boquilla^F reducidora^F

terminal
borne^F
Endableitung^F
terminal^M

low-tension distribution line
ligne^F de distribution^F à basse tension^F
Niedrigspannungsleitung^F
cables^M de baja tensión^F

transformer
transformateur^M
Transformator^M
transformador^M

supply point
point^M d'alimentation^F
Stromanschlußpunkt^M
cables^M de suministro^M

insulator
isolateur^M
Isolator^M
aislador^M

OVERHEAD CONNECTION
BRANCHEMENT^M AÉRIEN
FREILEITUNG^F
CONEXIÓN^F AÉREA

supply point
point^M d'alimentation^F
Stromanschlußpunkt^M
cables^M de suministro^M

customer's supply
branchement^M de l'abonné^M
Hauptanschluß^M
entrada^F del suministro^M

connection point
point^M de raccordement^M
Verbindungspunkt^M
conexión^F

phase conductor
conducteur^M de phase^F
Phase^F
conductor^M de fase^F

medium tension distribution line
ligne^F de distribution^F à moyenne tension^F
Mittelspannungsleitung^F
cables^M de tensión^F mediana

neutral conductor
conducteur^M neutre
Null-Leiter^M
conductor^M neutral

low-tension distribution line
ligne^F de distribution^F à basse tension^F
Niedrigspannungsleitung^F
cables^M de baja tensión^F

earth wire
conducteur^M de terre^F
Erdleitung^F
conexión^F a tierra^F

distributor service loop
branchement^M du distributeur^M
Verteilerschleife^F
cables^M de conexión^F

electricity meter
compteur^M d'électricité^F
Stromzähler^M
medidor^M

main switch
interrupteur^M principal
Hauptschalter^M
interruptor^M principal

main junction box
coffret^M de branchement^M
Wartungskasten^M
caja^F de servicio^M

distribution board
tableau^M de distribution^F
Verteilerkasten^M
tablero^M de distribución^F

fuse
fusible^M
Sicherung^F
fusible^M

ENERGY
ÉNERGIES

ENERGIE
ENERGÍA

757

NUCLEAR ENERGY
ÉNERGIE^F NUCLÉAIRE
KERNENERGIE^F
ENERGÍA^F NUCLEAR

NUCLEAR POWER STATION
CENTRALE^F NUCLÉAIRE
KERNKRAFTWERK^N
CENTRAL^F NUCLEAR

spent fuel storage bay
piscine^F de stockage^M du combustible^M irradié
Abklingbecken^N
fosa^F de almacenamiento^M de residuos^M de combustible^M

reactor building airlock
sas^M du bâtiment^M du réacteur^M
Luftschleuse^F des Reaktorgebäudes^N
esclusa^F de aire^M del edificio^M del reactor^M

spent fuel discharge bay
piscine^F de déchargement^M du combustible^M irradié
Entsorgungsbecken^N
fosa^F de descarga^F de residuos^M de combustible^M

turbine building
bâtiment^M de la turbine^F
Turbinengebäude^N
edificio^M de la turbina^F

generator
alternateur^M
Generator^M
generador^M

turbine
turbine^F
Turbine^F
turbina^F

transformer
transformateur^M
Transformator^M
transformador^M

condenser
condenseur^M
Kondensator^M
condensador^M

low-pressure steam
vapeur^F à basse pression^F
Niederdruckdampf^M
vapor^M a baja presión^F

separator steam release
sortie^F de la vapeur^F des séparateurs^M
Abdampfleitung^F
separador^M del escape^M de vapor^M

reheater
réchauffeur^M
Aufheizer^M
recalentador^M

turbine stop valve
vanne^F d'arrêt^M de la turbine^F
Turbinenabschaltventil^N
válvula^F de pare^M de la turbina^F

separator
séparateur^M
Kondensationskammer^F
separador^M

high-pressure steam inlet
entrée^F de la vapeur^F à haute pression^F
Hochdruckdampfeinlaß^M
toma^F de vapor^M a alta presión^F

ENERGY
ÉNERGIES

ENERGIE
ENERGÍA

dousing water valve
vanne^f d'arrosage^M
Kühlwasserventil^N
válvula^f de agua^f de rociado^M

dousing water tank
réservoir^M d'arrosage^M
Kühlwassertank^M
tanque^M de agua^f de rociado^M

steam generator room cooler
refroidisseur^M de la salle^f des générateurs^M de vapeur^f
Kühler^M für Dampfgeneratorraum^M
enfriador^M de la cámara^f del generador^M de vapor^M

steam generator
générateur^M de vapeur^f
Dampfgenerator^M
generador^M de vapor^M

reactor building
bâtiment^M du réacteur^M
Reaktorgebäude^N
edificio^M del reactor^M

deuterium oxide upgrading
reconcentration^f de l'oxyde^M de deutérium^M
Schwerwasseranreicherung^f
enriquecimiento^M del agua^f pesada

heat transport pump
pompe^f de caloportage^M
Wärmepumpe^f
bomba^f transportadora de calor^M

feeder header
collecteur^M du réacteur^M
Speisekopf^M
cargadora^f de combustible^M

reactor
réacteur^M
Reaktor^M
reactor^M

calandria
cuve^f du réacteur^M
Verdampferkörpermantel^M
calandria^f

fuelling machine
machine^f à combustible^M
Beschickungsmaschine^f
máquina^f abastecedora de combustible^M

control room
salle^f de commande^f
Steuerzentrale^f
sala^f de control^M

steam release pipes
tuyauterie^f de sortie^f de la vapeur^f des séparateurs^M
Abdampfleitungen^f
tubería^f de escape^M del vapor^M

main steam pipes
tuyauterie^f de vapeur^f primaire
Hauptdampfleitungen^f
tubería^f principal del vapor^M

main steam header
collecteur^M de vapeur^f primaire
Hauptdampfverteiler^M
cámara^f principal de vapor^M

condenser backwash outlet
sortie^f du reflux^M du condenseur^M
Kondensatauslaß^M
salida^f de la contracorriente^f

condenser cooling water inlet
entrée^f de l'eau^f de refroidissement^M du condenseur^M
Kondensatorkühlwassereinlaß^M
entrada^f del agua^f de enfriamiento^M del condensador^M

condenser backwash inlet
entrée^f du reflux^M du condenseur^M
Kondensateinlaß^M
entrada^f de la contracorriente^f

condenser cooling water outlet
sortie^f de l'eau^f de refroidissement^M du condenseur^M
Kondensatorkühlwasserauslaß^M
salida^f del agua^f de enfriamiento^M del condensador^M

GAS-COOLED REACTOR
RÉACTEUR^M AU GAZ^M CARBONIQUE
KOHLENDIOXIDREAKTOR^M
REACTOR^M DE BIÓXIDO^M DE CARBONO^M

fuelling machine
machine^F de chargement^M
Beschickungsmaschine^F
mecanismo^M de carga^F del combustible^M

concrete shielding
enceinte^F en béton^M
Betonmantel^M
resguardo^M de hormigón^M

control rod
barre^F de contrôle^M
Steuerstab^M
varilla^F de control^M

carbon dioxide gas coolant
gaz^M carbonique de refroidissement^M
Kohlendioxidkühlgas^N
gas refrigerante de bióxido de carbono

reactor core
cœur^M du réacteur^M
Reaktorkern^M
núcleo^M del reactor^M

heat exchanger
échangeur^M de chaleur^F
Wärmetauscher^M
intercambiador^M de calor^M

blower
soufflante^F
Gebläse^N
ventilador^M del evaporador^M

steam outlet
sortie^F de la vapeur^F
Dampfauslaß^M
salida^F de vapor^M

feedwater
alimentation^F en eau^F
Speisewasser^N
alimentación^F de agua^F

fuel: natural uranium
combustible^M: uranium^M naturel
Brennstoff^M: nichtangereichertes Uran^N
combustible^M: uranio^M natural

moderator: graphite
modérateur^M: graphite^M
Moderator^M: Graphit^M
moderador^M: grafito^M

coolant: carbon dioxide
caloporteur^M: gaz^M carbonique
Kühlmittel^N: Kohlendioxid^N
refrigerante^M: bióxido^M de carbono^M

concrete shielding
enceinte^F en béton^M
Betonmantel^M
resguardo^M de hormigón^M

steam generator
générateur^M de vapeur^F
Dampfgenerator^M
generador^M de vapor^M

pressurizer
pressuriseur^M
Druckerzeuger^M
compresor^M

steam outlet
sortie^F de la vapeur^F
Dampfauslaß^M
salida^F de vapor^M

feedwater
alimentation^F en eau^F
Speisewasser^N
alimentación^F de agua^F

control rod
barre^F de contrôle^M
Steuerstab^M
varilla^F de control^M

pump
pompe^F
Pumpe^F
bomba^F

pressurized heavy water
eau^F lourde sous pression^F
Schwerwasser^N unter Druck^M
agua^F pesada a presión^F

fuel
combustible^M
Brennelement^N
combustible^M

moderator tank
cuve^F du modérateur^M
Moderatortank^M
tanque^M moderador

cold heavy water
eau^F lourde froide
kaltes Schwerwasser^N
agua^F pesada de enfriamiento^M

safety tank
réservoir^M de sécurité^F
Sicherheitstank^M
tanque^M de seguridad^F

fuelling machine
machine^F de chargement^M
Beschickungsmaschine^F
máquina^F cargadora de combustible^M

fuel: natural uranium
combustible^M: uranium^M naturel
Brennstoff^M: nichtangereichertes Uran^N
combustible^M: uranio^M natural

moderator: heavy water
modérateur^M: eau^F lourde
Moderator^M: schweres Wasser^N
moderador^M: agua^F pesada

coolant: pressurized heavy water
caloporteur^M: eau^F lourde sous pression^F
Kühlmittel^N: Druckwasser^N
refrigerante^M: agua^F pesada a presión^F

761

NUCLEAR ENERGY
ÉNERGIE*F* NUCLÉAIRE
KERNENERGIE*F*
ENERGÍA*F* NUCLEAR

PRESSURIZED-WATER REACTOR
RÉACTEUR*M* **À EAU***F* **SOUS PRESSION***F*
DRUCKWASSERREAKTOR*M*
REACTOR*M* **DE AGUA***F* **A PRESIÓN***F*

concrete shielding
enceinte*F* en béton*M*
Betonmantel*M*
resguardo*M* de hormigón*M*

pressure vessel
pressuriseur*M*
Druckkessel*M*
recipiente*M* de presión*F*

steam generator
générateur*M* de vapeur*F*
Dampfgenerator*M*
generador*M* de vapor*M*

control rod
barre*F* de contrôle*M*
Steuerstab*M*
varilla*F* de control*M*

steam outlet
sortie*F* de la vapeur*F*
Dampfauslaß*M*
salida*F* de vapor*M*

feedwater
alimentation*F* en eau*F*
Speisewasser*N*
alimentación*F* de agua*F*

reactor core
cœur*M* du réacteur*M*
Reaktorkern*M*
núcleo*M* del reactor*M*

pump
pompe*F*
Pumpe*F*
bomba*F*

ENERGIE
ENERGÍA

ENERGY
ÉNERGIES

fuel: enriched uranium
combustible*M*: uranium*M* enrichi
Brennstoff*M*: angereichertes Uran*N*
combustible*M*: uranio*M* enriquecido

moderator: natural water
modérateur*M*: eau*F* naturelle
Moderator*M*: Wasser*N*
moderador*M*: agua*F* natural

coolant: pressurized water
caloporteur*M*: eau*F* sous pression*F*
Kühlmittel*N*: Druckwasser*N*
refrigerante*M*: agua*F* a presión*F*

BOILING-WATER REACTOR
RÉACTEUR^M À EAU^F BOUILLANTE
SIEDEWASSERREAKTOR^M
REACTOR^M DE AGUA^F HIRVIENTE

concrete shielding
enceinte^F en béton^M
Betonmantel^M
resguardo^M de hormigón^M

reactor tank
cuve^F du réacteur^M
Reaktortank^M
tanque^M del reactor^M

reactor core
cœur^M du réacteur^M
Reaktorkern^M
núcleo^M del reactor^M

steam outlet
sortie^F de la vapeur^F
Dampfauslaß^M
salida^F de vapor^M

circulation pump
pompe^F de recirculation^F
Umwälzpumpe^F
bomba^F de circulación^F

control rod
barre^F de contrôle^M
Steuerstab^M
varilla^F de control^M

dry well
enceinte^F sèche
Druckkammer^F
pozo^M seco

feedwater
alimentation^F en eau^F
Speisewasser^N
agua^F de alimentación^F

wet well
enceinte^F humide
Naßkammer^F
pozo^M

condensation pool
piscine^F de condensation^F
Kondensatorkühlwasserbecken^N
piscina^F para enfriamiento^M del condensador^M

fuel: enriched uranium
combustible^M: uranium^M enrichi
Brennstoff^M: angereichertes Uran^N
combustible^M: uranio^M enriquecido

moderator: natural water
modérateur^M: eau^F naturelle
Moderator^M: Wasser^N
moderador^M: agua^F natural

coolant: boiling water
caloporteur^M: eau^F bouillante
Kühlmittel^N: Siedewasser^N
refrigerante^M: agua^F hirviente

FUEL HANDLING SEQUENCE
SÉQUENCE^F DE MANIPULATION^F DU COMBUSTIBLE^M
BRENNELEMENTEBESCHICKUNG^F
SECUENCIA^F EN EL MANEJO^M DE COMBUSTIBLE^M

new fuel storage room
salle^F de stockage^M du combustible^M neuf
Lagerraum^M für neue Brennelemente^N
almacén^M de combustible^M nuevo

loading area
zone^F de chargement^M
Beschickungsbereich^M
sección^F de carga^F del combustible^M

fuelling machine
machine^F de chargement^M
Beschickungsmaschine^F
máquina^F cargadora de combustible^M

service building
bâtiment^M des services^M
Kraftwerksgebäude^N
zona^F de servicio^M

reactor
réacteur^M
Reaktor^M
reactor^M

port
hublot^M de chargement^M
Füllöffnung^F für neue Brennelemente^N
entrada^F de admisión^F de combustible^M

equipment lock
sas^M pour équipement^M
Materialschleuse^F
esclusa^F de materiales^M

accept machine
machine^F de déchargement^M
Annahmemaschine^F
máquina^F de descarga^F

spent fuel port
hublot^M de déchargement^M du combustible^M
irradié
Abgabeöffnung^F für verbrauchte
Brennelemente^N
entrada^F del residuo^M de combustible^M

elevator
élévateur^M
Aufzug^M
elevador^M

discharge bay
piscine^F de déchargement^M
Entsorgungsbecken^N
fosa^F descarga de residuos^M de combustible^M

storage tray
plateau^M de stockage^M
Lagergestell^N
recipiente^M para almacenamiento^M

failed fuel canning
gainage^M du combustible^M défectueux
Aufbewahrung^F schadhafter Brennelemente^N
envasado^M del residuo^M de combustible^M

reception bay
piscine^F de réception^F
Aufnahmebecken^N
fosa^F de recepción^F

transfer canal
canal^M de transfert^M
Überleitungstunnel^M
canal^M transportador

canned failed fuel
combustible^M défectueux sous gaine^F
Tonnen^F mit schadhaften Brennelementen^N
combustible^M fallido envasado

spent fuel storage bay
piscine^F de stockage^M du combustible^M irradié
Abklingbecken^N
fosa^F de desechos^M de combustible^M

failed fuel bay
piscine^F du combustible^M défectueux
Becken^N für schadhafte Brennelemente^N
fosa^F de combustible^M fallido

spacer
patin' d'espacement'
Distanzstück'
separador'

pressure tube
tube' de force'
druckfestes Außenrohr'
inyector' de píldoras'

end plate
grille' d'extrémité'
Abschlußplatte'
placa' terminal

fuel rod
crayon'
Brennstab'
inyector' unitario de alimentación'

fuel rod
crayon'
Brennstab'
inyector' unitario de alimentación'

bearing pad
patin' d'appui'
Lagerraster'
soporte'

fuel pellet
pastille' de combustible'
Brennstofftablette'
píldora' de combustible'

end plate
grille' d'extrémité'
Abschlußplatte'
placa' terminal

end cap
bouchon'
Endstück'
tapa'

NUCLEAR REACTOR
RÉACTEUR' NUCLÉAIRE
KERNREAKTOR'
CARGA' DEL REACTOR' NUCLEAR

reactor building
bâtiment' du réacteur'
Reaktorgebäude'
edificio' del reactor'

containment building
enceinte' de confinement'
Sicherheitshülle'
bloque' de contención'

fuel pellet
pastille' de combustible'
Brennstofftablette'
píldora' de combustible'

fuel bundle
grappe' de combustible'
Brennelement'
elemento' cargador de combustible'

spent fuel storage bay
piscine' de stockage' du combustible' irradié
Abklingbecken'
fosa' de desechos'

reactor vessel
calandre'
Reaktorkessel'
recipiente' del reactor'

pressure tube
tube' de force'
druckfestes Außenrohr'
inyector' de píldoras'

ENERGY
ÉNERGIES

ÉNERGIE
ENERGÍA

765

NUCLEAR ENERGY
ÉNERGIE*F* NUCLÉAIRE
KERNENERGIE*F*
ENERGÍA*F* NUCLEAR

PRODUCTION OF ELECTRICITY FROM NUCLEAR ENERGY
PRODUCTION*F* D'ÉLECTRICITÉ*F* PAR ÉNERGIE*F* NUCLÉAIRE
STROMERZEUGUNG*F* AUS KERNENERGIE*F*
PRODUCCIÓN*F* DE ELECTRICIDAD*F* POR MEDIO DE ENERGÍA*F* NUCLEAR

water turns into steam
transformation*F* de l'eau*F* en vapeur*F*
Wasser*N* verdampft
conversión*F* del agua*F* en vapor*M*

reactor
réacteur*M*
Reaktor*M*
reactor*M*

containment building
enceinte*F* de confinement*M*
Sicherheitshülle*F*
edificio*M*

dousing water tank
réservoir*M* d'arrosage*M*
Kühlwassertank*M*
tanque*M* de agua*F* de rociado*M*

transfer of heat to water
transmission*F* de la chaleur*F* à l'eau*F*
Wärmeabgabe*F* an Wasser*N*
transferencia*F* de calor*M* al agua*F*

sprinklers
gicleurs*M*
Sprinkler*M*
rociadores*M*

safety valve
soupape*F* de sûreté*F*
Sicherheitsventil*N*
válvula*F* de seguridad*F*

coolant transfers the heat to the steam generator
acheminement*M* de la chaleur*F* au générateur*M* de vapeur*F* par le caloporteur*M*
Kühlmittel*N* überträgt Wärme*F* an Dampfgenerator*M*
el refrigerante*M* transfiere el calor*M* al generador*M* de vapor*M*

heat production
production*F* de chaleur*F*
Wärmeerzeugung*F*
producción*F* de calor*M*

fission of uranium fuel
fission*F* de l'uranium*M*
Spaltung*F* des Uranbrennstoffs*M*
uranio*M* en fisión*F*

fuel
combustible*M*
Brennstoff*M*
combustible*M*

moderator
modérateur*M*
Moderator*M*
moderador*M*

coolant
caloporteur*M*
Kühlmittel*N*
refrigerante*M*

steam pressure drives turbine
entraînement^M de la turbine^F par la vapeur^F
Dampfdruck^M treibt Turbine^F an
la presión^F del vapor^M impulsa las turbinas^F

electricity transmission
transport^M de l'électricité^F
Stromfortleitung^F
transmisión^F de electricidad^F

voltage increase
élévation^F de la tension^F
Spannungserhöhung^F
ampliación^F del voltaje^M

turbine shaft turns generator
entraînement^M du rotor^M de l'alternateur^M
Turbinenwelle^F treibt Generator^M an
la flecha^F de la turbina^F hace girar el generador^M

electricity production
production^F d'électricité^F
Stromerzeugung^F
producción^F de electricidad^F

water cools the used steam
refroidissement^M de la vapeur^F par l'eau^F
Wasser^N kühlt Brauchdampf^M ab
el agua^F de un lago^M o de un río^M enfría el vapor^M utilizado

condensation of steam into water
condensation^F de la vapeur^F
Dampf^M kondensiert zu Wasser^N
el vapor^M se condensa en agua^F

water is pumped back into the steam generator
retour^M de l'eau^F au générateur^M de vapeur^F
Wasser^N wird zum Dampfgenerator^M zurückgepumpt
el agua^F regresa al generador^M de vapor^M

SOLAR ENERGY
ÉNERGIE*F* SOLAIRE
SONNENENERGIE*F*
ENERGÍA*F* SOLAR

SOLAR CELL
PHOTOPILE*F*
SOLARZELLE*F*
CELDA*F* SOLAR*F*

solar radiation
rayonnement*M* solaire
Sonnenstrahlung*F*
radiación*F* solar

antireflection coating
couche*F* antireflet
nichtreflektierende Beschichtung*F*
recubrimiento*M* antirreflectante

metallic contact grid
grille*F* métallique conductrice
Metallkontaktgitter*N*
reja*F* metálica de contacto*M*

positive region
région*F* positive
Plusbereich*M*
región*F* positiva

positive/negative junction
jonction*F* positif*M*/négatif*M*
PN-Übertragung*F*
junta*F*

negative contact
contact*M* négatif
Minuskontakt*M*
contacto*M* negativo

negative region
région*F* négative
Minusbereich*M*
región*F* negativa

positive contact
contact*M* positif
Pluskontakt*M*
contacto*M* positivo

FLAT-PLATE SOLAR COLLECTOR
CAPTEUR*M* SOLAIRE PLAN
FLACHKOLLEKTOR*M*
COLECTOR*M* SOLAR PLANO

solar radiation
rayonnement*M* solaire
Sonnenstrahlung*F*
radiación*F* solar

glass
vitre*F*
Glasabdeckung*F*
cristal*M*

coolant outlet
sortie*F* du caloporteur*M*
Kühlmittelauslaß*M*
salida*F* del refrigerante*M*

frame
coffre*M*
Rahmen*M*
armazón*M*

flow tube
tube*M* de circulation*F*
Durchflußrohr*N*
tubo*M* de circulación*F*

absorbing plate
plaque*F* absorbante
Absorber*M*
placa*F* de absorción*F*

coolant inlet
entrée*F* du caloporteur*M*
Kühlmitteleinlaß*M*
entrada*F* del refrigerante*M*

insulation
isolant*M*
Isolierung*F*
aislante*M*

SOLAR-CELL SYSTEM
CIRCUIT^M DE PHOTOPILES^F
SOLARZELLENSYSTEM^N
SISTEMA^M DE CELDAS^F SOLARES

solar cell panel
module^M de photopiles^F
Solarzellenprofil^N
panel^M de celdas^F solares

solar radiation
rayonnement^M solaire
Sonnenstrahlung^F
radiación^F solar

light bulb
lampe^F à incandescence^F
Glühbirne^F
lámpara^F incandescente

glass
vitre^F
Glasabdeckung^F
cristal^M

solar cell
photopile^F
Solarzelle^F
celda^F solar

fuse
fusible^M
Sicherung^F
fusible^M

frame
coffre^M
Rahmen^M
marco^M

diode
diode^F
Diode^F
diodo^M

negative contact
contact^M négatif
Minuskontakt^M
contacto^M negativo

terminal box
boîte^F électrique
Anschlußkasten^M
caja^F terminal

positive contact
contact^M positif
Pluskontakt^M
contacto^M positivo

battery
batterie^F d'accumulateurs^M
Batterie^F
acumulador^M

ENERGY
ÉNERGIES

ENERGIE
ENERGÍA

769

SOLAR ENERGY
ÉNERGIE^F SOLAIRE
SONNENENERGIE^F
ENERGÍA^F SOLAR

SOLAR FURNACE
FOUR^M SOLAIRE
SONNENOFEN^M
HORNO^M SOLAR

solar radiation
rayonnement^M solaire
Sonnenstrahlung^F
radiación^F solar

solar ray reflected
rayon^M solaire réfléchi
reflektierter Sonnenstrahl^M
rayo^M solar reflejado

reflecting surface
surface^F réfléchissante
Reflektionsfläche^F
espejo^M

ENERGIE
ENERGÍA

ENERGY
ÉNERGIES

parabolic mirror
miroir^M parabolique
Parabolspiegel^M
espejo^M parabólico

furnace
four^M
Ofen^M
horno^M

hill
pente^F
Anhöhe^F
colina^F

target area
foyer^M
Zielgebiet^N
punto^M de concentración^F

bank of heliostats
champ^M d'héliostats^M
Heliostatanordnung^F
terraplén^M de los helióstatos^M

tower
tour^F
Turm^M
torre^F

770

PRODUCTION OF ELECTRICITY FROM SOLAR ENERGY
PRODUCTION′ D'ÉLECTRICITÉ′ PAR ÉNERGIE′ SOLAIRE
STROMERZEUGUNG′ AUS SONNENENERGIE′
PRODUCCIÓN′ DE ELECTRICIDAD′ POR ENERGÍA′ SOLAR

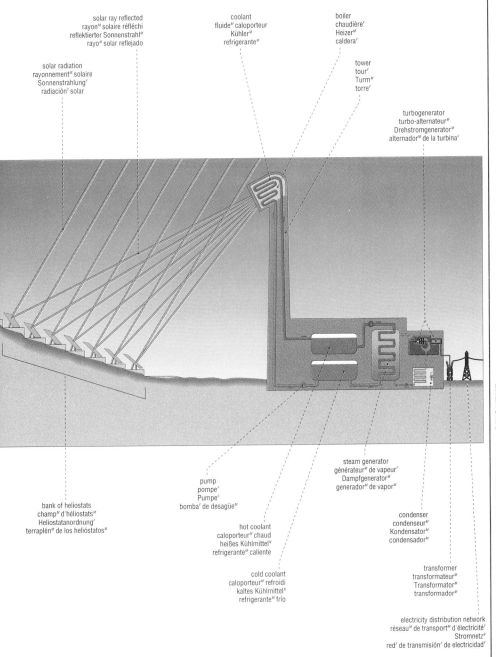

solar ray reflected
rayon^M solaire réfléchi
reflektierter Sonnenstrahl^M
rayo^M solar reflejado

coolant
fluide^M caloporteur
Kühler^M
refrigerante^M

boiler
chaudière′
Heizer^M
caldera′

solar radiation
rayonnement^M solaire
Sonnenstrahlung′
radiación′ solar

tower
tour′
Turm^M
torre′

turbogenerator
turbo-alternateur^M
Drehstromgenerator^M
alternador^M de la turbina′

bank of heliostats
champ^M d'héliostats^M
Heliostatanordnung′
terraplén^M de los helióstatos^M

pump
pompe′
Pumpe′
bomba′ de desagüe^M

hot coolant
caloporteur^M chaud
heißes Kühlmittel^N
refrigerante^M caliente

cold coolant
caloporteur^M refroidi
kaltes Kühlmittel^N
refrigerante^M frío

steam generator
générateur^M de vapeur′
Dampfgenerator^M
generador^M de vapor^M

condenser
condenseur^M
Kondensator^M
condensador^M

transformer
transformateur^M
Transformator^M
transformador^M

electricity distribution network
réseau^M de transport^M d'électricité′
Stromnetz^N
red′ de transmisión′ de electricidad′

ENERGY ÉNERGIES ENERGIE ENERGÍA

771

SOLAR ENERGY
ÉNERGIE^F SOLAIRE
SONNENENERGIE^F
ENERGÍA^F SOLAR

SOLAR HOUSE
MAISON^F SOLAIRE
SOLARHAUS^N
CASA^F SOLAR

solar collector
capteur^M solaire
Sonnenkollektor^M
colector^M solar

solar radiation
rayonnement^M solaire
Sonnenstrahlung^F
radiación^F solar

ventilation
ventilation^F
Lüftung^F
ventilación^F

Trombe wall
mur^M Trombe
Trombe-Wand^F
pared^F de Trombe

heat exchanger
échangeur^M thermique
Wärmetauscher^M
intercambiador^M de calor^M

circulating pump
pompe^F de circulation^F
Umwälzpumpe^F
bomba^F de circulación^F

water-heater tank
chauffe-eau^M
Wasserheizkessel^M
tanque^M calentador de agua^F

pool
piscine^F
Schwimmbecken^N
piscina^F

expansion tank
vase^M d'expansion^F
Expansionsgefäß^N
tanque^M de expansión^F

water main
eau^F de ville^F
öffentliche Wasserversorgung^F
suministro^M de agua^F

circulating pump
pompe^F de circulation^F
Umwälzpumpe^F
bomba^F de circulación^F

heat exchanger
échangeur^M thermique
Wärmetauscher^M
intercambiador^M de calor^M

storage tank
réservoir^M de stockage^M
Wasservorratstank^M
tanque^M de almacenamiento^M

filter
filtre^M
Filter^M
filtro^M

ENERGIE
ENERGÍA

ENERGY
ÉNERGIES

TROMBE WALL
MUR^M TROMBE
TROMBE-WAND^F
PARED^F DE TROMBE

warm air
air^M chaud
warme Luft^F
aire^M caliente

shutter
volet^M
Schließklappe^F
obturador^M para la circulación^F del aire^M

double glazing
double vitrage^M
Doppelverglasung^F
vidriado^M

air gap
intervalle^M d'air^M
Luftspalt^M
cámara^F de aire^M

absorbing surface
surface^F absorbante
Aufnahmefläche^F
superficie^F de absorción^F

concrete wall
mur^M en béton^M
Betonmauer^F
pared^F de hormigón^M

cold air
air^M frais
kalte Luft^F
aire^M frío

772

WIND ENERGY
ÉNERGIE^F ÉOLIENNE
WINDENERGIE^F
ENERGÍA^F EÓLICA

WINDMILL
MOULIN^M À VENT^M
WINDMÜHLE^F
MOLINO^M DE VIENTO^M

stock
bras^M
Schaft^M
larguero^M

sail
aile^F
Flügel^M
aspa^F

windshaft
arbre^M
Welle^F
eje^M de las aspas^F

cap
calotte^F
Windmühlenkappe^F
capucha^F giratoria

tower
tour^F
Turm^M
torre^F

floor
étage^M
Stockwerk^N
piso^M

gallery
galerie^F
Galerie^F
pasillo^M

fantail
gouvernail^M
Fächergerüst^N
molinete^F

sail cloth
voile^F
Segeltuchbespannung^F
lona^F

hemlath
cotret^M
Stabwerk^N
lama^F

sailbar
latte^F
Segelstange^F
travesaño^M

frame
cadre^M
Stabwerk^N
armazón^M

POST MILL
MOULIN^M PIVOT^M
BOCKMÜHLE^F
MOLINO^M DE PLATAFORMA^F GIRATORIA

rotor
rotor^M
Rotor^M
rotor^M

steps
escalier^M
Treppe^F
escalera^F

tail pole
queue^F
Stert^M
puntal^M trasero

post
pivot^M
Hausbaum^M
soporte^M de la plataforma^F

HORIZONTAL-AXIS WIND TURBINE
ÉOLIENNE*F* À AXE*M* HORIZONTAL
LÄNGSACHSENWINDTURBINE*F*
TURBINA*F* DE VIENTO*M* DE EJE*M* HORIZONTAL

hub
moyeu*M*
Nabe*F*
cubo*M*

nacelle
nacelle*F*
Zelle*F*
cubierta*F* del mecanismo*M*

blade
pale*F*
Rotorblatt*N*
aspa*F*

tower
tour*F*
Turm*M*
torre*F*

VERTICAL-AXIS WIND TURBINE
ÉOLIENNE*F* À AXE*M* VERTICAL
VERTIKALACHSENWINDTURBINE*F*
TURBINA*F* DE VIENTO*M* DE EJE*M* VERTICAL

guy wire
hauban*M*
Spannkabel*N*
tensor*M* de alambre*M*

strut
entretoise*F*
Verstrebung*F*
travesaño*M* de apoyo*M*

central column
axe*M* central
Mittelsäule*F*
columna*F* central

aerodynamic brake
aérofrein*M*
aerodynamische Bremse*F*
freno*M* aerodinámico

rotor
rotor*M*
Rotor*M*
rotor*M*

blade
pale*F*
Rotorblatt*N*
aspa*F*

base
socle*M*
Sockel*M*
base*F*

SUMMARY

SCHWERMASCHINEN
MAQUINARIA PESADA

HEAVY MACHINERY
ENGINS ET MACHINES

FIRE PREVENTION
PRÉVENTION^F DES INCENDIES^M
BRANDBEKÄMPFUNG^F
PREVENCIÓN^F DE INCENDIOS^M

HAND LAMP
LAMPE^F PORTATIVE
TASCHENLAMPE^F
REFLECTOR^M PORTÁTIL

FIREMAN
SAPEUR^M-POMPIER^M
FEUERWEHRMANN^M
BOMBERO^M

spotlight
projecteur^M
Strahler^M
bombilla^F reflectora

battery
pile^F
Batterie^F
acumulador^M

self-contained breathing apparatus
appareil^M de protection^F respiratoire
geschlossenes Atemschutzsystem^N
aparato^M de respiración^F autónomo

strap
sangle^F
Befestigungsriemen^M
correa^F

compressed-air cylinder
bouteille^F d'air^M comprimé
Druckluftflasche^F
tanque^M de aire^M comprimido

ladder and hose strap
attache^F pour tuyaux^M et échelles^F
Hakengurt^M für Leiter^F und Schlauch^M
correa^F para escalera^F y manguera^F

FIREMAN'S HELMET
CASQUE^M DE SAPEUR^M-POMPIER^M
FEUERSCHUTZHELM^M
CASCO^M DE BOMBERO^M

helmet
casque^M
Feuerschutzhelm^M
casco^M

reflective stripe
bande^F réfléchissante
Leuchtstreifen^M
banda^F reflectora

eye guard
visière^F
Gesichtsschutz^M
protector^M de ojos^M

chin strap
jugulaire^F
Kinnriemen^M
correa^F del casco^M

neck guard
protège-nuque^M
Nackenschutz^M
protector^M del cuello^M

chin guard
mentonnière^F
Kinnschutz^M
protector^M del mentón

helmet
casque^M
Feuerschutzhelm^M
casco^M

full face mask
masque^M complet
geschlossener Gesichtsschutz^M
máscara^F

air-supply tube
tube^M d'alimentation^F en air^M
Atemluftzufuhrschlauch^M
tubo^M de aire^M

pressure demand regulator
robinet^M de réglage^M de débit^M
Druckregler^M
regulador^M de presión^F

warning device
avertisseur^M sonore
Warngerät^M
alarma^F

fireproof and waterproof garment
vêtement^M ignifuge et hydrofuge
feuer- und wasserfeste Kleidung^F
vestido^M antifuego e impermeable

rubber boot
botte^F de caoutchouc^M
Gummistiefel^M
botas^F de caucho^M

FIRE ENGINE
VÉHICULES^M D'INCENDIE^M
FEUERWEHRAUTO^N
COCHE^M DE BOMBEROS^M

PUMPER
FOURGON^M-POMPE^F
PUMPLÖSCHFAHRZEUG^N
CAMIÓN^M BOMBA^F

suction hose
tuyau^M d'aspiration^F
Saugrohr^N
manguera^F de succión^F

fitting
pièce^F de jonction^F
Kupplung^F
conector^M

spotlight
projecteur^M orientable
Scheinwerfer^M
faro^M reflector

water cannon
lance^F-canon^M
Wasserkanone^F
cañón^M lanzaagua

control wheel
volant^M de manœuvre^F
Wasserhahn^M
volante^M de control^M

backstep
marchepied^M
Trittbrett^N
estribo^M trasero

storage compartment
coffre^F de rangement^M
Staufach^N
compartimiento^M de almacenamiento^M

water pressure gauge
manomètre^M
Wasserdruckanzeiger^M
manómetro^M

hydrant intake
orifice^M d'alimentation^F
Hydrantenanschluß^M
boca^F de agua^F

fire hose
tuyau^M de refoulement^M
Schlauchleitung^F
manguera^F de incendios^M

nozzle
lance^F
Strahlrohr^N
boquilla^F

dividing connector
pièce^f d'embranchement^M
Y-Verbindungsstück^N
separador^M de boca^f de agua^f

control panel
panneau^M de commande^f
Bedienkonsole^f
tablero^M de operaciónes^f

horn
corne^f de feu^M
Martinshorn^N
bocina^f

light bar
rampe^f de signalisation^f
Signalleiste^f
luces^f de emergencia^f

loudspeaker
haut-parleur^M
Lautsprecher^M
sirena^f

grab handle
poignée^f montoir^M
Haltegriff^M
asidero^M

hydrant intake
orifice^M d'alimentation^f
Hydrantenanschluß^M
boca^f de agua^f

fire hydrant wrench
clé^f de barrage^M
Hydrantenschlüssel^M
llave^f de boca^f de agua^f

AERIAL LADDER TRUCK
GRANDE ÉCHELLE^F
DREHLEITERFAHRZEUG^N
CAMIÓN^M DE ESCALELERA^F TELESCÓPICA

elevating cylinder
vérin^M de dressage^M
Hubzylinder^M
cilindro^M elevador

turntable mounting
tourelle^F
Drehscheibe^F
plataforma^F giratoria

telescopic boom
flèche^F télescopique
ausfahrbarer Leiterbaum^M
elevador^M telescópico

spotlight
projecteur^M orientable
Scheinwerfer^M
faro^M reflector

storage compartment
coffre^M de rangement^M
Staufach^N
compartimiento^M de almacenamiento^M

jack
stabilisateur^M
Stützausleger^M
soporte^M del plano^M fijo

PORTABLE FIRE EXTINGUISHER
EXTINCTEUR^M
HANDFEUERLÖSCHER^M
EXTINGUIDOR^M PORTÁTIL

trigger
gachette^F
Abzug^M
disparador^M

pin
goupille^F
Sicherungsstift^M
clavija^F

hose
tuyau^M
Schlauch^M
manguera^F

pike pole
gaffe^F
Einreißhaken^M
pica^F

tank
réservoir^M
Löschmittelbehälter^M
tanque^M

percussion bar
clé^F à percussion^F
Brecheisen^N
barra^F de percusión^F

SCHWERMASCHINEN
MAQUINARIA PESADA

HEAVY MACHINERY
ENGINS ET MACHINES

tower ladder
parc^M à échelles^F
Schiebeleiter^F
escalera^F telescópica

rotating light
gyrophare^M
Blaulicht^N
faro^M de destello^M

top ladder
échelle^F de tête^F
Oberleiter^F
tope^M de la escalera^F

ladder pipe nozzle
lance^F à eau^F
Leiterstrahlrohr^N
escalera^F con boquilla^F telescópica

fireman's hatchet
hache^F
Feuerwehrbeil^N
hacha^F de bombero^M

hook ladder
échelle^F à crochets^M
Hakenleiter^F
escalera^F de ganchos^M

HEAVY MACHINERY
ENGINS ET MACHINES

SCHWERMASCHINEN
MAQUINARIA PESADA

781

HEAVY VEHICLES
MACHINERIE^F LOURDE
SCHWERFAHRZEUGE^N
VEHÍCULOS^M PESADOS

BACKHOE LOADER
CHARGEUSE^F-PELLETEUSE^F
RADLADER^M
RETROEXCAVADORA^F CARGADORA^F

arm
bras^M
Baggerstiel^M
brazo^M

cab
cabine^F
Führerkabine^F
cabina^F

boom
flèche^F
Ausleger^M
elevador^M

bucket cylinder
vérin^M du godet^M
Schaufelzylinder^M
cilindro^M del cucharón^M

arm cylinder
vérin^M du bras^M
Baggerstielzylinder^M
cilindro^M del brazo^M

bucket lever
levier^M coudé
Schaufelarm^M
palanca^F del cucharón^M

back-hoe controls
manœuvre^F de la pelleteuse^F
Tiefräumerbedienteil^N
controles^M de la retroexcavadora^F

bucket
godet^M
Schaufel^F
cucharón^M

bucket hinge pin
articulation^F de la pelleteuse^F
Schaufelbolzengelenk^N
perno^M de articulación^F del cucharón^M

bucket tooth
dent^F de godet^M
Schaufelzahn^M
diente^M de cucharón^M

diesel engine
moteur^M diesel
Dieselmotor^M
motor^M diésel

boom cylinder
vérin^M de la flèche^F
Auslegerzylinder^M
cilindro^M del elevador^M

lift arm
bras^M de levage^M
Hubarm^M
brazo^M levantador

backward bucket
godet^M rétro
hintere Schaufel^F
cangilón^M trasero

lift-arm cylinder
vérin^M du bras^M de levage^M
Hubarmzylinder^M
cilindro^M del brazo^M levantador

backward bucket cylinder
vérin^M du godet^M rétro
hinterer Schaufelzylinder^M
cilindro^M del cangilón^M trasero

SCHWERMASCHINEN
MAQUINARIA PESADA

HEAVY MACHINERY
ENGINS ET MACHINES

front-end loader
chargeuse^F frontale
Schaufellader^M
cargador^M delantero

wheel tractor
tracteur^M
Radtraktor^M
tractor^M de ruedas^F

backhoe
pelleteuse^F
Tiefräumer^M
retroexcavadora^F

782

air-cleaner filter
filtre^M à air^M
Luftfilter^M
filtro^M de aire^M

diesel engine
moteur^M diesel
Dieselmotor^M
motor^M diésel

exhaust pipe
tuyau^M d'échappement^M
Auspuffrohr^N
tubo^M de escape^M

cab
cabine^F
Führerkabine^F
cabina^F

blade lift cylinder
vérin^M de levage^M de la lame^F
Schildhubzylinder^M
cilindro^M del elevador^M de la pala^F

sprocket wheel
barbotin^M
Antriebsrad^N
rueda^F catalina

blade
lame^F
Planierschild^N
pala^F

ripper cylinder
vérin^M de défonceuse^F
Aufreißerzylinder^M
cilindro^M de elevación^F del zanco^M

cutting edge
bord^M tranchant
Schneidkante^F
cuchilla^F de corte^M

shank protector
sabot^M de protection^F
Reißschenkelschutz^M
protector^M del zanco^M

frame push
bras^M du longeron^M
Schubrahmen^M
chasis^M de empuje^M

track
chenille^F
Gleiskette^F
oruga^F

ripper tip
pointe^F de dent^F
Aufreißerspitze^F
pico^M del zanco^M

track idler
roue^F folle
Spannrad^N
rueda^F guía^F

track roller frame
longeron^M de chenille^F
Kettenlaufwerkrahmen^M
bastidor^M de los rodillos^M

ripper tooth
dent^F de défonceuse^F
Aufreißerzahn^M
diente^M del zanco^M

blade
lame^F
Planierschaufel^F
pala^F

tracklaying tractor
tracteur^M à chenilles^F
Gleiskettenschlepper^M
tractor^M de orugas^F

ripper
défonceuse^F
Aufreißer^M
zanco^M

SCRAPER
DÉCAPEUSE^F
SCHRAPPER^M
RASPADOR^M

steering cylinder
vérin^M de direction^F
Lenkzylinder^M
cilindro^M de dirección^F

gooseneck
col-de-cygne^M
Schwanenhals^M
cuello^M de ganso^M

ejector
éjecteur^M
Auswerfer^M
eyector^M

draught tube
palonnier^M
Saugrohr^N
barra^F de arrastre^M

draught arm
brancard^M
Saugarm^M
brazo^M de arrastre^M

skip
benne^F
Schürfkübel^M
contenedor^M

cutting edge
lame^F racleuse
Schneidkante^F
cuchilla^F de corte^M

tractor engine
tracteur^M-remorqueur^M
Traktormotor^M
motor^M

GRADER
NIVELEUSE^F
STRASSENHOBEL^M
NIVELADORA^F

blade lifting mechanism
mécanisme^M de levage^M de la lame^F
Scharhubvorrichtung^F
mecanismo^M de elevación^F de la pala^F

cab
cabine^F
Führerkabine^F
cabina^F

exhaust stack
cheminée^F d'échappement^M
Auspuffrohr^N
tubo^M de escape^M

overhead frame
poutre^F-châssis^M
obenliegender Rahmen^M
chasis^M delantero

engine
moteur^M
Motor^M
motor^M

counterweight
contrepoids^M
Gegengewicht^N
contrapeso^M

driving wheels
roues^F motrices
Antriebsräder^N
ruedas^F de tracción^F

front axle
essieu^M avant
Vorderachse^F
eje^M delantero

turntable
cercle^M porte-lame^M
Schardrehkranz^M
corona^F rotatoria

blade
lame^F
Hobelschar^F
pala^F

front wheel
roue^F avant
Vorderrad^N
rueda^F delantera

blade rotation mechanism
mécanisme^M d'orientation^F de la lame^F
Schardrehvorrichtung^F
mecanismo^M de rotación^F de la cuchilla^F

hydraulic cylinder
vérin^M
Hydraulikzylinder^M
cilindro^M

HEAVY MACHINERY
MACHINERIE^F LOURDE
SCHWERMASCHINEN^F
MAQUINARIA^F PESADA

TIPPER TRUCK
CAMION^M-BENNE^F
HINTERKIPPER^M
CAMIÓN^M BASCULANTE

cab
cabine^F
Führerhaus^N
cabina^F

tipper body
benne^F basculante
Kippermulde^F
caja^F basculante

canopy
auvent^M
Stirnwand^F
cubierta^F protectora

diesel engine
moteur^M diesel
Dieselmotor^M
motor^M diésel

ladder
échelle^F
Leiter^F
escalerilla^F

rib
nervure^F
Verstärkungsrippe^F
cuaderna^F

frame
châssis^M
Rahmen^M
chasis^M

HYDRAULIC SHOVEL
PELLE^F HYDRAULIQUE
HYDRAULIK-HOCHLÖFFELBAGGER^M
PALA^F HIDRÁULICA

boom cylinder
vérin^M de la flèche^F
Auslegerzylinder^M
cilindro^M del elevador^M

boom
flèche^F
Ausleger^M
pluma^F

arm cylinder
vérin^M du bras^M
Baggerstielzylinder^M
cilindro^M del brazo^M

cab
cabine^F
Führerkabine^F
cabina^F

hinge pin
point^M d'articulation^F
Gelenk^N
perno^M de la bisagra^F

counterweight
contrepoids^M
Gegengewicht^N
contrapeso^M

arm
bras^M
Baggerstiel^M
brazo^M

diesel engine
moteur^M diesel
Dieselmotor^M
motor^M diésel

bucket cylinder
vérin^M du godet^M
Schaufelzylinder^M
cilindro^M del cucharón^M

pivot cab
tourelle^F
Schwenkbrückenstand^M
cabina^F giratoria

turntable
couronne^F d'orientation^F
Drehkranz^M
plato^M giratorio

frame
châssis^M
Rahmen^M
chasis^M

jack
stabilisateur^M
Heber^M
soporte^M del plano^M fijo

tooth
dent^F
Schaufelzahn^M
diente^M

digger bucket
godet^M chargeur
Baggerlöffel^M
cucharón^M excavador

MATERIAL HANDLING
MANUTENTION^F
LASTENFORTBEWEGUNG^F
MANEJO^M DE MATERIALES^M

TOWER CRANE
GRUE^F À TOUR^F
TURMKRAN^M
GRÚA^F TORRE^F

jib tie
tirant^M
Auslegerseil^N
tirante^M del pescante^M

travelling crab
chariot^M
Laufkatze^F
montacargas^M

jib
flèche^F
Ausleger^M
pescante^M

counterjib ballast
contrepoids^M
Gegenauslegerballast^M
contrapeso^M

crab pulley
poulie^F de chariot^M
Laufkatzenrolle^F
polea^F del montacargas^M

counterjib
contre-flèche^F
Gegenausleger^M
contrapluma^F

hoisting rope
câble^M de levage^M
Aufzugseil^N
cable^M de elevación^F

operator's cab
cabine^F de commande^F
Kranführerkabine^F
cabina^F de control^M

hoisting block
treuil^M de levage^M
Hubwinde^F
garrucha^F montacarga

tower mast
tour^F
Turmmast^M
torre^F

hook
crochet^M
Haken^M
gancho^M

counterweight
lest^M
Gegengewicht^N
contrapeso^M

crane runway
chemin^M de roulement^M
Kranbahn^F
riel^M de rodamiento^M

TRUCK CRANE
GRUE^F SUR PORTEUR^M
FAHRKRAN^M
GRÚA^F MÓVIL^M

elevating cylinder
vérin^M de dressage^M
Hubzylinder^M
cilindro^M elevador

telescopic boom
flèche^F télescopique
ausfahrbarer Baum^M
brazo^M telescópico

jack
stabilisateur^M
Stützarm^M
estabilizador^M

GANTRY CRANE
PORTIQUE^M
LAUFKRAN^M
GRÚA^F DE PÓRTICO^M

hoisting system
appareil^M de levage^M
Hubvorrichtung^F
sistema^M de elevación^F

jib
avant-bec^M
Ausleger^M
pescante^M

tower
pied^M
Turm^M
torre^F

running track
piste^F de roulement^M
Laufschiene^F
riel^M

FORKLIFT TRUCK
CHARIOT^M ÉLÉVATEUR
GABELSTAPLER^M
MONTACARGAS^M DE HORQUILLA^F

mast
mât^M
Führungsständer^M
mástil^M

crosshead
tête^F du vérin^M de levage^M
Kreuzkopf^M
cruceta^F de cabeza^F

lifting chain
chaîne^F de levage^M
Hubkette^F
cadena^F de elevación^F

carriage
tablier^M
Träger^M
portahorquilla^M

fork
bras^M de fourche^F
Gabel^F
horquilla^F

forks
fourches^F
Gabeln^F
horquillas^F

overhead guard
toit^M de protection^F
Schutzdach^N
guarda^F de protección^F superior

manœuvring lever
levier^M de manœuvre^F
Bedienhebel^M
palanca^F de maniobras^F

hydraulic system
système^M hydraulique
Hydraulik^F
sistema^M hidráulico

engine
moteur^M
Motor^M
motor^M

frame
châssis^M
Rahmen^M
chasis^M

WING PALLET
PALETTE^F À AILES^F
RÜCKSPRUNGPALETTE^F
TARIMA^F CON ALAS^F

top deckboard
plancher^M supérieur
obere Vertäfelung^F
plataforma^F

stringer
entretoise^F
Träger^M
larguerillo^M

entry
entrée^F
Einfahröffnung^F
entrada^F

double-decked pallet
palette^F à double face^F
Doppeldeck-Flachpalette^F
tarima^F de plataforma^F doble

bottom deckboard
plancher^M inférieur
untere Vertäfelung^F
plataforma^F inferior

BOX PALLET
PALETTE^F-CAISSE^F
GITTERBOXPALETTE^F
TARIMA^F DE CAJA^F

side
paroi^F
Seitenteil^N
costado^M

pallet
palette^F
Palette^F
tarima^F

single-decked pallet
palette^F à simple face^F
Einfachdeck-Flachpalette^F
tarima^F de plataforma^F sencilla

block
support^M
Klotz^M
soporte^M

half-side
demi-panneau^M
Halbseite^F
medio lado^M

HYDRAULIC PALLET TRUCK
GERBEUR[M]
HYDRAULISCHER PALETTENHUBWAGEN[M]
MONTACARGAS[M] HIDRÁULICO DE TARIMA[F]

pallet truck
transpalette[F] manuel
Palettenhubwagen[M]
carretilla[F] hidráulica

manœuvring lever
levier[M] de manœuvre[F]
Bedienhebel[M]
palanca[F] de maniobras[F]

mast
mât[M]
Führungsständer[M]
mástil[M]

steering lever
levier[M] de conduite[F]
Lenkhebel[M]
palanca[F] de dirección[F]

barrow
diable[M]
Sackkarren[M]
carretilla[F]

hydraulic cylinder
vérin[M] hydraulique
Hydraulikzylinder[M]
cilindro[M] hidráulico

forks
fourches[F]
Gabeln[F]
horquillas[F]

solid rubber tyre
bandage[M] de roue[F] caoutchoutée
Vollgummirad[M]
llanta[F] maciza

stabilizing leg
longeron[M] stabilisateur
Stabilisator[M]
barra[F] estabilizadora

steering axle
essieu[M] directeur
Lenkachse[F]
eje[M] de dirección[F]

frame
châssis[M]
Rahmen[M]
chasis[M]

roller
roulette[F]
Rolle[F]
rueda[F]

platform pallet truck
chariot[M] à palette[F]
Flachpalettenwagen[M]
plataforma[F] hidráulica

platform trolley
chariot[M] à plateau[M]
Handwagen[M]
plataforma[F] móvil

SCHWERMASCHINEN
MAQUINARIA PESADA

HEAVY MACHINERY
ENGINS ET MACHINES

SUMMARY

WAFFEN
ARMAS

WEAPONS
ARMES

STONE AGE WEAPONS
ARMES^F DE L'ÂGE^M DE PIERRE^F
WAFFEN^F IN DER STEINZEIT^F
ARMAS^F DE LA EDAD^F DE PIEDRA^F

polished stone hand axe
hache^F en pierre^F polie
polierter Steinfaustkeil^M
hacha^F de piedra^F pulida

flint arrowhead
pointe^F de flèche^F en silex^M
Pfeilspitze^F aus Feuerstein^M
punta^F de flecha^F de pedernal^M

flint knife
couteau^M en silex^M
Messer^N aus Feuerstein^M
cuchillo^M de pedernal^M

WEAPONS IN THE AGE OF THE ROMANS
ARMES^F DE L'ÉPOQUE^F ROMAINE
WAFFEN^F IN DER RÖMERZEIT^F
ARMAS^F DEL IMPERIO^M ROMANO

GALLIC WARRIOR
GUERRIER^M GAULOIS
GALLISCHER KRIEGER^M
GUERRERO^M GALO

ROMAN LEGIONARY
LÉGIONNAIRE^M ROMAIN
RÖMISCHER LEGIONÄR^M
LEGIONARIO^M ROMANO

helmet
casque^M
Helm^M
casco^M

crest
cimier^M
Helmbusch^M
penacho^M

shield
bouclier^M
Schild^M
escudo^M

cuirass
cuirasse^F
Küraß^M
loriga^F

gladius
glaive^M
Kurzschwert^N
espada^F

breeches
braies^F
Hose^F
pantalones^M

tunic
tunique^F
Tunika^F
túnica^F

javelin
javelot^M
Lanze^F
jabalina^F

shield
bouclier^M
Schild^M
escudo^M

spear
lance^F
Speer^M
lanza^F

sandal
sandale^F
Sandale^F
sandalia^F

WEAPONS
ARMES

WAFFEN
ARMAS

791

armet
armet^M
Helm^M
yelmo^M

vision slit
fente^F de vision^F
Sehschlitz^M
ranura^F de visión^F

pauldron
épaulière^F
Vorderflug^M
espaldarón^M

beaver
mentonnière^F
Kinnreff^N
barbote^M

breastplate
plastron^M
Bruststück^N
peto^M

rerebrace
brassard^M
Oberarmschiene^F
brafonera^F

skirt
braconnière^F
Vorderschürze^F
faldar^M

couter
cubitière^F
Armkachel^F
codal^M

tasset
tassette^F
Bauchreifen^M
escarcela^F

vambrace
canon^M d'avant-bras^M
Unterarmschiene^F
avambrazo^M

gauntlet
gantelet^M
Panzerhandschuh^M
guantelete^M

chain mail
cotte^F de mailles^F
Panzerschurz^M
cota^F de malla^F

poleyn
genouillère^F
Kniebuckel^M
rodillera^F

cuisse
cuissard^M
Diechling^M
quijote^M

greave
grève^F
Beinröhre^F
greba^F

sabaton
soleret^M
Bärlatsch^M
escarpe^M

poulaine
poulaine^F
Schnabel^M
escarpín^M

comb
crête^F
Scheitelstück^N
crestón^M

visor
visière^F
Visier^N
visera^F

skull
timbre^M
Helmglocke^F
celada^F

nose
nasal^M
Nase^F
nasal^M

brow reinforce
frontal^M
Stirn^F
frontal^M

ventail
ventail^M
Atemlöcher^N
ventalle^M

gorget
gorgerin^M
Halsberge^F
gola^F

beaver
mentonnière^F
Kinnreff^N
babera^F

BOWS AND CROSSBOW
ARCS^M ET ARBALÈTE^F
BOGEN^M UND ARMBRUST^F
ARCOS^M Y BALLESTA^F

**BOW
ARC^M
BOGEN^M
ARCO^M**

upper limb
branche^F supérieure
oberer Arm^M
rama^F superior

back
dos^M
Bogen^M
dorso^M

handle
poignée^F
Handgriff^M
empuñadura^F

bowstring
corde^F
Bogensehne^F
cuerda^F

nock
encoche^F
Nocke^F
muesca^F

lower limb
branche^F inférieure
unterer Arm^M
rama^F inferior

modern bow
arc^M moderne
moderner Bogen^M
arco^M moderno

arrow
flèche^F
Pfeil^M
flecha^F

bow
arc^M
Bügel^M
arco^M

**CROSSBOW
ARBALÈTE^F
ARMBRUST^F
BALLESTA^F**

groove
rainure^F
Rinne^F
canal^M

stirrup
étrier^M
Steigbügel^M
estribera^F

nut
noix^F
Nuß^F
nuez^F

tiller
arbrier^M
Abzugstange^F
cureña^F

pulley
poulie^F
Winde^F
polea^F

crank
manivelle^F
Drehschwengel^M
manivela^F

trigger
détente^F
Abzug^M
gatillo^M

pulley block
moufle^F
Rollkloben^M
cierre^M de polea^F

bolt
carreau^M d'arbalète^F
Bolzen^M
flecha^F

bowstring
corde^F
Bogensehne^F
cuerda^F

**WEAPONS
ARMES**

**WAFFEN
ARMAS**

THRUSTING AND CUTTING WEAPONS
ARMES^F BLANCHES
HIEB- UND STICHWAFFEN^F
ARMAS^F CORTANTES Y DE ESTOCADA^F

sabre
sabre^M
Säbel^M
sable^M

rapier
rapière^F
Rapier^N
espadín^M

broadsword
épée^F à deux mains^F
beidhändiges Schwert^N
espada^F de dos manos^F

stiletto
stylet^M
Stilett^N
estilete^M

poniard
poignard^M
Dolch^M
puñal^M

dagger
dague^F
Dolch^M
daga^F

machete
machette^F
Machete^F
machete^M

commando knife
couteau^M de combat^M
Kampfmesser^N
cuchillo^M de combate^M

hilted bayonet
baïonnette^F à poignée^F
Messerbayonett^N
bayoneta^F con empuñadura^F

fixed bayonet
baïonnette^F incorporée
aufgepflanztes Bayonett^N
bayoneta^F integral

plug bayonet
baïonnette^F à manche^M
Spundbayonett^N
bayoneta^F de mango^M

socket bayonet
baïonnette^F à douille^F
Tüllenbayonett^N
bayoneta^F de cubo^M

ARQUEBUS
ARQUEBUSE*F*
ARKEBUSE*F*
ARCABUZ*M*

ball
balle*F*
Kugel*F*
bala*F*

ramrod
baguette*F*
Ladestock*M*
cargador*M*

FLINTLOCK
PLATINE*F* À SILEX*M*
STEINSCHLOSS*N*
PEDERNAL*M*

powder flask
poire*F* à poudre*F*
Pulverhorn*N*
cebador*M*

steel
batterie*F*
Stahl*M*
eslabón*M*

pan cover
couvre-bassinet*M*
Pfanndeckel*M*
cubrecazoleta*F*

cock
chien*M*
Hahn*M*
martillo*M*

flint
silex*M*
Feuerstein*M*
pedernal*M*

steel spring
ressort*M* de batterie*F*
Stahlfeder*F*
resorte*M* del eslabón*M*

pan
bassinet*M*
Pfanne*F*
cazoleta*F*

trigger
détente*F*
Abzug*M*
gatillo*M*

SUBMACHINE GUN
PISTOLET*M* MITRAILLEUR*M*
MASCHINENPISTOLE*F*
METRALLETA*F*

front sight
guidon*M*
Korn*N*
punto*M* de mira*F*

cartridge chamber
boîte*F* de culasse*F*
Patronenkammer*F*
caja*F* del cerrojo*M*

rear sight
hausse*F*
Kimme*F*
alza*F*

barrel
canon*M*
Rohr*N*
cañón*M*

magazine catch
verrou*M* de chargeur*M*
Magazinhalter*M*
retén*M* del cargador*M*

magazine
chargeur*M*
Magazin*N*
cargador*M*

trigger guard
pontet*M*
Abzugbügel*M*
guardamonte*M*

trigger
détente*F*
Abzug*M*
gatillo*M*

pistol grip
poignée*F*-pistolet*M*
Pistolengriff*M*
pistolete*M*

butt plate
crosse*F*
Rückschlaghinderer*M*
culata*F*

WEAPONS
ARMES

WAFFEN
ARMAS

795

AUTOMATIC RIFLE
FUSIL^M AUTOMATIQUE
AUTOMATISCHES GEWEHR^N
FUSIL^M AUTOMÁTICO

front sight housing
protège-guidon^M
Kornhalter^M mit Korn^N
punto^M de mira^F

barrel jacket
manchon^M de refroidissement^M
Kühlmantel^M für den Lauf^M
manguito^M de enfriamiento^M

ejection port
fenêtre^F d'éjection^F
Hülsenauswurf^M
ventana^F de eyección^F

cartridge chamber
boîte^F de culasse^F
Patronenkammer^F
caja^F del cerrojo^M

barrel
canon^M
Rohr^N
cañón^M

rear sight
hausse^F
Kimme^F
alza^F

bolt assist mechanism
mécanisme^M d'assistance^F de la culasse^F
Schlagbolzenmechanismus^M
mecanismo^M asistido de descarga^F

charging handle
levier^M d'armement^M
Durchladegriff^M
palanca^F del cerrojo^M

flash hider
cache-flammes^M
Feuerdämpfer^M
cubrellama^M

handguard
garde-main^M
Handschutz^M
guardamano^M

trigger
détente^F
Abzug^M
gatillo^M

pistol grip
poignée^F-pistolet^M
Pistolengriff^M
pistolete^M

butt
crosse^F
Schulterstütze^F
culata^F

magazine
chargeur^M
Magazin^N
cargador^M

safety catch
verrou^M de sûreté^F
Sicherung^F
seguro^M

LIGHT MACHINE GUN
FUSIL^M MITRAILLEUR^M
LEICHTES MASCHINENGEWEHR^N
FUSIL^M AMETRALLADOR

flash hider
cache-flammes^M
Feuerdämpfer^M
cubrellama^M

barrel jacket
manchon^M de refroidissement^M
Kühlmantel^M für den Lauf^M
manguito^M de enfriamiento^M

rear sight
hausse^F
Kimme^F
alza^F

front sight housing
protège-guidon^M
Kornhalter^M mit Korn^N
punto^M de mira^F

carrying handle
poignée^F de transport^M
Tragegriff^M
empuñadura^F

cover
couvre-culasse^M
Deckel^M
cubierta^F

barrel
canon^M
Rohr^N
cañón^M

gas cylinder
cylindre^M des gaz^M
Gaskolben^M
cilindro^M del gas^M

trigger
détente^F
Abzug^M
gatillo^M

operating rod
tige^F de manœuvre^F
Schlagbolzen^M
barra^F de operación^F

bipod
bipied^M
Zweibein^N
bípode^M

pistol grip
poignée^F-pistolet^M
Pistolengriff^M
pistolete^M

butt
crosse^F
Schulterstütze^F
culata^F

WEAPONS
ARMES

WAFFEN
ARMAS

REVOLVER
REVOLVER[M]
REVOLVER[M]
REVÓLVER[M]

hammer
chien[M]
Hammer[M]
percutor[M]

barrel
canon[M]
Rohr[N]
cañón[M]

front sight
guidon[M]
Korn[N]
punto[M] de mira[F]

muzzle
bouche[F]
Mündung[F]
boca[F]

cylinder
barillet[M]
Trommel[F]
tambor[M]

trigger guard
pontet[M]
Abzugbügel[M]
guardamonte[M]

butt
crosse[F]
Kolben[M]
culata[F]

trigger
détente[F]
Abzug[M]
gatillo[M]

PISTOL
PISTOLET[M]
PISTOLE[F]
PISTOLA[F]

hammer
chien[M]
Hammer[M]
percutor[M]

rear sight
cran[M] de mire[F]
Kimme[F]
mira[F]

barrel
canon[M]
Rohr[N]
cañón[M]

front sight
guidon[M]
Korn[N]
punto[M] de mira[F]

magazine
chargeur[M]
Magazin[N]
cargador[M]

slide
glissière[F]
Schieber[M]
guía[F]

trigger guard
pontet[M]
Abzugbügel[M]
guardamonte[M]

trigger
détente[F]
Abzug[M]
gatillo[M]

magazine base
semelle[F] de chargeur[M]
Magazinabschluß[M]
base[F] del cargador[M]

butt
crosse[F]
Kolben[M]
culata[F]

magazine catch
arrêtoir[M] de chargeur[M]
Magazinhalter[M]
seguro[M] del cargador[M]

cartridge
cartouche[F]
Patrone[F]
cartucho[M]

**WEAPONS
ARMES**

**WAFFEN
ARMAS**

797

HUNTING WEAPONS
ARMES^F DE CHASSE^F
JAGDWAFFEN^F
ARMAS^F DE CAZA^F

CARTRIDGE (RIFLE)
CARTOUCHE^F (CARABINE^F)
PATRONE^F (GEWEHR^N)
CARTUCHO^M DE RIFLE^M

bullet
balle^F
Kugel^F
bala^F

nose
pointe^F
Spitze^F
nariz^F

core
noyau^M
Kern^M
núcleo^M

jacket
chemise^F
Mantel^M
revestimiento^M

case
douille^F
Hülse^F
casquillo^M

propellant
poudre^F
Treibladung^F
explosivo^M

primer
amorce^F
Zündhütchen^N
fulminante^M

cup
culot^M
Amboß^M
culote^M

RIFLE (RIFLED BORE)
CARABINE^F (CANON^M RAYÉ)
GEWEHR^N (GEZOGENER LAUF^M)
RIFLE^M

hammer
chien^M
Hammer^M
percutor^M

breechblock
bloc^M de culasse^F
Verschlußstück^N
bloque^M de cierre^M de la recámara^F

telescopic sight
lunette^F de visée^F
Zielfernrohr^N
mira^F telescópica

pistol grip
poignée^F
Kolbenhals^M
empuñadura^F

stock
crosse^F
Schäftung^F
culata^F

rear sight
hausse^F
Kimme^F
alza^F

trigger guard
pontet^M
Abzugbügel^M
guardamonte^M

lever
levier^M
Bügelhebel^M
palanca^F

trigger
détente^F
Abzug^M
gatillo^M

butt plate
plaque^F de couche^F
Rückschlaghinderer^M
cantonera^F

front sight
guidon^M
Korn^N
punto^M de mira^F

muzzle
bouche^F
Mündung^F
boca^F

ventilated rib
bande^F ventilée
Laufschiene^F
banda^F de ventilación^F

barrel
canon^M
Rohr^N
cañón^M

forearm
fût^M
Vorderschaft^M
caña^F

CARTRIDGE (SHOTGUN)
CARTOUCHE^F (FUSIL^M)
PATRONE^F (SCHROTFLINTE^F)
CARTUCHO^M DE ESCOPETA^F

crimping
sertissage^M
Faltverschluß^M
doblez^M hacia el interior^M

pellets
plombs^M
Schrot^M
carga^F de perdigones^M

base
culot^M
Boden^M
culote^M

primer
amorce^F
Zündhütchen^N
fulminante^M

plastic case
douille^F de plastique^M
Plastikhülse^F
revestimiento^M

wad
bourre^F
Pfropf^M
taco^M

charge
poudre^F
Ladung^F
explosivo^M

front sight
guidon^M
Korn^N
punto^M de mira^F

muzzle
bouche^F
Mündung^F
boca^F

barrel
canon^M
Rohr^N
cañón^M

SHOTGUN (SMOOTH-BORE)
FUSIL^M (CANON^M LISSE)
SCHROTFLINTE^F (GLATTER LAUF^M)
ESCOPETA^F

pistol grip
poignée^F
Pistolengriff^M
empuñadura^F

hammer
chien^M
Hammer^M
percutor^M

stock
crosse^F
Schäftung^F
culata^F

butt plate
plaque^F de couche^F
Rückschlaghinderer^M
cantonera^F

breechblock
bloc^M de culasse^F
Verschlußstück^N
bloque^M de cierre^M de recámara^F

trigger
détente^F
Abzug^M
gatillo^M

trigger guard
pontet^M
Abzugbügel^M
guardamonte^M

SEVENTEENTH-CENTURY CANNON
CANON^M DU XVIIe SIÈCLE^M
KANONE^F AUS DEM 17. JAHRHUNDERT^N
CAÑÓN^M DEL SIGLO^M XVII

MUZZLE-LOADING CANNON
BOUCHE^F À FEU^M
VORDERLADE-GESCHÜTZ^N
CAÑÓN^M DE AVANCARGA^F

button
bouton^M de culasse^F
Knopf^M
botón^M de la culata^F

chase
volée^F
langes Feld^N
caña^F

muzzle
bouche^F
Mündung^F
boca^F

base ring
plate-bande^F de culasse^F
Bodengesims^N
plaza^F de la culata^F

second reinforce
second renfort^M
zweiter Ring^M
segundo refuerzo^M

vent
lumière^F
Zündloch^N
cazoleta^F

first reinforce
renfort^M de culasse^F
erster Ring^M
refuerzo^M de la culata^F

astragal
astragale^M
Band^N
astrágalo^M

trunnion
tourillon^M
Lagerzapfen^M
gorrón^M

wheel
roue^F
Rad^N
rueda^F

cheek
flasque^M
Lafettenwand^F
gualdera^F

wedge
cale^F
Keil^M
calce^M

barrel
tube^M
Rohr^N
tubo^M

carriage
affût^M
Fahrgestell^N
cureña^F

WAFFEN
ARMAS

WEAPONS
ARMES

CROSS SECTION OF A MUZZLE-LOADING CANNON
COUPE^F D'UNE BOUCHE^F À FEU^M
QUERSCHNITT^M EINER VORDERLADUNG^F
CORTE^M TRANSVERSAL DE UN CAÑÓN^M DE AVANCARGA^F

vent
lumière^F
Zündloch^N
cazoleta^F

shot
boulet^M
Geschoß^N
bala^F

bore
âme^F
Rohr^N
alma^F

wad
bourre^F
Pfropf^M
taco^M

powder chamber
chambre^F à poudre^F
Pulverkammer^F
cámara^F de la pólvora^F

FIRING ACCESSORIES
ACCESSOIRES^M DE MISE^F À FEU^M
GESCHOSSZUBEHÖR^N
ACCESORIOS^M DE DISPARO^M

rammer
refouloir^M
Ladestock^M
atacador^M

linstock
boutefeu^M
Luntenstock^M
botafuego^M

worm
tire-bourre^M
Spirale^F
sacatrapos^M

ladle
lanterne^F
Ladeschaufel^F
cucharón^M

sponge
écouvillon^M
Schwamm^M
escobillón^M

PROJECTILES
PROJECTILES^M
PROJEKTILE^N
PROYECTILES^M

bar shot
boulet^M ramé
Stangenkugel^F
bala^F de barra^F

grapeshot
grappe^F de raisin^M
Kartätsche^F
metralla^F

solid shot
boulet^M
Vollgeschoß^N
bala^F sólida

hollow shot
boulet^M creux
Hohlladungsgeschoß^N
bala^F con perdigones^M

MODERN HOWITZER
OBUSIER^M MODERNE
MODERNE HAUBITZE^F
OBÚS^M MODERNO

recuperator cylinder
cylindre^M récupérateur
Vorholer^M
cilindro^M de recuperación^F

elevating arc
crémaillère^F de pointage^M
Zahnbogen^M
arco^M de elevación

recoil sleigh
glissoire^F de recul^M
Rohrrücklauf^M
patín^M de retroceso^M

breechblock operating lever assembly
levier^M de manœuvre^F de la culasse^F
Bedienungshebel^M für Verschlußblock^M
palanca^F de accionamiento^M de la recámara^F

recuperator cylinder front head
tête^F avant du cylindre^M récupérateur
Vorholervorderteil^N
cabeza^F delantera del cilindro^M
de recuperación^F

breechblock
culasse^F
Verschlußblock^M
bloque^M de cierre^M de la recámara^F

sliding breech
manchon^M de culasse^F
Schubkurbelverschluß^M
placa^F de la culata^F

firing shaft
arbre^M de mise^F à feu^M
Schlagbolzenschaft^M
eje^M de tiro^M

barrel
canon^M
Rohr^N
cañón^M

locking ring
cercle^M de verrouillage^M
Verschlußring^M
anillo^M de bloqueo^M

cradle
berceau^M
Wiege^F
cuña^F

carriage
affût^M
Fahrgestell^N
afuste^M

elevating handwheel
manivelle^F de pointage^M en hauteur^F
Handrad^N zur Höhenverstellung^F
manivela^F de elevación^F

firing lanyard
cordon^M tire-feu^M
Abzugsleine^F
cuerda^F de disparo^M

equilibrator
équilibreur^M
Gewichtsausgleicher^M
estabilizador^M

MORTAR
MORTIER[M]
MÖRSER[M]
MORTEROS[M]

MODERN MORTAR
MORTIER[M] MODERNE
MODERNER MÖRSER[M]
MORTERO[M] MODERNO

muzzle
bouche[F]
Mündung[F]
boca[F]

sight
appareil[M] de pointage[M]
Richtaufsatz[M]
mira[F]

elevating handle
manivelle[F] de pointage[M] en hauteur[F]
Höheneinstellhebel[M]
manivela[F] de elevación[F]

traversing handle
manivelle[F] de pointage[M] en direction[F]
Richtkurbel[F]
manivela[F] de dirección[F]

tube
tube[M]
Rohr[N]
tubo[M]

bipod
bipied[M]
Zweibein[N]
bípode[M]

baseplate
plaque[F] de base[F]
Grundplatte[F]
espolón[M]

drawbar
barre[F] d'attelage[M]
Zugstange[F]
barra[F] de tracción[F]

drawbar lock
verrou[M] de barre[F] d'attelage[M]
Zugstangenverschluß[M]
seguro[M] de la barra[F] de tracción[F]

towing eye
lunette[F]
Auge[N]
argolla[F] de remolque[M]

SEVENTEENTH-CENTURY MORTAR
MORTIER[M] DU XVIIe SIÈCLE[M]
MÖRSER[M] AUS DEM 17. JAHRHUNDERT[N]
MORTERO[M] DEL SIGLO[M] XVII

trail
crosse[F]
Schleppstange[F]
gualdera[F]

lifting handle
poignée[F] de soulèvement[M]
Hebegriff[M]
asa[F] de levantamiento[M]

spade
bêche[F]
Spaten[M]
pala[F]

float
flotteur[M]
Schwimmer[M]
flotador[M]

HAND GRENADE
GRENADE^F À MAIN^F
HANDGRANATE^F
GRANADA^F DE MANO^F

lead ball
bille^F de plomb^M
Bleikugel^F
bala^F de plomo^M

cover
tête^F
Mantel^M
cubierta^F

tape
ruban^M
Band^N
cinta^F

safety cap
capuchon^M de sûreté^F
Sicherungskappe^F
casquete^M de seguridad^F

fuse body
corps^M de la fusée^F
Zündergehäuse^N
espoleta^F

striker
percuteur^M
Schlagbolzen^M
percutor^M

spring
ressort^M
Feder^F
resorte^M

primer
amorce^F
Zündladung^F
cebador^M

detonator
détonateur^M
Sprengkapsel^F
detonador^M

bakelite® body
corps^M en bakélite®^F
Bakelitgehäuse^N
cuerpo^M de baquelita^F

bursting charge
charge^F explosive
Sprengladung^F
explosivo^M

base plug
bouchon^M de fermeture^F
Bodenstöpsel^M
culote^M

filling hole
bouchon^M de chargement^M
Fülloch^N
orificio^M de carga^F

BAZOOKA
BAZOOKA^M
PANZERFAUST^F
BAZUCA^F

tube
tube^M
Rohr^N
tubo^M

spring
ressort^M
Feder^F
resorte^M

rear sight
hausse^F
Kimme^F
alza^F

front sight
guidon^M
Korn^N
punto^M de mira^F

shoulder rest
épaulière^F
Schulterstütze^F
hombrera^F

front grip
poignée^F avant
vorderer Haltegriff^M
empuñadura^F delantera

RECOILLESS RIFLE
CANON^M SANS RECUL^M
RÜCKSTOSSFREIES GESCHÜTZ^N
FUSIL^M SIN RETROCESO

barrel
tube^M
Rohr^N
cañón^M

shoulder pad
épaulière^F
Schulterstütze^F
hombrera^F

firing mechanism
mécanisme^M de tir^M
Zündmechanismus^M
mecanismo^M de disparo^M

venturi fastening lever
levier^M de fixation^F de venturi^M
Feststellhebel^M für Venturidüse^F
palanca^F de fijación^F del venturi^M

front grip
poignée^F avant
vorderer Haltegriff^M
empuñadura^F delantera

trigger
détente^F
Abzug^M
gatillo^M

cocking lever
levier^M d'armement^M
Spannhebel^M
palanca^F de armar^F

anti-tank rocket
projectile^M antichar
panzerbrechendes Geschoß^N
bala^F antitanque

venturi
venturi^M
Venturidüse^F
venturi^M

TANK
CHAR^M D'ASSAUT^M
PANZER^M
TANQUE^M

gunner's sight
épiscope^M du tireur^M
Stand^M des Richtschützen^M
mira^F del tirador^M

antenna
antenne^F
Antenne^F
antena^F

machine gun
mitrailleuse^F
Maschinengewehr^N
ametralladora^F

commander's seat
poste^M de commandement^M
Kommandantenstand^M
asiento^M del comandante^M

periscopic sight
viseur^M périscopique
Rundblickperiskop^N
mira^F periscópica

ammunition stowage
casier^M à munitions^F
Munitionsbehälter^M
depósito^M de municiones^F

smoke bomb discharger
lance-pots^M fumigènes
Entschärfer^M für Rauchbomben^F
lanzador^M de bombas^F fumígenas

hatch
écoutille^F
Luke^F
escotilla^F

sprocket wheel
barbotin^M
Kettenrad^N
rueda^F motriz

driver's seat
poste^M de pilotage^M
Fahrerstand^M
asiento^M del piloto^M

engine
moteur^M
Motor^M
motor^M

fuel tank
réservoir^M à carburant^M
Treibstofftank^M
depósito^M del combustible^M

track shoe
chenille^F
Kettenschuh^M
zapata^F de la cadena^F

armoured plate
préblindage^M
Panzerplatte^F
placa^F blindada

armour
blindage^M
Panzer^M
blindaje^M

headlight
phare^M
Scheinwerfer^M
faro^M

track link
patin^M de chenille^F
Kettenplatte^F
patín^M de oruga^F

gun
canon^M
Geschützrohr^N
cañón^M

wheel
roue^F
Laufrolle^F
rueda^F

turret
tourelle^F mobile
Panzerturm^M
torreta^F giratoria

fume extractor
dégageur^M de fumée^F
Rauchabsauger^M
extractor^M de humo^M

SUBMARINE
SOUS-MARIN^M
UNTERSEEBOOT^N
SUBMARINO^M

propulsion machinery control room
poste^M de conduite^F de la propulsion^F
Kontrollraum^M für Antriebswerke^N
sala^F de control^M de máquinas^F de propulsión^F

upper rudder
gouvernail^M de direction^F
oberes Ruder^N
timón^M superior

pressurized chamber
sas^M d'accès^M arrière
Luftdruckkammer^F
cámara^F de compresión^F

steam generator
générateur^M de vapeur^F
Dampfgenerator^M
generador^M de vapor^M

propeller
hélice^F
Schraube^F
hélice^F

emergency electric motor
moteur^M électrique auxiliaire
Ersatzelektromotor^M
motor^M eléctrico de emergencia^F

turbogenerator
turbo-alternateur^M
Turboalternator^M
alternador^M de turbina^F

engine room
chambre^F des machines^F
Maschinenraum^M
sala^F de máquinas^F

diving plane
barre^F de plongée^F
Steuerbordtiefenruder^N
timón^M de inmersión^F

main electric motor
moteur^M électrique principal
Hauptelektromotor^M
motor^M eléctrico principal

electricity generating room
compartiment^M de la production^F d'électricité^F
Elektrizitätsraum^M
sala^F de producción^F de electricidad^F

nuclear boiler room
compartiment^M du réacteur^M
Kernreaktorraum^M
sala^F de la caldera^F nuclear

reactor
réacteur^M
Reaktor^M
reactor^M

radar antenna
antenne^F radar^M
Radarantenne^F
antena^F de radar^M

multipurpose antenna
antenne^F multifonction
Multifunktionsantenne^F
antena^F múltiple

attack periscope
périscope^M d'attaque^F
Angriffsperiskop^N
periscopio^M de ataque^M

conning tower
kiosque^M
Turm^M
torreta^F de mando^M

radio antenna
antenne^F radio^F
Funkantenne^F
antena^F de radio^F

computer room
salle^F des ordinateurs^M
Computerraum^M
sala^F de computación^F

navigation periscope
périscope^M de veille^F
Navigationsperiskop^N
periscopio^M de navegación^F

sail plane
gouvernail^M de plongée^F avant
Flügel^M des Kommandoturms^M
timón^M de buceo^M

torpedo room
chambre^F des torpilles^F
Torpedoraum^M
sala^F de torpedos^M

officers' quarters
logement^M des officiers^M
Offiziersquartiere^N
camarotes^M de los oficiales^M

galley
cuisine^F
Kombüse^F
cocina^F

dining room
salle^F à manger
Speiseraum^M
comedor^M

firing tube
tube^M lance-torpilles^M
Torpedorohr^N
tubo^M de disparo^M

torpedo
torpille^F
Torpedo^M
torpedo^M

operation control room
poste^M de commandement^M
Operationszentrale^F
sala^F de control^M de operaciones^F

VHF antenna
antenneF VHF
VHF-AntenneF
antenaF VHF

anti-aircraft missile
missileM antiaérien
FlugabwehrraketeF
misilM antiaéreo

antimissile self-defence
autodéfenseF antimissile
FlugkörperabwehrF
autodefensaF antimisil

helicopter hangar
hangarM pour hélicoptèresM
HubschrauberhangarM
hangarM de helicópteroM

helicopter
hélicoptèreM
HubschrauberM
helicópteroM

WEAPONS
ARMES

WAFFEN
ARMAS

missile stowage
stockageM des missilesM
RaketendepotM
depósitoM de misilesM

officers' quarters
logementM des officiersM
OffiziersquartiereM
camarotesM de los oficialesM

helicopter flight deck
hélisurfaceF
HubschrauberlandeplattformF
plataformaF de vueloM del helicópteroM

propellers
hélicesF
SchraubenF
hélicesF

shaft
arbreM
WelleF
ejeM

target detection radar
radar^M de détection^F
Radar^N zur Zielfolgung^F
radar^M de detección^F de blancos^M

surface surveillance radar
radar^M de veille^F de surface^F
Überwachungsradar^N
radar^M de vgilancia^F de superficie^F

telecommunication antenna
antenne^F de télécommunication^F
Telekommunikationsantenne^F
antena^F de telecomunicaciones^F

air search radar
radar^M de surveillance^F aérienne
Luftzielsuchradar^N
radar^M aéreo

turret
tourelle^F
Geschützturm^M
torreta^F

decoy launcher
lance-leurres^M
Köderlauncher^M
disparador^M de señuelo^M

surface-to-subsurface missile
missile^M anti-sous-marin
Boden-Unterwasser-Flugkörper^M
misil^M antisubmarino

hull sonar
sonar^M de coque^F
Rumpfsonar^M
sonar^M del casco^M

sea-to-sea missile
missile^M mer^F-mer^F
See-See-Flugkörper^M
misil^M mar^M a mar^M

diesel engines
moteurs^M diesel
Dieselmotoren^M
motores^M diésel

ship's launch
vedette^F
Motorbeiboot^N
lancha^F de motor^M

antenna
antenne[F]
Antenne[F]
antena[F]

flight deck
pont[M] d'envol[M]
Flugdeck[N]
cubierta[F] de vuelo[M]

catapult
catapulte[F]
Katapult[N]
catapulta[F]

air navigation device
balise[F] de navigation[F] aérienne
Flugnavigationsvorrichtung[F]
aparato[M] de navegación[F] aérea

jet blast deflector
déflecteur[M] de jet[M]
Düsenstrahlablenkfläche[F]
deflector[M] de viento[M] de los aviones[M]

surface surveillance radar
radar[M] de veille[F] de surface[F]
Überwachungsradar[N]
radar[M] de vigilancia[F] de superficie[F]

communication antenna
antenne[F] de communication[F]
Telekommunikationsantenne[F]
antena[F] de comunicaciones[F]

height finder
altimètre[M]
Höhensucher[M]
buscador[M] de altura[F]

air control radar
radar[M] de contrôle[M] aérien
Radar[N] zur Luftüberwachung[F]
radar[M] de control[M] aéreo

control tower
tour[F] de contrôle[M]
Kontrollturm[M]
torre[F] de control[M]

bridge
passerelle[F]
Brücke[F]
puente[M] de mando[M]

air search radar
radar^M de surveillance^F aérienne
Luftzielsuchradar^N
radar^M de búsqueda^F aérea

landing radar
radar^M d'appontage^M
Landeradar^N
radar^M de aterrizaje^M

deck crane
grue^F de bord^M
Bordkran^M
grúa^F de la plataforma^F

main deck
hangar^M
Hauptdeck^N
cubierta^F principal

elevator
ascenseur^M
Aufzug^M
ascensor^M

jet engine test area
zone^F d'essai^M des réacteurs^M
Testbereich^M für Düsentriebwerke^N
zona^F de prueba^F de motores^M de aviones^M

arrester wire
brin^M d'arrêt^M
Fangseil^N
cable^M de frenado^M

missile launcher
lance-missiles^M
Raketenwerfer^M
lanzamisiles^M

runway
piste^F d'atterrissage^M
Rollbahn^F
pista^F

landing deck
pont^M d'appontage^M
Landedeck^N
cubierta^F de aterrizaje^M

radar antenna
antenne^F radar^M
Radarantenne^F
antena^F de radar^M

rudder
gouvernail^M de direction^F
Seitenruder^N
timón^M

fin
dérive^F
Flosse^F
aleta^F

parachute
parachute^M
Fallschirm^M
paracaídas^M

tailplane
stabilisateur^M
Stabilisierungsflosse^F
estabilizador^M

exhaust nozzle
tuyère^F d'éjection^F
Düse^F
tubo^M de escape^M

turbo-jet engine
turboréacteur^M
Turboluftstrahltriebwerk^N
turborreactor^M

air brake
aérofrein^M
Bremsklappe^F
aerofreno^M

trailing edge flap
volet^M de bord^M de fuite^F
hintere Flügelklappe^F
alerón^M de hipersustentación^F

wing
aile^F
Flügel^M
ala^F

fuel tank
réservoir^M à carburant^M
Treibstofftank^M
depósito^M de combustible^M

leading edge flap
volet^M de bord^M d'attaque^F
Nasenklappe^F
alerón^M de hipersustentación^F

main landing gear
train^M d'atterrissage^M principal
Hauptfahrwerk^N
tren^M de aterrizaje^M principal

wing box
caisson^M de voilure^F
Flügelkasten^M
cajón^M del plano^M de sustentación^F

flap hydraulic jack
vérin^M de commande^F de volet^M
hydraulischer Klappenheber^M
gato^M hidráulico del alerón^M de curvatura^F

tanker aircraft
ravitailleur^M
Tankerflugzeug^N
avión^M nodriza^F

in-flight refuelling probe
perche^F de ravitaillement^M
Luftbetankungsausleger^M
manguera^F de abastecimiento^M en vuelo^M

air-to-air missile
missile^M air^M-air^M
Luft-Luft-Flugkörper^M
misil^M aire^M aire^M

missile launch rail
rail^M de lancement^M de missile^M
Raketenschiene^F
riel^M de lanzamiento^M de proyectiles^M

canopy
verrière^F
Kabinenhaube^F
cúpula^F de la carlinga^F

ejector seat
siège^M éjectable
Schleudersitz^M
asiento^M de eyección^F

radar unit
système^M radar^M
Radaranlage^F
unidad^F del radar^M

radome
radôme^M
Radom^N
radomo^M

front landing gear
train^M d'atterrissage^M avant
Bugfahrwerk^N
tren^M de aterrizaje^M delantero

engine air inlet
entrée^F d'air^M du moteur^M
Triebwerklufteinlauf^M
toma^F de aire^M del motor^M

MISSILES
MISSILES^M
FLUGKÖRPER^M
PROYECTILES^M

STRUCTURE OF A MISSILE
STRUCTURE^F D'UN MISSILE^M
AUFBAU^M EINES FLUGKÖRPERS^M
ESTRUCTURA^F DE UN MISIL^M

battery
pile^F
Batterie^F
batería^F

actuator
servomoteur^M
Aktuator^M
actuador^M

pilot
pilote^M
Autopilot^M
guía^{MF}

warhead
charge^F militaire
Gefechtskopf^M
ojiva^F

rate gyro
gyroscope^M
Meßkreisel^M
grado^M de rotación^F

fixed winglet
empennage^M fixe
stabiler Flügel^M
aleta^F fija

proximity fuse
fusée^F de proximité^F
Abstandszünder^M
espoleta^F de proximidad^F

rocket motor
propulseur^M
Raketenantrieb^M
motor^M del proyectil

infrared homing head
autodirecteur^M infrarouge
Infrarot-Zielsuchkopf^M
cabeza^F dirigida por rayos^M infrarrojos

rudder
gouverne^F
Ruder^N
timón^M

fin
empennage^M
Flosse^F
estabilizador^M

PRINCIPAL TYPES OF MISSILE
PRINCIPAUX TYPES^M DE MISSILES^M
DIE WICHTIGSTEN FLUGKÖRPER^M
PRINCIPALES TIPOS^M DE MISILES^M

surface-to-air missile
missile^M sol^M-air^M
Boden-Luft-Flugkörper^M
misil^M tierra^F aire^M

air-to-air missile
missile^M air^M-air^M
Luft-Luft-Flugkörper^M
misil^M aire^M aire^M

anti-radar missile
missile^M antiradar
Radarabwehrflugkörper^M
misil^M antiradar

anti-ship missile
missile^M antinavire
Seezielflugkörper^M
misil^M antibuques

surface-to-subsurface missile
missile^M anti-sous-marin
Boden-Unterwasser-Flugkörper^M
misil^M antisubmarino

anti-tank missile
missile^M antichar
Panzerabwehrflugkörper^M
misil^M antitanque

air-to-surface missile
missile^M air^M-sol^M
Luft-Boden-Flugkörper^M
misil^M aire^M tierra^F

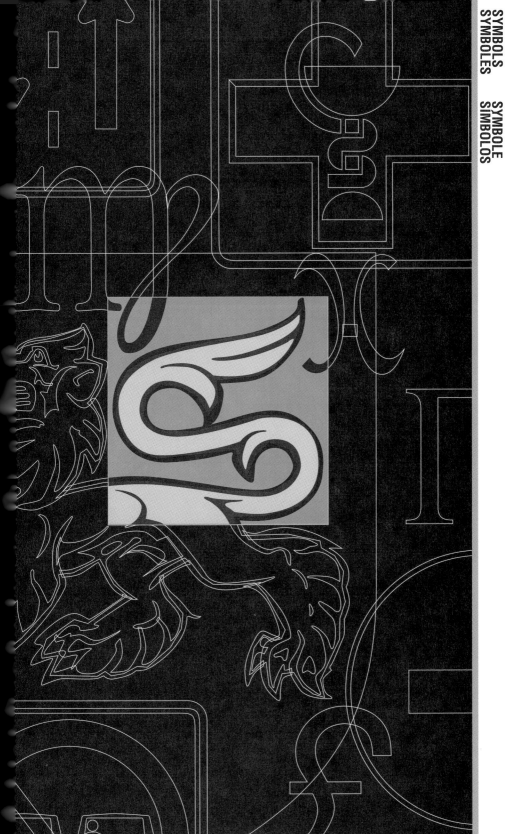

SUMMARY

SYMBOLE
SÍMBOLOS

SYMBOLS
SYMBOLES

HERALDRY
HÉRALDIQUE^F
HERALDIK^F
HERÁLDICA^F

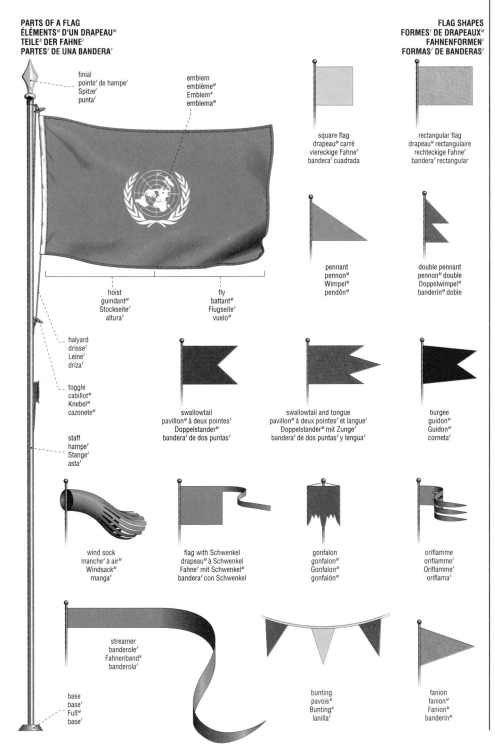

PARTS OF A FLAG
ÉLÉMENTS^M D'UN DRAPEAU^M
TEILE^N DER FAHNE^F
PARTES^F DE UNA BANDERA^F

finial
pointe^F de hampe^F
Spitze^F
punta^F

emblem
emblème^M
Emblem^N
emblema^M

hoist
guindant^M
Stockseite^F
altura^F

fly
battant^M
Flugseite^F
vuelo^M

halyard
drisse^F
Leine^F
driza^F

toggle
cabillot^M
Knebel^M
cazonete^M

staff
hampe^F
Stange^F
asta^F

wind sock
manche^F à air^M
Windsack^M
manga^F

flag with Schwenkel
drapeau^M à Schwenkel
Fahne^F mit Schwenkel^M
bandera^F con Schwenkel

gonfalon
gonfalon^M
Gonfalon^M
gonfalón^M

streamer
banderole^F
Fahnenband^N
banderola^F

base
base^F
Fuß^M
base^F

bunting
pavois^M
Bunting^N
lanilla^F

FLAG SHAPES
FORMES^F DE DRAPEAUX^M
FAHNENFORMEN^F
FORMAS^F DE BANDERAS^F

square flag
drapeau^M carré
viereckige Fahne^F
bandera^F cuadrada

rectangular flag
drapeau^M rectangulaire
rechteckige Fahne^F
bandera^F rectangular

pennant
pennon^M
Wimpel^M
pendón^M

double pennant
pennon^M double
Doppelwimpel^M
banderín^M doble

swallowtail
pavillon^M à deux pointes^F
Doppelstander^M
bandera^F de dos puntas^F

swallowtail and tongue
pavillon^M à deux pointes^F et langue^F
Doppelstander^M mit Zunge^F
bandera^F de dos puntas^F y lengua^F

burgee
guidon^M
Guidon^M
corneta^F

oriflamme
oriflamme^F
Oriflamme^F
oriflama^F

fanion
fanion^M
Fanion^M
banderín^M

SHIELD DIVISIONS
DIVISIONS_F_ **DE L'ÉCU**_M_
SCHILDPLÄTZE_M_
DIVISIONES_F_ **DE LOS ESCUDOS**_M_

dexter
dextre_F_
rechte Flanke_F_
tercio_M_ diestro

sinister
senestre_F_
linke Flanke_F_
tercio_M_ siniestro

dexter chief
canton_M_ dextre du chef_M_
rechtes Obereck_N_
cantón_M_ diestro del jefe_M_

sinister chief
canton_M_ senestre du chef_M_
linkes Obereck_N_
cantón_M_ siniestro del jefe_M_

chief
chef_M_
Schildhaupt_N_
jefe_M_

centre chief
point_M_ du chef_M_
Ort_N_
centro_M_ del jefe_M_

dexter flank
flanc_M_ dextre
rechte Hüftstelle_F_
flanco_M_ diestro

sinister flank
flanc_M_ senestre
linke Hüftstelle_F_
flanco_M_ siniestro

dexter base
canton_M_ dextre de la pointe_F_
rechtes Untereck_N_
cantón_M_ diestro de la punta_F_

centre point
centre_M_
Herzstelle_F_
corazón_M_

base
pointe_F_
Fußrand_M_
punta

sinister base
canton_M_ senestre de la pointe_F_
linkes Untereck_N_
cantón_M_ siniestro de la punta_F_

centre base
pointe_F_
Fußstelle_F_
centro_M_ de la punta_F_

EXAMPLES OF PARTITIONS
EXEMPLES_M_ **DE PARTITIONS**_F_
TEILUNGSBEISPIELE_N_
EJEMPLOS_M_ **DE PARTICIONES**_F_

per fess
coupé
geteilt
escudo_M_ cortado

per pale
parti
gespalten
escudo_M_ partido

per bend
tranché
schrägrechts geteilt
escudo_M_ tronchado

quarterly
écartelé
geviert
escudo_M_ acuartelado

EXAMPLES OF ORDINARIES
EXEMPLES_M_ **DE PIÈCES**_F_ **HONORABLES**
BEISPIELE_N_ **FÜR HEROLDSBILDER**_N_
EJEMPLOS_M_ **DE PIEZAS**_F_ **HONORABLES**

chief
chef_M_
Hauptrand_M_
jefe_M_

chevron
chevron_M_
Sparren_M_
cheurón_M_

pale
pal_M_
Pfahl_M_
palo_M_

cross
croix_F_
Kreuz_N_
cruz_F_

SYMBOLS
SYMBOLES

SYMBOLE
SÍMBOLOS

fleur-de-lis
fleur*F* de lis*M*
Lilie*F*
flor*F* de lis*F*

crescent
croissant*M*
Mond*M*
creciente*M*

lion passant
lion*M* passant
schreitender Löwe*M*
león*M* rampante

eagle
aigle*M*
Adler*M*
aguila*F*

mullet
étoile*F*
Stern*M*
estrella*F*

EXAMPLES OF METALS
EXEMPLES*M* **DE MÉTAUX***M*
BEISPIELE*N* **FÜR METALL***N*
EJEMPLOS*M* **DE METALES***M*

EXAMPLES OF FURS
EXEMPLES*M* **DE FOURRURES***F*
BEISPIELE*N* **FÜR PELZWERK***N*
EJEMPLOS*M* **DE FORROS***M*

argent
argent*M*
Silber*V*
plata*F*

or
or*M*
Gold*N*
oro*M*

ermine
hermine*F*
Hermelin*M*
armiño*M*

vair
vair*M*
Eishutfeh*N*
cerros*M*

EXAMPLES OF COLOURS
EXEMPLES*M* **DE COULEURS***F*
FARBBEISPIELE*N*
EJEMPLOS*M* **DE COLORES***M*

azure
azur*M*
blau
azur*M*

gules
gueules*M*
rot
gules*M*

vert
sinople*M*
grün
sinople*M*

purpure
pourpre*M*
purpur
púrpura*M*

sable
sable*M*
schwarz
sable*M*

SIGNS OF THE ZODIAC
SIGNES^M DU ZODIAQUE^M
TIERKREISZEICHEN^N
SIGNOS^M DEL ZODÍACO^M

FIRE SIGNS
SIGNES^M **DE FEU**^M
FEUERZEICHEN^N
SIGNOS^M **DE FUEGO**^M

Aries the Ram (March 21)
Bélier^M (21 mars)
Widder^M, Aries (21. März)
Aries, el Carnero (21 de marzo)

Leo the Lion (July 23)
Lion^M (23 juillet)
Löwe^M, Leo (23. Juli)
Leo, el León (23 de julio)

Sagittarius the Archer (November 22)
Sagittaire^M (22 novembre)
Schütze^M, Sagittarius (22. November)
Sagitario, el Arquero (22 de noviembre)

EARTH SIGNS
SIGNES^M **DE TERRE**^F
ERDZEICHEN
SIGNOS^M **DE TIERRA**^F

Taurus the Bull (April 20)
Taureau^M (20 avril)
Stier^M, Taurus (20. April)
Tauro, el Toro (20 de abril)

Virgo the Virgin (August 23)
Vierge^F (23 août)
Jungfrau^F, Virgo (23. August)
Virgo, la Virgen (23 de agosto)

Capricorn the Goat (December 22)
Capricorne^M (22 décembre)
Steinbock^M, Capricornus (22. Dezember)
Capricornio, la Cabra (22 de diciembre)

AIR SIGNS
SIGNES^M **D'AIR**^M
LUFTZEICHEN^N
SIGNOS^M **DE AIRE**^M

Libra the Balance (September 23)
Balance^F (23 septembre)
Waage^F, Libra (23. September)
Libra, la Balanza (23 de septiembre)

Aquarius the Water Bearer (January 20)
Verseau^M (20 janvier)
Wassermann^M, Aquarius (20. Januar)
Acuario, el Aguador (20 de enero)

Gemini the Twins (May 21)
Gémeaux^M (21 mai)
Zwillinge^M, Gemini (21. Mai)
Géminis, los Gemelos (21 de mayo)

WATER SIGNS
SIGNES^M **D'EAU**^F
WASSERZEICHEN^N
SIGNOS^M **DE AGUA**^F

Cancer the Crab (June 22)
Cancer^M (22 juin)
Krebs^M, Cancer (22. Juni)
Cáncer, el Cangrejo (22 de junio)

Scorpio the Scorpion (October 24)
Scorpion^M (24 octobre)
Skorpion^M, Scorpius (24. Oktober)
Escorpio, el Escorpión (24 de octubre)

Pisces the Fishes (February 19)
Poissons^M (19 février)
Fische^M, Pisces (19. Februar)
Piscis, los peces (19 de febrero)

SYMBOLS
SYMBOLES
SYMBOLE
SÍMBOLOS

SAFETY SYMBOLS
SYMBOLES*M* DE SÉCURITÉ*F*
WARN- UND GEBOTZEICHEN*N*
SÍMBOLOS*M* DE SEGURIDAD*F*

corrosive
matières*F* corrosives
ätzend
corrosivo

electrical hazard
danger*M* électrique
elektrische Spannung*F*
alto voltaje*M*

explosive
matières*F* explosives
explosionsgefährlich
explosivo

flammable
matières*F* inflammables
leicht entzündlich
inflamable

radioactive
matières*F* radioactives
radioaktiv
radioactivo

poison
matières*F* toxiques
Gift*N*
veneno*M*

PROTECTION
PROTECTION*F*
SCHUTZMASSNAHMEN*F*
PROTECCIÓN*F*

eye protection
protection*F* obligatoire de la vue*F*
Augenschutz*M* tragen
protección*F* de los ojos*M*

ear protection
protection*F* obligatoire de l'ouïe*F*
Gehörschutz*M* tragen
protección*F* de los oidos*M*

head protection
protection*F* obligatoire de la tête*F*
Schutzhelm*M* tragen
protección*F* de la cabeza*F*

hand protection
protection*F* obligatoire des mains*F*
Schutzhandschuhe*M* tragen
protección*F* de las manos*F*

feet protection
protection*F* obligatoire des pieds*M*
Schutzschuhe*M* tragen
protección*F* de los pies*M*

respiratory system protection
protection*F* obligatoire des voies*F* respiratoires
Atemschutz*M* tragen
protección del sistema*M* respiratorio

COMMON SYMBOLS
SYMBOLES[M] D'USAGE[M] COURANT
ALLGEMEINE ZEICHEN[N]
SÍMBOLOS[M] DE USO[M] COMÚN

buffet
casse-croûte[M]
Cafeteria[F]
cafetería[F]

telephone
téléphone[M]
Telefon[N]
teléfono[M]

restaurant
restaurant[M]
Restaurant[N]
restaurante[M]

men's toilet
toilettes[F] pour hommes[M]
Toiletten[F] (Herren[M])
Servicios[M] (Caballeros[M])

women's toilet
toilettes[F] pour dames[F]
Toiletten[F] (Damen[F])
Servicios[M] (Señoras[F])

access for physically handicapped
accès[M] pour handicapés[M] physiques
für Schwerbehinderte[M]
acceso[M] para minusválidos[M]

chemist's shop
pharmacie[F]
Apotheke[F]
farmacia[F]

no access for wheelchairs
ne pas utiliser avec une chaise[F] roulante
nicht für Rollstuhlfahrer[M]
prohibido usar silla[F] de ruedas[F]

first aid
premiers soins[M]
Erste Hilfe[F]
puesto[M] de socorro[M]

hospital
hôpital[M]
Krankenhaus[N]
hospital[M]

police
police[F]
Polizei[F]
policía[F]

taxi rank
transport[M] par taxi[M]
Taxi[N]
servicio[M] de taxis[M]

camping (tent)
camping*M*
Zeltplatz*M*
zona*F* para acampar

camping prohibited
camping*M* interdit
Zelten*N* verboten
prohibido acampar

camping (caravan)
caravaning*M*
Platz*M* für Wohnwagen*M*
zona*F* para caravanas*F*

camping (caravan and tent)
camping*M* et caravaning*M*
Platz*M* für Zelte*N* und Wohnwagen*M*
zona*F* para acampar y para caravanas*F*

picnics prohibited
pique-nique*M* interdit
Picknick*N* verboten
prohibido hacer comidas*F* campestres

picnic area
pique-nique*M*
Rastplatz*M*
zona*F* de comidas*F* campestres

petrol station
poste*M* de carburant*M*
Tankstelle*F*
gasolinera*F*

information
renseignements*M*
Information*F*
información*F*

information
renseignements*M*
Information*F*
información*F*

currency exchange
change*M*
Geldwechsel*M*
casa*F* de cambio*M*

lost property
articles*M* perdus et retrouvés
Fundbüro*N*
oficina*F* de objetos*M* perdidos

fire extinguisher
extincteur*M* d'incendie*M*
Feuerlöscher*M*
extintor*M* de incendios*M*

ROAD SIGNS
SIGNALISATION*F* ROUTIÈRE
VERKEHRSZEICHEN*N*
SEÑALES*F* DE CIRCULACIÓN*F*

MAJOR NORTH AMERICAN ROAD SIGNS
PRINCIPAUX PANNEAUX*M* NORD-AMÉRICAINS
DIE WICHTIGSTEN NORDAMERIKANISCHEN VERKEHRSZEICHEN*N*
PRINCIPALES SEÑALES*F* DE CIRCULACIÓN*F* NORTEAMERICANAS

stop at intersection
arrêt*M* à l'intersection*F*
Halt! Vorfahrt*F* gewähren
alto

no entry
accès*M* interdit
Verbot*N* der Einfahrt*F*
prohibido el paso*M*

give way
cédez le passage*M*
Vorfahrt*F* gewähren
ceda el paso*M*

one-way traffic
voie*F* à sens*M* unique
Einbahnstraße*F*
una vía*F*

direction to be followed
direction*F* obligatoire
vorgeschriebene Fahrtrichtung*F*
dirección*F* obligatoria

direction to be followed
direction*F* obligatoire
vorgeschriebene Fahrtrichtung*F*
dirección*F* obligatoria

direction to be followed
direction*F* obligatoire
vorgeschriebene Fahrtrichtung*F*
dirección*F* obligatoria

direction to be followed
direction*F* obligatoire
vorgeschriebene Fahrtrichtung*F*
dirección*F* obligatoria

no U-turn
interdiction*F* de faire demi-tour*M*
Wenden*N* verboten
prohibido dar vuelta*F* en U

passing prohibited
interdiction*F* de dépasser
Überholverbot*N*
prohibido adelantar

two-way traffic
circulation*F* dans les deux sens*M*
Gegenverkehr*M*
doble vía*F*

merging traffic
intersection*F* avec priorité*F*
Vorfahrt*F* an nächster Einmündung*F*
señal*F* de unión*M*

SYMBOLE
SÍMBOLOS

SYMBOLS
SYMBOLES

stop at intersection
arrêt[M] à l'intersection[F]
Halt! Vorfahrt[F] gewähren
alto

no entry
accès[M] interdit
Verbot[N] der Einfahrt[F]
prohibido el paso

give way
cédez le passage[M]
Vorfahrt[F] gewähren
ceda el paso[M]

one-way traffic
voie[F] à sens[M] unique
Einbahnstraße[F]
una vía[F]

direction to be followed
direction[F] obligatoire
vorgeschriebene Fahrtrichtung[F]
dirección[F] obligatoria

direction to be followed
direction[F] obligatoire
vorgeschriebene Fahrtrichtung[F]
dirección[F] obligatoria

direction to be followed
direction[F] obligatoire
vorgeschriebene Fahrtrichtung[F]
dirección[F] obligatoria

direction to be followed
direction[F] obligatoire
vorgeschriebene Fahrtrichtung[F]
dirección[F] obligatoria

no U-turn
interdiction[F] de faire demi-tour[M]
Wenden[N] verboten
prohibido dar vuelta[F] en U

passing prohibited
interdiction[F] de dépasser
Überholen[N] verboten
prohibido adelantar

two-way traffic
circulation[F] dans les deux sens[M]
Gegenverkehr[M]
doble vía[F]

priority intersection
intersection[F] avec priorité[F]
Vorfahrt[F] an nächster Einmündung[F]
cruce[M] con preferencia[F]

SYMBOLS
SYMBOLES

SYMBOLE
SÍMBOLOS

825

ROAD SIGNS
SIGNALISATION^F ROUTIÈRE
VERKEHRSZEICHEN^N
SEÑALES^F DE CIRCULACIÓN^F

MAJOR NORTH AMERICAN ROAD SIGNS
PRINCIPAUX PANNEAUX^M NORD-AMÉRICAINS
DIE WICHTIGSTEN NORDAMERIKANISCHEN VERKEHRSZEICHEN^N
PRINCIPALES SEÑALES^F DE CIRCULACIÓN^F NORTEAMERICANAS

bend to right
virage^M à droite^F
Rechtskurve^F
curva^F a la derecha^F

double bend
double virage^M
Doppelkurve^F
curva^F doble

roadway narrows
chaussée^F rétrécie
verengte Fahrbahn^F
estrechamiento^M del camino^M

slippery road
chaussée^F glissante
Schleudergefahr^F
camino^M resbaladizo

uneven surface
chaussée^F cahoteuse
unebene Fahrbahn^F
superficie^F irregular

steep hill
descente^F dangereuse
Gefälle^N
bajada^F pronunciada

falling rocks
chutes^F de pierres^F
Steinschlag^M
zona^F de derrumbes^M

no vehicles over height shown
limitation^F de hauteur^F
Verbot^N für Fahrzeuge^N über angegebene Höhe^F
altura^F máxima

signal ahead
signalisation^F lumineuse
Lichtzeichenanlage^F
semáforo^M

school zone
zone^F scolaire
Schule^F
zona^F escolar

pedestrian crossing
passage^M pour piétons^M
Fußgängerüberweg^M
paso^M de peatones^M

road works ahead
travaux^M
Baustelle^F
obras^F

bend to right
virage^M à droite^F
Rechtskurve^F
curva^F a la derecha^F

double bend
double virage^M
Doppelkurve^F
curva^F doble

road narrows
chaussée^F rétrécie
verengte Fahrbahn^F
estrechamiento^M del camino^M

slippery road
chaussée^F glissante
Schleudergefahr^F
camino^M resbaladizo

bumps
chaussée^F cahoteuse
unebene Fahrbahn^F
badén^M

steep hill
descente^F dangereuse
Gefälle^N
bajada^F pronunciada

falling rocks
chutes^F de pierres^F
Steinschlag^M
zona^F de derrumbes^M

no vehicles over height shown
limitation^F de hauteur^F
Verbot^N für Fahrzeuge^N über angegebene Höhe^F
altura^F máxima

traffic signals ahead
signalisation^F lumineuse
Lichtzeichenanlage^F
semáforo^M

school
zone^F scolaire
Schule^F
zona^F escolar

pedestrian crossing
passage^M pour piétons^M
Fußgängerüberweg^M
paso^M de peatones^M

road works ahead
travaux^M
Baustelle^F
obras^F

ROAD SIGNS
SIGNALISATION^F ROUTIÈRE
VERKEHRSZEICHEN^N
SEÑALES^F DE CIRCULACIÓN^F

MAJOR NORTH AMERICAN ROAD SIGNS
PRINCIPAUX PANNEAUX^M NORD-AMÉRICAINS
DIE WICHTIGSTEN NORDAMERIKANISCHEN VERKEHRSZEICHEN^N
PRINCIPALES SEÑALES^F DE CIRCULACIÓN^F NORTEAMERICANAS

level crossing
passage^M à niveau^M
Bahnübergang^M
paso^M a nivel^M

wild animals
passage^M d'animaux^M sauvages
Wildwechsel^M
cruce^M de animales^M salvajes

closed to pedestrians
accès^M interdit aux piétons^M
gesperrt für Fußgänger^M
prohibido el paso^M de peatones^M

closed to bicycles
accès^M interdit aux bicyclettes^F
gesperrt für Radfahrer^M
prohibido el paso^M de bicicletas^F

closed to motorcycles
accès^M interdit aux motocycles^M
gesperrt für Krafträder^N
prohibido el paso^M de motocicletas^F

closed to trucks
accès^M interdit aux camions^M
gesperrt für Kfz^N über 2,8t
prohibido el paso^M de camiones^M

MAJOR INTERNATIONAL ROAD SIGNS
PRINCIPAUX PANNEAUX^M INTERNATIONAUX
DIE WICHTIGSTEN INTERNATIONALEN VERKEHRSZEICHEN^N
PRINCIPALES SEÑALES^F DE CIRCULACIÓN^F INTERNACIONALES

level crossing
passage^M à niveau^M
Bahnübergang^M
paso^M a nivel^M

wild animals
passage^M d'animaux^M sauvages
Wildwechsel^M
cruce^M de animales^M salvajes

closed to pedestrians
accès^M interdit aux piétons^M
gesperrt für Fußgänger^M
prohibido el paso^M de peatones^M

closed to bicycles
accès^M interdit aux bicyclettes^F
gesperrt für Radfahrer^M
prohibido el paso^M de bicicletas^F

closed to motorcycles
accès^M interdit aux motocycles^M
gesperrt für Krafträder^N
prohibido el paso^M de motocicletas^F

closed to trucks
accès^M interdit aux camions^M
gesperrt für Kfz^N über 2,8t
prohibido el paso^M de camiones^M

FABRIC CARE
ENTRETIEN^M DES TISSUS^M
TEXTILPFLEGE^F
CUIDADO^M DE TELAS^F

do not wash
ne pas laver
nicht waschen
no se lave

hand wash in lukewarm water
laver à la main^F à l'eau^F tiède
Handwäsche^F in handwarmem Wasser^N
lávese a mano^F con agua^F tibia

machine wash in lukewarm water at a gentle setting/reduced agitation
laver à la machine^F à l'eau^F tiède avec agitation^F réduite
Hand- und Maschinenwäsche^F, Schonwaschgang^M
lávese en lavadora^F con agua^F tibia en el ciclo^M para ropa^F delicada

machine wash in warm water at a gentle setting/reduced agitation
laver à la machine^F à l'eau^F chaude avec agitation^F réduite
Hand- und Maschinenwäsche^F, Schonwaschgang^M
lávese en lavadora^F con agua^F caliente en el ciclo^M para ropa^F delicada

machine wash in warm water at a normal setting
laver à la machine^F à l'eau^F chaude avec agitation^F normale
Hand- und Maschinenwäsche^F, Normalwaschgang^M
lávese en lavadora^F con agua^F caliente, en el ciclo^M normal

machine wash in hot water at a normal setting
laver à la machine^F à l'eau^F très chaude avec agitation^F normale
Hand- und Maschinenwäsche^F, Normalwaschgang^M
lávese en lavadora^F con agua^F muy caliente, en el ciclo^M normal

do not use chlorine bleach
ne pas utiliser de chlorure^M décolorant
nicht chloren
no use lejía^F de cloro^M

use chlorine bleach as directed
utiliser un chlorure^M décolorant suivant les indications^F
chloren möglich
use lejía^F de cloro^M siguiendo las indicaciones^F

hang to dry
suspendre pour sécher
zum Trocknen^N hängen
cuelgue al aire^M libre después de escurrir

dry flat
sécher à plat
zum Trocknen^N legen
seque extendido sobre una toalla^F después de escurrir

tumble dry at medium to high temperature
sécher par culbutage^M à moyenne ou haute température^F
Wäschetrockner^M mit mittlerer bis hoher Temperatur^F
seque en secadora^F a temperatura^F de mediana a alta

tumble dry at low temperature
sécher par culbutage^M à basse température^F
Wäschetrockner^M mit niedriger Temperatur^F
seque en secadora^F a temperatura^F baja

drip dry
suspendre pour sécher sans essorer
tropfnaß hängen
cuelgue sin exprimir, dando forma^F a mano^F

do not iron
ne pas repasser
nicht bügeln
no use plancha^F

iron at low setting
repasser à basse température^F
bügeln bei niedriger Einstellung^F
use plancha^F tibia

iron at medium setting
repasser à moyenne température^F
bügeln bei mittlerer Einstellung^F
use plancha^F caliente

iron at high setting
repasser à haute température^F
bügeln bei hoher Einstellung^F
use plancha^F muy caliente

COMMON SCIENTIFIC SYMBOLS
SYMBOLES[M] SCIENTIFIQUES USUELS
ALLGEMEINE SYMBOLE[N] IN DEN WISSENSCHAFTEN[F]
SÍMBOLOS[M] CIENTÍFICOS COMUNES

MATHEMATICS
MATHÉMATIQUES[F]
MATHEMATIK[F]
MATEMÁTICAS[F]

subtraction
soustraction[F]
Subtraktion[F]
menos[M]

addition
addition[F]
Addition[F]
más[M]

multiplication
multiplication[F]
Multiplikation[F]
por[M]

division
division[F]
Division[F]
entre[M]

is equal to
égale
ist gleich
igual a

is not equal to
n'égale pas
ist ungleich
desigual a

is approximately equal to
égale à peu près
ist annähernd gleich
casi igual a

is equivalent to
équivaut à
ist äquivalent mit
equivalente a

is identical with
est identique à
ist identisch mit
idéntico a

is not identical with
n'est pas identique à
ist nicht identisch mit
no es idéntico a

plus or minus
plus ou moins
plus oder minus
más[M] o menos[M]

empty set
ensemble[M] vide
Leermenge[F]
conjunto[M] vacío

is greater than
plus grand que
ist größer als
mayor que

is equal to or greater than
égal ou plus grand que
ist gleich oder größer als
igual o mayor que

is less than
plus petit que
ist kleiner als
menor que

is equal to or less than
égal ou plus petit que
ist gleich oder kleiner als
igual o menor que

union
réunion[F]
Vereinigung[F]
unión[F]

intersection
intersection[F]
Durchschnitt[M]
intersección[F]

is contained in
inclusion[F]
echte Teilmenge[F] von
contenido en

percent
pourcentage[M]
Prozent[N]
porcentaje[M]

belongs to
appartenance[F]
Element[N] von
pertenece a

does not belong to
non-appartenance[F]
nicht Element[N] von
no pertenece a

integral
intégrale[F]
Integral[N]
integral

square root of
racine[F] carrée de
Quadratwurzel[F] aus
raíz[F] cuadrada de

sum
sommation[F]
Summe[F]
suma[F]

infinity
infini[M]
unendlich
infinito[M]

factorial
factorielle[F]
Fakultät[F]
factorial

GEOMETRY
GÉOMÉTRIE[F]
GEOMETRIE[F]
GEOMETRÍA[F]

degree
degré[M]
Grad[M]
grado[M]

minute
minute[F]
Minute[F]
minuto[M]

second
seconde[F]
Sekunde[F]
segundo[M]

pi
pi[M]
Pi[N]
pi

perpendicular
perpendiculaire[F]
Senkrechte[F]
perpendicular

acute angle
angle[M] aigu
spitzer Winkel[M]
ángulo[M] agudo

right angle
angle[M] droit
rechter Winkel[M]
ángulo[M] recto

obtuse angle
angle[M] obtu
stumpfer Winkel[M]
ángulo[M] obtuso

is parallel to
parallèle
ist parallel zu
es paralelo a

is not parallel to
non-parallèle
ist nicht parallel zu
no es paralelo a

male
mâle[M]
männlich
masculino[M]

female
femelle[F]
weiblich
femenino[M]

born
naissance[F]
geboren
nacimiento[M]

Rh+

blood factor positive
facteur[M] Rhésus positif
Rhesusfaktor[M] positiv
factor[M] RH positivo

Rh-

blood factor negative
facteur[M] Rhésus négatif
Rhesusfaktor[M] negativ
factor[M] RH negativo

†

died
mort[F]
gestorben
muerte[F]

CHEMISTRY
CHIMIE[F]
CHEMIE[F]
QUÍMICA[F]

—

negative charge
négatif[M]
negativ geladen
elemento[M] negativo

+

positive charge
positif[M]
positiv geladen
elemento[M] positivo

reversible reaction
réaction[F] réversible
reversible Reaktion[F]
reacción[F]

→

reaction direction
direction[F] d'une réaction[F]
Reaktionsrichtung[F]
dirección[F]

MISCELLANEOUS
SYMBOLES[M] **DIVERS**[M]
WEITERE SYMBOLE[N]
VARIOS

recycled
recyclé
wiederverwertet
recuperado

recyclable
recyclable
wiederverwertbar
recuperable

&

ampersand
esperluette[F]
Et-Zeichen[N]
y

®

registered trademark
marque[F] déposée
eingetragenes Warenzeichen[N]
marca[F] registrada

©

copyright
copyright[M]
Copyright[N]
copyright (derechos[M] de autor[M])

R𝒙

prescription
ordonnance[F]
verschreibungspflichtig
receta[F] médica

pause/still
pause[F]/arrêt[M] sur l'image[F]
Pause[F]
pausa[F]

stop
arrêt[M]
Stop[M]
paro[M]

rewind
rebobinage[M]
Rücklauf[M]
rebobinado[M]

play
lecture[F]
Spiel[N]
reproducción[F]

fast forward
avance[F] rapide
Vorlauf[M]
avance rápido

SYMBOLS
SYMBOLES

SYMBOLE
SÍMBOLOS

DIACRITIC SYMBOLS
SIGNES^M DIACRITIQUES
DIAKRITISCHE ZEICHEN^N
SIGNOS^M DIACRÍTICOS

acute accent
accent^M aigu
Accent^M aigu
acento^M agudo

umlaut
tréma^M
Umlaut^M
diéresis^F

grave accent
accent^M grave
Accent^M grave
acento^M grave

circumflex accent
accent^M circonflexe
Accent^M circonflexe
acento^M circunflejo

cedilla
cédille^F
Cedille^F
cedilla^F

tilde
tilde^M
Tilde^F
tilde^F

PUNCTUATION MARKS
SIGNES^M DE PONCTUATION^F
SATZZEICHEN^N
SIGNOS^M DE PUNTUACIÓN^F

semicolon
point^M-virgule^F
Semikolon^N
punto^M y coma^F

full stop
point^M
Punkt^M
punto^M

comma
virgule^F
Komma^N
coma^F

ellipsis
points^M de suspension^F
Fortführungspunkte^M
puntos^M suspensivos

colon
deux-points^M
Doppelpunkt^M
dos puntos^M

asterisk
astérisque^M
Sternchen^N
asterisco^M

quotation marks (French)
guillemets^M
Anführungszeichenn (französische)
comillas^F

single quotation marks
guillemets^M
halbe Anführungszeichen^N
comillas^F sencillas

quotation marks
guillemets^M
Anführungszeichen^N
comillas^F

dash
tiret^M
Gedankenstrich^M
guión^M largo

parentheses
parenthèses^F
runde Klammern^F
paréntesis^M

slash
barre^F oblique
Querstrich^M
diagonal^F

exclamation mark
point^M d'exclamation^F
Ausrufezeichen^N
admiración^F

question mark
point^M d'interrogation^F
Fragezeichen^N
interrogación^F

square brackets
crochets^M
eckige Klammern^F
corchetes^M

EXAMPLES OF CURRENCY ABBREVIATIONS
EXEMPLES^M D'UNITÉS^F MONÉTAIRES
BEISPIELE^N FÜR WÄHRUNGSABKÜRZUNGEN^F
EJEMPLOS^M DE ABREVIACIONES^F DE MONEDAS^F

$

dollar
dollar^M
Dollar^M
dólar^M

¢

cent
cent^M
Cent^M
centavo^M

€

EURO
EURO^M
EURO^M
EURO^M

£

pound
livre^F
Pfund^M
libra^F

¥

yen
yen^M
Yen^M
yen^M

F

franc
franc^M
Franc^M
franco^M

DM

Deutsche Mark
mark^M
Deutsche Mark^F
marco^M

Dr

drachma
drachme^F
Drachme^F
dracma^M

L

lira
lire^F
Lira^F
lira^F

Kr

krone
couronne^F
Krone^F
corona^F

IS

shekel
shekel^M
Schekel^M
shekel^M

Esc

escudo
escudo^M
Escudo^M
escudo^M

Pta

peseta
peseta^F
Peseta^F
peseta^F

Fl

florin
florin^M
Florin^M
florín^M

ENGLISH INDEX

A

a 537.
abacus 166, 167.
abdomen 78, 79, 81, 91, 108, 116, 118.
abdominal aorta 126, 132.
abdominal cavity 127, 128.
abdominal rectus 120.
abdominal segment 78.
aboveground pipeline 740.
absorbing plate 768.
absorbing surface 772.
abutment 176, 454, 455, 456.
abyssal hill 29.
abyssal plain 29.
abyssal plain 29.
acanthus leaf 167, 220.
acceleration lane 452.
accelerator pedal 430.
accent mark 539.
accept machine 764.
access door 709.
access for physically handicapped 822.
access gallery 747.
access panel 207.
access road 452, 502.
access shaft 752.
access window 529.
accessories 586, 672.
accessory box 568.
accessory gear box 501.
accessory pouch 684.
accessory shoe 391, 409.
accidentals 538.
accordion 536.
accordion bag 380.
accordion pleat 335.
account book 518.
Ace 695.
acetylene cylinder 306.
acetylene valve 306.
achene 62, 66.
acid precipitation 32, 33, 35.
acoustic ceiling 189.
acoustic guitar 546.
acoustic meatus 138, 139.
acoustic screen 406.
acromion 123.
acroterion 167, 168.
action lever 541.
action of wind 35.
active tracking 402.
actual temperature 213, 705.
actuator 814.
actuator arm 529.
actuator arm motor 529.
acute accent 832.
acute angle 830.
Adam's apple 116.
add in memory 523.
add key 523.
addition 830.
additional production personnel 412.
adductor muscle 92.
adhesive disc 85.
adhesive tape 725.
adipose tissue 129, 136.
adjustable antenna 722.
adjustable buckle 645.
adjustable catch 641.
adjustable channel 278.
adjustable clamp 234.
adjustable frame 277.
adjustable lamp 234.
adjustable seat 460.
adjustable shelf 521.
adjustable spanner 279.
adjustable strap 350.
adjustable support 661.
adjustable waist tab 322.
adjuster 728.
adjusting band 406.
adjusting lever 539.
adjusting ring 264.
adjusting screw 278, 306.
adjusting tube 659.
adjustment for horizontal-circle image 713.
adjustment for vertical-circle image 713.
adjustment pedal 591.
adjustment slide 323.
adjustment wheel 311.
administrative building 752.
adrenal gland 132.
advertising panel 474.
advertising poster 477.
adze 587, 681.

aerator 294, 295.
aerial 408, 427.
aerial ladder truck 780.
aerodynamic brake 774.
Africa 21.
Afro pick 368.
aft shroud 16.
afterbay 746, 747, 749, 750.
afterfeather 110.
aftermast 478.
agitator 258.
agricultural pollution 32.
aileron 498, 638.
air 437.
air bladder 89.
air brake 638, 812.
air brake handle 639.
air bulb shutter release 393.
air cap 304.
air chamber 298.
air compression unit 458.
air compressor 469.
air concentrator 370.
air conditioner 449.
air conditioner compressor 435.
AIR CONDITIONING 214.
air conditioning unit 415.
air control radar 810.
air cushion 352.
air data computer 500.
air filter 210, 272, 469.
air flow 590.
air gap 772.
air hole 385, 389.
air horn 440.
air hose 590, 627, 734.
air hose connection 304.
air inlet 443.
air inlet control 204.
air intake 14, 493, 501, 508.
air leg 734.
air mattress 687.
air navigation device 810.
air purifier 210.
air relief valve 743.
air scoop 445.
air sealing gland 543.
air search radar 809, 811.
air signs 820.
air space 14, 109.
air temperature 38.
air tube 209.
air valve 304, 590.
air vent 257.
air-cleaner filter 783.
air-inlet grille 370.
air-outlet grille 370.
air-pressure pump 710.
air-supply tube 777.
air-to-air missile 813, 814.
air-to-surface missile 814.
air/fuel mixture 436.
airbrush 590.
airbrush, cross section 590.
aircraft 722.
AIRCRAFT CARRIER 810.
aircraft maintenance truck 506.
airframe 637.
airlock 14.
AIRPORT 502, 504, 506.
airport 52.
airspeed indicator 639.
aisle 177.
ala 141.
alarm threshold display button 485.
alarm threshold setting 485.
albumen 109.
alcohol bulb 705.
alcohol column 705.
alidade 41, 713.
alidade level 713.
alighting board 82.
all-terrain vehicle 425.
alley 614, 618.
almond 63, 66.
alphanumeric keyboard 422, 530.
alpine skier 640.
ALPINE SKIING 640.
Altar 13.
altazimuth mounting 15.
alteration line 565.
alternator 434, 468.
altimeter 635, 639.
altitude clamp 720, 721.
altitude fine adjustment 720, 721.
altitude scale 19.
alto clef 537.
altocumulus 44.
altostratus 44.
alula 110.

aluminium layer 405.
alveolar bone 144.
AM antenna 400.
amble 101.
ambulatory 177.
American betting layout 700.
American corn bread 153.
AMERICAN FOOTBALL 602.
american football player 602.
American football, playing field 604.
american plug 309.
American roulette wheel 700.
American white bread 153.
AMERICAN/CANADIAN FOOTBALL 604.
amethyst 363.
ammunition stowage 805.
ampersand 831.
AMPHIBIANS 84.
amplification of seismic waves 714.
amplifier 402.
amplifier 714.
ampoule 725.
ampulla of fallopian tube 129.
anal cleft 117.
anal fin 87.
anal proleg 78.
analogue watch 706.
analytical balance 709.
ANCHOR 483.
anchor 656.
anchor pin 432.
anchor wires 738.
anchorage 661.
anchorage block 456.
anconeus 121.
andirons 205.
Andromeda 11.
anemometer 41.
Anik-E 418.
ANIMAL CELL 115.
ankle 116, 118.
ankle boot 357.
ankle sock 325, 344.
ankle-strap 356.
ankle/wrist weight 665.
announcer console 407.
annual ring 59.
annular combustion chamber 501.
annular eclipse 8.
annulet 167.
anode rod 297.
anorak 353.
ant 77.
Antarctic Circle 3.
Antarctica 20.
antefix 169.
antenna 16, 43, 78, 79, 80, 81, 91, 498, 508, 613, 805, 810.
antennae cleaner 80.
antennule 90.
anterior chamber 140.
anterior end 95.
anterior notch 139.
anterior root 135.
anterior tibial 120.
anterior tibial artery 126.
anterior view 120, 122.
anther 60.
anti-aircraft missile 808.
anti-friction pad 641.
anti-radar missile 814.
anti-ship missile 814.
anti-skating device 404.
anti-slip foot 302.
anti-slip shoe 661.
anti-tank missile 814.
anti-tank rocket 804.
anti-torque tail rotor 508.
anti-vibration handle 272.
anticline 737.
anticollision light 498.
anticyclone 38.
antihelix 139.
antimissile self-defence 808.
antireflection coating 768.
antiseptic 725.
antitragus 139.
anus 89, 92, 127, 128, 131.
aorta 125, 130.
aortic valve 125.
aperture 94.
aperture changer 717.
aperture diaphragm 717.
aperture door 16.
aperture scale 396.
aperture/exposure value display 396.

apex 83, 94, 143, 144.
apical foramen 144.
apocrine sweat gland 136.
apogee motor firing 419.
apogee passage 419.
apple 64.
apple 64.
appoggiatura 538.
appointment book 518.
approach 683.
approach ramp 456.
approach wall 492.
apricot 63.
apron 219, 220, 223, 502, 669.
apse 177.
apsidiole 177.
aquamarine 363.
Aquarius the Water Bearer (January 20) 820.
aquastat 209.
aquatic bird 111.
aquatic bird 111.
aqueous humour 140.
arc welder 305.
arc welding 305.
arcade 176.
arcades 172.
arch 14, 455, 649.
arch bridge 455.
arch dam 750.
arch dam, cross section 750.
arch of aorta 124, 125, 126.
arch of foot artery 126.
archboard 518.
archer 684.
Archer 13.
ARCHERY 684.
arches, types 174.
archipelago 51.
ARCHITECTURAL STYLES 166.
architrave 166, 168.
Arctic 20.
Arctic Circle 3, 47.
Arctic Ocean 21.
area of ice 620.
arena 654.
Arenberg parquet 200.
areola 129.
argent 819.
Aries the Ram (March 21) 820.
arm 100, 117, 119, 157, 220, 234, 264, 483, 535, 561, 568, 718, 727, 782, 785.
arm cylinder 782, 785.
arm elevator 404.
arm guard 602.
arm lock 668.
arm nut 568.
arm pad 609.
arm position 625.
arm rest 404.
arm slit 331.
arm stump 220.
ARMCHAIR 220.
armet 792.
armet 792.
armguard 684.
armhole 325.
armoire 225.
ARMOUR 792.
armour 805.
armoured flex 422.
armoured plate 805.
armpit 116, 118.
armrest 428, 429, 727.
armstand 624.
armstand dive 625.
arpeggio 539.
ARQUEBUS 795.
arrector pili muscle 136.
arrester wire 811.
arris 167.
arrow 684.
Arrow 11.
arrow 793.
arrow rest 684.
arteries 126.
artichoke 69.
articulated lorry with trailer 440.
articulated mannequin 592.
artificial fly 670.
artificial satellite 19.
ascending aorta 124.
ascending colon 131.
ash 386.
ash layer 25.
ashtray 386.
Asia 21.
asparagus 72.
asphalt 745.

835

ENGLISH INDEX

The terms in **bold type** correspond to an illustration; those in CAPITALS indicate a title.

The terms in **bold type** correspond to an illustration; those in CAPITALS indicate a title.

ENGLISH INDEX

The terms in **bold type** correspond to an illustration; those in CAPITALS indicate a title.

The terms in **bold type** correspond to an illustration; those in CAPITALS indicate a title.

The terms in **bold type** correspond to an illustration; those in CAPITALS indicate a title.

eyebrow stripe 109.
eyebrow tweezers 365.
eyelash 140.
eyelash curler 367.
eyelashes 107.
eyelet 230, 353, 354, 381, 569, 644.
eyelet tab 354.
eyelid 97.
eyepiece 390, 396, 409, 718, 719, 720, 721.
eyepiece holder 721.
eyeshadow 367.
eyestalk 83.

F

f 537.
F-1 engine 509.
FABRIC CARE 829.
fabric guide 256.
fabric structure 566.
façade 175.
face 116, 179, 275, 277, 579, 619, 677, 733, 736.
face mask 602, 609, 643.
face side 288.
face-off circle 608.
face-off spot 608.
facepiece 730.
faceplate 289, 290.
facial nerve 139.
facsimile machine 417.
factorial 830.
faculae 6.
Fahrenheit scale 705.
failed fuel bay 764.
failed fuel canning 764.
fairing 442, 445.
fairlead 630.
fairway 676.
fall 341.
fall front 226.
falling rocks 826, 827.
fallopian tube 128.
fallopian tubes 128.
fallout 35.
fallow land 148.
false rib (3) 123.
false tuck 349.
family tent 685.
fan 161, 162, 209, 212, 259, 501, 528.
fan belt 434.
fan brush 366, 589.
fan cable stays 456.
fan control 214.
fan duct 162.
fan heater 211.
fan housing 370.
fan motor 214.
fan thermostat 438.
fan trellis 263.
fang 96.
fanion 817.
fantail 773.
far turn 651.
FARM ANIMALS 150.
farmhouse 148.
farmhouse loaf 153.
FARMSTEAD 148.
farmyard 148.
fascia 166.
fast data entry control 555.
fast forward 411, 831.
fast forward key 411.
fast-forward button 403, 408, 420.
fastener binder 519.
fasteners 566.
fastening device 230.
fault 23.
fax machine 421.
feather crown 618.
feather stitch 571.
FEATURES OF HISTORICAL COSTUME 315, 316, 318.
feed dog 562.
feed lever 283.
feed pin 531.
feed table 162.
feed tube 251.
feeder header 759.
feeder lane 452.
feeder output tray 532.
feeding tube 160.
feedwater 760, 761, 762, 763.
FEET PROTECTION 730.
feet protection 821.
feet-first entry 624.
felt tip pen 588.

female 831.
female cone 58.
female ferrule 670.
FEMALE GENITAL ORGANS 128, 129.
female union nut 300.
femoral artery 126.
femoral nerve 133.
femoral vein 126.
femur 78, 80, 103, 122.
fence 148.
fencer 667.
FENCING 666.
fencing shoe 667.
fencing weapons 666.
fencing, parts of the weapon 666.
fencing, piste 666.
fencing, positions 667.
fencing, target areas 667.
fennel 72.
ferrule 304, 375, 675, 678.
FERRY 494.
ferryboat 491.
fertilizers 32.
FERTILIZING 156.
fertilizing 154.
fetlock 101.
fetlock joint 101.
fettling knife 585.
fiber 692.
fibula 102, 122, 315.
FIELD HOCKEY 607.
field judge 605.
field lens 718.
field lens adjustment 718.
fielder's glove 596.
fielders 599.
fifth 537.
fifth wheel 440.
figure skate 644.
figure ski 633.
figure skiing handle 633.
figure-eight knot 691.
filament 6, 60, 232.
filament support 233.
file 277, 688.
file guides 518.
filing box 517.
filler 384.
filler cap 271, 438, 440.
filler hole 256.
filler pipe 293.
fillet 166, 167.
filleting knife 242.
filling hole 804.
filling inlet 741.
film 390.
film advance mode 391.
film cassette chamber 390.
film disc 395.
film drying cabinet 398.
film guide rail 390.
film guide roller 390.
film leader 395.
film leader indicator 390.
film pack 395.
film recorder 527.
film rewind knob 391.
film rewind system 390.
film speed 391, 396.
film sprocket 390.
films 395.
filter 207, 247, 252, 255, 385, 772.
filter cover 730.
filter tip 384.
fin 210, 627, 633, 639, 812, 814.
fin-mounted tail unit 498.
finderscope 720, 721.
fine adjustment knob 718.
FINE BOOKBINDING 577, 578.
fine data entry control 555.
fine guidance system 16.
finely threaded screw 711.
finger 137.
finger 596.
finger board 535, 544, 547.
finger button 550.
finger flange 726.
fingerless mitt 327.
fingernail 137.
finial 230, 817.
finish 646.
finish line 654.
finishing 586.
finishing line 651.
finishing post 654.
fir needles 58.
FIRE ENGINE 778, 780.
fire hose 778.

fire hydrant 186.
fire hydrant wrench 779.
fire irons 205.
FIRE PREVENTION 777.
fire signs 820.
firebrick 204.
firebrick back 204.
fireman 777.
fireman's hatchet 781.
fireman's helmet 777.
fireplace 204.
fireplace 195, 204.
fireproof and waterproof garment 777.
fireproofing 198.
firing 585.
firing accessories 801.
firing chamber 585.
firing lanyard 802.
firing mechanism 804.
firing shaft 802.
firing tube 807.
firmer chisel 587.
first aid 822.
FIRST AID EQUIPMENT 726.
FIRST AID KIT 725.
first aid manual 725.
first base 597.
first baseman 597.
first dorsal fin 86.
first floor 194.
first floor 196.
first focal room 15.
first molar 144.
first officer's seat 500.
first premolar 144.
first quarter 6.
first reinforce 800.
first space 610.
first stage 509.
first valve slide 550.
first violins 556.
first-class cabin 498.
FISH 86, 88.
fish dish 238.
fish fork 240.
fish kettle 248.
fish knife 239.
fish scaler 688.
fish wire 311.
fish, anatomy 88.
fish, morphology 86.
fishbone stitch 571.
fisherman's knot 691.
Fishes 11.
fisheye lens 392.
fishhook 671.
fishhook 670.
FISHING 670, 672.
fishing jacket 672.
fishing wear 672.
fishnet stocking 344.
fishplate 466.
fishplate bolt 466.
fission of uranium fuel 766.
FITNESS EQUIPMENT 663, 664.
fitted sheet 224.
fitting 778.
fittings 301.
five-number bet 700.
fivepin 683.
fixative 592.
fixed arch 455.
fixed base 282.
fixed bayonet 794.
fixed blade 578.
FIXED BRIDGES 454, 456.
fixed distance marking 505.
fixed jaw 279, 282.
fixed platform 739.
fixed weight 559.
fixed winglet 814.
fixed-roof tank 741.
fixing bath 399.
flag 606.
flag shapes 817.
flag with Schwenkel 817.
flag, parts 817.
flagstone 263.
flail mower 158.
flail mower 154.
flame adjustment wheel 386.
flame spreader 307.
flammable 821.
flank 101, 108, 179, 579.
flanker 605.
flanking tower 180.
flap 322, 380, 649.
flap hydraulic jack 812.
flap lever 500.

flap pocket 320, 322, 339.
flare 6, 738.
flare joint 300.
flare nut spanner 279.
flash bulb 393.
flash hider 796.
flashcube 393.
flashing 205.
flashing light 471.
flashtube 393.
flat 538.
flat brush 589.
flat end pin 231.
flat mirror 14, 720.
flat part 567.
flat roof 182.
flat sheet 224.
flat shuttle 573.
flat stitches 571.
flat tip 276.
flat truck 473.
flat washer 278.
flat-back brush 368.
flat-plate solar collector 768.
flatbed 441.
flesh 62, 63, 64.
FLESHY FRUITS 62, 65.
fleshy leaf 70.
FLESHY POMES 64.
FLESHY STONE FRUITS 63.
fletching 684.
fleur-de-lis 819.
flews 106.
flex 256, 260, 268, 271, 310, 370, 374.
flex sleeve 283, 305.
flex support 256.
flexible hose 260, 735.
flexible hose connection 735.
flexible rubber hose 298.
flexible skirt 493.
flexible tube 726.
flies 188.
flight 625, 698.
flight bag 382, 637.
FLIGHT DECK 500.
flight deck 498, 508, 510, 810.
flight information board 505.
flight instruments 635.
flight management computer 500.
flight of stairs 201.
flights 624.
flint 307, 795.
flint arrowhead 791.
flint knife 791.
flintlock 795.
flip turn 622, 623.
flip-flop 357.
float 216, 485, 672, 803.
float ball 293.
float clamp 216.
floater 626.
floating bridge 457.
floating crane 490.
floating head 374.
floating rib 122.
floating roof 741.
floating sleeve 316.
floating-roof tank 741.
floodlight 414.
floodlight on pantograph 414.
floor 205, 616, 617, 773.
floor brush 260.
floor drain 215.
floor joist 198, 199.
floor tile 286.
floor-level electric convector 210.
flooring strip 200.
floppy disc 529.
floppy disc drive 526, 528.
florin 832.
flotation section 486.
flow 493.
flow bean 740.
flow tube 768.
flower 57.
flower bed 263.
flower bud 57.
FLOWER, STRUCTURE 60.
flowering 61.
flue 297, 542.
flue hat 297.
flue pipe 542.
fluff trap 259.
fluid adjustment screw 304.
fluke 483.
fluorescent tube 232.
fluorescent tube 233.
flush 695.

The terms in **bold type** correspond to an illustration; those in CAPITALS indicate a title.

The terms in **bold type** correspond to an illustration; those in CAPITALS indicate a title.

845

The terms in **bold type** correspond to an illustration; those in CAPITALS indicate a title.

The terms in **bold type** correspond to an illustration; those in CAPITALS indicate a title.

The terms in **bold type** correspond to an illustration; those in CAPITALS indicate a title.

The terms in **bold type** correspond to an illustration; those in CAPITALS indicate a title.

The terms in **bold type** correspond to an illustration; those in CAPITALS indicate a title.

The terms in **bold type** correspond to an illustration; those in CAPITALS indicate a title.

ENGLISH INDEX

851

The terms in **bold type** correspond to an illustration; those in CAPITALS indicate a title.

The terms in **bold type** correspond to an illustration; those in CAPITALS indicate a title.

The terms in **bold type** correspond to an illustration; those in CAPITALS indicate a title.

The terms in **bold type** correspond to an illustration; those in CAPITALS indicate a title.

The terms in **bold type** correspond to an illustration; those in CAPITALS indicate a title.

The terms in **bold type** correspond to an illustration; those in CAPITALS indicate a title.

The terms in **bold type** correspond to an illustration; those in CAPITALS indicate a title.

white balance sensor 409.
white cabbage 73.
white cap 626.
white cue ball 673.
white flag 626.
white light 488.
white line 104, 452.
white matter 135.
white spot ball 673.
white square 696.
white stone 697.
white tape 618, 619.
white wine glass 237.
white-tailed deer 105.
whole wheat bread 153.
wholemeal bread 153.
whorl 83, 94.
wicker basket 635.
wicket 599.
wicket 599.
wicket gate 753.
wicketkeeper 599.
wide-angle lens 392.
wigwam 165.
wild animals 828.
willow 598.
winch 630.
wind 38.
wind 629.
wind abeam 629.
wind arrow 38.
wind chest 543.
wind chest table 543.
wind deflector 440.
wind direction 38.
wind direction and speed 38.
wind duct 543.
WIND ENERGY 773, 774.
wind guard 634.
wind indicator 628.
WIND INSTRUMENTS 548, 550.
wind sock 817.
wind speed 38.
wind supply 543.
wind trunk 543.
wind vane 41.
windbag 536.
windcheater 320, 321.
winder 706.

winder house 735.
winding adjustment 718.
winding mechanism 231, 707.
winding shaft 736.
winding tower 735.
windmill 773.
WINDOW 203.
window 194, 195, 253, 255, 379,
   399, 427, 429, 477, 498, 631.
WINDOW ACCESSORIES 228, 230.
window awning 685.
window curtain 228.
window tab 518.
window winder handle 429.
windscreen 14, 426, 440, 442, 445,
   498, 500.
windscreen wiper 431.
windscreen wiper 426.
windscreen wiper blade 431.
windshaft 773.
wine waiter corkscrew 244.
wing 78, 108, 316, 426, 440, 499,
   511, 637, 638, 670, 812.
wing attack 611.
wing box 812.
wing covert 108.
wing defence 611.
wing forward 606.
wing membrane 112.
wing nut 279.
wing pallet 787.
wing rib 498.
wing slat 499.
wing vein 79.
wing, bird 110.
winglet 499.
wings 112, 189.
wings, bat 112.
wingtip 637, 638.
winning line 702.
winter 8.
winter solstice 8.
winze 736.
wiper arm 431.
wiper blade rubber 431.
wiper control 430.
wire 641, 658, 663, 714.
wire beater 250.
wire brush 553.

wire cutter 311.
wire frame 689.
wire sling 681.
wire stripper 311.
wire stripper 311.
wisdom tooth 144.
wishbone boom 631.
withers 100, 106.
wok 248.
wok set 248.
WOMEN'S CLOTHING 330, 332, 334,
   336, 338, 340, 342, 344, 346, 348.
women's toilet 822.
wood 288, 677.
WOOD CARVING 586.
wood chip wagon 472.
wood chisel 275.
wood engraving 581.
WOOD FLOORING 200.
wood flooring 199.
**wood flooring on cement screed
   200.**
**wood flooring on wooden base
   200.**
wood flooring types 200.
wood storage space 204.
wood, golf 678.
wood-based materials 288, 289.
woodcut 581.
wooden bar 661.
wooden modelling tools 585.
woods 52.
woodstrip flooring 200.
woodwind family 548.
woofer 401.
word correction 525.
worker, honeybee 80.
worker, honeybee 81.
working area 16.
working pressure gauge 306.
worm 575, 801.
wrapover dress 333.
wrapover skirt 334.
wrapover top 337.
wrapper 384.
wrist 106, 112, 117, 119, 137.
wrist sling 681.
wrist strap 640, 642.
wrist-length glove 327.

wristband 602, 615.
write protect notch 529.
writing brush 389.
writing case 378.
WRITING INSTRUMENTS 389.

X

X-band antenna 49.
xylophone 554.
xylophone 556.

Y

Y-branch 301.
Y-tube 726.
yard 478.
yard line 604.
yarn 692.
yarn ball 596.
yarn clip 569.
yarn feeder 569.
yarn guide 569.
yarn rod 569.
yarn tension unit 569.
yellow ball 673.
yellow onion 70.
yen 832.
yoke 230, 320, 324, 337.
yoke skirt 334.
yolk 109.
yurt 165.

Z

zenith 16.
zenith S-band antenna 49.
zester 242.
zip 350, 365, 382, 685.
zip fastener 566.
zip fastener 321.
zip line 565.
zither 535.
zona pellucida 128.
zoom lens 392, 409, 414.
zygomatic bone 122.

FRENCH INDEX

Les termes en **caractères gras** renvoient à une illustration, ceux en CAPITALES indiquent un titre.

Les termes en **caractères gras** renvoient à une illustration, ceux en CAPITALES indiquent un titre.

Les termes en **caractères gras** renvoient à une illustration, ceux en CAPITALES indiquent un titre.

ciseaux(m) de sûreté(f) 365.
ciseaux(m) sculpteurs 369.
citerne(f) 742, 743.
cithare(f) 535.
citron(m) 65.
citrouille(f) 69.
civière(f) 726.
clairon(m) 550.
clapet(m) 293, 294, 568.
clapet(m) de non-retour(m) 306.
clapet(m) de retenue(f) 216.
claque(f) 353, 355.
clarinette(f) 548.
clarinette(f) basse 556.
clarinettes(f) 556.
classeur(m) 519.
classeur(m) à clapets(m) 520.
classeur(m) à soufflets(m) 378.
classeur(m) mobile 521.
classification(f) de Hubble 9.
claveau(m) 174.
clavette(f) 290.
clavicule(f) 122.
clavier(m) 530.
clavier(m) 420, 422, 526, 527, 540,
   555, 683.
clavier(m) à pédales(f) 542.
clavier(m) accompagnement(m) 536.
clavier(m) alphanumérique 422, 530.
clavier(m) chant(m) 536.
clavier(m) de grand orgue(m) 542.
clavier(m) de positif(m) 542.
clavier(m) de récit(m) 542.
clavier(m) manuel 543.
clavier(m) numérique 422, 530, 709.
claviers(m) manuels 542.
clayette(f) 254.
clé(f) 290, 549.
clé(f) à chaîne(f) 299.
clé(f) à cliquet(m) 279.
clé(f) à crémaillère(f) 299.
clé(f) à fourches(f) 279.
clé(f) à molette(f) 279.
clé(f) à percussion(f) 780.
clé(f) à sangle(f) 299.
clé(f) à tuyau(m) 299.
clé(f) coudée à tuyau(m) 299.
clé(f) d'ut(m) 537.
clé(f) de barrage(m) 779.
clé(f) de bocal(m) 548.
clé(f) de bras(m) 668.
clé(f) de contact(m) 271.
clé(f) de fa(m) 537.
clé(f) de mandrin(m) 281.
clé(f) de sol(m) 537.
clé(f) de voûte(f) 174, 177.
clé(f) mixte 279.
clé(f) polygonale 279.
clé(f) polygonale à têtes(f) fendues
   279.
clés(f) 537.
client(m) 417.
clignotant(m) 441.
clignotant(m) arrière 443.
CLIMATISATION(F) 214.
climatiseur(m) 449.
climatiseur(m) de fenêtre(f) 214.
climats(m) continentaux 45.
climats(m) de montagne(f) 45.
climats(m) de montagne(f) 45.
CLIMATS(M) DU MONDE(M) 45.
climats(m) polaires 45.
climats(m) subarctiques 45.
climats(m) subarctiques 45.
climats(m) subtropicaux 45.
climats(m) tempérés 45.
climats(m) tropicaux 45.
clin foc(m) 481.
cliquet(m) 276, 281, 573, 706, 707.
clitoris(m) 128.
cloche(f) 329.
clocher(m) 175.
clocheton(m) 175, 176, 181.
cloison(f) 65, 141, 685, 697, 701.
cloison(f) de citerne(f) 742.
cloison(f) longitudinale 742.
cloison(f) transversale 742.
clôture(f) 148.
clôture(f) en lattis(m) 263.
clou(m) 275.
clou(m) 104.
clou(m) millésimé 466.
club-house(m) 651.
coach(m) 425.
coccinelle(f) 77.
coccyx(m) 122.
Cocher(m) 11.
cocheur(m) d'allée(f) 678.

cocheur(m) de sable(m) 678.
cochonnet(m) 682.
cockpit(m) 628.
code(m) 524.
code(m) des produits(m) 709.
cœur(m) 125.
cœur(m) 64, 88, 92, 97, 130, 204,
   615, 695.
cœur(m) de croisement(m) 467.
cœur(m) du réacteur(m) 760, 762,
   763.
coffre(m) 226, 427, 768, 769.
coffre(m) à bagages(m) 449.
coffre(m) d'appareillage(m) 458.
coffre(m) de rangement(m) 440, 778,
   780.
coffret(m) 410.
coffret(m) de branchement(m) 757.
coiffe(f) 57, 577, 670.
coiffeuse(f) 292.
COIFFURE(F) 328, 368, 370.
coiffure(f), accessoires(m) 369.
coin(m) 542, 577, 669.
coin(m) de patinoire(f) 608.
coinceur(m) 681.
coinceur(m) 680.
coing(m) 64.
col(m) 341.
col(m) 27, 319, 322, 324, 352, 410,
   678.
col(m) banane(f) 341.
col(m) berthe(f) 342.
col(m) cagoule(f) 342.
col(m) châle(m) 341.
col(m) chemisier(m) 341.
col(m) chinois 342.
col(m) Claudine 341.
col(m) cravate(f) 342.
col(m) de l'utérus(m) 128.
col(m) italien 324.
col(m) marin(m) 342.
col(m) officier(m) 342.
col(m) pointes(f) boutonnées 324.
col(m) polo(m) 342.
col(m) roulé 326, 338, 342, 642.
col(m) tailleur(m) 330, 341.
col(m) transformable 319.
col(m)-de-cygne(m) 201.
col-de-cygne(m) 784.
colette(f) 363.
collant(m) 344.
collant(m) fantaisie(f) 349.
collant(m) sans pied(m) 353.
collatéral(m) 177.
collatérale(f) 135.
colle(f) 200.
collecteur(m) 753.
collecteur(m) d'appareil(m) 215.
collecteur(m) d'échappement(m) 435,
   438, 439.
collecteur(m) d'évacuation(f) 215.
collecteur(m) de graisse(f) 253.
collecteur(m) de vapeur(f) primaire
   759.
collecteur(m) du réacteur(m) 759.
collecteur(m) principal 215, 216.
collerette(f) 318, 341.
collet(m) 57, 144, 205, 240, 241, 283,
   483, 579.
collet(m) de l'axone(m) 135.
collet(m) repoussé 300.
collier(m) 248, 641, 653.
collier(m) coupe-feu(m) 205.
collier(m) de perles(f), longueur(f)
   matinée(f) 361.
collier(m) de serrage(m) 40, 663.
collier(m) de serrage(m) du casque(m)
   512.
collier(m) de soirée(f) 361.
collier(m)-de-chien(m) 361.
colliers(m) 361.
colline(f) 27.
colline(f) abyssale 29.
Colombe(f) 13.
colombin(m) 584.
côlon(m) ascendant 131.
côlon(m) descendant 131.
côlon(m) pelvien 131.
côlon(m) transverse 131.
colonne(f) 24, 36, 166, 168, 169, 283,
   393, 399, 477, 545, 561, 579, 621,
   700, 701.
colonne(f) ascendante 208.
colonne(f) avec capuchon(m) 37.
colonne(f) d'air(m) 298.
colonne(f) d'alcool(m) 705.
colonne(f) de mercure(m) 705.
colonne(f) de production(f) 740.

colonne(f) de radiateur(m) 208.
colonne(f) de stabilisation(f) 738.
colonne(f) de ventilation(f) 215.
colonne(f) de ventilation(f) principale
   215.
colonne(f) descendante 208.
colonne(f) montante d'eau(f) chaude
   215.
colonne(f) montante d'eau(f) froide
   215.
colonne(f) vertébrale 89, 122, 134.
cols(m), types(m) 341, 342.
columelle(f) 94.
combattant(m) 668.
combinaison(f) 325, 351, 643.
combinaison(f) de nuit(f) 350.
combinaison(f) de ski(m) 640, 642.
combinaison(f) de vol(m) 635.
combinaison(f) gagnante 702.
combinaison(f)-jupon(m) 345.
combinaison(f)-pantalon(m) 336.
combiné(m) 347, 420, 422.
combiné(m) 2 dans 1 368.
combiné(m) bucco-dentaire 373.
combiné(m)-culotte(f) 347.
combustible(m) 761, 766.
combustible(m) défectueux sous
   gaine(f) 764.
**combustible(m) nucléaire,
   manipulation(f) 764.**
combustible(m): uranium(m) enrichi
   762, 763.
combustible(m): uranium(m) naturel
   760, 761.
combustion(f) 436, 437, 501.
COMÈTE(F) 9.
commande(f) amovible 253.
commande(f) au pied(m) 561.
commande(f) d'accélération(f) 272.
commande(f) d'aérofrein(m) 639.
commande(f) d'alimentation(f) en
   oxygène(m) 639.
commande(f) d'arrêt(m) 411.
commande(f) d'avance(f) rapide 411.
commande(f) d'éjection(f) de la
   cassette(f) 409, 411.
commande(f) d'éjection(f) de la pile(f)
   409.
commande(f) d'enregistrement(m)
   411.
commande(f) d'essuie-glace(m) 430.
commande(f) d'insertion(f) du
   papier(m) 523.
commande(f) de barrières(f) 471.
commande(f) de chauffage(m) 430.
commande(f) de dossier(m) 428.
commande(f) de largage(m) de
   câble(m) 639.
commande(f) de largage(m) de la
   verrière(f) 639.
commande(f) de lecture(f) 411.
commande(f) de marche(f) arrière 397.
commande(f) de marche(f) avant 397.
commande(f) de marge(f) 525.
commande(f) de mémoire(f) 396.
commande(f) de panneau(m) solaire
   42.
commande(f) de positionnement(m)
   du specimen(m) 717.
commande(f) de rebobinage(m) 411.
commande(f) de réglage(m) macro(f)
   409.
commande(f) de remise(f) à zéro(m)
   411.
commande(f) de sélection(f) de
   l'ouverture(f) 717.
commande(f) de sélection(f) manuelle
   397.
commande(f) de température(f) 254.
commande(f) de ventilateur(m) 214.
commande(f) de virage(m) et
   d'inclinaison(f) latérale 639.
commande(f) de vitesse(f) 250.
commande(f) de volume(m) 420.
commande(f) de volume(m) de la
   sonnerie(f) 420.
commande(f) de volume(m) du
   récepteur(m) 420.
commande(f) des freins(m) 636.
commande(f) du chariot(m) 569, 718.
commande(f) du rétroviseur(m) 429.
commande(f) électrique de
   paiement(m) 702.
commande(f) électrique du zoom(m)
   409.
commande(f) mémoire(f) 420.
commandes(f) de la bande(f) vidéo
   409.
commandes(f) de montage(m) 409.

commandes(f) de préréglage(m) 411.
commandes(f) de prise(f) de vue(f) 409.
commandes(f) du magnétoscope(m)
   411.
commandes(f) du pilote(m)
   automatique 500.
commencement(m) du patron(m) 569.
commissure(f) labiale 142.
commode(f) 226.
communication(f) par réseau(m) 527.
communications(f) aériennes 417.
communications(f) individuelles 417.
communications(f) industrielles 417.
communications(f) maritimes 417.
communications(f) militaires 417.
communications(f) routières 417.
commutateur(m) 310, 397.
commutateur(m) d'entrée(f) 402.
commutateur(m) de fonctions(f) 402.
commutateur(m) marche(f)/arrêt(m)
   391.
commutateur(m) mono(f)/stéréo(f)
   402.
compartiment(m) à fret(m) 499.
compartiment(m) bagages(m) 458.
compartiment(m) de la production(f)
   d'électricité(f) 806.
compartiment(m) de première classe(f)
   498.
compartiment(m) des instruments(m)
   43.
compartiment(m) des voitures(f) 494.
compartiment(m) du réacteur(m) 806.
compartiment(m) touriste 499.
compartiment(m) voyageurs(m) 458.
compartiment(m)-couchette(f) 440.
compas(m) 619.
compas(m) d'épaisseur(f) 583.
**compas(m) magnétique liquide
   484.**
**compas(m) magnétique liquide,
   coupe(f) 485.**
compensateur(m) de poussée(f) latérale
   404.
**complexe(m) hydroélectrique
   746.**
compluvium(m) 170, 171.
composeuse(f) 527.
compresse(f) stérilisée 725.
compresseur(m) 212, 517.
compresseur(m) centrifuge 501.
compresseur(m) d'air(m) 469.
compresseur(m) du climatiseur(m) 435.
compression(f) 436, 437, 501.
compression(f)/admission(f) 436.
comprimé(m) 725.
compte-pose(m) 399.
compte-rangs(m) 568.
compte-touches(m) électrique 666.
compte-tours(m) 431.
compteur(m) 215, 403.
compteur(m) d'électricité(f) 757.
compteur(m) kilométrique 431.
comptoir(m) d'enregistrement(m) 504.
comptoir(m) de renseignements(m)
   504.
comptoir(m) de vente(f) des billets(m)
   504.
concentration(f) du faisceau(m) 717.
concombre(m) 69.
Concorde(m) 19.
condensation(f) 35.
condensation(f) de la vapeur(f) 767.
condenseur(m) 717, 718, 758, 771.
conditionnement(m) d'air(m) 494.
CONDITIONNEMENT(M) PHYSIQUE,
   APPAREILS(M) 664.
conducteur(m) 652.
conducteur(m) de phase(f) 757.
conducteur(m) de terre(f) 757.
conducteur(m) du thermocouple(m)
   297.
conducteur(m) en faisceau(m) 756.
conducteur(m) neutre 757.
conduit(m) 543.
conduit(m) auditif 138.
conduit(m) de chauffage(m) 259.
conduit(m) de distribution(f) vertical
   206.
conduit(m) de la glande(f) 96.
conduit(m) de raccordement(m) 204.
conduit(m) hydraulique 156, 157, 158.
conduit(m) lactifère 129.
conduite(f) à la terre(f) 741.
conduite(f) d'admission(f) principale
   741.
conduite(f) d'admission(f) secondaire
   741.
conduite(f) d'alimentation(f) 215.

Les termes en **caractères gras** renvoient à une illustration, ceux en CAPITALES indiquent un titre.

Les termes en **caractères gras** renvoient à une illustration, ceux en CAPITALES indiquent un titre.

Les termes en **caractères gras** renvoient à une illustration, ceux en CAPITALES indiquent un titre.

Les termes en **caractères gras** renvoient à une illustration, ceux en CAPITALES indiquent un titre.

FRENCH INDEX

875

Les termes en **caractères gras** renvoient à une illustration, ceux en CAPITALES indiquent un titre.

Les termes en **caractères gras** renvoient à une illustration, ceux en CAPITALES indiquent un titre.

Les termes en **caractères gras** renvoient à une illustration, ceux en CAPITALES indiquent un titre.

FRENCH INDEX

Les termes en **caractères gras** renvoient à une illustration, ceux en CAPITALES indiquent un titre.

Les termes en **caractères gras** renvoient à une illustration, ceux en CAPITALES indiquent un titre.

Les termes en **caractères gras** renvoient à une illustration, ceux en CAPITALES indiquent un titre.

repose-bras(m) 404.
repose-pied(m) 727.
repose-pied(m) du passager(m) 443, 444.
repose-pied(m) du pilote(m) 443, 444.
repositionnement(m) 525.
repousse-chair(m) 365.
reprise(f) d'air(m) 206, 207.
REPTILE(M) 96.
réseau(m) d'oléoducs(m) 740.
réseau(m) de transport(m) d'électricité(m) 771.
réseau(m) national 416.
réseau(m) nerveux 144.
réseau(m) privé 416.
réseau(m) téléphonique 417.
réserve(f) d'eau(f) 373.
réserve(f) de papier(m) 532.
réservoir(m) 216, 247, 386, 399, 543, 689, 746, 747, 748, 749, 750, 751, 780.
réservoir(m) à carburant(m) 440, 468, 508, 805, 812.
réservoir(m) à essence(f) 442.
réservoir(m) à grain(m) 160.
réservoir(m) à toit(m) fixe 741.
réservoir(m) à toit(m) flottant 741.
réservoir(m) auxiliaire 441.
réservoir(m) d'air(m) comprimé 469.
réservoir(m) d'alcool(m) 705.
réservoir(m) d'arrosage(m) 759, 766.
réservoir(m) d'azote(m) liquide 717.
réservoir(m) d'eau(f) 210.
réservoir(m) d'essence(f) 272.
réservoir(m) d'huile(f) 272.
réservoir(m) d'hydrogène(m) liquide 509.
réservoir(m) d'oxygène(m) liquide 509.
réservoir(m) de brut(m) 744.
réservoir(m) de chasse(f) d'eau(f) 292.
réservoir(m) de fluide(m) 212.
réservoir(m) de kérosène(m) 509.
réservoir(m) de mercure(m) 705.
réservoir(m) de sécurité(f) 761.
réservoir(m) de stockage(m) 772.
réservoir(m) externe 510.
réservoir(m) magmatique 25.
réservoir(m) propane(m) 449.
réservoir(m) tampon(m) 740.
réservoirs(m) 511.
résistance(f) hydraulique 664.
résonnateur(m) 406.
ressort 234, 278, 290, 294, 389, 659, 804.
ressort(m) athlétique 665.
ressort(m) compensateur de fil(m) 562.
ressort(m) d'échappement(m) 541.
ressort(m) de batterie(f) 795.
ressort(m) de rappel(m) 432.
ressort(m) de soupape(f) 434, 543.
ressort(m) de suspension(f) 258, 469.
ressort(m) de tension(f) 431, 665.
ressort(m) en spirale(f) 231.
restaurant(m) 185, 190, 494, 822.
rétenteur(m) 653.
Réticule(f) 13.
réticule(m) 718.
réticulum(m) endoplasmique 115.
rétine(f) 140.
retombées(f) 35.
retour(m) 521.
retour(m) de chariot(m) 525.
retour(m) de l'eau(f) au générateur(m) de vapeur(f) 767.
RETOURNER LA TERRE(F) 156.
retourner la terre(f) 154.
retrait(m) 524.
rétroviseur(m) 430, 440, 442, 444.
rétroviseur(m) extérieur 426.
réunion(f) 830.
réverbère(m) 186.
revers(m) 322, 323, 341, 354.
revers(m) à cran(m) aigu 322.
revers(m) cranté 319, 320.
revêtement(m) 198, 199, 619, 741.
revêtement(m) de sécurité(f) 512.
revêtement(m) intérieur 433.
revêtement(m) thermique 510.
revêtement(m), matériaux(m) 286.
REVOLVER(M) 797.
rez-de-chaussée(m) 194.
rez-de-chaussée(m) 197.
rhéostat(m) 309.
rhino-pharynx(m) 141.
rhubarbe(f) 72.

ribosome(m) 115.
richelieu(m) 354.
rideau(m) 229.
rideau(m) 229, 414.
rideau(m) ballon(m) 229.
rideau(m) bonne femme(f) 228.
rideau(m) brise-bise(m) 228.
rideau(m) coulissé 228.
rideau(m) d'obturateur(m) 390.
rideau(m) de fer(m) 188.
rideau(m) de scène(f) 188, 189.
rideau(m) de vitrage(m) 228.
rideau(m) festonné 228.
rideau(m) pare-vent(m) 14.
rideaux(m) croisés 229.
rideaux(m), types(m) 228.
ridoir(m) 630.
riflouir(m) 587.
rift(f) 28.
rigole(f) 682.
rimaye(f) 26.
rinceau(m) 220.
ring(m) 669.
risberme(f) 748.
rive(f) externe 104.
rive(f) interne 104.
rivet(m) 242, 278.
rivière(f) 51.
rivière(f) souterraine 24.
riz(m) 152.
robe(f) 741.
robe(f) à crinoline(f) 318.
robe(f) à paniers(m) 317.
robe(f) à tournure(f) 316.
robe(f) bain(m)-de-soleil(m) 332.
robe(f) chemisier(m) 333.
robe(f) de maison(f) 333.
robe(f) enveloppe(f) 333.
robe(f) fourreau(m) 332.
robe(f) princesse(f) 334.
robe(f) taille(f) basse 332.
robe(f) tee-shirt(m) 351.
robe(f) trapèze(f) 332.
robe(f) tunique(f) 333.
robe(f)-manteau(m) 332.
robe(f)-polo(m) 333.
robes(f), types(f) 332.
robinet(m) 294.
robinet(m) 292.
robinet(m) d'acétylène(m) 306.
robinet(m) d'arrêt(m) 293, 296, 298.
robinet(m) d'arrêt(m) général 215.
robinet(m) d'oxygène(m) 306.
robinet(m) de réglage(m) de débit(m) 777.
robinet(m) de vidange(f) 297, 741.
robinet(m) flotteur à clapet(m) 293.
robinet(m) relais(m) 689.
robinets(m) de carburant(m) 500.
robot(m) de cuisine(f) 251.
roc(m) 714.
rocaille(f) 263.
roches(f) d'intrusion(f) 23.
roches(f) ignées 23.
roches(f) métamorphiques 23.
roches(f) sédimentaires 23.
rochet(m) 281, 706, 707.
Roi(m) 695, 696.
romaine(f) 73.
romarin(m) 74.
rond pronateur(m) 120.
rond-point(m) 52.
ronde(f) 538.
rondeau(m) 584.
rondelle(f) 608.
rondelle(f) 294, 641, 642.
rondelle(f) à denture(f) extérieure 278.
rondelle(f) à denture(f) intérieure 278.
rondelle(f) à ressort(m) 278.
rondelle(f) conique 293.
rondelle(f) de fibre(f) 300.
rondelle(f) plate 278.
rondelles(f) 278.
rondiste(m) 363.
rongeur(m), mâchoire(f) 98.
ros(m) 572.
rosace(f) 546.
rose(f) 175.
rose(f) des vents(m) 484.
rosée(f) 37.
rosette(f) 167, 289, 290.
rostre(m) 90.
rotonde(f) 190.
rotor(m) 161, 290, 437, 753, 773, 774.
rotor(m) anticouple 508.
rotule(f) 103, 122, 282.
roue(f) 433.

roue(f) 270, 427, 440, 727, 753, 800, 805.
roue(f) à rayons(m) 652.
roue(f) avant 147, 784.
roue(f) d'échappement(m) 706, 707.
roue(f) d'engrenage(m) 280, 575.
roue(f) d'entraînement(m) 575.
roue(f) de centre(m) 706, 707.
roue(f) de champ(m) 706.
roue(f) de poulie(f) 230.
roue(f) de pression(f) 158.
roue(f) de sécurité(f) 476.
roue(f) de support(m) 445.
roue(f) de turbine(f) 752.
roue(f) dentée 445, 573.
roue(f) folle 783.
roue(f) Francis 754.
roue(f) Kaplan 754.
roue(f) libre 448.
roue(f) motrice 147, 707.
roue(f) Pelton 754.
roue(f) petite moyenne 706, 707.
roue(f) pivotante 727.
roues(f) motrices 784.
rouge(m) 700, 701.
rouge(m) à lèvres(m) 366.
Rouges(m) 697.
rough(m) 676.
rouleau(m) 304.
rouleau(m) 231, 270, 369, 583, 702.
rouleau(m) à pâtisserie(f) 245.
rouleau(m) à vernir 282.
rouleau(m) conditionneur 158.
rouleau(m) d'encrage(m) 581.
rouleau(m) de pellicule(f) 395.
rouleau(m) principal 572.
roulette(f) 563.
roulette(f) 260, 383, 553, 582, 645, 788.
roulette(f) américaine 700.
roulette(f) de pâtissier(m) 245.
roulette(f) française 701.
route(f), coupe(f) 450.
route(f) 52, 452.
route(f) d'accès(m) 502.
route(f) secondaire 52.
ruban(m) 566, 711, 804.
ruban(m) adhésif 607.
ruban(m) blanc 618.
ruban(m) correcteur 515.
ruban(m) de caoutchouc(m) 677.
ruban(m) de tissu(m) adhésif 725.
rubis(m) 363, 706.
ruche(f) 82.
ruche(m) 109.
ruché(m) 349.
rue(f) 52, 184, 190.
RUE(F), COUPE(F) 186.
RUGBY(M) 606.
rugby(m), terrain(m) 606.
ruisseau(m) 676.
ruissellement(m) 32, 34.
russule(f) verdoyante 55.
rutabaga(m) 71.

S

sable(m) 748, 819.
sablier(m) 244.
sablière(f) 469.
sablière(f) double 198.
sabot(m) 104.
sabot(m) 101, 441, 633, 656.
sabot(m) à 1 doigt(m) 99.
sabot(m) à 2 doigts(m) 99.
sabot(m) à 3 doigts(m) 99.
sabot(m) à 4 doigts(m) 99.
sabot(m) de protection(f) 783.
sabot(m), face(f) plantaire 104.
SABOTS(M), TYPES(M) 99.
sabre(m) 666, 794.
sabreur(m) 667.
sac(m) 59.
sac(m) à bandoulière(f) 380.
sac(m) à dos(m) 680.
sac(m) à provisions(f) 381.
sac(m) accordéon(m) 380.
sac(m) besace(f) 380.
sac(m) boîte(f) 381.
sac(m) cartable(m) 380.
sac(m) de golf(m) 679.
sac(m) de vol(m) 382.
sac(m) fourre-tout(m) 380, 382.
sac(m) marin(m) 381.
sac(m) polochon(m) 381.
sac(m) pour accessoires(m) 684.
sac(m) seau(m) 381.
sacoche(f) 448.
sacrum(m) 122, 123.

SACS(M) À MAIN(F) 380.
sacs(m) de couchage(m) 687.
Sagittaire(m) 13.
Sagittaire(m) (22 novembre) 820.
saharienne(f) 338.
saillant(m) 178.
saisie(f) des données(f) 717.
SAISONS(F), CYCLE(M) 8.
saladier(m) 238.
salamandre(f) 85.
salière(f) 238.
salle(f) 189.
salle(f) à manger 195, 460, 496, 807.
salle(f) d'embarquement(m) 505.
SALLE(F) DE BAINS(M) 292.
salle(f) de bains(m) 194, 195.
salle(f) de bal(m) 497.
salle(f) de commande(f) 746, 759.
salle(f) de commandes(f) 14.
salle(f) de contrôle(f) 16.
salle(f) de contrôle(f) des machines(f) 742.
salle(f) de prière(f) 172, 173.
salle(f) de projection(f) 16.
salle(f) de réception(f) 172, 173.
salle(f) de répétition(f) 188.
salle(f) de séjour(m) 195.
SALLE(F) DE SPECTACLE(M) 188.
salle(f) de stockage(m) du combustible(m) neuf 764.
salle(f) des cartes(f) 494.
salle(f) des gradateurs(m) 412.
salle(f) des machines(f) 496, 746, 747.
salle(f) des ordinateurs(m) 807.
salle(f) des pas(m) perdus 462.
salle(f) du treuil(m) 735.
salle(f) polyvalente 412.
salomé(m) 356.
salon(m) 195, 496.
salopette(f) à bretelles(f) croisées 351.
salopette(f) à dos(m) montant 350.
salsifis(m) 71.
sandale(f) 356, 791.
sandalette(f) 357.
Sandow®(m) 685, 686.
sangle(f) 428, 614, 634, 649, 651, 660, 664, 679, 777.
sangle(f) d'amortissement(m) 729.
sangle(f) de brancard(m) 653.
sangle(f) de nuque(f) 729.
sangle(f) élastique 382.
sangle(f) serre-vêtements(m) 383.
sangle(f) sous-ventrière 653.
sanglon(m) 649.
sanguine(f) 583.
sapeur(m)-pompier(m) 777.
saphir(m) 363.
sarcloir(m) 266.
sarment(m) 61.
sarrazin(m) 152.
sarriette(f) 74.
sas(m) 14, 493, 510.
sas(m) d'accès(m) arrière 806.
sas(m) du bâtiment(m) du réacteur(m) 758.
sas(m) du laboratoire(m) 511.
sas(m) pour équipement(m) 764.
satellite(m) 416.
satellite(m) à défilement(m) 43.
satellite(m) artificiel 19.
SATELLITE(M) DE TÉLÉDÉTECTION(F) 48.
satellite(m) géostationnaire 42.
SATELLITE(M) MÉTÉOROLOGIQUE 42.
satellite(m) Radarsat 49.
satellites(m) 4.
SATELLITES(M) DE TÉLÉCOMMUNICATIONS(F) 418.
satellites(m) de télécommunications(f), exemples(m) 418.
satin(m) 576.
Saturne 5.
saucière(f) 238.
sauge(f) 74.
saumon(m) d'aile(f) 638.
saupoudreuse(f) 246.
saut(m) à la perche(f) 657.
saut(m) à la perche(f) 655.
saut(m) en hauteur(f) 657.
saut(m) en hauteur(f) 654.
sauterelle(f) 77, 733.
sauteur(m) 635.
sauteuse(f) 249.
sautoir(m) 361.
sautoir(m), longueur(f) opéra(m) 361.
savane(f) 45.

Les termes en **caractères gras** renvoient à une illustration, ceux en CAPITALES indiquent un titre.

Les termes en **caractères gras** renvoient à une illustration, ceux en CAPITALES indiquent un titre.

Les termes en **caractères gras** renvoient à une illustration, ceux en CAPITALES indiquent un titre.

Les termes en **caractères gras** renvoient à une illustration, ceux en CAPITALES indiquent un titre.

GERMAN INDEX

Fettgedruckte Wörter beziehen sich auf eine Illustration; Wörter in GROSSBUCHSTABEN sind Überschriften.

Fettgedruckte Wörter beziehen sich auf eine Illustration; Wörter in GROSSBUCHSTABEN sind Überschriften.

Fettgedruckte Wörter beziehen sich auf eine Illustration; Wörter in GROSSBUCHSTABEN sind Überschriften.

GERMAN INDEX

K

Fettgedruckte Wörter beziehen sich auf eine Illustration; Wörter in GROSSBUCHSTABEN sind Überschriften.

GERMAN INDEX

Fettgedruckte Wörter beziehen sich auf eine Illustration; Wörter in GROSSBUCHSTABEN sind Überschriften.

Fettgedruckte Wörter beziehen sich auf eine Illustration; Wörter in GROSSBUCHSTABEN sind Überschriften.

Fettgedruckte Wörter beziehen sich auf eine Illustration; Wörter in GROSSBUCHSTABEN sind Überschriften.

914

Rollgabelschlüssel(m) 299.
Rollkloben(m) 793.
Rollkragen(m) 338, 342, 642.
Rollkragenpullover(m) 326.
Rollkugel(f) 526.
Rollmechanismus(m) 231.
Rollo(n) 231.
Rollo-Fallstab(m) 231.
Rollostoff(m) 231.
Rollring(m) 293.
ROLLSCHUH(M) 645.
Rollschweller(m) 542.
ROLLSTUHL(M) 727.
Rollstuhl(m) 461.
Rollstuhlfahrer(m) 822.
ROM-Modul(n) 528.
Romagna-Salat(m) 73.
Römerpantolette(f) 357.
RÖMISCHES WOHNHAUS(N) 170.
Rondiste(f) 363.
Rondistenfacette(f), obere 363.
Rondistenfacette(f), untere 363.
Rose(f) 105.
Rosenkohl(m) 73.
Rosennerv(m), großer 133.
Rosenschliff(m) 362.
Rosenstock(m) 105.
Rosenvene(f), große 126.
Rosette(f) 167, 175, 289, 290, 294, 295.
Rosmarin(m) 74.
Rösselsprung(m) 696.
Rost(m) 255.
Rostrum(n) 90.
rot 819.
Rot(n) 697.
Rotationsschiene(f) 15.
Rotes Meer(n) 21.
Rotor(m) 161, 290, 753, 755, 773, 774.
Rotorblatt(n) 508, 774.
Rotorkopf(m) 508.
Rotormast(m) 508.
Rotornabe(f) 508.
Rotstrahl(m) 410.
Rotunde(f) 190.
Rouge(n) 700, 701.
Rougepinsel(m) 366.
Roulette(f) 582.
Roulette(n), amerikanisches 700.
Roulette(n), französisches 701.
Roulettekessel(m) 701.
Roulettekugel(f) 701.
Roulettespielplan(m), amerikanischer 700.
Roulettespielplan(m), französischer 701.
ROULETTESPIELTISCH(M) 700.
Royal Flush(m) 695.
Royalstange(f) 479.
Rübe(f) 71.
Rübenhacke(f) 266.
Rubin(m) 363.
Rückansicht(f) 95, 121, 123, 129.
Rücken(m) 101, 106, 108, 117, 119, 174, 239, 240, 241, 242, 277, 322, 386, 577.
Rücken(m), ozeanischer 28.
Rückenflosse(f), erste 86.
Rückenflosse(f), zweite 86.
Rückengürtel(m) 330.
Rückenlage(f) 621.
Rückenlasche(f) 653.
Rückenlehne(f) 220, 223, 428, 445, 727.
Rückenmark(n) 89, 134, 135.
Rückenmarkshaut(f), harte 134, 135.
Rückenmittelschlitz(m) 322.
Rückenmuskel(m), breiter 121.
Rückenpanzer(m) 96.
Rückenpolster(m) 653.
Rückenschlitz(m), seitlicher 322.
Rückenschwimmen(n) 623.
Rückenspange(f) 322.
Rückenteil(n), verstellbares 726.
Rückenverstärkung(f) 644.
Rückfeld(n) 614.
Rückfeldrichter(m) 605.
Rückfeldschiedsrichter(m) 603.
Rückgrat(m) 670.
Rückholfeder(f) 432.
Rücklagenstütze(f) 641.
Rücklauf(m) 208, 831.
Rücklauf-Taste(f) 403.
Rücklaufboden(m) 161.
Rücklauftaste(f) 408, 420.
Rücklaufverschraubung(f) 208.
Rücklicht(n) 441, 446.

Rückruftaste(f) 396.
Rucksack(m) 680.
Rückschläger(m) 614, 616, 618.
Rückschlaghinderer(m) 795, 798, 799.
Rückschlagventil(n) 216.
Rückseite(f) 363.
Rücksitzbank(f) 428.
Rückspiegel(m) 430, 442.
Rücksprungpalette(f) 787.
Rückspulknopf(m) 391.
Rückspultaste(f) 411.
Rückstellknopf(m) 706, 711.
Rückstelltaste(f) 403, 411, 421.
Rückstrahler(m) 441, 445, 446.
rückwärts 624.
Rückwurflinie(f) 599.
Ruder(m) 492, 496, 511, 664, 742, 814.
Ruder(n), oberes 806.
Ruderblatt(n) 628.
Ruderboote(n) 632.
Rudergerät(n) 664.
RUDERN(N) 632.
Rudern(n) 632.
Ruf(m), nächster 422.
Ruffinisches Körperchen(n) 136.
Rufnummernregister(n) 420.
Rufnummernregister(n) für automatische Wahl(f) 420.
RUGBY(N) 606.
Rugbyball(m) 606.
Rührbesen(m) 250.
Rührbesen(m) 250.
Rührschüssel(f) 250.
Rührschüsseln(f) 245.
Rührwerk(n) 258.
Rumpf(m) 117, 119, 445, 499, 628, 639, 698.
Rumpfleitwerk(n) 498.
Rumpfsonar(m) 809.
rund 56.
Rundblickperiskop(n) 805.
Rundbogen(m) 174.
Rundbürste(f) 368.
runde Bahn(f) 275.
Rundeisen(n) 581.
RUNDFUNK(M): SPRECHERRAUM(M) UND REGIERAUM(M) 407.
Rundfunkempfänger(m) 400, 402.
Rundfunknetz(n), privates 416.
Rundkopf(m) mit Schlitz(m) 276.
Rundmuskel(m), großer 121.
Rundmuskel(m), kleiner 121.
Rundstricknadel(f) 567.
Rungentasche(f) 441.
Rüschen(f) 349.
Rüschenhöschen(n) 349.
Rüschenstrumpfhose(f) 349.
Rüssel(m) 79.
russischer Pumpernickel(m) 153.
RÜSTUNG(F) 792.
Rutengriff(m) 671.
Rutenschwellkörper(m) 127.
Rutsche(f) 736.

S

S-Bahn(f) 464.
S-Band Antenne(f) 43.
S-Band hochbündelnde Antenne(f) 42.
S-Band Rundstrahlantenne(f) 42.
S-Bogen(m) 548.
Saal(m) 496.
Saatgutbehälter(m) 158.
Säbel(m) 666, 794.
Säbel- und Degenfechten(n) 666.
Säbelfechter(m) 667.
Sackkarren(m) 788.
SÄEN(N) 158.
Säen(n) 154.
Safarijacke(f) 338.
Safety(m), linker 603.
Safety(m), rechter 603.
Safetyback(m), linker 605.
Safetyback(m), rechter 605.
Sägeblatt(n) 277, 285.
Sägeblatthöhenverstellung(f) 285.
Sägekette(f) 272.
Sagittalschnitt(m) 127, 128, 129, 142.
Sagittarius 820.
Sähkelle(f) 268.
Saite(f) 541, 544, 545.
Saitenaufhängung(f) 547.
Saitenbezug(m) 540.
Saitenhalter(m) 544.
SAITENINSTRUMENTE(N) 544, 546.
Salamander(m) 85.

Salatgabel(f) 240.
Salatschale(f) 238.
Salatschleuder(f) 243.
Salatschüssel(f) 238.
Salatteller(m) 238.
Salbei(m) 74.
Saling(f) 478, 628.
Salto(m) 625.
Saltostellung(f) 624.
Salz(m) 46.
Salzstreuer(m) 238.
Salzsumpf(m) 30.
Samen(m) 62, 63, 64, 65, 66, 67.
Samenanlage(f) 60.
Samenbläschen(n) 127.
Samenleiter(m) 127.
Samenmantel(m) 63.
Samenschale(f) 152.
Samenstrang(m) 127.
Sammellinsen(f) 722.
Sammelrohr(n) 162.
Sammelschiene(f) 747.
Sammeltrichter(m) 40.
Samtkropfband(n) 361.
Sand(m) 748.
Sand- oder Staubsturm(m) 39.
Sand-Wedge(m) 678.
Sandale(f) 357, 791.
Sandalette(f) 356.
Sandbank(f) 30.
Sandblattfeilen(f) 365.
Sandinsel(f) 30.
Sandkasten(m) 469.
Sandwüste(f) 46.
SANITÄRINSTALLATION(F) 292, 294, 296, 298, 299, 300.
SANITÄRINSTALLATIONSSYSTEM(N) 215.
Saphir(m) 363.
Sarong(m) 334.
Satellit(m) 416, 419.
SATELLIT(M), ERDERKENNUNGSGEODÄTISCHER 48.
Satellit(m), geostationärer 42.
Satellit(m), polarumlaufender 43.
Satelliten(m) 418.
Satelliten(m), Umlaufbahn(f) 43.
Satelliten-Direktempfang(m) 416.
Sattel(m) 649.
Sattel(m) 320, 324, 337, 397, 446, 544, 546, 547, 648, 651, 661.
Satteldach(n) 182.
Sattelgurt(m) 649.
Sattelkupplung(f) 440.
Sattelplatz(m) 651.
Sattelpolster(n) 649.
Sattelrock(m) 334.
Sattelschlepper(m) 440.
Sattelstütze(f) 446.
Satteltasche(f) 448.
Satteltuch(n) 651.
Sattelzug(m) 440.
Saturn(m) 5.
Satztische(m) 219.
SATZZEICHEN(N) 832.
Sau(f) 151.
Sauciere(f) 238.
Sauerstoffdruck-Stelleinrichtung(f) 512.
Sauerstoffflasche(f) 306.
Sauerstoffventil(n) 306.
Sauerstoffzufuhranzeige(f) 639.
Sauerstoffzufuhrregler(m) 639.
Saugarm(m) 784.
Saugpinsel(m) 260.
Saugrohr(m) 260, 434, 747, 753, 778, 784.
Saugzubehör(n) 260.
Säule(m) 24, 36, 166, 168, 169, 393, 399, 455, 573, 574, 578, 579, 621.
Säule(f), bedeckte 37.
Säulenordnung(f), dorische 167.
Säulenordnung(f), ionische 166.
Säulenordnung(f), korinthische 167.
Saum(m) 231, 565, 598.
Saummaß(n) 563.
Saumrand(m) 104.
Savanne(f), tropische 45.
Saxhorn(n) 551.
Saxophon(n) 548.
Saxophon(n) 548.
Scanner(m) 526.
Schaber(m) 582.
Schabracke(f) 229.
SCHACH(N) 696.
Schachbrett(n) 696.
Schachtelfalte(f) 228.
Schachtfördergerüst(n) 736.

Schachtgebäude(n) 734.
Schachtsumpf(m) 736.
Schädel(m) 88, 102, 116, 134.
Schadstoffbelastung(f) im Boden(m) 32.
Schadstoffbelastung(f) im Wasser(n) 32.
Schaf(m) 150.
Schaffnertisch(m) 461.
Schafstall(m) 149.
Schaft(m) 110, 166, 275, 276, 281, 483, 562, 567, 568, 573, 609, 615, 632, 652, 658, 675, 677, 684, 698, 773.
Schaftführung(f) 653.
Schaftstiefel(m) 357.
Schäftung(f) 798, 799.
Schäkelband(n) 483.
Schale(f) 64, 65, 66, 92, 109, 383.
SCHALE(F), EINKLAPPIGE 94.
Schale(f), obere 641.
Schale(f), untere 641.
SCHALE(F), ZWEIKLAPPIGE 95.
Schalenhaut(f) 109.
Schalensitz(m) 428.
Schäler(m) 242.
Schälfurnier(m) 288.
Schalkragen(m) 341.
Schallbecher(m) 542.
Schallbecherstütze(f) 549.
Schallbrett(m) 175.
Schalldämpfer(m) 439.
Schalloch(n) 544.
Schallplatte(f) 404.
Schallrille(f) 404.
Schallrose(f) 546.
Schalotte(f) 70.
Schalter(m) 254, 255, 280, 283, 285, 309.
Schalter(m), einpoliger 312.
Schalter(m), zweipoliger 312.
Schalterabdeckplatte(f) 309.
Schalthebel(m) 430, 447, 448.
Schaltpedal(n) 443, 444.
Schaltpult(m) 16.
Schalttafel(f) 210, 214.
Schaltuhr(f) 255.
Schaltung(f), elektronische 233.
Schaltzug(m) 448.
Schambein(n) 116, 118.
Schamhügel(m) 128.
Schamlippe(f), große 128, 129.
Schamlippe(f), kleine 128, 129.
Schamotteplatte(f) 204.
Schamottestein(m) 204.
Schanzkleid(n) 478.
Schar(n) 156.
Schärbaum(m) 575.
Schardrehkranz(m) 784.
Schardrehvorrichtung(f) 784.
Scharfeinsteller(m) 399.
Scharfeinstellung(f) 409, 720, 721.
Schärfentiefenknopf(m) 391.
Schärfentiefenskala(f) 392.
Scharfsteller(m) 399.
Scharfstellrad(n), zentrales 719.
Scharfstellring(m) 719.
Scharhubvorrichtung(f) 784.
Scharnier 202.
Scharnier(n) 203, 225, 253, 257, 378, 382, 404, 429, 443, 585, 719.
Scharwachturm(m) 178, 181.
Schatten(m) 706.
Schaufel(f) 640, 642, 681, 782.
Schaufel(f), hintere 782.
Schaufelarm(m) 782.
Schaufelblatt(n) 753.
Schaufelbolzengelenk(n) 782.
Schaufellader(m) 782.
Schaufelradbagger(m) 733.
Schaufelzahn(m) 782, 785.
Schaufelzylinder(m) 782, 785.
Schaufelzylinder(m), hinterer 782.
Schaukelstuhl(m) 221, 223.
Schaum(m) 30.
Schaumanzeiger(m) 743.
Schaumgummiisolierung(f) 287.
Schaumgummimatratze(f) 687.
Schaumgummipolsterung(f) 729.
Scheckheft(n) 379.
Scheckhülle(f) 379.
Scheibe(f) 157, 203, 583, 663.
Scheiben(f) 251.
Scheibenbremse(f) 432.
Scheibenbremse(f) 442.
Scheibenegge(f) 157.
Scheibenegge(f) 154.
Scheibengardine(f) 228.
Scheibenkopf(m) 584.
Scheibensech(m) 156.

Fettgedruckte Wörter beziehen sich auf eine Illustration; Wörter in GROSSBUCHSTABEN sind Überschriften.

Fettgedruckte Wörter beziehen sich auf eine Illustration; Wörter in GROSSBUCHSTABEN sind Überschriften.

Fettgedruckte Wörter beziehen sich auf eine Illustration; Wörter in GROSSBUCHSTABEN sind Überschriften.

Fettgedruckte Wörter beziehen sich auf eine Illustration; Wörter in GROSSBUCHSTABEN sind Überschriften.

Fettgedruckte Wörter beziehen sich auf eine Illustration; Wörter in GROSSBUCHSTABEN sind Überschriften.

Fettgedruckte Wörter beziehen sich auf eine Illustration; Wörter in GROSSBUCHSTABEN sind Überschriften.

GERMAN INDEX

Fettgedruckte Wörter beziehen sich auf eine Illustration; Wörter in GROSSBUCHSTABEN sind Überschriften.

Fettgedruckte Wörter beziehen sich auf eine Illustration; Wörter in GROSSBUCHSTABEN sind Überschriften.

Los términos en **negrita** corresponden a una ilustración; los que aparecen en MAYÚSCULAS indican un título.

Los términos en **negrita** corresponden a una ilustración; los que aparecen en MAYÚSCULAS indican un título.

Los términos en **negrita** corresponden a una ilustración; los que aparecen en MAYÚSCULAS indican un título.

SPANISH INDEX

círculo(m) 25 698.
círculo(m) central 601, 610, 611, 620.
círculo(m) de canasta(f) 611.
círculo(m) de espera(f) 597.
círculo(m) de la estación(f) 38.
círculo(m) de lanzamiento(m) 654, 655.
círculo(m) de reanudación(f) del juego(m) 608.
círculo(m) de saque(m) inicial 608.
círculo(m) doble 698.
círculo(m) exterior 620.
círculo(m) polar antártico 3.
círculo(m) polar ártico 3, 47.
círculo(m) triple 698.
cirrocúmulos(m) 44.
cirros(m) 44.
cirrostratos(m) 44.
ciruela(f) 63.
Cisne 11.
cisterna(f) del retrete(m) 292.
cisterna(f), camión(m) 742.
cisterna(f), vagón(m) 743.
cítara(f) 535.
citoplasma(m) 115, 128.
cítrico(m), corte(m) de un 65.
CÍTRICOS(M), FRUTOS(M) CARNOSOS 65.
cítricos(m), principales variedades(f) 65.
ciudad(f) 51.
CIUDAD(F), CENTRO(M) 184.
cizalla(f) 578.
clarín(m) 550.
clarinete(m) 548.
clarinete(m) bajo 556.
clarinetes(m) 556.
clasificación(f) de Hubble 9.
clasificador(m) de fuelle(m) 378.
clave(f) 174, 177.
clave(f) de do 537.
clave(f) de fa 537.
clave(f) de sol 537.
clave(f), modelo(m) 38.
clavera(f) 104.
claves(f) 537.
clavícula(f) 122.
clavija(f) 540, 544, 545, 546, 780.
clavija(f) de afinación(f) 547.
clavija(f) de tensión(f) 552.
clavija(f) hendida 290.
clavijero(m) 540, 544.
clavo(m) 275.
clavo(m) 104, 680.
clavo(m) fechador 466.
claxon(m) 444.
claxón(m) 430.
climas(f) de alta montaña(f) 45.
climas(f) subárticos 45.
climas(m) continentales 45.
climas(m) de alta montaña(f) 45.
CLIMAS(M) DEL MUNDO(M) 45.
climas(m) polares 45.
climas(m) subárticos 45.
climas(m) subtropicales 45.
climas(m) templados 45.
climas(m) tropicales 45.
clip(m) 230.
clip(m) de ajuste(m) 233.
clitoris(m) 128.
cloroplasto(m) 115.
cobertera(f) inferior de la cola(f) 109.
cobertera(f) superior de la cola(f) 109.
coberteras(f) 108.
coberteras(f) grandes 110.
coberteras(f) medias 110.
coberteras(f) pequeñas 110.
coberteras(f) primarias 110.
coberteras(f) primarias medias 110.
cobertizo(m) 148, 193, 263.
cobertizo(m) de la parada(f) 186.
cobertizo(m) del andén(m) 464.
cobertizo(m) para ovejas(m) 149.
cocción(f) 585.
cóccix(m) 122.
COCHE(M) DE BOMBEROS(M) 778, 780.
coche(m) familiar 425.
Cochero 11.
cocina(f) 689.
cocina(f) 171, 195, 460, 807.
cocina(f) de a bordo(m) 498.
cocina(f) eléctrica 255.
cocina(f) pequeña 195.
COCINA(F), UTENSILIOS(M) DE 242, 244, 246, 248.
cocina(f), utensilios(m) de 688.
cóclea(f) 139.
coco(m) 66.
codal(m) 792.

codaste(m) 742.
codera(f) 602, 609.
código(m) 524.
código(m) del producto(m) 709.
codillo(m) 106, 108.
codo(m) 106, 112, 117, 119, 206, 376.
codo(m) de 45 grados(m) 301.
codo(m) de 90 grados(m) 301.
cofia(f) cónica 318.
COHETE(M) 509.
cohetes(m) impulsores 510.
cojín(m) 224.
cojín(m) para sellos(m) 516.
cojinete(m) 106, 376, 468.
cojinete(m) carpal 106.
cojinete(m) de rodamiento(m) 753.
cojinete(m) digital 106, 107.
cojinete(m) estéril de gasa(f) 725.
cojinete(m) móvil 631.
cojinete(m) palmar 106.
cojinete(m) plantar 107.
col(f) de China(f) 73.
col(f) rizada 73.
cola(f) 91, 96, 97, 101, 106, 107, 112, 200, 499, 579, 641, 642, 643, 645, 670.
cola(f) de polvo(m) 9.
cola(f) gaseosa 9.
colador(m) 251, 296.
COLAS(F), TIPOS(M) 498.
colchón(m) 657, 726.
colchón(m) aislante 687.
colchón(m) de aire(m) 687.
colchón(m) de espuma(f) 687.
colchón(m) de muelles(m) 224.
colchoneta(f) 657.
colchonetas(f) y camas(f) 687.
colector(m) 40, 741, 753.
colector(m) de grasa(f) 253.
colector(m) solar 772.
colector(m) solar plano 768.
coles(f) de Bruselas 73.
colgante(m) 236.
coliflor(f) 69.
colilla(f) 386.
colina(f) 27, 770.
colina(f) abisal 29.
colinabo(m) 71.
collar(m) 304.
collar(m) cortafuego 205.
collar(m) de 5 hilos(m) 361.
collar(m) de perforación(f) 737.
collar(m) de una vuelta(f) 361.
collares(m) 361.
collarín(m) 205, 279, 283, 663.
collarino(m) 167.
colleja(f) 73.
colmena(f) 82.
colmena(f) 149.
colmillo(m) 96, 98, 144.
colmillos(m) de elefante(m) 99.
colmillos(m) de jabalí(m) verrugoso 99.
colmillos(m) de morsa(f) 99.
COLMILLOS(M): TIPOS(M) MÁS COMUNES 99.
colon(m) ascendente 131.
colon(m) descendente 131.
colon(m) sigmoideo 131.
colon(m) transverso 131.
color(m) 695.
color(m) vaporizado 590.
colores(m), ejemplos(m) 819.
columela(f) 94.
columna(f) 24, 36, 166, 168, 169, 236, 399, 455, 545, 561, 700, 701.
columna(f) central 393, 774.
columna(f) con capuchón(m) 37.
columna(f) de alcohol(m) 705.
columna(f) de control(m) 500.
columna(f) de mercurio(m) 705.
columna(f) de soporte(m) 738.
columna(f) de tensión(f) 562.
columna(f) vertebral 89, 122, 134.
coma(f) 832.
COMBATE(M), AVIÓN(M) 812.
combinación(f) 345.
combinación(f) 94.
combinación(f) con sostén(m) 345.
combinación(f) ganadora 702.
combustible(m) 761, 766.
combustible(m) en vuelo(m), reaprovisionamiento(m) 813.
combustible(m) fallido envasado 764.
combustible(m) para aviones(m) 745.
combustible(m), elemento(m) cargador 765.
combustible(m): uranio(m) enriquecido 762, 763.

combustible(m): uranio(m) natural 760, 761.
combustión(f) 436, 437, 501.
comedor(m) 195, 460, 496, 807.
comedor(m), vagón(m) 460.
COMETA(M) 9.
comienzo(m) de lectura(f) 405.
comillas(f) 832.
comillas(f) sencillas 832.
comisura(f) labial 142.
comodín(m) 695.
compartimiento(m) para almacenamiento(m) 449.
compartimiento(m) para el casete(m) 411.
compartimiento(m) para el equipo(m) 458.
compartimiento(m) para equipaje(m) 458.
compartimiento(m) para la casete(f) 409.
compartimientos(m) 82.
compartimiento(m) 701.
compartimiento(m) de almacenamiento(m) 778, 780.
compartimiento(m) de pasajeros(m) 493.
compartimiento(m) del cable(m) de la batería(f) 415.
compartimiento(m) del casete(m) 403.
compartimiento(m) del equipo(m) técnico 415.
compartimiento(m) para almacenamiento(m) 397.
compartimiento(m) para el disco(m) 405.
compartimiento(m) para mantequilla(f) 254.
compartimiento(m) para queso(m) y crema(f) 254.
compás(m) 537.
compás(m) del volumen(m) 413.
compensador(m) de flotación(f) 627.
compensador(m) gráfico de sintonización(f) 400.
complejo(m) hidroeléctrico 746.
completamente nublado 39.
complexo(m) mayor 121.
compluvio(m) 170, 171.
componentes(m) 400.
COMPONENTES(M) BÁSICOS 528, 530.
compresión(f) 436, 437, 501.
compresión(f)/admisión(f) 436.
compresor(m) 212, 517, 761.
compresor(m) centrífugo 501.
compresor(m) de aire(m) 469.
compresor(m) de la turbina(f) 501.
compresor(m) del aire(m) acondicionado 435.
compuerta(f) 490, 747, 752.
compuerta(f) de llenado(m) 493.
compuerta(f) de toma(f) 753.
compuerta(f) del aliviadero 746.
compuerta(f) del tanque(m) 743.
compuerta(f) inferior 492.
computador(m) de gestión(f) de vuelo(m) 500.
computador(m) de vuelo(m) 500.
común fruncida 340.
comunicación(f) por computador(m) 417.
COMUNICACIÓN(F) POR SATÉLITE DE TRANSMISIÓN(F) 416.
comunicación(f), unidades(f) 526.
comunicaciones(f) aéreas 417.
comunicaciones(f) industriales 417.
comunicaciones(f) marítimas 417.
comunicaciones(f) militares 417.
comunicaciones(f) personales 417.
COMUNICACIONES(F) POR TELÉFONO(M) 420, 422.
comunicaciones(f) terrestres 417.
comunicaciones(f), terminal(m) 422.
con aletilla(f) 342.
con chorrera(f) 342.
con hombrera(f) 340.
concentrador(m) de aire(m) 370.
concha(f) 83, 92, 139, 220, 553.
CONCHA(F) BIVALVA 95.
concha(f) del apuntador(m) 188.
CONCHA(F) UNIVALVA 94.
Concorde 19.
CONCURSO(M) DE SALTOS(M), EQUITACIÓN(F) 646.
concurso(m) de velocidad(f) 646.
concurso(m) profesional 646.
condensación(f) 35.

condensador(m) 717, 718, 758, 771.
cóndilo(m) externo 123.
cóndilo(m) interno 123.
condominios(m) 187.
conducto(m) 590.
conducto(m) de aire(m) caliente 259.
conducto(m) de aire(m) comprimido 590.
conducto(m) de desviación(f) 501.
conducto(m) de distribución(f) vertical 206.
conducto(m) de monedas(f) 702.
conducto(m) de salida(f) de aire(m) 501.
conducto(m) deferente 127.
conducto(m) del aire(m) 543.
conducto(m) del veneno(m) 96.
conducto(m) eyaculador 127.
conducto(m) galactóforo 129.
conducto(m) principal 206.
conducto(m) principal de gas(m) 186.
conducto(m) radicular 144.
conducto(m) secundario 206.
conducto(m) semicircular lateral 139.
conducto(m) semicircular posterior 139.
conducto(m) semicircular superior 139.
conducto(m) sudorífero 136.
conductor(m) 652.
conductor(m) de fase(f) 757.
conductor(m) neutral 757.
conductor(m) transversal 161.
conector(m) 300, 312, 406, 778.
conector(m) de expansión(f) 528.
conector(m) de línea(f) cargada 757.
conector(m) de salida(f) 547.
conector(m) del desagüe(m) 215.
conector(m) en T del desagüe(m) 298.
conexión(f) 697, 756, 757.
conexión(f) a tierra(f) 757.
conexión(f) aérea 757.
conexión(f) de seguridad(f) del traje(m) 512.
conexión(f) eléctrica 207, 213.
conexión(f) eléctrica a tierra(f) 741.
conexión(f) en T 301.
conexión(f) en U 301.
conexión(f) en Y 301.
conexión(f) para el módem(m) 528.
conexión(f) para el teclado(m) 528.
conexión(f) para el vídeo(m) 528.
conexión(f) para la impresora(f) 528.
conexión(f) para la manguera(f) de aire(m) 304.
conexión(f) para la red(f) 528.
conexión(f) para unidad(f) de disco(m) 528.
conexión(f) para unidades(f) periféricas 528.
conexiones(f) 301.
conexiones(f) 41.
conexiones(f) de transición(f) 301.
conexiones(f) mecánicas 300.
conexiones(f), árbol(m) 740.
CONEXIONES(F), FONTANERÍA(F) 298.
confidente(m) 221.
configuración(f) de almacenamiento(m) 48.
CONFIGURACIÓN(F) DEL LITORAL(M) 30.
configuración(f) topográfica 28.
conformación(f) 692.
congelador(m) incorporado 254.
cónico 183.
CONÍFERA(F) 58.
conjuntiva(f) 140.
conjunto(m) de la colmena(f) 82.
conjunto(m) de montañas(f) 51.
conjunto(m) deportivo 351.
conjunto(m) vacío 830.
CONJUNTOS(M) INSTRUMENTALES, EJEMPLOS(M) 558.
conmutador(m) de intensidad(f) 309.
connector(m) en T 298.
cono(m) 24, 410.
cono(m) de admisión(f) 501.
cono(m) de penumbra(f) 8.
cono(m) de sombra(f) 8.
cono(m) femenino 58.
cono(m) masculino 58.
cono(m) piromético 585.
conopial(m) 174.
consejero(m) de producción(f) 412.
consejeros(m) musicales 412.
consigna(f) 462.
consola(f) 542.
consola(f) 545.

936

Los términos en **negrita** corresponden a una ilustración; los que aparecen en MAYÚSCULAS indican un título.

Los términos en **negrita** corresponden a una ilustración; los que aparecen en MAYÚSCULAS indican un título.

descanso(m) del macillo(m) 541.
descanso(m) del pie(m) 727.
descapotable(m) 425.
descompresor(m) 627.
desenganchador(m) 291.
desenganchador(m) manual 641.
desértico 45.
desfiladero(m) 24.
deshuesador(m) de frutas(f) 246.
DESIERTO(M) 46.
desierto(m) arenoso 46.
desierto(m) rocoso 46.
desigual a 830.
desnivel(m) 193.
despachador(m) de hojas(f) de afeitar 374.
despacho(m) de camareros(m) 461.
despejado 39.
despensa(f) 195.
desplantador(m) 268.
despliegue(m) completo 419.
despliegue(m) de la antena(f) del radar(m) 49.
despliegue(m) del panel solar 419.
despliegue(m) del panel(m) solar 48.
despliegue(m) del reflector(m) del este(m) 419.
destacador(m) 515.
destilador(m) para asfalto(m) 745.
destinos(m) 463.
destorcedor(m) 672.
destornillador(m) 276.
destornillador(m) 688.
destornillador(m) de crucela(f) 688.
destornillador(m) de trinquete(m) 276.
desviación(f) 301.
desyerbador(m) 268.
detección(f) de ondas(f) sísmicas 714.
detector(m) de alta tensión(f) 310.
detector(m) de continuidad(f) 310.
detector(m) de tensión(f) 310.
detonador(m) 804.
devanadera(f) 575.
devanador(m) 575.
devanador(m) 671.
devanador(m) de bobinas(f) 575.
devolución(f) de monedas(f) 422.
devolución(f) de monedas(f) rechazadas 702.
devolvedor(m) 683.
diablo(m) 306.
diadema(f) 729.
diafragma(m) 130, 401, 406.
diafragma(m) de expansión 485.
diafragma(m) de iris(m) 390.
diafragma(m) de vacío(m) 435.
diagonal(f) 832.
diagonal(m) 756.
diagrama(m) de la circulación(f) 124.
diagramas(m) de tejidos(m) 576.
diamante(m) 363, 451, 597, 695.
diamante(m), corte(m) 363.
diana(f) 698.
diapasón(m) 539, 544, 547, 707.
diapositiva(f) 397.
diapositiva(f) 397.
diapositivas(f), proyector(m) 397.
diastema(f) 98.
dibujo(m) 350, 570.
dibujo(m) de la superficie(f) de rodadura(f) 433.
DIBUJO(M) Y PINTURA(F) 588, 590, 592.
diente(m) 96, 158, 159, 160, 162, 240, 268, 277, 284, 369, 445, 785.
diente(m) de cucharón(m) 782.
diente(m) de la charnela(f) 95.
diente(m) de león(m) 73.
diente(m) del zanco(m) 783.
DIENTES(M) 144.
dientes(m) 566, 644.
dientes(m) de la leva(f) 562.
dientes(m), cepillo(m) de 373.
diéresis(f) 832.
diésel(m) 745.
diésel(m) para barcos 745.
difusor(m) 396.
DIGESTIVO, APARATO(M) 131.
dijes(m) 364.
dinamo(f) 446.
dinamómetro(m) 709.
dintel(m) 175, 202, 204.
diodo(m) 769.
dióxido(m) 33.
dique(m) 25, 490.

dique(m) de machones(m), corte(m) transversal 751.
dique(m) de operación(f) 752.
dique(m) de terraplén(m), corte(m) transversal 748.
dique(m) inerte 752.
dique(m) seco 490.
dirección(f) 465, 831.
dirección(f) de la Meca(f) 173.
dirección(f) de los puntos(m) 488.
dirección(f) del viento(m),medición(f) 41.
dirección(f) obligatoria 824, 825.
dirección(f) y velocidad(f) del viento(m) 38.
dirección(m) del viento(m) 38.
directorio(m) telefónico 516.
disco(m) 251, 284, 404, 608, 658.
disco(m) 157, 284, 285, 432, 433, 529, 583, 663, 712.
disco(m) compacto 405.
disco(m) compacto 408.
disco(m) compacto, lector(m) 405.
disco(m) de ajuste(m) de ascención(f) recta 720, 721.
disco(m) de ajuste(m) de declinación(f) 720, 721.
disco(m) de articulación(f) 440.
disco(m) de caucho(m) 404.
disco(m) de tensión(f) 562, 569.
disco(m) desviador de calor(m) 232.
disco(m) duro, unidad(f) 529.
disco(m) flexible 529.
disco(m) flexible pequeño 529.
disco(m) giratorio 250.
disco(m) microondas(f) 415.
disco(m) óptico 527.
disco(m) tapador 158.
disco(m) y martillo(m) (lanzamiento(m)) 654.
disco(m), freno(m) 432.
discontinuidad(f) de Mohorovicic 22.
discontinuidad(f) de Gutenberg 22.
discos(m), pulverizador(m) 157.
diseño(m) 586.
diskette(m) 526.
disparador(m) 264, 780.
disparador(m) de cable(m) 393.
disparador(m) de pago(m) 702.
disparador(m) de señuelo(m) 809.
disparador(m) neumático 393.
disparo(m), accesorios(m) 801.
disposición(f) de los bolos(m) 683.
dispositivo(m) antideslizante 404.
dispositivo(m) de protección(f) 549.
dispositivo(m) para enmarcar 578.
distancia(f) recorrida 711.
DISTANCIA(F), MEDICIÓN(F) 711.
distribución(f) al consumidor(m) 755.
distribución(f) por redes(f) de cable(m) 416.
distribuidor(m) de calor(m) 209.
distribuidora(f) de billetes(m) de transferencia(f) 475.
distrito(m) 52.
divisiones(f) de los escudos(m) 818.
divisores(m) 519.
do(C) 537.
doble 646.
doble caja(f), camión(m) tractor(m) 440.
doble caña(f) 549.
doble cero(m) 700.
doble filo(m), tijeras(f) para entresacar 369.
doble fuelle(m) 536.
doble techo(m) 685.
doble toldo(m) 686.
doble vía(f) 824, 825.
doble(m) bemol 538.
doble(m) cero 700.
doble(m) sostenido 538.
doblez(m) 341, 565.
doblez(m) hacia el interior(m) 799.
doceava costilla(f) 122.
docena(f) (1 a 12) 700, 701.
docena(f) (13 a 24) 700, 701.
docena(f) (25 a 36) 700, 701.
dólar(m) 832.
DOMINÓ(M) 695.
domo(m) de vidrio(m) 484.
dórico, orden(m) 167.
dormitorio(m) 194, 195, 460, 685.
dormitorio(m) principal 194.
dorsal(f) oceánica 28.
dorsal(m) ancho 121.
dorso(m) 143, 288, 793.

dorso(m) del pie(m), arteria(f) del 126.
dos pares(m) 695.
dos puntos(m) 832.
dos tiempos(m), motor(m) 436.
dos(m) doble 695.
dosel(m) 229.
dosel(m) fruncido 229.
dosel(m) plisado 229.
dosel(m) plisado de canotillo(m) 229.
doselera(f) 228.
doseles(m), tipos(m) de 229.
Douglas, saco(m) de 128.
dovela(f) 174.
dovelaje(m) 175.
dracma(m) 832.
Dragón 11.
drapeado 343.
driver(m), palo(m) núm. 1 678.
driza(f) 480, 817.
drupéolo(m) 62.
ducha(f) 194.
ducha(f) de teléfono(m) 292.
ducha(f) y bañera(f) 215.
duna(f) 30.
duna(f) compleja 46.
duna(f) parabólica 46.
dunas(f) longitudinales 46.
dunas(f) paralelas 46.
dúo(m) 558.
duodeno(m) 131.
duramadre(f) 134, 135.
duramen(m) 59.

E

eclipse(m) anular 8.
ECLIPSE(M) DE LUNA(F) 8.
ECLIPSE(M) DE SOL(M) 8.
eclipse(m) parcial 8.
eclipse(m) total 8.
eclíptica(f) 3.
eclisa(f) 466.
eco(m) 722.
ECOLOGÍA(F) 31, 32, 34.
ecuador(m) 3, 47.
ecuador(m) celeste 3.
EDAD(F) DE PIEDRA(F), ARMAS(F) 791.
edificio(m) 766.
edificio(m) comercial 185.
edificio(m) de apartamentos(m) 185, 187.
edificio(m) de la administración(f) 752.
edificio(m) de la turbina(f) 758.
EDIFICIO(M) DE OFICINAS(F) 190.
edificio(m) de oficinas(f) 184, 185.
edificio(m) del reactor(m) 759, 765.
edificio(m) público 52.
edredón(m) 224.
efectos(m) especiales video\digital 413.
efluvio(m) 216.
eje(m) 251, 290, 374, 468, 564, 575, 584, 645, 707, 808.
eje(m) de cuchillas(f) 156.
eje(m) de declinación(f) 14.
eje(m) de dirección(f) 788.
eje(m) de la rueda(f) 447.
eje(m) de las aspas(f) 773.
eje(m) de tiro(m) 802.
eje(m) de toma(f) de fuerza(f) 156, 159, 162.
eje(m) del cepillo(m) 373.
eje(m) del pedal(m) 448.
eje(m) delantero 784.
eje(m) horizontal, turbina(f) de viento(m) 774.
eje(m) polar 14.
eje(m) propulsor 492.
eje(m) vertical, turbina(f) de viento(m) 774.
el agua(f) de un lago(m) o de un río(m) enfría el vapor(m) utilizado 767.
el agua(f) regresa al generador(m) de vapor(m) 767.
el cuatro 632.
el cuatro con timonel(m) 632.
el dos 632.
el dos con timonel(m) 632.
el galope(m) 101.
el paso(m) 101.
el paso(m) de andadura(f) 101.
el refrigerante(m) transfiere el calor(m) al generador(m) de vapor(m) 766.
el trote(m) 101.
el vapor(m) se condensa en agua(f) 767.
elástico(m) 224, 382.

ELECTRICIDAD(F) 309, 310, 312, 746, 748, 750, 752, 754, 756.
electricidad(f), transmisión(f) 757.
electricista(m), herramientas(f) de 310, 311.
electrodo(m) 232, 305.
electrodo(m) central 439.
electrodo(m) de masa(f) 439.
ELECTRODOMÉSTICOS, APARATOS(M) 250, 252, 254, 256, 257, 258, 260.
electrodos(m) 233.
electrodos(m) de encendido(m) 209.
electrones(m), cañón(m) 410.
ELECTRONES(M), MICROSCOPIO(M) 717.
elemento(m) calorífero 207, 209.
elemento(m) cargador de combustible(m) 765.
elemento(m) cargador de combustible(m) 765.
elemento(m) horizontal 756.
elemento(m) negativo 831.
elemento(m) positivo 831.
ELEMENTOS(M) BÁSICOS DE UN PLANO(M) 195.
elevación(f) 193.
elevación(f) continental 29.
elevador(m) 160, 161, 764, 782.
elevador(m) del brazo(m) 404.
elevador(m) telescópico 780.
embalse(m) 746, 748, 749, 750, 751, 752.
embalse(m) de la presa(f) 747.
embarcación(f) de emergencia 739.
emblema(m) 596, 817.
embocadura(f) del cable(m) 256.
émbolo(m) 159, 726.
embrague(m) de espacios(m) 525.
embudo(m) 243.
embutidor(m) 251.
empacadora(f) de heno(m) 159.
empacadora(f) de heno(m) 155.
empalizada(f) 181, 263, 646, 647.
empalmadura(f) 692.
empalme(m) de rieles(m) 466.
empalme(m) hidráulico 147.
empaque(m) 741.
empaquetadura(f) 294.
empate(m) de la boquilla(f) 550.
empeine(m) 325.
empella(f) 353, 355.
empujacutículas(m) 365.
empuje(m) 455.
empuñaderas(f) 665.
empuñadura(f) 281, 375, 596, 615, 633, 658, 665, 666, 670, 677, 679, 684, 793, 796, 798, 799.
empuñadura(f) del carro(m) 568.
empuñadura(f) delantera 804.
empuñaduras(f) para esquí(m) 633.
empuñaduras(f) para esquí(m) de figuras(f) 633.
en escalera(f) 362.
en espiral(f) 250.
en flor(f) 61.
en pendiente(f) 182.
en prisión(f) 700, 701.
en tijera(f) 362.
ENCAJE(M) DE BOLILLOS(M) 570.
encañado(m) 263.
encendedor(m) 307, 386.
encendido(m) 271.
encendido(m) \ apagado 408.
encendido(m) \ apagado(m) \ volumen(m) 408.
enceradora(f) 358.
enchufe(m) 255, 280, 309, 310, 400, 401, 406, 408, 485, 561, 585.
enchufe(m) con control(m) de tiempo(m) 255.
enchufe(m) de recarga(f) 374.
enchufe(m) del termómetro(m) 253.
enchufe(m) hembra(f) 400.
enchufe(m) para auriculares(m) 408.
enchufe(m) y selector(m) desmontables 253.
encía(f) 142, 144.
ENCUADERNACIÓN(F) ARTÍSTICA 578.
ENCUADERNACIÓN(F) ARTÍSTICA(F) 577.
encuadernación(f) en rústica 578.
endocarpio(m) 63, 64.
eneldo(m) 74.
ENERGÍA(F) EÓLICA 773, 774.
ENERGÍA(F) NUCLEAR 758, 760, 762, 764, 766.
energía(f) nuclear, producción(f) de electricidad(f) 766.
ENERGÍA(F) SOLAR 768, 770, 772.

939

Los términos en **negrita** corresponden a una ilustración; los que aparecen en MAYÚSCULAS indican un título.

SPANISH INDEX

Los términos en **negrita** corresponden a una ilustración; los que aparecen en MAYÚSCULAS indican un título.

950

Los términos en **negrita** corresponden a una ilustración; los que aparecen en MAYÚSCULAS indican un título.

poste(m) 201, 464, 471, 604, 613, 618, 626, 669.
poste(m) con tablas(f) 646.
poste(m) de canasta(f) 611.
poste(m) de dobles(m) 614.
poste(m) de individuales(m) 614.
poste(m) de la grúa(f) 743.
poste(m) de llegada(f) 654.
poste(m) de salto(m) 657.
poste(m) del asiento(m) 446.
poste(m) del radar(m) 742.
poste(m) extensible, taladro(m) 734.
poste(m) indicador 651.
postigos(m) interiores 231.
poterna(f) 179, 181.
potro(f) 659.
pozo(m) 763.
pozo(m) ciego(m) 736.
pozo(m) de acceso(m) 752.
pozo(m) de extracción(f) 736.
pozo(m) marino 740.
pozo(m) principal 734.
pozo(m) seco 763.
pradera(f) 149.
prado(m) 148.
precio(m) total 709.
precio(m) unitario 709.
precipitación(f) 34, 35.
precipitación(f) ácida 32, 33, 35.
precipitación(f) radiactiva 35.
PRECIPITACIONES(F) 36.
precisión(f), balanza(f) 709.
premaxilar(m) 86.
premolar(m) 98.
premolares(m) 144.
prensa(f) 579.
prensa(f) 578, 579.
prensa(f) de aguafuerte(f) 581.
prensa(f) de cajos(m) 579.
prensa(f) de contactos(m) 398.
prensa(f) de tornillo(m) 579.
prensa(f) en C 282.
prensa(f) litográfica 583.
prensapapel(m) 531.
prensatelas(m) 562.
prensatelas(m) 561, 562.
preparación(f) del eclipse(m) 419.
prepucio(m) 101, 106, 127.
presa(f) 749.
presa(f) 668, 746.
presa(f) de arco(m), corte(m) transversal 750.
presa(f) de brazo(m) 668.
presa(f), corte(m) transversal 749.
presidente(m) 666.
presilla(f) 323, 324, 688.
presilla(f) de estaquilla(f) 685, 686.
presilla(f) de la manga(f) 319.
presilla(f) del cinturón(m) 319.
presillas(f) 515.
presión(f) 663.
presión(f) barométrica 38.
presión(f) barométrica a nivel(m) del mar(m) 38.
presión(f) del aire(m), medición(f) 41.
PRESIÓN(F), MEDICIÓN(F) 710.
pretina(f) 320, 323.
pretina(f) con broches(m) 350.
pretina(f) elástica 321, 325.
PREVENCIÓN(F) DE INCENDIOS(M) 777.
primavera(f) 8.
primer árbitro(m) 613.
primer escalón(m) 201.
primer espacio(m) 610.
primer jugador(m) 620.
primer molar(m) 144.
primer pistón(m) móvil 550.
primer premolar(m) 144.
primer recinto(m) focal 15.
primera base(f) 597.
primera etapa(f) 509.
primera falange(f) 103.
primera vía(f) de clasificación(f) 465.
primera(f) 667.
PRIMEROS AUXILIOS(M), EQUIPO(M) 726.
primeros violines(m) 556.
principales señales(f) de circulación(f) internacionales 827, 828.
principales señales(f) de circulación(f) norteamericanas 824, 825, 826, 828.
principales tipos(m) de intercambios(m) 450.
principales tipos(m) de lentes(f) 377.

principales variedades(f) de bayas(f) 62.
principales variedades(f) de frutos(m) carnosos con hueso(m) 63.
principio(m) de la película(f) 395.
prisma(f) 390.
prisma(m) de Porro 719.
PRISMÁTICOS(M) BINOCULARES 719.
proa(f) 497, 628, 631, 637.
probador(m) de contactos(m) con tierra(f) 310.
probóscide(m) 79.
procesador(m) digital de sonido(m) 528.
procesamiento(m) de la información(f) 722.
proceso(m) de maduración(f) 61.
procesos(m) ciliares 140.
producción(f) de calor(m) 766.
producción(f) de electricidad(f) 767.
producción(f) de electricidad(f) por energía(f) solar 771.
producción(f) de electricidad(f) por generador(m) 755.
producción(f) de electricidad(f) por medio de energía(f) nuclear 766.
producción(f) de electricidad(f), etapas(f) 755.
producción(f), plataforma(f) 738.
productor(m) 412, 415.
productor(m) técnico 412, 415.
productos(m) del refinado(m) 744.
productos(m) lácteos 33.
productos(m) petroquímicos 745.
profundidad(f) del hipocentro(m) 23.
profundo(m) derecho 603, 605.
profundo(m) izquierdo 603, 605.
profundo(m) libre 605.
programador(m) 257, 258, 259.
prohibido acampar 823.
prohibido adelantar 824, 825.
prohibido dar vuelta(f) en U 824, 825.
prohibido el paso(m) 825.
prohibido el paso(m) 824.
prohibido el paso(m) de bicicletas(f) 828.
prohibido el paso(m) de camiones(m) 828.
prohibido el paso(m) de motocicletas(f) 828.
prohibido el paso(m) de peatones(m) 828.
prohibido hacer comidas(f) campestres 823.
prohibido usar silla(f) de ruedas(f) 822.
pronador(m) redondo 120.
pronaos(m) 168, 169.
propulsor F-1(m) 509.
propulsor J-2(m) 509.
propulsor(m) 49, 160, 509, 510, 512.
propulsor(m) de maniobras(f) 511.
propulsor(m) de proa(f) 497.
propulsor(m) radial 512.
proscenio(m) 188.
próstata(f) 127.
protección del sistema(m) respiratorio 821.
protección(f) 821.
protección(f) contra el vaho(m) 721.
protección(f) contra la luz(f) 16.
protección(f) de la cabeza(f) 821.
protección(f) de las manos(f) 821.
protección(f) de los oídos(m) 821.
protección(f) de los ojos(m) 821.
protección(f) de los pies(m) 821.
protector(m) 255, 268, 319, 598, 659, 669, 698, 726.
protector(m) abdominal 609.
protector(m) bucal 669.
protector(m) de brazo(m) 684.
protector(m) de la barbilla(f) 443.
protector(m) de la correa(f) 283.
protector(m) de la culata(f) 549.
protector(m) de la garganta(f) 595.
protector(m) de oídos(m) 729.
protector(m) de ojos(m) 777.
protector(m) de piernas(f) 609.
protector(m) del brazo(m) 602, 609.
protector(m) del cable(m) 280, 283, 305.
protector(m) del cuello(m) 609, 777.
protector(m) del mentón 777.
protector(m) del motor(m) 442.
protector(m) del pie(m) 595.
protector(m) del quemador(m) 634.
protector(m) del tendón(m) 644.

protector(m) del zanco(m) 783.
protector(m) facial 609, 643.
protector(m) genital 602, 609.
protector(m) lumbar 602.
protector(m) para las costillas(f) 602.
protector(m) pectoral 684.
protector(m) solar 512.
protoneurona(f) 135.
protórax(m) 78.
protuberancia(f) 6.
provincia(f) 51.
próxima llamada(f) 422.
proyección(f) cilíndrica 50.
proyección(f) cónica 50.
proyección(f) en círculo(m) 668.
proyección(f) interrumpida 50.
proyección(f) plana 50.
proyección(f) primera de cadera(f) 668.
proyección(f), pantalla(f) 397.
proyecciones(f) del mapa(m) 50.
PROYECTILES(M) 814.
proyectiles(m) 801.
proyector(m) auxiliar 16.
proyector(m) de altura(f) máxima 41.
proyector(m) de diapositivas(f) 397.
proyector(m) de luz(f) difusa 414.
proyector(m) múltiple 16.
proyector(m) sobre el pantógrafo(m) 414.
psicrómetro(m) 41.
púa(f) 535.
púa(f) de muelle(m) 157, 272.
pubis(m) 116, 118.
puente(m) 52, 109, 230, 376, 452, 491, 544, 546, 650, 719.
puente(m) colgante 456.
puente(m) de arco(m) 455.
puente(m) de carga(f) para contenedores(m) 490.
puente(m) de ensamblaje(m) 547.
puente(m) de los altos(m) 540.
puente(m) de los bajos(m) 540.
PUENTE(M) DE MANDO(M) 500.
puente(m) de mando(m) 494, 495, 497, 810.
puente(m) de pontones(m) 457.
puente(m) de portal(m) 455.
puente(m) de señales(f) 464.
puente(m) de tablero(m) inferior 455.
puente(m) de tablero(m) intermedio 455.
puente(m) de tablero(m) superior 455.
puente(m) de viga(f) 454.
puente(m) de viga(f) de un tramo(m) 454.
puente(m) de viga(f) de varios tramos(m) 454.
puente(m) desmontable tipo(m) Bailey 457.
puente(m) elevador 457.
puente(m) giratorio 457.
puente(m) levadizo 180.
puente(m) levadizo doble 457.
puente(m) levadizo sencillo 457.
puente(m) peatonal 464.
puente(m) transportador 457.
puente(m) voladizo 454.
puentes(m) de arco(m), tipos 455.
puentes(m) de tirantes(m) 456.
puentes(m) de viga(f), tipos(m) 454.
PUENTES(M) FIJOS 454, 456.
PUENTES(M) MOVIBLES 457.
puerco(m) 70.
PUERTA(F) 202.
puerta(f) 429.
puerta(f) 16, 173, 225, 253, 259, 427, 449, 498, 617, 685, 686, 709.
puerta(f) a la nave(f) de carga(f) 510.
puerta(f) abatible 195.
puerta(f) automática 504.
puerta(f) convencional 202.
puerta(f) corrediza 202.
puerta(f) de acceso(m) a la rejilla(f) de las luces(m) 412.
puerta(f) de entrada(f) 202.
puerta(f) de proa(f) 493, 494.
puerta(f) del congelador(m) 254.
puerta(f) del fogón(m) 204.
puerta(f) del refrigerador(m) 254.
puerta(f) del vestíbulo(m) 461.
puerta(f) lateral 477.
puerta(f) plegable 194, 202, 292.
puerta(f) trasera 195, 470.
puertas(f), tipos(m) de 202.
PUERTO(M) 490.
puesta(f) en marcha(f) 532, 569.

puesta(f) en órbita(f) 419.
puesto(m) de bombeo(m) 453.
puesto(m) de información(f) 504.
puesto(m) de socorro(m) 822.
pujamen(m) 631.
pulgar(m) 112, 137, 327, 596.
pullman(m) de ocho plazas(f) 425.
pulmón(m) 97.
pulmón(m) derecho 124, 130.
pulmón(m) izquierdo 124, 130.
pulpa(f) 62, 63, 64, 65, 144.
pulpejo(m) 104.
pulsera(f) de dijes(m) 364.
PULVERIZACIÓN(F) 157.
pulverización(f) 154.
pulverizador(m) 257, 264, 265, 590.
pulverizador(m) de agua(f) 426.
pulverizador(m) de discos(m) 157.
pulverizador(m) de discos(m) 154.
puñal(m) 794.
puño(m) 315, 324, 596, 615, 640, 642, 666, 727.
puño(m) de amura(f) 631.
puño(m) de escota(f) 631.
puño(m) de la puerta(f) 427.
puño(m) para gemelos(m) 339.
punta 818.
punta grabadora(f) 714.
punta(f) 30, 57, 72, 239, 240, 241, 242, 275, 276, 277, 284, 291, 305, 323, 325, 375, 384, 389, 544, 562, 567, 633, 640, 642, 658, 671, 678, 684, 697, 698, 817.
punta(f) de caja(f) cuadrada (Robertson) 276.
punta(f) de cruz(f) (Phillips) 276.
punta(f) de diamante(m) 225.
punta(f) de flecha(f) de pedernal(m) 791.
punta(f) de hoja(f) plana 276.
punta(f) de la plancha(f) 256.
punta(f) de plástico(m) 370.
punta(f) de sujeción(f) 540.
punta(f) del ala(f) 637.
punta(f) del bastón(m) 643.
punta(f) del cuello(m) 324, 341.
punta(f) del esquí(m) 642.
punta(f) delantera 680.
punta(f) seca 582, 583.
puntal(m) 199, 553, 757.
puntal(m) derecho 606.
puntal(m) izquierdo 606.
puntal(m) trasero 773.
puntales(m) de refuerzo(m) 198.
punteo(m) 586.
puntera(f) 277, 355, 641, 644, 645.
puntera(f) protectora 730.
puntera(f) reforzada 644.
puntero(m) 719.
punto(m) 565, 695, 832.
punto(m) de apoyo(m) variable 624.
punto(m) de cambio(m) 467.
punto(m) de concentración(f) 770.
punto(m) de cruz(f) 571.
punto(m) de escapulario(m) 571.
punto(m) de espiga(f) 571.
punto(m) de inserción(f) 684.
punto(m) de interés 52.
punto(m) de malla(f) 567.
punto(m) de mira(f) 719, 795, 796, 797, 798, 799, 804.
punto(m) de montaje(m) 501.
punto(m) de musgo(m) 567.
punto(m) de nudos(m) 571.
punto(m) de ochos(m) 567.
punto(m) de pénalty 601.
punto(m) de respiguilla(f) 567.
punto(m) de salida(f) 676.
punto(m) de saque(m) 608.
punto(m) y coma(f) 832.
punto(m), tipos(m) de 567.
puntos(m) de cruz(f) 571.
puntos(m) de malla(f) 571.
puntos(m) de montado(m) 567.
puntos(m) de relleno(m) 571.
puntos(m) de relleno(m) sueltos 571.
puntos(m) suspensivos 832.
puntos(m), tipos(m) de 571.
PUNTUACIÓN(F), SIGNOS(M) 832.
punzón(m) 570, 585, 688.
pupila(f) 107, 140.
pupila(f) vertical 96.
purificador(m) de aire(m) 210.
puro(m) 384.
púrpura(m) 819.
putter(m) 677.
putter(m) 678.

Los términos en **negrita** corresponden a una ilustración; los que aparecen en MAYÚSCULAS indican un título.

Los términos en **negrita** corresponden a una ilustración; los que aparecen en MAYÚSCULAS indican un título.

Los términos en **negrita** corresponden a una ilustración; los que aparecen en MAYÚSCULAS indican un título.

SPANISH INDEX

955

Y

y 831.
yardas(f) 604.
yelmo(m) 792.
yelmo(m) 792.
yema(f) 70, 109, 137.
yema(f) axilar 57.
yema(f) terminal 57.
yen(m) 832.
yeyuno(m) 131.
yugo(m) 364.
yunque(m) 138.
yurta(f) 165.

Z

zafiro(m) 363.
zaguero(m) izquierdo 613.
zamarra(f) 321.
zampoña(f) 536.
zanahoria(f) 71.
zanco(m) 783.
zángano(m) 81.
zanja(f) 733.

zapata(f) 293, 294, 295, 432, 441, 678.
zapata(f) antideslizante 302, 661.
zapata(f) de goma(f) 302.
zapata(f) de la cadena(f) 805.
zapata(f) hidrostática 14.
zapatera(f) de alambre(m) 358.
zapatilla(f) 598, 656, 662.
zapatilla(f) con tacos(m) 595.
zapatilla(f) de ballet(m) 356.
zapatilla(f) de tenis(m) 615.
zapatillas(f) de esgrima(f) 667.
zapato(m) a la polaca 318.
zapato(m) con tacos(m) 602.
zapato(m) de calle(f) 355, 356.
zapato(m) de cordones(m) 354.
zapato(m) de correa(f) 356.
zapato(m) de golf(m) 679.
zapato(m) de tacón(m) 318.
zapato(m) de tacón(m) alto 356.
zapato(m) de tacón(m) alto con
  presillas(f) 356.
zapato(m) de tenis(m) 355.
zapato(m) de vestir 355.
zapato(m) deportivo 352.
ZAPATOS(M) 354.

zarcillo(m) 61.
zarpa(f) 198, 199.
zócalo(m) 199, 201, 707.
zócalo(m) de la bañera(f) 292.
ZODÍACO(M), SIGNOS(M) 820.
zona(f) 610.
zona(f) central 611.
zona(f) comercial 190.
zona(f) de alta presión(f) 38.
zona(f) de anotación(f) 604.
zona(f) de asteroides(m) 4.
zona(f) de ataque(m) 608, 613.
zona(f) de atención(f) 597.
zona(f) de baja presión(f) 38.
zona(f) de cambio(m) 612.
zona(f) de circulación(f) 502.
zona(f) de comidas(f) campestres 823.
zona(f) de convección(f) 6.
zona(f) de defensa(f) 608, 613.
zona(f) de derrumbes(m) 826, 827.
zona(f) de estacionamiento(m) 503.
zona(f) de gol(m) 606.
zona(f) de la portería(f) 608.
zona(f) de pelos(m) absorbentes 59.
zona(f) de precipitación(f) 38.

zona(f) de prueba(f) de motores(m) de
  aviones(m) 811.
zona(f) de radiación(f) 6.
zona(f) de recreo(m) 496.
zona(f) de saque(m) derecha 614.
zona(f) de saque(m) izquierda 614.
zona(f) de servicio(m) 503, 613, 764.
zona(f) de trabajo(m) 16.
zona(f) de traspaso(m) de carga(f) 743.
zona(f) de tres segundos(m) 610.
zona(f) débil de la hoja(f) 666.
zona(f) defensiva 611.
zona(f) del hoyo(m) 676.
zona(f) escolar 826, 827.
zona(f) fuerte de la hoja(f) 666.
zona(f) libre 613.
zona(f) media 666.
zona(f) neutral 603, 605, 608.
zona(f) ofensiva 611.
zona(f) para acampar 823.
zona(f) para acampar y para
  caravanas(f) 823.
zona(f) para caravanas(f) 823.
zona(f) pelúcida 128.
zona(f) verde 184.
zoom(m) 392, 414.